LIBERATION THEOLOGY:
A DOCUMENTARY HISTORY

LIBERATION THEOLOGY: A DOCUMENTARY HISTORY

Edited with Introductions, Commentary, and Translations by

ALFRED T. HENNELLY, S. J.

ORBIS BOOKS

Maryknoll, New York 10545

The Catholic Foreign Mission Society of America (Maryknoll) recruits and trains people for overseas missionary service. Through Orbis Books, Maryknoll aims to foster the international dialogue that is essential to mission. The books published, however, reflect the opinions of their authors and are not meant to represent the official position of the society.

For permission to reprint material, grateful acknowledgment is made to the following: *Cross Currents* for Juan Luis Segundo, "The Future of Christianity in Latin America"; *Our Sunday Visitor* for Cardinal Alfonso Lopez Trujillo, "Liberation, a Permanent Value"; *Christianity & Crisis* (537 West 121st St., New York, NY 10027), for Jürgen Moltmann, "An Open Letter to José Míguez Bonino" (copyright 1976); *The Ecumenist* for "German Theologians and Liberation Theology"; Michael Novak, for his article "Liberation Theology and the Pope"; Meyer Stone Books for Harvey Cox, "Oneness and Diversity," from *The Silencing of Leonardo Boff;* *America* for Alfred Hennelly, "The Red Hot Issue: Liberation Theology"; *The New York Times* for Alan Riding, "Pope Shifts Brazilian Church to Right"; and SPCK, the British publishers of Leonardo Boff, *Jesus Christ Liberator.*

Every attempt was made to locate those who hold rights for the works in this book.

Manuscript editor: William E. Jerman

Library of Congress Cataloging-in-Publication Data

Liberation theology: a documentary history/edited with
  introductions, commentary, and translations [by] Alfred T. Hennelly.
    p. cm.
  Includes bibliographical references.
  ISBN 0-88344-592-1. – ISBN 0-88344-593-X (pbk.)
  1. Liberation theology – History of doctrines – Sources.
I. Hennelly, Alfred T.
BT83.57.L487 1990
230'.2'09045 – dc20   89-28484
                                                       CIP

For my brother Bob, Joan, and the children

and for Bridget and Kathleen McTiernan

Contents

Preface

One of the most astonishing and lasting phenomena in the Catholic Church during the second half of the twentieth century has been the efflorescence of a new approach to theology, that is now known throughout the world as the theology of liberation. This theology is astonishing because its deepest insights did not spring from the minds of scholars in the great universities of the First World, but rather from small communities of the poorest and least literate men and women in Latin America and eventually in many other parts of the Third World in Africa and Asia. Its endurance is shown by the fact that its message has grown brighter in clarity and depth as it has spread throughout the world, while some of the many new theologies of the First World have flickered and grown dimmer as the years have passed.

My own acquaintance with this theology began in the late sixties when I came across some writings of the Peruvian theologian Gustavo Gutiérrez. The words of Keats from some forgotten course flashed before me — "then felt I like some watcher of the skies, when a new planet swims into his ken" — and I have followed this movement with great interest in the intervening years. Here I can only sketch a few of the major reasons for this continuing interest.

For the first time in history, liberation theology has created an opportunity for the voice of the poor — the mute and invisible four-fifths of the world — to be heard clearly and loudly in every corner of the planet. It is a voice of intense urgency and a powerful challenge, especially to the Christian churches of the First World, and also to its theologians, who have not made it a priority over the past five centuries, despite the fact that it is a central concern of the Bible. For these four billion human beings represent starkly and unambiguously the poor, the orphan, the widow, and the stranger who were identified time and again by the prophets of Israel as *the* place to encounter and to know Yahweh. These four billion also clearly epitomize the "least of my brothers and sisters," to whose suffering Jesus of Nazareth called his followers to respond as the ultimate test of their commitment and eternal destiny (Matt. 25).

From another perspective, the importance of liberation theology lies in the fact that it has integrated, extensively and profoundly, the struggle for justice as an essential feature of every method, theme, and context of theology. This too is of the utmost significance for the First World, which is dominated today by individualism on the personal level and various forms of nationalism on the social level. Along with this emphasis on the positive centrality of justice, liberation theology employs a methodology of ideology-criticism, that is, the unmasking of oppressive ideas and attitudes in both society and the Christian churches. Thus, it employs a needed "hermeneutic of suspicion" regarding the many ways in which the churches, either consciously or unconsciously, preach a gospel of social justice but actually justify or even grant religious legitimation to ideas or policies that are oppressive or alienating, and thus opposed to the freedom of the gospel of Jesus of Nazareth.

Many other aspects of liberation theology could be added here, but I believe they will emerge with great clarity throughout the pages of this volume. For these and other reasons I was immediately interested when the idea of this collection of the key documents regarding the history of liberation theology was first proposed to me. I want to emphasize that the original idea for the book was the brainchild of Robert Ellsberg, editor-in-chief of Orbis Books, and I am very grateful to him for his guidance and encouragement in bringing to birth what turned out to be a very large infant.

I would like also to thank Dean Brackley, Alexander Wilde, and Lee Cormie, who helped me with suggestions for this volume. Invaluable help was provided to me by the staff of the Woodstock Theological Center Library at Georgetown University, the libraries of the Catholic University of America, Fordham University, the Maryknoll Fathers, and the Library of Congress, especially its Latin American department. I am indebted, moreover, to the Jesuit community at Fordham University and its staff, who tirelessly photocopied documents, as well as to the Woodstock Theological Center community for welcoming me to their home during trips to Washington over the years.

My greatest and deepest gratitude, however, must be reserved for those who did the most to make this volume possible. They are, once again, the impoverished people of Latin America and the many Christians, including theologians, who have committed themselves with great conviction and courage to their cause. My fondest hope at the moment is that this book may help in some way for all of these to draw nearer to the freedom in the Spirit promised to them in the gospel of Jesus of Nazareth.

General Introduction

Twenty years ago, at a time when Latin American theology was just beginning to be referred to as a "theology of liberation," a Latin American theologian was asked to explain the major difference between this new approach and so-called traditional theology, that is, theology as it was usually understood in the centers of learning in Europe and the United States. After a brief pause for reflection, the theologian answered the question as follows: "Let me put it this way. European theology may best be described as 'prologues in search of courage.' Latin American theology, on the other hand, should be characterized as 'courage with primitive weapons.' "

Reflecting on this description now, the emphasis on courage appears as indispensable as ever. If the danger of exile, torture, or assassination is not as frequent today, there is still continual and organized opposition, which results in removal from universities, seminaries, or study centers, and also an unending barrage of personal attacks and crude distortions of liberation theology. It is important to emphasize right from the beginning of this volume that I do not think this opposition and conflict is going to end in some form of reconciliation in the foreseeable future. When one identifies with the interests of the poor, one will undoubtedly come into conflict with the interests of other sectors of society, and their allies in the churches. It is no wonder, then, that in his *Spirituality of Liberation* Jon Sobrino emphasizes the virtue of fortitude, which "can be translated as the refusal to abandon the poor in their sufferings. And these same poor—by what they give and what they ask—inspire us with that fortitude, the strength to remain steadfast in persecution."[1]

If we turn, however, to the other element in our description of liberation theology, it is clear that enormous change has taken place with regard to the once "primitive" weapons. In every nation of Latin America, a great maturing process has occurred with regard to liberation theology, epitomized by the fact that the really "interesting" theology is now flowing from the South to be translated for eager readers in Europe and the United States, and later also for many readers in the Third World. These developments in liberation theology will be discussed in more detail throughout this book.

In giving a preliminary evaluation of this recent theology, I believe that it is impossible to deny that it is the most significant and influential theological movement in the Catholic Church since the Second Vatican Council. Personally, I would go much further and understand it as representing a completely new epoch in church history, following the bishops at Vatican II who emphasized that today "we can speak of a new age in human history" (*Gaudium et Spes*, no. 54). Thus, I am in complete agreement with the division of the church's relationship with society into three distinct eras. In the first centuries, it adopted a posture of social protest against the social order. Then, during the many centuries of the Constantinian era, it fulfilled a function of the conservation of the status quo. Finally, the historical moment has arrived for the church to adopt a role of social construction. Leonardo and Clodovis Boff stress that "the end and aim of the theology of liberation is to serve as an echo of and response to this immense challenge facing the church."[2]

From another perspective, I have concluded that liberation theology should be understood as the cutting edge of theological reflection in the entire Third World, which now constitutes more than eighty percent of humanity, and which is inexorably increasing that percentage as each day passes. For these four billion persons, then, liberation theology represents the "missing voice" in the entire history of post-Constantinian theology — that is, the voice of the poor and the victims of oppression throughout the world. Considering their numbers, combined in many areas of the world with an exuberant religious vitality and creativity, I am willing to wager that liberation theology will continue to be the most significant influence in the world church for the foreseeable future.

THE RETRIEVAL OF HISTORY

An important first step in understanding liberation theology is to recognize *its distinctiveness* from other forms of theology, such as those in Europe, and its profound rootedness in the soil of Latin America, that is, in the world of the poor. Of course, like any Roman Catholic theology, it received the riches of tradition through the Eurocentric church of the past, of which Hilaire Belloc boldly proclaimed: "The Church is Europe, and Europe is the Church." But its most original and truly creative characteristic is, as Gustavo Gutiérrez has emphasized incessantly, to see the world "from the underside of history" — that is, from the perspective of the poor and suffering, the losers in history, and to respond to this vision by searching for effective strategies to transform the "structures of sin" that are the root causes of their suffering.

Rebecca Chopp has published an interesting study comparing the approach of two European theologians, Johannes B. Metz and Jürgen Moltmann, with that of two Latin Americans, Gustavo Gutiérrez and José Míguez Bonino, and has produced an excellent statement of what I am discussing:

Liberation theology, in sum, both continues and radically departs from modern theology. As a continuation, liberation theology represents a radical engagement of Christianity with the world, with the intent to represent human freedom and God's gratuitous activity in the questions and issues of the day. As a radically new paradigm and departure from modern theology, liberation theology reflects and guides a Christianity that is identified with those who suffer, that represents a freedom of transformation, and that proclaims a God whose love frees us for justice and faith.[3]

Another key element for understanding liberation theology is the recognition that it did not fall on Latin America like some meteor from the skies, but had forerunners in Latin American history going back to the time of the conquest. The historian Enrique Dussel, who is director for the Center for the Study of Church History in Latin America (CEHILA), has clearly delineated the stages of Latin American theology.

The first epoch he mentions is that of a "prophetic theology" from 1511 to 1553. This consisted of a few powerful voices that vehemently protested and condemned the enslavement and brutal oppression of Amerindians by the conquistadores. In November 1511, one of them, the Dominican Antonio de Montesinos, preached a powerful sermon attacking the oppressive rule of the Spaniards and presenting a passionate defense of the rights of the Amerindians. One of his listeners, Bartolomé de las Casas, was so galvanized by these words that he was converted to the cause of the Amerindians and spent his entire life speaking and writing prodigiously on their behalf. As Dussel points out, "this prophetic conversion of a thinker who would afterward be so prolific in his writings as well as so profound and practical in his conclusions could be considered the birth of the Latin American theology of liberation."[4]

A reaction, designated as "the theology of colonial Christendom" (1553-1808), began with the founding of the first universities in the New World. The resultant academic theology not only ceased to denounce the continuing crimes against the Amerindians, but eventually succeeded in creating a "sacred canopy" that provided an ideological justification for their oppression. Even in this period, however, prophetic exceptions and glimmers of a liberating theology broke forth in the work of José de Acosta in Peru and the labors of the Jesuits in constructing the communal Amerindian settlements known as the "reductions."

The next epoch (1808-1831) comprised the years of struggle for independence throughout Latin America, and is considered by Dussel to have produced another genuine liberation theology, which he calls "a political theology of emancipation." This movement was certainly not academic or scholarly, but reflected the efforts of a wide variety of leaders to provide a theological justification for the wars of independence and religious motivation to take part in the struggle. Because of the chaos created by war, this theology was not published in books but rather in tracts, sermons, pamphlets, speeches, and other forms of ad hoc literature.

The fourth and fifth periods consisted of a conservative "neocolonial theology" (1831-1930), as well as by a period marked by a moderately progressive "New Christendom" mentality (1930-1962). Although this latter period did not break with its dependency on Europe, it did succeed in providing an *essential infrastructure* for a truly Latin American theology. The major achievements included the following: widespread promotion of the Catholic Action movement; the rapid multiplication of theological faculties and theological journals in the universities; the founding of many centers for the study of the social sciences; the founding of youth, social, and labor organizations; the creation of political parties, such as the Christian Democrats; and finally the formation of the Latin American bishops' conference (CELAM) in 1955, and the beginning of the continentwide conference of religious (CLAR) in 1958.

As regards the sixth period, that of modern liberation theology, my chronology differs considerably from Dussel's. My chronology is built into the table of contents at the beginning of this book and can be consulted there. Also, at the beginning of each section of the book, I will give a survey of the background and important events. Thus it would be redundant to include the same information here in the introduction.

BEGINNINGS OF LIBERATION THEOLOGY

At this point, I will discuss three key components of liberation theology's initial phase, all of which had their beginnings in the mid to late 1950s. These include: (1) the formation of basic ecclesial communities (called CEBs in both Spanish and Portuguese); (2) the development of the educational method known as conscientization (*concientização*) by the Brazilian Paulo Freire; and (3) a growing awareness in the universities of the ideologies used by both state and church to legitimate injustice.

The basic ecclesial communities are small groups of Catholics, usually coordinated by lay leaders, who meet regularly for services of prayer, worship, and communal reflection on both their religious and secular lives. They also stress sharing, communication, mutual assistance, and friendship, thus creating what they are proud to call real and active communities, in contrast to the passive, anonymous religious experience they had before the advent of the CEBs. They have great interest in the Bible, and apply it to their personal and communal lives by means of Freire's technique of conscientization, which has no real equivalent in English but is perhaps closest to the concept of "consciousness-raising." In the process of teaching literacy to peasants, Freire intended also to liberate them from socio-cultural enslavement by becoming aware of their own dignity and rights, aware, too, of the real causes of their oppression, and of the urgent need to become active agents of their own destiny in seeking avenues of change. Obviously, this did not please governments that preferred peasants to accept passively their designation as brutes or animals, and Freire has been exiled from a number of Latin American countries, including his homeland, Brazil.

Those who have observed or studied the basic ecclesial communities express their relationship to liberation theology in one of two ways. Some assert that "the base communities are liberation theology put into practice"; others state that "liberation theology emerges from the experience and reflection of the base communities." To me it appears obvious that these two assertions are by no means in opposition to each other but rather are clear evidence that there is an ongoing and profound dialectical relationship between the base communities and liberation theology, resulting in a symbiosis that stimulates growth and maturation in both partners in the dialectic. At any rate, the pastoral plans of the Brazilian bishops for new forms of community and Freire's experiments in education and conscientization go back to the 1950s, thus providing a reasonable basis for dating the genesis of liberation theology to that period.

All this receives further confirmation from the third component, Juan Luis Segundo's experience with university faculty and students. Here is how he presents his own recollection of liberation theology's beginnings:

Contrary to the most common assumption, Latin American theology, without any precise title, began to have clearly distinctive features at least ten years before Gustavo Gutiérrez's well-known book, *A Theology of Liberation*. This was a kind of baptism, but the baby had already grown old. The real beginning came simultaneously from many theologians working in countries and places in Latin America, even before the first session of Vatican II.[5]

Segundo then goes on to describe in detail how faculty, students, and professionals in the politically autonomous Latin American universities met together and began to unmask the ideologies used by both governments and churches to legitimate the inhuman condition of most of the population in their countries.

CONTENT AND METHOD

Granted this rather brief account of the origins and stages of liberation theology, important questions still remain. What is this theology all about? What is its content and substance? And what kind of method does it employ in its theological reflection? In responding to these questions I will first discuss content and then turn to the issue of theological method.

By far the most important background experience of liberation theology is the widespread experience of poverty, the impoverishment of many millions of persons because of domestic and foreign socio-economic systems. This means that the vast majority of Latin Americans live in a state of permanent destitution, of mortal danger, because of chronic deficiencies in food, potable water, sanitation, decent shelter, as well as in even the rudiments of health care, literacy, and education. Because of this mortal danger, Jürgen Moltmann has referred to the vast urban slums that surround the great Latin American cities as "circles of death." The theologians of Latin America cannot escape these ubiquitous circles, and thus a certain passion and urgency is characteristic of all their writings.

In reaction to this massive enslavement, liberation theology also places great emphasis on themes of freedom and liberation, such as the exodus in the Old Testament or Jesus' mission of bringing liberation to captives in the New Testament. This entails liberation especially from the social and structural sinfulness described above, but it also consistently emphasizes the very profound roots of personal sinfulness. A concrete example of this is evident in the pedagogy of the basic ecclesial communities, which aims at overcoming the sense of fatalism that has been imposed on the poor and enables them to become free and creative actors in the fulfillment of their own destiny. Connected with this is the realization that it is in this world, not in some other "religious" realm, that men and women are called to act, to fulfill God's will, and to advance the kingdom of God.

Another way of expressing this is to note that in liberation theology there is a powerful current of historical consciousness, along with an openness to personal and social change and an opposition to a static or fixed worldview or social order. This has led liberation theology to an analysis of its own historical context and to an awareness of its situation of dependency and domination, along with a determination to search for strategies to break out of these shackles.

From all that has been said so far, it should be evident that liberation theology places considerable emphasis on the social nature of human existence. Such a stance puts it in sharp opposition to the religious sensibility of the United States, for example, which is more characterized by radical individualism. A social consciousness emphasizes the effects for good or ill of one's environment and social status on the most basic assumptions of one's worldview, including the religious or theological perspective, and devotes considerable attention to a careful critique of unexamined ideologies. It emphasizes, too, that human society is a "social construction,"[6] not a fixed creation of God or nature, and thus can be reconstructed in ways that promise greater justice and participation.

Thus, it was inevitable that liberation theology should turn more and more to the social sciences, both for macro- and microanalysis of the theologian's social context, as well as for possible models and strategies for social change and even radical transformation of societies that frustrate the liberty and well-being of their members. It was also inevitable in their context that Latin Americans should enter into dialogue with Marxism, which offers the most comprehensive alternative to capitalism on both the analytic and strategic levels in the contemporary world.

Other characteristic theological themes or emphases of liberation theology can only be touched on briefly at this point. Major emphasis is given to the biblical notion of the kingdom of God, a vision of societal existence marked by justice, peace, and loving collaboration. This does not mean an idolatrous baptism of any one polis as the kingdom, as some facile criticisms suggest, but rather the recognition, in the example of Jon Sobrino, that states that murder their own citizens with impunity are certainly further from the kingdom of God than states that abjure and punish such activity.[7] Other major concepts include the universality of God's grace in the world (that is, it is not limited to the various channels of the Christian churches), the close relationship between liberation or salvation from personal sin and from oppressive social structures, and a very strong insistence that the essence of Christianity consists in love.

A final word should be added about spirituality, understood as the interior life of prayer, worship, and union with God integrated with one's whole life. Liberation theology is often charged with neglecting this dimension of Christian life because of its interest in secular affairs; paradoxically, however, liberation theology stresses the importance of an authentic spiritual life even more than traditional theology. The paradox is resolved when it is seen that the commandment of love mentioned above is inextricably linked in liberation theology with the demands of social justice and with a praxis that emphasizes action of some kind in the struggle for justice. As in so many other areas of liberation theology, this does not constitute a novelty but rather a retrieval of an authentically biblical spirituality.

At this point, I will move to the question of theological method and begin with the book of Gustavo Gutiérrez, *A Theology of Liberation.*[8] Gutiérrez defines his own method as critical reflection on praxis in the light of the word of God and insists on the point mentioned earlier that this does not involve a new content but a *new way* of doing theology. In describing his approach further, he notes that the Christian and the Christian community are called by their religious belief to a praxis that involves "real charity, action, and commitment to the service of men and women." In the Latin American context the most striking sign of the times is clearly that of massive human suffering, and so the praxis is further qualified as the attempt to eliminate such suffering. Theology, then, is a reflection on this definite praxis and so is referred to as a "second step."

But this reflection must be critical, both of society and of the church itself in the light of the Bible. Thus, its goal is to free both these institutions from various forms of ideology, idolatry, and alienation, while at the same time preventing pastoral practice from degenerating into unreflective activism.

Another influential theologian, Juan Luis Segundo, has added clarity to the discussion on method by utilizing the "hermeneutic circle" — that is, the continuing interaction between the text of the Bible and its interpretation in various periods or contexts. This method involves "the continuous change in the interpretation of the Bible, which is dictated by the continuing changes in our present-day reality, both individual and societal." If present reality is to change, one must be to some extent dissatisfied with it and thus raise questions about it that are "rich enough, general enough, and basic enough to force us to change our customary perceptions of life, death, knowledge, society, politics, and the world in general."[9] Once these new and more profound questions are posed to the scriptural texts, it is essential that our interpretations of the texts change also; otherwise, the new questions would either receive no answers or else answers that are conservative and useless.

Within the hermeneutic circle, Segundo distinguishes four crucial steps:

> *First* there is our way of experiencing reality, which leads us to ideological suspicion. *Secondly* there is the application of our ideological suspicion to the whole ideological superstructure in general and to theology in particular. *Thirdly* there comes a new way of experiencing theological reality that leads us to exegetical suspicion — that is, to the suspicion that the prevailing interpretation of the Bible has not taken important pieces of data into account. *Fourthly* we have our new hermeneutic — that is, our new way of interpreting the fountainhead of our faith (i.e., Scripture) with the new elements at our disposal.[10]

It is important to note that for Segundo the first stage of the circle always involves the experience of a definite problem and an act of will or commitment to find a solution to the problem. As he expresses it, "a hermeneutic circle in theology always presupposes a profound human commitment, a partiality that is consciously accepted — not on the basis of theological criteria of course, but on the basis of human criteria."[11] For understanding the circle more concretely, it may be helpful for North American readers to refer to the experience of North Americans who spend some time in a Third World country or in a very poor section of their own country and afterward arrive at a more critical view of their own government's policies or the actions and teachings of their own church with regard to these areas.

At any rate, it is clear from the above that Segundo is in agreement with Gutiérrez on the priority of praxis in theological reflection. He also agrees with him regarding the "critical" nature of the reflection, although his method, utilizing the hermeneutic circle, is more detailed and nuanced than that of Gutiérrez.

WHO ARE THE LIBERATION THEOLOGIANS?

In the most profound sense, it is fundamentally the poor of the world who are the real authors of liberation theology. That is the reason for beginning Part I of this volume with documents on conscientization as well as the basic ecclesial communities and other forms of religious organizations of the poor. In this setting occurred one of the most extraordinary events in the twenty centuries of Christianity, as the teeming multitudes of the poor began to speak in their own voice and express their own freedom and dignity by increasingly full participation in both church and society. To use Gutiérrez's definition of theology, it was the reflection of the poor upon their own praxis of suffering and struggle in the light of the word of God that created the theology of liberation, just as it provided the essential material for the final documents of the bishops' conference at Medellín in 1968.

This phenomenon is clearly recognized in the introduction to liberation theology by Clodovis and Leonardo Boff. They begin by observing that "liberation theology is a cultural and ecclesial phenomenon by no means restricted to a few professional theologians. It is a way of thinking that embraces most of the membership of the church, especially in the Third World."[12] The authors then analyze in detail three levels of participation in theology, the popular, the pastoral, and the professional. Without going into the details of the eight different areas of analysis for each level, we may summarize by saying that the Boff brothers place great emphasis on the communal and the integrating nature of the levels of reflection. The nature of this integration, they continue, "is seen most clearly at church conferences, where you can find pastoral ministers—bishops, priests, religious, and lay persons—telling of their problems, Christians from base communities recounting their experiences, and theologians contributing their insights, deepening the meaning of events under discussion and drawing conclusions from them."[13] In this introduction I will confine myself to the professional theologians, and stress those whose books are available in English.

Certainly the best-known theologian is Gustavo Gutiérrez, a diocesan priest born in Lima, Peru, in 1928. The very title of the liberation movement is taken from his book, *A Theology of Liberation*, first published in Peru in 1971, and since translated into many languages around the world. The genius of this work was to gather together many different strands regarding method and different themes in theology and to provide a kind of blueprint—sketchy in some areas and needing revision in others—of the new theology that was developing from the new experiences of Latin Americans. It thus provided both a compendium of liberation theology and a point of departure for the work of other theologians. Gutiérrez also founded and directs the de las Casas Institute for the study of Amerindian religion and culture in Lima, where he also teaches and works with a number of religious organizations. He has also lectured widely on the world scene and published a number of other books, of which the most important are *The Power of the Poor in History* and *We Drink from Our Own Wells*.[14]

Another very important figure in the liberation movement is the Franciscan priest, Leonardo Boff, who was born in Concordia, Brazil, in 1938. In 1972 he published a book entitled *Jesus Christ Liberator*, which provided an excellent model of the rethinking of a classic tract of theology from the liberation viewpoint.[15] Since then he has become the most prolific of the liberation theologians, writing very profoundly on a large number of diverse topics. Other well-known works of Boff include *Liberating Grace, The Maternal Face of God, Passion of Christ, Passion of the World*, and *Church: Charism and Power*,[16] all of which will be discussed later in this book. Aside from his writing, teaching and lecturing, Boff is editor of *Revista Eclesiástica Brasileira*, the most important theological periodical in Brazil, is a member of the theological commission for the Brazilian Bishops' Conference, and is religious editor for Vozes, an important publishing firm. Boff, in short, richly deserves his reputation as the most prominent and talented theologian in the Portuguese-speaking world.

I have already referred to the work on methodology of a Jesuit priest, Juan Luis Segundo, who was born in Montevideo, Uruguay, in 1925. While studying in Europe, he published an important study of the person in the works of Nicolai Berdyaev for his doctorate at the University of Paris. Since then, he has worked in dialogue with professional groups in Montevideo and has taught theology at the universities of Harvard, Chicago, Toronto, Montreal, Birmingham, and São Paulo. His many works include *A Theology for Artisans of a New Humanity* (five volumes), *The Hidden Motives of Pastoral Action, Theology and the Church*, and *Jesus of Nazareth Yesterday and Today*[17] (five volumes). The last-named work is his most comprehensive (1400 dense pages in the Spanish edition) and is clearly his masterwork, placing him in the very first rank of Latin American theologians.

Jon Sobrino is another Jesuit priest who has worked most of his life teaching philosophy and theology at José Simeón Cañas University in San Salvador, El Salvador. Born to a Basque family in Barcelona during the Spanish Civil War, he studied at St. Louis University for an engineering degree and in Sankt Georgen, Frankfurt, for his doctorate in theology. He first came to world attention with his *Christology at the Crossroads*,[18] which he later elaborated on in *Jesus in Latin America*. More recently, Sobrino has published two other important works, *The True Church and the Poor* and *Spirituality of Liberation*.[19] The latter work had been long awaited because of his numerous articles on spirituality, published in various Latin American periodicals.

The most influential Protestant liberation theologian is clearly José Míguez Bonino, who was born in Santa Fe, Argentina, in 1924. He pursued his theological studies in Buenos Aires, Emory University, and Union Theological Seminary in New York. He is an important ecumenical figure, having served on the World Council of Churches, and having lectured widely throughout Latin America and in many other parts of the world. The book that first brought him to prominence was entitled *Doing Theology in a Revolutionary Situation*.[20] Since that time, he has also published *Christianity and Marxists* and *Toward a Christian Political Ethics*, and edited *Faces of Jesus*.[21] More information and insight into these authors and many other aspects of liberation theology may be found in the documents, introductions, and commentaries that follow in the rest of this volume.

CONCLUSION

In concluding this introduction to the basic features of liberation theology, it seems appropriate to recall what I stated at the beginning. This approach to theology from the viewpoint of the poor and suffering of the world, its condemnation of their suffering as totally opposed to the kingdom of God preached by Jesus Christ, and its unambiguous call for bold and profound changes in the political and socio-economic structures of sin that perpetuate that suffering, was destined from the beginning to generate opposition and conflict from other sectors of society that seek to maintain the status quo or even to increase their share of economic and political power.

It must also be emphasized that powerful sectors of the Christian churches have opposed liberation theology, on the basis of a broad spectrum of political and theological reasons. This book is meant to constitute a record of both the positive and negative evaluations of the movement that I believe have been most influential historically in the past quarter of a century.

It is, moreover, important to stress that the controversy is far more than a debate within the halls of academe or a squabble between competing groups in the churches. The "preferential option for the poor" espoused by liberation theology and endorsed by the Latin American bishops at Puebla translates today into choosing life for the poor rather than death, in the same urgent way this choice was presented to the people of Israel in the Book of Deuteronomy. And that option is also addressed to all those who own much of the world's resources as a direct and very blunt challenge to convert both their hearts and their institutions to respond to the cause of the poor. For these reasons, and many others that could be mentioned, I believe that a compilation of documents scattered in many languages and in a great variety of sources is an urgent necessity for a more profound understanding of this theology today and for the decades to come.

NOTES

1. Jon Sobrino, *Spirituality of Liberation: Toward Political Holiness* (Maryknoll, N.Y.: Orbis Books, 1988), p. 97.

2. Leonardo and Clodovis Boff, *Liberation Theology: From Dialogue to Confrontation* (San Francisco: Harper and Row, 1986), p. 14.

3. Rebecca S. Chopp, *The Praxis of Suffering: An Interpretation of Liberation and Political Theologies* (Orbis Books, 1986), p. 153.

4. Enrique Dussel, *Liberación y cautiverio: Debates en torno al método de la teología en América Latina* (Mexico City: Imprenta Venecia, 1976), p. 35. Dussel's account of the stages of theology occupies pp. 19-68.

5. Juan Luis Segundo, *The Shift within Latin American Theology* (Toronto: Regis College Press, 1983), p. 2.

6. The general use of this term is usually attributed to Peter Berger and Thomas Luckman, *The Social Construction of Reality: A Treatise in the Sociology of Knowledge* (Garden City, N.Y.: Doubleday, 1967).

7. This statement was made by Jon Sobrino in a conversation at the Woodstock Theological Center, Georgetown University, in 1982.

8. *A Theology of Liberation: History, Politics, and Salvation* (Orbis Books, 1973). The discussion of method and quotes are found in chapter 1, pp. 3-19.

9. Juan Luis Segundo, *The Liberation of Theology* (Orbis Books, 1976), p. 8.

10. Ibid., p. 9.

11. Ibid., p. 13.

12. Leonardo and Clodovis Boff, *Introducing Liberation Theology* (Orbis Books, 1987), p. 11.

13. Ibid., p. 15.

14. *The Power of the Poor in History: Selected Writings* (Orbis Books, 1983); *We Drink from Our Own Wells: The Spiritual Journey of a People* (Orbis Books, 1984).

15. Orbis Books, 1978.

16. *Liberating Grace* (Orbis Books, 1979); *The Maternal Face of God: The Feminine and Its Religious Expression* (San Francisco: Harper and Row, 1987); *Passion of Christ, Passion of the World* (Orbis Books, 1987); *Church: Charism and Power: Liberation Theology and the Institutional Church* (New York: Crossroad, 1985).

17. *A Theology for Artisans of a New Humanity* (Orbis Books, 1973-74); *The Hidden Motives of Pastoral Action: Latin American Reflections* (Orbis Books, 1978); *Theology and the Church: A Response to Cardinal Ratzinger and a Warning to the Whole Church* (New York: Seabury, 1985); *Jesus of Nazareth Yesterday and Today* (Orbis Books, 1984-88).

18. *Christology at the Crossroads* (Orbis Books, 1978); *Jesus in Latin America* (Orbis Books, 1987).

19. *The True Church and the Poor* (Orbis Books, 1984); *Spirituality of Liberation: Toward Political Holiness* (Orbis Books, 1988).

20. Philadelphia: Fortress, 1975.

21. *Christians and Marxists: The Mutual Challenge of Revolution* (Grand Rapids: Eerdmans, 1976); *Toward a Christian Political Ethics* (Philadelphia: Fortress, 1983); *Faces of Jesus: Latin American Christologies* (Orbis Books, 1984).

LIBERATION THEOLOGY:
A DOCUMENTARY HISTORY

PART I

SEEDS OF A LIBERATING THEOLOGY
(1950s–1962)

The decade of the 1950s in the United States was characterized by a general prosperity and a certain aura of tranquility and even somnolence during the Eisenhower administration. An element of excitement, hope, and idealism was added to the continuing prosperity in 1960 with the inauguration of John Fitzgerald Kennedy, whose unique blend of youth, contagious energy, and inspiring leadership led many Americans to dream new dreams and undertake new commitments both at home and abroad. For American Catholics the election provoked joy and a profound sense of pride, for the charismatic Kennedy was also the first Roman Catholic to be elected to the presidency of the United States. To a lesser but still significant degree, the predominantly Catholic Latin America shared in this euphoria, especially when the young president unveiled his plan for an Alliance for Progress throughout Latin America.

Angelo Roncalli, who became Pope John XXIII, was also destined to leave an indelible imprint on the church and the secular world when he ascended to the throne of Peter in 1958, at the death of Eugenio Pacelli (Pope Pius XII). In contrast to the somewhat aloof and aristocratic Pacelli, "good Pope John" was clearly a man of peasant origins and simple piety. He soon won the affection of the world with his good humor, genuine warmth, and openness to everyone he met. Many concluded that this friendly man would go down in history as a mere "transition pope" because of his advanced years, yet he profoundly startled the church (and especially the Roman Curia) less than a year after the death of Pius XII, on January 25, 1959, by summoning an ecumenical council of bishops from all parts of the world. The Second Vatican Council (1962–1965) turned out to be one of the most important events in the entire history of the church.

Although he was not known as an intellectual, Pope John had another surprise in store for the church when he published two encyclical letters, "Christianity and Social Progress" (*Mater et Magistra;* May 15, 1961) and

"Peace on Earth" (*Pacem in Terris;* April 11, 1963). These writings certainly changed the course of Catholic social thought and also profoundly influenced the council, for John had moved the church's thinking from domestic issues to a vision of the entire planet and to a truly global social analysis and prescriptions for reform.

These events also exercised a profound influence on the church in Latin America. There were other events that did not attract much attention in the United States but deeply affected the Latins. One was American involvement in the overthrow of a reformist government in Guatemala in 1954, which awakened antagonisms still smoldering from a long history of American interventions, especially in Central America. Another was the victory of the Cuban revolution, with the entrance of Fidel Castro and his guerilla band into Havana in 1959. Although Fidel's rule became increasingly autocratic, many seized upon it as a symbol of real change and a model of independence from American imperialism.

As regards the development of liberation theology, however, I believe that there was one phenomenon or realization in the Latin American church that was crucial. This was the awareness, gradually and painfully emerging into consciousness, that for centuries it had been a "mirror" church, reflecting the experience, pastoral approaches, and theological works of Europe and to a lesser extent of the United States. In the 1950s it took the first hesitant steps on a new and unexplored path, a path leading to the formation of a "source" church—that is, one that drew its inspiration and sustenance from its own historical and cultural experience, from its own pastoral needs and challenges, and, as a result of all this, from its own unique approach to the practice of Christian reflection that is called theology. It was only later (in 1971, to be exact) that this indigenous type of reflection began to be referred to as the "theology of liberation."

It is of the utmost importance, moreover, to note the most crucial element in this new form of consciousness. That element is a profound realization that, unlike the United States and Europe, Latin America constituted an enormous ocean of poverty with a few islands of extravagant wealth and conspicuous consumption. Theologically speaking, this horror was gradually recognized as a situation of sin, and sin that was "mortal," because it continued incessantly to bring death to millions of human beings. As a direct consequence of this, the church gradually arrived at a fundamental pastoral option which would have profound and far-reaching implications, that is, the "preferential option for the poor." This option will be analyzed further in many of the pages of this book.

In this first chapter, I have selected three articles that graphically represent the beginnings of Latin America's transition from a mirror church to a source church, and thus deserve to be referred to as "seeds of a liberating theology": (1) the educational process known as "conscientization," developed by Paulo Freire as a method of literacy training and later adapted for use by the church; (2) various experiments in Brazil with new forms of church organization that gradually came to be known as "basic ecclesial communities" (BECs), as analyzed by the Dutch missionary and scripture scholar, Carlos Mesters, and (3) an early example by Juan Luis Segundo of the kind of indigenous theological reflection that was taking place even before the Second Vatican Council and more than a decade before the use of the term "liberation theology."

1

Paulo Freire
"Conscientizing as a Way of Liberating"
(1970)

*Paulo Freire was born in Recife in the desperately poor northeast section of
Brazil. He became a lawyer, and took a position as counsel for local labor
unions. In the course of this work, he took part in numerous adult education
seminars for workers, and this finally led him to his lifetime vocation as an
educator, especially in the area of literacy programs for adults. His technique
of conscientization is described in his best-known work,* The Pedagogy of the
Oppressed *(New York: Seabury, 1973). The following article by Freire is taken
from* LADOC *Keyhole Series 1 (Washington, D. C.: U. S. Catholic Conference, n. d.). The informal style of the article is explained by the fact that it is
a taped version of a talk given by Freire in Rome in 1970 and published in the
March 1971 isssue of the Mexican quarterly,* Contacto.

A discussion of conscientization calls for a number of preliminary remarks, and I would like to begin today by telling where that great mouthful
of a word "conscientization" came from.

Many people, especially in Latin America and the United States, insist
that I invented that strange word, because it is a central idea in my thoughts
on education. But I didn't. The word was born during a series of round
table meetings of professors at the Brazilian Institute of Higher Studies
(ISEB), which was created after the "liberating" revolution of 1964, under
the wing of the Ministry of Education.

The word was excogitated by some one of the professors there, but I
really can't remember who. Anyway, it came out of our group reflections.
I recall, among others who met there with us, Prof. Alvaro Pinto, a great
philosopher who wrote a book, *Science and National Reality,* and a more
recent one entitled *Science, Awareness and Existence.* There was also a sociologist, Professor Guerreiro, who is presently at the University of Cali-
fornia.

I used to compare notes regularly with all of them, and it was there at the ISEB that for the first time I heard the word "conscientization." As soon as I heard it, I realized the profundity of its meaning, since I was fully convinced that education, as an exercise in freedom, is an act of knowing, a critical approach to reality. It was inevitable, then, that the word became a part of the terminology I used thereafter to express my pedagogical views, and it easily came to be thought of as something I had created.

Helder Camara was the one who popularized the term and gave it currency in English. Thus, thanks to him rather than to me, the word caught on in Europe and in the United States.

In 1965 I wrote an article for the review *Civilisation et Développement* entitled "Education and Conscientization." But it was Helder Camara who, as I have said, in his wanderings about the world, popularized the word so that it is a commonplace today in the United States, where a great number of articles are being written about conscientization. Nonetheless, I am more and more convinced that the word should really be used in its Brazilian form, *conscientização,* and spelled that way. That is why I entitled an article I recently wrote in English "The Conscientização Progress," not "The Conscientization Process."

What is *conscientization?* I have noticed that conscientization is frequently taken to be synonymous with the French expression *prise de conscience,* yet the two must be carefully distinguished. To show why, let me define the scope of each of them. As a matter of fact, conscientization is possible only because a *prise de conscience* is possible. If human beings were not able to *become aware,* there wouldn't be any conscientization.

Well then, what is this conscientization?

One of the distinguishing traits of humankind is that only it can stand off from the world and the reality of things around it. Only humankind can stand at a distance from a thing and admire it.

As they objectivize or admire a thing (admire is taken here in the philosophical sense of ad-miring, looking at), humans are able to consciously act on the objectivized reality. That, precisely, is the human praxis, the action-reflection on the world, on reality. And yet, in their approach to the world, humans have a preliminary moment in which the world, the objective reality, doesn't yet come to them as a knowable object of their critical consciousness. In other words, in their spontaneous approach to the world, the normal, basic human attitude is not a critical, but an ingenuous one.

Not that there is no knowledge of reality at this spontaneous stage: but what we don't have yet is a critical attitude. There is one kind of perception of reality that gives us a real, if limited, knowledge of it: the Greeks called it *doxa* (mere opinion, or belief). Knowledge that stays at the level of mere *doxa* and goes no further to the level of a task (the reality's reason for being, as Mao Tse-tung would say) never becomes full knowledge, it is not a *logos* of reality.

To become aware, then, all it takes is to be a human being. All it takes is to be human to seize reality in the dialectical relations that flow between humankind and the world, the world and humankind; those relations are so intimate that we really shouldn't talk about humankind and *world,* but just about humankind, or perhaps world-human. This first level of apprehension of reality is what the French mean by *prise de conscience.* The taking awareness of reality exists precisely because as situated beings—closed beings, in Gabriel Marcel's words—human beings are with and in the world, gazing at it.

This *prise de conscience* is not yet conscientization, however. Conscientization is a *prise de conscience* that goes deeper; it is the critical development of a *prise de conscience.* Hence, conscientization implies going beyond the spontaneous phase of apprehension of reality to a critical phase, where reality becomes a knowable object, where the human takes an epistemological stance and tries to know. Thus, conscientization is a probing of the ambience, of reality. The more persons conscientize themselves the more they unveil reality and get at the phenomenic essence of the object they stand in front of, to analyze it. For that same reason, conscientization without a praxis, i. e., without action-reflection as two paired, dialecticized elements permanently constituting that special way of being in the world (or transforming it), is peculiar to human beings.

Conscientization implies a historical commitment. Conscientization, then, is a commitment in time. In fact, there is no conscientization without historical commitment. So that conscientization is also a historical awareness. It is a critical insertion into history. It means that humans take on a role as subjects making the world, remaking the world; it asks humans to fashion their existence out of the material that life offers them. The more they are conscientized, the more they exist.

The mere fact of finding oneself oppressed will move a step ahead and become a process of liberation only if this discovery leads to a historical commitment that means involvement. For involvement is more than commitment: it is a critical insertion into history in order to create it, to mold it. And so, when oppressed individuals see they are oppressed, if they do not set out to do something to transform the concrete oppressing reality, they are not historically committed, and they thus are not really conscientized.

Conscientization implies, then, that when I realize that I am oppressed, I also know I can liberate myself if I transform the concrete situation where I find myself oppressed. Obviously, I can't transform it in my head: that would be to fall into the philosophical error of thinking that awareness "creates" reality, I would be decreeing that I am free by my mind. And yet, the structures would continue to be the same as ever—so that I wouldn't be free. No, conscientization implies a critical insertion into a process, it implies a historical commitment to make changes. That is why conscientization bids us to adopt a utopian attitude toward the world, an attitude that turns the one conscientized into a utopian agent. Before going any further, let me explain what I mean by that word "utopian."

The acts of denouncing and announcing. For me, utopian does not mean something unrealizable, nor is it idealism. Utopia is the dialectization in the acts of denouncing and announcing—denouncing the dehumanizing structure and announcing the structure that will humanize. Hence it is also a historical commitment. A utopia supposes that we know critically. It is an act of knowledge. For I cannot denounce the dehumanizing structure unless I get at it and know it. Nor can I announce, either, unless I know. But—this is important—between the moment of an announcement and the accomplishment of it there is a great difference: the announcement is not the announcement of a project, but of an ante-project. Because the ante-project becomes a project only through a historical praxis. Besides, between the ante-project and the moment of accomplishing or concretizing the project, a period intervenes that we call historical commitment. For this reason, only utopians—and revolutionaries too, to the extent that they are utopians (what was Marx but a utopian? what was Che Guevara if not a utopian?)—can be prophetic and hopeful.

Only those who announce and denounce, who are permanently committed to a radical process of transforming the world so that human beings can be more, only they can be prophetic. Reactionaries, oppressors, cannot be utopian, they cannot be prophetic, and because they cannot be prophetic, they cannot have hope.

What future have oppressors but to preserve their present status as oppressors? What scope for denouncing can oppressors have, other than the denunciation of those who denounce them? What scope for announcing do oppressors have, other than the announcement of their myths? And what can be the hope of those who have no future?

I see a great possibility here for a theology, the utopian theology of hope. The utopian posture of the denouncing, announcing, historically committed Christians who are convinced that the historical vocation of humankind is not to adapt, not to bend to pressures, not to spend 90 percent of their time making concessions in order to salvage what we call the historical vocation of the church. We humans have an unbelievable historical vocation, and we cannot jeopardize it for any one fact, nor can we compromise it for any single, isolated problem, because the church has the whole world. Why, then, risk one's entire historical task over any single fact? That would be, not to be utopian, but to be, literally, Machiavellian, horribly Machiavellian. It would be to concede, and to forfeit one's soul in the concession.

CONSCIENTIZATION RESHAPES REALITY

Conscientization clearly has to do with utopia. The more we are conscientized, the more we become, by the commitment that we assume to change things, announcers and denouncers. This commitment ought to be permanent, though, because if after denouncing a dehumanizing structure and announcing a more human one, after committing ourselves with reality (after all, the project is going to be accomplished only if we work at it), after understanding the project and being convinced of its importance (being conscientized about it), if we were then to stop being utopian, we would simply bureaucratize ourselves. This is the danger inherent in any revolution, once it ceases to be permanent. One masterly way to avoid that danger is by a cultural revolution, that dialecticalization which has no yesterday, today, or tomorrow, and which avoids becoming static because it is an ongoing effort for change.

That's what conscientization is: a seizing of reality; and for that very reason, for the very utopian strain that permeates it, we can call it a reshaping of reality. Conscientization demythologizes. Obvious and impressive as the fact may be, an oppressor can never conscientize for liberation. (How would I possibly demythologize if I am an oppressor?) A humanizing endeavor can only be an endeavor to demythify. Conscientization, then, is the most critical approach conceivable to reality, stripping it down so as to get to know it and know the myths that deceive and perpetuate the dominating structure.

One might protest: "But how can we ever find the process, the how of conscientization?"

The how of it brings up an important point, one that seems to me to be the essential difference between education as a means of domination and education as a means of liberation.

An education that is used to domesticate merely transfers knowledge, as the educator passes on his thirst for knowing to his pupils, who, passively, receive that knowledge. In that sort of relationship, conscientization is impossible. We can see a certain incipient conscientization in it, though, despite that education, in the way the students react, because the natural intentionality of human awareness cannot be thwarted by any educator's domesticating purpose.

A conscientizing—and therefore liberating—education is not that transfer of neatly wrapped knowledge in which there certainly is no knowledge; it is a true act of knowing. Through it, both teacher and pupils simultaneously become knowing subjects, brought together by the object they are knowing. There is no longer one who thinks, who knows, standing in front of others who admit they don't know, that they have to be taught. Rather, all of them are inquisitive learners, avid to learn.

EDUCATION FOR FREEDOM

Those who propagate the superstructure's myths are, equivalently, bringing the superstructure itself right into the infrastructure—and thereby conditioning the infrastructure, too. In any serious changeover, such as a revolution, the myths from the previous structure will carry over and continue to influence the new governmental structure. Unless we critically grasp this fact, we will never understand how, even after an infrastructure has been changed, people will continue to think as they did before.

An understanding of this dialectic and this sort of subdetermination (which Marx certainly had) will persuade us that a mechanistic view of social changes is no good. Someone with a mechanistic approach would expect that if the infrastructure were changed, the superstructure would automatically be changed too—but that is not what happens. That was the problem that baffled Lenin, after the Soviet Revolution; Stalin wrestled with it—and solved it finally by shooting down the peasants. It is the dilemma facing Fidel Castro today with his peasants, though it is not so crucial for him. It is also the problem that Mao Tse-tung had and has, but he came up with the most genial solution of the century: China's cultural revolution.

What is cultural action? What is a cultural revolution? In generic terms, but in the good sense of the phrase, it is the way we culturally attack culture. It means to see culture always as a problem and not to let it become static, becoming a myth and mystifying us.

Whereas education, in practice, too often merely inverts the praxis and domesticates students by pumping myths into them, education for freedom, on the other hand, strives to expose that inversion of praxis at the moment it occurs, so that it will not take place. A noble objective, indeed. But how to do it? As we turn our attention to see our misdirected praxis, we fix our eyes on, as the object of our knowledge, that domesticating capability of an inversion of praxis, the very prostituting of our transforming action. At that moment our act of knowing illuminates the action that is the source of our knowing. And right there we have the permanent, constant dynamic of our attitude toward culture itself.

Otherwise we risk falling into an elitist position, hence one that is neither liberating, nor human, nor humanizing. But even supposing that we avoid that pitfall, how are we to undertake a program of cultural action, or of education for freedom, when we know that people are all the while being dominated through the so-called mass media—which are really means for sending messages rather than for communicating, for propagandizing and domesticating rather than for liberating. We must save that word from the distortion being done to it. The term communications media is being made to cover a wholesale invasion by slogans. But communications is not sloganizing: it is something completely different. As all of us recognize, cultural action for freedom is ultimately a kind of action.

Let's turn, for a moment, to the desperate situation of the peasants in northeast Brazil. Their awareness of what is going on is so primitive that they are wholly unable to get a structural view of reality. They are incapable of envisaging their plight as a result, in the world they live in. Yet even a peasant is a man, and any man wants to explain the reality around him. How can he? one might ask. What reasons can he find? How does his dulled brain conceive his wretched lot?

Normally, he will try to size up his situation. He will look for causes, the reasons for his condition, in things higher and more powerful than man.

One such thing is God, whom he sees as the maker, the cause of his condition. Ah, but if God is responsible, man can do nothing. Many Christians today, thanks be to God, are vigorously reacting against that attitude, especially in Brazil. But as a child, I knew many priests who went out to the peasants saying: "Be patient. This is God's will. And anyway, it will earn heaven for you." Yet the truth of the matter is that we have to earn our heaven here and now, we ourselves. We have to build our heaven, to fashion it during our lifetime, right now. Salvation is something to achieve, not just to hope for. This latter sort of theology is a very passive one that I cannot stomach.

How could we make God responsible for this calamity? As if Absolute Love could abandon man to constant victimization and total destitution. That would be a God such as Marx described.

THE IMPOTENCE OF THE OPPRESSED

Whenever men make God responsible for intolerable situations, for oppression, then the dominating structures help to popularize that myth. If God is not the cause, they whisper, then destiny must be. Human reason at this level easily becomes fatalistic; it sits back and sighs: "Nothing can be done about it."

Sometimes another scapegoat is found, and it too is a myth spread by the dominating structure: the helplessness of the oppressed. The dominated mind looks inward and decides that it is totally unable to cope with its misery: it concludes that it is impotent. A Presbyterian clergyman from the United States once told me that the whites in his country say God made the blacks inferior. It was a fine example of what the author of the book *Picture of the Colonized Contrasted with the Picture of the Colonizer* meant when he wrote: "The oppressor always draws a picture of the oppressed." For the oppressed mind in its desperate plight, I repeat, there seems to be nothing that can be done.

For the critical mind, though, for the mind that conscientizes itself, beyond this situation there is the future, what we must do, the thing we must create, the historical futurity we have to bring into being; and to do that, we must change whatever it is that prevents the humanization of our fellow humans.

As we examine the structures and the reasons why they are so intolerable, as we expose the oppressive situation, we are forced to a decision: we either commit ourselves or we don't—but we will have to answer to our consciences for our choice. The process of conscientization leaves no one with his arms folded. It makes some unfold their arms. It leaves others with a guilty feeling, because conscientization shows us that God wants us to act.

As I conscientize myself, I realize that my brothers who don't eat, who don't laugh, who don't sing, who don't love, who live oppressed, crushed and despised, who *are* less each day, are suffering all this because of some reality that is causing it. And at that point I join in the action historically by genuinely loving, by having the courage to commit myself (the term is used here in its psychological sense). A North American theologian has called those rationalizations "fake generosities," because to escape my guilt feelings I go in for philanthropy, I seek compensation by almsgiving, I send a check to build a church, I make contributions: land for a chapel or a monastery for nuns, hoping in that way to buy my peace. But peace cannot be purchased, it is not for sale; peace has to be lived. And I can't live my peace without commitment to humans, and my commitment to them can't exist without their liberation, and their liberation can't exist without the final transformation of the structures that are dehumanizing them. There is only one way for me to find peace: to work for it, shoulder to shoulder with my fellow human beings.

FEAR OF FREEDOM

It is very interesting to observe how in the seminars I have given in various countries, two attitudes are produced. Often I am violently attacked because many people, when they hear me, start to despoil themselves — and their almost immediate second reaction is to strike back at whoever made them do that. Observing this process can be extremely interesting.

A similar process takes place with very simple persons, too. Many of them run away from freedom. Oppression is so potent a thing that it produces fear of freedom. That fear crops up whenever any discussion or even mention of freedom makes them already feel it as a threat. But freedom isn't something that is given. It is something very arduous, because nobody gives freedom to anyone else, no one frees another, nobody can even free himself all alone; humans free themselves only in concert, in communion, collaborating on something wrong that they want to correct. There is an interesting theological parallel to this: no one saves another, no one saves himself all alone, because only in communion can we save ourselves — or not save ourselves. You don't save me, because my soul, my being, my conscious body is not something that A or B can save. We work out our salvation in communion. Each one of us must set out in quest of his salvation, we must do it ourselves. I don't mean that God hasn't saved us by the divine presence in history: I'm talking now on the human level.

CONSCIENTIZATION: A PAINFUL BIRTH

Bringing together all the things I have said, we see that conscientization is a painful birth. There is no palliative for it like those exercises that women use to avoid birth pangs. Conscientization also involves an excruciating moment, a tremendously upsetting one, in those who begin to conscientize themselves, the moment they start to be reborn. Because conscientization demands an Easter. That is, it demands that we die to be reborn again. Christians must live their Easter, and that too is a utopia. Those who don't make their Easter, in the sense of dying in order to be reborn, are not real Christians. That is why Christianity is, for me, such a marvelous doctrine. People have accused me of being a communist, but no communist could say what I have just said. I never had any temptation to cease being, to stop existing. The reason is that I am not yet completely a Catholic; I just keep on trying to be one more completely, day after day. The condition of being is to go on being. I have never yet felt that I had to leave the church, or set aside my Christian convictions, in order to say what I have to say, or go to jail—or even refuse to. I just feel passionately, corporately, physically, with all my being, that my stance is a Christian one because it is 100 percent revolutionary and human and liberating, and hence committed and utopian. And that, as I see it, must be our position, the position of a church that must not forget it is called by its origins to die shivering in the cold. This is a utopia; it is a denunciation and an announcement with a historical commitment that adds up to heroism in love.

Each of us has to give witness, and conscientization is a summons to do that: to be new each day. Hence it is peace, and it enables us to understand others.

Conscientization could never be an imposition on others or a manipulation of them. I cannot impose my opinions on someone else; I can only invite others to share, to discuss. To impose on others my way of not being would be a real contradiction. For loving is not only a free act, it is an act for freedom. And love that cannot produce more freedom is not love.

2

Carlos Mesters
"The Use of the Bible in Christian Communities of the Common People"
(1981)

Carlos Mesters is a Carmelite who has spent most of his life working with the basic ecclesial communities of Brazil. He has a degree in scriptural studies and has concentrated on the function of the Bible in these communities. He is also a prolific author and has conducted workshops on the base communities in many countries throughout Latin America. This article is from Sergio Torres and John Eagleson, eds., The Challenge of Basic Christian Communities *(Maryknoll, N. Y.: Orbis Books, 1981), pp. 197-210.*

PRELIMINARY OBSERVATIONS

LIMITATIONS OF THIS REPORT

The information I am going to pass along to you is limited for several reasons. First of all, I am going to talk to you only about Brazil because I am not that familiar with the rest of Latin America. Second, I am going to talk only about the Catholic Church in Brazil because I know relatively little about other Christian churches. I am just now beginning to make an acquaintance with them. Third, my report is limited by the fact that there is this "opening up" process now going on in Brazil. That may well force me to rethink a lot of the things I am going to say about the past twelve years or so in Brazil. Finally, my report is limited by my own eyesight. Even though I wear glasses and have good intentions, I find it hard to grasp certain sides of reality—the political side in particular. That may be due to the fact that when I got my education the social sciences and their findings were not a part of the picture.

THE IMPORTANCE OF THE BIBLE IN GRASSROOTS CHRISTIAN COMMUNITIES

The Bible is very important in the life and growth of grassroots communities. But its importance must be put in the right place. It's something like the motor of an automobile. Generally the motor is under the hood, out of sight. It is not the steering wheel. The history of the use of the Bible in grassroots communities is a bit like the history of car motors. Way back when the first cars came out, the motor was huge. It was quite obvious and made a lot of noise. It also wasted a lot of gasoline and left little room for passengers. Today the motors are getting smaller and smaller. They are more powerful, but they are also quieter and better hidden. There's a lot more leg room and luggage room in the car. Much the same is true about the Bible and its function in the life of Christian communities. The Bible is supposed to start things off, to get them going; but it is not the steering wheel. You have to use it correctly. You can't expect it to do what it is not meant to do.

MY RELATIVE OPTIMISM

Perhaps what I am going to say to you may seem a trifle optimistic. If so, it is something like the optimism of a farmer watching the grain surface above ground. A storm may come later and wipe out the whole crop. But there is room for optimism, and it's good to be optimistic.

INTRODUCING THE ISSUE: THREE BASIC SITUATIONS

FIRST SITUATION

In Brazil there are many groups meeting to focus on the Bible. In this case the motivating occasion for the group is some pious exercise or special event: a feast day, a novena, a brotherhood week, or what have you. The people meet on the parish level. There is no real community context involved. The word of God is the only thing that brings them together. They want to reflect on God's word and put it into practice.

SECOND SITUATION

In Brazil some groups are meeting within a broader context. They are meeting on the level of the community and its life. I once went to give a course to the people in such a community. In the evening the people got together to organize the course and establish basic guidelines. In such groups you generally get questions such as these: "How do you explain the Apocalypse? What does the serpent stand for? What about the fight between David and Goliath?"

The questions, you see, are limited to the Bible as such. No hint of their own concerns, no hint of real-life problems, no hint of reality, no hint of problems dealing with the economic, social, and political life. Even though they are meeting as a community, the real-life problems of the people are not brought up.

THIRD SITUATION

To introduce the third situation, I am going to tell you a typical story about my experience in this area. I was invited to give a course in Ceará, in northeast Brazil. The group was made up of about ninety farmers from the backlands and the riverbanks. Most of them couldn't read. In the evening we met to get things organized. They asked me about a dozen basic questions, but these are the ones I remember:

1. What about these community activities we are engaged in? Are they just the priest's idea? Are they communism? Or do they come from the word of God?

2. What about our fight for land? (Most of them had no land. But they had plenty of problems and fights on their hands.) What about our labor struggles and our attempts to learn something about politics? What does the word of God have to say about all that?

3. What about the gospel message? Does it have to do just with prayer, or is it something more than that?

4. The other day, in a place where there was a big fight going on between the landlord and his tenants, this priest came, said Mass, and explained the gospel in a way that made the landlord right. Then the local priest of the parish read the same gospel and explained it in a way that made the tenant farmers right. So who really is right?

5. The landlord gives catechism lessons that teach subservience and bondage. In our community we have a catechetics of liberation, and the landlord persecutes us for it. So how do we settle the matter and figure it all out? We want to know whether the Bible is on our side or not!

Here we have three basic situations. In the first situation the group involved comes together solely for the sake of discussing the Bible; the Bible is the only thing that unites them and they stick to it. In the second situation the people focus on the Bible, too, but they come together as a community. In the third situation we have a community of people meeting around the Bible who inject concrete reality and their own situation into the discussion. Their struggle as a people enters the picture. So we can formulate the basic picture of Figure 1.

We find three elements in the common people's interpretation of the Bible: the Bible itself, the community, and reality (i.e., the real-life situation of the people and the surrounding world). With these three elements they seek to hear what the word of God is saying. And for them the word of God is not just the Bible. The word of God is within reality and it can be discovered there with the help of the Bible. When one of the three elements is missing, however, interpretation of the Bible makes no progress and enters into crisis. The Bible loses its function.

When the three elements are present and enter the process of interpretation, then you get the situation that I encountered when I gave a course in Ceará. The people asked me to tell them the stories of Abraham, Moses,

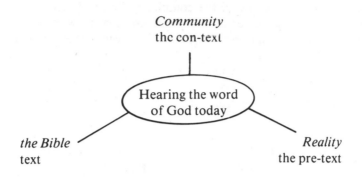

Jeremiah, and Jesus. That is what I did. But in their group discussions and full meetings, the Bible disappeared. They hardly ever talked about the Bible. Instead they talked about real life and their concrete struggles. So at the nightly review the local priest asked them what they had learned that day. They quickly got to talking about real life. No one said anything about the Bible. Ye gods, I thought to myself, where did I go wrong? This is supposed to be a course on the Bible and all they talk about is real life. Should I feel upset and frustrated, or should I be satisfied? Well, I decided to take it easy and feel satisfied because the Bible had achieved its purpose. Like salt, it had disappeared into the pot and spiced the whole meal.

It's like what happens when you take a sponge and dip it in a little bowl of water. The water is soaked up and disappears inside the sponge. At the end of the nightly review the people were asked what they had learned from the biblical explanations. They squeezed the sponge a bit and let a few drops of water out. I could see that the sponge was filled with water. At the final ceremony for the week, which lasted four hours, they squeezed the sponge completely and everything inside came out. I realized that when the three elements are integrated—Bible, community, real-life situation— then the word of God becomes a reinforcement, a stimulus for hope and courage. Bit by bit it helps people to overcome their fears.

CONCLUSIONS

1. When the community takes shape on the basis of the real-life problems of the people, then the discovery of the Bible is an enormous reinforcement.

2. When the community takes shape only around the reading of the Bible, then it faces a crisis as soon as it must move on to social and political issues.

3. When the group closes itself up in the letter of the biblical text and does not bring in the life of the community or the reality of the people's struggles, then it has no future and will eventually die.

4. These three factors or situations characterize the use of the Bible by the common people and reveal the complexity involved. The three situations can be successive stages in a single ongoing process, or they can be antagonistic situations that obstruct and exclude each other. It all depends on how the process is conducted.

5. It doesn't matter much where you start. You can start with the Bible, or with the given community, or with the real-life situation of the people and their problems. The important thing is to do all you can to include all three factors.

SOME OBSTACLES AND HOW THE PEOPLE ARE SURMOUNTING THEM

It is not always easy to integrate all three factors in the interpretation of the Bible. There are many obstacles along the way that the people are trying to surmount in various ways.

MANY DON'T KNOW HOW TO READ

Many people don't know how to read, and the Bible is a book! Sometimes no one in the group knows how to read. They are inventing ways to get around this problem. They are using song and story, pictures and little plays. They are thus making up their own version of the "Bible of the poor." Thanks to songs, for example, many people who have never read the Bible know almost every story in it.

SLAVISH LITERALISM

Another obstacle is slavery to the letter or fundamentalism. This usually occurs when the Bible is read in dissociation from a real-life community and concrete situation. The circle closes and the letter becomes a source of further oppression rather than of liberation.

The Bible is ambiguous. It can be a force for liberation or a force for oppression. If it is treated like a finished monument that cannot be touched, that must be taken literally as it is, then it will be an oppressive force.

Three things can help to overcome this obstacle. The first is the good sense of the people. In one community composed of blacks and other farmers the people were reading the Old Testament text that forbade the eating of pork. The people raised the question: "What is God telling us today through this text?" Their conclusion was: "Through this text God today is ordering us to eat the flesh of pork." How did they arrive at such a contrary conclusion? They explained: "God is concerned first and foremost with life and health. In those times eating the flesh of pork was very dangerous to people's health. It was prohibited in God's name because people's lives had to be protected. Today we know how to care of pork meat, and the only thing we have to feed our children are the piglets in our yards. So in this text God is bidding us to eat the flesh of pork."

A second thing of great importance in breaking through enslavement to the letter is the ongoing action of a local church that takes sides with the poor. The ongoing movement of the church in this direction is helping to ensure that questions focused exclusively on the letter of the biblical text gradually give way to others. Literalist questions are falling from the tree like dry leaves to make room for new buds. The larger complex of a local church that sides with the poor and joins their fight for justice is very important in correctly channeling the people's interpretation of the Bible.

The third thing has to do with the various devices of a fairly simple kind. For example, we can show people that many of the things we talk about in words cannot be taken literally. Symbolism is an integral part of human language. In many instances the first step toward liberation comes for people when they realize that they need not always take the biblical text literally. They discover that "the letter kills, the Spirit gives life." This realization unlocks the lid and lets new creativity out.

THE CONCEPTION OF TIME

Another problem or obstacle is the people's conception of time. Often folks will ask questions like these: "Did Abraham come before or after Jesus Christ? Did David live before or after Cabral discovered America? Was it Jesus Christ who created the world?" Such questions may seem to indicate a great deal of confusion to us, but I think not. Apart from a certain amount of ignorance about the content of the Bible, I don't think it is a matter of confusion at all. Instead it is an expression of their circular conception of time. In such a conception you don't know exactly what comes at the beginning and what comes at the end. A simple explanation will not suffice to change this view of time, because it is a cultural problem rather than a problem of mere ignorance. In their minds the people simply don't have a peg on which to hang a concept of linear time.

How do we help them to overcome this obstacle? How do we unroll the carpet of time in their consciousness? Perhaps the best way we can help is to help them discover their own ongoing journey in their lives today. We can help them to recover the memory of their own history, of struggles lost and forgotten. We can help them to begin to recount their own history. In Goiás a group of farmworkers was asked: "How did the Bible come about?" An old farmer gave this reply: "I know. It was something like this. Suppose fifty years from now someone asks how our community arose. The people will reply: In the beginning there was nothing here. . . ." Thanks to his own concrete journey in life, the old farmworker perceived that the Bible had arisen from narrative accounts, from stories people told to others about their history. He realized that the Bible was the collective memory that gave a people its identity.

DEPENDENCE ON INFORMATIONAL KNOWLEDGE AND THE LEARNED EXPERT

You often hear people say something like this: "I don't know anything. You or Father should do the talking. You're the ones who know things. We folks don't know anything." In the past we members of the clergy expropriated the Bible and got a monopoly on its interpretation. We took the Bible out of the hands of the common people, locked it with a key, and then threw the key away. But the people have found the key and are beginning again to interpret the Bible. And they are using the only tool they have at hand: their own lives, experiences, and struggles.

Biblical exegetes, using their heads and their studies, can come fairly close to Abraham; but their feet are a long way from Abraham. The common people are very close to Abraham with their feet. They are living the same sort of situation. Their life process is of the same nature and they can identify with him. When they read his history in the Bible, it becomes a mirror for them. They look in that mirror, see their own faces, and say: "We are Abraham!" In a real sense they are reading their own history, and this becomes a source of much inspiration and encouragement. One time a farmworker said this to me: "Now I get it. We are Abraham, and if he got there then we will too!" From the history of Abraham he and his people are drawing the motives for their courage today.

Now here is where the danger comes in. Some teacher or learned expert may come along. It might be a pastoral minister, a catechist, or an exegete. This expert may arrive with his or her more learned and sophisticated approach and once again expropriate the gains won by the people. Once again they grow silent and dependent in the presence of the teacher or expert. Our method is logical. It involves a reasoning process, a careful line of argument. We say it is scientific. When the people get together to interpret the Bible, they do not proceed by logical reasoning but by the association of ideas. One person says one thing; somebody else says another thing. We tend to think this approach has little value, but actually it is just as scientific as our approach! What approach do psychoanalysts use when they settle their patients into a chair or couch? They use the free association of ideas. And this method is actually better than our "logical" method. Our method is one for teaching information; the other is one for helping people to discover things themselves.

LACK OF TACT ON THE PART OF PASTORAL AGENTS

Another obstacle that crops up at times is the lack of tact on the part of pastoral workers among the people. They are in a hurry and have no patience. They ride roughshod over some of the natural resistance that people have to our interpretations of the Bible. One time a nun went to give a course on the Old Testament. Halfway through she had to close down the course because no one was showing up. The people said: "Sister is destroying the Bible!" A certain priest offered an explanation of the exodus. Many people never came back. "He is putting an end to miracles," they complained.

Meddling with the faith of the people is very serious business. You must have deep respect and a delicate touch. You must try to feel as they would and intuit their possible reaction to what you are going to say. The people should be allowed to grow from the soil of their own faith and their own character. They should not be dragged along by our aggressive questions.

ERUDITE LANGUAGE

Another obstacle is erudite language, abstruse words. We talk a difficult idiom, and the language of translations is difficult. Today, thank God, various efforts are being made to translate the Bible into more popular terms. Nothing could be more desirable. People now feel that they are getting the point at least. The first and most basic requirement is that people talk in such a way that their listeners can understand them. It sounds simple enough, but often it is very hard to do.

Another important point is that we must not lose the poetry of the Bible. We must not reduce it to concepts. The Bible is full of poetry, and poetry is more than a matter of words. It is the whole way of seeing and grasping life.

FROM CONFRONTATION TO PRACTICAL ECUMENISM

Another problem crops up on the grassroots level with "fundamentalist" groups. They head for people's homes with the Bible in their hands and make it clear that they have the only right answer. This leads to a defensive reaction and sectarian apologetics. It is hard to foster any ecumenism around the Bible in such an atmosphere.

In some areas, however, practical biblical ecumenism is growing from other starting points. Roman Catholics and Protestants are meeting each other and working together in labor unions, in fights for land ownership, and in other real-life struggles. Gradually other sectarian issues are taking a back seat to practical ecumenism.

CHARACTERISTICS OF THE PEOPLE'S INTERPRETATION
OF THE BIBLE

In a sense we can say that the tabernacle of the church is to be found where the people come together around the word of God. That could be called the church's "holy of holies." Remember that no one was allowed to enter the holy of holies except the high priest, and he was allowed in only once a year! In this holy of holies no one is master—except God and the people. It is there that the Holy Spirit is at work; and where the Spirit is at work, there is freedom. The deepest and ultimate roots of the freedom sought by all are to be found there, in those small community groups where the people meet around the word of God. One song in Ceará has this line: "It is the tabernacle of the people. Don't anyone touch it!" Certain characteristics are surfacing in this tabernacle, and I should like to point them out here.

The things I am going to mention now are not fully developed and widespread. They are more like the first traces of dawn in the night sky. We are dipping our finger into the batter to savor how the cake will taste when it is baked and ready. The following characteristics are just beginning to surface here and there in the ongoing journey of various communities. I think they are very important.

THE SCOPE OF THE BIBLICAL MESSAGE

In the eyes of the common people the word of God, the gospel message, is much broader than just the text itself. The gospel message is a bit of everything: Bible, community, reality. For the common people the word of God is not just in the Bible; it is also in the community and in their real-life situation. The function of the Bible, read in a community context, is to help them to discover where God is calling them in the hubbub of real life. It is as if the word of God were hidden within history, within their struggles. When they discover it, it is big news. It's like a light flicking on in their brains. When one leper in Acre made this discovery, he exclaimed: "I have been raised from the dead!" He used the idea of resurrection to express the discovery he had made.

Theologians say that reality is a *locus theologicus.* The common people say: "God speaks, mixed into things." A tinker defined the church this way: "The church is us exchanging ideas with each other to discover the idea of the Holy Spirit in the people." If it hadn't come from Antonio Pascal, I would have said it came from St. Augustine. But it came from Antonio Pascal. It is us exchanging ideas with each other to discover the idea of the Holy Spirit in the people. Not in the church, in the people!

So you see, when they read the Bible, basically they are not trying to interpret the Bible; they are trying to interpret life with the help of the Bible. They are altering the whole business. They are shifting the axis of interpretation.

THE UNITY OF CREATION AND SALVATION

The common people are recovering the unity or oneness of creation and salvation, which is certainly true in the Bible itself. The Bible doesn't begin with Abraham. It begins with creation. Abraham is not called to form some group apart. Abraham is called to recover for all peoples the blessing lost by the sin of Adam. This is the oneness between life and faith, between transforming (political) activity and evangelization, that the people are concretely achieving in their praxis.

THE REAPPROPRIATION OF THE BIBLE

The Bible was taken out of the people's hands. Now they are taking it back. They are expropriating the expropriators: "It is our book! It was written for us!" It had always been "Father's book," it seemed. Now it is the people's book again.

That gives them a new way of seeing, new eyes. They feel at home with the Bible and they begin to link it with their lives. So we get something very interesting. They are mixing life in with the Bible, and the Bible in with life. One helps them to interpret the other. And often the Bible is what starts them developing a more critical awareness of reality. They say, for example: "*We* are Abraham! *We* are in Egypt! *We* are in bondage! *We* are David!" With the biblical data they begin to reflect on their real-life situation. The process gradually prompts them to seek a more objective knowledge of reality and to look for a more suitable tool of analysis elsewhere. But it is often the word of God that starts them moving.

The rediscovery of the Bible as "our book" gives rise to a sense of commitment and a militancy that can overcome the world. Once they discover that God is with them in their struggles, no one can really stop them or deter them. One farmworker from Goiás concluded a letter this way: "When the time comes for me to bear my witness, I will do so without any fear of dying." That is the kind of strength that is surfacing. A sort of resurrection is taking place, as I suggested earlier.

We who have always had the Bible in hand find it difficult to imagine and comprehend the sense of novelty, the gratitude, the joy and the commitment that goes with their reading of the Bible. But that is why these people generally read the Bible in the context of some liturgical celebration. Their reading is a prayer exercise. Rarely will you find a group that reads the Bible simply for better understanding. Almost always their reading is associated with reflection on God present here and now, and hence with prayer. They live in a spirit of gratefulness for God's gift.

HISTORY AS A MIRROR

Another characteristic I hinted at already is the fact that the Bible is not just history for the people; it is also a mirror. Once upon a time we used to talk about the Bible as "letter" and "symbol." Today we might do well to talk about it as "history" and "mirror." The common people are using it as a mirror to comprehend their own lives as a people.

We who study a great deal have a lot more trouble trying to grasp the point of images and symbols. If we want to get a handle on symbolic language, we have to go through a whole process of "demythologizing." We have to go through a long process of study to get the point of the symbol. To us images are opaque glasses; we can't see through them at all. To see at all, we have to punch out the glass and smash it. To the common people in Brazil, an image or symbol is a pair of glasses with a little dust or frost on it. They just wipe them a bit and everything is as clear as day.

I don't think we pay enough attention to this educational item. We are awfully "Europeanized" in our training. Take the question of the historicity of a text. I think you have to approach it very differently, or worry about it differently, when you are dealing with ordinary people. Very often pastoral workers are talking about the Bible and they ask questions like these: "Did that really happen? Did Jesus walk on top of the water? Were there only five loaves and two fishes?" They think that this is the most important problem that the people have with the text in front of them. I don't think so. Once, in Goiás, we read the passage in the New Testament (Acts 17:19) where an angel of the Lord came and freed the apostles from jail. The pastoral worker asked his people: "Who was the angel?" One of the women present gave this answer: "Oh, I know. When Bishop Dom Pedro Casaldáliga was attacked in his house and the police surrounded it with machine guns, no one could get in or out and no one knew what was going on exactly. So this little girl sneaked in without being seen, got a little message from Pedro, ran to the airport, and hitched a ride to Goiana where the bishops were meeting. They got the message, set up a big fuss, and Dom Pedro was set free. So that little girl was the angel of the Lord. And it's really the same sort of thing."

The people don't always take things literally. They are far smarter than you would think. Our question simply will have to take more account of the way that ordinary people understand history. They are far more capable of understanding symbols than we assume.

DISLOCATIONS

Gustavo spoke earlier of the irruption of the poor. When there are only five persons in a room, then each one can be pretty much at ease. When fifty more persons enter the room, then the original five find themselves a bit crowded and some moving around has to take place. Well, the common people have entered the precincts of biblical interpretation and they are causing much shifting and dislocation.

A Shift in Standpoint

First of all, the Bible itself has shifted its place and moved to the side of the poor. One could almost say that it has changed its class status. This is important. The place where the people read the Bible is a different place. We read the Bible something like the wealthy car owner who looks out over the top of his car and sees a nice chrome finish. The common people read the Bible something like the mechanic under the car who looks up and sees a very different view of the same car.

The common people are discovering things in the Bible that other readers don't find. At one session we were reading the following text: "I have heard the cries of my people." A woman who worked in a factory offered this commentary: "The Bible does not say that God has heard the praying of the people. It says that God has heard the cries of his people. I don't mean that people shouldn't pray. I mean that people should imitate God. Very often we work to get people to go to church and pray first; and only then will we pay heed to their cries." You just won't find that sort of interpretation in books.

The Bible has changed its place, and the place where the common people read the Bible is different. It is the place where one can appreciate the real import of Jesus' remark: "I thank thee, Father . . . that thou has hidden these things from the wise and understanding and revealed them to babes; yea, Father, for such was thy gracious will" (Matt. 11:25–26). If you take sides with the poor, you will discern things in the Bible that an exegete does not see. All of us have a slight blind spot that prevents us from seeing certain things.

FROM BIBLICAL TEXT TO REAL LIFE

Another shift mentioned earlier has to do with the fact that the word of God has moved in a certain sense from the Bible to real life. It is in the Bible but it is also in real life — especially in real life. So we come to the following conclusion: the Bible is not the one and only history of salvation; it is a kind of "model experience." Every single people has *its own* history of salvation.

Clement of Alexandria said: "God saved the Jews in a Jewish way, the barbarians in a barbarian way." We could go on to say: "God saves Brazilians in a Brazilian way, blacks in a black way, Indians in an Indian way, Nicaraguans in a Nicaraguan way, and so on." Each people has its own unique history. Within that history it must discover the presence of God the Liberator who journeys by its side. The scope of this particular dislocation is most important.

FROM MEANING IN ITSELF TO MEANING FOR US

Another dislocation is to be found in the fact that emphasis is not placed on the text's meaning in itself but rather on the meaning the text has for the people reading it. At the start people tend to draw any and every sort of meaning, however well or ill founded, from the text. Only gradually, as they proceed on their course in life, do they begin to develop an interest in the historical import and intrinsic meaning of the text. It is at this point that they can benefit greatly from a study of the material conditions of the people in biblical times: that is, their religious, political, and socio-economic situation. But they do so in order to give a better grounding to the text's meaning "for us." In this framework scientific exegesis can reclaim its proper role and function, placing itself in the service of the biblical text's meaning "for us."

FROM ABSTRACT UNDERSTANDING TO A COMMUNITY SENSE

The common people are doing something else very important. They are reintroducing faith, community, and historical reality into the process of interpretation. When we studied the Bible back in the seminary in the old days, we didn't have to live as a real community or really know much about reality. We didn't even have to have faith. All we needed was enough brains to understand Greek and Hebrew and to follow the professor's line of reasoning.

Now the common people are helping us to realize that without faith, community, and reality we cannot possibly discover the meaning that God has put in that ancient tome for us today. Thus the common people are recovering something very important: the *sensus ecclesiae* ("sense of the church"). The community is the reasonance chamber; the text is a violin string. When the people pluck the string (the biblical text), it resonates in the community and out comes the music. And that music sets the people dancing and singing. The community of faith is like a big pot in which Bible and community are cooked just right until they become one tasty dish.

FROM NEUTRALITY TO TAKING SIDES

The common people are also eliminating the alleged "neutrality" of scholarly exegesis. No such neutrality is possible. Technology is not neutral, and neither is exegesis.

CLEARING UP OVERLY SPIRITUALIZED CONCEPTS

The common people are giving us a clearer picture of concepts that have been excessively spiritualized. Let me give just one example. Pope Paul VI once delivered an address in which he warned priests not to become overly preoccupied with material things. He urged them to show greater concern for spiritual things. One farmworker in Goiás had this comment: "Yes, the pope is quite right. Many priests concern themselves only with material things, such as building a church or decorating it. They forget spiritual things, such as food for the people!"

That is what the people are doing with such notions as grace, salvation, sin, and so forth. They are dusting them off and showing us that these notions have to do with solid, concrete realities of life.

PUTTING THE BIBLE IN ITS PROPER PLACE

Finally, the common people are putting the Bible in its proper place, the place where God intended it to be. They are putting it in second place. Life takes first place! In so doing, the people are showing us the enormous importance of the Bible and, at the same time, its relative value—relative to life.

PROBLEMS, CHALLENGES, REQUIREMENTS

There are many problems, difficulties, and failings associated with the interpretation of the Bible by the common people. But every good tree has a strong, solid limb that can be pruned when the time comes. The point is that its roots are okay. The common people are reading and interpreting the Bible as a new book that speaks to them here and now. And this basic view of the Bible is the view that the church fathers of the past had when they interpreted the Bible.

Here I simply want to enumerate a few further points that need greater attention.

1. There is the danger of subjectivistic interpretation. This can be combated in two ways: by more objective grounding in the literal sense of the Bible and by reading the Bible in community.

2. It is possible to read the Bible solely to find in it a confirmation of one's own ideas. In this case the biblical text loses its critical function. Community-based reading and interpretation help to overcome this tendentious use of the Bible. In addition, people must have a little humility and a little signal-light in their brains that calls them up short when they are tempted to absolutize their own ideas.

3. People may lack a critical sense in reading and interpreting the biblical text. They may be tempted to take the ancient text and apply it mechanically to today, without paying any serious attention to the difference in historical context.

4. The above three points underline the proper and necessary function of scientific exegesis. Exegesis is being called upon to concern itself, not with the question it raises, but with the questions that the common people are raising. In many cases the exegete is like the person who had studied salt and knew all its chemical properties but didn't know how to cook it. The common people don't know the properties of salt well, but they do know how to season a meal.

5. We need biblical interpretation that will reveal the material living conditions of the people in the Bible. We need a materialist reading and interpretation of the Bible, but not a narrow and confined reading. It must be broad and full.

6. We urgently need to give impetus to ecumenism on the grassroots

level. It is a hard and challenging task, but a beginning has been made here and there.

7. The Bible is a book derived from a rural environment. Today we live in an urban environment. Rereading the Bible today here in São Paulo, in this urban reality, presents no easy task of interpretation.

8. There is the matter of revolutionary effectiveness and gratitude for the Father's gift. This is another matter that needs further exploration.

9. Criticism can be derived from the word of God to foster transforming action.

Juan Luis Segundo, S. J.
"The Future of Christianity in Latin America" (November 1962)

This article is a talk that Fr. Segundo gave to a group of Catholic students in Paris, and very obviously reflects the context of Latin America and the requirements for evangelization there and not the context of Europe. This development represents a real beginning of liberation theology. It should also be noted that 1962 was the year in which he published the book Función de la Iglesia en la realidad rioplatense *[The function of the church in the area of the Plate River] (Montevideo: Barreiro y Ramos, 1962). The very title of this book shows that at this time he was writing a distinctively* Latin American *ecclesiology. Given the amount of time required for writing and then publishing a book, the book must have been begun at least a year and probably two years before its publication. It has not been translated into English. The English translation for the article below is taken from* Cross Currents, *13 (Summer 1963), pp. 273-81. The original French text appeared in* Lettres *[Paris] (November 1962).*

Latin America is a world on the move. The speed of its movement can be measured only from within. Unfortunately, what the visitor sees and what is printed abroad about Latin America is usually "local color" — precisely that aspect of our society which is not changing. The swiftness of social change in a continent without the traditions that are the strength of Western civilization in Europe is not easy to understand.

Nevertheless, Latin America is a *Western* world on the move; here again the view of a foreigner may be distorted by exotic local color associated with the area. It is part of the West that is evolving; our peoples participate in Western culture; they have read the same books and have been brought up in the same way. Despite some variations of temperament or character, as from one region to another in any country, basically they are not very different. This is the Western world; it is the culture of the West that is changing in Latin America — and changing at great speed.

Finally, Latin America is a *Christian* world on the move. Our religion is involved in this change. And it is precisely the speed and depth of this movement changing Latin America that pose very difficult problems for the Christian — deeper problems, or at least more obvious problems than those posed elsewhere. Change calls for a reaction; one has to respond with a clear vision of what one wants. There is change elsewhere, but it is slower; in Latin America we are obliged to reflect on how to impress Christian concepts on new institutions, on the freshly minted realities of this new world.

This movement confronts Christians with three obvious and basic problems that must be carefully solved:

1. The breakdown of closed societies — the impossibility of maintaining Christian ghettos or of preserving the "Christian environment."

2. The compromised relationship between Christian institutions and the social relationships of an existing system; this is something that is inevitably bound up with the task of maintaining, not church institutions as such (parishes, dioceses, etc.), but civic institutions in which Christians will feel at home, with a mentality and program that is apparently Christian (religious schools, Christian political parties and trade unions, Catholic universities and newspapers).

3. Christian action in a pluralistic world. Christians are not alone; change touches everyone in these countries. The Christian must know how to act alongside others who have other ideologies, other ways of thinking. Since our continent is going through a revolutionary process at breakneck speed, Christians must consciously face the problem of how they will work with others and to what point they should collaborate.

Obviously, these problems are not peculiar to Latin America; they are the same as those posed elsewhere. After I spoke in these terms to some North Americans going to work in Latin America, a surprised Canadian exclaimed, "But that's the problem in Quebec." Yes, and in many other places; it is the situation of Christianity as it faces the modern world. That is why I located Latin America in a larger Western and Christian world process. Local differences in dress and custom matter little; the problems we face are the same ones that concern Christians everywhere — at least everywhere a Christian spirit has been incarnated in a specific culture to the point of being identified with it. The problem of Christendom challenged by the evolution of history is especially acute in Latin America mainly because of the rate of change.

The breakdown of closed societies is illustrated by a story from Father Desqueyrat's *La Crise Religieuse des Temps Modernes*, in which it is supposed that a new pastor is appointed to the parish of Ars, famous for its earlier incumbent, Jean Baptiste Vianney. What would this new pastor find? The same village, the same houses, and so on — apparently much the same as at the time of the saint. But he could no longer use the pastoral approach of the Curé d'Ars, which was that of a rather simple man. The saint had discovered that there was one sin at Ars—dancing. His pastoral duty was clear: to get at the cause of this evil, and the cause was obviously the violin player in the village; without music, there was no dancing and therefore no occasion of sin. The Curé d'Ars simply paid the violin player to go away— to provide an occasion for sin in another village.

Father Desqueyrat asks what changes the new pastor would find today. One decisive change is that there is a violin player in every house—that is, there is a radio (and, increasingly, television). One cannot pay this violin player to go elsewhere; he is already inside. It is as if the village were actually in a big city, by means of the radio. The modern world uproots persons because of the power of its mass media in communicating ideas and images. The closed society of the village no longer exists at Ars; rural citizens no longer have to come to the city to be overwhelmed with distractions and contradictory appeals; even in the country they participate in the life of the city.

With the demise of the closed societies, their Catholic atmosphere and power to form the inhabitants of the village have also disappeared. Today they all have many ideologies in front of them, as available as in a shop window, and they can choose the one they like. Just as the parishioners of Ars could choose to sin if they wished, today everyone reached by modern means of communicating ideas can choose among various ideologies. All this applies to Latin America, with its tremendous migrations to large cities; the development of São Paulo, Rio de Janeiro, and Buenos Aires has been amazing. Even without migration, radio broadcasts produce similar results in the villages. In the modern world there are nothing but uprooted people, for whom every possibility is open.

The comment of a Spanish bishop about the effect of movies is also appropriate. He simply reminded us that movies tend to make their viewers passive, and this passivity encouraged by movie-going influences people; it encourages them to acquire new habits and customs different from those they would naturally acquire in their own surroundings. In a country like Spain movies have a tremendous impact on the urban masses; their traditions and characteristic national customs are replaced by an international lifestyle that is closer to that of Hollywood than that of Madrid. If movies and the other communications media make their audiences passive to the world about them, how can Christianity deal with this phenomenon of "massification"? The opportunity we once had to christianize the persons of a closed society is all but gone. We must react against massification and maintain a critical sense in the face of those images of life in other surroundings where there are other ideologies. But among those masses who go to the movies, how many will learn to take a critical attitude, not passive but active? Only a minority. In that case, we must be satisfied with the formation of a minority.

Among these masses, therefore, we must discover those who are open to education, a minority. This minority may be the only group to remain Christian in any consistent way, because they alone will be able to evaluate the ideas, customs, or new habits which the mass media present. If we want to hold on to the masses, however, institutions will be needed to provide sufficient social pressure to keep them within the confines of Christendom. But such institutions will have to be paid for in one way or another; that is what is meant by referring to the compromising character of Christian institutions.

A related point is made by Canon Jacques Leclercq when he speaks of the situation of Christians today in a world that must meet its needs with the help of everyone. Previously a nation could resolve its affairs by itself. But if we are to think seriously today of the problems of hunger, disease, education, and popular culture, we realize that it is necessary to deal with them on a world scale, and an appeal for their solution should be made to everyone. This awareness should impress on Christians the fact that they are a minority in the world.

For the first time in history Christians face the reality that if they are going to collaborate in the building of a world in the making, they must do so as members of a minority. Unfortunately, too many Christians are not prepared to collaborate in a world where they are not the dominant group. If they cannot govern, many withdraw, assuming that they are the majority, and if this Christian majority is not heard, the world will fall apart. But today Christians cannot control the world in this way; if they withdraw, the world will simply do without them. Are Christians prepared to live in such a society? Can they act with loyalty as a minority in the construction of a new order that will not be built according to Christian principles?

All this is quite relevant to conditions in Latin America, where a social revolution is underway. It is inconceivable that this revolution should take place without the participation of the people most interested in it—socialists, communists, atheists, and others—who do not have the same ideas as Christians. Latin America today is already a pluralistic world, even if some 90 percent of the population in most countries has been baptized. Will Latin American Christians, formed in the mentality of a dominant Christendom, be able to adjust quickly enough in this moment of rapid change?

Let us take a closer look at the three problems I mentioned by considering the example of my own country, Uruguay. It is a small country, to be sure; it was created as a buffer state between Argentina and Brazil, which were continuously at war. England found this solution particularly useful; here was a nation that provided a bit of "English soil" between the two great powers. Uruguay was a state created out of nothing, so to speak, and at independence it had only a hundred thousand inhabitants. The three million people there today are for the most part European immigrants of the last hundred years from Spain, Italy, and France. These people came from Christian countries and almost all were Christians. However, a laicist constitution was introduced about 1917, establishing a system of public schools. Reliable statistics are hard to come by in Uruguay, but it is rea-sonable to accept the estimate that at present about 60 percent of the population is baptized.

What has happened? In less than half a century a once entirely Christian people has either stopped being baptized or has come to look on baptism as nothing but a social ceremony. This rapid dechristianization means an uprooting of traditions, a widespread phenomenon in the modern world. Immigration has only speeded up the process, especially as religion has had little to offer in a period of dislocation. The same conditions may be pointed out in Argentina, although there are provinces in that country which retain ancient Catholic traditions. For practical purposes, we can assume the basic process of dechristianization is going on in all the large cities of Latin America.

At one time social pressure could be regarded as an assistant in the work of christianization; it was a kind of "machine to make Christians." Cer-tainly, a real pressure existed in certain closed Christian groups, in Christian schools and villages, for example. But as soon as this machine stopped functioning there seemed nothing left of the old traditions of Catholic countries. Dechristianization has been much quicker than in Europe; priests accustomed to relying on this "machine to make Christians" have within their lifetime seen a country like Uruguay change from a 100 percent Catholic population to one that is only 60 percent baptized, and the general pastoral reaction has been that of panic. An effort has been made to main-tain a superficial contact with these who have left the church; nothing has been thought out because the people drifted away almost overnight, and all the pastor could think of doing was to be sympathetic, *gavacho*. People found their priests as sympathetic as ever, but that did not make them any more Christian.

There was nothing to replace the pastoral customs of an older Christian society. When Brazil was without priests for almost twenty years, the Chris-tians of Brazil became adherents of spiritism; the machine had broken down. European Christianity withstood the challenge of pagan Greece and Rome, and overcame the mystery religions that sprang up in the West. The persistence of tribal rites, most often in corrupt form, represented a similar challenge to Brazilian Christianity, but the latter did not have the same interior resources. It had only a borrowed life, lent by the social pressure within an omnipresent Christendom. This is the difference between a Chris-tianity living on its own strength and a Christendom living within imposed structures.

Nothing has yet taken the place of the pastoral theology of older Chris-tian ages. But a choice must be made; we must decide what is authentically Christian in Latin America. A new beginning is required, planting a Chris-tianity that would be deeply rooted in the human structure of society. If we continue the old approaches, if priests try to maintain superficial con-tacts with people so that they will go to church and receive the sacraments from time to time, we have not made a pastoral choice between an authentic Christianity, able to develop by itself, and a Christian world that will endure only as long as certain externally Christian structures may survive.

Take the situation in Haiti when Bishop Paul Robert, arriving at the diocese of Gonaives, found a situation like that in Brazil. There were blacks of African origin who mixed Christianity with spiritism; Christians brought little statues of the saints with them to Mass. The bishop finally decided to fight this syncretism, and begin the christianization of his diocese over again, no matter how difficult it would be. He called all the Catholics together and told them, "I am your bishop. You are going to leave here with me all the little statues that you have and you are not going to have any more until I tell you. All this must stop; do as I say." He was aware that the majority would not obey him. To all who surrendered their little statues he gave a card saying "Roman Catholic." The next day he said, "Only those who have the card can attend Mass." With the help of those who had obeyed him, the bishop believed that one could try to evangelize the others. Those who surrendered their statues are capable of learning because they can see that Christianity is something more than they had known. The others thought they already understood the words of Christ; when the priests told them, "Listen, the saints are not the same as God," they said, "Of course not, everyone knows that," and went on as before. As long as they do not admit that they are *not* Christians, they cannot be evangelized.

Bishop Robert and several priests of his diocese have since been expelled from Haiti for "having tried to destroy national cultural traditions" of the country. In fact, this reaction on the part of the government is said to have been due chiefly to Dictator François Duvalier's personal attachment to voodooism. Some say that the method of Bishop Robert was too violent, too radical, but a choice must be made, one way or another.

Another example may be studied in the suburbs of the big cities where the people from the country come in search of work. Although they soon become a dechristianized mass, they continue to take their children to be baptized. In at least one diocese religious instruction of the parents was made a condition for the baptism of their children. This is another way of forcing a decision, because parents who do not want to be instructed, who find it not worth the trouble, no longer get their children baptized. Again it is a way of beginning over, of making a distinction between what may become deep Christian commitment and what is often merely superficial religiosity and social habit. If we wish to plant the seeds for an authentic Christianity, there is a price to be paid for it, for we will no longer have that social framework within which the officially Catholic population can lead its life. If serious conditions are set down for membership in the church, it will no longer be possible to hold on to those Christian masses that make Latin America the only continent in the world with a Catholic majority.

But to make this choice there must be a theology which can account for it, and we do not have such a theology. Why do I say this? Because we need an answer to a burning and practical question: Can you let children go without baptism? The theology I learned does not permit it. And so we let an official and almost automatic Christendom go on and on. There seems to be no theology which permits us to choose authentic Christianity; our theology was apparently created with the idea of a stable Christian West in mind, a society in which one knew perfectly how grace acts through the sacraments, within the visible church. It does not tell us very much about how grace acts outside the sacraments and outside the visible church.

If the choice I am discussing has as its consequence that a large number of those whom we now list as Christians will be left outside the visible church ("only those with the card, 'Roman Catholic,' can enter; the other 85 percent must stay outside"), we need a theology that will discuss what is going to happen to those souls from the point of view of salvation. After all, we do not want to create a perfect church if this perfection is going to bring about the damnation of others. How are we to decide? We do not have an adequate theology and that is why the choice is not made.

After considerable hesitation, one bishop, faced with this agonizing choice, finally said, "Baptize even when . . ." That is, let the parents go without religious instruction; let them continue in an official and external relationship to Christianity. In effect, he said, "Give up evangelizing them." The speed of dechristianization has not made it possible for the Christian West to create a theology for a post-Christian society. But if we have to abandon official Christendom, what then?

If no other choice can be made, we just accept the implications of a policy of holding on to our Christian masses. This means the perpetuation — and even further development — of Christian institutions that maintain pressure on Christians so that they will remain Christians. Catholic schools, Catholic universities, the Catholic press, Christian trade unions and political parties — all these institutions continue to make persons Christians, even if it is with the help of an external machine. But ultimately this policy is pursued at the price of compromising Christianity.

Defensively oriented Christian institutions are, obviously, not always alive to the spirit of our times. They can only be kept in being by political and economic alliances that are especially noticeable in Latin America, where such relations are quite visible. Everyone knows, for example, that certain Catholic universities are supported by industrialists. When one of these industrialists hears that someone has spoken about the church's social doctrine in a way that may be interpreted as a criticism against capitalism, he telephones the rector, "Excuse me, but the subsidy I have been giving to the university will not be possible in the future." Compromising relationships with politically and emotionally charged ideas are involved in the maintenance of Christian institutions throughout Latin America. There is no real tradition of independent administration, or of more or less impersonal organization, as in the more developed nations of western Europe or North America. Everything is signed, first name and last; it is always known who the person is who is paying for something.

Every choice implies a price to be paid, but the greatest price for a Christian is to stop evangelizing. It seems to me that there is no Christian evangelization in Latin America any more. What do I mean by that? For centuries, generation after generation became Christian by being born into Christian families, living in Christian environments; they were simply given or loaned to the church for their religious education. The church taught children the catechism; it prepared their intellectual framework. I say "intellectual framework" because you know what children are given in catechism: the summary of twenty centuries of the church's answers to heresies is crammed into their heads so that they will not go astray in later life. Formulas developed by Catholic minds over a period of almost two millennia are handed out in a few months to children preparing for their first communion, and then they are left on their own. The church then leaves them to society, which will make them religious in the sense that they will attend Mass and receive the sacraments; to a certain degree it is the social structure that makes them Christian.

It is this situation I have in mind when I speak of the absence of Christian evangelization. There was a time when Christianity was the religion of converts; they went to the source of Christianity, and decided to adhere to the basic message of the Gospel. But this has not been the case for centuries. Father Desqueyrat reminds us that when religious life no longer finds support in the social environment, it can only be maintained in a personal, heroic, interiorly enlightened form. It becomes impossible to be Christian except through a conversion to Christianity; persons will no longer bother about Christianity unless they have sought contact with Christian sources. They must find there the strength to be a Christian *despite* the social environment.

In Latin America the time is fast approaching when there will no longer be Christians except through evangelization. But to our great amazement we are beginning to realize that we do not know how to evangelize any longer. When someone comes and asks, "Why should I be a Christian?," you are apt to say, "But, of course, my friend, in order to be good, courageous, and generous." Then he says, "I am; I am just like you. You know me; what's the difference between us?" What are you to answer? "Well, yes, we are nearly the same; but I think you don't really accept the assumption of the Blessed Virgin and the infallibility of the pope. But, yes, be yourself."

Is that the Good News? The Assumption and papal infallibility? No, of course not. But then what does it mean to evangelize? What is Christianity? We don't know any more, and we answer with old formulas, listing heresies that we have memorized inside out. But all these things are intellectual abstractions. In its first centuries Christianity had a special power of its own which we desperately need to rediscover. At that time it was a matter of developing a truly Christian spirit. What happened in those early days of the church? If we reread the Acts of the Apostles we will find the example of the Apostle Philip baptizing the representative of the Queen of Ethiopia before that functionary had what we would today consider an elementary notion of Christian doctrine. It is important to realize that these early Christians knew absolutely nothing about such things as papal infallibility, but they knew what it was be a Christian. At any rate, it is through them that Christianity has come down to us rather than the spiritism that the masses of Brazilian Christians pass on to their children.

We have lost the force of early Christians. Our words do not express Christianity, but merely express the fact that our social structures have Christian trimmings. And in Latin America, the very words we use in evangelization have been corrupted; try to speak of charity, poverty, or the afterlife, and you will be told, "Go away; we know all about your Christianity!"

Unfortunately, they do know. Every word of the Christian message has been used to support the status quo of Christendom, but Christianity itself has been compromised by this attempt to maintain control of the masses, preserving Christian institutions by political means or through alliances with social conservatism. All this is justified on the basis that without this economic power and political influence it would be impossible to preach Christianity to the masses, but this only means that it would be impossible to maintain the social machine as a "machine to make Christians." How can we talk of Christianity with words that will reach human beings, with words that are not betrayed by these realities? In Latin America, more than elsewhere, the concern to guard Catholic institutions by every possible means has compromised the very words by which Christianity must be expressed.

The choice has still to be made to distinguish between what is authentically Christian and what is not. I believe that the pressure of reality is going to force Latin America and the church to come to a decision. It is precisely at the moment where earthly kingdoms disappear around us that the kingdom of Christ really begins. I believe that in this truth lies the hope for Latin America.

PART II

FROM VATICAN II TO MEDELLÍN
(1962-1968)

The Second Vatican Council began on October 11, 1962, and finally came to a close more than three years later on December 7, 1965. Although that is not the subject of this book, there can be little doubt that the council rather unexpectedly developed into one of the most significant events in the whole history of the Roman Catholic Church. Indeed, the German Jesuit, Karl Rahner, believed that it constituted one of the two most important transformations in that history. The first occurred at the beginning of the second century, when the church ceased to be a Jewish sect and began the long process of achieving its own identity in Europe and later in the lands influenced or even colonized by Europe. It was not until the passage of almost two millennia, according to Rahner, that the second great transformation took place during the council. This conclusively marked the end of the Eurocentric church and its gradual metamorphosis into what Rahner referred to as the "world church."

In this volume I will not include any texts from Vatican II, since these are readily available in many editions and also in many commentaries. Rather, the emphasis at this point will fall on analyzing the relationship between the council and the Catholic Church in Latin America. Most historians of the council conclude that the Latin American bishops made few significant contributions to its deliberations, yet it is also certain that Latin America was much more profoundly influenced by it than any other region of the church.

A key actor in facilitating this influence was the dynamic Manuel Larraín, bishop of Talca, Chile, at whose suggestion the Latin American bishops decided to hold a meeting concerning the council at Medellín, Colombia, from August 26 to September 2, 1968. The title conferred on these deliberations was "The Church in the Present-Day Transformation of Latin America in Light of the Council." As a consequence, the Medellín conference was understood by many to be an "application" of Vatican II to the Latin American *realidad* or socio-cultural context.

However, Pablo Richard, the Chilean director of a theological center in San José, Costa Rica, has argued persuasively that Medellín was not so much an application of Vatican II as a profound "reinterpretation" of the council in the light of its own social and theological experience and practice, which differed in a number of very significant points from the experience and practice of Europe. Richard encapsulates three of these differences very succinctly:

> The European church was confronted with the problem of "faith and science" and entered a process of secularization, declericalization, and demythologization. The Latin American church faced the problem of "faith and revolution" and entered a process of liberation.
>
> In Europe the theological challenge to the church was the structural *atheism* of modern society and its proclamation of the *death of God*. In Latin America the theological challenge was *exploitation* and *underdevelopment* which was causing the *death of the human being*.
>
> As it dealt with the modern world, the European church came to feel how far away it was from that world and sought to bring about a *reconciliation*. The Latin American church, by contrast, felt too *identified* with the modern world and thus sought to *break away* from it.[1]

It also appears to me that not all the documents of Vatican II were considered of equal importance in the Latin American reinterpretation of the council. Clearly of primary importance was the Pastoral Constitution on the Church in the Modern World (*Gaudium et Spes*), which was one of the last documents approved on December 7, 1965, the final day of the council. Much of the disagreement and conflict that has continued for more than two decades over the proper interpretation of the council has revolved around the issue of whether the earlier decrees, such as the ones on the church and on the liturgy, should be reinterpreted in the light of the Pastoral Constitution's new and far-reaching conception of the positive and essential role of the church in the transformation of human society and human history. And this applies to the whole Catholic Church today as much as it does to Latin America.

During the council and soon after the publication of his chef d'oeuvre, "Peace on Earth," Pope John XXIII died, on June 3, 1963, "mourned by a larger percentage of the population of the world — Catholic, Protestant, Jewish, Moslem, agnostic, and atheist — than any pope in the entire history of the world," as John Dwyer expresses it in his *Church History*.[2] Although he possessed a more reticent and introspective personality than the jovial and ebullient Roncalli, Giovanni Montini (Paul VI) assumed the reins of the papacy and exercised cautious but firm leadership in bringing the Second Vatican Council to a successful conclusion.

Of great importance, also, for the Latin Americans was the fact that

Pope Paul continued along the trail of progressive social teaching that had been pioneered by his predecessor in the papacy. Just over a year after the end of the Vatican Council, on March 26, 1967, Pope Paul published an encyclical letter "On the Development of Peoples" (*Populorum Progressio*). This ringing plea for social justice and fundamental changes for the impoverished masses of the Third World was widely acclaimed worldwide, although the situation of these countries continued to grow worse in the two decades that followed its publication. This was sorrowfully pointed out by John Paul II in an encyclical letter marking the twentieth anniversary of *Populorum Progressio* and updating the Vatican's analysis of the major obstacles to development. Later on in the book, we will present some excerpts from this encyclical.

On the Latin American political scene, perhaps the most significant event during the years between the councils was the coup d'état and consequent military government that seized power in Brazil on March 31, 1964. Given Brazil's great size and potential leadership role in the southern hemisphere, this event cast a menacing shadow of militarism and repression over Latin America, along with a new type of totalitarian ideology called the "National Security State." This theory postulated a state of "permanent war" against the forces of godless communism, during which violations of human rights and even the right to life itself were justified to ensure ultimate victory. Unfortunately, a number of other nations followed the "Brazilian Model" in this respect.

Since, as we have seen earlier in this section, liberation theology called for a fundamental option for the poor, and since the poor in Latin America were always the first and the most brutalized victims of repression, the Brazilian *golpe* served as a literally terrifying harbinger of the fierce opposition and savage violence that would be visited on those who were allied with the poor. And so the Latin American church entered into a new age of martyrs as thousands of Christians — laypersons, religious, priests, bishops — gave their lives for the "crime" of following out Christianity's basic commandment of love.

We may also note briefly that the conference at Medellín in 1968 occurred toward the end of the First Decade of Development sponsored by the United Nations. By that time it was clear that this well-meaning attempt was a failure. The bishops at Medellín clearly understood this as they denounced "the international monopolies and the international imperialism of money" as well as the "institutionalized violence" that plagued their countries. Their response was a *cri de coeur* till then unparalleled in documents of the church's magisterium: "Such a situation demands global, bold, urgent and profoundly renovating transformations."

Finally, in the spring and summer of 1968, revolutionary enthusiasm broke out in various parts of the world, profoundly influencing the global *Zeitgeist*. This fervor erupted in the form of demonstrations, sit-ins, university takeovers, and riots in Europe, the United States, and many other areas of the world. In Latin America, fuel was added to these flames by the activities and writings of two men who became revolutionary heroes, Ernesto (Che) Guevara and the Colombian priest, Camilo Torres. Torres had left the priesthood and joined guerilla forces as a sign of true Christian love, and died in battle in the Santander mountains of Colombia on February 15, 1966. Che Guevara, a guerilla major and veteran of Castro's revolution in Cuba, sought to extend it to the Latin American mainland. On October 8, 1967, he was wounded and taken prisoner in the mountains of Bolivia and, on the following day, was executed by Bolivian soldiers in the village of Quebrada del Yuro. Both men posed a challenge to the conscience of many Christians, and they are still seen by many in Latin America as models of revolutionary fervor, even unto death.

NOTES

1. Pablo Richard, *Death of Christendoms, Birth of the Church* (Maryknoll, N.Y.: Orbis Books, 1987).
2. John Dwyer, *Church History: Twenty Centuries of Catholic Christianity* (New York: Paulist Press, 1985), p. 387.

4

Roberto Oliveros Maqueo
"Meeting of Theologians at Petrópolis"
(March 1964)

This selection contains an account of a meeting on the question of a Latin American theology that was held in March 1964, considerably before the end of the Vatican Council and its crucial Pastoral Constitution on the Church in the Modern World. The principal speakers were Juan Luis Segundo, Lucio Gera, and Gustavo Gutiérrez. The different approaches to the Latin American context are obvious, and at this point Gutiérrez presents the most comprehensive approach. The text is from Roberto Oliveros Maqueo, S.J., Liberación y teología: Génesis y crecimiento de una reflexión (1966–1976) *[Liberation and theology: origins and growth of a reflection], published by the Center for Theological Reflection (CRT) in Mexico City. The book has not been translated into English; the following translation is my own.*

Up to the time of the Second Vatican Council, Latin American theologians contributed little to the universal church. The powerful and fruitful missionary activities among our peoples contrasted sharply with the lack of profound theological reflection on Christian faith within Latin America. One could go on referring to Bartolomé de Las Casas and his urgent pleas, as well as to others such as Antonio de Valdevieso, who was bishop of Nicaragua from 1544–1550.

To a large extent, however, Latin American theologians were merely repeating the thought of the great masters of European theology. One has only to peruse the program for theological studies and the textbooks at the seminary level until Vatican II to become aware of the continuous dependency of theological reflection on the schools of thought in Europe, a dependency that was justified because of unity, orthodoxy, and the universality of the so-called classic theology. How marvelous was the power and creativity of the European thinker, how paltry that of the Latin American theologian!

The first years of the 1960s were characterized by an awareness of social conditions in Latin America and also by the opportunity for meeting together that Vatican II provided for bishops and some theologians. This occurred in an ecclesial atmosphere of openness and creative theological reflection, as well as of great uncertainty, which stimulated some theologians of our countries to begin meeting together and reflecting theologically on their own unique context and their own culture. An example of this is the first meeting of Latin American theologians that took place in Petrópolis, in the state of Rio de Janeiro, Brazil, in March 1964. The following is a statement of its objectives:

1. To provide an occasion for a group of South American and Mexican theologians to get to know each other and to exchange ideas.

2. By means of this group to awaken an active interest in theological faculties and professors of theology for exploring the horizons and clarifying the assumptions of research *concerned with Latin America* [emphasis in original text]. The idea is that this meeting could be the point of departure for theological research on the problems of the Latin church.

3. To consider themes for discussion, persons to invite, and so forth, for a possible course of 20–30 days in July 1964 for Latin American theologians along with three or four of the leading European theologians.

4. To choose some themes for possible pastoral letters of the Latin American episcopate (this was suggested by various bishops from CELAM).

In effect, therefore, this meeting at Petrópolis was the beginning of many conferences summoned to probe more deeply the theological and pastoral issues proper to Latin America. There were other theological meetings that took place throughout 1965, providing an idea of the theologico-pastoral movement that was beginning: a conference in Havana, Cuba, July 14–16, on the topic of pastoral renewal, with talks by Segundo Galilea and Luis Maldonato, among others; another meeting in Bogotá, Colombia, from June 14 to July 9, also on pastoral issues, with talks by Juan Luis Segundo and Cassiano Floristán; and finally one in Cuernavaca, Mexico, from July 4 to August 14, with presentations by Ivan Illich and Segundo Galilea.

At the Petrópolis meeting, which included experts from a variety of disciplines regarding the Latin American situation, the most important presentations were by Juan Luis Segundo, Lucio Gera, and Gustavo Gutiérrez. Here I will briefly present some points that give an idea of the development of topics.

Segundo's talk, "Theological Problems of Latin America," began with the fact of social change in Latin America. The first of three aspects to be considered was the process of urbanization; the second, the multiplication of the means of communication; and the third, "the growth of revolutionary social consciousness." His basic question was: "Are we evangelizing?" He then goes on to develop this topic, pointing out erroneous or deficient understandings of evangelization that have impeded the pastoral task of the church. "In Latin America," Segundo asserts, "the basic watchword is a minimum of demands, so as to maintain a maximum of adherents, and also to keep Christians separated as far as possible from non-Christians, in order to preserve their identity as Christians." Segundo ends with an analysis of Pauline thought on grace and the sacraments, from which he concludes that the sacraments should not be administered without previous evangclization.

Speaking on the theological problems of Latin America, Lucio Gera focuses on the task of theology: "First of all, I began by asking myself what is the function of theology and of the theologian in Latin America." He points out the limitations and the excessive work that the theologian faces in Latin America, and also the lack of sufficient personnel in this field. He then stresses the theologian's need to be integrated into the work of the church body; he is convinced that awareness of this body and the functions its different organs perform in unison within the church will be very fruitful both for the theologian and the pastor. He believes that the opposition between pastor and theologian should be overcome by emphasizing their complementarity.

Concretely, Gera affirms that the function of the theologian is "to bring the word to a rational level." He then points out the need for wisdom in theologians' reflections, so that they do not confuse their own approach with that of a mere rationalist. Finally, he moves on to the question of the teaching of theology, which is the occupation of most Latin American theologians. He adverts to serious deficiencies in the manner of teaching theology in the seminaries, and asserts that the solution of these problems involves a profound change in the *life* of the seminary: "There is, of course, a doctrinal function of the theologian, that of scholarly teaching. But true change would mean a renovation not only of the teaching but of the whole lifestyle of the seminary. Thus it is important in Latin America to move to a kind of seminary that is really new."

We have observed in the seminaries of many regions in Latin America that Gera's "whole lifestyle" has been taken very seriously. He ends his presentation by suggesting that theologians descend from their olympian heights and become involved with the people, so that they may understand them and thus express their message within a proper context.

The presentation of Gustavo Gutiérrez was the most substantive in the conference, both as regards theological content and also its Latin American perspective. His talk opened up directions of study and of expression that would eventually become the theology of liberation.

In the talk, he did not attempt to analyze a theme, but rather to open up new pathways. The question with which he begins his talk is: How do we establish a saving dialogue with the human being in Latin America? In order to answer this question, he asserts that the first step is to study the human being in Latin America. For such an investigation he points out three separate and clearly differentiated groups: (1) the popular masses, which comprise the majority of the population; (2) an intellectual, technocratic elite; and (3) the conservative oligarchy. He briefly discusses the characteristics of each group, and gives special attention to the actions of the groups with relation to their salvation: "In the first place, I think it is necessary to undertake an examination from a religious point of view and from a salvific point of view, and to analyze the most profound options of these different types of human beings."

Here we have in embryo what will later be called theology's critical function with regard to the praxis of Christians, and also how we discover our most profound options precisely in our praxis. After examining the conduct typical of the different groups of Latin Americans, he moves on to the need for studying the praxis, the pastoral action, and the present options for the church, since these will reveal a great deal about the way it understands the faith: "Moving on from what has been said, a second thing I wish to discuss and propose as a theme for study is a theological critique of the pastoral options that have already been adopted in Latin America."

The first pastoral approach that he studies is that of "Christendom," of which there are two types. The first belongs to the period of colonization; the second and more advanced type is that which creates institutions of Christian inspiration. Gutiérrez goes on to show the value and the limitations of this pastoral approach.

The second approach, which is called "spiritualistic," is marked by the attempt to form militant Christians from the elite classes in small and very select communities. This "elitism" will be rejected by the current of liberation theology, strongly committed to the common people.

After his survey and critique, Gutiérrez suggests a new pastoral focus: the "status of humanity touched by grace vis-à-vis the church as institution." Avenues of study include first an investigation of how the word of God comes to human beings, then the question of the salvation of those outside the church, and finally an inquiry into what is the fundamental essence of Christian life. The last point is treated in some detail, since it is the core of his misgivings as he ponders the question of the mission of the church in the context of Latin America. It is still only a sketch, marked by a certain hesitation. Four years later he will publish a book on pastoral approaches in Latin America, which will provide the basis for understanding his ecclesiology and the proper theological focus for pastoral action in Latin America. But in the Petrópolis conference the basic intuition was already present.

The last theological issue he probes more deeply is "the process of social recovery being experienced in Latin America." This includes three issues: the first is how to reconcile the revolutionary struggle in Latin America with the preaching of paschal kenosis [emptying]; secondly, the question of violence; thirdly, the question of birth control. These points are only sketched briefly, but they are seen to be the most typical and the most necessary for the church in Latin America.

The conference at Petrópolis had the aura of a beginning, a combination of conciliar language and a growing consciousness of the enormous task that still needed to be accomplished. One senses the deep seriousness of the ecclesial and human issues upon which they were just beginning to reflect.

5

Third World Bishops
"A Letter to the Peoples
of the Third World"
(August 15, 1967)

*This letter was published five months after Pope Paul VI issued his encyclical "On the Development of Peoples" (*Populorum Progressio*) and was clearly intended as a response going beyond the recommendations of that document. It represents the thinking of eighteen bishops from ten nations, and is included here because the majority of the bishops were from Latin America, including the well-known Archbishop of Olinda and Recife, Dom Helder Camara. The document did not receive much attention in the First World, perhaps because of its endorsement of socialism. The text is taken from* Beyond Honesty and Hope, *published in 1970 by Maryknoll Publications, pp. 1-12.*

1. We are bishops from some of the nations that are struggling and fighting toward higher development. We wish to raise our anxious voices to join with the plea that Pope Paul VI issued in his encyclical *Populorum Progressio*, to spell out to our priests and our faithful their duties, and to offer some words of encouragement to all our brothers in the underdeveloped world.

THE WORLD'S PROLETARIAT

2. Our churches, located in the countries of the Third World, are enmeshed in the conflict that brings various groups into confrontation. It is not just a confrontation between the East and the West. It is a confrontation between three large groups of people: the Western powers that became affluent in the last century, the two great Communist countries that have been transformed into great powers, and finally the Third World that is still trying to escape the domination of the great powers and to achieve its own free development. The latter group includes certain social classes,

48

races, and peoples within the developed nations, who have not yet won the right to a life that is truly human. An irresistible impulse drives these people on to better themselves and to free themselves from the forces of oppression.

While most nations have managed to achieve political independence, few peoples are yet free economically. Equally rare are those nations where social equality reigns; and this is an indispensable precondition for true brotherhood because peace cannot exist without justice. The peoples of the Third World are the proletariat of humanity today. They are exploited by the great nations; and their very existence is threatened by those who, because they are more powerful, arrogate to themselves the right to make all the decisions and policies for peoples that are less affluent than they are. But the fact is that our peoples are not less upright and just than the great nations of this world.

A NEW APPRAISAL OF REVOLUTION

3. In the present pageant of world history we find revolutions in progress or already effected, and there is nothing surprising about this. All the powers that are now established in the world were born in an era of revolution that dates back to the near or distant past. In short, they were spawned through a breakaway from a system that no longer insured the common good, and through the establishment of a new order that was better equipped to provide this common good.

Not all revolutions are necessarily good. Some are nothing more than palace revolts that do nothing to change the oppression suffered by the people. Some do more harm than good, "fostering new injustices" (*Populorum Progressio,*31). Atheism and collectivism, to which certain movements feel bound, offer grave dangers to humanity. But history shows us that certain revolutions were necessary, and that they have produced good effects after their temporary flirtation with antireligious sentiments. There is no better proof of this than the fact that the French Revolution of 1789 allowed people to proclaim the rights of man (see *Pacem in Terris*).

Many of our nations have felt obliged to effect these profound changes, or feel so now. What then should be the attitude of Christians and the churches in the face of this situation? Paul VI had already cleared the road for us through his encyclical *Populorum Progressio*.

4. From the viewpoint of doctrine, the church knows that the gospel calls for the first and most radical revolution: conversion, the thoroughgoing transformation from sin to grace, from egotism to love, from haughtiness to humble service. This conversion is not simply interior and spiritual; it involves the whole man corporeally and socially as well as spiritually and personally. It has a communitarian aspect that is fraught with consequences for society as a whole. It concerns not only our life on earth but also our eternal life in Christ, who is drawing all persons to himself on high. That,

in the eyes of Christians, is what total development means. For this reason the gospel, either openly or covertly, either within the church or outside it, has always been the most powerful force behind the profound transformations that have taken place in the last twenty centuries.

5. In its journey through history on earth, however, the church has almost always been tied up with the political, social, and economic *system* which, at a given moment, insured the common good or at least a certain social order. On the other hand, churches have been seen to be so tied up with the *system* that they seemed to be wedded to it in marriage. But the church is not wedded to any system, whatever it might be. It is not now wedded to the "international imperialism of money" (*Populorum Progressio*, 26) any more that it was wedded to royalism or feudalism in the past or will be wedded to some form of socialism in the future. We need only look at history to see that the church has survived the collapse of many powers that once were thought to protect it or to use it. The current social doctrine of the church, reaffirmed by Vatican II, has already rescued it from the clutches of monetary imperialism—one of the forces to which it seemed bound for some time in the past.

NEW TIES WITH THE PEOPLE

6. After Vatican II energetic voices were raised, demanding that the church end its earthly collusion with money interests. This collusion had been denounced on various sides, and a few bishops[1] had already set the right example. We ourselves are duty-bound to examine our situation in this regard, and to free our churches from all enslavement to international financial interests. We cannot serve God and mammon.

7. Faced with the present course of monetary imperialism, we must recall to ourselves and our faithful the admonition which the seer of Patmos directed to the Christians of Rome. That great city had been prostituted by wealth and luxury, which she had amassed by oppressing other nations and engaging in slave trade; and now she was on the verge of collapse. Saint John's message rang out: "Come out, my people, come away from her, so that you do not share in her crimes and have the same plagues to bear" (Apoc. 18:4).

8. Insofar as the church maintains its essential and perduring ties—that is, its fidelity to Christ and communion with him in the gospel—it is never bound up with any given social, political, or economic system. When a system ceases to promote the common good and favors special interests, the church must not only denounce injustice but also break with the evil system. It must be prepared to work with another system that is juster and more suited to the needs of the day.

9. This holds true for Christians, for their leaders in the hierarchy, and for the churches. We do not have perduring cities in this world, since our leader Jesus chose to suffer outside the city (Heb. 13:12-14). Hopefully we

shall be prompt to share our goods in common, "for these are sacrifices that please God" (Heb. 13:16). Even if we are not able to do this willingly and out of love, it is to be hoped that we will at least recognize the hand of God in those events that correct our prodigal hearts and force us to such sacrifices (Heb. 12:5-7).

10. We do not judge or condemn those who now or in the past have felt obliged before God to go into exile in order to safeguard their own faith or that of their descendants. The only ones to be condemned are those who drive people out by taking their lands or oppressing them materially and spiritually.

Christians and their pastors should remain with the people, in the land that is theirs. History shows that it is not beneficial in the long run for people to go into exile from their own land. They should either defend their land against unjust aggressors from abroad, or else accept the governmental changes that are effected in their country. It is wrong for Christians not to be in solidarity with their country and its people in the moment of trial. This is particularly true if they are rich, and if their only real reason for leaving is to preserve their riches and their privileges. To be sure, an individual or a family may be obliged to emigrate in order to find work; that is part of the right to emigrate (see *Pacem in Terris*, part one). But the mass exodus of Christians can cause regrettable results. It is in their own land and among their own people that Christians are normally summoned by God to live out their lives, acting in concert with their fellow humans of whatever religion and thus bearing witness to the love that Christ bears for all.

11. We priests and bishops have an even more pressing obligation to remain in our own locale, for we are the representatives of the Good Shepherd. Far from running away when mercenaries threaten, the good shepherd remains with his people and is ready to lay down his life for his own (John 10:11–18). Jesus did tell his apostles to move from city to city (Matt. 10:23), but that was only when they were being persecuted individually for the faith. It is a different matter when we are talking about wars of revolution that affect a whole nation, with whom a pastor should feel bound in solidarity. In the latter cases a pastor should remain among his people. If the whole nation decides to go into exile, then their pastor may choose to follow them. But he cannot save himself alone, or with a handful of profiteers and frightened souls.

THE SOCIAL DIMENSION OF PROPERTY

12. Beyond this, Christians and their pastors should know how to recognize the hand of the Almighty in those events that occur sporadically— when the powerful are dethroned and the lowly are exalted, when the rich are sent away empty-handed and the needy are filled. Today "the world insistently calls for recognition of man's full dignity and for social equality

among all classes."² Christians and all persons of good will cannot but go along with this demand, even if it means that they must give up their privileges and their personal fortunes for more equitable distribution in the social community.

The church is in no way the protector of large property interests. Like Pope John XXIII, it demands that property be shared among all since it has a social destiny.³ In his encyclical *Populorum Progressio* (n. 23) Paul VI recalls the words of Saints John and Ambrose: "If a man who was rich enough in this world's goods saw one of his brothers in need, but closed his heart to him, how could the love of God be living in him?" (1 John 3:17); "The earth belongs to everyone, not just to the rich."

13. All the church fathers, both those in the East and those in the West, reiterate the sentiments of the gospel. In his homily against riches, Saint Basil presents this dialogue with a miser:

> "Share the crop you have harvested with your fellow men, for tomor-row it will have rotted. What abominable avarice it is to let it rot before giving it to the needy!"
>
> "How do I do injury to others," asks the miser, "by not giving them what is mine?"
>
> "Which goods belong to you? Where did you get them from? You are like the man at the theater who wants to keep others from the performance, who wants to derive exclusive enjoyment from a per-formance that everyone has a right to see. That is how the rich are. They say that they are the rightful owners of goods that belong to all, goods that they have expropriated for themselves simply because they were the first to lay their hands on them. If each person kept only what was necessary for day-to-day needs and gave the rest to the needy, there would be no more poverty or extravagant luxury. The food that you hoard belongs to the hungry. The clothes in your ward-robe belong to the naked. The shoes that are growing old in your house belong to those who have none. The money you have buried belongs to the poor. You are oppressing people whom you could help. . . . It is not your avarice but your unwillingness to share that con-demns you."

JUST REWARDS FOR HUMAN LABOR

14. Taking account of the necessary preconditions for material progress in some areas, the church in the last hundred years has tolerated capitalism, its loans at a legitimate interest rate, and its other mechanisms that are hardly in conformity with the moral code of the prophets and the gospel. But it cannot help but rejoice over the appearance of another social system that is less at variance with this moral code. Tomorrow's Christians must

follow the lead of Paul VI, retracing the Christian roots that lie behind the moral values of solidarity and fraternity (see *Ecclesiam Suam*). Christians must show that "authentic socialism is Christianity lived to the full, in basic equality and with a fair distribution of goods."[4]

Instead of opposing it, we must learn to accept joyfully a form of societal life that is better adapted to our times and more in tune with the spirit of the gospel. In this way we will prevent people from equating God and religion with those things that oppress the workers and the poor: that is, feudalism, capitalism, and imperialism. These inhuman systems have spawned other systems that proposed to free peoples, but ended up by oppressing them in the snares of total collectivism and religious persecution.

God and authentic religion, however, have nothing to do with the mammon of iniquity in any of its forms. On the contrary, they are always on the side of those who seek to build a more equitable and fraternal society among the family of God's children.

15. With pride and joy the church greets a new humanity, which does not honor money accumulated in the hands of the few but money distributed among workers, manual laborers, and farmers. For it is nothing without Jesus of Nazareth, who continues to give it life and vitality, and who spent so many years at manual labor to reveal the eminent dignity of workers. "Labor is infinitely superior to money," remarked one bishop at the council.[5] And another bishop, from a socialist country, pointed out this:

If workers do not succeed somehow in becoming proprietors of their own labor, structural reforms will be fruitless. Even if they sometimes receive a higher salary in another economic system, that is not enough to satisfy them. Today workers are becoming more and more aware of the fact that work forms a part of the human person. And since the human person cannot sell himself or be sold, the buying and selling of labor is a form of slavery. Human society is evolving along this new line of thought, even indeed within that system which is thought not to be as sensitive as we are to the dignity of the human person: that is, the Marxist system.[6]

16. So the church is happy to see the development of new societal forms in which labor finds its rightful place — at the top. The church, both Eastern and Western, made the mistake of adapting itself to the pagan juridical principles that were inherited from ancient Rome. As Archbishop Borovoi remarked at the assembly of the World Council of Churches:

Of all Christian cultures, Byzantine Christianity did most to sanction outright social evil. It docilely adopted the whole social heritage of the pagan world and gave it sacramental blessing. Under the cloak of ecclesiastical tradition, the civil law of the pagan Roman Empire was

preserved for more than a thousand years in Byzantium and in medieval Europe. Since the sixteenth century, when my country, Russia,
began to regard herself as the heir of Byzantium, it has been preserved
there too. But this is radically opposed to the social tradition of primitive Christianity and the Greek Fathers, to the missionary preaching
of our Lord, and to the perduring message of the Old Testament
prophets.[7]

17. Let no one bother to look for political motives as the reason for these
words. Our only source is the word of him who spoke to the prophets and
the apostles. The Bible and the gospel label as sin against God any blow
against the dignity of humankind, created in God's likeness. It is within this
obligatory framework of respect for the human person that atheists of good
will are now joining with believers to serve humanity in its quest for justice
and peace. We, for our part, can unhesitatingly offer words of encouragement to all, for all will need much courage and energy for the urgent task
that lies before us. Only this effort can save the Third World from poverty
and hunger, and from the catastrophe of nuclear war. As Paul VI remarked
at the United Nations, we must never again have war: "Away with arms!"[8]

THE TASK BEFORE US

18. The poor nations and the poor in the nations, over whom we have
been appointed shepherds, know from experience that they must count on
themselves and their own initiatives more than on the help of the rich. To
be sure, some affluent nations and some rich people in different nations
do provide appreciable aid to our peoples. But it would be a delusion to
wait passively for a change of heart in those who, as our father Abraham
warns us, "will not be convinced even if someone should rise from the
dead" (Luke 16:31).

It is primarily up to the poor nations and the poor of other nations to
effect their own betterment. They must regain confidence in themselves.
They must educate themselves and overcome their illiteracy. They must
work zealously to fashion their own destiny. They must develop themselves
by utilizing all the media that modern society places at their disposal, such
as schools and printed materials. They must open their ears to those who
can awaken and shape the conscious awareness of the masses and, in particular, listen to their pastors.

The latter, for their part, must dispense the word of truth and the gospel
of justice in its entirety. The militant laity in apostolic movements must learn
to appreciate and implement the exhortation Pope Paul VI addressed to
them: "The laity have the duty of using their own initiative and taking action
in this area—without waiting passively for directives and precepts from others. They must try to infuse a Christian spirit into people's mental outlook
and daily behavior, into the laws and structures of the civil community.

Changes must be made; present conditions must be improved. And the transformations must be permeated with the spirit of the gospel" (*Populorum Progressio*, 81). Finally, the working classes and the poor must get together, for only unity will enable the poor to demand and achieve real justice.

19. The people are hungering for truth and justice, and those who are entrusted with the task of teaching and educating them should do so with enthusiasm. Certain erroneous viewpoints must be wiped away without delay. No, it is not God's will that a few rich people enjoy the goods of this world and exploit the poor. No, it is not God's will that some people remain poor and abject forever. No, religion is not the opiate of the people; it is a force that exalts the lowly and casts down the proud, that feeds the hungry and sends the sated away empty. Of course Jesus warned us that the poor will always be with us (see John 12:8); but that is because there will always be rich people who expropriate to themselves the goods of this world and because there will always be certain inequalities resulting from differing degrees of capability and other unavoidable factors. But Jesus also teaches us that the second commandment is equal to the first, since we cannot love God without loving our fellow humans. We shall all be judged by the same standard: "I was hungry and you gave me food . . . in so far as you did it to one of the least of these brothers of mine, you did it to me" (Matt. 25: 35-40).

All the great religions and philosophies of the world echo this sentiment. The Qur'ān spells out the last and ultimate test to which humans must submit when they are judged by Allah. What is that test? "Have you redeemed the captive, fed the orphan in his need or the beggar on your doorstep, and lived your life as a rod of mercy?" (Sura 90, 11:18).

20. It is our duty to share our food and all our goods. If some try to monopolize for themselves what others need, then it is the duty of public authority to carry out the distribution that was not made willingly. As Paul VI reminds us in *Populorum Progressio*:

> If certain landed estates impede the general prosperity because they are extensive, unused, or poorly used, or because they bring hardship to peoples or are detrimental to the interests of the country, the common good sometimes demands their expropriation. Vatican II affirms this emphatically. At the same time it clearly teaches that income thus derived is not for our capricious use, and that the exclusive pursuit of personal gain is prohibited. Consequently, it is not permissible for citizens who have garnered sizable income from the resources and activities of their own nation to deposit a large portion of their income in foreign countries for the sake of their own private gain alone, taking no account of their country's interests; in doing this they clearly wrong their country [n. 24].

In like manner, we cannot allow rich foreigners to come and exploit our impoverished peoples under the pretext of developing commerce and industry; nor can we allow rich nationals to exploit their own nation. These things incite the exasperating strains of excessive nationalism, which is hostile to authentic collaboration between nations.

21. What is true for individuals is also true for nations. Today, unfortunately, there is not truly worldwide government that could effect justice among the nations and an equitable distribution of earthly goods. The economic system presently in force allows the affluent nations to keep getting richer even when they offer a modicum of aid to the poor nations; the latter, in the meantime, keep getting poorer. These poor nations have the right to press, with all the legitimate means at their disposal, for the establishment of a world government where all nations without exception would be represented, and which would have the competence to demand and even force an equitable distribution of the earth's goods. That is an indispensable precondition for world peace (see *Pacem in Terris* and *Populorum Progressio*).

22. Within each nation, workers have a right and a duty to form real trade unions, so that they may press for and defend their rights. These rights include a just wage, paid vacations, social security, family allotments, and management participation. It is not enough for these rights to be recognized on paper by the law. The laws must be implemented, and government must exercise its powers in this area to serve the working class and the poor.

Governments must face up to the task of stopping class warfare. Contrary to popular belief, this warfare is often incited by the rich; and they keep it up by exploiting the worker through inadequate wages and inhuman working conditions. It is a subversive war that has been craftily waged throughout the world for a long time by money interests, annihilating whole nations in the process. It is high time that the poor, supported and guided by their legitimate governments, defend their right to live. When God appeared to Moses, it was said to him: "I have seen the miserable state of my people in Egypt, I have heard their appeal to be free of their slave drivers. ... I mean to deliver them" (Ex. 3:7). Jesus took all humanity upon himself to lead it to eternal life. And the earthly foreshadowing of this is social justice, the first form of brotherly love. When Jesus freed humankind from death through his resurrection, he brought all human liberation movements to their fullness in eternity.

23. Some of us here directed a particular passage of the gospel to our peoples last year.[9] Motivated by the same concern and prompted by the same spirit, all of us now reiterate that passage to the people of the underdeveloped world. "We urge you to remain strong and fearless, to act as the leaven of the gospel in the world, taking strength from the words of Christ, 'Stand erect, hold your heads high because your liberation is near at hand' (Luke 21: 28)."

Signed by:

Helder Camara, Archbishop of Olinda and Recife, Brazil
João Batista da Mota, Archbishop of Vitoria, Brazil

Luis Gonzaga Fernandez, Auxiliary Bishop of Vitoria, Brazil
Georges Mercier, Bishop of Laghouat, Algeria
Michel Darmancier, Bishop of Wallis and Futuna, Oceania
Amand Hubert, Vicar Apostolic for Latins, Heliopolis, Egypt
Angelo Cuniberti, Vicar Apostolic of Florencia, Colombia
Severino Marino de Aguiar, Bishop of Pesqueira, Brazil
Franjo Franić, Bishop of Split, Yugoslavia˙
Francisco Austregésilo de Mesquita, Bishop of Afogados da Ingazeira, Brazil
Gregorio Haddad, Melkite Auxiliary Bishop of Beirut, Lebanon
Manuel Pereira da Costa, Bishop of Campina Grande, Brazil
Charles van Melckebeke, Bishop of Ning-Hsia, China and Apostolic Visitor for Overseas Chinese, Singapore
Antônio Batista Fragoso, Bishop of Crateús, Brazil
Etienne Loosdregt, Vicar Apostolic of Ventiane, Laos
Waldir Calheiros de Novais, Bishop of Barra do Pirai-Volta Redonda, Brazil
Jacques Grent, Bishop of Tual, Indonesia
David Picão, Bishop of Santos, Brazil

NOTES

1. *Populorum Progressio* [n. 32] cites the example of the late lamented bishop of Talce, Chile: Manuel Larraín, Pastoral Letter, *Desarrollo: Exito o Fracaso en América Latina*, 1965.
2. Address at the council by Patriarch Maximos IV Saigh, October 27, 1964.
3. *Mater et Magistra*, n. 119.
4. Address at the council by Maximos IV Saigh, September 28, 1965.
5. Address at the council by Georges Hakim, Melkite archbishop of Galilea, November 10, 1964.
6. Franjo Franić, bishop of Split, Yugoslavia, October 4, 1966.
7. WCC, "Church and Society," Geneva, July 12, 1966.
8. Paul VI at the United Nations in New York, October 4, 1965.
9. Manifesto of the bishops of Northeast Brazil, Recife, July 1, 1966.

6

Latin American Priests
"*Populorum Progressio* and Latin American Realities" (November 1967)

A seminar for priests was sponsored by the Social Department of CELAM (Latin American Bishops' Conference) and conducted in Chile during October-November 1967. The theme of their discussion was again Paul VI's encyclical and its meaning for Latin America. A total of thirty-eight priests from Argentina, Bolivia, Brazil, Chile, Colombia, Ecuador, El Salvador, Guatemala, Mexico, Nicaragua, Panama, Paraguay, Peru, and Uruguay signed the following communiqué. The document shows the attitudes of priests, the church's pastoral agents who are in the most immediate daily contact with the people. It also manifests a poignant sense of urgency regarding what the priests refer to as "the heartrending reality of Latin America," an urgency that was a major characteristic of liberation theology from its inception. This text is taken from Between Honesty and Hope, *pp. 70–73.*

We thirty-eight priests have participated in this seminar to study the new encyclical of Pope Paul VI and the realities of life in Latin America. Now we wish to share with fellow priests the disquieting thoughts and reflections that were raised by our study.

We do not propose to present a systematic exposition of principles, a thoroughgoing diagnosis of the existing situation, or a finished program. We simply wish to make our presence known at this critical hour for Latin America, to raise our voice in defense of the justice proclaimed by the gospel, and to contribute to the process of taking stock, which the present hour demands.

1. We are confronted by the anguished condition of our peoples and by the impatience of those who see violence as the only way to obtain justice. Caught in this situation, we feel the urgency and the necessity of two different pleas: on the one hand, the cries of the oppressed who do not live

in freedom because they do not possess the basic prerequisites for a decent existence; on the other hand, the appeal of Paul VI to work for humankind's fully rounded development into "persons of peace."

2. Our peoples have economic, political, and social problems that place them in a state of hopelessness and that are gradually closing the door on the possibility of living freely and decently. The new brand of slavery, which weighs heavy on the Latin American masses, strikes at the deepest parts of humankind. It prevents persons, not only from sharing in the goods that are rightfully theirs, but also from being capable of being the masters of their own destiny.

By the same token, the lack of access to material, educational, and cultural benefits creates a state of dependency on the economic, political, and cultural levels. It permits small oligarchies, whose power extends beyond geographical frontiers, to use the structures of society to their own benefit while placing obstacles in the way of the total transformation now called for throughout Latin America.

This state of injustice has so far prevented our countries from becoming integral national communities, which they must be if there is to be real freedom. It has also ruled out sovereignty for our people, by which they might be able to open their hearts to all human beings everywhere.

We cannot fail to underline the following truths. The present situation is the result of a society based solely on the "profit motive," a society that has subordinated human dignity and rights to economic advances, a society that has placed economic power in the hands of a small minority, and thus spawned "the international imperialism of money" (Pius XI) and a "despicable economic system" (Paul VI).

3. When we look at the heartrending reality of Latin America, we cannot help but fear for the fate of Paul VI's encyclical. It has already aroused sharp criticism from the ranks of liberalist capitalism. We fear that it may be shelved in the recesses of some dusty archive instead of becoming a prophetic clarion call to restore justice and freedom to the peoples who are working for their own betterment. This restoration must be accomplished if humanity is to avoid the tragic fate of renewed destruction. We appreciate the compelling urgency of Paul VI's courageous and realistic words, of the commitment undertaken by CELAM at Mar del Plata, and of the recent declaration by various bishops from the underdeveloped world. All these actions commit the church wholeheartedly to the task of bettering the human lot and winning true freedom for humankind.

4. Persons of good will, the oppressed in particular, expect the church to adopt a clearcut and appropriate outlook. They expect us to be consistent with our teachings, to be free in adopting positions, and to be generous in our actions. Only then will we be able to stimulate an effort on behalf of all humankind at this critical juncture in history.

5. Our mission is the same mission that Christ had. If we are to carry out this mission, then our priestly presence must be one of service (partic-

ularly to the oppressed) rather than one of wielding power. It has often seemed to be the latter in the past.

The church must be involved in human activity as the leaven in the dough. But it must be free from compromising entanglements that would prevent it from being a beacon of hope for the peoples of the world. Thus it must avoid entanglement with those who wield economic, political, and social power, and it cannot be the accomplice of those who try to block necessary structural changes and the restoration of rights to the dispossessed.

Granting this, *we are deeply concerned* over the faint impact of the encyclical *Populorum Progressio* on certain Christian sectors of the business world that wield economic, social, and political power, and on certain ecclesiastical circles of Latin America. It is vitally important, we feel, that there be a serious effort to make all of us priests aware of the present condition of underdevelopment on our continent, and of the guidelines and solutions that *Populorum Progressio* has put forward on the doctrinal level.

We deplore the fact that every attempt to regain just rights, sometimes violent in cast because there seems to be no other recourse, is labeled communism when, in fact, it is simply rebellion against a situation of injustice that is no longer tolerable. It pains us that the truth about these protests is distorted to favor the groups in control, who own most of the communications media.

We recognize the need for a more earnest effort on the church's part to eliminate the contradiction between the social doctrine it preaches and the unevangelical lifestyle it sometimes leads. We must increase the number of priests who will devote themselves to the ministry of the poor.

We want Catholic universities (which have for the most part been slow to face up to the real situation in Latin America and to the dictates of Vatican II and *Populorum Progressio*) to immerse themselves in the work of rapid and total change that Latin America needs. They should devote themselves primarily to studying and interpreting the complex situation of the continent. Only in this way will these halls of study be loyal to the cause of justice. Only in this way will their alumni become active protagonists of oppressed peoples seeking to mold their own destiny.

We cannot share the attitude of misunderstanding and sometimes even oppression that is directed against those who seriously and honestly express their thoughts on matters that are open to discussion.

We respect and hope to encourage the initiative of the laity in the process of change that Latin America must undergo. It must be left to them to form groups and movements that are Christian in inspiration. We deem it inadvisable for such groups to be confessional in character, with the result that civic institutions and movements are dependent on the hierarchy; for such an approach will divide Christians and imprison doctrine in fixed molds.

We are convinced that there is an urgent need to accelerate our study of

Latin America within a pastoral framework, so that the appeals of the pope and the episcopate may be incorporated into a pastoral outlook of continental, national, and diocesan dimensions. Such study will be valid and effective only if it is allied with teamwork that is multinational and polyvalent.

We express our thanks and appreciation to all those pastors and lay persons who have fought hard for the authentic human betterment of the oppressed, often encountering misunderstanding in the process.

Finally *we are fully aware* of our primordial priestly task. It is to form lay people who are deeply Christian and wholly committed to the building of a new social order that is more just and more human, that is at the service of each and every human being everywhere.

7

Gustavo Gutiérrez
"Toward a Theology of Liberation"
(July 1968)

In the month before the Medellín conference began in 1968, Gustavo Gutiérrez delivered this talk at a meeting of priests and laity held July 21-25 at Chimbote, Peru. The historian, Pablo Richard, describes it thus: "Roberto Oliveros provides a good summary of how liberation theology developed before Medellín. A key point in this development was Gustavo Gutiérrez's conference in Chimbote, Peru, in July 1968, 'Hacia una teología de la liberación.' This conference marked the explicit break, the qualitative leap, from a worldvision tied to a 'developmentalist' kind of practice to one tied to a practice of 'liberation'" (Death of Christendoms, Birth of the Church *[Maryknoll, N.Y.: Orbis Books, 1987], p. 145).*

This English text was translated by me from a mimeographed copy of the talk, which is in the archives of the De Las Casas Institute in Lima, Peru. I am indebted to Fr. Jeffrey Klaiber, S.J., a professor of Peruvian history, in Lima, for obtaining a copy for this volume. As far as I know, this is the first time it will be printed in English.

As Christians come in contact with the acute problems that exist in Latin America, they experience an urgent need to take part in solutions to them. They run the risk, however, of doing this without a reexamination of their own basic doctrinal principles, a situation that can lead to dead ends and to action that is ultimately sterile.

In this talk I will distance myself from concrete issues in order to analyze these basic doctrinal principles. Actually, the distancing is only apparent, since the following reflections can only be understood within a broader and richer approach that includes pastoral action and even political action.

INTRODUCTION

First of all, let us examine what we mean by *theology*. Etymologically speaking, theology is a treatise or discourse about God—which really does not tell us very much. The classic meaning of theology is an intellectual understanding of the faith—that is, the effort of the human intelligence to comprehend revelation and the vision of faith. But faith means not only truths to be affirmed, but also an existential stance, an attitude, a commitment to God and to human beings. Thus faith understands the whole of life theologically as faith, hope, and charity.

If, then, we say that faith is a commitment to God and human beings, and affirm that theology is the intellectual understanding of faith, we must conclude that faith is an understanding of this commitment. It is an understanding of this existential stance, which includes the affirmation of truths, but within a broader perspective.

Faith is not limited to affirming the existence of God. No, faith tells us that God loves us and demands a loving response. This response is given through love for human beings, and that is what we mean by a commitment to God and to our neighbor.

Consequently, when we speak about theology, we are not talking about an abstract and timeless truth, but rather about an existential stance, which tries to understand and to see this commitment in the light of revelation.

But precisely because faith is above all an existential stance, it admits a differentiation according to circumstances and the different approaches to the commitment to God and human beings. To say that faith is a commitment is true for all ages, but the commitment is something much more precise: I commit myself here and now. The commitment to God and to human beings is not what it was three centuries ago. Today I commit myself in a distinctive manner.

When we speak of theology, we mean a theology that takes into account its variation according to time and circumstances. From this we can deduce three characteristics:

1. Theology is a progressive and continuous understanding, which is variable to a certain extent. If it were merely the understanding of abstract truth, this would not be true. If theology is the understanding of an existential stance, it is progressive, it is the understanding of a commitment in history concerning the Christian's location in the development of humanity and the living out of faith.

2. Theology is a reflection—that is, it is a second act, a turning back, a re-flecting, that comes after action. Theology is not first; the commitment is first. Theology is the understanding of the commitment, and the commitment is action. The central element is charity, which involves commitment, while theology arrives later on.

This is what ancient authors said with regard to philosophy: "Primum vivere, deinde philosophare—first you must live, and then philosophize." We have interpreted this as first *la dolce vita*, and then some reflection if I have time. No, the principle is much more profound: philosophy, like theology, is a second act.

The pastoral consequences of this are immense. It is not the role of theology to tell us what to do or to provide solutions for pastoral action. Rather, theology follows in a distinctive manner the pastoral action of the church and is a reflection upon it.

3. If it is the intellectual understanding of a commitment, theology is an endeavor that must continuously accompany that commitment. The pastoral action of the church will be a commitment to God and the neighbor, while theology will accompany that activity to provide continual orientation and animate it. Every action of ours must be accompanied by a reflection to orient it, to order it, to make it coherent, so that it does not lapse into a sterile and superficial activism.

Theology, therefore, will accompany the pastoral activity of the church — that is, the presence of the church in the world. It will accompany that activity continuously, to help it to be faithful to the word of God, which is the light for theology.

But, I insist, the first and fundamental objective is the commitment of Christians. One should not ask of theology more than it can give. Theology is a science, and like any discipline, has a modest role in the life of human beings. The first step is action. As Pascal expressed it: "All the things in this world are not worth one human thought, and all the efforts of human thought are not worth one act of charity."

Theology is on the level of thought and reflection, and there is no theology that is the equivalent of an act of charity. The central issue is charity, commitment, action in the world. All this is what we understand by theology.

There is talk today of a theology of human liberation. Using this or other expressions, the theme has become a major preoccupation of the magisterium of the church in recent years.

If faith is a commitment to God and human beings, it is not possible to live in today's world without a commitment to the process of liberation. That is what constitutes a commitment today. If participation in the process of human liberation is the way of being present in the world, it will be necessary for Christians to have an understanding of this commitment, of this process of liberation.

This process constitutes what has been called since the council a "sign of the times." A sign of the times is not primarily a speculative problem — that is, a problem to be studied or interpreted. For the reasons noted above, a sign of the times is first of all a call to action and secondly a call to interpretation. A sign of the times calls Christians to action.

The process of liberation is a sign of the times. It is a call to action at the same time that it is a new theme for reflection, new because it is a global term for the problems contained within it. Thus there is a certain deficiency in the attempts that are being made with regard to a theology of liberation, which is clearly evident in the conclusions of the meetings at Mar del Plata and Itapoan, both of which leave me dissatisfied.

We will have to be much more concrete, but we will also be dependent on the progress of the science of economics for a more precise knowledge regarding the national and Latin American reality. A genuine theology of liberation can only be a team effort, a task which has not yet been attempted.

I will limit myself therefore to a sketch, to recalling a few paths of inquiry, as is suggested by my title, "Toward a Theology of Liberation." It really is *toward*. I believe we will have to go much further, but we can only achieve that through collaboration as a number of concepts become more precise.

We understand theology, then, as an intellectual understanding of the faith. But faith is above all a commitment to God and the neighbor. Although it implies the affirmation of truths, Christian truth nevertheless has the particular character of being a truth that is thought but that first of all is done. "To do the truth," the gospel text requires, and that is proper to Christian truth.

In this sketch we will consider three areas along the following lines:
1. the statement of the question
2. human liberation and salvation
3. the encounter with God in history.

1. THE STATEMENT OF THE QUESTION

The gospel is primarily a message of salvation. The construction of the world is a task for human beings on this earth. To state the question of a theology of liberation means, therefore, to ask about the meaning of this work on earth, the work that human beings perform in this world vis-à-vis the faith. In other words, what relationship is there between the construction of this world and salvation?

A theology of liberation, then, will have to reply first of all to this question: Is there any connection between constructing the world and saving it? The question is an old one and has an answer that can be considered the traditional one. Perhaps it is also the one we received in our Christian training and is more or less the following:

The world is a stage on which the drama of salvation takes place, where we are placed to decide if we will be saved or not. Consequently, human life is a "test," and we save or condemn ourselves by our actions. In this perspective the nature of the act itself is secondary.

A work is good if it functions religiously, if it "edifies," as we used to say. For example, a novel is good if it has a "religious" value—that is, if it teaches a religious or moral principle. The question of the book's literary value is secondary, since what is important is that it is useful in teaching its readers to be more moral, more chaste, and the like. A film is good to the extent that it has a "religious" purpose, to the extent that it "edifies."

College libraries used to contain books that were very deficient from a literary standpoint, but "helped" to understand the gospel. That and not their literary value was the important thing. We arrived at the extreme position of condemning as morally evil works that the rest of the world considered to be good and of high literary quality. The authentic works were in our view "evil," while the poor works, which nobody read, were considered good because they "edified." What was important in this approach was to do things for the love of God, as we see in this act of charity, which we still read in prayer books: "to love my neighbor as myself for love of You." The fundamental objective was to place oneself in the presence of God, for this automatically gave value to the work. It did not matter if one was an economist or a beautician, as long as everything was done for the love of God. The content of the act was of no concern, since the important thing in this life was to say yes or no to the Lord and to live in a moral way.

Work from this perspective had value if it was a sacrifice; the more sacrificial, the greater the value. The more useless it was, the more sacrificial, since even one's intelligence was sacrificed. A God who crushes us, a life in the beyond that devalues the present life, a supernaturalized theology that swallows up natural values, all this is what we have lived for a long time. This has prevented us from appreciating the things of this world. But that is precisely the question: Do these things have a value in themselves? Is there a relationship between the kingdom of God and human work as such?

Father Häring remarks on this point: "Christian morality has been dominated by occasions of sin and complicity." The world is full of complicity and occasions of sin; that is the real world. Fear of this has led Christians to lose interest in their earthly tasks, since preoccupation with the absolute has left no place for the ephemeral, the contingent, and the temporal. We are well aware that the Marxist and humanist critique of contemporary Christianity points out that there is something contradictory in our attitude. We have always said that we have only one economy of salvation for human beings, that we have a global view of the human person, that as the pope said at the United Nations and repeated in *Populorum Progressio*, the church is an expert in humanity. But often Christians, with their gaze fixed on the world beyond, manifest little or no commitment to the ordinary life of human beings.

We say that the human person is our fundamental concern, but the contemporary non-Christian humanist believes correctly that Christianity is not interested in human values. In a well-known text, Engels says:

Christianity and socialism proclaim the proximate liberation of humanity from slavery; but Christianity proclaims it in the next life, not here on earth. That is the difference. We are both agreed that humanity has to be liberated; however, for Christians it is later on, while for us it is now.

The absolute salvation provided by God in the hereafter, which diminishes the present life, has led to a very peculiar outlook: human institutions will be considered important if they are oriented to the hereafter. All other institutions have no value because they will pass away.

The church as institution is oriented to the hereafter, to the absolute. Only that which favors religion is considered good. A government is considered good if it aids the church, or if it provides money to build churches and schools. Goodness is measured by generosity to the church, because the church, as an instrument of salvation in the hereafter, is the only thing that will remain. In a somewhat paradoxical manner, therefore, we have a church that preaches "my kingdom is not of this world" ending up very comfortably ensconced in that world.

This position, this way of looking at reality, constitutes a brake on the presence and action of human beings in this world. But in our time we are in a new situation, which has been adopted by the Vatican Council. I believe that there are basically two factors that have created this new situation.

The first is the rise of science in the fifteenth and sixteenth centuries. Previously, nature has appeared to human beings fundamentally as a reflection of the glory of God. It was also seen as a kind of participation in the transcendence of God, so that nature received the same kind of reverent fear that was proper to God. At the present time, however, nature appears as dominated by science and technology as well as by human beings, so that, as the Vatican Council expressed it, "many benefits once looked for, especially from heavenly powers, man has now enterprisingly procured for himself" (*Gaudium et Spes*, no. 33). All this entails an enormous change in our outlook.

A second factor, derived from the first one, is that the human person has become the agent of his or her own destiny and the one responsible for his or her own development in history. This realization has occurred at approximately the same time as the growth of science. It begins with the reflection of Descartes, "I think, therefore I am," a reflection that starts with the human person.

While previous philosophy began with the object, exterior to humanity, Descartes begins with the human being. This tendency is accentuated by Immanuel Kant, for whom the world is a chaos, where the human being creates order by means of the well-known categories. This process will be referred to as a Copernican revolution, with the emphasis placed on the human being. As the affirmation of human subjectivity, it is tremendously important.

A key figure for understanding our era is certainly Hegel, who takes up the affirmation of subjectivity and brings it one step further: the human person is the agent of history, but, even more, history is nothing else than the process of human liberation. Since it is a history of human emancipation, the human being creates history by self-liberation. To liberate oneself, to emancipate oneself, is to create history. This idea will be taken up by Karl Marx within an economic framework,

Father Teilhard de Chardin provides a very beautiful image to describe this process. He sees the history of humanity more or less in the following way. In an early stage, people were in the hold of a ship, but they did not know they were in a ship. They had never left the hold, but remained in its obscure depths. What did they do there? They quarreled among themselves until one day someone climbed the stairs, went to the bridge, and discovered that they were in a machine that moved, that had a motor. It was at that moment that human beings became aware of an active role in history. From that moment on, they said, it was not a question of drifting, but of piloting. That is, human beings had learned that it was necessary to pilot the ship, not to drift in history but to direct it.

It is a question, then, of human liberation, of human emancipation throughout history, which will pass through radical social change, revolution, and even beyond these. Therefore, the question changes. It is not merely a matter of knowing the meaning of earthly action, but of knowing the meaning of human liberation in the perspective of faith, and what faith can say not only to human action in this world but to human liberation. What relationship exists between the kingdom of God and human emancipation?

A text from *Populorum Progressio* is very significant in this respect: "It is a question, rather, of building a world where all persons, no matter what their race, religion, or nationality, can live a fully human life, freed from servitude imposed on them by other human beings or by natural forces over which they have no control" (no. 47). Thus it is a question of constructing a world where human beings are free and in which freedom is not an empty word.

It means that theology faces the sign of the times, which is human liberation, and scrutinizes it profoundly. This leads us to take a definite perspective in judging economic and political domination. When we talk of economic domination, we touch the sore point, especially if we say that what is important is to free the human person, as the pope says, from every form of domination, whether it be natural or human. Economic and political domination not only imprison people economically, but they also prevent them from being human. Thus we must commit ourselves with respect to this great sign of the times.

Perhaps we are not sufficiently attentive to the completely new language of *Populorum Progressio*, which asserts that a global view of humanity is something proper to the church. If you ask Christians what is proper to the church, they will say: grace, the sacraments, but not the global vision of humanity. Are we passing from a theocentric theology to one that is anthropocentric? I think it is much more exact to say that we are passing from a theology that concentrated excessively on a God located outside this world to a theology of a God who is present in this world. That would be a Christian anthropocentrism. One would have to agree with the Protestant theologian Karl Barth, who said: "From the moment God became man, the human being is the measure of all things."

One of the classic texts of Paul VI, presented December 7, 1965, concerned anthropocentrism. In reply to the accusation that the council was excessively anthropocentric, the pope replied that it was a question of God present in history and present in the midst of human beings.

Thus our own question is posed. The theology of liberation means establishing the relationship that exists between human emancipation — in the social, political, and economic orders — and the kingdom of God.

2. HUMAN LIBERATION AND SALVATION

Pope Paul VI said that what the church can appropriately contribute is a global vision of the human being and of humanity, a vision that situates the process of development within the human vocation. This had been affirmed by *Gaudium et Spes*, and a reading of the texts will show us the theological progress that was accomplished by *Populorum Progressio*.

Gaudium et Spes, no. 34, reads: "Throughout the course of the centuries, human beings have labored to better the circumstances of their lives through a monumental amount of individual and collective effort. To believers, this point is settled: such human activity is in accord with God's will." This text shows that all that we do is a response to the will of God.

But Paul VI goes much further. In *Populorum Progressio* he adds clarity and profundity to the conciliar text: "In the design of God, all human beings are called upon to develop and fulfill themselves, for every life is a vocation" (no. 15). Human beings are called upon to develop themselves. In this perspective, we understand development as liberation, with all that implies, even in the economic sphere.

Human emancipation is included within this vocation. The vocation, as we know, is to communion with God, to being a child of God — it is to this that we have been called (Eph. 1:5). To have a vocation means to have been created and chosen to be children of God.

But the pope is careful to say that it is not a question of an individual vocation or of individual salvation. Rather, all human beings are called to this full development, which in the strong biblical sense we call convocation. Human beings are convoked and the process of development lies within that convocation. "All are called to this fullness of development" (*Populorum Progressio*, no. 17).

If this is true, if full, integral, and authentic development liberates human beings, then it is included within the human vocation. Development, therefore, is not a stage previous to evangelization, which we refer to with the incorrect word, "preevangelization." Rather development (and this is the new theological contribution of *Populorum Progressio*) is situated within one's vocation and thus of one's communion with God. It is not a previous step, but forms part of the process of salvation, because it is a vocation. Salvation, therefore, affects the whole human being.

The call of God includes all of reality and provides us with a radical change of outlook, a new way of evaluating the things of this world. This world is not a trampoline to leap upward to God, nor is it a stage on which to play a role—that is, a reality that does not interest us but allows us to be spiritual beings and to choose within it to be good or evil. No. If development is human fulfillment, it is part of our vocation, and all things have value.

There are not static obligations of charity that are somehow independent of the content of my actions of love. The world is not a "test," nor is it a stage. The work of constructing the world, the work itself which is brought to realization, has a salvific value. If development exists within our vocation, it has the value of salvation. Not only what is done for the love of God, but everything which contributes to growth in humanity, as *Populorum Progressio* says, everything which makes a person more human and contributes to human liberation, contains the value of salvation and communion with the Lord. In other words, and this vocabulary is new in the church, integral development is salvation.

What *Populorum Progressio* calls integral development is what we refer to theologically as salvation. Let us consider a text from *Populorum Progressio* (no. 21) which, together with no. 47, is one of the most important in the encyclical. Paul VI begins with the definition of development given by Fr. Lebret: it is to pass from less human conditions to more human conditions.

"Less human conditions: the lack of material necessities for those who are without the minimum essential for life, the moral duties of those who are mutilated by selfishness." That is less human. "Less human" also means "oppressive social structures, whether due to the abuses of ownership or to the abuses of power, to the exploitation of workers or to unjust transactions." Thus "less human" are oppressive structures, something Christians are generally unaware of. The structure itself is oppressive, although naturally human beings are responsible for it. But let us not say too quickly that we can only change the structures by changing human beings. Faced with contemporary humanism, which desires a change of structures, we are sometimes content to recall that human beings are inclined to sin. Certainly everything is connected, and it is right for a global vision to show the connections between these different aspects. But that global vision should not say that first we must change human beings in order afterward to change the structures. After Marx, it is no longer possible to say first change the human beings and then the structures. Our global vision must be able to see everything in a synthetic way. Human behavior is conditioned by the structures that human beings have created. It is a question, then, of simultaneous action on human beings and structures.

As regards the passage from less human to more human, the pope moves step by step: "More human: the passage from misery toward the possession of necessities, victory over social scourges," in this case scourges not of a personal kind but of structures. Also more human is "the growth of knowledge, the acquisition of culture." More human is "increased esteem for the dignity of others, turning toward the spirit of poverty." I think we have to understand this spirit of poverty correctly. "Poor in spirit," like the word "aggiornamento," are ambiguous expressions. *Aggiornare*, for example, has two meanings: to bring up to date, and to adjourn until tomorrow. Some have labored to "bring the church up to date" and others have tried to adjourn the council "until tomorrow." We could say that Christians today are divided into two sectors, which correspond to the two meanings of aggiornamento. Something similar happens with the phrase "poor in spirit," which I will clarify later on.

More human is "cooperation for the common good, the will and desire for peace." More human, too, is the acknowledgment by human beings of absolute values and of God. Finally and especially, more human is "faith, a gift of God accepted by the good will of human beings and unity in the charity of Christ, who calls us all to share as sons in the life of the giving God, the Father of all" (*Populorum Progressio*, no. 21).

More human is grace, more human is faith, more human is to be a child of God. Consequently, we can say that integral development, authentic emancipation, and human liberation are, for the pope, salvation. Actually, in this section Paul VI is sketching the whole process of development, which proceeds from material and moral misery toward the grace of God. This is development, which is also a task and a call to action.

I emphasize that the work of building the earth is not a preceding stage, not a stepping stone, but already the work of salvation. The creation of a just and fraternal society is the salvation of human beings, if by salvation we mean the passage from the less human to the more human. Salvation, therefore, is not purely "religious."

In all this, the pope and the council are only retrieving the most ancient tradition of the church, which I will now recall and illustrate by two biblical themes that will serve simply as examples.

First of all, there is the relationship between creation and salvation. This is a general theme that is not secondary but in a certain sense dominant throughout the Bible.

In a rather simplistic exegesis, creation is presented as the explanation of what now exists. This is not false, but it is insufficient. In the Bible, creation appears not as a stage previous to the work of salvation but rather as the first salvific act. "God chose us before the salvation of the world" (Eph. 1:3). Creation is included in the process of salvation, which is God's self-communication. The religious experience of Israel is above all a history, but a history that is nothing else but the prolongation of the creative act. Thus the Psalms speak of Yahweh as simultaneously creator and savior (see Psalm 136). The God who has made a cosmos out of chaos is the same one who acts in the history of salvation. The redemptive work of Christ is presented also in a context of creation (John, chap. 1). Creation and salvation have a Christological meaning: in him everything has been created, and everything has been saved (see Col. 1:15-20).

From this perspective, when we say that the human person is fulfilled by prolonging the work of creation through labor, we are affirming that he or she is located first of all within the work of salvation. To subdue the earth, as Genesis prescribes, is a work of salvation. To labor to transform this world is to save it. As Marx had clearly seen, work as a humanizing element normally tends through the transformation of nature to construct a society that is more just and worthy of human beings. The Bible makes us understand the profound meaning of this effort. The construction of the temporal city is not simply a stage of humanization or preevangelization, as theology used to say until recent years. It is to place oneself completely in a salvific process, which includes the whole person. Every offense, every humiliation, every alienation of human labor is an obstacle to the work of salvation.

A second great biblical theme has similar implications. It is the theme of the messianic promises—that is, of the events that announce and accompany the coming of the Messiah. It is not an isolated theme, but like the first one extends throughout the Bible. It has a vital presence in the history of Israel and thus takes its place in the emergence of the people of God.

The prophets announce a kingdom of peace. But peace supposes the establishment of justice, the defense of the *rights of the poor*, the punishment of oppressors, a life without the fear of being enslaved by others. A poorly conceived spiritualization has often made us forget the human task and the power to transform unjust structures that the messianic promises contain. The elimination of misery and exploitation is a sign of the coming of the messiah.

In the Gospel of Luke we read: "The Spirit of the Lord is upon me, because he has appointed me to preach good news to the poor. He has sent me to proclaim release to captives and recovering of sight to the blind." Christ will add later: "Today the Scripture has been fulfilled in your hearing" (4:18). What is it that is being fulfilled? The Spirit has anointed him to preach the gospel to the poor, proclaim liberation to captives, sight to the blind, freedom to the oppressed, and to proclaim the Lord's year of grace.

We have deeply interiorized a framework for interpreting the Bible: as Christians we must understand everything the Old Testament says about the temporal order as belonging to the spiritual plane. This spiritual outlook would begin with the New Testament. Thus we translate "to preach good news to the poor" as meaning that we should tell the poor in spirit that they should hope in God. "To preach liberation to captives" means to speak to the captives about sin. "The recuperation of sight by the blind" means that they do not see God. "Freedom to the oppressed" means those oppressed by Satan.

In reality all these expressions have a meaning that is direct and clear. For example, let us take "to proclaim a year of grace." This becomes clear if we refer to Leviticus 25:10, which says that a just society must be established. *Populorum Progressio* says the same thing: When it is left simply to economic laws freely to organize human life, then we begin to have rich and poor. If the economy is given free rein, the distance between them increases. That is what happened in the past, in the time of Leviticus. For that reason, the "year of grace" was created, when all would have to go back to the starting point, when all would leave aside what they possessed and begin anew.

We have said that everything in the Old Testament was purely secular and thus required transformation into a more religious framework, but this is not true. Certainly there is a religious significance, but the messianic promise means something integral and global, which affects the whole person.

If we understand salvation as something with merely "religious" or "spiritual" value for my soul, then it would not have much to contribute to concrete human life. But if salvation is understood as passing from less human conditions to more human conditions, it means that messianism brings about the freedom of captives and the oppressed, and liberates human beings from the slavery that Paul VI referred to (*Populorum Progressio* no. 47).

The sign of the coming of the messiah is the suppression of oppression: the messiah arrives when injustice is overcome. When we struggle for a just world in which there is not servitude, oppression, or slavery, we are signifying the coming of the messiah. Therefore the messianic promises bind tightly together the kingdom of God and better living conditions for human beings or, as Paul VI said, more human living conditions. An intimate relationship exists between the kingdom and the elimination of poverty and misery. The kingdom comes to suppress injustice.

These are two biblical themes, then, creation/salvation and the messianic promises, which demonstrate the extent to which the encyclical of Paul VI is anchored in revelation and the word of God. Consequently, the pope can say that human development "constitutes a summary of all our duties." If then we can understand integral development as passing from less human conditions to more human conditions, and if within the most human elements we include grace, faith, and divine filiation, then we comprehend profoundly why it can be said that working for development is the summary of all our duties.

3. THE ENCOUNTER WITH GOD IN HISTORY

Gaudium et Spes (no. 45) tells us the following: "The Lord is the goal of human history, the focal point of the longings of history and of civilization, the center of the human race, the joy of every heart, and the answer to all its yearnings."

If there is a finality inscribed in history, then the essence of Christian faith is to believe in Christ, that is, to believe that God is irreversibly committed to human history. To believe in Christ, then, is to believe that God has made a commitment to the historical development of the human race.

To have faith in Christ is to see the history in which we are living as the progressive revelation of the human face of God. "Who sees me sees the Father." This holds to a certain extent for every human being according to the important text of Matthew 25, which reminds us that an action on behalf of a human being is an action on behalf of God. If you gave food and drink, you gave it to me; if you denied it, you denied it to me.

The encounter with God takes place in the encounter with our neighbor; it is in the encounters with human beings that I encounter God. Therefore, to have faith is to live in view of tomorrow, which is an encounter with the Lord. To have faith is to journey in history, for the life of faith is a project aimed at the future. To live complacently in the present entails nostalgia for the past and is already growing old.

To use an image from Teilhard de Chardin, God is not at our back, pushing us along on our journey. God is before us, revealed in the thousands of faces of human beings in the different circumstances of life. As Péguy says: "The faith that I love is hope," the hope of encountering God in my encounters with human beings.

Christ is the place of interchange, for in him a human person gives a human face to God and God gives a divine face to human beings. The historic adventure and the meaning of history will be the revelation of God. To believe in Christ, therefore, is to believe at the same time in history. To believe in eschatology, in the final times, is the motor of the historical process.

Faith from this perspective is thus the horizon and also the motivating force of all human behavior at the same time that it divinizes it. The encounter with Christ takes place in the neighbor, so that the key question is: Who is my neighbor?

The parable of the Good Samaritan is clear. Christ is asked: Who is my neighbor? Then the Lord tells a story that on a superficial level teaches that the neighbor is the one who is on the road—that is, the wounded man. But Christ reverses the question at the end: Which of these three was a neighbor to the other? To be a Christian is to draw near, to make oneself a neighbor, not the one I encounter in my journey but the one in whose journey I place myself. The neighbor is the one to whom I draw near, and I am an agent of history.

There are roads in life in which we will always encounter neighbors. If I take the road of human liberation, I will encounter millions of neighbors. The free human person is the one who constructs emancipation and salvation. It is certain that I find God in my neighbor, but as I draw near, I make him or her my neighbor. The last person to pass the wounded man made of him a neighbor.

I leave aside other aspects of the parable, which are interesting in describing this encounter with God, but that is enough. If we are correct, faith energizes and activates within history, since there is no way of encountering God outside history. Christians cannot hide in some dead end of history in order to watch it passing them by.

That the encounter with God occurs in the neighbor is a classic biblical theme. Matthew 25 is a clear text, but the whole Old Testament teaches it: whatever you do for the stranger, the widow, and the orphan has an effect upon God. Those are the three types of the poor: the stranger rejected by a nationalist people, the widow who has no one to support her, and the orphan, left without the aid of parents.

Faith energizes my actions in history and makes me take that history seriously, since it is impossible to be a Christian outside history. At present one should not fear to say that. It is an understanding of what a contemporary commitment is—that is to say, one cannot be a Christian in these times without a commitment to liberation. To be a Christian in our epoch, it is necessary to commit oneself in one way or other in the process of human emancipation.

But at the same time that faith radicalizes my commitment and makes it ever more profound, it also relativizes every human work. There is, therefore, a dialectic between radicalization and relativization.

Faith relativizes human work, because it prevents me from being content with what I am doing or what others are doing. Faith will continually move me further ahead. If God is before us, our journey will never cease. To a certain extent, a Christian remains unsatisfied, for the process of human liberation is never ending.

The radicalization and relativization of my task in history is a dialectical interplay that will comprise my originality as a Christian. It will keep me from falling into sectarianism or being content with my human efforts, but it will also permit me to undertake that task with radical seriousness.

No. 43 of *Gaudium et Spes* poses the question of the relationship between faith and life, and tells us that faith leads us to take our worldly task with great seriousness. It reminds us that faith that is not intertwined with life will be useless. On the other hand, it can be helpful to refer to the second part of no. 43: "Nor, on the contrary, are they any less wide of the mark who believe that religion consists in acts of worship alone and in the discharge of certain moral obligations, and who imagine they can plunge themselves into earthly affairs in such a way as to imply that these are altogether divorced from religious life." Faith should nourish and criticize our commitment in history. We should take up our commitment to the process of change, to revolution, to human emancipation in the light of faith.

CONCLUSION

In closing let us consider two well-known texts in the light of what we have been discussing. The first is from Karl Marx:

> The social principles of Christianity preach the need of a dominating class and an oppressed class. And to the latter class they offer only the benevolence of the ruling class. The social principles of Christianity point to heaven as the compensation for all the crimes that are committed on earth. The social principles of Christianity explain all the viciousness of oppressors as a just punishment either for original sin or other sins, or as trials that the Lord, in infinite wisdom, inflicts on those the Lord has redeemed. The social principles of Christianity preach cowardice, self-hatred, servility, submission, humility—in a word, all the characteristics of a scoundrel [1847, MEGA 1, 6, p. 278].

How could we have presented such an image of Christianity?
The other is a text from Isaiah:

> For behold I create new heavens and a new earth; and the former things shall not be remembered and come into mind. [We will have changed reality in such a way that no one will remember the past. The result is a global change of structures.] But be glad and rejoice forever in that which I create: for behold, I create Jerusalem rejoicing, and her people a joy. I will rejoice in Jerusalem, and be glad in my people; no more shall be heard in it the sound of weeping and the cry of distress or an old man who does not fill out his days. . . . They shall build houses and inhabit them; they shall plant vineyards and eat their fruit. They shall not build and another inhabit; they shall not plant and another eat; for like the days of a tree shall the days of my people be, and my chosen shall long enjoy the work of their hands [65: 17-22].

This very concrete reality is the kingdom of God. In it children will not die in a few days. The people will not work for others but for themselves, the city will be called a "rejoicing" and her people a "joy."

How could we have transformed this into what was described in the text of Marx? Unfortunately, both images are true, from different perspectives. Although the messianic promises refer to concrete material things, Marx's vision of over a century ago continues to be repeated by human beings today.

The issue, then, is whether we are capable of realizing the prophecy of Isaiah and of understanding the kingdom of God in its integral reality, or whether we are going to give the counter-testimony that is reflected in the statements of Marx. This is precisely what is at stake in our epoch.

8

Provincials of the Society of Jesus
"The Jesuits in Latin America"
(May 1968)

The expectations and specific plans of the members of an influential religious order is the theme of this document. The Jesuit provincials for all of Latin America met in Rio de Janeiro, Brazil, May 6–14, 1968, and summarized their deliberations in this letter sent to all members of the Society. With respect to liberation theology, it is interesting to note the Jesuits' expression of their basic apostolic mission: "In all our activities, our goal should be the liberation of persons from every sort of servitude that oppresses them" (no. 3). The source for this document is Between Honesty and Hope, *pp. 144–50.*

1. Meeting here with our Father General, we Jesuit provincials direct this communiqué to all the Jesuits in Latin America: superiors, priests, brothers, and students. We wish to share with you the outlooks and commitments we have arrived at in our collective examination of conscience, taken in the Lord's presence. We have been spurred to this examination by the teachings of the council, by the words of Pope Paul's encyclical *Populorum Progressio*, by the statements of our bishops, and by the letter of our Father General on the social apostolate in Latin America.

A DISGRACEFUL SITUATION

2. Most Latin Americans find themselves in a state of poverty, the injustice of which cries to heaven for vengeance (*Populorum Progressio*, no. 30). The alienated masses in the rural and urban areas are increasing at an accelerated rate. Native groups are subject to de facto racial discrimination. The same dialectic of violence is encouraged by those who reject the thoroughgoing reforms needed as by those who despair of a peaceful solution.

Traditional society is disappearing along with its specific culture. A new society is being born: industrial, urban, democratic, pluricultural, socialized,

77

secularized, laicized. Its lifestyles know no geographical frontiers, and it is challenging or even rejecting the values and structures that once predominated. At the same time we are seeing the growth of an affluent civilization, now threatened by materialism. On the other side of the coin, the continuing progress of science and technology, and the increasingly conscious initiatives of the people at large, offer new reasons for hope.

3. The social problem of Latin America is the problem of humankind itself. The epoch in which we are living is a critical moment in the history of salvation. For this reason we propose to give this problem absolute priority in our apostolic strategy; indeed we intend to orient our whole apostolate around it. In this way we hope to participate, as best we can, in the common quest of all peoples (whatever their ideology may be) for a freer, more just, and more peaceful society. We want the Society to be actively present in the temporal life of humankind today: having as its sole criterion the gospel message as interpreted by the church, exercising no power in civil society and seeking no political goals, seeking solely to shape the consciences of individuals and communities.

We are aware of the profound transformation this presupposes. We must break with some of our attitudes in the past to reestablish ties with our humanist tradition: "The human being fully alive is the glory of God" (Saint Irenaeus).

We want to avoid any attitude of isolation or domination that may have been ours in the past. We want to adopt an attitude of service to the church and to society, rejecting the overtones of power that have often been attributed to us. We proclaim our desire to cooperate with the clergy and the laity in a joint pastoral effort, to look for the new collaborative structures on which our work might be based.

In all our activities, our goal should be the liberation of humankind from every sort of servitude that oppresses it: the lack of life's necessities, illiteracy, the weight of sociological structures which deprive it of personal responsibility over life itself, the materialistic conception of history. We want all our efforts to work together toward the construction of a society in which all persons will find their place, and in which they will enjoy political, economic, cultural, and religious equality and liberty.

We are counting on you as we undertake this effort to divest ourselves of any aristocratic attitude that may have been present in our public positions, in our style of life, in the selection of our audience, in our dealings with lay co-workers, and in our relations with the wealthy classes.

4. If our apostolate is truly motivated by an open and evangelical spirit, it will almost certainly arouse reactions. We shall not provoke such reactions by a partisan stance, but shall continue to preach the gospel to the poor no matter what reactions may be unleashed.

We are convinced that all humanity is yearning for peace, even amid its fratricidal conflicts. We want to be faithful to the evangelical spirit that was embodied in John XXIII's encyclical, the very title of which was significant:

Pacem in Terris. So we promise to work for bold reforms that will radically transform existing structures (*Populorum Progressio,* no. 32), regarding this as the only way to promote social peace. Violent attitudes are inauthentic if they are based on utopian dreams, frustration, or hatred rather than on conscientious reflection and Christian love. They evade the real issue if they neglect here-and-now action, with the sacrifices it entails. Passive attitudes, too, can be inauthentic when based on ignorance, inertia, fear, or lack of interest in others. In all its activities the Society of Jesus will summon Christians to reflection and love, urging them to fulfill their temporal commitments.

SOCIETAL LIFE AND CHRISTIAN LIVING

5. In spreading the spiritual and sacramental life, in preaching the gospel and performing all our other pastoral activities, we must make a special effort to preclude and eliminate the dissociation that crops up in the lives of many Christians. We often find a complete chasm between their private life and their professional life; there is no room for love or a sense of sin in the latter.

Persons are saved or damned, depending on the import of their life for the common history of humankind. The integration of societal life within the Christian way of life calls for theological and philosophical reflection that will take in the whole world and its pressing problems. The task of teachers of philosophy and theology, in particular, is to teach the global vision of humankind that the church itself has (*Populorum Progressio,* no. 13), so as to prepare priests and laypersons for their apostolate in the world of today. This formation should include a sound grounding in the sciences that deal with human nature.

FOCUS ON HUMAN NEEDS

6. Since our work is based on the most critical human and religious needs of this continent, we propose first of all to allocate a part of our apostolic resources to the growing mass of those who are most neglected.

For several years now we have been establishing study and action centers in the provinces of Latin America. These centers study the aspects relative to the development of the local region in a Christian perspective, serving as our contribution to structural change. We have decided to consolidate them into Centers of Research and Social Action, and to bolster them with greater resources and personnel. Their specific mission will be to awaken personal awareness and to orient outlook and actions in the right direction, through research, publications, training courses, and advisory work.

Within such centers and elsewhere too, other Jesuits are working to train peasant and labor leaders, to establish cooperatives and labor unions, and to foster civic and community action. Material-aid centers have also been established throughout the continent, and some Jesuits have dedicated their lives to working among the poor in rural parishes. We intend to allocate more Jesuits to this work, our aim always being to turn responsibility over to the people themselves so that they can take charge of their own liberation.

We are convinced that the Society of Jesus in Latin America must take a clear stand in defense of social justice, supporting those who lack the basic tools of education, which are so essential for development. Hence we must offer marginal groups the chance for an education, so that they may be able to contribute their talents to the life of the nation. We wish to encourage and perfect educational programs for the people at large, providing a solid education to all. Our tradition in education will find a fruitful modern direction through this effort.

In addition to these activities, the Society finds another thrust to be fully in accord with its underlying spirit. It is the vocation to an apostolate of being present to the people and bearing witness among them, sharing their life of poverty. Such an apostolate is truly authentic, but the forms of this presence may vary according to circumstances. It may involve pastoral work among grassroots communities, collaboration with the diocesan clergy in revamping the parish apostolate, or manual labor in the factories if this type of apostolate seems necessary among marginally Christian groups. Experience will show us whether it is advisable to form a distinctive religious community for Jesuits who work in this ministry, so that they may be united with the Society as a whole.

In all these ways our Society will demonstrate its desire to share the life of our people. Our communities will feel the influence of this presence, and the whole Society will feel invited to give clearer witness to poverty in its buildings and style of life.

TOWARD A SOCIAL APOSTOLATE

7. Allocating a part of our resources to the people is not enough. We also want all forms of the Society's apostolate to be integrated into a social apostolate, without losing their specific orientation.

Education, for example, is a major factor for social change. We think it is most important that our schools and universities accept their role as active agents of national integration and social justice in Latin America. We will not have development for all until we have integral education for all.

Our education centers should be awakening an awareness that the whole community benefits from their services, and that the whole community should therefore join in providing the resources they need to carry out their task. These centers should permit capable aspirants to participate at every educational level, without regard to social class or wealth.

Up to now most of our students have come to us to get personal training that would ensure them a place in the present social order. For the most part we have fallen in with this individualistic outlook and its attendant traces of class prejudice (*Letter of the Father General on the Social Apostolate in Latin America*). The present situation in Latin America calls for some radical changes. First and foremost we must instill an attitude of service to society in our students and a genuine concern for marginal groups. Our students must participate in the transformation of present-day society and in the work of bettering the human condition.

We should also do what we can to see to it that our students engage in some real social service before graduation. This service should form part of the school curriculum. In this way the families of our students will commit themselves to working with us in our concern for societal problems.

As far as our universities are concerned, the recentness of their establishment and the difficult task of maintaining them make them truly difficult apostolic enterprises. Their academic and economic difficulties are aggravated even more by the fact that they must now provide high quality training and research, and that they should provide a broader-based opportunity for education to all. We feel that our universities should excel in the sciences relating to human nature, since these have a vital role to play in the overall project of changing our society. In our universities there should be a group of education experts who would serve the educational interests of the community.

We must not forget that a lack of equal educational opportunities lies at the base of the unjust social structures in Latin American countries. We must do all we can to offer as many scholarships and other aids as possible, so that education may be within the reach of all. And for the same reason, we must also engage in serious studies to ensure a fairer distribution of funds in government educational budgets.

Finally, in this area of education we feel that it would be advisable for all the Jesuit provinces in Latin America to get together in pilot projects so as to carry out the ideas set forth in the preceding paragraphs.

FORMING ADULT CONSCIENCES

8. Absorbed in its apostolate to children and adolescents, the Society of Jesus in many parts of Latin America may well have dedicated insufficient time and effort to forming the consciences of adults. Adults in every walk of life must be the active promoters of social change: intellectuals, business owners, labor organizers, artists, businessmen, professionals in their service to society.

And we must not only work *for* the laity, we must also work *with* them. By virtue of their real priesthood, they are called to the apostolate; and we must help them to channel their immense energies into the work of transforming our continent.

THE MASS MEDIA

9. The communications media are powerful and far-reaching instruments for promoting cultural awareness and social consciousness. They should therefore be accorded new importance in our apostolate. It would be difficult for us to find a more effective tool for educating the masses of the people. If we do not use these media, it is doubtful that our voice will be heard at all by atheists and fallen-away Christians. The statistics indicating the average amount of time a person in Latin America devotes to these media each week leave no doubt as to their importance. They will be of decisive importance in inculcating human values and in promoting new types of organizational and living styles that will help to create the new order we seek.

OUR PERSONAL CONVERSION

10. As we come to the close of this communiqué, we must stress the fact that our participation in the creation of a new social order presuppose a deep, inner conversion within each one of us. As Pope Paul VI indicated, a humanism closed in upon itself and impervious to spiritual values is essentially inhuman (*Populorum Progressio,* no. 42). We will never manage to construct a more humane society if we cannot bring to it the support of God. This is the type of support that the world expects from us above all. We priests and religious should ask ourselves in all seriousness: Are we capable of responding to the world's expectations? Are our faith and charity equal to the anxiety-ridden appeals of the world around us? Do we practice self-denial sufficiently, so that God is able to flood us with light and energy? Does personal prayer have its proper place in our life, so that we are united with God in this great human task that cannot succeed without God? Can the Society keep within its ranks those members who do not want to pray or who do not have a real and personal prayer life?

We provincials of the Society have thought seriously about these questions, and we pose them now to all the Jesuits of Latin America with a sense of earnestness and urgency. The new commitments, which we have spelled out here, will ultimately depend on our response to these questions.

THE RESPONSIBILITY OF SUPERIORS

11. We realize that the directives of this letter presuppose a profound reworking of our apostolate and our personal life. We also realize that it presupposes changes in our decision-making process as provincials. We have no delusions about the fact that such a thoroughgoing reform will not be accomplished in a short time. But we are pledged to carry it through as

quickly as possible. We are depending on you to assist this process through your labors, your reflections, and your prayers.

In this way, hopefully, the Society of Jesus in Latin America will be able to undergo the necessary conversion with God's grace. It then will be able to carry out the responsibilities it faces at this critical juncture in the continent's history—*ad majorem Dei gloriam.*

9

Peruvian Organizations
"The Role of the Laity"
(June 1–2, 1968)

Nineteen different organizations concerned with the apostolate of the laity in Peru met in the Peruvian city of Naña on June 1–2, 1968. Their objectives were to discuss the topics that were to be discussed two months later in the Medellín conference, and to offer their suggestions to the Peruvian bishops. Noteworthy is the fact that the lay persons are critical not only of society but also of the church. Thus, while insisting on the need for them to participate in the church's work of evangelization, sanctification, and service, they continue as follows: "It is of fundamental importance for this work that relations with the hierarchy not be kept on the level of command and compliance, but on the interpersonal and community level." This document is also important symbolically, because it points to the fact that the church of the future in Latin America is going to depend on the full participation and responsible leadership of the laity. This report is found in Between Honesty and Hope, *pp. 151–55.*

As was originally planned, we discussed two basic aspects of lay involvement: (1) the role of the laity in the world; and (2) the role of the laity in ecclesial structures.

This agenda gave rise to related questions, which were discussed amicably by those present. It led us to believe that we would have to reform our way of living Christianity in our daily lives. To begin with, faith prompts us to affirm that the Lord is present in every human happening and encounter, and to see in the "signs of the times" God's concrete call to humankind of a particular time and region. One conclusion to be drawn from this affirmation is that the only authentic response to God's love is fraternal love, which must be put into action. Love demands a perduring effort on our part to keep our neighbors and their concrete needs before our eyes. And since it is apparent that the ills afflicting our fellow countrymen have social roots, we can only live as Christians by participating actively in the work of changing the structures that condition societal life.

So we should like to spell out some of the ideas that express our present outlook and our effort to come closer to the Lord's wishes.

FUNCTION OF THE LAITY IN THE WORLD

COMMITMENTS TO SOCIAL CHANGE

Lay persons cannot evade their commitment to social change. They must involve themselves in this effort.

Every human being of good will is committed to changing a social order that is cruelly unjust. To refuse such a commitment would be to make oneself an accomplice of injustice. If Christians do not commit themselves to changing a system that prevents most persons from achieving personal fulfillment, then they are not helping humanity to live out its vocation and attain union with God. In short, uncommitted lay persons are betraying their mission to serve the progress of human history.

Thus the outlook of Christians cannot be restricted to personal religious practices or to an individualistic morality; they cannot fail to reexamine their conduct within the framework of the structures prevailing in this world. If they failed to do this, they would be bearing witness against the gospel. They must confront the reality of today with the reality of the gospel, living always as wayfarers open to change and ever on the move.

So the question: How many authentic Christian lay persons do we find today? Well, some lay persons fail to fulfill their Christian duty out of ignorance or lack of awareness. Some adopt a negative attitude toward change and put obstacles in its path. Some pretend to assist in the process of change, but they do so from a narrow sectarian outlook; they consider themselves to be the only bearers of truth, and they deprecate any solution offered by non-Catholic groups. Others adopt a paternalistic attitude, regarding themselves as messengers of truth to the rest of humankind as if these others lacked any trace of Christian inspiration.

VIOLENCE

Commitment to change often confronts lay persons with the whole problem of violence. Traditionally Christians have regarded violent tactics as the extreme reaction of oppressed groups who are the victims of an unjust social order. They have not tended to regard as violent the maintenance of an inhuman order by the oppressors themselves. They have noted the sporadic violence of the oppressed, but not the continuing everyday violence of oppressors.

It is our opinion that the real violence of the present day is the intolerable and perduring violence of an institutionalized nature. This seems clear from the facts before us: the rate of infant mortality, the lack of daily sustenance, the wage level and salary policy, the whole scheme of charitable contributions and international economic relationships.

There are instances where the violence of the oppressed can be justified, and lay persons can adopt this course when prior analysis suggests that it will be an effective course of action. Of course it is not possible to rule out error in such judgments, and there is always a risk involved in such a course of action.

POVERTY

The poverty situation, we feel, is the product of unjust socio-economic structures. Our people in Peru endure their harsh lot only by relying on the escapes of alcoholism, coca addiction, and alienation. Faced with this intolerable situation, we feel that we must change our style of living. We are members of the church, and we are also the products of a society that has taught us to look coldly on the impoverished plight of our brother Peruvians. In the light of the present situation and our faith, we feel it is not enough to give up luxuries, we must also give up some necessities. It is not enough to avoid giving scandal, we must also draw nearer to the poor. We cannot just dedicate a small portion of our time to the poor; we must dedicate our working and leisure hours to the cause of the poor, for only then will we be able to change the situation radically.

The limits of self-sacrifice must be set by real love, not by the standards of a society that tends to maintain the present situation. And the real import of all our actions must be sought for in the love of our Lord himself. He has shared this love with us, and we must learn to grow in it. Saint Paul suggests the outlines of this love:

> If I give away all that I possess, piece by piece, and if I even let them take my body to burn it, but am without love, it will not do me any good whatever [1 Cor. 13:3].

> Remember how generous the Lord Jesus was: he was rich, but he became poor for your sake, to make you rich out of his poverty [2 Cor. 8:9].

We, too, must become poor in order to save the poor from poverty.

FUNCTION OF THE LAITY IN ECCLESIAL STRUCTURES

NEED FOR CHRISTIAN COMMUNITY

We cannot continue to grow in the life of faith without living in a Christian community. It is in this community that our commitment to structural change (i.e., our task as citizens of the world) runs into the commitment which God demands of us through the Bible and the signs of the times.

The love of the Christian community is important for lay persons because it replaces their individualistic moral values (individual salvation) with community-centered moral values. Through the Christian community, lay persons can take on the real life of the people of God in all its dimensions.

Lay persons have a right and a duty to offer an interpretation of the signs of the times. And this interpretation should be picked up by the church so that it may work out a pastoral program that measures up to the needs of the historical moment in which we live. The lay person, then, shares the task of preaching the gospel and turning it into a truly historical message. In addition, the lay person will also participate in the church's pastoral task of forming Christians within the Christian community.

ANALYZING THE REAL SITUATION

The presentation of the gospel message presupposes a solid knowledge of the real situation in which its audience lives. Social, political, and economic factors must be part of this knowledge, insofar as they affect human lives. To attain such knowledge, there must be a thoroughgoing analysis of the situation in which the church and today's humankind are living.

The spiritual life of the community and the individual must be guided by the signs of the times, on the basis of such factual analysis. A spirituality that is unconcerned about temporal realities is always alienating to the extent that it does not induce Christians to love the ones who are living through the same moment of history. The Christian community should help its members to discern, interpret, and respond to the signs of the times. Historical situations and happenings send out a call to us and expect a response from us. Today's situation calls for poverty and fellowship on our part; we must join the cause of the oppressed, working on behalf of full human development.

RELATIONS WITH THE HIERARCHY

As we noted above, the lay person must participate in the church's work of evangelization, sanctification, and service. It is of fundamental importance for this work that relationships with the hierarchy not be kept on the level of command and compliance, but on the interpersonal and community level where these tasks are carried out in different ways. We see difficulties involved here because the positions of both the priest and the lay person are now in constant flux—due to the fact that the church has only recently begun to adapt itself to our concrete historical situation. By virtue of their practical experience and their place in the world, lay persons have sufficient guidelines to judge how the message is to be presented; and the hierarchy should always take this into account. Any critical evaluation of this nature should take place within the framework of the Christian community.

SOLIDARITY WITH THE PEOPLE'S POVERTY

Our apostolic organizations, as visible signs of Christ's love, must avoid all manner of scandalous ostentation—in our activities, buildings, furnishings, and styles of life. And such ostentation must be judged in terms of the scandalous poverty of our compatriots rather than in our own terms. Our organizations must somehow get close to the poor, because only close experience will teach us the great magnitude of the problems that afflict the majority of the people. We must therefore reform the structures of our organizations so that such contact really takes place. So long as the church and its individual members do not actually share the problems of the people—lack of basic necessities, insecurity, unemployment, etc.—they cannot really identify with "the joys and the hopes, the griefs and the anxieties, of persons of this age, especially those who are poor" (*Gaudium et Spes*, no. 1).

10

Second General Conference of Latin American Bishops "The Church in the Present-Day Transformation of Latin America in the Light of the Council" (August 26–September 6, 1968)

There can be little doubt that the Medellín conference marked a momentous watershed in the history of the church in Latin America, analogous but with significant differences to the effect of the Second Vatican Council on the universal church. The most significant difference was not that Medellín discovered the world of the poor, for that discovery and a subsequent option to struggle on their behalf is obvious in all the documents in this section, and all these documents preceded Medellín. Rather, in my opinion its importance was to institutionalize in its decrees the experience and practice of a significant number of Catholics in every stratum of the church from peasants to archbishops. It thus provided legitimation, inspiration, and pastoral plans for a continentwide preferential option for the poor, encouraging those who were already engaged in the struggle and exhorting the entire church, both rich and poor, to become involved.

It would be impossible to analyze all the Medellín documents in a volume of this kind. At this point, I will merely include the five most significant parts of the conference, together with their titles, and let the documents speak for themselves. However, one last event of great symbolic value should be mentioned. On August 24, 1968, Pope Paul VI delivered the opening address to the conference, marking the first time a pope had ever set foot in the New World. Whatever its intention, it surely illustrated dramatically that the Latin American church was embarking on a new voyage with its destination still not clearly in sight.

The selections here are taken from Second General Conference of Latin American Bishops, The Church in the Present-Day Transformation of Latin America in the Light of the Council: II Conclusions *(second edition, Wash-*

ington, D.C.: Division for Latin America — United States Catholic Conference, 1973).

MESSAGE TO THE PEOPLES OF LATIN AMERICA

OUR WORD, A SIGN OF COMMITMENT

The Second General Conference of the Latin American Episcopate to the peoples of Latin America: "Grace and peace from God, our Father, and from the Lord Jesus Christ."[1]

Upon finishing the work of this Second General Conference we wish to direct a message to the peoples of our continent.

We want our word as pastors to be a sign of commitment.

As Latin Americans we share the history of our people. The past definitively identifies us as Latin Americans; the present places us in a decisive crossroads, and the future requires of us a creative labor in the process of development.

LATIN AMERICA, A COMMUNITY IN TRANSFORMATION

Latin America, in addition to being a geographical reality, is a community of peoples with its own history, with specific values and with similar problems. The confrontation and the solutions must acknowledge this history, these values and these problems.

The continent harbors very different situations, but requires solidarity. Latin America must be one and many, rich in variety and strong in its unity.

Our countries have preserved a basic cultural richness, born from ethnic and religious values that have flourished in a common conscience and have borne fruit in concrete efforts toward integration.

Its human potential, more valuable than the riches hidden in its soil, makes of Latin America a promising reality brimming with hope. Its agonizing problems mark it with signs of injustice that wound the Christian conscience.

The multiplicity and complexity of its problems overflow this message.

Latin America appears to live beneath the tragic sign of underdevelopment that not only separates our brothers and sisters from the enjoyment of material goods, but from their proper human fulfillment. In spite of the efforts being made, there is the compounding of hunger and misery, of illness of a massive nature and infant mortality, of illiteracy and marginality, of profound inequality of income, and tensions between the social classes, of outbreaks of violence and rare participation of the people in decisions affecting the common good.

THE CHURCH, THE HISTORY OF LATIN AMERICA, AND OUR CONTRIBUTION

As Christians we believe that this historical stage of Latin America is intimately linked to the history of salvation.

As pastors, with a common responsibility, we wish to unite ourselves with the life of all of our peoples in the painful search for adequate solutions to their multiple problems. Our mission is to contribute to the integral advancement of humankind and of human communities of the continent.

We believe that we are in a new historical era. This era requires clarity in order to see, lucidity in order to diagnose, and solidarity in order to act.

In the light of the faith that we profess as believers, we have undertaken to discover a plan of God in the "signs of the times." We interpret the aspirations and clamors of Latin America as signs that reveal the direction of the divine plan operating in the redeeming love of Christ, which bases these aspirations on an awareness of fraternal solidarity.

Faithful to this divine plan, and in order to respond to the hopes placed in the church, we wish to offer that which we hold as most appropriate: a global vision of humanity, and the integral vision of Latin Americans in development.

Thus we experience solidarity with the responsibilities that have arisen at this stage of the transformation of Latin America.

The church, as part of the essence of Latin America, despite its limitations, has lived with our peoples the process of colonization, liberation, and organization.

Our contribution does not pretend to compete with the attempts for solution made by other national, Latin American, and world bodies; much less do we disregard or refuse to recognize them. Our purpose is to encourage these efforts, accelerate their results, deepen their content, and permeate all the process of change with the values of the gospel. We would like to offer the collaboration of all Christians, compelled by their baptismal responsibilities and by the gravity of this moment. It is our responsibility to dramatize the strength of the gospel, which is the power of God.[2]

We do not have technical solutions or infallible remedies. We wish to feel the problems, perceive the demands, share the agonies, discover the ways, and cooperate in the solutions.

The new image of the Latin American requires a creative effort: public authorities, promoting with energy the supreme requirements of the common good; technicians, planning concrete means; families and educators, awakening and orienting responsibility; the people incorporating themselves in the efforts for fulfillment of the spirit of the gospel, giving life with the dynamism of a transforming and personalizing love.

THE CHALLENGE OF THE PRESENT MOMENT: POSSIBILITIES, VALUES, CONDITIONS

Our peoples seek their liberation and their growth in humanity, through the incorporation and participation of everyone in the very conduct of the personalizing process.

For this reason, no sector should reserve to itself exclusively the carrying out of political, cultural, economic, or spiritual matters. Those who possess the power of decision-making must exercise it in communion with the desires and options of the community. In order that this integration respond to the nature of the Latin American peoples, it must incorporate the values that are appropriate to all and everyone, without exception. The imposition of foreign values and criteria would constitute a new and grave alienation.

We count upon elements and criteria that are profoundly human and essentially Christian, an innate sense of the dignity of all, a predilection to fraternity and hospitality, a recognition of woman and her irreplaceable function in the society, a wise sense of life and death, the certainty of a common Father in the transcendental destiny of all.

This process requires of all our nations the surmounting of mistrust, the purification of exaggerated nationalism, and the solution of their conflicts.

We consider it irreconcilable with our developing situation to invest resources in the arms race, excessive bureaucracy, luxury, and ostentation, or the deficient administration of the community.

The firm denunciation of those realities in Latin America that constitute an affront to the spirit of the gospel also forms part of our mission.

It is also our duty to give recognition to and to stimulate every profound and positive attempt to vanquish the existing great difficulties.

YOUTH

In this transformation, Latin American youth constitute the most numerous group in the population and show themselves to be a new social body with their own ideas and values desiring to create a more just society. The youthful presence is a positive contribution that must be incorporated into society and the church.

COMMITMENTS OF THE LATIN AMERICAN CHURCH

During these days we have gathered in the city of Medellín, moved by the spirit of the Lord, in order to orient once again the labor of the church in a spirit of eagerness for conversion and service.

We have seen that our most urgent commitment must be to purify ourselves, all of the members and institutions of the Catholic Church, in the spirit of the gospel. It is necessary to end the separation between faith and life, "because in Christ Jesus . . . only faith working through love avails."[3]

This commitment requires us to live a true scriptural poverty expressed in authentic manifestations that may be clear signs for our peoples. Only poverty of this quality will show forth Christ, Savior of humankind, and disclose Christ, the Lord of history.[4]

Our reflections have clarified the dimensions of other commitments, which, allowing for modifications, shall be assumed by all the people God:

— To inspire, encourage and press for a new order of justice that incorporates all persons in the decision-making of their own communities;

— To promote the constitution and the efficacy of the family, not only as a human sacramental community, but also as an intermediate structure in function of social change;

— To make education dynamic in order to accelerate the training of mature persons in their current responsibilities;

— To encourage the professional organizations of workers, which are decisive elements in socio-economic transformation;

— To promote a new evangelization and intensive catechesis that reach the elite and the masses in order to achieve a lucid and committed faith;

— To renew and create new structures in the church that institutionalize dialogue and channel collaboration between bishops, priests, religious, and laity;

— To cooperate with other Christian confessions, and with all persons of good will who are committed to authentic peace rooted in justice and love.

The concrete results of these deliberations and commitments we give to you in detailed and hopeful form in the final documents that follow this message.

A FINAL CALL

We call to all persons of good will that they cooperate in truth, justice, love, and liberty, in this transforming labor of our peoples, the dawn of a new era.

In a special way we direct ourselves to the church and Christian communities that share our same faith in Jesus Christ. During this conference our brothers of these Christian confessions have been taking part in our work and in our hopes. Together with them we shall be witnesses of this spirit of cooperation.

We wish also to caution, as a duty of our conscience, as we face the present and future of our continent, those who direct the destinies of public order. In their hands is the possibility of an administrative conduct that liberates from injustice and acts as a guide to an order having for its end the common good, that can lead to the creation of a climate of confidence and action that Latin Americans need for the full development of their lives.

By its own vocation, Latin America will undertake its liberation at the cost of whatever sacrifices, not in order to seal itself off but in order to open itself to union with the rest of the world, giving and receiving in a spirit of solidarity.

We find dialogue with our brothers and sisters of other continents who find themselves in a similar situation to ours to be most important for our work. United in difficulties and hopes, we can make our presence in the world a force for peace.

We remind other peoples who have overcome the obstacles we encounter today that peace is based on the respect for international justice, justice which has its own foundation and expression in the recognition of the political, economic, and cultural autonomy of our peoples.

Finally, we have hope that the love of God the Father, who manifests himself in the Son, and who is spread abroad in our hearts by the Holy Spirit, will unite us and always inspire our actions for the common good.[5]

Thus we hope to be faithful to the commitments that we have made in these days of reflection and common prayer, in order to contribute to the full and effective cooperation of the church in the process of transformation that is being lived in our America.

We hope also to be heard with understanding and good will by all persons with whom we commune in the same destiny and the same aspirations.

All our work and this same hope we place under the protection of Mary, Mother of the Church and Patroness of the Americas, in order that the reign of God may be realized among us.

We have faith:

in God
in human beings
in the values
and the future of Latin America.

"The grace of our Lord Jesus Christ, the charity of God, and the fellowship of the Holy Spirit be with you all."[6]

MEDELLÍN, SEPTEMBER 6, 1968

NOTES

1. See 1 Cor. 1:3.
2. See Rom. 1:16.
3. See Gal. 5:6.
4. See 2 Cor. 8:9.
5. See Rom. 5:5.
6. 2 Cor. 13:14.

INTRODUCTION TO THE FINAL DOCUMENTS

1. The Latin American church, united in the Second General Conference of its Bishops, has chosen as the central theme of its deliberations the Latin

Americans who are living a decisive moment of their historical process. In making this choice, it has in no way "detoured from," but has actually "returned to" humankind,[1] aware that "in order to know God, it is necessary to know humanity."[2]

The church has sought to understand this historic moment in the life of Latin America in the light of the word, who is Christ, in whom the human mystery is made manifest.[3]

2. This assessment of the present naturally turns our scrutiny to the past. Upon examining it, the church can verify with joy that the work has been carried forward generously, and it expresses its gratitude to all those who have laid the foundations of the gospel in our lands; to those who have been active and present through charity to the different cultures, especially to the Amerindians of the continent; to all who have continued the educational work of the church in our urban and rural areas. At the same time, it must acknowledge that throughout the course of history not all its members, clergy and lay, have always been faithful to the Holy Spirit. A glance at the present joyously confirms the dedication of many members and also the frailty of its own messengers.[4] The Church accepts history's judgment on its chiaroscuro past and assumes the full historical responsibility that befalls it in the present.

3. It is certainly not enough to reflect, to be more discerning, and to speak. Action is required. The present has not ceased to be the hour of the word, but it has already become, and with dramatic urgency, the time for action. It is the moment to exercise creativity and imagination in inventing the action that must be performed and brought to term with the boldness of the Holy Spirit and the balance of God. This assembly has been invited "to take decisions and establish programs only under the condition that we are disposed to carry them out as a personal commitment even at the cost of sacrifice."[5]

4. Latin America is obviously under the sign of transformation and development; a transformation that, besides taking place with extraordinary speed, has come to touch and influence every level of human activity, from the economic to the religious.

This indicates that we are on the threshold of a new epoch in the history of our continent. It appears to be a time full of zeal for full emancipation, of liberation from every form of servitude, of personal maturity and of collective integration. In these signs we perceive the first indications of the painful birth of a new civilization. And we cannot fail to see in this gigantic effort toward a rapid transformation and development an obvious sign of the Spirit who leads the history of individuals and of peoples toward their vocation.[6] We cannot but discover in this force, daily more insistent and impatient for transformation, vestiges of the image of God in humankind as a powerful incentive. Progressively this dynamism leads us to an even greater control of nature, a more profound personalization and fellowship and also toward an encounter with God who ratifies and deepens those values attained through human efforts.

5. The fact that the transformation affecting our continent had made an impact on the whole person appears as a sign and a demand. In fact, we Christians cannot but acknowledge the presence of God, who desires to save the whole person, body and soul.[7]

For all of us who possess the first fruits of the Spirit, we too groan inwardly as we wait for our bodies to be set free.[8] God has raised Christ from the dead, and therefore also, all those who believe in him. Christ, actively present in our history, foreshadows his eschatological action not only in the impatient human zeal to reach total redemption, but also in those conquests which, like prophetic signs, are accomplished by humankind through action inspired by love.[9]

6. Just as Israel of old, the first people (of God) felt the saving presence of God when God delivered them from the oppression of Egypt by the passage through the sea and led them to the promised land, so we also, the new people of God, cannot cease to feel God's saving passage in view of "true development, which is the passage for each and all, from conditions of life that are less human, to those that are more human. **Less human:** the material needs of those who are deprived of the minimum living conditions, and the moral needs of those who are mutilated by selfishness. **Less human:** the oppressive structures that come from the abuse of ownership and of power, and from exploitation of workers or from unjust transactions. **More human:** overcoming misery by the possession of necessities; victory over social calamities; broadening of knowledge; the acquisition of cultural advantages. **More human also:** an increase in respect for the dignity of others; orientation toward the spirit of poverty; cooperation for the common good; the will for peace. **More human still:** acknowledgment, on our part, of the supreme values and of God who is their source and term. **More human, finally:** and especially, faith, the gift of God, accepted by humans of good will and unity in the charity of Christ, who calls us all to participation, as sons and daughters in the life of the living God who is the father of all human beings."[10]

7. In this transformation, which evinces an eager desire to integrate the scale of temporal values in a global vision of Christian faith, we become aware of the "original vocation" of Latin America: "a vocation to create a new and ingenious synthesis of the old and the new, the spiritual and the temporal, that which others have bequeathed us and that which is our own creation."[11]

8. In this General Assembly of the Latin American bishops the mystery of Pentecost has been renewed. Together with Mary, the Mother of the Church, who by her patronage has aided this continent since its first evangelization, we have implored the light of the Holy Spirit and, persevering in prayer, have been nourished by the bread of the word and the eucharist. This word has been the object of earnest meditation. The goal of our re-

flection was to search for a new and more dynamic presence of the church in the present transformation of Latin America, in the light of the Second Vatican Council, which was the theme assigned to this conference.

Three broad areas over which our pastoral care extends have been considered in relation to the process of continental transformation:

In the first place, the promotion of individuals, and of the peoples of the continent toward the values of justice and peace, of education and the family.

Secondly, an evangelization adapted to needs, and a process of maturation of the faith of the masses and the elites by means of catechesis and the liturgy.

Finally we touched upon those problems dealing with the members of the church that require greater unity and pastoral action by means of visible structures, also adapted to the new conditions of the continent.

The following conclusions express the fruit of the work of the Second General Conference of Latin American bishops in the hope that all the people of God, encouraged by the Holy Spirit, commit themselves to its complete fulfillment.

NOTES

1. See Paul VI, *Closing Address of the Second Vatican Council,* December 7, 1965.
2. Ibid.
3. Vatican Council II, *Gaudium et Spes,* no. 22.
4. Ibid., no. 43.
5. Most Rev. Eugenio de Araujo Sales, *The Church in Latin America and Human Promotion,* August 28, 1968.
6. See Paul VI, *Populorum Progressio,* no. 15.
7. See *Gaudium et Spes,* no. 3.
8. See Rom. 8:22-23.
9. *Gaudium et Spes,* no. 38.
10. Paul VI, *Populorum Progressio,* nos. 20-21.
11. See Paul VI, *Homily on the Ordination of Priests for Latin America,* July 3, 1966.

DOCUMENT ON JUSTICE

PERTINENT FACTS

1. There are in existence many studies of the Latin American people.[1] The misery that besets large masses of human beings in all our countries is described in all these studies. That misery, as a collective fact, expresses itself as injustice which cries to the heavens.[2]

But what perhaps has not been sufficiently said is that in general the efforts which have been made have not been capable of assuring that justice be honored and realized in every sector of the respective national communities. Often families do not find concrete possibilities for the education of their children. The young demand their right to enter universities or centers of higher learning for both intellectual and technical training; the women, their right to a legitimate equality with men; the peasants, better conditions of life; or if they are workers, better prices and security in buying and selling; the growing middle class feels frustrated by the lack of expectations. There has begun an exodus of professionals and technicians to more developed countries; the small businessmen and industrialists are pressed by greater interests and not a few large Latin American industrialists are gradually coming to be dependent on the international business enterprises. We cannot ignore the phenomenon of this almost universal frustration of legitimate aspirations, which creates the climate of collective anguish in which we are already living.

2. The lack of socio-cultural integration, in the majority of our countries, has given rise to the superimposition of cultures. In the economic spheres systems flourished which consider solely the potential of groups with great earning power. This lack of adaptation to the characteristics and to the potentials of all our people, in turn, gives rise to frequent political instability and the consolidation of purely formal institutions. To all of this must be added the lack of solidarity which, on the individual and social levels, leads to the committing of serious sins, evident in the unjust structures which characterize the Latin American situation.

DOCTRINAL BASES

3. The Latin American church has a message for all persons on this continent who "hunger and thirst after justice." The very God who creates human beings in the divine image and likeness, creates the "earth and all that is in it for the use of all humans and all nations, in such a way that created good can reach all in a more just manner,"[3] and gives them power to transform and perfect the world in solidarity.[4] It is the same God who, in the fullness of time, sends the Son in the flesh, so that he might come to liberate all persons from the slavery to which sin has subjected them:[5] hunger, misery, oppression, and ignorance—in a word, that injustice and hatred which have their origin in human selfishness.

Thus, for our authentic liberation, all of us need a profound conversion so that "the kingdom of justice, love, and peace" might come to us. The origin of all disdain for humankind, of all injustice, should be sought in the internal imbalance of human liberty, which will always need to be rectified in history. The uniqueness of the Christian message does not so much consist in the affirmation of the necessity for structural change, as it does in the insistence on the conversion of men and women, which will in turn bring about this change. We will not have a new continent without new and reformed structures, but, above all, there will be no new continent without new human beings who know how to be truly free and responsible according to the light of the gospel.

4. Only by the light of Christ is the mystery of humankind made clear. In the economy of salvation the divine work is an action of integral human development and liberation, which has love for its sole motive. Humankind is "created in Christ Jesus,"[6] fashioned in him as a "new creature."[7] By faith and baptism the creature is transformed, filled with the gift of the Spirit, with a new dynamism, not of selfishness, but of love, which compels human beings to seek out a new, more profound relationship with God, their fellow humans, and created things.

Love, "the fundamental law of human perfection, and therefore of the transformation of the world,"[8] is not only the greatest commandment of the Lord; it is also the dynamism which ought to motivate Christians to realize justice in the world, having truth as a foundation and liberty as their sign.

5. This is how the church desires to serve the world, radiating over it a light and life which heals and elevates the dignity of the human person,[9] which consolidates the unity of society[10] and gives a more profound reason and meaning to all human activity.

Doubtless, for the church, the fullness and perfection of the human vocation will be accomplished with the definitive inclusion of each human being in the passover or triumph of Christ, but the hope of such a definitive realization, rather than lull, ought to "vivify the concern to perfect this earth. For here grows the body of the new human family, a body which even now is able to give some kind of foreshadowing of the new age."[11] We do not confuse temporal progress and the kingdom of Christ; nevertheless, the former, "to the extent that it can contribute to the better ordering of human society, is of vital concern to the kingdom of God."[12]

The Christian quest for justice is a demand arising from biblical teaching. All humans are merely humble stewards of material goods. In the search for salvation we must avoid the dualism which separates temporal tasks from the work of sanctification. Although we are encompassed with imperfections, we are persons of hope. We have faith that our love for Christ and for our brothers and sisters will not only be the great force liberating us from injustice and oppression, but also the inspiration for social justice, understood as a whole of life and as an impulse toward the integral growth of our countries.

PROJECTIONS FOR SOCIAL PASTORAL PLANNING

6. Our pastoral mission is essentially a service of encouraging and educating the conscience of believers, to help them to perceive the responsibilities of their faith in their personal life and in their social life. This

Second Episcopal Conference wishes to point out the most important demands, taking into account the value judgments that the latest documents of the magisterium of the church have already made concerning the economic and social situation of the world of today, which applies fully to the Latin American continent.

DIRECTION OF SOCIAL CHANGE

7. The Latin American church encourages the formation of national communities that reflect a global organization where all of the peoples but more especially the lower classes have, by means of territorial and functional structures, an active and receptive, creative and decisive participation in the construction of a new society. Those intermediary structures—between the person and the state—should be freely organized, without any unwarranted interference from authority or from dominant groups, in view of their development and concrete participation in the accomplishment of the total common good. They constitute the vital network of society. They are also the true expression of the citizens' liberty and unity.

The Family

8. Without ignoring the unique character of the family, as the natural unit of society, we are considering it here as an intermediary structure, inasmuch as the families as a group ought to take up their function in the process of social change. Latin American families ought to organize their economic and cultural potential so that their legitimate needs and hopes be taken into account, on the levels where fundamental decisions are made, which can help or hinder them. In this way they will assume a role of effective representation and participation in the life of the total community.

Besides the dynamism generated in each country by the union of families, it is necessary that governments draw up legislation and a healthy and up-to-date policy governing the family.

Professional Organization

9. The Second Latin American Episcopal Conference addresses itself to all those who, with daily effort, create the goods and services which favor the existence and development of human life. We refer especially to the millions of Latin American men and women who make up the peasant and working class. They, for the most part, suffer, long for and struggle for a change that will humanize and dignify their work. Without ignoring the totality of the significance of human work, here we refer to it as an intermediary structure, inasmuch as it constitutes the function which gives rise to professional organization in the field of production.

Business Enterprises and the Economy

10. In today's world, production finds its concrete expression in business enterprises, industrial as well as rural; they constitute the dynamic and

fundamental base of the integral economic process. The system of Latin American business enterprises, and through it the current economy, responds to an erroneous conception concerning the right of ownership of the means of production and the very goals of the economy. A business, in an authentically human economy, does not identify itself with the owners of capital, because it is fundamentally a community of persons and a unit of work, which is in need of capital to produce goods. A person or a group of persons cannot be the property of an individual, of a society, or of the state.

The system of liberal capitalism and the temptation of the Marxist system would appear to exhaust the possibilities of transforming the economic structures of our continent. Both systems militate against the dignity of the human person. One takes for granted the primacy of capital, its power and its discriminatory utilization in the function of profit-making. The other, although it ideologically supports a kind of humanism, is more concerned with collective humanity, and in practice becomes a totalitarian concentration of state power. We must denounce the fact that Latin America sees itself caught between these two options and remains dependent on one or another of the centers of power which control its economy.

Therefore, on behalf of Latin America, we make an urgent appeal to the business leaders, to their organizations, and to the political authorities, so that they might radically modify the evaluation, the attitudes, and the means regarding the goal, organization, and functioning of business. All those financiers deserve encouragement who, individually or through their organizations, make an effort to conduct their business according to the guidelines supplied by the social teaching of the church. That the social and economic change in Latin America be channeled toward a truly human economy will depend fundamentally on this.

11. On the other hand this change will be essential in order to liberate the authentic process of Latin American development and integration. Many of our workers, although they gradually become conscious of the necessity for this change, simultaneously experience a situation of dependence on inhuman economic systems and institutions: a situation which, for many of them, borders on slavery, not only physical but also professional, cultural, civic, and spiritual.

With the clarity which arises from human knowledge and human hopes, we must reiterate that neither the combined value of capital nor the establishment of the most modern techniques of production, nor economic plans will serve humankind efficiently if the workers, the "necessary unity of direction" having been safeguarded, are not incorporated with all of the thrust of their humanity, by means of "the active participation of all in the running of the enterprise, according to ways which will have to be determined with care and on a macroeconomic level, decisive nationally and internationally.[13]

Organization of Workers

12. Therefore, in the intermediary professional structure the peasants' and workers' unions, to which the workers have a right, should acquire sufficient strength and power. Their associations will have a unified and responsible strength, to exercise the right of representation and participation on the levels of production and of national, continental, and international trade. They ought to exercise their right of being represented, also, on the social, economic, and political levels, where decisions are made which touch upon the common good. Therefore, the unions ought to use every means at their disposal to train those who are to carry out these responsibilities in moral, economic, and especially in technical matters.

Unity of Action

13. Socialization, understood as a socio-cultural process of personalization and communal growth, leads us to think that all the sectors of society, but in this case, principally the social-economic sphere, should, because of justice and fellowship transcend antagonisms in order to become agents of national and continental development. Without this unity, Latin America will not be able to succeed in liberating itself from the neocolonialism to which it is bound, nor will Latin America be able to realize itself in freedom, with its own cultural, socio-political, and economic characteristics.

Rural Transformation

14. The Second Episcopal Conference wishes to voice its pastoral concern for the extensive peasant class, which, although included in the above remarks, deserves urgent attention because of its special characteristics. If it is true that one ought to consider the diversity of circumstances and resources in the different countries, there is no doubt that there is a common denominator in all of them: the need for the human promotion of the peasants and Amerindians. This uplifting will not be viable without an authentic and urgent reform of agrarian structures and policies. This structural change and its political implications go beyond a simple distribution of land. It is indispensable to make an adjudication of such lands, under detailed conditions which legitimize their occupation and insure their productivity for the benefit of the families and the national economy. This will entail, aside from juridical and technical aspects not within our competence, the organization of the peasants into effective intermediate structures, principally in the form of cooperatives; and motivation toward the creation of urban centers in rural areas, which would afford the peasant population the benefits of culture, health, recreation, spiritual growth, participation in local decisions, and in those which have to do with the economy and national politics. This uplifting of the rural areas will contribute to the necessary process of industrialization and to participation in the advantage of urban civilization.

Industrialization

15. There is no doubt that the process of industrialization is irreversible and is a necessary preparation for an independent economy and integration into the modern worldwide economy. Industrialization will be a decisive factor in raising the standard of living of our countries and affording them better conditions for an integral development. Therefore it is indispensable to revise plans and reorganize national macroeconomies, preserving the legitimate autonomy of our nation, and allowing for just grievances of the poorer nations and for the desired economic integration of the continent, respecting always the inalienable rights of the person and of intermediary structures, as protagonists of this process.

POLITICAL REFORM

16. Faced with the need for a total change of Latin American structures, we believe that change has political reform as its prerequisite.

The exercise of political authority and its decisions have as their only end the common good. In Latin America such authority and decision-making frequently seem to support systems which militate against the common good or which favor privileged groups. By means of legal norms, authority ought effectively and permanently to assure the right and inalienable liberties of the citizens and the free functioning of intermediary structures.

Public authority has the duty of facilitating and supporting the creation of means of participation and legitimate representation of the people, or if necessary the creation of new ways to achieve it. We want to insist on the necessity of vitalizing and strengthening the municipal and communal organization, as a beginning of organizational efforts at the departmental, provincial, regional, and national levels.

The lack of political consciousness in our countries makes the educational activity of the church absolutely essential, for the purpose of bringing Christians to consider their participation in the political life of the nation as a matter of conscience and as the practice of charity in its most noble and meaningful sense for the life of the community.

INFORMATION AND CONSCIENTIZATION

17. We wish to affirm that it is indispensable to form a social conscience and a realistic perception of the problems of the community and of social structures. We must awaken the social conscience and communal customs in all strata of society and professional groups regarding such values as dialogue and community living within the same group and relations with wider social groups (workers, peasants, professionals, clergy, religious, administrators, etc.).

This task of conscientization and social education ought to be integrated into joint pastoral action at various levels.

18. The sense of service and realism demands of today's hierarchy a greater social sensitivity and objectivity. In that regard there is a need for direct contact with the different social-professional groups in meetings which provide all with a more complete vision of social dynamics. Such encounters are to be regarded as instruments which can facilitate a collegial action on the part of the bishops, guaranteeing harmony of thought and activities in the midst of a changing society.

The national episcopal conference will implement the organization of courses, meetings, etc., as a means of integrating those responsible for social activities related to pastoral plans. Besides priests, and interested religious and laypersons, invitations could be extended to heads of national and international development programs within the country. In like manner the institutes organized to prepare foreign apostolic personnel, will coordinate their activities of a pastoral-social nature with the corresponding national groups; moreover, opportunities will be sought for promoting study weeks devoted to social issues in order to articulate social doctrine applying to our problems. This will allow us to effect public opinion.

19. "Key persons" deserve special attention; we refer to those persons at a decision-making level whose actions effect changes in the basic structures of national and international life. The episcopal conference, therefore, through its commission on social action or pastoral service, will support, together with other interested groups, the organization of courses of study for technicians, politicians, labor leaders, peasants, managers, and educated persons of all levels of society.

20. It is necessary that small basic communities be developed in order to establish a balance with minority groups, which are the groups in power. This is possible only through vitalization of these very communities by means of the natural innate elements in their environment.

The church—the people of God—will lend its support to the downtrodden of every social class so that they might come to know their rights and how to make use of them. To this end the Church will utilize its moral strength and will seek to collaborate with competent professionals and institutions.

21. The Commission of Justice and Peace should be supported in all our countries at least at the national level. It should be composed of persons of a high moral caliber, professionally qualified and representative of different social classes; it should be capable of establishing an effective dialogue with persons and institutions more directly responsible for the decisions which favor the common good and detect everything that can wound justice and endanger the internal and external peace of the national and international communities; it should help to find concrete means to obtain adequate solutions for each situation.

22. For the implementation of their pastoral mission, the episcopal conferences will create commissions of social action or pastoral service to develop doctrine and to take the initiative, presenting the church as a catalyst

in the temporal realm in an authentic attitude of service. The same applies to the diocesan level.

Furthermore, the episcopal conferences and Catholic organizations will encourage collaboration on the national and continental scene with non-Catholic Christian churches and institutions, dedicated to the task of restoring justice in human relations.

"Caritas" which is a church organization[14] integrated in the joint pastoral plan, **will not be** solely a welfare institution, but rather will **become operational** in the developmental process of Latin America, as an institution authentically dedicated to its growth.

23. The church recognizes that these institutions of temporal activity correspond to the specific sphere of civic society, even though they are established and stimulated by Christians. In actual concrete situations this Second General Conference of Latin American bishops feels it its duty to offer special encouragement to those organizations which have as their purpose human development and the carrying out of justice. The moral force of the church will be consecrated, above all, to stimulate them, not acting except in a supplementary capacity and in situations that admit no delay.

Finally, this second conference is fully aware that the process of socialization, hastened by the techniques and media of mass communication, makes these means a necessary and proper instrument for social education and for conscientization ordered to changing the structures and the observance of justice. For the same reason this conference urges all, but especially laypersons, to make full use of mass media in their work of human promotion.

NOTES

1. See the synthesis of this situation in the Work Paper of the Second Conference of Latin American bishops, nos. 1-9.
2. See Paul VI, *Populorum Progressio,* no. 30.
3. See Vatican Council II, *Gaudium et Spes,* no. 69.
4. See Gen. 1:26; *Gaudium et Spes,* no. 34.
5. See John 8:32-35.
6. See Eph. 2:10.
7. See 2 Cor. 5:17.
8. See *Gaudium et Spes*, no. 38.
9. Ibid., no. 41.
10. Ibid., no. 42
11. Ibid., no. 39.
12. Ibid.
13. Ibid., no. 68.
14. See *Populorum Progressio,* no. 46.

DOCUMENT ON PEACE

THE LATIN AMERICAN SITUATION AND PEACE

1. "If development is the new name for peace,"[1] Latin American underdevelopment, with its own characteristics in the different countries, is an unjust situation which promotes tensions that conspire against peace.

We can divide these tensions into three major groups, selecting, in each of these, those variables which constitute a positive menace to the peace of our countries by manifesting an unjust situation.

When speaking of injustice, we refer to those realities that constitute a sinful situation; this does not mean, however, that we are overlooking the fact that at times the misery in our countries can have natural causes which are difficult to overcome.

In making this analysis, we do not ignore or fail to give credit to the positive efforts made at every level to build a more just society. We do not include this here because our purpose is to call attention to those aspects which constitute a menace or negation of peace.

TENSIONS BETWEEN CLASSES AND INTERNAL COLONIALISM

2. **Different forms of marginality.** Socio-economic, cultural, political, racial, religious, in urban as well as rural sectors;

3. **Extreme inequality among social classes.** Especially, though not exclusively, in those countries which are characterized by a marked biclassism, where a few have much (culture, wealth, power, prestige) while the majority has very little. The Holy Father describes this situation when directing himself to the Colombian rural workers; "social and economic development has not been equitable in the great continent of Latin America; and while it has favored those who helped establish it in the beginning, it has neglected the masses of native population, which are almost always left at a subsistence level and at times are mistreated and exploited harshly."[2]

4. **Growing frustrations.** The universal phenomenon of rising expectations assumes a particularly aggressive dimension in Latin America. The reason is obvious: excessive inequalities systematically prevent the satisfaction of the legitimate aspirations of the ignored sectors, and breed increasing frustrations.

The same low morale is obtained in those middle classes which, when confronting grave crises, enter into a process of disintegration and proletarization.

5. **Forms of oppression of dominant groups and sectors.** Without excluding the eventuality of willful oppression, these forms manifest themselves most frequently in a lamentable insensitivity of the privileged sectors

to the misery of the marginated sectors. Thus the words of the pope to the leaders: "That your ears and heart be sensitive to the voices of those who ask for bread, concern, justice. . ."[3]

It is not unusual to find that these groups, with the exception of some enlightened minorities, characterize as subversive activities all attempts to change the social system which favors the permanence of their privileges.

6. **Power unjustly exercised by certain dominant sectors.** As a natural consequence of the above-mentioned attitudes, some members of the dominant sectors occasionally resort to the use of force to repress drastically any attempt at opposition. It is easy for them to find apparent ideological justifications (anticommunism) or practical ones (keeping "order") to give their action an honest appearance.

7. **Growing awareness of the oppressed sectors.** All the above results are even more intolerable as the oppressed sectors become increasingly aware of their situation. The Holy Father referred to them when he said to the rural workers: "But today the problem has worsened because you have become more aware of your needs and suffering, and you cannot tolerate the persistence of these conditions without applying a careful remedy."[4]

The static picture described in the above paragraphs is worsened when it is projected into the future: basic education will increase awareness, and the demographic explosion will multiply problems and tensions. One must not forget the existence of movements of all types interested in taking advantage of and irritating these tensions. Therefore, if today peace seems seriously endangered, the automatic aggravation of problems will produce explosive consequences.

INTERNATIONAL TENSIONS AND EXTERNAL NEOCOLONIALISM

8. We refer here particularly to the implications for our countries of dependence on a center of economic power, around which they gravitate. For this reason, our nations frequently do not own their goods, or have a say in economic decisions affecting them. It is obvious that this will not fail to have political consequences, given the interdependence of these two fields.

We are interested in emphasizing two aspects of this phenomenon.

9. **Economic aspect.** We analyze only those factors having greater influence on the global and relative impoverishment of our countries, and which constitute a source of internal and external tensions.

a) **Growing distortion of international commerce.** Because of the relative depreciation of the terms of exchange, the value of raw materials is increasingly less in relation to the cost of manufactured products. This means that the countries which produce raw materials — especially if they are dependent upon one major export — always remain poor, while the industrialized countries enrich themselves. This injustice clearly denounced by *Populorum Progressio*,[5] nullifies the eventual positive effect of external aid and constitutes a permanent menace against peace, because our countries sense that "one hand takes away what the other hand gives."[6]

b) **Rapid flight of economic and human capital.** The search for security and individual gain leads many members of the more comfortable sectors of our countries to invest their money in foreign countries. The injustice of such procedures has already been denounced categorically by the encyclical *Populorum Progressio.*[7] To this can be added the loss of technicians and competent personnel, which is at least as serious and perhaps more so than the loss of capital, because of the high cost of training these people and because of their ability to teach others.

c) **Tax evasion and loss of gains and dividends.** Some foreign companies working in our country (also some national firms) often evade the established tax system by subterfuge. We are also aware that at times they send their profits and dividends abroad, without contributing adequate reinvestments to the progressive development of our countries.

d) **Progressive debt.** It is not surprising to find that in the system of international credits, the true needs and capabilities of our countries are not taken into account. We thus run the risk of encumbering ourselves with debts whose payment absorbs the greater part of our profits.[8]

e) **International monopolies and international imperialism of money.** We wish to emphasize that the principal guilt for economic dependence of our countries rests with powers, inspired by uncontrolled desire for gain, which leads to economic dictatorship and the "international imperialism of money"[9] condemned by Pope Pius XI in *Quadragesimo Anno* and by Pope Paul VI in *Populorum Progressio.*

10. **Political aspect.** We here denounce the imperialism of any ideological bias that is exercised in Latin America either indirectly or through direct intervention.

TENSIONS AMONG THE COUNTRIES OF LATIN AMERICA

11. We here denounce the particular phenomenon of historico-political origin that continues to disturb cordial relations among some countries and impedes truly constructive collaboration. Nevertheless, the integration process, well understood, presents itself as a commanding necessity for Latin America. Without pretending to set norms of a truly complex, technical nature, governing integration, we deem it opportune to point out its multi-dimensional character. Integration, in effect, is not solely an economic process; it has a broader dimension reflected in the way in which it embraces man in his total situation: social, political, cultural, religious, racial.

Among the factors that increase the tensions among our countries we underline:

12. **An exacerbated nationalism in some countries.** The Holy Father[10] has already denounced the unwholesomeness of this attitude, especially on

a matter where the weakness of the national economies requires a union of efforts.

13. **Armaments.** In certain countries an arms race is under way that surpasses the limits of reason. It frequently stems from a fictitious need to respond to diverse interests rather than to a true need of the national community. In that respect, a phrase of *Populorum Progressio* is particularly pertinent: "When so many communities are hungry, when so many homes suffer misery, when so many persons live submerged in ignorance ... any arms race becomes an intolerable scandal."[11]

DOCTRINAL REFLECTION

CHRISTIAN VIEW OF PEACE

14. The above-mentioned Christian viewpoint on peace adds up to a negation of peace such as Christian tradition undersands it.

Three factors characterize the Christian concept of peace:

a) Peace is, above all, a work of justice.[12] It presupposes and requires the establishment of a just order[13] in which persons can fulfill themselves as human beings, where their dignity is respected, their legitimate aspirations satisfied, their access to truth recognized, their personal freedom guaranteed; an order where persons are not objects but agents of their own history. Therefore, there will be attempts against peace where unjust inequalities among individuals and nations prevail.[14]

Peace in Latin America, therefore, is not the simple absence of violence and bloodshed. Oppression by power groups may give the impression of maintaining peace and order, but in truth it is nothing but the "continuous and inevitable seed of rebellion and war."[15]

"Peace can only be obtained by creating a new order which carries with it a more perfect justice among persons."[16] It is in this sense that integral human development, the path to more human conditions, becomes the symbol of peace.

b) Secondly, peace is a permanent task.[17] A community becomes a reality in time and is subject to a movement that implies constant change in structures, transformation of attitudes, and conversion of hearts.

The "tranquility of order," according to the Augustinian definition of peace, is neither passivity nor conformity. It is not something that is acquired once and for all. It is the result of continuous effort and adaptation to new circumstances, to new demands and challenges of a changing history. A static and apparent peace may be obtained with the use of force; an authentic peace implies struggle, creative abilities, and permanent conquest.[18]

Peace is not found, it is built. The Christian is the artisan of peace.[19] This task, given the above circumstances, has a special character in our continent: thus, the people of God in Latin America, following the example of Christ, must resist personal and collective injustice with unselfish courage and fearlessness.

c) Finally, peace is the fruit of love.[20] It is the expression of true fellowship among human beings, a union given by Christ, prince of peace, in reconciling all persons with the Father. Human solidarity cannot truly take effect unless it is done in Christ, who gives peace that the world cannot give.[21] Love is the soul of justice. Christians who work for social justice should always cultivate peace and love in their hearts.

Peace with God is the basic foundation of internal and social peace. Therefore, where this social peace does not exist, there will we find social, political, economic, and cultural inequalities, there will we find the rejection of the peace of the Lord, and a rejection of the Lord himself.[22]

THE PROBLEM OF VIOLENCE IN LATIN AMERICA

15. Violence constitutes one of the gravest problems in Latin America. A decision on which the future of the countries of the continent will depend should not be left to the impulses of emotion and passion. We would be failing in our pastoral duty if we were not to remind the conscience, caught in this dramatic dilemma, of the criteria derived from the Christian doctrine of evangelical love.

No one should be surprised if we forcefully reaffirm our faith in the productiveness of peace. This is our Christian ideal. "Violence is neither Christian nor evangelical."[23] Christians are peaceful and not ashamed of it. They are not simply pacifists, for they can fight,[24] but they prefer peace to war. They know that "violent changes in structures would be fallacious, ineffectual in themselves, and not conforming to human dignity, which demands that the necessary changes take place from within—that is to say, through a fitting awakening of conscience, adequate preparation and effective participation of all, which the ignorance and often inhuman conditions of life make it impossible to assure at this time."[25]

16. As Christians believe in the productiveness of peace in order to achieve justice, they also believe that justice is a prerequisite for peace. They recognize that in many instances Latin America finds itself faced with a situation of injustice that can be called institutionalized violence, when, because of a structural deficiency of industry and agriculture, of national and international economy, of cultural and political life, "whole towns lack necessities, live in such dependence as hinders all initiative and responsibility as well as every possibility for cultural promotion and participation in social and political life,"[26] thus violating fundamental rights. This situation demands all-embracing, courageous, urgent, and profoundly renovating transformations. We should not be surprised, therefore, that the "temptation to violence" is surfacing in Latin America. One should not abuse the patience of a people that for years has borne a situation that would not be acceptable to anyone with any degree of awareness of human rights.

Facing a situation which works so seriously against human dignity and against peace, we address ourselves, as pastors, to all the members of the Christian community, asking them to assume their responsibility in the promotion of peace in Latin America.

17. We would like to direct our call in the first place to those who have a greater share of wealth, culture, and power. We know that there are leaders in Latin America who are sensitive to the needs of the people and try to remedy them. They recognize that the privileged many times join together, and with all the means at their disposal pressure those who govern, thus obstructing necessary changes. In some instances, this pressure takes on drastic proportions, which result in the destruction of life and property.

Therefore, we urge them not to take advantage of the pacifist position of the church in order to oppose, either actively or passively, the profound transformations that are so necessary. If they jealously retain their privileges, and defend them through violence, they are responsible to history for provoking "explosive revolutions of despair."[27] The peaceful future of the countries of Latin America depends to a large extent on their attitude.

18. Also responsible for injustice are those who remain passive for fear of the sacrifice and personal risk implied by any courageous and effective action. Justice, and therefore peace, conquer by means of a dynamic action of awakening (conscientization) and organization of the popular sectors, which are capable of pressing public officials who are often impotent in their social projects without popular support.

19. We address ourselves finally to those who, in the face of injustice and illegitimate resistance to change, put their hopes in violence. With Paul VI we realize that their attitude "frequently finds its ultimate motivation in noble impulses of justice and solidarity."[28] Let us not speak here of empty words which do not imply personal responsibility and which isolate persons from the fruitful nonviolent actions that are immediately possible.

If it is true that revolutionary insurrection can be legitimate in the case of evident and prolonged "tyranny that seriously works against fundamental human rights, and which damages the common good of the country,"[29] whether it proceeds from one person or from clearly unjust structures, it is also certain that violence or "armed revolution" generally "generates new injustices, introduces new imbalances, and causes new disasters; one cannot combat a real evil at the price of a greater evil."[30]

If we consider, then, the totality of the circumstances of our countries, and if we take into account the Christian preference for peace, the enormous difficulty of a civil war, the logic of violence, the atrocities it engenders, the risk of provoking foreign intervention, illegitimate as it may be, the difficulty of building a regime of justice and freedom while participating in a process of violence, we earnestly desire that the dynamism of the awakened and organized community be put to the service of justice and peace.

Finally, we would like to make ours the words of our Holy Father to the newly ordained priests and deacons in Bogotá, when he referred to all the suffering and said to them: "We will be able to understand their afflictions and change them, not into hate and violence, but into the strong and peaceful energy of constructive works."[31]

PASTORAL CONCLUSIONS

20. In the face of the tensions which conspire against peace, and even present the temptation of violence; in the face of the Christian concept of peace, which has been described, we believe that the Latin American episcopate cannot avoid assuming very concrete responsibilities; because to create a just social order, without which peace is illusory, is an eminently Christian task.

To us, the pastors of the church, belongs the duty to educate the Christian conscience, to inspire, stimulate and help orient all the initiatives that contribute to the human formation. It is also up to us to denounce everything which, opposing justice, destroys peace.

In this spirit we feel it opportune to bring up the following pastoral points:

21. To awaken in individuals and communities, principally through the mass media, a living awareness of justice, infusing in them a dynamic sense of responsibility and solidarity.

22. To defend the rights of the poor and oppressed according to the gospel commandment, urging our governments and upper classes to eliminate anything which might destroy social peace: injustice, inertia, venality, insensibility.

23. To favor integration, energetically denouncing the abuses and unjust consequences of the excessive inequalities between poor and rich, weak and powerful.

24. To be certain that our preaching, liturgy, and catechesis take into account the social and community dimensions of Christianity, forming persons committed to world peace.

25. To achieve in our schools, seminaries, and universities a healthy critical sense of the social situation and foster the vocation of service. We also consider very efficacious the diocesan and national campaigns that mobilize the faithful and social organizations, leading them to a similar reflection.

26. To invite various Christian and non-Christian communities to collaborate in this fundamental task of our times.

27. To encourage and favor the efforts of the people to create and develop their own grassroots organizations for the redress and consolidation of their rights and the search for true justice.

28. To request the perfecting of the administration of justice, whose deficiencies often cause serious ills.

29. To urge a halt and revision in many of our countries of the arms race that at times constitutes a burden excessively disproportionate to the legitimate demands of the common good, to the detriment of desperate social necessities. The struggle against misery is the true war that our nations should face.

30. To invite the bishops, the leaders of different churches and all persons of good will of the developed nations to promote in their respective spheres of influence, especially among political and financial leaders, a consciousness of greater solidarity facing our underdeveloped nations, obtaining among other things, just prices for our raw materials.

31. On the occasion of the twentieth anniversary of the solemn declaration of human rights, to interest universities in Latin America to undertake investigations to verify the degree of its implementation in our countries.

32. To denounce the unjust action of world powers that works against self-determination of weaker nations who must suffer the bloody consequences of war and invasion, and to ask competent international organizations for effective and decisive proceedings.

33. To encourage and praise the initiatives and works of all those who in the diverse areas of action contribute to the creation of a new order which will assure peace in our midst.

NOTES

1. See Paul VI, *Populorum Progressio,* no. 87.
2. See Paul VI, *Address to the Peasants,* Mosquera, Colombia, August 23, 1968.
3. See Paul VI, *Homily of the Mass on Development Day,* Bogotá, August 23, 1968.
4. See Paul VI, *Address to the Peasants,* Mosquera, Colombia, August 23, 1968.
5. See Paul VI, *Populorum Progressio*, nos. 56-61.
6. Ibid., no. 56.
7. Ibid., no. 24.
8. Ibid., no. 54.
9. Ibid., no. 26.
10. Ibid., no. 62.
11. Ibid., no. 53.
12. See Vatican Council II, *Gaudium et Spes,* no. 78.
13. See John XXIII, *Pacem in Terris,* no. 167, and Paul VI, *Populorum Progressio,* no. 78.
14. See Paul VI, *Message of January 1st, 1968.*
15. Ibid.
16. See Paul VI, *Populorum Progressio,* no. 76.
17. See *Gaudium et Spes,* no. 78.
18. See Paul VI, *Christmas Message 1967.*
19. See Matt. 5:9.
20. See *Gaudium et Spes,* no. 78.

21. See John 14:27.

22. See Matt. 25:31-46.

23. See Paul VI, *Homily of the Mass on Development Day,* Bogotá, August 23, 1968; idem, *Opening Address at the Second General Conference of Latin American Bishops,* Bogotá, August 24, 1968.

24. See Paul VI, *Message of January 1, 1968.*

25. See Paul VI, *Homily of the Mass on Development Day,* Bogotá, August 23, 1968.

26. See Paul VI, *Populorum Progressio,* no. 30.

27. See Paul VI, *Homily of the Mass on Development Day,* Bogotá, August 23, 1968.

28. Ibid.

29. See Paul VI, *Populorum Progressio,* no. 31.

30. Ibid.

31. See Paul VI, *Address to New Priests and Deacons,* Bogotá, August 22, 1968.

DOCUMENT ON THE POVERTY OF THE CHURCH

LATIN AMERICAN SCENE

1. The Latin American bishops cannot remain indifferent in the face of the tremendous social injustices existent in Latin America, which keep the majority of our peoples in dismal poverty, which in many cases becomes inhuman wretchedness.

2. A deafening cry pours from the throats of millions of men and women asking their pastors for a liberation that reaches them from nowhere else. "Now you are listening to us in silence, but we hear the shout which arises from your suffering," the pope told the campesinos in Colombia.[1]

And complaints that the hierarchy, the clergy, the religious, are rich and allied with the rich also come to us. On this point we must make it clear that appearance is often confused with reality. Many causes have contributed to create this impression of a rich hierarchical church. The great buildings, the rectories and religious houses that are better than those of the neighbors, the often luxurious vehicles, the attire, inherited from other eras, have been some of those causes.

The system of taxes and tuition to support clergy and maintain educational endeavors has become discredited and has led to the formation of erroneous opinions about the amount of money received.

To this has been added the exaggerated secrecy in which the finances of high schools, parishes, and dioceses have been shrouded, favoring a mysterious atmosphere which magnifies shadows to gigantic proportions and helps to create fictions. Besides, isolated cases of reprehensible opulence have been generalized.

All this has helped substantiate the argument that the Latin American church is rich.

3. The reality of the very great number of parishes and dioceses that are extremely poor, and the exceeding number of bishops, priests, and religious who live in complete deprivation and give themselves with great abnegation to the service of the poor, generally escapes the appreciation of many and does not succeed in dissipating the prevailing distorted image.

Within the context of the poverty and even of the wretchedness in which the great majority of the Latin American people live, we, bishops, priests, and religious, have the necessities of life and a certain security, while the poor lack that which is indispensable and struggle between **anguish** and **uncertainty.** And incidents are not lacking in which the poor feel that their bishops, or pastors and religious, do not really identify themselves with them, with their problems and afflictions, that they do not always support those who work with them or plead their cause.

DOCTRINAL MOTIVATION

4. We must distinguish:

a) Poverty, as a lack of the goods of this world necessary to live worthily as human beings, is in itself evil. The prophets denounce it as contrary to the will of the Lord and most of the time as the fruit of human injustice and sin.

b) Spiritual poverty is the theme of the poor of Yahweh.[2] Spiritual poverty is the attitude of opening up to God, the ready disposition of one who hopes for everything from the Lord.[3] Although he values the goods of this world, he does not become attached to them and he recognizes the higher value of the riches of the kingdom.[4]

c) Poverty as a commitment, through which one assumes voluntarily and lovingly the conditions of the needy of this world in order to bear witness to the evil it represents and to spiritual liberty in the face of material goods, follows the example of Christ who took to Himself all the consequences of our sinful condition[5] and who "being rich became poor"[6] in order to redeem us.

5. In this context a poor church:

— denounces the unjust lack of this world's goods and the sin that begets it;

— preaches and lives in spiritual poverty, as an attitude of spiritual childhood and openness to the Lord;

— is itself bound to material poverty. The poverty of the church is, in effect, a constant factor in the history of salvation.

6. All members of the church are called to live in evangelical poverty, but not all in the same way, as there are diverse vocations to this poverty, that tolerate diverse styles of life and various modes of acting. Among religious themselves, although they all have a special mission to witness within the church, there will be differences according to personal charismas.

7. Against this background, it will be necessary to reemphasize strongly

that the example and teaching of Jesus, the anguished condition of millions of the poor in Latin America, the urgent exhortations of the pope and of the council, place before the Latin American church a challenge and a mission that it cannot sidestep and to which it must respond with a speed and boldness adequate to the urgency of the times.

Christ, our savior, not only loved the poor, but rather "being rich he became poor," he lived in poverty. His mission centered on advising the poor of their liberation and he founded his church as the sign of that poverty among men and women.

The church itself has always tried to fulfill that vocation, notwithstanding "very great weaknesses and flaws in the past."[7] The Latin American church, given the continent's conditions of poverty and underdevelopment, experiences the urgency of translating that spirit of poverty into actions, attitudes, and norms that make it a more lucid and authentic sign of its Lord. The poverty of so many brothers and sisters cries out for justice, solidarity, open witness, commitment, strength, and exertion directed to the fulfillment of the redeeming mission to which it is committed by Christ.

The present situation, then, demands from bishops, priests, religious and laypersons the spirit of poverty which, "breaking the bonds of the egotistical possession of temporal goods, stimulates the Christian to order organically the power and the finances in favor of the common good."[8]

The poverty of the church and of its members in Latin America ought to be a sign and a commitment—a sign of the inestimable value of the poor in the eyes of God, an obligation of solidarity with those who suffer.

PASTORAL ORIENTATIONS

8. Because of the foregoing, we wish the Latin American church to be the evangelizer of the poor and one with them, a witness to the value of the riches of the kingdom, and the humble servant of all our people. Its pastors and the other members of the people of God have to correlate their life and words, their attitudes and actions, to the demands of the gospel and the necessities of the people of Latin America.

PREEMINENCE AND SOLIDARITY

9. The Lord's distinct commandment to "evangelize the poor" ought to bring us to a distribution of resources and apostolic personnel that effectively gives preference to the poorest and most needy sectors and to those segregated for any cause whatsoever, animating and accelerating the initiatives and studies that are already being made with that goal in mind.

We, the bishops, wish to come closer to the poor in sincerity and fellowship, making ourselves accessible to them.

10. We ought to sharpen the awareness of our duty of solidarity with the poor, to which charity leads us. This solidarity means that we make

ours their problems and their struggles, that we know how to speak with them. This has to be concretized in criticism of injustice and oppression, in the struggle against the intolerable situation that a poor person often has to tolerate, in the willingness to dialogue with the groups responsible for that situation in order to make them understand their obligations.

11. We express our desire to be very close always to those who work in the self-denying apostolate with the poor in order that they will always feel our encouragement and know that we will not listen to parties interested in distorting their work.

Human advancement has to be the goal of our action on behalf of the poor and it must be carried out in such a manner that we respect their personal dignity and teach them to help themselves. With that end in mind we recognize the necessity of the rational structuring of our pastoral action and the integration of our efforts with those of other entities.

TESTIMONY

12. We wish our houses and style of life to be modest, our clothing simple, our works and institutions functional, without show or ostentation.

We ask priests and faithful to treat us in conformity with our mission as fathers and pastors, for we desire to renounce honorable titles belonging to another era.

13. With the help of all the people of God we hope to overcome the system of fees, replacing it with other forms of financial cooperation not linked to the administration of the sacraments.

The administration of diocesan or parish properties has to be entrusted to competent laypersons and put to better use for the welfare of the whole community.[9]

14. In our pastoral work we will trust above all in the strength of God's word; when we have to employ technical means we will seek those most adequate to the environment in which they will be used and will put them at the disposal of the community.[10]

15. We exhort priests also to give testimony of poverty and detachment from material goods, as so many do, particularly in rural areas and poor neighborhoods. With great diligence we will procure for them a just though modest sustenance and the necessary social security. To this end we will seek to establish a common fund among all the parishes and the diocese itself; also among the dioceses of the same country.[11]

We encourage those who feel themselves called to share the lot of the poor, living with them and even working with their hands, in accord with the decree *Presbyterorum Ordinis.*[12]

16. The religious communities by virtue of their special vocation ought to witness to the poverty of Christ. We encourage those who feel themselves called to form among their members small communities, truly incarnated

in the poor environment; they will be a continual call to evangelical poverty for all the people of God.

We hope also that religious communities will be able more and more to effect the sharing of their goods with others, especially with the most needy, dividing among them not only superfluities, but also necessities, and disposed to put at the disposal of the human community the buildings and instruments of their work.[13] The distinction between what belongs to the community and what pertains to the work will facilitate this distribution. It will likewise permit the searching for new forms to accomplish those works, in whose administration or ownership other members of the Christian community will participate.

17. These authentic examples of detachment and freedom of spirit will make the other members of the people of God give a similar witness to poverty. A sincere conversion has to change the individualistic mentality into another one of social awareness and concern for the common good. The education of children and youth at all levels, beginning in the home, ought to include this fundamental aspect of the Christian life.

This feeling of love of neighbor is evinced when one studies and works above all with the intention of performing a service for the community; when one organizes power and wealth for the benefit of the community.

SERVICE

18. No earthly ambition impels the church, only its wish to be the humble servant of all.[14]

We need to stress this spirit in Latin America.

We want our Latin American church to be free from temporal ties, from intrigues and from a doubtful reputation; to be "free in spirit as regards the chains of wealth,"[15] so that its mission of service will be stronger and clearer. We want it to be present in life and in secular works, reflecting the light of Christ, present in the construction of the world.

We want to recognize all the value and legitimate autonomy of temporal works; aiding them we do not wish to take away their substance or divert them from their distinctive ends.[16]

We desire sincerely to respect all persons and listen to them in order to serve them in their problems and afflictions.[17] Thus, the church, carrying on the works of Christ, "who made himself poor for us, being rich in order to enrich us with his poverty,[18] will present before the world a clear and unmistakable sign of the poverty of its Lord.

NOTES

1. See Paul VI, *Address to the Peasants,* Mosquera, Colombia, August 23, 1968.
2. Luke 1:46-55.
3. See Matt. 5:3.

4. See Amos 2:6-7; Jer. 5:28; Micah 6:12-13; Isa. 10:2.

5. See Phil. 2:5-8.

6. See 2 Cor. 8:9.

7. See Paul VI, *Ecclesiam Suam,* no. 50.

8. See Paul VI, *Homily of the Mass on Development Day,* Bogotá, August 23, 1968.

9. See Vatican Council II, *Presbyterorum Ordinis,* no. 17.

10. See Vatican Council II, *Gaudium et Spes,* no. 69.

11. *Presbyterorum Ordinis,* no. 21.

12. Ibid., no. 8.

13. *Gaudium et Spes* no. 69.

14. Ibid., no. 3; Paul VI, *Closing Address of Vatican Council II,* December 7, 1965.

15. See Paul VI, *Opening Address to Latin American Bishops' Assembly,* Bogotá, August 24, 1968.

16. See *Gaudium et Spes,* no. 36.

17. Ibid., nos. 1-3.

18. See 2 Cor. 8:9.

PART III

PROGRESS AND OPPOSITION
(1968–1973)

The five years that followed the bishops' conference at Medellín have been characterized by some Latin American writers as a time of "euphoria." This estimate is based on "signs of the times," which seemed to offer new possibilities for a just society (the interpretation by many of the socialist government in Chile in 1970) and for a new church dedicated to the service of the poor (the flurry of activity, conferences, workshops, and teaching spreading the message of Medellín to all Latin America).

In my view, however, it is more illuminating to view the period as a time of extraordinary paradox or, as indicated in the title of this chapter, of a curious dialectic between diffusion and resistance to the documents of Medellín. It must be remembered that a number of the 130 bishops at the conference disagreed with what had occurred there, and that there were substantial divergences among most of the bishops with regard to the "real meaning of Medellín." I will discuss this paradox first with regard to the church and then, briefly, with regard to secular society.

First of all, the paradox just mentioned can be expressed succinctly as follows. This was a period of enormous activity and vitality in order to spread the liberating message of Medellín from the Rio Grande of Mexico to Cape Horn. At the same time, however, the period witnessed the emergence from the very beginning of a powerful and well-organized opposition to key directions of Medellín and to liberation theology, which had followed those directions.

As regards liberation theology, I would evaluate this epoch as the most creative in its entire history thus far. Since there is by now an avalanche of literature in the field, I will mention only the most significant authors. Leading the field, of course, is Gustavo Gutiérrez, whose *A Theology of Liberation* was published (in Spanish) in 1971. In it, Gutiérrez provides a model of his definition of theology as "critical reflection upon praxis in the light of the word of God," for his liberating theology (part 4 of the book)

121

occurs only after a careful perusal of statements from all elements of the church regarding their experience or praxis (part 3 of the book). The lasting value of the volume was that it provided a panoramic survey or map of the field, which later collaborators could follow, develop, or even correct. Little attention, however, has been given to the fact that the theology of Gutiérrez had already come to the attention of theologians throughout the world the year before, when his article "Notes for a Theology of Liberation" was published in the very scholarly and influential journal, *Theological Studies* (June 1970).

In another very significant event, the large Portuguese-speaking area of Latin America discovered a powerful voice from the heart of Brazil when the Franciscan Leonardo Boff published his *Jesus Christ Liberator* in 1972.[1] Though comparatively young, Boff has published prolifically on a great number of theological themes. The selection below (no. 15) is important because it is an excellent summary of his priorities or methodology. They do not apply only to christology; indeed, his application of this approach to the church was what led to difficulties with the Congregation for the Doctrine of the Faith a few years later.

Another theologian of major stature worldwide, Juan Luis Segundo, contributed greatly to the process of diffusion by completing his 5-volume *Artisans for a New Humanity* series with the publication of *Our Idea of God* (1973), *The Sacraments Today* (1974), and *Evolution and Guilt* (1974).[2] Along with this, he completed another theological work in 1970, *De la sociedad a la teología*,[3] and the very influential and controversial pastoral work, *The Hidden Motives of Pastoral Action*.[4] In my opinion, Segundo is the most rigorous, profound, and original of the Latin American liberation theologians.

Two other authors who should be mentioned in this period are Enrique Dussel and Segundo Galilea. In 1972 Dussel published the first edition of a history that incorporated many insights of liberation theology, *A History of the Church in Latin America: Colonialism to Liberation (1492–1972)*.[5] He has published many other books and articles in the field of history as well as important works in the fields of philosophy and ethics.

Segundo Galilea, a Chilean priest, also published in 1972 a book on spirituality, *Contemplación y apostolado*,[6] and followed that with *Espiritualidad de la liberación* in 1974.[7] Unfortunately, such works were not translated into English at that time, thus leading North American theologians to assert that liberation theology had no spirituality. The reality, however, was the opposite; one of the primordial insights of liberation theology was that spirituality was the door through which theology must pass if it is to leave the classroom and enter the real lives of human beings. (It should be added that, in the past few years, a number of Galilea's books have finally appeared in English.)[8]

A final untranslated work that is of great significance is the volume, *Fe cristiana y cambio social en América Latina*. This is a collection of the talks presented in a conference held July 8–16 in El Escorial, Spain, in which most of the leading liberation theologians participated.[9] In the context of diffusion, this meeting not only brought these theologians into personal contact with European scholars, but it was also an occasion for Latin Americans to meet with colleagues as well as publishers, journalists, and other interested persons from their own region. Although it drew considerable attention and controversy in Spain and Europe, the event passed unnoticed in the United States. The North Americans would have to wait another three years for their own introduction to their neighbors, which would not take place until August 1975, in Detroit.[10]

The dialectic mentioned at the beginning of this chapter was also in operation from the first days following Medellín, although the activities and publications of the opponents of liberation theology did not loom so large in the public eye. The general coordination of the campaign throughout Latin America was directed by Cardinal Alfonso López Trujillo, such a powerful figure throughout Latin America and in Rome that some Vaticanologists have him marked as a future pope. López became auxiliary bishop of Bogotá, Colombia, in 1971, and archbishop of Medellín, Colombia, in 1979. On February 2, 1983, Pope John Paul II elevated him to the rank of cardinal, the highest position in the Catholic hierarchy next to the papacy.

This brings us to one of the most crucial events in this period, and also in the whole history of liberation theology. The Latin American bishops' conference (CELAM) had been a prophetic voice at least since the end of the Second Vatican Council and had been on quite friendly terms with the liberation theologians. However, during the sixteenth ordinary assembly of CELAM, held November 15–23, 1972, in Sucre, Bolivia, López Trujillo was elected general secretary of CELAM, a post which he held until 1979, when he became president of CELAM. In 1983, when he retired as president, his followers were firmly in control of the conference, and continued to implement his policies, which have been consistently opposed to liberation theology and to the major advances of Medellín.

I would emphasize that this is truly an astonishing spectacle: within the brief space of four years, an organization that was speeding along the road of implementation of Medellín was suddenly thrown into reverse gear, with a great shock to all involved. Furthermore, López Trujillo successfully recruited other persons and institutions as allies in the struggle. One of the principal ones is the Jesuit Roger Vekemans, who left Chile in some haste in 1970 after the election of Salvador Allende and relocated in Bogotá. By 1972 he had created an organization called CEDIAL (Center for the Study of Development and Integration in Latin America) and had also founded a publication called *Tierra Nueva* ("New Earth"), institutions which both appear to have as one of their major purposes the launching of continual attacks on liberation theology. A last key player is the Brazilian Franciscan, Boaventura Kloppenburg, incidentally a former teacher of Leonardo Boff, who has written a number of books critical of liberation theology, especially with regard to its understanding of the nature of the church.[11] All this gives clear evidence that the battle for a liberating theology will continue to be fought for a long time in the years ahead.

If we turn to a look at secular society, it is clear that the experience of Chile was paradigmatic for the entire continent. The election of Allende and a socialist government in 1970 did appear to be a promise of a more just society for many Chileans and other Latin Americans. However, the opposition quickly rallied and the United States government played a major role in waging "economic war," while the Central Intelligence Agency funneled money into the opposition parties and directed the action from behind the scenes. This led in 1973 not only to the overthrow of the government, but also to the murder of Allende and thousands of Chilean citizens in the days that followed the coup. Almost immediately too, General Augusto Pinochet inaugurated a military dictatorship in Chile, which maintains an iron grip on the Chilean people at this writing. All in all, it was a shameful blot upon the historical record of the United States, which continues to view the Americas as "our" hemisphere and to deny to other countries their basic human right of national sovereignty.

NOTES

1. *Jesus Christo Libertador: Ensaio de Cristologia crítica para o nosso tempo* (Petrópolis: Vozes). English translation, *Jesus Christ Liberator: A Critical Christology for Our Time* (Orbis Books, 1978).

2. English translation, Orbis Books.

3. Buenos Aires: Carlos Lohlé.

4. Buenos Aires: Búsqueda. English translation, Orbis Books, 1978.

5. *Historia de la Iglesia en América Latina: Coloniaje y liberación 1492–1972* (Barcelona: Nova Terra, 1972). The English translation was published by Eerdmans in 1981.

6. Bogotá: Indo-American Press, 1972.

7. Santiago: ISPAJ. Part of this book was translated in *Following Jesus* (Orbis Books, 1981).

8. See, for example, *The Beatitudes: To Evangelize as Jesus Did* (Orbis Books, 1984) and *Spirituality of Hope* (Orbis Books, 1989).

9. Salamanca: Sígueme, 1973.

10. See Sergio Torres and John Eagleson, eds., *Theology in the Americas* (Orbis Books, 1976).

11. See especially *The People's Church: A Defense of My Church* (Chicago: Franciscan Herald Press, 1973).

11

Bishops of Peru
"Justice in the World"
(1971)

It was noted earlier in this book that the Latin American bishops contributed very little of lasting significance to the deliberations of the Second Vatican Council. Thus, it is astonishing to note, just a few years after the council, how confident and outspoken the Peruvian bishops' conference has become. This paper was presented as a contribution to the world synod of bishops held in Rome in November 1971. The text is taken from IDOC International *(December 11, 1971), pp. 2-18.*

INTRODUCTION: OUR NATIONAL REALITY

THE PERUVIAN EXPERIENCE

1. The Peruvian church finds itself in a country which is at a crossroads in its history, when our people's willingness to forge a more just society has become evident. The experience which we are living, with its positive aspects and its ambiguities, provide us with a definite contribution to be offered to the community of nations and churches in the world. The history of each people is the common patrimony in the joint history of all humanity according to God's saving design.

SITUATION OF DEPENDENCY

2. With the nations of the Third World we share the fact that we are the victims of systems that exploit our natural resources, that control our political decisions, that impose on us the cultural domination of their values and their consumer civilization. This situation, which was denounced by the Latin American episcopacy in Medellín, is reinforced and supported by the internal structures of our own nations, where there is increasing economic, social, and cultural inequality, where politics are perverted so that instead of serving the common good, only a few are favored.

WILLINGNESS TO CHANGE

3. We also share the struggle for liberation with these countries. In our own nation, because of historical circumstances, an aspiration for liberation is arising on every level. It is the result of the misery of marginal persons, of their being organized into pressure groups, and of their struggle; it is the effect also of interpreting our reality as a subproduct of the capitalistic development of Western society, which is considered the center of the system. This interpretation leads those who hold political power today to initiate measures which can begin to break internal and external domination. These are, for example, the attempt to recuperate our natural resources, the bringing home of capital and the control of foreign exchange, agrarian reform, the creation of labor communities, the reform of education, the support of social mobilization. These measures are designed: (a) to reaffirm our sovereignty; (b) to put the control of the economy in the hands of the state; (c) to provide for a more just distribution of income among the peasant sectors; (d) to augment the participation of labor in the profits, management, and ownership of businesses; (e) to increase the capability of critical judgment in order to confront creatively the answers that Peruvians are giving their environment and historic destiny; and (f) to permit the participation of people as the agents of their own liberation.

EXTERNAL PRESSURES

4. The forces of domination become more evident as greater effort for change is expended. External pressure increases in its repressive measures by means of economic sanctions in the international market, by controlling loans and other types of aid. News agencies and the communication media, which are controlled by the powerful, do not express the rights of the weak and deform reality by filtering information in a self-interested manner.

INTERNAL PRESSURES

5. Resistance to change is also manifested by internal pressures: the dominant groups fight so as not to lose their privileges; they hold back their capital so as to put obstacles in the path of change, obviously belittling the human lives which will be affected by the consequent unemployment; the individualistic values of a consumer society determine the reticent attitudes of the middle class; the popular sector, alienated so long by a history of domination, are unable to find their path and their sense of participation, since they have been disoriented by repressive policies or by the dishonest manipulation of political groups. These sectors, falsely stimulated by the consumer society, frequently look only for the personal development which can lift them out of their situation, without searching for the solidarity of their class in an effort of group advancement. The presence of Christians

is ambiguous: some manifest determined support of the measures for change, and even demand a greater radicalization, while others pretend to justify, on the basis of their faith, the defense of their privileges, because they lack the wider vision of a solidarity based on the gospel.

EXPERIENCE OF THE CHURCH

6. In this situation certain options favoring the oppressed arise within the Christian community, bringing identification with their problems, their struggle, their aspirations. Many Christians see their commitment as illumined by a theology, based on faith, which interprets the present situation as sinful and a negation of God's plan, and which moves them to a commitment to liberation as an answer to the Lord who calls us to construct history. The church thus discovers the inevitable political implications of its presence, and that it cannot announce the gospel in a situation of oppression without moving consciences with the message of Christ the liberator. It sees in evangelical poverty the expression of its solidarity with the oppressed and the denunciation of sin in the oppressive consumer society which creates artificial needs and superfluous expenses. It perceives the urgency of becoming aware of the world's problems in order to be faithful to its mission, since today, as in the past, it tends to live enclosed with its own internal problems and runs the risk of not being a sign if it continues to be absent from the anguish and worry which human beings face.

FOR A JUST WORLD

JUSTICE AND HOLINESS

7. The problem of justice in the world is "the central problem for world society today" (Roman document for the preparation of the Synod), and the realization of interpersonal justice is at the heart of the biblical message. To work justice is to know, that is, to love God (see 1 John 2:29). When justice does not exist among humans, God is ignored. That is why Medellín says that "Where unjust social, political, economic, and cultural inequalities are found, there is a rejection of the Lord's gift of peace, and even more, a rejection of the Lord himself" (Medellín, *Peace,* 14).

Justice, understood as holiness, a gift of the Lord, is the basic foundation of social justice. But this is at the same time a necessary and irreplaceable answer to the first. To struggle to establish interpersonal justice is to begin to be just before the Lord; the love of God and the love of neighbor are inseparable.

LIBERATION AND SALVATION

8. To construct a just society in Latin America and in Peru is to be liberated from the present situation of dependency, oppression, and plun-

der in which the great majority of our people live. On the one hand, liberation implies the rupture with all that keeps persons from self-fulfillment, as an individual and in community; on the other hand, it means the construction of a new society which is more human and fraternal.

The salvation of Christ does not stop at political liberation, but the latter has its place and true meaning within the total liberation incessantly announced by sacred Scripture, fulfilling in human beings their true dignity as sons and daughters of God (see Medellín, *Justice,* 3). A people of God who will promote all persons and the whole person (p. 14) is what God wants and humanity hopes for (see *Gaudium et Spes,* 11).

For the Peruvian ecclesial community this implies opting for the oppressed and marginal peoples as personal and communal commitment. This option does not exclude any individual from our charity; rather opting for those who today experience the most violent forms of oppression is for us an efficacious way of also loving those who, possibly unconsciously, are oppressed themselves by their very situation of being oppressors.

PARTICIPATION IN THE PROCESS OF LIBERATION

9. Humanity should be the artisan of its own destiny (see *Populorum Progressio,* 15), responsible before history, creator of its own culture and civilization, an act which becomes more urgent in the process of sociopolitical change which we are living. This means that persons should have a real and direct participation in the revolutionary action against structures and oppressive attitudes and for a just society for all. This participation will be made manifest by the awakening of critical consciousness and by the activity which demands that channels for participation in decision-making be created. Only thus can we avoid the myth of a formal democracy which hides a situation of injustice: "Actually, if beyond juridical laws a more profound sense of respect and service of one another is lacking, and even of an equality before the law, it could serve as an alibi for flagrant discrimination, for constant exploitation, for effective deceit" (*Octogesima Adveniens,* 23). This participation goes beyond the limits of law or governmental organisms, even if these were designed to favor it, because we must prevent popular participation from being channeled along a predetermined line or under political leadership. It should be a creative and autonomous process. In addition, there is no political participation without economic participation. That is why we must affirm that work provides a legitimate and primordial title of property over goods. This implies a new, fundamentally humanistic conception of the economic process, which surpasses the capitalist model, where capital was privileged and work was considered as marketable.

As a consequence of this conception of work, it follows that it is necessary that the exclusive and private ownership of the means of production be eliminated and an idea of social property be promoted, an idea which will more effectively fit the true meaning of human labor and the universal goal of all goods. God the creator has destined all goods for all human beings. Still more, the management of business should be patrimony of all who labor within it, as a specific way to be mobilized and to participate socially. Therefore, not only should the predominance of capital over labor be avoided, but so should paternalism and the possible manipulation by leaders and business persons, and the concern for laborers in less-favored businesses should be promoted for the good of the whole country.

A NEW SOCIETY

10. What has been said before and the experience lived by our people lead us to reject capitalism, in its economic expression as well as in its ideological basis, which favors individualism, profit, and the exploitation of humanity by humanity. We should therefore aim toward the creation of a qualitatively different society. By this we understand a society wherein the "willingness of justice, of solidarity and equality" reigns, one that will respond to "generous aspirations and the search for a more just society" and where "values, particularly freedom, responsibility, and an openness to things spiritual, which will guarantee the integral development of humankind," will be realized (*Octogesimo Anno,* 31).

In order that this kind of a society be developed, it is necessary that the education of all the people include the social and communal meaning of human life, in the total context which includes culture, economics, politics, and the whole society. That is why many Christians today recognize in socialist currents "certain aspirations which they hold within themselves in the name of their faith" (*Octogesima Adveniens,* 31). Education thus conceived will lead to the creation of a new human being and a new society — social humankind and a communal society, where democracy is real through the effective political participation of the members of a society, through the human concept and realization of work, through the submission of capital to the needs of the whole society. Consequently, a society so understood excludes certain historical socialisms, which we do not accept because of their bureaucracy, their totalitarianism, or their militant atheism.

PROPOSALS TO THE SYNOD

11. In the face of the situation of injustice represented by the kind of education generally found in the countries of the Third World, and especially in Latin America, because of its class consciousness and its orientation to form dependent, individualistic, and passive beings,

We propose that the church reject this kind of education and commit the efforts and resources dedicated to education to a liberating orientation.

12. In the face of the situation of injustice lived by a great number of ethnic-cultural groups, defined as "indigenous or native," who are trampled

upon with no recognition of their minimal rights as human beings, and consequently, with grave danger to their cultural and even biological survival,

We propose that the church demand that their basic rights be recognized: (a) reaffirming the human reality of the native and the maximal respect due his culture, which demands the right to be recognized legally as persons and as groups, the right to the ownership of the lands they need and have inhabited from time immemorial, the right to live with dignity and the right to be "different"; (b) considering it the obligation of the church to discover, know, and appreciate the values of these ethnic groups, which reflect the presence of God and the incarnation of Christ in history; and (c) being convinced that the church has the obligation to see that justice is done toward the Amerindians as the sole base for the truth, the love, and the peace of the Good News: Christ.

13. When governments arise which are trying to implant more just and human societies in their countries,

We propose that the church commit itself to giving them its backing; contributing to the elimination of prejudice; recognizing the aspirations they hold, and encouraging the search for their own road toward a socialist society which will have a humanist and Christian content; recognizing the right to expropriate property and resources, when ownership causes grave harm to the country (*Populorum Progressio*, 24), even when the unjust accumulation of riches has been accomplished within a legal framework.

14. In the face of the repressive policies of any government, particularly when, in the name of Christian civilization, any government uses violence and even torture on the persons who are fighting for the liberation of their peoples,

We propose that the church condemn these repressive methods, that it recognize the right these persons have to fight for justice, and that it should manifest solidarity with their ideals, even though it may not always approve of their methods.

15. In the face of the developed nations' withdrawal of investments in those countries that condition foreign investment to their national political objectives, as they fight for their autonomy but find their development delayed by the withdrawals which prevent the creation of work, and cause hunger, misery, and unemployment,

We propose that the universal church denounce this treason of human fellowship, taking advantage of an international forum to express its protest.

We also propose that the synod denounce the pseudo neutrality of countries which use their banking systems to favor the flight, accumulation, and protection of capital, and carry out policies that impoverish countries like ours.

In addition, *we propose* that the national churches of powerful nations become aware that their actions and omissions are factors in the activity exercised by their nations as dominators of other peoples, and that consequently they should exert their best effort to fight this situation by denouncing it and exercising moral and social influence to overcome it, for example, by censuring the sale of arms to the nations of the Third World and the arbitrary criteria used to determine international loans.

16. Given the situation of injustice and sin, which is that millions of human beings live in subhuman conditions while huge economic resources are spent in an uncontrolled arms race meant to maintain situations of domination, aggravated in the case of nuclear arms, and this not just because of the resources thus consumed and by the potential danger, but because of the damage testing has already done to humanity,

We propose that the universal church fully denounce this situation in general terms as well as in the specific cases where these arms are used by powerful countries to oppress poor peoples.

17. Regarding space conquest — even though it is recognized that it can generate great technological progress, it is a cause for worry to see it carried out as political competition, thus unnecessarily duplicating costs, as well as presenting a danger that this technological progress be used for the massive destruction of humanity, or to benefit exclusively the centers of world power by reinforcing a situation of domination,

We propose that the universal church demand that the powers committed to the race for the conquest of space integrate their efforts and that it ask that new discoveries be used for the good of all humanity.

IMPLICATIONS ON A NATIONAL LEVEL

18. We give our support and encouragement to those Christians who have opted for the popular sectors and are carrying out and living this option by identifying with their problems, their struggle, their hopes. In the face of structural changes in our country, we say that necessary sacrifices must be preceded by a personal example of austerity. So Christ taught us.

19. Observing the manipulative and depersonalizing mentality of many public functionaries and employees, especially in the provinces, we point out that these attitudes and conduct not only contradict the possibility of justice, but also the effort they are exerting to break the old structures and build a new society. The same contradiction is expressed by indolence, routine, a lack of mystique.

20. In the face of the attitudes of the authorities who are closest to the people, who are more concerned about repressing the criticism of internal inconsistencies — which are natural to any process of change — than about examining the denunciations objectively, we think it opportune to point out that the times demand new attitudes and the search for new ways of exerting authority.

21. In the face of the racial and cultural discrimination that our rural inhabitants still suffer, of the marginal status of women, especially in the mountains, we must remind everyone that we are all persons, children of

the same Father, destined for the same salvation and liberation.

22. In the face of the fact that an agrarian reform, although attempting to present a just answer to problems, could still generate new situations of injustice, such as distributing farms exclusively to the workers who are employed at the time of the partition—something which can generate great discrepancies among the new owners of rich and poor farm lands, since it can exclude from the process large sectors of peasants who are not employed,

We propose that this problem be considered in the plan for reform, searching creatively for types of property which can benefit the largest possible number of peasants, as well as duly guarding the social end of property by establishing the legal mechanisms which can best serve all of society.

23. The communities of workers have been created in an effort to reconcile the interests of capital and labor within the capitalist enterprise, thus allowing gradually the workers' participation in management and ownership of the means of production. This innovation was made by the decision of the government, without the participation of the workers, who are being asked to mold themselves to a measure, which because it is radically different from previous experience, goes beyond what is possible and generates frustration and inadequacy. It is therefore urgent that the roles of workers and management be redefined, within a process of change which, because it is open, is capable of generating its own mechanisms and a dynamism which can bring a complete reevaluation of human work in a new society.

THE CHURCH: SACRAMENT OF UNITY IN THE WORLD

24. In a world and a humanity marked by sin and characterized by its consequences, which are injustice, deprivation, exploitation, and oppression, the unity which Christ asked of the Father (John 17:21), is the vocation of the whole world (Col. 1:20; Eph. 1:4-10) and the task of the church which will thus appear as the sacrament of the world's unity (*Lumen Gentium,* 1 and 48). The unity of humankind will be possible only through a justice effective for all.

25. The church is the sacrament of this unity, of the final synthesis of history, of the world, and of humanity (Rom. 8:22ff.), of the total and universal salvation which is already operating in the hearts of men and women and in their reality. The sacrament of the world in its hopes for peace, for justice, for solidarity, for a communion of humankind with itself and with God (*Populorum Progressio,* 13), the church defines itself as the people of God on the way, searching (*Lumen Gentium,* 8).

26. The church is conceived as a sacrament of salvation (*Lumen Gentium,* 8) and as a human community that recognizes, proclaims, and celebrates Jesus as the savior of humanity (*Lumen Gentium,* 8), and it discovers, with

new insight, its mission of announcing the kingdom (*Ad Gentes,* 1,5), the meaning of its evangelical action and of temporal promotion, as well as the roles and tasks of its members.

27. A church defined from the viewpoint of the Latin American world demands of us a redefinition as a community of faith in a world marked by various forms of oppression. In other words, the problem of Latin American believers is faith and a revolutionary commitment, faith and political action. The relationship between eschatology and politics is given when the attempt to create a liberating historical project is made; that is, one that looks for the creation of a just, fraternal, and unified society and of a truly new humanity. Human history acquires a meaning and orientation which is new, with the novelty which is Christ himself in the world. It is not a matter of asking faith and the church for a model of society, for an outline of a scientific interpretation of reality, or for criteria for political options.

28. In addition, the gospel preached authentically to the oppressed necessarily brings them to awareness; that is, it sharpens their perception of themselves, and this with full economic, social, and political implications and with the incentive to struggle for justice.

29. It is in the concrete framework of a world struggling for its liberation that the Peruvian community of faith questions itself and redefines itself as the messenger of Christ who has come to reveal to us the full meaning of history, and it renews its heart through the call of the Lord in the signs and demands of liberation for authenticity, for generosity, and for fidelity.

ROLE OF THE CHURCH

EVANGELIZATION

30. The presence and the action of the church has an inevitable political implication, since it is impossible to preach the gospel without becoming committed to the struggle against the situation of domination. From a doctrinal and explanatory pastoral practice the transfer must be made to an authentic assimilation of the gospel which can transform life. The gospel, far from favoring the evasion of temporal responsibilities, leads us to fulfill and live them in the Lord.

AUTHENTICITY

31. The contribution of the church to the process of change demands a profound internal renewal of its way of working. Therefore: (a) it should be in such shape that it can exercise a role of prophetic and energetic denunciation of the forces which in one way or another, directly or indirectly, impede the process of change in favor of the people; and (b) the sectors of the church (bishops, priests, religious, laity) who have made a serious commitment, often for a lifetime, and who with deeds more than

words are trying to identify with the people in their struggle for a full liberation, deserve support.

POVERTY

32. So that the ecclesiastical community can participate in the process of change, it is necessary that it take upon itself an effective poverty as a means of identification and as a protest. Its word and action will be practically annulled until it suppresses the economic gap that separates a people sunk in misery from a church famed for its wealth. This implies: (a) that it assume the sense of evangelical poverty as an expression of solidarity, as a denunciation of a nonevangelical situation and as a challenge to a society which tarnishes its Christian name by calling itself so; and (b) that it search for ways of implementing common ownership of church goods as a concrete way of socializing and integrating our material resources, our energies, our capabilities and possibilities, both individual and communal, in order to construct a more just and human society.

EDUCATION

33. During a process of social transformation there can arise a discrepancy between structural changes and changes in attitude or mentality. Thus, on the one hand, a mentality accustomed to economic privileges finds it difficult to adjust to the sacrifices demanded by a process for social justice while on the other hand, a popular sector which has been accustomed to alienation during a long history of domination, finds it difficult to discover for itself a way of participating. The church's responsibility in this sphere becomes very grave when we add, to the enormous geographical challenge and to the isolation of many of our people, the obstacles arising from inertia, selfishness, exploitation. This demands:
   a. that the church, through the correct channels, develop the theological thought which can inspire the commitment of Christians and which offers the basis, from faith, to interpret the process we are living;
   b. that the teaching congregations seriously and urgently review the concrete forms of educational presence in the light of the new demands and needs of the people; they should enrich their mission with new expressions of educational-pastoral action;
   c. that church groups and associations, through due channels, renew themselves by creating a critical consciousness in their members and new fields of activity;
   d. that leaders be formed urgently, recalling that for the building of peace and justice, humankind (God's image) should be made responsible for its own destiny and that of the human community;
   e. that the church mobilize its human resources for adult education, preferably informally and deschooled; this implies wide collaboration with

national plans for "conscientization" and literacy. It also implies the denunciation of the use of the communication media for propaganda which encourages selfishness and uncontrolled consumption, both of which militate against the sociability and friendliness necessary to the society to which we aspire;

f. that while considering the possibilities of the common ownership of our goods, we begin studying now the implication and the contribution we can make toward the system of "nuclearization."

The church's role is to inform and encourage the reign of justice, and to change humankind from within by creating for it a new scale of values and the sense of coresponsibility for the creation of a new society.

APPENDIX

THE APOSTOLIC VICARIATES OF THE JUNGLE FACE SITUATIONS OF INJUSTICE

In the name of those who "have no voice," but who suffer silently the most subhuman consequences of a system of domination and exploitation wielded by intranational and extranational power centers (economic, political, scientific, etc.) who decide the fate of peoples in an unjust and unequal competition, we wish to serve as a loudspeaker for the numerous tribes of the Peruvian Amazon, who are crying out desperately in tongues which "civilized and/or Christian" people do not want to or cannot understand:

"We are human beings and we have a right to be recognized as such; therefore we demand the legal status which as persons and as a group is still denied us.

"We have a right to the land which from time immemorial we have inhabited, where we were born and where we have buried our elders; therefore we demand legal property titles which are still denied us.

"We have a right to life; therefore we demand that we be permitted to survive and to live with dignity.

"We have a right to be different; therefore we demand that we be respected as persons and groups, which is now denied us.

"We have a right to be considered a part of the Peruvian nation without being enslaved; therefore we demand the autonomy, equality, and liberty which up to the present have been denied us."

These cries express the existence of a situation of injustice which denies fundamental human rights and threatens the cultural and even the biological survival of numerous ethnic groups.

In the face of this injustice, the church, through its Apostolic Vicars, to whom it has confided the responsibility of announcing and effecting Christian justice: (a) reaffirms the human reality of the natives and the maximal respect due their culture; (b) considers it a fundamental obligation (as a church) to discover, know, and appreciate the values of these ethnic groups who demonstrate the presence of God and of Christ incarnate in their history; and (c) is convinced that it is its primordial duty to realize justice among the Amerindians, as the sole basis for the truth, the love, and the peace of the Good News: Christ.

COMMITMENTS AS A CHURCH

Therefore, the Peruvian church makes severe denunciations and commits itself to exert all its influence to effect substantial changes in regard to:

a. the lack of legal protection suffered by the majority of the aborigines in the Peruvian Amazon, who have no legal rights, no adequate legislation, and no documentation of citizenship;

b. the invasion, resettlement, and systematic expropriation of lands which the Amerindians have inhabited from time immemorial, which they suffer since they have no property titles;

c. the assaults and injustices (rarely sanctioned) to which the Amerindians are subjected by the abuse of authority, by deceit, theft, and subhuman exploitation;

d. insufficient medical attention, both preventive and curative, needed by the Amerindians as they face biological disintegration, caused or augmented by their contact with the national community.

REQUESTS GOVERNMENT ACTION

In conclusion, the episcopacy urges the government:

1. To promulgate soon the Law of Native Communities, which will give the natives minimal effective guarantees; legal protection and proper documentation as Peruvian citizens, and legal property titles and real ownership of the lands they have long inhabited. The amount of land should be sufficient according to the ecological characteristics of the zone and according to their traditional culture.

2. (a) To maintain greater control and better selection criteria for the military and civil authorities in the zones where the natives live, in order to avoid the frequent abuse of authority, (b) to control more effectively the abundant and indiscriminate inflow of persons who are not included in the colonization programs, and (c) to review seriously the Amerindian policies of certain colonization programs for the jungle.

3. (a) To provide the Division of Native Communities with sufficient budget, personnel, and authority so that, as an official government organism, it can defend the rights and denounce the injustices committed against Amerindians, and (b) to establish a Department of Native Communities in the zones of greatest Amerindian concentration.

4. To intensify medical and public health attention so as to assure the survival of these groups, especially through programs of vaccination and preventive medicine.

12

Synod of Bishops
"Justice in the World"
(November 30, 1971)

This was the second general assembly of the synod of bishops that had been inaugurated by Vatican II in its Decree on the Bishops' Pastoral Office in the Church, no. 5: "Bishops from various parts of the world, chosen through ways and procedures established or to be established by the Roman Pontiff, will render specially helpful assistance to the supreme pastor of the church in a council to be known by the proper name of Synod of Bishops. Since it will be acting in the name of the entire Catholic episcopate, it will at the same time demonstrate that all the bishops in hierarchical communion share in the responsibility for the universal church." The selection published here contains the introduction and the first section on "Justice and the World Society," which clearly shows the influence of the bishops of Latin America and other parts of the Third World. The text is taken from Joseph Gremillion, ed., The Gospel of Peace and Justice *(Maryknoll, N.Y.: Orbis Books, 1976), pp. 513-29.*

INTRODUCTION

1. Gathered from the whole world, in communion with all who believe in Christ and with the entire human family, and opening our hearts to the Spirit who is making the whole creation new, we have questioned ourselves about the mission of the people of God to further justice in the world.

2. Scrutinizing the "signs of the times" and seeking to detect the meaning of emerging history, while at the same time sharing the aspirations and questionings of all those who want to build a more human world, we have listened to the word of God that we might be converted in the fulfilling of the divine plan for the salvation of the world.

3. Even though it is not for us to elaborate a very profound analysis of the situation of the world, we have nevertheless been able to perceive the serious injustices which are building around the human world a network of domination, oppression, and abuses which stifle freedom and keep the

greater part of humanity from sharing in the building up and enjoyment of a more just and more united world.

4. At the same time we have noted the inmost stirring moving the world in its depths. These are facts constituting a contribution to the furthering of justice. In associations of men and women, and among peoples themselves, there is arising a new awareness which shakes them out of any fatalistic resignation and spurs them on to liberate themselves and to be responsible for their own destiny. Movements are seen which express hope in a better world and a will to change whatever has become intolerable.

5. Listening to the cry of those who suffer violence and are oppressed by unjust systems and structures, and hearing the appeal of a world that by its perversity contradicts the plan of its creator, we have shared our awareness of the church's vocation to be present in the heart of the world by proclaiming the Good News to the poor, freedom to the oppressed, and joy to the afflicted. The hopes and forces which are moving the world in its very foundations are not foreign to the dynamism of the gospel, which through the power of the Holy Spirit frees humankind from personal sin and from its consequences in social life.

6. The uncertainty of history and the painful convergences in the ascending path of the human community direct us to sacred history; there God has been revealed to us, and has made known to us, as it is brought progressively to realization, the plan of liberation and salvation, which is once and for all fulfilled in the paschal mystery of Christ. Action on behalf of justice and participation in the transformation of the world fully appear to us as a constitutive dimension of the preaching of the gospel, or, in other words, of the church's mission for the redemption of the human race and its liberation from every oppressive situation.

JUSTICE AND WORLD SOCIETY

CRISIS OF UNIVERSAL SOLIDARITY

7. The world in which the church lives and acts is held captive by a tremendous paradox. Never before have the forces working for bringing about a unified world society appeared so powerful and dynamic; they are rooted in the awareness of the full basic equality as well as of the human dignity of all. Since human beings are members of the same human family, they are indissolubly linked with one another in the one destiny of the whole world, in the responsibility for which they all share.

8. New technological possibilities are based upon the unity of science, on the global and simultaneous character of communications, and on the birth of an absolutely interdependent economic world. Moreover, persons are beginning to grasp a new and more radical dimension of unity; for they perceive that their resources, as well as the precious treasures of air and water—without which there cannot be life—and the small delicate bio-

sphere of the whole complex of all life on earth, are not infinite, but on the contrary must be saved and preserved as a unique patrimony belonging to all humankind.

9. Paradox lies in the fact that within this perspective of unity the forces of division and antagonism seem today to be increasing in strength. Ancient divisions between nations and empires, between races and classes, today possess new technological instruments of destruction. The arms race is a threat to humankind's highest good, which is life; it makes poor peoples and individuals yet more miserable, while making richer those already powerful; it creates a continuous danger of conflagration, and in the case of nuclear arms, it threatens to destroy all life from the face of the earth. At the same time new divisions are being born to separate individuals from their neighbors. Unless combatted and overcome by social and political action, the influence of the new industrial and technological order favors the concentration of wealth, power, and decision-making in the hands of a small public or private controlling group. Economic injustice and lack of social participation keep persons from attaining their basic human and civil rights.

10. In the last twenty-five years a hope has spread through the human race that economic growth would bring about such a quantity of goods that it would be possible to feed the hungry at least with the crumbs falling from the table, but this has proved a vain hope in underdeveloped areas and in pockets of poverty in wealthier areas, because of the rapid growth of population and of the labor force, because of rural stagnation and the lack of agrarian reform, and because of the massive migratory flow to the cities, where the industries, even though endowed with huge sums of money, nevertheless provide so few jobs that not infrequently one worker in four is left unemployed. These stifling oppressions constantly give rise to great numbers of "marginal" persons, ill-fed, inhumanly housed, illiterate, and deprived of political power as well as of the suitable means of acquiring responsibility and moral dignity.

11. Furthermore, such is the demand for resources and energy by the richer nations, whether capitalist or socialist, and such are the effects of dumping by them in the atmosphere and the sea that irreparable damage would be done to the essential elements of life on earth, such as air and water, if their high rates of consumption and pollution, which are constantly on the increase, were extended to the whole of humankind.

12. The strong drive toward global unity, the unequal distribution, which places decisions concerning three-quarters of income, investment, and trade in the hands of one-third of the human race—namely, the more highly developed part—the insufficiency of a merely economic progress, and the new recognition of the material limits of the biosphere—all this makes us aware of the fact that in today's world new modes of understanding human dignity are arising.

THE RIGHT TO DEVELOPMENT

13. In the face of international systems of domination, the bringing about of justice depends more and more on the determined will for development.

14. In the developing nations and in the so-called socialist world, that determined will asserts itself especially in a struggle for forms of claiming one's rights and self-expression, a struggle caused by the evolution of the economic system itself.

15. This aspiring to justice asserts itself in advancing beyond the threshold at which begins a consciousness of enhancement of personal worth (cf. *Populorum Progressio*, 15; A.A.S. 59, 1967, p. 265) with regard both to the whole person and the whole humankind. This is expressed in an awareness of the right to development. The right to development must be seen as a dynamic interpenetration of all those fundamental human rights upon which the aspirations of individuals and nations are based.

16. This desire, however, will not satisfy the expectations of our time if it ignores the objective obstacles which social structures place in the way of conversion of hearts, or even of the realization of the ideal of charity. It demands on the contrary that the general condition of being marginal in society be overcome, so that an end will be put to the systematic barriers and vicious circles which oppose the collective advance toward enjoyment of adequate remuneration for the factors of production, and which strengthen the situation of discrimination with regard to access to opportunities and collective services from which a great part of the people are now excluded. If the developing nations and regions do not attain liberation through development, there is a real danger that the conditions of life created especially by colonial domination may evolve into a new form of colonialism in which the developing nations will be the victims of the interplay of international economic forces. That right to development is above all a right to hope according to the concrete measure of contemporary humanity. To respond to such a hope, the concept of evolution must be purified of those myths and false convictions which have up to now gone with a thought-pattern subject to a kind of deterministic and automatic notion of progress.

17. By taking their future into their own hands through a determined will for progress, the developing peoples — even if they do not achieve their final goal — will authentically manifest their own personalization. And in order that they may cope with the unequal relationships within the present world complex, a certain responsible nationalism gives them the impetus needed to acquire an identity of their own. From this basic self-determination can come attempts at putting together new political groupings allowing full development to these peoples; there can also come measures necessary for overcoming the inertia which could render fruitless such an effort — as in some cases population pressure; there can also come new

sacrifices which the growth of planning demands of a generation which wants to build its own future.

18. On the other hand, it is impossible to conceive true progress without recognizing the necessity—within the political system chosen—of a development composed both of economic growth and participation; and the necessity too of an increase in wealth implying as well social progress by the entire community as it overcomes regional imbalance and islands of prosperity. Participation constitutes a right which is to be applied both in the economic and in the social and political field.

19. While we again affirm the right of persons to keep their own identity, we see ever more clearly that the fight against a modernization destructive of the proper characteristics of nations remains quite ineffective as long as it appeals only to sacred historical customs and venerable ways of life. If modernization is accepted with the intention that it serve the good of the nation, persons will be able to create a culture which will constitute a true heritage of their own in the manner of a true social memory, one which is active and formative of authentic creative personality in the assembly of nations.

VOICELESS INJUSTICES

20. We see in the world a set of injustices which constitute the nucleus of today's problems and whose solution requires the undertaking of tasks and functions in every sector of society, and even on the level of the global society toward which we are speeding in this last quarter of the twentieth century. Therefore we must be prepared to take on new functions and new duties in every sector of human activity and especially in the sector of world society, if justice is really to be put into practice. Our action is to be directed above all at those individuals and nations which because of various forms of oppression and because of the present character of our society are silent, indeed voiceless, victims of injustice.

21. Take, for example, the case of migrants. They are often forced to leave their own country to find work, but frequently find the doors closed in their faces because of discriminatory attitudes, or, if they can enter, they are often obliged to lead an insecure life or are treated in an inhuman manner. The same is true of groups that are less well off on the social ladder such as workers and especially farm workers who play a very great part in the process of development.

22. To be especially lamented is the condition of so many millions of refugees, and of every group of people suffering persecution—sometimes in institutional form—for racial or ethnic origin or on tribal grounds. This persecution on tribal grounds can at times take on the characteristics of genocide.

23. In many areas justice is seriously injured with regard to persons who are suffering persecution for their faith, or who are in many ways being

ceaselessly subjected by political parties and public authorities to an action of oppressive atheization, or who are deprived of religious liberty either by being kept from honoring God in public worship, or by being prevented from publicly teaching and spreading their faith, or by being prohibited from conducting their temporal affairs according to the principles of their religion.

24. Justice is also being violated by forms of oppression, both old and new, springing from restriction of the rights of individuals. This is occurring both in the form of repression by political power and of violence on the part of private reaction, and can reach the extreme of affecting the basic conditions of personal integrity. There are well-known cases of torture, especially of political prisoners, who besides are frequently denied due process or who are subjected to arbitrary procedures in their trial. Nor can we pass over the prisoners of war who even after the Geneva Convention are being treated in an inhuman manner.

25. The fight against legalized abortion and against the imposition of contraceptives and the pressures exerted against war are significant forms of defending the right to life.

26. Furthermore, contemporary consciousness demands truth in the communications systems, including the right to the image offered by the media and the opportunity to correct its manipulation. It must be stressed that the right, especially that of children and the young, to education and to morally correct conditions of life and communications media is once again being threatened in our days. The activity of families in social life is rarely and insufficiently recognized by state institutions. Nor should we forget the growing number of persons who are often abandoned by their families and by the community: the old, orphans, the sick, and all kinds of persons who are rejected.

The Need for Dialogue

27. To obtain true unity of purpose, as is demanded by world society, a mediatory role is essential to overcome day by day the opposition, obstacles, and ingrained privileges which are to be met with in the advance toward a more human society.

28. But effective mediation involves the creation of a lasting atmosphere of dialogue. A contribution to the progressive realization of this can be made by persons unhampered by geopolitical, ideological, or socio-economic conditions or by the generation gap. To restore the meaning of life by adherence to authentic values, the participation and witness of the rising generation of youth is as necessary as communication among peoples.

13

Chilean Bishops
"Declaration of the Bishops of Chile"
(April 22, 1971)

The context of this document and the next one is that of the socialist government of the Marxist Salvador Allende, which extended from his election in 1970 to his death and the overthrow of the government by military forces on September 11, 1973. Earlier, a group of Chilean priests known as "The 80" who lived among the working class held a workshop in April 1971, advocating Christian participation in the implementation of socialism in Chile. On April 16, 1971, under the leadership of the Jesuit Gonzalo Arroyo, they issued a "Declaration of the 80." This document stated the following:

Socialism, which is characterized by social appropriation of the means of production, paves the way for a new economy that makes possible autonomous development at a more accelerated level and overcomes the division of society into antagonistic classes. But socialism is not just a new economy. It should also generate new values that will pave the way for a society that evinces more fellowship and brotherhood. In this society the workers will shoulder their proper role with new dignity.

They also emphasize socialism's relationship to Christianity:

As Christians we do not see any incompatibility between Christianity and socialism. Quite the contrary is true. As the Cardinal of Santiago said last November: "There are more evangelical values in socialism than there are in capitalism." The fact is that socialism offers new hope that humanity can be more complete, and hence more evangelical—that is, more conformed to Jesus Christ, who came to liberate us from any and every form of bondage."

Six days later, on April 22, 1971, the bishops of Chile issued their own declaration, which presented their views on socialism and also replied specifically to

143

the Declaration of the 80. Although the bishops declare that they are not competent to make political or economic decisions, and that fundamental human rights have been violated in both Marxist socialism and capitalism, they appear hesitant to make an option for socialism. As theologians later pointed out, this is really equivalent to an option for the existing capitalist system. The bishops' document is taken from John Eagleson, ed., Christians and Socialism: The Christians for Socialism Movement in Chile *(Maryknoll, N.Y.: Orbis Books, 1975), pp. 12-15. The text of the "Declaration of the 80" is also found in the same volume, pp. 3-6.*

Gathered together at our annual plenary session, we the bishops of Chile have examined the present-day situation of the country. As a result of that examination, we want to issue the following statements:

1. The church sees itself as the people of God. Its particular mission, in its opinion, is to proclaim and live out the gospel of the risen Jesus Christ in every age and place.

2. Faced with the situation that Chile is experiencing at this present moment, Christians must take as their own the overall option that was affirmed by the Latin American episcopate at Medellín. This option should be the basic criterion for their outlook and their activities. According to this option asserted at Medellín, fidelity to the gospel of Jesus Christ today requires Christians to commit themselves to thoroughgoing and urgently needed social transformations.

3. To us who live in Chile today, the implementation of socialism is being proposed as a concrete way of effecting these transformations. There are sound reasons for believing that the socialism that is being proposed is predominantly Marxist in its inspiration.

4. As Vatican II reminds us, the church, by virtue of its mission and its area of competence, is not tied to any political system. Its mission is to incarnate in every age and in every situation the good news of complete liberation for the human person and for human society. It is not competent to make pronouncements on contingent solutions of a political or economic nature. But it does have authority to denounce anything in these solutions that is ambivalent in itself, that might delude or enslave humankind. And it is also obliged to proclaim and promote anything that would safeguard the dignity and transcendence of the human person.

5. An option for socialism of a Marxist cast poses legitimate questions. It is a system that already has concrete embodiments in history. In these concrete embodiments we find that fundamental rights of the human person have been trodden under foot just as they have been in concrete embodiments of the capitalist system. We find similar ways of proceeding that are just as condemnable. The church, which has been sent by God to serve and liberate humankind, cannot remain indifferent to this fact.

6. We feel that the needs and the rights of our people call for, and should make possible, a sincere effort by all those who claim to be com-

mitted to their liberation, so that this liberation is effected in a rapid and thoroughgoing way. This poses the whole question of dialogue: its possibility, its scope, and its underlying conditions.

7. The church is looking for dialogue and it invites others to it. Dialogue is always fruitful when the indispensable conditions for it are verified: sincerity, honesty, mutual respect. But the most pressing reason for dialogue is to be found in the expectations that the people nurture. They cannot wait hopefully forever. Nor can they be sacrificed to ideological schemes that are alien to their own original place in history.

8. To the legitimate government of Chile we reiterate the position that comes to us from Christ: that is, respect for its authority and collaboration in its effort to serve the people. Any and every effort to fashion a more human society, to eliminate poverty by promoting the common good over private interest, demands the support of those who are committed to human liberation as Christians are. The democratic tradition of this country permits us to say that this support can and should be offered through serious-minded criticism with a genuine concern for the common good.

9. The active and vigorous presence of Christians in all the organisms connected with the life of the nation, and their increased effort in every sector, would seem to be urgent imperatives flowing from their real commitment to the country.

10. We greatly appreciate the repeated statements of the president of the republic in which he has sought to respect and safeguard the rights of the religious conscience. We thank him for this cordial and considerate attitude, and we offer the same considerateness and cordiality in return.

Recently a group of priests issued a declaration, and it has been widely commented on in the communications media. With regard to their declaration we feel obliged to make the following points:

1. Like any citizen, a priest is entitled to have his own political option. But in no case should he give this option the moral backing that stems from his character as a priest. For this reason we continue to follow the tradition of the Chilean church as exemplified by Cardinal Caro and Bishop Manuel Larraín. We have always insisted, and we will continue to insist, that our priests abstain from taking partisan political positions in public. To act otherwise would be to revert to an outdated clericalism that no one wants to see around again.

2. If the political option of the priest is presented as a logical and inescapable consequence of his Christian faith, as it was in this case, then it implicitly condemns every other option and it is an attack on the liberty of other Christians.

3. When the political option of the priest is made public, then it threatens to disrupt the unity of the Christian people with their pastors. As Vatican II points out: "In building the Christian community priests are never to put themselves at the service of any ideology or human faction. Rather as

heralds of the gospel and shepherds of the church, they must devote themselves to the spiritual growth of the Body of Christ" (*Presbyterorum Ordinis*,
no. 6).

4. The situation that has arisen does not affect our esteem for the priests
in question. Nor does it diminish our high regard for the apostolic work
they, along with many others, are performing among the working class. We
have touched upon this matter in our declaration only because of the wide
repercussions that their own document has had.

Finally, we reiterate and renew our hope in the liberating presence of
Christ in the midst of the historical process through which we are now
living. May he give us light so that we can discern and support his activity
where he is struggling on behalf of the poor and the suffering. May he give
us the energy of his love so that we can place it in the service of our common
task: that is, making Chile a family where every person has food, respect,
and happiness.

14

Christians for Socialism
"Final Document of the Convention"
(April 30, 1972)

This document is the best synthetic presentation of the position of the Christians for Socialism. As far as I can judge, it never claimed to be an essay in liberation theology, although the opponents of liberation theology have had frequent recourse to it over the years as ammunition for their attacks. The text must be understood within the atmosphere of "euphoria" that prevailed in the early years of the 1970s, as was noted at the beginning of the introduction to this section. Thus, there are statements regarding a sweeping tide of socialism and liberation that is said to be engulfing all of Latin America. A somewhat naive attitude toward existing forms of Marxist socialism, its tendency toward totalitarian politics, its new forms of class privileges, and its new bonds of dependency, run throughout the document without any critical lenses at all. Finally, the theology of the document is very rudimentary, and appears totally at the service of the Marxist project. The text is taken from Christians and Socialism *(section 13, above), pp. 160–75.*

More than four hundred in number, we are Christians who have come to Santiago from all the countries of Latin America. The delegates have included lay persons, ministers, priests, and nuns; and there are observers from the United States, Quebec, and Europe. With a clear realization of the injustice pervading the socioeconomic structures of our continent, we wanted to ponder, in light of our common faith, what we can and should do at this point in history from within the concrete set of circumstances we face.

We wish to identify ourselves clearly as Christians. We are pondering our faith and reexamining our love for the oppressed from the basic standpoint of the liberation process now going on among our people and of our own real-life commitment to the task of constructing a socialist society. Most of us work with industrial laborers, peasants, or the unemployed. These persons are suffering the pangs of poverty, constant frustration, and neglect on the economic, social, cultural, and political levels. There is so much we have to do. We must do it together with these persons, and we must do it right away.

We have come together in Santiago at the same time that the Third World convention of UNCTAD is taking place here. That group is discussing a problem which is growing more acute every day. A relatively small sector of humanity is making greater progress and growing richer every day; but the price for their progress is the oppression of two-thirds of the human race. What pricks the consciousness of the exploited peoples most is the realization that their precarious economy results from the growing wealth and well-being of the great powers. Our poverty is the other side of the coin, the reflection of the growing wealth of the exploiter classes throughout the world.

How are we to confront this clear-cut situation of injustice? One thing, at least, is clear: the peoples dominated by imperialist capitalism must unite to break away from the situation of oppression and plunder to which they are subject. But this unity, which seems so logical, is not easy to attain because their dependence on foreign elements fosters disunity; and in direct or subtle ways this disunity is fostered by imperialism. United here from all over Latin America, and in the presence of the UNCTAD convention, we Christians wish to send out an appeal to the exploited social classes and countries under foreign domination; we urge them to unite to defend their rights, and not to beg for aid.

The economic and social structures of our Latin American countries are grounded on oppression and injustice, which in turn is a result of our capitalist dependence on the great power centers. In each of our nations small minorities serve the cause of international capitalism and its accomplices. Using every means in their power, they seek to maintain a situation that was created to benefit themselves. This structural injustice is in fact violence, whether it be open or disguised.

Those who have exploited the weak for centuries, and who wish to keep doing this, use de facto violence against them. This violence is often veiled under the guise of a fallacious order and a fallacious legality, but it is violence and injustice nonetheless. It is not human, and hence, it is not Christian.

But the diagnosis is not enough. By his example Christ taught us to live what he preached. Christ preached human solidarity and proclaimed that love should configure all our social structures. Even more importantly, he *lived out* his message of liberation to its ultimate consequences. He was condemned to death. The power brokers in his nation saw his message of liberation, and the real-life love to which he bore witness, as a serious threat to their economic, social, religious, and political interests. Today, as always, the Spirit of Christ is actively giving impetus to history. It shows up in solidarity, in the unselfish commitment of those who struggle for liberty and evince authentic love for their oppressed sisters and brothers.

The structures of our society must be transformed from the roots up. The task is more necessary today than ever before because those who benefit from the unjust order in which we live are defending their class interests in an aggressive way. They use all the means at their disposal— propaganda, subtle ways of dominating popular consciousness, defense of a discriminatory legal setup, frequent repression, and dictatorship if necessary—to prevent a revolutionary transformation from taking place. Only by gaining economic and political power will the exploited class be able to construct a society that is qualitatively different from the existing one: that is, a socialist society—without oppressors or oppressed, in which everyone will have the same possibilities for human fulfillment.

The revolutionary process is in full swing in Latin America. Many Christians have made a personal commitment to it. But many more Christians, imprisoned in mental inertia and categories that are suffused with bourgeois ideology, regard this process fearfully and insist on taking the impossible pathway of reformism and modernization. The Latin American process is all-embracing and one in character. We Christians do not have a peculiar political approach of our own to offer, and we do not wish to have such an approach. The realization that the process is all-embracing and one in character makes us comrades, uniting all those who struggle in a common task. Our revolutionary commitment has enabled us to rediscover the import of Christ's liberative work. That work gives human history its underlying unity. Framing political liberation in a broader and more radical context, it enables us to grasp its true sense and import. Christ's liberation necessarily shows up in liberating events of history, but it is not limited to such events. It indicates the limitations of these events and, even more importantly, leads them toward their complete fulfillment. The real reductionists, who diminish Christ's work, are those who want to separate it from the pulsing course of history where individual and social classes struggle to liberate themselves from the oppression to which other individuals and classes subject them. The real reductionists are those who are unwilling to recognize the fact that Christ's liberation is a thoroughgoing liberation from every sort of exploitation, plunder, and alienation.

We commit ourselves to the task of fashioning socialism because it is our objective conclusion, based on the concrete experience of history and on a rigorous, scholarly analysis of the facts, that this is the only effective way to combat imperialism and to break away from our situation of dependence.

The construction of socialism is not accomplished by vague denunciations or by appeals to good will. It presupposes an analysis that will reveal the mechanisms which really move society, that will lay bare the existing oppression, and that will unmask and name all those persons and things which oppress the laboring class in open or subtle ways. Above all, it presupposes participation in the struggle that pits the exploited class against its oppressors. Authentic charity cannot gloss over the struggle unleashed by those who exploit the people and who seek to defend or increase their own privileges.

We publicize our reflections because we believe that they can help to inspire other Christians and persons of good will to reflect along with us and to set out in quest of some way to radically transform the structures that now prevail our continent.

PART ONE

1. THE LATIN AMERICAN REALITY: A CHALLENGE FOR CHRISTIANS

1.1. The socio-economic, political, and cultural situation of the peoples of Latin America poses a challenge to our Christian conscience. Unemployment, malnutrition, alcoholism, infant mortality, illiteracy, prostitution, ever growing inequality between rich and poor, racial and educational discrimination, exploitation, and so forth: these are the factors that go to make up a situation of institutionalized violence in Latin America.

1.2. To begin with, it is clear that this reality is not the inevitable product of natural inadequacies, much less of some "inexorable" destiny or some implacable "God" who is a stranger to the human drama. On the contrary, it is a process determined by the will of human beings.

1.3. The human "will" in question is that of a privileged minority. It has made possible the construction and maintenance of an unjust society — capitalist society — based on exploitation, profit, and competition.

1.4. This unjust society is objectively grounded on the capitalist production-centered relationships, which necessarily give rise to a class-based society.

1.5. Colonialist and neocolonialist capitalism is the economic structure that shapes the reality of Latin American countries. In its higher phase, this capitalist structuring leads to imperialism and its auxiliary factors, which operate through many different mechanisms: military and economic aggression, alliances between repressive governments, multinational organizations, cultural domination, the presence of the CIA and the State Department, and so forth.

1.6. Within each country imperialism operates in complicity with the ruling classes or the national bourgeoisie who are dependent on the capitalist setup. The ruling classes, in turn, are allied with the institutional church.

1.7. One of the last resorts of imperialism is dictatorships and governments of a fascist cast, which spawn repression, torture, persecution, political crimes, and so forth.

1.8. The desperate struggle of imperialism poses economic obstacles to those countries that have opted for socialism. This is true in the case of Cuba and of Chile.

1.9. Imperialism tries to keep the people disunited. It sets Christians against Marxists with the intention of paralyzing the revolutionary process in Latin America.

1.10. False models of economic growth, implemented at the expense of the laboring class and the peasantry, try to distract the people from the real overall goals of the revolution. This is true, for example, of the developmental models worked up for Brazil and Mexico.

1.11. Using all the communication and education media, the forces of imperialism and the ruling classes in the nation impose a dependent form of culture on the people. This culture disguises and justifies the situation of domination. In addition, it forms human beings who are resigned to their alienation. It also stimulates the oppressed to patronize and exploit others in turn.

1.12. The historical process of a class-based society and imperialist domination inevitably leads to confrontation between the classes. Despite the fact that this confrontation becomes clearer every day, it is denied by oppressors. Meanwhile the exploited classes are progressively discovering and adopting a new revolutionary consciousness.

1.13. The growing acuteness of the class struggle makes it clear that there are only two possible alternatives in Latin America today: dependent capitalism with its resultant underdevelopment, or socialism. At the same time the happenings within each country reveal the historical failure and the impossibility of any middle-ground position between capitalism and socialism, and of any kind of reformism.

1.14. Some leftist national movements have importance for the revolution. But they prove to be inadequate if they do not lead to socialism within the framework of the liberation process now going on in Latin America.

1.15. Whether we realize it or not, the present position of every human being on this continent — and hence of the Christian — is determined by the historic dynamism of the class struggle within the process of liberation.

1.16. Christians who are personally committed to the revolutionary process recognize the ultimate failure of any Christian "third way" in the social realm. Hence they make every effort to insert themselves into the one and only history of liberation that belongs to our continent.

1.17. The intensification of the class struggle represents a new stage in the politico-ideological struggle, and it rules out any pretension to neutrality or apoliticism. The intensification of the class struggle gives the revolutionary process in Latin America its true dimension of totality.

1.18. Scientific analysis and revolutionary commitment to the struggle of the exploited necessarily bring out the real-life elements at work in the present situation: that is, production-based relationships, capitalist expropriation of surplus value, class struggle, ideological struggle, and so forth.

1.19. In this context, the Cuban revolution and the Chilean transition toward socialism propose a return to the wellsprings of Marxism and a criticism of traditional Marxist dogmatism.

1.20. With the help of all the analytic devices provided, by Marxism in particular, the common people are realizing the need to set out for a real takeover of power by the working class. Only this will make it possible to fashion an authentic socialism, which so far is the only way to achieve total liberation.

2. ATTEMPTS AT LIBERATION IN LATIN AMERICA

2.1. A common process of liberation is under way in Latin America. It is in the tradition provided by Bolívar, San Martín, O'Higgins, Hidalgo, José Martí, Sandino, Camilo Torres, Che Guevara, Néstor Paz, and others. It is a second war for independence, bringing together the revolutionary forces of a continent who share a common past — colonization — and a common present — exploitation and poverty.

2.2. The dependent form of capitalism that reigns in Latin America necessarily spawns the laboring classes: industrial workers, manual workers, and peasants. As such, these classes constitute the social base that is objectively revolutionary. They also pose an urgent task of politicization, so that they may gradually acquire the power to destroy the capitalist system and replace it with a more just and comradely society.

2.3. Numerous attempts at liberation have cropped up throughout the continent, particularly since the Cuban revolution. They are similar in form insofar as they represent a breakaway from dependence and a fight against imperialism. They take on different forms in accordance with the diversity of the various nations in which they take place.

2.4. Despite their differing tactics, these attempts at liberation tend to unify at a higher level. They bear witness to a desire to develop a new strategy which will combine the revolutionary forces in a common attempt at liberation.

2.5. The revolutionary process demands that we overcome sterile divisions between different leftist groups in Latin America, divisions that are fostered and manipulated by imperialism.

2.6. Urged on by the spirit of the gospel, Christians are joining proletarian groups and parties and accepting the same rights and duties as other revolutionaries. Christians committed to socialism see the national and continental proletariat as the vanguard of the liberation process in Latin America.

2.7. The growing mobilization of the people makes new demands upon us: for example, overcoming such things as sectarianism, bureaucratism, corruption in high places, and the inculcation of bourgeois values.

3. CHRISTIANS AND THE PROCESS OF LIBERATION IN LATIN AMERICA

3.1. Some Christians are beginning to realize that the reality of Christianity (its institutional forms, its theologies, its consciousness) is not outside this confrontation between the exploited and their exploiters. On the contrary, it is marked by colonialism and, in many cases, it is allied with our dependent brand of capitalism.

3.2. Groups of Christians, motivated by their faith, are making a revolutionary commitment to the people in growing numbers. And it is evident that they are having greater impact on this continent.

3.3. At the same time Christian and non-Christian groups are showing greater interest in noting and analyzing the sociological impact that Christianity has had and continues to have on the social configuration of the Latin American continent—in both a positive and a negative sense.

3.4. Increasing numbers of Christians are discovering the historical relevance of their faith through their political activity on behalf of the construction of socialism and the liberation of the oppressed on this continent. The Christian faith shows up with new vitality and relevance as a factor for criticism and liberation.

3.5. Real-life praxis alongside the proletariat is destroying ethical and emotional blocks within Christians that have prevented them from committing themselves to the class struggle. By virtue of their historical weight, these blocks are a particularly important aspect of the cultural and educational revolution.

3.6. Priests and ministers are making a growing commitment to the poor, the oppressed, and the working class. Enlightened by a new type of theological reflection, they are discovering that their specific mission has new dimensions. Their personal commitment induces them to take on a political responsibility, which is required if they are to effectively display the love for the oppressed that is demanded by the gospel. It also immerses them in the prophetic thrust that is part and parcel of the process of divine revelation. Sometimes grouped together in specific organizations of their own, they represent a positive contribution to the Latin American process of liberation.

3.7. There is a growing awareness that revolutionary Christians must form a strategic alliance with Marxists within the liberation process on this continent. Such a strategic alliance goes beyond the tactical alliances of a temporary or short-run nature. It signifies a common journey toward liberation in history through joint political action. This identification with Marxists in political action within history does not mean that Christians are abandoning their faith. To them it represents revitalized faith in the future of Christ.

PART TWO

1. SOME ASPECTS OF OUR REVOLUTIONARY COMMITMENT

1.1. Revolutionary commitment entails a comprehensive historical project: the transformation of society. Generosity and good will are not enough. Political action calls for a scientific analysis of reality. There is a constant interaction between political activity and critical analysis. This particular brand of analysis has its own peculiar scientific rationale, which is qualitatively different from the rationale of the bourgeois social sciences.

1.2. The social structure of our countries is based on production relationships (predominantly capitalistic and dependent on worldwide capitalism), which are grounded on the exploitation of workers. Recognition of the class struggle as a fundamental fact enables us to arrive at an overall interpretation of the structures of Latin America. Revolutionary praxis discloses that any objective, scientific interpretation must resort to class analysis as a key.

1.3. Socialism presents itself as the only acceptable option for getting beyond a class-based society. The fact is that social classes are a reflection of the economic base which, in a capitalist society, sets up an antagonistic division between the possessors of capital and those who are paid for their labor. The latter must work for the former, and thus they are an object of exploitation. Only by replacing private ownership with social ownership of the means of production do we create objective conditions that will allow for the elimination of class antagonism.

1.4. The takeover of power that will lead to the construction of socialism has need of a theory that will criticize capitalist society. Laying bare the contradictions of Latin American society, this theory reveals the objective revolutionary potential of the working classes. The latter are exploited by the system; at the same time, however, they have the capacity to transform it.

1.5. To attain socialism we need not only a critical theory but also the revolutionary praxis of the proletariat. This entails a change of consciousness. That is to say, the present gap between the societal reality and the consciousness of the workers must be overcome. To effect this change in consciousness, we must unmask and denounce the ideological mystifications of the bourgeoisie. In this way the people will identify the structural causes of their wretchedness and conceive the possibility of eliminating them. At the same time, however, this change of consciousness requires popular parties and organisms, and a strategy that will lead to a takeover of power.

1.6. The construction of socialism is a creative process that has nothing to do with dogmatic schemas or an uncritical stance. Socialism is not a complex of historical dogmas but a constantly developing critical theory of the conditions of exploitation and a revolutionary praxis. Operating through the takeover of power by the exploited masses, this praxis leads to social appropriation of the means of production and financing, and to comprehensive, rational economic planning.

1.7. Inadequate comprehension of the rationale proper to the class struggle has led many Christians to a defective kind of political involvement. Failing to appreciate the structural mechanisms of society and the necessary contributions of a scientific theory, they try to deduce their political approach from a certain kind of humanistic conception: for example, the "dignity of the human person," "liberty," and so forth; this is accompanied by political naiveté, activism, and voluntarism.

2. Christianity and the Ideological Struggle

2.1. The class struggle is not restricted to the socio-economic level. It extends to the ideological realm as well. The ruling class fabricates a set of ideological justifications which impede recognition of this struggle. The ideology of the ruling classes, spread among the people by the communication and education media, produces a false consciousness in the dominated class. This false consciousness acts as a restraint on revolutionary action.

2.2. For this reason, revolutionary action places great value on the ideological struggle and regards it as an essential component. Its aim is to liberate the consciousness of the oppressed.

2.3. The dominant ideology takes in certain Christian elements which bolster it and diffuse it through vast segments of the Latin American population. At the same time, the dominant ideology to some extent finds its way into the expression of Christian faith—in particular, into Christian social doctrine, theology, and church organizations. One of the central tasks of the ideological struggle is to identify and unmask these ideological justifications that are supposedly Christian.

2.4. The deeper core of the faith which we profess, and which is Christ's gratuitous gift, requires us to be critical of the ideological use to which it is put—often in subtle and unnoticed ways. The task of unmasking this sort of use, in which the Christian faith is impoverished and made to serve certain interests, is an exigency of the gospel itself. But it also requires a satisfactory scientific methodology and a real-life commitment to the poor, the oppressed, and the working class. The aim is not to use the faith as a tool for other political ends, rather, it is to restore its pristine evangelical dimension to it. On our continent that task is an urgent one, because the ideological use which people make of the faith paralyzes its liberative, evangelical force that is so important right now.

2.5. The dominant culture imposes an image of the human being as someone who is summoned to accept an already established order. The latter is presented as the objective order, which is founded on human nature itself and which finds expression in natural laws and natural rights. Existing inequalities, dependence, the division of labor, and the chasm between the people and political power are presented as the natural necessities of society. This hides the fact that these relationships are rooted in the capitalist system itself, and it undermines the tendency to look for radical, all-pervasive change.

2.6. The dominant culture imposes an individualistic conception of humankind, picturing the human being with capabilities, tasks, and goals that are purely individual. In its various forms—liberalism, humanism, and personalism, for example—this culture presents itself as the defender of personal liberty, private property, free trade, open competition, and love reduced to the interpersonal plane entirely. In this way it conceals the structural features of social relationships and the contradictions engendered by the system.

2.7. The culture of the prevailing system imposes a "spiritualistic" idea of humankind. It explains human behavior and history as if they were grounded mainly on moral ideas and attitudes, as if the ills of the world were based solely on ideological or moral deviations of a purely individual cast. Without at all denying the creativity and the moral worth of the individual person, we feel that the prevailing culture diverts attention away from scientific study of the economic and social mechanisms which fundamentally govern the movement of history. It conceals the fundamental role of structures in the oppression of individuals and nations. It hides the basic impact of the economic factor, of class relationships in particular, on human political, cultural, and religious life. Hence it sloughs off the idea of seeking change through a transformation of the economic system.

2.8. Using the gospel in a partial and distorted way, the dominant culture imposes a pacifist notion of society. It describes the contrasts, the forms of dependence, the division of labor, and the privileges of some as so many forms of pluralism and complementarity required for order and the common good. Hence it promotes "collaboration" and "dialogue" among the classes and the nations. In this way it conceals the conflict-ridden nature of the relationships between classes and peoples, and of any authentic process of liberation. It disguises the institutionalized violence of the prevailing system, reserving the label "violence" for the struggle against the dominant class and in favor of revolution. In this way it ultimately retards any authentic communion between human beings.

2.9. The underlying basis for most persons' unawareness of the class struggle is the class struggle itself. It works all the more effectively when it works without the oppressed taking note of its influence and its mechanisms.

2.10. To a large extent, the alliance between Christianity and the ruling classes explains the historical forms that Christian awareness has taken. Hence Christians must take a definite stand on the side of the exploited in order to break this alliance. Such a stand, verified in concrete praxis, will enable us to discover a revitalized Christianity. In a sincere effort to be faithful to the gospel, we can recover the revolutionary, conflictive character of its pristine inspiration.

3. FAITH AND REVOLUTIONARY COMMITMENT

3.1. One of the most important discoveries being made by many Christians today is the convergence between the radicality of their faith and the radicality of their political commitment. The radicality of Christian love and its required note of efficaciousness impels them to recognize the specific rationale of the political realm, and to accept the full and logical implications of the tie-up between revolutionary action and scientific analysis of historic reality.

3.2. The real-life presence of faith in the very heart of revolutionary praxis provides for a fruitful interaction. The Christian faith becomes a critical and dynamic leaven for revolution. Faith intensifies the demand that the class struggle move decisively toward the liberation of all humankind — in particular, of those who suffer the most acute forms of oppression. It also stresses our orientation toward a total transformation of society rather than merely a transformation of economic structures. Thus, in and through committed Christians, faith makes its own contribution to the construction of a society that is qualitatively distinct from the present one, and to the appearance of the new humanity. The specific nature of the Christian contribution should not be viewed as something prior to revolutionary praxis, as something ready-made that Christians bring with them to the revolutionary struggle. Rather, in the course of their real-life experience in that struggle, faith reveals its capacity to provide creative contributions which neither Christians nor anyone else could have foreseen outside the revolutionary process.

3.3. But revolutionary commitment also has a critical and motivating function vis-à-vis the Christian faith. It criticizes the open and the more subtle forms of complicity between the faith and the dominant culture during the course of history. It gives new impetus to the faith insofar as it compels the Christian faith to set out on new and unforeseen pathways in order to maintain its vitality. Christians involved in the process of liberation vividly come to realize that the demands of revolutionary praxis force them to rediscover the central themes of the gospel message — only now they are freed from their ideological dress.

3.4. The real context for a living faith today is the history of oppression and of the struggle for liberation from this oppression. To situate oneself within this context, however, one must truly participate in the process of liberation by joining parties and organizations that are authentic instruments of the struggle of the working class.

3.5. Christians involved in revolutionary praxis discover the liberative power of God's love, of Christ's death and resurrection. They discover that their faith is not the acceptance of the world already made and a history already determined; that it is an existence which creates a new world of fellowship and a historical effort seeded by Christian hope.

3.6. In real-life commitment to the revolution, Christians learn to think and to live in terms of history and conflict. They discover that a love which brings about transformation is lived out in antagonism and confrontation, and that the definitive goal is approached and constructed in history. They begin to realize that no neutrality is possible in the struggle to create a different society, that the humanity of tomorrow is fashioned in the struggles of today. Finally, they discover that the unity of the church comes about through the unity of humanity. Hence the revolutionary struggle, which reveals the superficial unity of the church today, is fashioning the authentic unity of the church of tomorrow.

3.7. Reflection on the faith ceases to be abstract speculation outside commitment in history. Revolutionary praxis comes to be recognized as the matrix that will generate a new theological creativity. Thus theological thinking is transformed into critical reflection in and on liberation praxis — in a context of permanent confrontation with the exigencies of the gospel.

Theological reflection assumes that an indispensable prerequisite for carrying out its task is a socio-analytical methodology that is capable of critically grasping the conflictive nature of historical reality.

3.8. This leads Christians, in a spirit of authentic faith, to a new reading of the Bible and Christian tradition. It poses the basic concepts and symbols of Christianity anew, in such a way that they do not hamper Christians in their commitment to the revolutionary process but rather help them to shoulder these commitments in a creative way.

CONCLUSION

We leave this convention and return to our tasks with a revitalized spirit of personal commitment. We take as our own the words of Che Guevara, which we have put into practice to some extent during these past few days:

> Christians should opt definitively for the revolution — particularly on this continent where the Christian faith is so important among the masses of the people. But in the revolutionary struggle Christians cannot presume to impose their own dogmas or to proselytize for their churches. They come without any intention of evangelizing Marxists and without cowardly concealing their faith to assimilate themselves to the latter.
>
> When Christians dare to give full-fledged revolutionary witness, then the Latin American revolution will be invincible; because up to now Christians have allowed their doctrine to be used as a tool by reactionaries.

15

Leonardo Boff
"Toward a Christology of Liberation"
(1972)

The importance of the work of the Brazilian Franciscan, Leonardo Boff, has already been discussed in the introduction to this chapter. In general, liberation theology has followed Boff in emphasizing a christology that exists in a profound symbiosis with a liberating spirituality, as in the later works of Jon Sobrino and Juan Luis Segundo. Thus, its major emphasis is on a "christology from below"—that is, with its normative criteria derived from the teachings and actions of the Jesus of history. Another dominant feature is the centrality given to Jesus' preaching of the kingdom of God, a kingdom understood as being realized partially but efficaciously in history, thus conferring a lasting value on human freedom and creativity in laboring for this kingdom in the present life. This excerpt is from Boff's Jesus Christ Liberator: A Critical Christology for Our Time *(Maryknoll, N.Y.: Orbis Books, 1978), pp. 43–48. The original Portuguese edition was published by Editorial Vozes, Petrópolis, in 1972, making this one of the earliest scholarly books in the field of liberation theology.*

The hermeneutic reflections developed up to this point ought to have made it clear that we cannot simply speak *about* Jesus as we would speak about other objects. We can only speak *with him as starting point*, as persons touched by the significance of his reality. We come to him with that which we are and have, inserted into an unavoidable socio-historical context. We see with our eyes the figure of Christ and reread the sacred texts that speak of him and had him as starting point. Consequently, a christology thought out and vitally tested in Latin America must have characteristics of its own. The attentive reader will perceive them throughout this book. The predominantly foreign literature that we cite ought not to delude anyone. It is with preoccupations that are ours alone, taken from our Latin American context, that we will reread not only the old texts of the New Testament but also the most recent commentaries written in Europe. The facts will be situated within other coordinates and will be situated within an appropriate horizon.

Our sky possesses different stars that form different figures of the zodiac by which we orient ourselves in the adventures of faith and of life. Here are a few characteristics of such a christology.

THE PRIMACY OF THE ANTHROPOLOGICAL ELEMENT OVER THE ECCLESIASTICAL

The special focus in Latin American is not so much the church but the human person that it should help, raise up, and humanize. In Latin American theological thought, there reigns an accentuated ecclesiological skepticism: here the church reproduced models and structures imported from Europe. Very little creativity was allowed the faith that, lived and tested in our milieu, could have expressed itself naturally and with greater liberty within structures having peculiarly Latin American characteristics. The general horizon was one that dogmatically interpreted canon law and juridically interpreted dogma. This basically impeded healthy attempts to create a new incarnation of the church outside the inherited traditional framework of a Greco-Roman understanding of the world.

The future of the Catholic Church, given the diminution of the European population, is undeniably in Latin America. It is in the more anthropological vision, in the new human person being elaborated here, that we can gather elements to nourish a new, renewed Christian reflection. What are the great expectations among the people to which the faith can address itself, announcing the joyful news? We must be aware of the connection between question and answer if we want to offer a reflection that will heal reality where it hurts.

THE PRIMACY OF THE UTOPIAN ELEMENT OVER THE FACTUAL

The determining element in the Latin American person is not the past (our past is a European past, one of colonization) but the future. Herein lies the activating function of the utopian element. Utopia ought not to be understood as a synonym for illusion and flight from present reality. As recent studies in philosophy and theology have revealed, utopia is born in the springs of hope. It is responsible for models that seek a perfecting of our reality, models that do not allow the social process to stagnate, or society ideologically to absolutize itself, models that maintain society permanently open to ever increasing transformation.[1] Faith promises and demonstrates as realized in Christ a utopia that consists in a world totally reconciled, a world that is the fulfillment of what we are creating here on earth with feeling and love. Our work in the construction of a more fraternal and humanized world is theoretically relevant: it builds and slowly anticipates the definitive world promised and demonstrated as possible by Jesus Christ.

THE PRIMACY OF THE CRITICAL ELEMENT OVER THE DOGMATIC

The general tendency of persons, and in particular of institutions, is to stagnate in an existential arrangement that was successful during a specific period. Then there emerge the mechanisms of self-defense and the dogmatic mentality that fears and represses every kind of criticism that looks to the proper functioning of all institutions and to that continuous opening to the future that a society ought always protect at the risk of losing the rhythm of history. This explains the primacy of the critical element in Latin American theological reflection. Many ecclesiastical traditions and ecclesial institutions were functional at one time but today have become obsolete. They are centers of a conservatism that locks the door to a dialogue between faith and the world, the church and society. Criticism refines and purifies the core of the Christian experience so that it can be made incarnate within the historical experience we are living.

THE PRIMACY OF THE SOCIAL OVER THE PERSONAL

Latin American society is most afflicted by the problem of the marginalization of immense portions of the population. The question cannot be posed merely within the dimensions of a personal conversion. There are structural evils that transcend individual ones. The church is, whether it likes it or not, involved in a context that transcends it. What will be its function? Shall it be oil or sand within the social mechanism? On the other hand, it ought not to create its own little world within the great world. It ought to participate, *critically*, in the global upsurge of liberation that Latin American society is undergoing. Like Jesus, it ought to give special attention to the nobodies and those without a voice. It ought to accentuate particularly the secular and liberating dimensions contained in the message of Christ. It should emphasize the future kingdom is growing between the wheat and the cockle, not for a few privileged persons, but for all.

THE PRIMACY OF ORTHOPRAXIS OVER ORTHODOXY

The weakness in the classical christology of the manuals resides precisely in that wherein it considers itself to be strong: its theological-philosophical systematization. It did not lead to an ethic and a comportment that was typically Christian. The fundamental theme of the synoptic Gospels, on following Christ, has been poorly thematized and translated into concrete attitudes. Orthodoxy, that is, correct thinking about Christ, occupied primacy over orthopraxis, correct acting in the light of Christ.

It was also for this reason that, although the church preached Christ the liberator, it generally was not the church that liberated or supported liberation movements. Not rarely has the church left active, participating

Christians as complete orphans. This has resulted in recent years in the continuous exodus from the church of the best minds and most active forces. We know nevertheless that for Christ and for the primitive church the essential did not consist in the reduction of the message of Christ to systematic categories of intellectual comprehension but in creating new habits of acting and living in the world. This praxiological moment of the message of Christ is especially perceptible in Latin American theological reflection.

CONCLUSION: BEGINNING WITH JESUS CHRIST, TO SPEAK IN SILENCE

In our christological study we will try to reflect with Jesus Christ as the starting point and within the wide horizon opened up in the above pages. We can no longer be scientifically ingenuous and acritical. Whether we wish it or not, we are inheritors of the christological discussions of the last decades, though the questions will be framed within our Latin American horizons. What we say here with words about Christ and his message is nothing compared with that which faith discerns and gratefully embraces. "Be quiet, recollect yourself, because it is the Absolute," said Kirkegaard, and Bonhoeffer repeated it as he began his treatise on Jesus Christ.[2]

"Concerning things that we cannot speak of," commanded Wittgenstein, "we ought to be silent."[3] Nevertheless, we ought to speak of Jesus Christ, not with a view to defining him but rather ourselves, not the mystery but our position when confronted with the mystery. Every scholar of Jesus Christ has the experience witnessed by the ardent mystic St. John of the Cross:

> There is much concerning Christ that can be made more profound, since he is such an abundant mine with many caverns full of rich veins, and no matter how much we tunnel we never arrive at the end, nor does it ever run out; on the contrary, we go on finding in each cavern new veins and new riches, here and there, as St. Paul witnessed when he said of the same Christ: "In Christ all the jewels of wisdom and knowledge are hidden" (Col. 2:3).[4]

NOTES

1. See "Utopia" by the Concilium General Secretariat in *The Problem of Eschatology* (*Concilium*, 41: New York: Paulist Press, 1969), pp. 149–65; M. Demaison, "The Christian Utopia," in *Concilium*, 59 (New York: Herder, 1970), pp. 42–58.

2. "Christologie," in *Gesammelte Schriften* (*1927–44*) (Munich: Kaiser, 1958–61), 3:167.

3. L. Wittgenstein, *Tractatus logico-philosophicus* (São Paulo, 1967), 7:129; English translation, *Tractatus logico-philosophicus* (New York: Humanities Press, 1963).

4. *Obras de São João da Cruz* (Petrópolis: Vozes, 1960), 2:201; in English see *The Collected Works of St. John of the Cross* (Washington, D.C.: ICS, 1972).

16

Cardinal Alfonso López Trujillo
"Liberation, a Permanent Value"
(1977)

I have referred to the importance of the role of Cardinal López Trujillo and of his election as Secretary General of CELAM in November 1972. It should be noted that his opposition to liberation theology is considerably more nuanced than other more open attacks against it. Throughout this article, he basically accepts Jesus' role as liberator of the poor, but interprets these concepts in a way that either softens or eradicates their meaning. For example, Jesus "is situated beyond alternatives, particularly revolution or violence against the established order," and "the poor in the gospel do not constitute a class per se but a quality of availability." Liberation theologians see this as an attempt to co-opt liberation theology by introducing a supposedly "authentic" version of it which eliminates all threats to the status quo and thus prohibits all activities or policies that foster real social change. The article cited here is from Liberation or Revolution? *(Huntington, Ind.: Our Sunday Visitor, 1977), pp. 14–27. The original edition was published by Ediciones Paulinas in Bogotá.*

LIBERATION: A HISTORY OF SALVATION

Liberation is a value which underlies all the Scriptures. We can verify the etymology of certain terms: *gaal-padah*, in Hebrew, means to buy as well as to liberate. In the ethnic context of Palestine, it supposedly meant that you should rescue the one who had been sold[1] by paying for him.

In Greek, these ideas are usually expressed by *apolutrosis*: as in the rescue of a captive, in Exodus: "I will rescue you by my outstretched arm and with mighty acts of judgment. Know that I am Yahweh [the Lord]."

This idea is translated as *redemptio* in Latin, which more precisely means *to liberate*. This term is most relevant for modern humankind. Among redemption, liberation, and salvation, then, there exists the most intimate connection.[2]

YAHWEH, THE LIBERATOR

God is revealed in action. History is the starting point when God manifests a relationship with humankind. God is revealed as a liberator; God was understood as such, through a special human and religious experience. God answers the cries of the children of Israel who had been made slaves.[3] Passover is a great event of liberation: "I have come down to rescue them from the hands of the Egyptians."[4]

In the famous theophany of the burning bush that never consumes itself, Moses asks God to reveal the divine name, since a name, in Hebrew thought, is equivalent to the person himself. And God answers: *Eheyéh asher éheyéh*[5] (I am who I am). This expression can be translated in other ways: "I am who is" (Vulgate). In consequence of this we speak of "biblical metaphysics" (Gilson). It has also been translated as "I am what I am," or "I am who am," just as if God were refusing to respond, by leaving the divine name in mystery. This particular expression, for another people, would mean: "I am your companion in the alliance," or "I am with you in all circumstances." There is another more suggestive and "heavy" interpretation: "I will be the one that I will be," or "what I will be." God is designated as an act, toward us, for us. What God is, the people will experience through God's deeds, through God's acts. Congar's own interpretation is: "I will be what you will see me to be," that is to say, "I will be your liberator."

We must take into account that this liberation, through which the people are liberated, is in itself a salvific and religious event that encompasses social and political dimensions, yet in the deep exposition of the Bible it will not run out of these dimensions. It is a reality to come into the promised land, but it is a development that in itself is an announcement, an open symbol toward new realities.

The messianic expectation of an intervening liberator grows proportionately with the disasters and chains of slavery in Israel. "I am the one who speaks with justice," or "I am a great liberator." We can explain the ambiguity of the messianic expectation or the detectable deviations toward a political and earthly messianism. Christ's temptations are described in this context.

CHRIST, THE LIBERATOR

Christ in the synagogue of Nazareth begins his mission by collecting and making concrete all the hopes of his people. It is the realization of the promise: "The Spirit of the Lord is upon me; therefore he has anointed me. He has sent me to bring glad tidings to the poor, to proclaim liberty to captives, recovery of sight to the blind, and release to prisoners, to announce a year of favor from the Lord. . . . Today's Scripture passage is fulfilled in your hearing."[6] The text that Christ cites is taken from Isaiah, as an echo of the hopes Israel cherished during its captivity. Christ presents himself as a liberator.

When John the Baptist (who was in prison at the time) sent some of his disciples to ask Jesus if he was the Messiah, Christ, in response, gives concrete signs of liberation: "The blind recover their sight, cripples walk, lepers are cured. ... Blessed is the one who finds no stumbling block in me."[7] Obscurity, darkness, and shadows of death are the metaphoric expression of the slavery of sin.

POLITICAL MESSIANISM AND THE POOR

Who is the messiah, the Christ, and who are the poor? Is Christ a Zealot who seeks radical change by means of violence, by means of struggle against legitimate authorities? Does he impatiently seek the "kingdom," and does he want to speed his mission by means of violence? If this were true, his message of liberation could be concentrated in the political, economic, and social domains. There are some persons who sincerely make this interpretation of Christ, either directly or tacitly. They argue that Christ died because he was accused of being an agitator and he was sentenced by Roman power. He criticized the established order and he judged the powerful landlords. Some of his disciples were Zealots, including perhaps Peter who was supposed to carry a weapon. Jesus lashes the traders from the temple; he stigmatizes the social injustices of his time.[8] Some authors bring up the argument: "The kingdom of God has suffered violence and the violent take it by force."[9]

Or is Christ an ultimate pacifist, an adversary of all resistance and of all change? His love and forgiveness regarding his enemies[10] would evince this. He forbids the use of weapons, he lets them imprison him without resistance, and he rejects those who want him to become a king.

NEITHER GUERILLA NOR PACIFIST

Christ is neither a guerilla nor a pacifist. With accuracy Cullman comments on these viewpoints, saying they are simplistic.[11] Jesus' stand is not simplistic. He is situated beyond alternatives, particularly revolution or violence against the established order. His message must be understood in relation to a hope for his kingdom. He takes upon himself a critical attitude against the already existent institutions, which are perishable, irresponsible, though he respects tradition and asks his followers to observe it.[12] Thus he asks for the betterment and purification of tradition. He exposes injustices, but he is not oriented toward the destruction of "order" or toward a reform of institutions or structures; neither is he caught in immobility. He preaches on a fundamental conversion from love, according to the present kingdom. For that particular reason, he does not accept political messianisms. Therefore, he conceives his messianic identity as threatened.[13] He is the son of man, the suffering servant, not the leader or the warrior. He will enter Jerusalem riding a donkey, not on the back of a lively mount in the Roman style.

Not for the sake of diplomacy but for his faithfulness to the kingdom, his position ranks beyond political antagonisms. Hans Küng, who is not suspicious of "integrism," comments:

> Jesus preached neither theories nor laws . . . but the kingdom of God. Certainly he was not a man who belonged in the priestly establishment (Sadduccees). He was neither a political revolutionary (Zealot); neither did he proclaim a national or worldly theocracy, but the immediate and endless lordship of God on top of the world . . . ; it is more ethical than the moralists and more revolutionary than the very revolutionaries; he has come to fulfill God's will, as a supreme and immediate law.[14]

IDENTIFYING "POOR" AND "PROLETARIAN": LAMENTABLE CONFUSION

Who are the poor? There is a growing trend to identify the poor with the "proletarians," with those persons who—according to Marx—carry within themselves the meaning of history and who, in the final stage of the class struggle, will rise against those who have spoiled and oppressed them. The rich through their injustices are training their own gravediggers, as it was written in the manifesto of the Communist Party.

The poor will be categorized by social classes, according to Mao:

> In a society made of classes, where each person exists as a member of a definite social class, the only escape is revolution, which is an insurrection, an act of violence used by one class to defeat the other class [because] it happens the same way with all the reactionaries; if you do not hit him, he does not fall . . . : as a rule of thumb, where the broom does not reach, the dust will not disappear by itself.

When this identification occurs between the "poor" and the "proletariat," which is very common nowadays, there are almost immediate consequences: to be of the party of the poor is to fight in order to make the rich fall.

It must be well understood that this position can be politically necessary, but we cannot accept the idea of its coming directly as a command from the gospel. Giulio Girardi's presentation is a clear synthesis of the ideas discussed about this subject: "We must love everybody, but not everyone in the same way; you love the oppressed by liberating them; you love the oppressors by fighting them. . . . Love has to be like a classifying device to become universal."[15]

THE POOR, ACCORDING TO THE BIBLE

In the Scriptures there is a series of words to define the poor, humble, quiet, needy. Poverty is a state of life and also an attitude of approach and availability regarding the kingdom, the word.

The poor in the gospel do not constitute a "class" per se, but a quality of availability, who usually coexist in a situation of economic crisis. The *anawim* are measured according to the kingdom on how they live with a liberated heart in hopes of reaching it. The lord liberates and announces his gospel to them with love.

It would be dangerous to minimize the elements of real poverty by "making spiritual" what in the Scriptures appears as a virtue, because it belongs to the poor. The poor are also the oppressed, the humble, the enslaved, and for the most part — it is recorded in the *Biblical Theology Dictionary* by Bauer in that context — "the rich, the powerful, and the violent ones who are to be blamed for causing this evil." However, there is a sort of later evolution and clarification. In times of captivity and postcaptivity, an important change in the concept of poverty is triggered. Since then, according to Bauer, poverty will be synonymous with humility and surrender to God. In this context the poor are now the pious ones, in a counterbalance with the "heartless rich and the powerful ones." That is why the poor person is "God's servant, who fears Yahweh, the just, for whose rights and whom God protects."

THE POOR IN SPIRIT

When Jesus says: "Blessed are the poor in spirit," by poverty he means an attitude of total orientation to God. The absence of property is really included, because material possessions enslave persons and take their liberty away from the true meaning that they should give to their life. The true support, the true security, the treasure that counts is the Lord. It is the same idea in Sophonias: "But I will leave as a remnant in your midst a people humble and lowly, who shall take refuge in the name of the Lord."

THE POOR IN APOSTOLIC LITERATURE

In St. James's epistle there are similar vibrations. One finds constant preaching of the prophet favoring the poor. The poor deserve respect. They must be sought out in contrast to the rich. We must look at them with acceptance,[16] because: "Did not God choose those who are poor in the eyes of the world to be rich in faith?[17] Are not the rich exploiting you? They are the ones who haul you into the courts. . ."[18]

From the eschatological perspective, with the sort of eschatology that has already begun, then we are already in the "last days."[19] St. James points out: "Now, then, you rich persons, cry and yell for all the affliction that will be coming upon you. Your riches are rotten and your garments have become moth-eaten. . . . Behold, the wages that you have not paid to the peasants who reaped your fields cry out as a protest; and the shouts of the field workers have reached the ears of the Lord."[20] In this last expression there is a clear reference to Exodus 22:22.

JUSTICE IN THE PROPHETS

In the prophets of Israel moral doctrine is featured by a key word, justice (*tzedaka*), the meaning of which goes widely beyond the legal aspect, and means completeness. Above all, justice is the ontological completeness of one being—in other words, holiness. In fact, in the Scriptures, justice and holiness are terms difficult to keep apart. Justice also includes—as it obviously seems apparent in Amos—some aspects that have to do with its present meaning. In the preaching of the prophets, one sees a striking inequality of the scandalous inequities restored after the children of Israel came into Canaan.

The damnation for accumulation of wealth, for exploitation, is also a constant factor in Hosea and Isaiah. The new Sion, the messianic times, become a hope that will overcome all kinds of enslavement. Then there will be no more comments about iniquity against God or against humans.[21] In this context, justice is not a gift of God exclusively, but it is also founded in human efforts.

True sainthood cannot exist without dynamic effort in seeking justice: "Woe to you, Scribes and Pharisees, you frauds! You pay tithes on mint and herbs and seeds, while neglecting the weightier matters of the law: justice and mercy and good faith."[22]

PROPHETS DETEST EXPLOITATION

The right of the socially powerless is improved upon by the prophets. The right to work and the certainty of not being exploited appears quite clearly: "You shall not defraud a poor and needy hired servant, whether he be one of your own countrymen or one of the aliens who live in your communities. You shall pay him each day's wages, since he is poor and looks forward to them."[23]

Prophets are like sentries for the rights of those who have nothing to show in an interplay of reciprocities, such as widows and orphans. Luxury and vanity are an insult to the poor.[24] If sacrifices, canticles,[25] and abstinence do not go alongside justice, they are not good and are displeasing to God. Knowing God is to understand the suffering of the poor[26] in a generous way and with a sense of alliance that surmounts the rupture of sin.

ALIENATING RICHES

In the New Testament this doctrine is treated again: "Looking after orphans and widows in their distress and keeping oneself unspotted by the world make for pure worship without stain before our God and Father."[27]

The theme of justice — through the reality of friendship — is presented in a new dimension of the covenant. The lack of pity and tenderness for the poor is narrated by St. Luke in a marvelous way in chapter 16 of his Gospel. Lazarus is the strong symbol of the needy poor. Lazarus is not a beggar; he is a poor man (*ptōchos*), whose needs contrast with the food on the splendid table of the rich man. His riches isolate him, enslave him, make him feel as lacking lucidity. There is an abyss of separation. According to Father Pierre Bigo, between the two worlds, that of the poor and the rich, there is no communication.

Lazarus belonged to the dog's world, which according to the symbolism in Scripture, is a synonym of punishment and damnation. In this parable the rich man used his riches for himself and ignored the misery of the poor. Christ points out how deep is the isolation of the rich.

WORSHIP OF MONEY

In Christ's preaching, preaching against the rich whom he calls "unfortunate," we find a relationship to the theme of idolatry as it existed in the old covenant. Riches are a form of idolatry: the idolatrous person is the one who assigns an absolute value to something that did not have the value before. The unique absolute is God. Wealth is a form of idolized cult. From another viewpoint, it is an institution, a lack of availability. Its chains are heavy. An alienated rich person is also alienating.

Poverty is a liberator. Human agility permits a response. It gives the poor an approach to God and to others. The beatitude of poverty in St. Matthew's Gospel and his clear reference to the poverty of the spirit is something quite demanding. Obviously he wanted to emphasize — not to forget or to relegate to a secondary level — the fact that it was not enough to be really poor because of lack of possessions but to stress that one should consent to this lack of possessions up to a certain point. Here this is not the case of differentiating — as we do it in modern times — poverty as an evangelic command and destitution. Christians in their special vocation can sometimes play the role of the destitute as a protest against misery in a perspective of authentic awareness.

All this should be very deeply understood in all its meanings. Then it will be easier to make the necessary distinction between this Christian viewpoint and the clear conception of the "proletarian class" in Marxism with all its dialectics of class struggle, necessary for its existence as "a class."

THE PASCHAL WEEK: A MYSTERY OF LIBERATION

The paschal event is a mystery of freedom: "Christ liberated us so that we can be free."[28] He liberates us in truth[29] from sin, from death, from our own selfishness, and he makes us spiritual persons who live in the Spirit.

Easter to us means a new creation. By virtue of the exaltation of the Lord, we are new creatures who march toward the completeness of our being, in a similar way to Christ, the perfect image of the Father. Therefore, and also by virtue of Easter, we are "God's image." Re-created by the death and resurrection of Christ, we are integrally liberated. This liberation comes into all the aspects of our being and necessarily transforms the structures of sin. The inner conversion expresses a rapport to what is social. Converts, recreated in love, know their way to their brothers and sisters through new forms of unity and of meaningful solidarity.

HUMANKIND LIBERATED THROUGH JUSTICE

"True justice and holiness" are the essential qualities of a new human being. We live as one immersed in the fertile stream of a continuous rebirth, which gets us nearer the realization of the promise. Therefore, it is more of a reality when we talk about the person-we-will-be than when we talk about the person-we-are-today. The true person is a possible conquest to the grace of God. The new person St. Paul talks about is not the "new person" introduced by Marxism, though in both we find the echoes of liberation. It is a Marxist feature, as shown by Gaston Fessard, to use Christian categories, as persons today use a certain terminology which seems eloquent, but which has been coined by Marx. The problem arises when we try to determine in which of the two systems true liberation exists, and whether or not in the end the promise of Marxist liberation constitutes a new alienation which denies the promise and leads away from it.

HUMANKIND LIBERATED THROUGH HOPE

Christians are also liberated through hope and must explain with reasons this fact. Jürgen Moltmann points out:

> By means of this hope in the future of God, this world of ours remains free, for the sake of faith, among all the temptations of self-redemption or self-production by means of work, and it opens up to a loving alienation, which is like a servant, in favor of a humanization of the circumstances, in favor of the realization of the right in the light of the divine right which is coming. But this means that the hope for resurrection has to trigger a new manner to understand the world.[30]

LIBERATION: OPEN TO GOD AND HUMANS

Easter enables us to see the very sense of freedom, which is possible only by the approach to God and others. We are free when we know the way to enter into communion with others, supported and prodded by means of a deep communion with Christ. It is false to claim that there is a choice by means of which we should choose between being true to God or to humankind, just as if the first option would make servants of us, or subjects.

Van Buren's intuition, not necessarily conditioned by his pragmatism, is stated in this fashion:

> Easter is a somewhat real experience which in fact the disciples had. It was one experience of Jesus and of his freedom in a way that was absolutely new to them . . . ; they felt themselves beginning to share that liberty of existing for their neighbors. . . . The statement: Jesus is the Lord . . . liberates from enslavement the center of relative loyalty. . . . His own history will not be seen, but the history of all humankind, in the light of the unique history of Jesus of Nazareth and Easter. . . . The disciples found themselves caught in something like the freedom of Jesus himself, transformed into free beings even to face death without fear.[31]

LIBERATION AND LIBERATIONS

Liberation calls for terms of relationship. For the nonbeliever, anything surmountable can be called fear, anguish, economic exploitation, political restraint, manipulation. Marx used to say that he wanted to go down to the very roots of these alienations. We are not going to deny these actualities. Not to lament them limits one's vision. Christians insert these relationships into a vision of faith and they should not be afraid to talk about liberation from sin, which is a form of slavery compared to the liberty of Christ.

Human beings tortured by fear and anguish, by mistrust and self-interest, divided into hostile classes when they are seen in reference to the freedom of Christ, which is the measure, are either in a condition of sin or they suffer its consequences. Therefore, we have hope in the life of Christ: "Just as in Adam all die, so in Christ all will come to life again."[32] That is to say, we are liberated in Christ because of his death and resurrection. St. Athanasius, in *De Incarnatione* (chapter 20), argues that Christ really rose from the dead in order to give freedom to the Christians, a freedom to love even one's enemies. According to Van Buren, the church is the people who share this liberty and are aware of its source.

LIBERATION OF THE BELIEVER

Christian Easter was founded on Israel's Easter, but it surmounted the latter. It leads to victory in a dramatic fight between light and dark for the liberation of that complete being called human, body and soul, present and social. And that victory is possible through our faith.[33] Let us be true in confessing our hope because the author of the promise is true. In the solemn presentation of Christ, he promises liberation to all those who are brokenhearted: "The messiah will come to heal broken hearts." The full liberty of Christ is a liberating principle of everything that makes a captive of any human being.

Thus, we understand the promise: "It was for liberty that Christ freed us." "That is why, if the son frees you, you will really be free."[34] It is Christ who gives freedom. Liberty is a gift, a grace, that implies our collaboration. Today we usually talk about liberty as something we can obtain by our own efforts, because we thinking of another kind of liberty.

MOTIVATION FOR A THEOLOGY OF LIBERATION

An authentic theology of liberation has to be founded on immovable pillars of faith. Otherwise, one would become too suspicious if the theology seemed to be an emotional pretext for plotting a social revolution. Our vision of faith has to enlighten reality. The problem is not in elaborating a theology of liberation, but in the manner in which it is done, in the orientation given to it, and the purpose to which it leads. Very often we are concerned with political subjects covered under a surface of a calculated theological vocabulary. Robert Bosc formulated certain reservations about this: "A theology of revolution seems to me to be an inadequate term. It would be much better to talk about a theology for times of revolution."[35]

NOTES

1. See Lev. 25:3, 37.
2. Claude Tremontant, *The Teaching of Jesus of Nazareth*, pp. 13–15.
3. Exod. 2:23–25; 3:7–11.
4. Exod. 3:8.
5. Exod. 3:14.
6. Luke 4:18–19, 21.
7. Matt. 11:2–6.
8. Luke 16:19; 6:24.
9. Matt. 11:12.
10. Matt. 5:44–45.
11. Oscar Cullman, *Jesus and the Revolutionaries of his Times*. This is a magnificent study of this subject.
12. Matt. 23:3, 23.
13. Matt. 4:10; Mark 8:27.
14. *Concilium*, extra issue, December 1970, p. 238.
15. Giulio Girardi, "Christian Life and Earthly Commitment," 5th Week of Theology, University of Deusto, pp. 126–27.
16. James 2:3.
17. James 2:5.
18. James 2:6.
19. 2 Cor. 6:2.
20. James 5:1–5.
21. Isa. 1:26; 11:9; Jer. 31:23.
22. Matt. 23:23.

23. Deut. 24:14–15.
24. James 1:11–20.
25. Amos 5:23.
26. Jer. 22:13.
27. James 1:27.
28. Gal. 5:1; Rom. 6:3–11; Col. 2:12.
29. John 8:32.
30. Jürgen Moltmann, *Theology of Hope*, pp. 434–35.
31. Van Buren, *The Secular Meaning of the Gospel*, p. 16.
32. 1 Cor. 15:22.
33. John 5:4.
34. John 8:36.
35. Robert Bosc, in *The Pastoral View on Politics*, p. 71.

PART IV

PREPARING FOR PUEBLA
(1973 – 1979)

At the outset of this period, a certain foreboding and anxiety clouded the atmosphere in both secular society and the church. The trend toward military dictatorships, dramatized for the whole world in the orgy of bloodshed in Chile in 1973, spread through the continent, resulting in a gradual loss of human rights and an escalation of unbridled terror that moved from exile, imprisonment, torture, to murder, and finally to the grotesque fate of the *desaparecidos* or "disappeared"—multitudes of human beings who simply vanished from the face of the earth, leaving relatives and friends to agonize for years and even lifetimes about their fate. A chronicle of these events up to the year 1979 has been provided in grim detail by the North American journalist, Penny Lernoux, in *Cry of the People* (Garden City, N.Y.: Doubleday, 1980). This brutality continued and even worsened throughout the decade.

As regards the church and liberation theology, a major focus of controversy began to dominate the picture, as both friends and enemies of that theology and of Medellín made plans and initiated activities to influence the next bishops' conference, scheduled to take place in 1978. However, because of the death of Pope Paul VI in 1978, followed soon after by the death of his successor, Pope John Paul I, the conference was postponed until January-February 1979, and was scheduled to be held in the city of Puebla, Mexico.

Since Bishop López Trujillo and his supporters had assumed control of the bishops' conference (CELAM), they were in an advantageous position to extend the scope of their attack on liberation theology and at the same time to take control of the preparations and actual agenda for the Puebla conference. The strategy for expanding the attack was based on an opening to conservative circles in Europe, especially among the German bishops. This process had its beginning in February 1973, at a meeting in Bogotá between German Bishop Franz Hengsbach, a board member of the relief organization *Adveniat*, and a group of Latin American bishops and theologians, headed by Bishop López Trujillo. At this meeting, careful plans were drawn up to launch an attack against liberation theology in Europe, especially in Germany and Italy. The execution and success of these plans are treated in an article by the Canadian theologian, Gregory Baum (no. 21); thus I will not repeat this information here.

As regards the counterattack by the liberation forces, it is important to keep in mind three developments during this period, one at the grassroots level, one at the level of the intellectual quality of theology itself, and finally one that reached beyond Latin America and to many areas of the world church. On the popular level, theology was communicated through the pastoral and liturgical activities of the Christian base communities, so that theology took on a popular character and spread far beyond small circles of Christians and prophetic minorities.

Before moving to the second and third developments, I want to stress the new *approaches* of the liberation movement, since its advocates could no longer rely on the network of the bishops' conference to disseminate their views. One of the first examples of the wider appeal of liberation theology came with the dedication of an entire 1974 issue of the influential international journal *Concilium* to Latin American representatives of the liberation movement, including Leonardo Boff, José Míguez Bonino, Joseph Comblin, Enrique Dussel, Segundo Galilea, Gustavo Gutiérrez, Ronaldo Muñoz, Juan Luis Segundo, and Raúl Vidales. The French Dominican, Claude Geffré, who was coeditor of the volume with Gustavo Gutiérrez, wrote an introduction to the volume, included below (no. 17).

At the same time liberation theologians began to extend their influence through international conferences, such as the one at El Escorial, Spain, in 1972. Before long they moved north, first to Mexico City, on August 11–15, 1975, and then to the very heart of the "colossus of the North," in Detroit, Michigan, August 17–24, 1975. The results of both conferences were made available to a much wider audience by the publication of large volumes. The Mexico City book, entitled *Liberación y Cautiverio,* was not translated into English and received very little attention in the United States.[1] The account of the Detroit meeting was published in *Theology in the Americas,*[2] and numerous articles about it appeared in periodicals, especially in the religious press. As a participant in the 1975 meeting, I can attest to the deep and lasting effect it had on the many North Americans in attendance.

In December 1975 another quite unexpected impetus was given to the liberation movement when Pope Paul VI published his Apostolic Exhortation "On Evangelization in the Modern World," which gave extensive treatment to the subject of liberation and also to the question of Christian base communities. The relevant sections of this document are included below (no. 18). Another discussion of liberation theology by the Vatican's International Theological Commission was published in 1977 (no. 20). A final indicator in this period of the interest in liberation theology on a world level may be seen in a debate between two leading Protestant theologians, which was conducted in public and between continents in March 1976 (no. 19).

At this point, I will survey the intellectual development of works on liberation theology that were published during this period. Some new faces on the theological scene appeared in El Salvador in the persons of Ignacio Ellacuría and Jon Sobrino, both professors of theology at the Jesuit university in San Salvador. Ellacuría's book on political theology appeared in 1974,[3] and his area of special interest lies in the philosophical foundations of liberation theology.

His colleague, Jon Sobrino, produced a widely read and controversial *Cristología desde Latinoamerica* in 1976, which was translated into English in 1978 under the title *Christology at the Crossroads* (Orbis Books). Besides his specialty in christology, which he continues, Sobrino has also published widely in the area of spirituality, which he sees as an essential complement to his christological work.

Leonardo Boff continued his scholarly works with a study of grace from a liberation perspective, *Liberating Grace*, in 1976 (English translation, Orbis Books, 1979). In 1977 he published what is certainly one of his most profound and comprehensive works, and also the one most deeply affected by the liberation outlook, *Passion of Christ, Passion of the World*, which unfortunately was not translated into English until a full ten years had passed (Orbis Books, 1987). His brother and co-author in some works, Clodovis Boff, contributed an important and closely reasoned book, *Theology and Praxis* (Orbis Books, 1987), the most profound study of the epistemological foundations of liberation theology.

Other significant works included Roberto Oliveros Maqueo's *Liberación y teología: Génesis y crecimiento de una reflexión 1966-1976*, which was a very valuable history of the early development of liberation theology (see no. 4 in this volume), published in 1977 and not translated into English. In the area of Scripture, where there is a great need of scholarship from the liberation perspective, books were published by J. Severino Croatto, *Exodus: A Hermeneutics of Freedom* (1978; Orbis Books, 1981) and by Francisco López Rivera, *Biblia y sociedad: Cuatro estudios exegéticos* (1977). A work that analyzed in depth one of the most dangerous ideologies in South (and North) America is José Comblin's *The Church and the National Security State* (Orbis Books, 1979). Finally, one of the most significant works of this period was Juan Luis Segundo's *The Liberation of Theology* (Orbis Books, 1976), a profound discussion of the key questions of method and hermeneutics.

In concluding this section, I must return again to the immediate preparations for the Puebla conference. As the conference drew nearer, the lightning rod for controversy and debate became the "Preparatory Document" that had been written by CELAM, under the close supervision of

López Trujillo, Vekemans, and others. While it was intended to control the conference (and to lead to the repudiation of liberation theology), the result was spectacularly different: the PD, as it came to be known, generated an enormous process of conscientization throughout Latin America as all kinds of groups, from scholarly seminars to base communities, reflected upon it and argued about it. In general, the document was rejected, even by the conservative bishops of Colombia. But it produced a great number of alternative agendas from all sectors of the church. Thus, ironically, a document aimed at control of the conference actually opened it up to valuable contributions from every sector of the church, causing it to become a much more participatory and democratic event than the Medellín conference.

NOTES

1. *Liberación y cautiverio: Debates en torno al método de la teología en America Latina* (Mexico City: Imprenta Venecia, 1976).
2. Sergio Torres and John Eagleson, eds., *Theology in the Americas* (Maryknoll, N.Y.: Orbis Books, 1976).
3. English translation, *Freedom Made Flesh: The Mission of Christ and His Church* (Maryknoll, N.Y.: Orbis Books, 1976).

17

Claude Geffré
"A Prophetic Theology"
(1974)

Claude Geffré is a French Dominican who co-edited this volume of Concilium *with Gustavo Gutiérrez. It was the first time in its history that* Concilium *published a volume whose articles were written entirely by Latin Americans. The editorial is taken from* Concilium 96: The Mystical and Political Dimension of the Christian Faith *(New York: Herder and Herder, 1974), pp. 7–16.*

There are now so many books, theses, articles, and research projects on the "theology of liberation" that it is just impossible to keep up with them. I would even go so far as to say that it has become something of a myth for European theologians trying to break the bounds of a traditional theology. But there is a great danger of taking up some topics of liberation theology and separating them from the particular socio-ecclesial reality of their origins. The word "liberation" is becoming a magic amulet for theological enterprises concerned with contexts outside Latin America. But one thing is certain: it is a would-be universal theology if one is not taking part in the struggles of those Christians actually engaged in liberating the South American continent. It is also very difficult to judge it critically from without, inasmuch as the very originality of this form of theological discourse depends on its indissolubility from real practice. Hence, in this special issue of *Concilium*, we have given Latin American theologians an exclusive opportunity to make known their views.

Therefore the articles in this issue should be read as bearing witness to a prophetic theology arising from a particular ecclesial experience, and as a question addressed to the European theology for which *Concilium* is too exclusively a medium. It will be seen that the various articles in this issue, contributed by a team of theologians centering on Gustavo Gutiérrez, are not intended to make up an issue on Latin America, but to show from various angles how the historical practice of a specific church can be an impetus for a new understanding of faith in Jesus Christ. All these theologians are "theologians of liberation." Of course there is no point in examining their articles for a mere reworking of a theme often written on in Europe: that of the relations between "faith and political commitment." Politics is only one of the fields of application for a dynamic faith. In his own way each author tries to show how, on the basis of the specific experience of the Christian communities of Latin America, there is now evident a new connection between the mystical and political dimensions of Christian faith. That was the main intention of this special issue and it appears as an explicit theme in the articles by Segundo Galilea, Gustavo Gutiérrez, Ronaldo Muñoz, and José Míguez Bonino. Yet, inevitably and significantly, almost all these authors have said something about that special topic of the theology of liberation: the relations between a historical practice of liberation and eschatological salvation. Hence we decided that the general title of this issue should be: "Praxis of Liberation and Christian Faith."

Rather than engage in a critical commentary on the articles in this number, it is important to know how to take the impact of a theology that is not only different and provocative, but sometimes even unjust in regard to certain theologies originating in Europe and North America. But as Europeans we run the risk, with another theological perspective and another practice, of making ill-considered judgments. One of the major contributions of this issue is certainly that of asking us for a more lively awareness of the special and therefore relative nature of our European theology. By way of introduction, all I shall do here is to spell out some of the lessons that most impressed me on reading the subsequent pages.

DISTANCING FROM WESTERN THEOLOGIES

It seems permissible to claim that the episcopal conference at Medellín in 1968, as far as the Latin American church was concerned, was comparable to Vatican II in its implications for the universal church. The process which had been maturing for some years among Christians increasingly aware of the challenge to their faith posed by the injustice prevalent on the South American continent broadened and began to express itself theologically.

The critical discovery of the world of the oppressed, as a result of a new scientific consciousness, gradually led to a radical questioning of the existing way of living, understanding, and proclaiming of faith. How were people to be Christians in the midst of an exploited and dependent continent, subject to the violence of the established order, under the sign of capitalist domination? How were they to live and conceive the faith within a dynamic movement inspiring and building a more just and fraternal society? The answers to these questions offered by some Christian communities in Latin America start from a position of commitment to the "historical practice of liberation," a practical version of the liberating love of Christ.

In connection with this very special socio-political context, Latin American theologians clearly distance themselves from what has been termed a "neo-integrism," which is developing at present in the U.S.A. and some European countries, in order to compensate for the liberal excesses provoked by Vatican II. But, more surprisingly, they criticize even more radically the various "progressive" theologies of the Western world—whether "secularization theologies" or "political theology." They share the defect of unconsciously playing the game of Western capitalist society.

Paradoxically, the secularization theologies, which claim to be progressive because they accept the profane nature and autonomy of the modern world, sin by conformism in regard to the neo-liberal societies of the West. Under the pretext that the church no longer exerts a sociological influence on modern societies, Christianity surrenders its historical efficacy in favor of the transformation of society and the world, and runs the risk of taking refuge in the inwardness of faith. As for German political theology, even though it insists on the historical responsibility of the church as a court of critical judgment for society as a whole, it remains an abstract and reformist theology, which refuses to pronounce on the alternative of socialism or capitalism on the pretext that the eschatological absolute relativizes any practical theological option.

The theology of liberation (see Segundo's article in this issue) wishes to show that the eschatological aspect, far from relativizing the present, connects it to the absolute. It sees in the neutrality of theology towards political choices the influence of the Lutheran thesis of justification by faith without works. In fact Latin American theology deliberately sets out to be a committed theology, both militant and even partisan. It cannot remain neutral in regard to "left" or "right" political positions. Hence it reproaches European theology for its supposed neutrality which, on the pretext of affirming the relativity of the political and absoluteness of the religious, offers an ideological justification of the established system of the capitalist West. European theologians want to develop a universal theology, which will be valid for the whole church. For Latin American theologians, theology should always start from actual historical practice—for example, the liberation movement on the South American continent. For them, too, a general theology of liberation is quite meaningless.

A NEW WAY OF THEOLOGIZING

The fact that Latin American theology is grounded in a historico-practical context of liberation seriously modifies the traditional conception of theology as understanding of faith. On the one hand, it is a theology defined as critical reflection on historical practice in the light of faith. On the other hand, it is a theology that not only addresses itself to interpreting the content of revelation but tries to answer the question, What is to be done?

European theology tries to reformulate the gospel message for today from the basis of the challenge to faith posed by the nonbeliever. For Latin

American theology the challenge does not come primarily from the non-believer but from the nonperson: that is, from the one whom the existing social order does not recognize as such: the poor, the exploited, the ones who are hardly aware that they are exploited (see Gutiérrez's article). The crucial problem for theology is therefore to know how to announce God as the Father in a nonhuman world. Hence theology engages in critical reflection on the historical practice of liberation in confrontation with the word of God lived in faith. In this critical task, theology intends to draw on all the resources of a scientific analysis of the social situation of the Latin American continent, and in particular a Marxist analysis.

Whereas traditional theology started from revelation in order to decide the value of Christian practice, in this case participation in the historical practice of liberation has its own legitimacy and becomes a location of theology by virtue of a reinterpretation of the gospel message, and of a more radical commitment of Christians to revolutionary activity. Distancing itself from an idealist and universal theology claiming to offer an understanding of faith outside an actual context of commitment, this new theology reflects on faith as historical practice: that is, on liberation in regard to this or that situation of oppression as a partial realization of that total and definitive liberation to which Christ bears witness. Therefore it is not only a question of revealing the social and political implications of the gospel in regard to this or that actual situation, but of making effective participation in the process of liberation the occasion for verifying theological discourse.

Because there can be no hiatus between faith and social practice, it is practice that will judge the truth of a theology. Clearly such a tendency can awaken a suspicion that in making practice the occasion of truth there is a risk of finishing up with a political manipulation of faith or a political reduction of the gospel. Several contributors to this issue are well aware of that danger. But they all seem to base their answer to it on a theology of the Holy Spirit. It is the Holy Spirit who inspires the activity of the Christian community and who shows Christians the substance of evangelical charity in this or that historical situation. We should juxtapose a theology based on revelation to one based on practice. God is revealed through, in, and by liberation struggles undertaken by all the poor of the South American continent.

Inasmuch as it is a reflection *in* and *on* practice by those engaged in it, this theology cannot remain content with offering a new theoretical interpretation of Christianity for today. It must address itself to actual problems. It does not answer only the questions, What is to be believed? and What is to be said? It wants to answer the question, What is to be done? This is obviously wholly revolutionary measured against a certain type of theology that considers Christianity mainly as a doctrinal content, hardly ever as action. There is a displacement of the central concern of theology, which is no longer exclusively the *intellectus fidei*, but an understanding of action in the name of Christ: that is, the perception of the forms that love should assume in a specific situation.

That also modifies the conventional conception of professional theologians. They cannot be merely an exegete and expert on church tradition. They should also be fundamentally concerned to have as rigorous as possible a knowledge of the process of liberation in Latin America. Of course such knowledge is inseparable from an effective part in revolutionary struggles for the liberation of the poor.

Theologians who carry out their theoretical research work independently of actual commitment, as happens in Europe, are inconceivable in Latin America. If this new type of theologian is not defined only as a revelation expert, it is clear that this theology is no longer the quasi-exclusive monopoly of clerics who have had many years of training. It is accessible to all the laity participating in Christian communities which are politically committed and which examine their activity critically. But in fact, despite the fact that this possibility is in theory available to the laity, the pioneers of "liberation theology" are almost exclusively priests.

In any case, whatever its limitations and technical inexactitudes we should pay great attention to the rise of this new theology, which puts in question the theology of the Western world as the dominant ideology of the universal church. As Dussel says: "After the major 'Christian theology' (from the fourth to the fifteenth century) and 'modern European theology' (from the sixteenth century to the twentieth) there appears the 'theology of liberation' of the periphery and the oppressed, with whose onset the entire traditional theology begins its paschal movement into the perspective of the poor."

A NEW THEOLOGY OF SALVATION

All the contributors to this issue have examined according to their individual standpoints the process of liberation as a sign of eschatological salvation. Yet Latin American theology is not only a theology *of* liberation or a theology *about* liberation, but a theology which deliberately stands up *for* liberation. We should welcome it as a stimulating and provoking phenomenon in contradistinction to our usual way of posing the question of salvation in Jesus Christ.

Latin American theologians are trying to work out a new image of Jesus Christ and a new conception of salvation by taking as their hermeneutical location the process of liberation occurring at present on the South American continent. That is to say, they reject an abstract theology of liberation which could only take into account the permanent human condition — the state of humankind subject to death, suffering, and sin. This type of theology did in fact act as an ideological warning to all those who are trying to maintain the *status quo*. A "theology of liberation" in general is meaningless. That is why the theologies of liberation are content to be provisional, partial, and tentative. They are not easily exportable products which can be used to legitimize Christian activity in other socio-political contexts.

However, these new theologies have a prophetic value in relation to the reinterpretation of Christian salvation which is at present taking place within the church. Almost everywhere today people are thinking about the connections between "human liberation and salvation in Jesus Christ." And Latin American theology reminds us opportunely that the relation between liberation and salvation is meaningful if it is located historically. In other words, the total and definitive liberation of Christ is always mediated in partial historical liberations.

The necessity for Christian theology in this last quarter of the twentieth century to show forth the bond between the liberation movements in which millions of persons are engaged as the coming of the kingdom of God is not an example of a new ecclesiastical opportunism. In the good sense it is a "sign of the times." The most precious contribution of Latin American theology, rooted as it is in a historical practice of liberation, is to allow us a new understanding of the concept of the "kingdom of God." As Boff remarks in his article, the kingdom of God is not only a spiritual reality but a universal revolution of the structures of the old world. That is exactly why it is offered as good news for the poor. The kingdom of God is not intended to be another world but this old world transformed into a new world, a new order of all the things of this world.

It is right to insist on the antimessianism of Jesus, on the fact that Jesus avoided the temptation of power during his earthly life. As Boff demonstrates very well in his article, Jesus' temptations stand for a rejection of the "regionalization" of the kingdom, of the reduction of the totality of the kingdom to a particular "province" of this world. But traditional theology argued incorrectly from that to a spiritualization of the kingdom of God and to a total political neutrality of the gospel. There was also too much insistence on the absoluteness of the eschatological future of the kingdom, so much so that there was also too much relativization of the historical examples of human liberation which anticipate the total human liberation as a gift of Christ.

In fact Christ's refusal to be a political messiah is politically significant in itself. That means that Christ does not relieve persons of the weight of their historical responsibility for a transformation of the world and society in the direction of God's design. Jesus' historical destiny taken seriously shows us that he did not preach a purely inward kingdom or a salvation which has to do only with the human condition in general, even if it is also true that he did not put forward for us any actual evangelical model which could inspire a Christian politics of liberation today. It is just as true that he came into conflict with the established order of his times and that his death was a political event. In other terms Jesus gave a historical actuality to the kingdom of God of which he was the witness and of which the mystery of the resurrection was the definitive epiphany.

Hence the effort of all the poor, whether Christians or not, of Latin America to liberate themselves from economic, political, and cultural oppression does not respond merely to a political demand. It is a demand of faith becoming actuality. It is one of the ways of putting the kingdom of God into practice in history. Of course there can be no identification between the totality of the kingdom of God and such a process of historical liberation. But there is continuity between the two, for the kingdom of God is already present "in a mysterious form" in the arena of history.

The kingdom of God is not wholly available on one occasion but is made incarnate in historical mediations which affect all levels—political, economic, social, and religious—of human reality. The coming of the kingdom is in fact good news for the whole of creation. The Latin American theologians would not hesitate to say that the news of the future kingdom does not make vain the historical struggle of human beings for their own liberation. Instead it radicalizes it inasmuch as it reveals its transcendent relevance.

A NEW KIND OF SPIRITUALITY

To the extent that political liberation is lived as a sign of eschatological liberation, we are becoming aware of a new connection between the mystical and political dimensions of the Christian faith. In all the articles in this issue, despite their variety, it is relatively easy to discern the essentials of a new kind of spirituality which all Christians would do well to consider seriously.

The point of the faith for Latin Americans Christians is one with the concern to take seriously the historical implication of Jesus and his salvation—and precisely for the weakest of all, those whose part Christ took. In this way Christians enter into the conflict-ridden and complex world of the poor as a basic choice of their loyalty to the Lord (see the articles by Galilea and Gutiérrez).

This experience of faith on the basis of the world of the poor opens up new horizons for Christian mysticism. The spirituality of liberation may be discerned in the dialectic of loyalty to Jesus and commitment to the poor. In Latin America works of faith are identified with the practice of liberation and are also the actual fruits of life in the Spirit. The contributions in this issue will show how the experience of evangelical conversion as a continual breaking with the egotistic sufficiency of the "old person" in order to enter as a "new person" into the world of the "other," in order to transform it, becomes for Latin American Christians the exercise of liberating love.

To commit oneself to the process of liberation is for Christians a new way of identifying themselves with Christ and constitutes a novel Christian experience, full of promise and possibility, but also of difficulties and disappointments. In fact for many Latin American Christians, liberating commitment corresponds to an authentic spiritual experience in the original,

biblical sense of the term: it is living in the Spirit who causes us to acknowledge ourselves in a free and creative way to be sons and daughters
of the Father and brothers and sisters of all human beings.

It is not a question of denying other traditionally valid dimensions of
Christian contemplation but rather of rediscovering, by means of integration, the biblical, historical, and committed dimensions of contemplation —
dimensions which have been forgotten by Christians. This mystical experience presents indivisibly a double dimension of one and the same original
event: the meeting with the person of Christ and the experience of the
presence of Christ in one's brother or sister, above all in the "least" of
them. The second encounter is the sacrament of the first. Hence it is not
a matter of putting contemplation at the service of liberation but of developing its own qualities and, in this case, its biblical dimension of commitment. To speak in those terms is to put the socio-political dimension at the
heart of Christian mystical experience, as one of its essential constituents.
In fact encounter with Christ necessarily occurs through the mediation of
the poor who are an exploited class, a forgotten race, a marginalized culture.

The foregoing are a few very fragmentary reflections suggested by the
various contributions to the present issue, which may be of some help to
those irritated or puzzled in regard to the present theme. While retaining
our critical freedom, we should heed this witness of a prophetic theology
which puts in question our conventional ways of thinking and our theological self-sufficiency. Behind this theology in process of formation, we must
hear the cry of the poor. And what is trying to find its voice and way in
Latin America may indeed prefigure what will arise tomorrow in Africa
and Asia. The "theologies of liberation" certainly represent an opportunity
for the universal church. And what the theology of the Western world might
well be tempted to disregard as an "antitheology" could become the condition of its own renewal.

18

Pope Paul VI
Selections from
"On Evangelization in the Modern World"
(December 8, 1975)

This was the first time that liberation theology and base communities (for some reason referred to by their French name, communautés de base*) were referred to in a papal document. Many considered it a very thoughtful and well-balanced treatment, and were disappointed that it was not published as an encyclical rather than as an apostolic exhortation, which is a step lower in theological importance. The texts are taken from Pope Paul VI, "On Evangelization in the Modern World" (Washington, D.C.: U.S. Catholic Conference, 1976), sections 25–39 and 57–58.*

25. In the message which the church proclaims there are certainly many secondary elements. Their presentation depends greatly on changing circumstances. They themselves also change. But there is the essential content, the living substance, which cannot be modified or ignored without seriously diluting the nature of evangelization itself.

26. It is not superfluous to recall the following points: to evangelize is first of all to bear witness, in a simple and direct way, to God revealed by Jesus Christ, in the Holy Spirit; to bear witness that in the incarnate word being has been given to all things and all persons have been called to eternal life. Perhaps this attestation of God will be for many the unknown God[1] whom they adore without naming, or whom they seek by a secret call of the heart when they experience the emptiness of all idols. But it is fully evangelizing in manifesting the fact that for the human beings the creator is not an anonymous and remote power; he is the Father: "that we should be called children of God; and so we are."[2] And thus we are one another's brothers and sisters in God.

27. Evangelization will also always contain—as the foundation, center, and at the same time summit of its dynamism—a clear proclamation that,

in Jesus Christ, the Son of God made man, who died and rose from the dead, salvation is offered to all, as a gift of God's grace and mercy.[3] And not an immanent salvation, meeting material or even spiritual needs, restricted to the temporal desires, hopes, affairs, and struggles, but a salvation which exceeds all these limits in order to reach fulfillment in a communion with the one and only divine Absolute: a transcendent and eschatological salvation, which indeed has its beginning in this life but which is fulfilled in eternity.

28. Consequently evangelization cannot but include the prophetic proclamation of a hereafter, a human being's profound and definitive calling, in both continuity and discontinuity with the present situation: beyond time and history, beyond the transient reality of this world, and beyond the things of this world, of which a hidden dimension will one day be revealed — beyond humankind itself, whose true destiny is not restricted to the temporal aspect but will be revealed in the future life.[4] Evangelization therefore also includes the preaching of hope in the promises made by God in the new covenant in Jesus Christ, the preaching of God's love for us and of our love for God; the preaching of brotherly love for all persons — the capacity of giving and forgiving, of self-denial, of helping one's brother and sister — which, springing from the love of God, is the kernel of the gospel; the preaching of the mystery of evil and of the active search for good. The preaching likewise — and this is always urgent — of the search for God through prayer which is principally that of adoration and thanksgiving, but also through communion with the visible sign of the encounter with God which is the church of Jesus Christ; and this communion in its turn is expressed by the application of those other signs of Christ living and acting in the church which are the sacraments. To live the sacraments in this way, bringing their celebration to a true fullness, is not, as some would claim, to impede or to accept a distortion of evangelization: it is rather to complete it. For in its totality, evangelization — over and above the preaching of a message — consists in the implantation of the church, which does not exist without the driving force which is the sacramental life culminating in the eucharist.[5]

29. But evangelization would not be complete if it did not take account of the unceasing interplay of the gospel and of concrete human life, both personal and social. This is why evangelization involves an explicit message, adapted to the different situations constantly being realized, about the rights and duties of every human being, about family life without which personal growth and development is hardly possible,[6] about life in society, about international life, peace, justice, and development — a message especially energetic today about liberation.

30. It is well known in what terms numerous bishops from all the continents spoke of this at the last synod, especially bishops from the Third World, with a pastoral accent resonant with the voice of the millions of sons and daughters of the church who make up those peoples. Peoples, as

we know, engaged with all their energy in the effort and struggle to over-come everything which condemns them to remain on the margin of life: famine, chronic disease, illiteracy, poverty, injustices in international rela-tions and especially in commercial exchanges, situations of economic and cultural neocolonialism sometimes as cruel as the old political colonialism. The church, as the bishops repeated, has the duty to proclaim the liberation of millions of human beings, many of whom are its own children — the duty of assisting the birth of this liberation, of giving witness to it, of ensuring that it is complete. This is not foreign to evangelization.

31. Between evangelization and human advancement — development and liberation — there are in fact profound links. These include links of an an-thropological order, because the human being to be evangelized is not an abstract being but is subject to social and economic questions. They also include links in the theological order, since one cannot dissociate the plan of creation from the plan of redemption. The latter plan touches the very concrete situations of injustice to be combatted and of justice to be restored. They include links of the eminently evangelical order, which is that of charity: How in fact can one proclaim the new commandment without pro-moting, in justice and in peace, true, authentic, human advancement? We ourself have taken care to point this out, by recalling that it is impossible to accept "that in evangelization one could or should ignore the importance of the problems so much discussed today, concerning justice, liberation, development, and peace in the world. This would be to forget the lesson which comes to us from the gospel concerning love of our neighbor who is suffering and in need."[7]

The same voices which during the synod touched on this burning theme with zeal, intelligence, and courage have, to our great joy, furnished the enlightening principles for a proper understanding of the importance and profound meaning of liberation, such as it was proclaimed and achieved by Jesus of Nazareth and such as it is preached by the church.

32. We must not ignore the fact that many, even generous Christians who are sensitive to the dramatic questions involved in the problem of liberation, in this wish to commit the church to the liberation effort are frequently tempted to reduce its mission to the dimensions of a simply temporal project. They would reduce its aims to a human-centered goal; the salvation of which it is the messenger would be reduced to material well-being. Its activity, forgetful of all spiritual and religious preoccupation, would become initiatives of the political or social order. But if this were so, the church would lose its fundamental meaning. Its message of liberation would no longer have any originality and would easily be open to mono-polization and manipulation by ideological systems and political parties. It would have no more authority to proclaim freedom as in the name of God. This is why we have wished to emphasize, in the same address at the opening of the synod, "the need to restate clearly the specifically religious finality of evangelization. This latter would lose its reason for existence if

it were to diverge from the religious axis that guides it: the kingdom of
God, before anything else, in its fully theological meaning."[8]

33. With regard to the liberation which evangelization proclaims and
strives to put into practice, one should rather say this:

— it cannot be contained in the simple and restricted dimension of economics, politics, social or cultural life; it must envisage the whole human
being, in all aspects, right up to and including openness to the absolute,
even the divine Absolute;

— it is therefore attached to a certain concept of human nature, to a
human view it can never sacrifice to the needs of any strategy, practice, or
short-term efficiency.

34. Hence, when preaching liberation and associating itself with those
who are working and suffering for it, the church is certainly not willing to
restrict its mission only to the religious field and dissociate itself from
human temporal problems. Nevertheless it reaffirms the primacy of its spiritual vocation and refuses to replace the proclamation of the kingdom by
the proclamation of forms of human liberation; it even states that its contribution to liberation is incomplete if it neglects to proclaim salvation in
Jesus Christ.

35. The church links human liberation and salvation in Jesus Christ, but
it never identifies them, because it knows through revelation, historical
experience, and the reflection of faith that not every notion of liberation is
necessarily consistent and compatible with an evangelical vision of humankind, of things, and of events; it knows too that in order that God's kingdom
should come, it is not enough to establish liberation and to create well-
being and development.

And what is more, the church has the firm conviction that all temporal
liberation, all political liberation — even if it endeavors to find its justification in such or such a page of the Old or New Testament, even if it claims
for its ideological postulates and its norms of action theological data and
conclusions, even if it pretends to be today's theology — carries within itself
the germ of its own negation and fails to reach the ideal that it proposes
for itself, whenever its profound motives are not those of justice in charity,
whenever its zeal lacks a truly spiritual dimension and whenever its final
goal is not salvation and happiness in God.

36. The church considers it to be undoubtedly important to build up
structures which are more human, more just, more respectful of the rights
of the person, and less oppressive and less enslaving, but it is conscious
that the best structures and the most idealized systems soon become inhuman if the inhuman inclinations of the human heart are not made whole-
some, if those who live in these structures or who rule them do not undergo
a conversion of heart and of outlook.

37. The church cannot accept violence, especially the force of arms —
which is uncontrollable once it is let loose — and indiscriminate death as
the path to liberation, because it knows that violence always provokes viol-

ence and irresistibly engenders new forms of oppression and enslavement, which are often harder to bear than those from which they claimed to bring freedom. We said this clearly during our journey in Colombia: "We exhort you not to place your trust in violence and revolution: that is contrary to the Christian spirit, and it can also delay instead of advancing that social uplifting to which you lawfully aspire."[9] "We must say and reaffirm that violence is not in accord with the gospel, that it is not Christian; and that sudden or violent changes of structures would be deceitful, ineffective of themselves, and certainly not in conformity with the dignity of the people."[10]

38. Having said this, we rejoice that the church is becoming ever more conscious of the proper manner and strictly evangelical means that it possesses in order to collaborate in the liberation of many. And what is it doing? It is trying more and more to encourage large numbers of Christians to devote themselves to human liberation. It is providing these Christian "liberators" with the inspiration of faith, the motivation of fraternal love, a social teaching which true Christians cannot ignore and which they must make the foundation of their wisdom and of their experience in order to translate it concretely into forms of action, participation, and commitment. All this must characterize the spirit of a committed Christian, without confusion with tactical attitudes or with the service of a political system. The church strives always to insert the Christian struggle for liberation into the universal plan of salvation, which it itself proclaims.

What we have just recalled comes out more than once in the synod debates. In fact we devoted to this theme a few clarifying words in our address to the Fathers at the end of the Assembly.[11]

It is to be hoped that all these considerations will help to remove the ambiguity which the word "liberation" very often takes on in ideologies, political systems, or groups. The liberation which evangelization proclaims and prepares is the one which Christ himself announced and gave to humankind by his sacrifice.

39. The necessity of ensuring fundamental human rights cannot be separated from this just liberation which is bound up with evangelization and which endeavors to secure structures safeguarding human freedoms. Among these fundamental human rights, religious liberty occupies a place of primary importance. We recently spoke of the relevance of this matter, emphasizing "how many Christians still today, because they are Christians, because they are Catholics, live oppressed by systematic persecution! The drama of fidelity to Christ and of the freedom of religion continues, even if it is disguised by categorical declarations in favor of the rights of the person and of life in society!"[12]. . .

57. Like Christ during the time of his preaching, like the Twelve on the morning of Pentecost, the church too sees before it an immense multitude of persons who need the gospel and have a right to it, for God "wants everyone to be saved and reach full knowledge of the truth."[13]

The church is deeply aware of its duty to preach salvation to all. Knowing that the gospel message is not reserved to a small group of the initiated, the privileged or the elect but is destined for everyone, it shares Christ's anguish at the sight of the wandering and exhausted crowds "like sheep without a shepherd" and it often repeats his words: "I feel sorry for all these people."[14] But the church is also conscious of the fact that, if the preaching of the gospel is to be effective, it must address its message to the heart of the multitudes, to communities of the faithful whose action can and must reach others.

58. The last synod devoted considerable attention to these "small communities," or *communautés de base*, because they are often talked about in the church today. What are they, and why should they be the special beneficiaries of evangelization and at the same time evangelizers themselves?

According to the various statements heard in the synod, such communities flourish more or less throughout the church. They differ greatly among themselves, both within the same region and even more so from one region to another.

In some regions they appear and develop, almost without exception, within the church, having solidarity with its life, being nourished by its teaching, and united with its pastors. In these cases they spring from the need to live the church's life more intensely, or from the desire and quest for a more human dimension such as larger ecclesial communities can only offer with difficulty, especially in the big modern cities which lend themselves both to life in the mass and to anonymity. Such communities can quite simply be in their own way an extension on the spiritual and religious level—worship, deepening of faith, fraternal charity, prayer, contact with pastors—of the small sociological community such as the village, etc. Or again their aim may be to bring together for the purpose of listening to and meditating on the word, for the sacraments and the bond of the agape, groups of persons who are linked by age, culture, civil state, or social situation: married couples, young people, professional people, etc., persons who already happen to be united in the struggle for justice, charitable aid to the poor, human advancement. In still other cases they bring Christians together in places where the shortage of priests does not favor the normal life of a parish community. This is all presupposed within communities constituted by the church, especially individual churches and parishes.

In other regions, on the other hand, *communautés de base* come together in a spirit of bitter criticism of the church, which they are quick to stigmatize as "institutional" and to which they set themselves up in opposition as charismatic communities, free from structures and inspired only by the gospel. Thus their obvious characteristic is an attitude of fault-finding and of rejection with regard to the church's outward manifestations: its hierarchy, its signs. They are radically opposed to the church. By following these lines their main inspiration very quickly becomes ideological, and it rarely happens that they do not quickly fall victim to some political option or current of thought, and then to a system, even a party, with all the attendant risks of becoming its instrument.

The difference is already notable: the communities which by their spirit of opposition cut themselves off from the church, and whose unity they wound, can well be called *communautés de base*, but in this case it is a strictly sociological name. They could not, without a misuse of terms, be called ecclesial *communautés de base*, even if, while being hostile to the hierarchy, they claim to remain within the unity of the church. This name belongs to the other groups, those which come together within the church in order to unite themselves to the church and to cause the church to grow.

These latter communities will be a place of evangelization, for the benefit of the bigger communities, especially the individual churches. And, as we said at the end of the last synod, they will be a hope for the universal church to the extent:

—that they seek their nourishment in the word of God and do not allow themselves to be ensnared by political polarization or fashionable ideologies, which are ready to exploit their immense human potential;

—that they avoid the ever present temptation of systematic protest and a hypercritical attitude, under the pretext of authenticity and a spirit of collaboration;

—that they remain firmly attached to the local church in which they are inserted, and to the universal church, thus avoiding the very real danger of becoming isolated within themselves, then of believing themselves to be the only authentic church of Christ, and hence of condemning the other ecclesial communities;

—that they maintain a sincere communion with the pastors whom the Lord gives to the church, and with the magisterium, which the Spirit of Christ has entrusted to these pastors;

—that they never look on themselves as the sole beneficiaries or sole agents of evangelization—or even the only depositaries of the gospel—but, being aware that the church is much more vast and diversified, accept the fact that this church becomes incarnate in other ways than through themselves;

—that they constantly grow in missionary consciousness, fervor, commitment, and zeal;

—that they show themselves to be universal in all things and never sectarian.

On these conditions, which are certainly demanding but also uplifting, the ecclesial *communautés de base* will correspond to their most fundamental vocation: as hearers of the gospel proclaimed to them and privileged beneficiaries of evangelization, they will soon become proclaimers of the gospel themselves.

NOTES

1. See Acts 17:22-23.
2. 1 John 3:1; see Rom. 8:14-17.

3. See Eph. 3:8; Rom. 1:16. See Sacred Congregation for the Doctrine of the Faith, *Declaratio ad fidem tuendam in mysteria Incarnationis et SS. Trinitatis e quibusdam recentibus erroribus* (February 21, 1972); AAS, 64 (1972), pp. 237-41.

4. See 1 John 3:2; Rom. 8:29; Phil. 3:20-21. See Second Vatican Ecumenical Council, Dogmatic Constitution on the Church, *Lumen Gentium*, 48-51; AAS, 57 (1965), pp. 53-58.

5. See Sacred Congregation for the Doctrine of the Faith, *Declaratio circa Catholicam Doctrinam de Ecclesia contra nonnullos errores hodiernos tuendam* (June 24, 1973); AAS, 65 (1973), pp. 396-408.

6. See Second Vatican Ecumenical Council, Pastoral Constitution on the Church in the Modern World, *Gaudium et Spes*, 47-52; AAS, 58 (1966), pp. 1067-74; Paul VI, Encyclical Letter *Humanae Vitae*; AAS, 60 (1968), pp. 481-503.

7. Paul VI, Address for the Opening of the Third General Assembly of the Synod of Bishops (September 27, 1974); AAS, 66 (1974), p. 562.

8. Ibid.

9. Paul VI, Address to the Campesinos of Colombia (August 23, 1968); AAS, 60 (1968), p. 623.

10. Paul VI, Address for the "Day of Development" at Bogotá (August 23, 1968); AAS, 60 (1968), p. 627; see St. Augustine, *Epistola* 229 (PL 33, 1020).

11. Paul VI, Address for the Closing of the Third General Assembly of the Synod of Bishops (October 26, 1974); AAS, 66 (1974), p. 637.

12. Address given on October 15, 1975, *L'Osservatore Romano* (October 17, 1975).

13. 1 Tim. 2:4.

14. Matt. 9:36; 15:32.

19

Jürgen Moltmann
"An Open Letter to José Míguez Bonino"
(March 29, 1976)

In 1975 a leading Protestant liberation theologian, José Míguez Bonino, dean of the Evangelical Institute for Theological Studies in Buenos Aires, published a book entitled Doing Theology in a Revolutionary Situation *(Philadelphia: Fortress). Despite the fact that he referred to Jürgen Moltmann as "the theologian to whom liberation theology is most indebted and with whom it has the closest affinity," he sharply criticized Moltmann's theology (pp. 144-50). A highly respected professor of theology at the University of Tübingen and one not noted for timidity, Moltmann replied publicly in an "Open Letter to José Míguez Bonino" in* Christianity and Crisis *with an equally trenchant criticism of Míguez Bonino's own theology and social analysis. In the letter he first faults Míguez Bonino for being too provincial by stressing his Latin American context, and then takes him to task for not being Latin American enough, but rather too European. Moltmann is also very wary of the Latin Americans' revolutionary enthusiasm and strongly defends his own version of democratic socialism.*

The text is taken from Christianity and Crisis *(March 29, 1976), pp. 57-63.*

Dear Friend: I have read through your book *Doing Theology in a Revolutionary Situation* in one sitting, and I am as deeply moved by it as I am disturbed. I have learned something from it about the history and the present situation of Latin America. The "theology of liberation" has become more understandable for me as seen in the context in which it lives. But I have learned even more about the history of Europe as it appears to the eyes of a Latin American and about the effect European "political theology" has on others in another situation.

After Hugo Assmann's announcement at the Geneva conference of 1973 that "incommunication" was to take the place of dialogue with European theologians because they are Europeans, my readiness to deal with his criticism, as you can understand, was somewhat diminished. But you want to sharpen the criticism of Metz and me in order to carry the dialogue forward (p. 146), not to break it off. That is an invitation.

I believe that European theologians would misunderstand Latin Americans if they were to remain silent any longer. Confrontations can shatter a dialogue, but they can also lead the participants out of superficial friendliness into a deeper community. After you, Rubem Alves, Juan Segundo, Gustavo Gutiérrez, and Hugo Assmann have made crystal clear what you find dissatisfying in us and what in our theology seems so irrelevant for your situation and then also for our own situation, I would like to begin to clarify what we find dissatisfying in you and what we actually are expecting from you.

The "theology of liberation" wants to be an indigenous theology that frees itself from the European tradition and North Atlantic theology in order to give its full attention to the unmistakable experiences and tasks of Latin America. That is a necessary historical process of liberation, as can be observed also in Africa and Asia. The sooner it is accomplished, the more European theologians will be able to learn from others.

But the destruction of European theological imperialism should not lead to the provincialization of theology. If that were to happen, we in Europe would be able to abandon the rest of the world and Christianity as a whole and occupy ourselves with our own concerns and traditions. The destruction of that imperialism can lead in a meaningful way only to the construction of a common world theology at the expense of the one-sided "Western theology." The tendencies toward a narrow provincialism with blinders are already strong enough among us. They should not be strengthened by an "incommunication" policy from outside.

Persons who know their own historical and socio-economic borders are eager to experience that which is different and strange as it encounters them beyond their borders. *African theology* confronted us with something really new, for the African modes of thought have been entirely unfamiliar to us ever since Aristotle. *Japanese theology*, done in the Buddhist context, forces Western activists again and again to fundamental reorientations of their interests and thought forms. In *North American black theology* we have encountered new forms of communication through the language and music of an oppressed community.

But up to now scarcely anything comparable has come out of Latin America. We hear severe criticism of Western theology and of theology in general—and then we are told something about Karl Marx and Friedrich Engels, as if they were Latin American discoveries. Nothing against Marx and Engels, but the one was born in Trier and the other in Barmen, and both occupy an important vantage point in European history. And they are not just a disadvantage but an advantage to this history. They will not be totally unknown to European theologians. Later on I want to try to clarify this phenomenon of ideological re-import.

"WHERE IS LATIN AMERICA IN IT ALL?"

One gets a quite ambiguous impression as regards the Latin American theological criticism of European theology: one is first criticized intensely, and then, to one's surprise, finds that in the end the critics confirm with their own words exactly the same thing that one oneself had said. Rubem Alves in his *A Theology of Human Hope* criticizes the "theology of hope" as too transcendental in the definition of divine promise and too negative in the judgment of the present. Over against this he wants to emphasize the future as coming out of the pregnancy of the historical present, as Leibniz and Bloch had maintained. But because he cannot present the future of history as the virgin birth of the present, in the end he must ask about the "father" who has begotten the child and has engendered the present with hope. Therefore he speaks of the divine promise and of the language of freedom and ends at the point where the "theology of hope" already was.

Juan Segundo ("The Choice between Capitalism and Socialism as the Theological Crux," *Concilium,*October 1974) lodges against "political theology" the criticism that by means of its eschatological hope it would simply relativize all absolute experiences and ideologies and would validate only nonbinding anticipations, analogies, and designs directed at the wholly other eschatological future. In this respect he has indeed read only half, for Bonhoeffer and Barth had already spoken constantly of the stimulation and intensification of historical hopes through the eschatological hope, not to speak of Metz and me. But he is right, of course, in maintaining that in his messianic actions Jesus did not "deabsolutize" but rather—according to our experiences, an activity that is a bit "unwise"—"absolutized." To be sure, the individual event of liberation or salvation does not gain in this way a "causal character" for the kingdom of God—even Pelagius never would have said that—but rather the kingdom attains a causal character for the experienced event of liberation, for all messianic activity realizes the possibilities that have been made possible through the inbreaking of the messianic time (Luke 4:18ff.). To this extent the messianic kingdom is the subject of its historical realization and not vice versa. But precisely this "absolutizes" the relative or brings the unconditioned into the conditioned.

If Segundo had remained with this point, one would have had to accept it self-critically. However, at the end of his article he relativizes his own conception by speaking of a "fragile, partial causality that not infrequently errs and must be initiated anew" and by saying that in history "it is the eschatological kingdom at stake, even if perhaps merely in a fragmentary way." In this way he has only replaced the critical expressions "anticipation," "design," and "analogy" by the expression "fragment." That is truly not a "radical criticism of even the most progressive European theologies," as he suspects, since they have all used the expression "fragment" in this context—and in my opinion much too often.

You have the same problems in *Doing Theology in a Revolutionary Situation.* Your Barthianism always lets you distinguish neatly between what God does and what human beings do. But at the same time, you reproach Barth, the Europeans, and thus, in the same breath, also yourself for not overcoming this dualism through a new, historical-dialectical way of thinking.

Over against me and European theology you would like to "materialize" the kingdom of God from a historical perspective and block the retreat to a neutral "critical function" in theology. Good, one says to oneself, this is a new orientation that we, consciously or unconsciously, have not seen clearly enough. But then one reads your summary of your own thoughts and, behold, everything you have criticized in the "political theology" of Metz and Moltmann is again in place.

You present the positive relationship between the kingdom of God and human undertaking in history as calling, invitation, and impulse to engagement. Our concrete historical options should "correspond" to the kingdom (true to Barth). You describe the critical connection of the judgment of God to the whole of our human efforts (true to Luther). Finally, you speak of the "utopian function" of Christian eschatology, of Christian faith as stimulus and challenge for revolutionary action, and of the eschatological faith that makes meaningful the investment of life for the building of a temporal, imperfect order, and of the resurrection of the dead as the triumph of God's love and of God's solidarity with all human beings in which the imperfect is perfected (true to Moltmann). One can also read all of this in Bonhoeffer, Barth, Gollwitzer, Metz, and other Europeans. One is, therefore, inclined to agree fervently with you, but then ask what sense your criticism has after all.

Gustavo Gutiérrez's *A Theology of Liberation* is often viewed by Latin American and European theologians as the first theology in the Latin American perspective. The reader is expectant; one would like to discover Latin America in this book. As magnificent as the book is otherwise, in this respect the reader is disappointed. Gutiérrez presents the process of liberation in Latin America as the continuation and culmination of the European history of freedom. One gets a glimpse into this history of freedom by being enlightened about Kant and Hegel, Rousseau and Feuerbach, Marx and Freud. The "secularization process" is portrayed in detail through the work of Gogarten, Bonhoeffer, Cox, and Metz. This is all worked through independently and offers many new insights—but precisely only in the framework of Europe's history, scarcely in the history of Latin America. Gutiérrez has written an invaluable contribution to European theology. But where is Latin America in it all?

It is not easy to interpret these impressions, for they are truly not meant as remonstrances or counter-criticism. Presumably we Europeans have a wrong expectation. Latin American theologians become interesting in Europe and the United States only when they offer something new, which is then, as you and Assmann complain, made fashionable as a "consumer good" in order to overcome one's own boredom. That is paternalistic—to act as if the young should entertain and cheer up the old. It can easily lead to oedipal reactions when those who profess to be "young" want to get free from those who consider themselves "old."

Is it true that in the relationship of the Europeans to the Latin American theologians there is still at work unconsciously the relationship between homeland and colonial land, mother church and daughter church? It would really be more meaningful to work in concert at a new construction of theology rather than in a rivalry to try to pass each other by on the "left" or the "right" or in the "middle," and in the process step on each other's toes.

TURNING TOWARD THE PEOPLE

The second problem, to which I have already referred, has to do with the use of Marxism by Latin American theologians. We are speaking now not about how often, with the joy of missionary discovery, it is introduced and interpreted to those Europeans who live in the land of Marx and Engels but rather about the way it is employed theologically. First let us consider the reception of Marxism in Latin America from a historical perspective.

You and Gutiérrez have described impressively the various historical epochs of your continent. After the phase of conquest and colonization for God and the king of Spain in the age of European imperialism, there followed the phase of national liberation from Spain and Portugal in the nineteenth century—partly as a consequence of the developing civil nationalism in Europe. Today we see the initial phases of the social and political liberation of the people from Western economic imperialism and from subjection to class rule by military dictatorship. That is, the proletarian revolution has begun, but again in the train of socialistic movements and their theories in Europe.

The history of Latin America, in contradistinction to that of Africa and Asia, is obviously more persistently defined by the European history of rule and revolution. Even now the necessary socialistic revolution for the proletariat remains in this framework. Whereas China, which was only briefly and never completely ruled by the West, found quite early through Mao its own Chinese way to socialism, there are still scarcely any beginnings of a peculiarly Latin American way to socialism. At any rate this is what one would conclude from the writings of the liberation theologians.

To be sure, they recommend that theologians in the whole world turn to a Marxist class analysis in order to stand in the concrete history of their people. But they do not carry through this class analysis with respect to the history of their own people; they only quote a few basic concepts of Marx. And they do this in such a general way that one learns only something about the fruits of the theologians' reading and scarcely anything about the struggle of the Latin American people. In them one reads more about the sociological theories of others, namely Western socialists, than about the history or the life and suffering of the Latin American people. One is called upon to opt, in a moral alternative, for the oppressed against the oppressors and to accept Marxism as the right prophecy of the situation.

Now it is simply not the case that European theologians prefer to remain politically neutral and to theorize only on the universal plane, as they have been accused. But it is one thing to be involved in an incisive analysis of

the historical situation of the people and quite another thing to make dec-
lamations of seminar-Marxism as a worldview. Whoever assumes that sociology can be a substitute for a deficient contact with the working and
suffering people (J. B. Metz, *Stimmen der Zeit*, 192, 1974, p. 809)—which
is not meant to be imputed to anyone—practices a sociology about the
people but does not tell the history of the people as his/her own history.
Marxism and sociology do not yet bring a theologian into the people but,
at least at first, only into the company of Marxists and sociologists.

On the other hand, moral appeals and biblical language about the poor
also do not bring the theologian where he/she belongs. Theology as pure
theology, and even theology that has been extended and broadened to
Marxism and socialism, remains in its own circle. The true radical change
that is necessary is still ahead of both the "political theologians" in the
European context and the "liberation theologians" in the Latin American
context. In my opinion they can enter in a thoroughly mutual way into this
change—namely, a radical turn toward the people.

It is also not a particularly impressive indication of solid socio-political
analysis or of good judgment when, in the discussion of the actual function
of "political theology" and of the words that Metz and I myself use, it is
maintained that "in Europe, for instance, they immediately are integrated
into the developmentalist, technological, liberal ideology adopted by the
Common Market and its orbit in relation to the Third World" (Míguez
Bonino, p. 80). As the sociologists of knowledge make clear, such suspicion
of ideology can be advanced in any context and at any time, but in this case
the author unfortunately adduces not the slightest shade of evidence. The
conclusion that "orthopraxis, rather than orthodoxy, becomes the criterion
for theology" (p. 81) is a literal quote from Metz, who was just charged
with propounding the ideology of the Common Market. And that "theology
has to stop explaining the world and to start transforming it" (p. 81) stood
already in 1964 in the *Theology of Hope* (p. 74) of the no less suspect
Moltmann. Both sentences, however, could well be true; therefore I have
no desire to enter into a dispute about them.

ASSESSING THE HISTORICAL SITUATION

The most decisive difference between the Latin American theology of
liberation and political theology in Western Europe lies in the assessment
of the various historical situations. I believe that there is an extensive una-
nimity about what is necessary in terms of world politics. But the various
countries, societies, and cultures do not live synchronously at the same point
in history. Therefore, according to each concrete situation, there are diverse
ways to realize what is generally good for all.

Many Latin American theologians believe that they are living in a "revolutionary situation." Others make a more skeptical judgment of their situation and speak, as does Rubem Alves, of a "prerevolutionary situation."

One cannot say much about this from a European vantage point. But it is clear that there are two issues involved when, on the one hand—in view of the ever more harsh economic imperialism of the North Atlantic nations and of the brutal military dictatorships it supports—one speaks of the *necessity* of a socialistic revolution and when, on the other hand—in view of the awakening of the people—one speaks of the *possibility* of such a revolution. The necessity of a speedy and radical transformation of the socioeconomic conditions can be understood by everyone as indisputable. But what use is the best revolutionary theory when the historical subject of the revolution is not at hand or is not yet ready? The subject of revolutionary liberation can only be the oppressed, exploited people themselves.

The intellectuals and the students are certainly not the subject. They can at most throw the revolutionary sparks into the dried up and parched woods. But if the people are not "burning" and do not rise up, the most beautiful sparks are of no use. The sparks then become sectarian candles around which elite circles gather ceremoniously in order to confirm themselves. One is justified in speaking of a revolutionary situation only when the common misery is generally experienced, when it is unbearable, when the one necessary thing is recognized, and when the potential to realize what is necessary is at hand and ready.

If we take these indicators and apply them to the situation *in* Europe, then we cannot speak realistically of a "revolutionary" or "prerevolutionary" situation. There was, it is true, a time in the 1960s during the student revolt, the anti-Viet Nam war movement, and "socialism with a human face" when one could point to such a situation and to concrete alternatives to the existing system. But it became clear that the most beautiful revolutionary theories found no basis in the people and therefore remained without a subject.

The elite cadre of ideologists developed a "socialism for the people," but the "socialism of the people" did not see the light of day. The reactions of the people were therefore rather hostile. The people had quite a realistic view of the privileges of the students who were able to demonstrate during working hours, and were thus not interested in their slogans. The so-called leftist theoreticians did not suffer from a manifest loss of reality, as they were reproached by the conservative theologians, but rather from a lack of contact with the people.

It is understandable in our country that the people are not interested in an ideological imperialism. Obviously there are conditions in which long trains wait only on the locomotives to lead them to the destination. But there are also times in which the locomotive departs so quickly that the couplings are torn apart and the train remains motionless on the track. Then, for better or for worse, the locomotive must come back and couple itself to the train again.

To say it without images, it seems more important to maintain a connection with the people than to travel alone into the paradise of the future. It is more important to live and to work in and with the people than to relish the classless society in the correct theories. Of course this sounds like a compromise, but it is not, for a concrete step is of more worth than the most beautiful idea of possibilities.

DEMOCRATIC SOCIALISM

The concept I consider the most realistic and at the same time pregnant with future in Europe is *democratic socialism*. It corresponds to the tradition of the German worker movement. Besides Marx there is also Lassalle; that is, besides the economic liberation from exploitation there is also the struggle for the universal right to vote and to participate in governance, the struggle for political liberation. It also corresponds to the European history of freedom. Without the French civil revolution there would have been no socialist revolution. From the historical perspective the reverse is also true: without socialism, no democracy.

In the European countries—and here I include also the United States— one cannot develop socialism at the cost of democracy. No one would be ready to sacrifice the freedoms that have already been won, freedom of the press, freedom to vote, right to express one's opinions, freedom to strike, freedom of movement, right to trial, etc., however imperfect and one-sided they may be. At least no one would be ready to give up these freedoms and rights for new dreams.

But many are ready to transfer these democratic rights and freedoms over to economic conditions and to struggle with the unions for the democratization of the economy. The direct leap from feudalism to socialism is not possible in Western Europe. In Western Europe Russian socialism continues to have the scent of czarism. There are also East European countries that have not experienced a civil revolution but have simply passed over this stage of historical development. In the West their socialism has the appearance of Prussian military socialism or feudal bureaucratic socialism, in any case a state socialism without a democratized state.

There are countries that, while maintaining intact the whole apparatus of state control, change over from a rightist dictatorship to a leftist dictatorship. Portugal has been standing on the threshold of this danger and perhaps Peru also. This way makes no sense for us. Whoever has tasted a bit of political freedom no longer believes the theories by which a dictatorship, be it rightist or leftist, tries to justify itself. For such a person the real situation is plain.

Socialism without democracy, economic justice without realization of human rights, are not hopes among our people. Democratic socialism must advance on both fields at once, on the way of the democratization of political institutions and on the way of the socialization of economic conditions. It will engage itself in the midst of positive issues and of the real potentialities at hand. Working with the trade unions to give everyone the right to participate in decisions, it will divide economic power and distribute it in such a way that the people will have control over it. It will try to change its political organizations from ideological parties into people's parties, for it is more important to represent the interests of the little people, the mass of the employed and the unemployed, than to chase after the phantom of pure theory.

Whether this democratic way to socialism will be successful and whether it could work in a liberating way for the countries of the Third World, is something that remains to be seen. Guarantees cannot be given, and no one would maintain that this would be the only right and infallible orthopraxis. But we should take this direction in our situation since the reverse way — from socialism to democracy — has produced such few satisfying results among us.

This certainly does not preclude others in their own situation from taking another course and under certain conditions seeking to overcome class rule and dictatorship of the right by a temporary leftist dictatorship, a protective and transitional dictatorship for the building up of socialism and democracy. In specific emergency situations this probably cannot be excluded as *ultima ratio*, even though the price is always rather high. But in any case it should be assumed that the one way from democracy to democratic socialism and the other way from socialism to social democracy do not mutually exclude each other but rather converge.

I am aware that with this statement I am laying myself open to the charge of being a "convergence theoretician," a term that stimulates a neurosis about one's profile on both sides of divided Germany. But I do not think that I am thereby withholding anything from the freedom and the humanity of the people. In the end the only thing that is at stake in socialism and democracy is that the people become the subject of their own history of freedom and human beings attain their unhindered humanity.

THE COMMON GOAL

Orthopraxis is a dangerous word if by it is meant that the practice of life should be dogmatized and made uniform. In the different political situations and in the different historical times in which we actually live, the right thing and the timely thing that must be done appear differently. But the goal can only be one and common to all. The goal lies in a world society in which human beings no longer live against but with each other. Latin American orthopraxis will have a different face than West European orthopraxis. But of crucial importance within the difference is the common prospect. Should it not be possible to acknowledge and with all criticism also to appreciate each other mutually?

I would like to close this letter with comments on two incidents that are deeply troubling to me at the moment.

1. In December 1974, thirty-two leading Protestant church officials greeted the power grab of the military junta in Chile as "God's answer to the prayers of all believers who see in Marxism a satanic power." This

declaration is so atrocious that it cannot be passed over in painful silence. Whoever expects the "fulfillment of his prayers" from the terror of tyranny does not pray in the name of the crucified messiah of the people. The God of Jesus Christ does not answer the prayers of those who believe in him through the execution of more than ten thousand poor people. With this declaration the "believers" who were referred to and their alleged "Protestant church officials" expose themselves as adherents of a murderous political religion that has nothing in common with Christianity.

The God of the Chilean military junta is the political idol Moloch. Whoever brings his/her thank-offering to him separates him/herself from every Christian community. That is religious fascism. "Satanic powers" can only be overcome by the risen Christ, not through another satan. By declaring Marxism to be a "satanic power" one makes out of Christ an anti-communist satan. Christianity throughout the whole world will have to repent for the perverse declaration of those thirty-two "Protestant church officials" in Chile. It will have to turn away from such apostasy and toward new obedience.

2. In January 1975 the socialist government of Yugoslavia discontinued the world-renowned journal *Praxis* and dismissed from the university eight Belgrade teachers, all members of the *Praxis* circle. *Praxis* was the last center of democratic socialism in Europe in which Eastern and Western socialists could work together. Ernst Bloch and Jürgen Habermas were Western co-editors. The self-governance of workers and democratic socialism obviously became dangerous to Moscow's state socialism, even in Yugoslavia. With this one of the few European lights that burn for socialists and democrats in common is extinguished. Dogmatism and bureaucratism rule. Nothing could be more opportune for the technocrats of capitalism. Now the managers and the rulers of the people can be counted among them and of their kind, and they will divide the purse between themselves.

Today our hope can point to only a few positive "signs of the times." The signs of destruction are increasing. Our hope can no longer afford to be childish and enthusiastic. In common resistance against evil and the flunkies that serve death, it must become mature and steady. However we analyze our situation, hope is faithfulness to the resurrection and therefore perseverance in the cross. One learns this among the people, in the community of the poor, among those who are heavy laden and hungering after righteousness.

In the community of the "people of the beatitudes" I greet you.

20

International Theological Commission "Declaration on Human Development and Christian Salvation" (September 1977)

The International Theological Commission was established as an adjunct to render assistance to the Vatican Congregation for the Doctrine of the Faith in 1969. It was intended to provide the pope and the Congregation with the consultative and advisory services of theological, scriptural, and liturgical experts representative of various schools of thought. The document displays great sympathy with liberation theology's concern for the poor and oppressed. However, it is very cautious and timid in accepting development and work for justice (the modern forms of love of neighbor) as a necessary part of the human response to God's grace in the contemporary world. The text is from the United States Catholic Conference, Washington, D.C., 1977.

WORLD POVERTY AND INJUSTICE AS SPRINGBOARD FOR A THEOLOGICAL MOVEMENT

The Second Vatican Council reminded the church of its ceaseless duty to "scrutinize the signs of the times and to interpret them in the light of the gospel."[1] A special incentive to carry out this injunction was provided by the documents emanating from the Second General Assembly of the Latin American Episcopal Conference (CELAM) held in 1968 in Medellín, Colombia: the church hears the outcries of poor peoples and makes itself the interpreter of their oppressive conditions. The church's worldwide solicitude in response to the challenge hurled by oppression and hunger is shown not only by papal documents — *Mater et Magistra, Pacem in Terris, Populorum Progressio, Octogesima Adveniens* — but also by documents of the Synod of Bishops held in Rome in 1971 (*Justice in the World*) and in 1974. Pope Paul VI once again highlighted the church's urgent duty in this regard with his apostolic exhortation of December 8, 1975, *Evangelization in Today's World.*[2]

These circumstances must be taken into account if the theological treatises on these issues are to be understood. Although they have a scholarly face, their primary source is not theoretical, scientific effort. They are not presented in the first instance as a "written" theology; they struggle to preserve close contact with the day-to-day existence of overburdened men and women and with the concrete injunction to action that challenges the church in this factual situation. They intend to give public expression to the cries of our poor, anguished brothers and sisters—specifically, to hunger, disease, unjust profit, exile, oppression. Add to this the inhuman living conditions of all those who own only what they wear, sleep at night in the streets, live and die there, lack basic medical care. For Christians enlightened by the gospel, these "signs of the times" are an exceptionally sharp stimulus to bend every effort, in the name of Christian faith, to free their brothers and sisters from inhuman living conditions. This attention to the needy, this affinity with all the oppressed, are singularly expressed and exemplified by the biblical words "justice," "liberation," "hope," "peace."

This witness to solicitude for the poor, a witness supported by the gospel of Jesus Christ,[3] is something of a ceaseless spiritual leaven in all the pertinent theological treatises; it obviously inspires their theological reflections and political options. A spiritual experience arouses innate forces whereby the pressures of Christian love are transformed into commands effective for action by means of human reflection and scientific analysis.

Both elements, a basic spiritual experience and theological and scientific reflection, are mutually complementary and consequently fashion a vital unity. But we must be careful not to confound the two elements. No one, therefore, should condemn these various theological systems if he is not listening at the same time to the cries of the poor and seeking more acceptable ways to respond. On the other hand, we must ask whether the types of theological reflection currently in vogue are, in their actual methodology, the only way of responding appropriately to yearnings for a more human world of brothers and sisters. The point is, every theology has service for its function, and so must at times undergo needed changes and corrections, if these help it to achieve its primary commission more effectively.

A NEW TYPE OF THEOLOGY AND ITS DIFFICULTIES

The theological treatises of which we have spoken stem from conditions in which human persons are oppressed, are slavishly subject to others in economic, social, and political life, and yearn for freedom. This existential human story is not accepted as an unchangeable destiny; it is understood as a "creative" process that looks to a larger freedom in all sectors of life and ultimately to the fashioning of a "new humanity." To change inhuman conditions is seen as a divine demand, as God's will: Jesus Christ, who by his redemptive action freed human persons from sin in all its forms, offers a new basis for human fellowship.

This way of thinking, which is the springboard for the theological treatises of which we are speaking, gives them a special form that is in a sense new. God reveals this mysterious plan in actual events; and the more intimately Christians enter into concrete situations and the historical progression of events, the more appropriately they respond to God's word. In consequence, the Christian recognizes the profound unity that links the divine history of salvation accomplished through Jesus Christ to efforts undertaken for the welfare and rights of humankind.

Although secular history and salvation history should not be regarded as simply identical, still the relationship between the two is to be conceived in the first instance as a unity. Their distinction may not be extended to a dualism in which history and salvation would be represented as indifferent one to the other. In fact, human activity acquires an entirely new value in history, a theological value, in that it builds up a more human society; for the construction of a just society is, in a sense, the inauguration of God's kingdom in anticipation.[4] Therefore Christian faith is understood principally as a historical praxis whereby socio-political conditions are changed and renewed.

This way of thinking contains many elements of great value; for it is indeed true that Christians should have a richer understanding of the total unity that their calling to salvation involves.[5] Nor can we doubt that faith, in its Scriptural sense, can be fructified and perfected only by deeds. Moreover, the Second Vatican Council reminds us[6] that the Holy Spirit is active in world history; even outside the visible church the preludes to faith, that is, the truths and rules of right reason about God and the common good, which are a kind of foundation for the Christian religion, are found to some extent.[7]

Nevertheless, in some theological movements these elemental data are interpreted in a one-sided fashion that is open to objection. The unity that links world history and salvation history may not be so conceived that it tends to consolidate the gospel of Jesus Christ, which as a supernatural mystery is altogether unique and beyond human intelligence,[8] with secular history. Nor can it mean that the boundaries between church and world are utterly effaced.

In a similar vein, the world in its historical existence is indeed the place where God's saving plan is unfolding—but not in such a way that the force and dynamism of God's word consist totally in its function of stimulating social and political change. And so faith's praxis is not reducible to changing the conditions of human society; for besides laying injustice bare, faith's praxis includes such things as conscience formation, change in mental attitude, adoration of the true God and of our Savior Jesus Christ in distinction from all forms of idolatry. Consequently, "faith as praxis" should not be interpreted in such a way that one's involvement in politics embraces and governs all human efforts and actions totally and "radically." Two points call for clarification here:

1. Political controversy, which is customarily linked with confrontation, should not be carried to the point where it obscures or obliterates peace and reconciliation as the objective and fruit of Christian activity, and what takes priority is an increase of antagonism and the onset of violence.

2. It must remain beyond dispute that for the Christian politics is not the final ground that gives ultimate meaning to all of life; it is not an absolute in the Christian eon; and so its nature is to be an instrument, a servant. Overlook this, and human freedom is threatened by movements that promote dictatorial control. Although theology is oriented in part toward praxis, its more prominent function is to seek understanding of God's word; for whatever engages it, theology must be able to distance itself from a concrete situation, which is almost always attended by various pressures and compulsions to action. It is from the principles of Catholic teaching on faith and morals that we can derive the light to make correct judgments about what has to be done to acquire eternal salvation without risk of losing the freedom of God's children. Only in this way is theology tied to truth; only in this way can it preserve the sovereign authority of God's word and the altogether unique character of that word. And so we have to take special care not to fall into a unidimensional vision of Christianity that would adversely affect christology and ecclesiology, our view of salvation and of Christian existence, even theology's proper function. Prophetic charges of injustice and urgent appeals to make common cause with the poor have to do with situations that are highly complex in nature, have roots in history, and depend on social and political realities. Even a prophetic judgment on the circumstances of a time calls for assured reasons or criteria. That is why the different theological treatments of liberation must deal simultaneously with theories that come from the social sciences, which study objectively what the "outcry of the people" expresses.

Theology, however, cannot deduce concrete political norms sheerly from theological principles; and so the theologian cannot settle profound sociological issues by theology's specific resources. Theological treatises, which strive to build a more human society, must take into account the risks that the use of sociological theories involves. In every instance these theories must be tested for their degree of certitude, inasmuch as they are often no more than conjectures and not infrequently harbor explicit or implicit ideological elements that rest on debatable philosophical assumptions or on an erroneous anthropology. This is true, for instance, of significant segments of analyses inspired by Marxism and Leninism. Anyone who employs such theories and analyses should be aware that these do not achieve a greater degree of truth simply because theology introduces them into its expositions. In fact, theology ought to recognize the pluralism that exists in scientific interpretations of society and realize that it cannot be fettered to any concrete sociological analysis.

BIBLICAL-THEOLOGICAL FACETS

Since the theological treatises we have been discussing often appeal to sacred Scripture, we should take care to uncover what the Old and New

Testaments have to say about the relationship between salvation and human welfare, between salvation and human rights. Obviously, our reflections here must be incomplete. On the other hand, we must avoid the anachronism that would read contemporary ideas back into the Bible.

OLD TESTAMENT

To determine the relationship between divine salvation and human development, practically everyone now cites the exodus story. The reason is, the exodus from Egypt[9] is actually a salvation event of capital importance in the Old Testament: liberation from foreign tyranny and from works forced by public powers. Nevertheless, "liberation" in the Old Testament is not totally situated in the removal from Egypt and the return from exile; for the liberation is oriented to the covenant worship solemnized on Mount Sinai,[10] and apart from that orientation it loses its specific meaning. The Psalms themselves, when they deal with need and protest, with aid and thanks, reveal forms of prayer that express salvation and "liberation."[11] There distress is identified not only with social affliction but also with hostility, injustice, blameworthy fault, as well as with that to which this leads: the threat that is death and the void death represents. Less significance, therefore, is placed on felt needs in individual instances; more important is the convincing experience that only God can bring deliverance and salvation.

Consequently, one should not speak of Old Testament salvation in its relation to human rights and welfare without simultaneously revealing the complete theological argumentation: it is not humankind but Yahweh who effects change. Besides, as long as the exodus lasted, in the desert, it was especially for the spiritual liberation and purification of the people that God provided.

A moving instance of an effort inspired by God's revelation to improve conditions of human living is the rebuke to the social order sounded by the prophets, especially in Amos.[12] Later prophets take up and enlarge the theme initiated by Amos, as when they cry "woe" on those who own large estates.[13] In powerful language Hosea censures the absence of human solidarity.[14] Isaiah explicitly includes widows and orphans among those who must be protected.[15] He threatens that the Lord will take away from Jerusalem "the powerful and the strong"—that is, the more potent leaders in the society[16]; he complains about possessions accumulating in the hands of a few[17] or, more broadly, about the oppression of the poor by the rich.[18] But he is clearly far from calling for revolt against the oppressors, even though this theme is discoverable in Old Testament writings.[19] Presentiment of impending disaster keeps a program for a more equitable society from making its appearance.[20] The prophets believe that there are many different ways of succoring society in its needs. But instead of an optimism supposedly supported by a theology of history, they show a large measure of skepticism on human ability actually to fashion a different world.

Such a change must be preceded by a way of acting that is proper to interior conversion and justice. "Cease to do evil, learn to do good; seek justice, assist the oppressed, defend the fatherless, plead for the widow."[21] It is God who must give human beings the power to bring about a greater degree of justice in the social sphere: in the last analysis Yahweh alone can efficaciously provide for human rights and welfare, especially of the oppressed.[22] God works salvation beyond the good or evil designs of humans.

In this connection, the prophets do recognize something akin to the "corrupt system." As they see it, however, we may not reduce everything to the point where evil is only a sign and effect of society's unjust structures or where we could hope to correct abuses simply by abolishing possessions. Over and above this, we must keep in mind the personal element, which determines the process of "liberation" for the Old Testament. This is particularly exemplified and confirmed by the principle of individual responsibility.[23]

Some significant passages of the Old Testament disclose partial visions of a new society, no longer arranged along the lines of pervasive contemporary structures.[24] Many Psalms speak expressly of God as liberator of the oppressed and defender of the poor.[25] While freeing the people of Israel from oppression, God demands of them that they remove all human oppression.[26] God's lordship, once it comes, will eliminate all tyranny among human beings.

In the Old Testament, however, this hope is long not distinguished with sufficient clarity from concrete history and does not bear on realities which transcend that history. Even down to our own time, a fair number of ideologies of a "secularized" salvation look for these promises of God to be realized within the limits of history, and simply in consequence of man's activity; but this, we have seen, the Old Testament rejects. Lastly, we should recall that in the apocalyptic passages of the later Old Testament the hope of a life after this life and the theology of history commend in remarkable fashion the human being's experience of weakness and of God's omnipotence.

NEW TESTAMENT

The New Testament takes up significant elements of the Old[27] or presupposes them.[28] As the discourse on the Beatitudes shows strikingly,[29] the Old Testament insistence on conversion and renewal of the human spirit is intensified, and in the New Testament these demands can be quite effectively realized by the power of the Holy Spirit. Still the impression remains — and it has been stated time and again — that the New Testament is not primarily concerned about the social sphere and human togetherness.

Possibly the unique newness of the Christian message initially tempered concern for questions that involved worldly duties. The personal love of the incarnate God for this new people was so transcendently important that questions prompted by temporal existence could not take priority (recall only the expectation of God's kingdom). With the spotlight on the mystery of our suffering and risen Lord, sheerly human needs could assume less urgency. The political situation of the Roman empire prevented Christians from turning their minds freely and extensively to the world.

However, this is not the place to explain in detail how Jesus' Good News and New Testament ethics imparted many directive norms and patterns of human conduct which were capable of inspiring a "social critique." Enough that we think of the command to love neighbor and enemy,[30] of the exhortatory and threatening words to the wealthy and the glutted,[31] of the obligation to care for the poor and the weak[32] and the admonition to all to help others,[33] of avoiding the temptation to exercise control over others[34] — on the ground that all human beings are brothers and sisters.[35]

Moreover, the New Testament discloses in the faithful a disposition to welcome "institutional" forms of Christian charity. Examples are the contributions taken up for Jerusalem[36] and the arrangement for the ministries of "diaconate" and charitable aid.[37] But it is clear that such "institutional" helps, at least in the beginning, were restricted to the ambit of the Christian communities and were quite undeveloped.

The New Testament also attaches great significance to the element of liberation, but we must be uncommonly careful to uncover its genuine sense. St. Paul's words about the new freedom are closely linked to his message on justification; and so liberation as such is not a theme severed from his other themes. The salvific work of Jesus Christ opened even the inner chambers of the human heart; so it is easy to be mistaken about what constitutes true denial of human freedom, true slavery. The announcing of justification shows with consummate clarity that the human person is prey to evil powers.

Authentic, complete liberty is impossible without the primary liberation[38] from death and perishability (*sarx*), from the power of sin and from the law (note also the "elements of the world"). "It is with this freedom that Christ has set us free."[39]

Liberation from these powers, however, brings a fresh freedom, in consequence of which we can, in the spirit of Jesus Christ, be effective in love so as to serve our brothers and sisters.[40] Here surely we have a foreshadowing of what God will accomplish as a gift to the just when God judges the whole story of humankind. The justice of God, through the spirit and by its power, bestows a liberating action that enables us to work what is good, an action that finds its perfection through love.

And so, when the New Testament speaks of "the liberation that brings freedom,"[41] the freedom that is grace, moral stimulus, and eschatological promise, these utterances are inserted into the proclamation of justification. Only if they rest on this foundation do they acquire their full force and power. Only if we bring our reflections to these depths can we understand

and actualize the stimulus the New Testament offers Christians for liberating activity.

In the light of the New Testament, society is not genuinely changed unless human beings are reconciled with God and with one another. Only if they become a new creation by conversion and justice can the conditions of human life be adequately and steadily improved. Human rights and welfare, therefore, human liberation, are not situated in the category of "having," but primarily within the boundaries that comprise "being"—including, of course, the implications that flow therefrom for shaping all the situations of human living.

SYSTEMATIC AND THEOLOGICAL REFLECTIONS

GOD AS LIBERATOR AND HUMAN LIBERATING ACTION

It has been noted that not all the Old Testament affirmations on liberation can be extended in every respect to the New Testament situation. The revelation given us in Christ divides the uninterrupted process of salvation history into two periods: promise and fulfillment. But both Testaments are at one in the conviction that God alone, precisely as supreme and utterly free Lord, administers human welfare; only God is properly liberator. This becomes clear, however, only when the needs of men and women are not reduced simply to their economic and material problems, only when we grasp the complete spectrum of their risk-laden, corrupt situation. Still, the unshakable proposition "God alone really frees" should not be interpreted as a kind of myth (as if we were talking about a *deus ex machina*); such a myth can only increase the indolence, inactivity, and apathy of those in straitened circumstances. Genuine faith does not condone inhuman living conditions, does not countenance them. God does not come to us in the violent hurricane of a revolution, but by grace God strengthens the human mind and heart so that they sharpen their conscience and, led by a living faith, build a more just world. To achieve this, however, the *whole* person must be freed from *all* the powers of evil. That is why an effectual change of mind and heart (*metanoia*) and a renewal of love for God and neighbor bring about actual liberation. But full liberation, according to Christian belief, is not accomplished in the course of earthly events, in history. For history leads to a "new earth" and to the "city of God"; consequently, until this fulfillment is realized, every liberating activity has a transitory character—and at the Last Judgment it will have to undergo its own ultimate testing.[42]

The relevance of our reflections, however, should not be restricted to spiritual reformation or incitement to assist individuals; for there is a kind of "injustice that assumes institutional shape," and as long as this obtains, the situation itself calls for a greater degree of justice and demands reforming. Our contemporaries are no longer convinced that social structures have been predetermined by nature and therefore are "willed by God," or that they have their origin in anonymous evolutionary laws. Consequently, the Christian must ceaselessly point out that the institutions of society originate also in the conscience of society, and that men and women have a moral responsibility for these institutions.

We may dispute how legitimate it is to speak of "institutional sin" or of "sinful structures," since the Bible speaks of sin in the first instance in terms of an explicit, personal decision that stems from human freedom. But it is unquestionable that by the power of sin injury and injustice can penetrate social and political institutions. This is why, as we have pointed out, even situations and structures that are unjust have to be reformed.

Here we have a new consciousness, for in the past these responsibilities could not be perceived as distinctly as they are now. From this perspective justice means a basic reverence for the equal dignity of all men; it means that radical human rights develop satisfactorily and are protected[43]; it means an assured equity in the distribution of those goods that are especially needful for human living.[44]

CONCRETE RELATIONSHIP BETWEEN HUMAN DEVELOPMENT AND DIVINE SALVATION

Reflection on the relationship between the salvation which God effects and the liberating action of humankind reveals the need to determine with greater exactness the relationship between human development and divine salvation, between the building up of the world and eschatological fulfillment. As is clear from the proofs we have adduced, human activity and Christian hope may be neither utterly divorced—on one side the world of earth exclusively, on the other a life to come utterly severed from the world—nor seen in terms of an "evolutionary optimism," as if God's lordship and human progressive construction of the world were one and the same thing.

Even the pastoral constitution *Gaudium et Spes* makes a distinction between the growth of God's kingdom and human progress as between the work of divinization and the work of humanization, or as between the order of divine grace and the order of human activity.[45] Indeed it speaks first of the affinity between the two: the service of humankind on earth "makes ready the material of heaven's kingdom."[46] The good fruits of our diligent activity—cleansed, however, of all sordidness, lit up and transfigured—we shall discover afresh in the kingdom of God, so that it is not only love that will remain[47] but love's labor as well.[48] Eschatological hope, therefore, ought to find its expression even in the structures of secular life.[49] That is why the council speaks not only of this world's passing away but of its transformation as well.[50] The earthly city and the heavenly city ought to penetrate each other, under faith's guidance, with due respect for their distinction and their harmonious union.[51] These ideas are summed up in the decree *Apostolicam Actuositatem* on the apostolate of the laity:

> Christ's redemptive work, while of its nature directed to the salvation of men and women, involves also the renewal of the whole temporal order. The church has for mission, therefore, not only to bring to men and women the message of Christ and his grace, but also to saturate and perfect the temporal sphere with the spirit of the gospel. . . . The two spheres, spiritual and temporal, distinct though they are, are so linked in the single plan of God that he himself purposes in Christ to take up the whole world again into a new creation, initially here on earth, completely on the last day.[52]

These passages persuade us that the vindication of justice and participation in the process of transforming the world should be regarded "as a constitutive element of the preaching of the gospel."[53] The words "constitutive element (*ratio constitutiva*) are still the subject of controversy. If we look at their strict meaning, it seems more accurate to interpret them as meaning an integral part, not an essential part.[54] Besides, the texts cited from the Second Vatican Council have commonly been explained as favoring a *harmony* between eschatological salvation and the human effort to build a better world. It is useful, therefore, while maintaining unyieldingly the unity that links the two, to spell out again, with even sharper clarity, the distinction between them.

The very resistance of earthly situations to positive change for the better, the power of sin and some ambiguous effects of human progress[55] teach us to recognize with even greater clarity within the very unity of salvation history an abiding difference between the kingdom of God and human development, as well as the mystery of the cross, without which no activity becomes genuinely salvific.[56] But if, while preserving the unity, it is the difference that is highlighted, this does not introduce a so-called dualism. In fact, this more penetrating vision helps us to carry out the task of promoting human welfare and justice with a greater measure of endurance, steadfastness, and confidence; it can also keep us from being thrown into confusion if our efforts prove ineffective.

This unifying connection and this difference in the relationship between human development and Christian salvation in their existential shape indeed demand further serious research; and this surely has a high priority among the tasks of today's theology. But the basic character of that unity cannot be overturned, for it is rooted at reality's very core.

On the one hand, existential history is in a way the locus where the world is so deeply transformed that it reaches as far as the mystery of God; and that is why love and its fruits abide. It is ultimately for this reason that there can be a link between salvation and human welfare, between salvation and human rights. But they are not linked to perfection, because the eschatological fulfillment "takes away" existential history.

On the other hand, the kingdom of God "directs" history and utterly transcends all the possibilities of earthly fulfillment; it presents itself, therefore, as the action of God. This involves a certain break with that world, no matter what perfection we recognize therein. This discontinuity in our individual stories we experience as death, but the same discontinuity precisely as "transformation" touches the whole of history: it is the world's "destruction."

In our pilgrim state this "dialectic," which finds expression in these two irreducible principles, cannot be dissolved and ought not be removed. In particular, however, the eschatological fulfillment for which we still yearn (the "eschatological reserve") is the reason why the relationship between God's kingdom and history cannot be described as either a monism or a dualism; and so from the very nature of this relationship we have to hold its definition in abeyance.

In any event, the relationship between the message of eschatological salvation and the shaping of historical time to come cannot be established univocally, by walking a single line, eyes fixed on harmony alone or difference alone. Perhaps this is what the words in Luke mean: "the kingdom of God is not coming with outward show; nor will they say 'Lo, here it is!' or 'There!' For behold, the kingdom of God is in the midst of you."[57] The *Pastoral Constitution on the Church in the Modern World* suggests another consequence of this basic relationship between history and salvation: "We do not know when the earth and humanity are to be consummated; nor do we know how the universe is to be transformed."[58]

Here surely lies the formal solution to our problem—a solution commended by the principal acts of revelation. In the concrete working-out of this relationship, however, we can discover many ways of realizing it, ways that have different, distinct shapes. The correct choice of means appropriate to this solution in various periods of history and, for example, in areas that belong to the First, Second, and Third Worlds will call for different procedures. What is effective in sections of Europe and North America that have a highly developed industrial economy does not have the same significance on continents and in areas of the world where most of the people are hungry. And still, however considerable the differences, we may not infringe on the above-mentioned basic relationship between human development and Christian salvation.

In this matter we have unambiguous criteria at hand. The basic relationship is disturbed, for example, if the practice of social and political liberation has such priority that divine worship, prayer, the eucharist and other sacraments, individual ethics and all questions about final human destiny (death and eternal life), and the exhausting struggle within history against the powers of darkness[59] take second place. On the other hand, in situations of poverty and injustice those truths of the faith must be proclaimed and practiced in such a way as not to corroborate a frequent reproach: the church disguises human distress, does no more than lull the poor in their very afflictions. Offering authentic relief is something totally different from raising hopes futilely comforting, hopes that only blunt the feeling of anguish.

RELATIONSHIP BETWEEN HUMAN DEVELOPMENT AND SALVATION IN THE CHURCH'S COMMISSION

To commend the significance of the church for the world is also to stress pointedly that the community which is church is always concretely circumstanced and that in these circumstances political options have already been taken. The church, though a special kind of community, must always remember that its life is ceaselessly lived on a stage where candidates for power compete with one another, where power is exercised in concrete ways, where power is linked to ideologies.

The church "is not bound exclusively and inseparably to any race or nation, to any one particular way of life, to any customary pattern of living, old or new."[60] In virtue of its origin, supernatural character, religious mission, and eschatological hope, it cannot be confounded with any sociopolitical system or linked with it by necessary, unbreakable ties.

If the church must be careful not to be entrapped by the power seekers, no more ought it surrender to sheer neutrality or unsympathetic detachment and retire to a purely nonpolitical role. It is a fact that in many parts of today's world the church is so dreadfully restricted that its witness to faith is invited in other forms, forms no less prophetic; primary among these are suffering in the footsteps of our Lord and silence by coercion.

The church cannot allow itself the cunning stratagems that characterize politics, but it must take care to anticipate the political consequences of its actions and its omissions. It can share in the blame when it does not denounce the situation of the poor and the oppressed, of those who suffer injustice — much more if it covers over such a situation and leaves it unchanged.

And so the church, on the model of the Old Testament prophets, should sharpen its conscience, so as to make a critique of the social order under the guidance of faith. A strong kinship with the poor ("poor" in its largest sense; e.g., those who are afflicted by any serious spiritual, psychological, or material wants) and effective assistance to them have been from olden times among the principal functions of the church and all its members. In our day, however, this task has become the preeminent witness to a living faith; for many outside the church, it is an inestimable criterion of the church's credibility.

To build up and shape the social and political order is a task committed in a special way to the laity.[61] But the church as a whole — represented particularly by the ministerial functions of the supreme pontiff, bishops, priests, and deacons — may not keep silent in conditions where human dignity and elementary human rights are crushed. This granted, the whole church is under obligation to express its convictions quickly and courageously.

But in many individual circumstances it is possible for Christians to opt freely among different paths that lead to the one same goal.[62] In consequence, Christians cannot utterly avoid controversy on social and political issues. "Where Christians exercise different options and on the face of it are apparently in disagreement, the church asks that they try to understand one another's positions and reasons with kindliness and appreciation."[63] Without concealing one's own convictions, each should try by persuasion and encouragement to contribute to the realization of the common objective. Where opinions differ, therefore, Christians may never forget this maxim of Vatican II: "The bonds that unite the faithful are more powerful than anything that divides them."[64]

Nevertheless, the church's unity is seriously imperiled if the differences that exist between social "classes" are taken up into a systematic "class struggle." Where you have those "class" differences, you can hardly avoid conflict. Christians are recognized in the first instance by the way they try to solve such tensions: they do not persuade the masses to destroy violence by counterviolence; rather, they try to effect change by, e.g., shaping human consciences, entering into discussion, initiating and supporting nonviolent action.[65] Nor may the Christian bypass the primary end: reconciliation.

We must also guard against the danger that social and political hostilities might supersede all else, so that, e.g., Christians of divergent positions no longer celebrate the eucharist together or shut one another out of their eucharist. The point is, political options may not become so contentious as to damage the universality of the Christian message of salvation. This message is to be carried to all, even the rich and the oppressors; for the church ought not exclude any human person from its love.

The church should constantly remind persons that politics does not have a kind of absolute value, and should be increasingly concerned to strip politics of such value. An exclusive political option, intolerant of any other option, becomes despotic and subverts the very nature of politics. It is the church's obligation—a duty it cannot forgo—to oppose the dictatorial claims of a state which would maintain that all the dimensions of human living fall under its sole control.

It is true that in such circumstances the church at times finds it difficult or impossible to manifest its mind in the public forum. Still, it does its duty surpassingly well if, in imitation of its Lord, it responds to such situations by courageous protest, by silent suffering, even by martyrdom in its various shapes. But even in such extreme situations the Christian liberation that leads to freedom cannot be totally fettered. This is our sovereign comfort; here is the high point of our confidence.

CONCLUSION

In dealing with these questions, we become strikingly aware of the diverse situations that confront the local churches within the Church catholic;

and this diversity is a cause for concern. Social, cultural, and political differences can at times weigh upon us with such increasing heaviness that our common unity in faith, the centrality of faith, seems no longer capable of overcoming our tensions and our rendings.

In our discussions we too were able to observe with some clarity the varying situations in which different peoples live. Now, no one in the church speaks simply for oneself; and so all of us should listen to the cries of our brothers and sisters, all those all over the world who are treated with injustice, are oppressed by tribulations, suffer from poverty, are distressed by hunger. Here too we can learn from one another, so as to keep ourselves from repeating afresh the mistaken solutions that have plagued the history of the church and of human societies (e.g., when politics is divinized).

In this effort it is the Spirit of Christ that links us all. In this connection, the church's unity and catholicity amid the variety of its peoples and of human cultures is simultaneously a gift to us and a claim on us. What has been laboriously achieved, however, must not be facilely jeopardized. This is particularly the case with all issues touching the relationship between human development and Christian salvation.

NOTES

1. *Gaudium et Spes*, 4.
2. See notes 30–38.
3. See Luke 4:18ff.
4. Sometimes *Gaudium et Spes*, 39, is referred to (a new earth and a new heaven).
5. See ibid., 10, 11, 57, 59, 61; *Ad Gentes*, 8; *Populorum Progressio*, 15–16.
6. See *Gaudium et Spes*, 22, 26, 38, 41, 57; *Dignitatis Humanae*, 12.
7. See First Vatican Council, Dogmatic Constitution *Dei Filius* (DS 3005).
8. Ibid.
9. See Exod. 1–24.
10. See Exod. 24.
11. See, e.g., Ps. 18.
12. Amos 2:6f.; 3:10; 5:11; 6:4ff.; 8:4ff.
13. See Isa. 5:8f.; Micah 2.
14. Hos. 4:1f.; 6:4, 6; 10:12.
15. Isa. 1:17, 23; 10:1f.
16. Isa. 3:1ff.; 1:21ff.; 10:1ff.
17. Isa. 5:8.
18. Isa. 1:21ff.; 3:14ff.
19. See Judg. 9:22f.; 1 Kings 12.
20. See Joel 3:1f.
21. Isa. 1:16f.
22. See Isa. 1:24ff.; Exod. 3:7–9; Ps. 103:6, 72:12ff.; Deut. 10:17ff.
23. See Ezek. 18; Jer. 31:29ff.
24. See, e.g., Isa. 55:3–5; Exod. 34:40–48; Jer. 31:31ff.
25. See Ps. 9:10; 72:146; Judith 9:11.

26. See Exod. 22:10; Lev. 9:13, 18, 33; Deut. 10:18; 24:14; Ps. 82:2–4.

27. See, e.g., Isa. 61:1 in Luke 4:16ff.

28. See Mark 12:29ff. and Lev. 19:18.

29. See Matt. 5:3–12.

30. See Luke 6:35; Matt. 25:31–46.

31. E.g., Luke 6:24ff.; Matt. 6:24; 1 Cor. 11:20ff.; Luke 12:16ff.; James 2:1ff.; 5:1ff.

32. See Luke 6:20; 1 Cor. 12:22ff.

33. Mark 10:2; Luke 12:33.

34. See Mark 10:42–45; Matt. 20:25–28; Luke 22:25–27.

35. See Matt. 23:8; 25:41ff.

36. See 2 Cor. 8:1ff.

37. See 1 Cor. 12:28; 15:15; Rom. 12:7; 16:1; Phil. 1:1; 1 Tim. 3:8, 12.

38. See Rom. 5–7.

39. Gal. 5:1.

40. See Gal. 5:6, 13.

41. See Gal. 5:1.

42. See Matt. 25.

43. See Schema Pontificae Commissionis a Iustitia et Pace, *The Church and Human Rights*, Vatican City, 1975.

44. See *Populorum Progressio*, 21.

45. See *Gaudium et Spes*, 36, 38, 40, 42, 43, 58; *Apostolicam Actuositatem*, 7.

46. *Gaudium et Spes*, 38.

47. See 1 Cor. 13:8.

48. See *Gaudium et Spes*, 39.

49. See *Lumen Gentium*, 35.

50. See *Gaudium et Spes*, 38, 39.

51. See *Lumen Gentium*, 36.

52. *Apostolicam Actuositatem*, 5, 7.

53. Synod of Bishops, 1971, "Justice in the World," Vatican ed., p. 5.

54. This was the interpretation given by the synod, 1974.

55. *Apostolicam Actuositatem*, 7.

56. *Gaudium et Spes*, 22, 78.

57. Luke 17:20ff.

58. *Gaudium et Spes*, 39.

59. Ibid., 13b.

60. Ibid., 58; see *Lumen Gentium*, 9; *Gaudium et Spes*, 42.

61. *Apostolicam Actuositatem*, 7; *Lumen Gentium* 31, 37; *Gaudium et Spes*, 43.

62. *Gaudium et Spes*, 43, develops this viewpoint.

63. Paul VI, *Octogesima Adveniens*, 50.

64. *Gaudium et Spes*, 92.

65. We cannot treat here at greater length further questions with regard to force or violence.

21

Gregory Baum
"German Theologians and Liberation Theology"
(May 1978)

In November 1977 a group of German theologians made public a statement of protest against the attacks made on liberation theology by some Latin American bishops and especially by some bishops and relief organizations in West Germany. Included among the signers of the statement were some of the most distinguished names in contemporary theology: Karl Rahner, Herbert Vorgrimler, Johannes B. Metz, Norbert Greinacher, Martin Niemoller, Helmut Gollwitzer, Ernst Käsemann, and Paulus Engelhardt. The statement was published in English in Cross Currents, *28 (Spring 1978), pp. 66-70.*

In the accompanying article, Gregory Baum discusses the West German statement as well as the negative reactions it elicited in German churches and political circles. He concludes that the document has been of great value, since it clearly revealed to the world the ecclesiastical campaign against liberation theology as well as the plans that had been made to secure that theology's condemnation in the forthcoming Puebla bishops' conference. The text is taken from The Ecumenist, *16 (May-June 1978), pp. 49-51.*

In November 1977 Karl Rahner joined a group of German theologians who protested against the ecclesiastical campaign to discredit the theology of liberation and various movements in Latin America related to it. The group of theologians included Johannes Baptist Metz, Norbert Greinacher, and Herbert Vorgrimler, all of whom are known to the English-speaking world through translations. The memorandum signed by this group related the facts of this campaign and brought out in particular the involvement of Bishop Hengsbach. Bishop Hengsbach is the president of the important assistance program for Latin America, called Adveniat, organized by the German bishops. It collects vast sums of money to help the church on the impoverished Latin American continent. Bishop Hengsbach is in charge of the distribution of these funds. Bishop Hengsbach is also the co-founder of a committee that aims at the destruction of liberation theology. Some of the funds of Adveniat are used to promote this cause. The purpose of the campaign is to achieve the ecclesiastical condemnation of liberation theology at the coming meeting of the Latin American Bishops' Conference meeting at Puebla, Mexico, in October 1978.

To understand the present conflict in the church we recall that in 1968 the Latin American Bishops' Conference meeting at Medellín, Colombia, affirmed the theology of liberation and assumed a position in favor of the liberation of the Latin American peoples from social misery, dependence, and tutelage. The bishops then acknowledged the oppression inflicted on the people of their continent as "social sin" and proclaimed that the redemption of Jesus Christ included the liberation of the people from this state of affairs. The bishops analyzed the economic forces that kept the people of Latin America in perpetual misery and accepted what economists have called the "theory of dependency." According to this theory, present corporate capitalism inevitably makes the industrialized center of the system feed upon the periphery. The periphery is the source of raw materials and cheap labor, and offers an extended market for goods produced at the center; and thus whatever money the center invests in the periphery, or even extends to it by way of cheap loans and assistance, inevitably produces increased returns for the center. At Medellín the Latin American bishops questioned the language of development and adopted the perspective of liberation. They recognized the "institutionalized violence" the system inflicts upon the people and in this manner encouraged the radical movements in Latin America.

Since then, most countries in Latin America have come to be ruled by military governments which defend the present economic system, even though it serves only a small minority on the continent. In the name of national security, these governments suppress civil liberties; with the help of large police forces they inhibit the freedom of expression and the freedom of association. These governments are particularly distressed at the left wing of the Catholic Church and at the Protestant groups that have joined the liberation struggle in Latin America. In many countries the church is under great pressure: lay persons, priests, and in some instances, bishops have been sent to prison, tortured, and some have disappeared altogether. At the same time, there are some bishops in the church who approve of the governments' efforts to crush the Catholic left.

CONTENT OF THE MEMORANDUM

The memorandum of the German theologians reveals the facts of the ecclesiastical campaign against liberation theology. Active in it are particularly Archbishops López Trujillo of Bogotá and D. Castrillon of Pereira, Colombia. Since Trujillo is the secretary of the Latin American Bishops'

Conference (CELAM), his group wields powerful influence in the church. It is assisted by the notorious Father Roger Vekemans, the director of the Center of Studies for Development and Integration in Latin America (CEDIAL) in Bogotá, Colombia. Vekemans has been one of the principal fighters against liberation theology. He plays a central role in the Committee on Church and Liberation, which has been set up to bring together bishops and theologians of Latin America and Europe to fight the influence of liberation theology and develop a more "spiritual" theological approach that does not interfere with economic and political matters. The German memorandum reveals what is well known to North American readers of the *National Catholic Reporter*, that Father Roger Vekemans is receiving large sums of money from the CIA to help him in the campaign to discredit critical theology and foster a piety among Latin Americans that makes them accept the sufferings of life with patience and long for eternal salvation. Father Roger Vekemans also receives money from Adveniat. He is supported by some ecclesiastical institutions, such as Opus Dei, in his effort to neutralize the critical spirit in Catholicism.

The Committee on Church and Liberation was created in February 1973 when Bishop Hengsbach, the president of Adveniat, was visiting a group of Latin American bishops and theologians in Bogotá, Colombia. Since then, the committee has met in October 1973, June 1974, and April 1975. None of the theologians who authored the theology of liberation were ever invited to attend. These gatherings were planning meetings to promote the campaign against critical thought in the church. From March 2 to 6, 1976, the committee organized a large meeting at Rome, under the chairmanship of Hengsbach and Trujillo, which was largely financed with German money. The proceedings of this conference, available at the Centre Oecuménique de Liaison International, Paris, are briefly summarized in the German memorandum. The papers given at the conference oppose all reinterpretations of the Christian faith that have social and political impact. They regard as principal enemy of the church the advocates of liberation theology and the group called "Christians for Socialism." They accuse these theologians of making use of a Marxist analysis of society (even though papal and episcopal documents have fully recognized the usefulness of this analytical method; see *Octogesima Adveniens*) and consider their influence on the church as a dangerous disease that could lead to radical social upheaval.

What this campaign against liberation theology does not admit is that the new, critical spirit has profoundly influenced theological and spiritual writings in the church everywhere and even found expression in papal and episcopal documents. In Latin America, beginning with Medellín, several episcopal documents from a variety of countries have adopted the liberation perspective. This perspective was acknowledged in principle by the Third Synod of Bishops held in Rome in 1971, in the document "Justice in the World." In the same year Pope Paul VI wrote a now famous letter to Archbishop Roy of Quebec City, *Octogesima Adveniens*, in which he acknowledges the enormous attraction of socialism on Catholics in many parts of the world. The pope recognizes the desire of these Catholics to participate with their fellow men and women in the building of a society beyond capitalism: and he even presents a nuanced picture of Marxism, distinguishing between doctrinaire and nondoctrinaire forms and restricting the church's condemnation to doctrinaire Marxism alone.

The purpose of the present campaign against liberation theology is to provoke an ecclesiastical condemnation of the new trend at the next meeting of the Latin American Bishops' Conference at Puebla, Mexico, in October 1978. This reveals the importance of the German theologians' memorandum. They want to alert the public and more especially the Latin American bishops to the nature of the present campaign and the funds with which it is supported.

UNFAVORABLE REACTION

The German memorandum made three specific points: it revealed the militant campaign against liberation theology financed largely by German money; it protested that Bishop Hengsbach, president of Adveniat, was at the same time the main instigator of the campaign and supported it with funds collected for Adveniat; and, third, it complained that in the distribution of German money in Latin America "nonpolitical" groups are favored — that is, the groups that do not criticize the existing order.

The memorandum caused a great deal of excitement in Germany. On the whole, it was not well received. The ecclesiastical institutions and the Catholic press sponsored by them interpreted the memorandum as an attack against Adveniat. One headline read: "Terror against Adveniat." The Catholic press and the official declarations of ecclesiastics misrepresented the memorandum; they alleged that the German theologians had accused Adveniat of giving money *only* to conservative, compliant Catholic groups. They made no reference to the militant campaign against liberation theology; they were totally silent about the curious fact that Bishop Hengsbach, president of Adveniat, is the driving force behind the committee; and they distorted the complaint of the memorandum that Adveniat tended to favor conservative Catholic enterprises. The official German church simply replied that Adveniat has offered help to critical groups in Latin America, including some of the priests engaged in popular education who were later imprisoned and shot by military governments. The memorandum, it was argued, was based on wrong information.

Because of this reaction, the original signers of the memorandum made a second public statement a few weeks later, in which they insist that their protest was not an attack on Adveniat. On the contrary, they realize the important role which Adveniat plays in the pastoral tasks of the Latin American church. The memorandum only attacked the ecclesiastical campaign against liberation theology and the use of Adveniat money to fund it. In this context, the German theologians asked for Bishop Hengsbach's resignation as president of Adveniat.

Nor was the memorandum welcome in the secular German press. At this time the German government is deeply involved in repressing the critical voices of the left and, in the name of the struggle against communist infiltration, has passed legislation that severely limits the civil liberties of Germans, especially those working for the government, which in Germany includes a wide section of the population, from teachers to railway employees. The press is behind the government in this repression; it tends to interpret all criticism of the present system as subversive activity and communist influence. It is quite common in Germany today to be summoned to the police and be examined in regard to one's political views and to the meetings one has attended in the past; some citizens are even cross-examined in regard to the views of their relatives and the meetings they have attended. These police inquiries extend into the Catholic and Protestant churches in Germany. In this political situation, the memorandum convinced the general public that the troublemakers and the critics of the system have penetrated the Christian churches. There are even voices in Germany today seriously claiming that the social teaching of German Catholicism has been affected by Marxism and is moving in a dangerous direction. (For such a view, see R. Weiler, "Catholic Social Teaching in the German Language Countries," *Christianity and Socialism*, ed. Metz/Jossua, *Concilium*, 105, 1977, pp. 50-57.)

Still, the German memorandum fulfilled a very useful service in the universal church. It informed concerned Catholics everywhere of the ecclesiastical campaign against liberation theology and made them aware of the plan to have this theology rejected by the next meeting of the Latin American Bishops' Conference at Puebla, Mexico. The draft documents written for this meeting have been composed in a spirit hostile to liberation theology. The Latin American bishops may of course reject these documents and compose their own. We recall that this was in fact the procedure at Vatican Council II. What is not clear, however, is to what extent the Latin American bishops stand under pressure from their governments and to what extent they fear that the defense of Medellín's perspective could lead to greater repression. Who knows what will happen at Puebla! But despite the military governments and despite the "spiritualizers" of the Christian gospel, the church goes on praying every day: "Thy kingdom come; thy will be done on earth as it is in heaven." The church believes that the earth is the place where the divine will, which is justice, is to be done.

22

Third General Conference
of the Latin American Bishops
"Evangelization in Latin America's
Present and Future"
(Puebla de los Angeles, Mexico,
January 27-February 13, 1979)

Space does not allow commentary on the Puebla Conference itself. The full official text and a number of excellent descriptions and commentaries are readily available in John Eagleson and Philip Scharper, eds., Puebla and Beyond: Documentation and Commentary *(Maryknoll, N.Y.: Orbis Books, 1979). Pope John Paul II delivered this address in the Palafoxiano Seminary in Puebla de los Angeles, Mexico, on January 28, 1979. The text includes (with the exception of an introductory paragraph) the Pope's complete remarks in Section I, "Teachers of the Truth," which aroused the most discussion, controversy, and press reports, accurate or not. The text may be found in* Puebla and Beyond, *pp. 59-64.*

POPE JOHN PAUL II, SELECTIONS FROM "OPENING ADDRESS AT THE PUEBLA CONFERENCE" (JANUARY 28, 1979)

TEACHERS OF THE TRUTH

It is a great consolation for the universal pastor to see that you come together here, not as a symposium of experts or a parliament of politicians or a congress of scientists or technologists (however important such meetings may be), but rather as a fraternal gathering of church pastors. As pastors, you keenly realize that your chief duty is to be teachers of the truth: not of a human, rational truth but of the truth that comes from God. That truth includes the principle of authentic human liberation: "You will know the truth, and the truth will set you free" (John 8:32). It is the one and only truth that offers a solid basis for an adequate "praxis."

I, 1. Carefully watching over purity of doctrine, basic in building up the Christian community, is therefore the primary and irreplaceable duty of the pastor, of the teacher of faith — in conjunction with the proclamation of the gospel. How often this was emphasized by St. Paul, who was convinced of the seriousness of carrying out this obligation (1 Tim. 1:3-7, 18-20; 2 Tim. 1:4-14)! Besides oneness in charity, oneness in truth ever remains an urgent demand upon us. In his Apostolic Exhortation *Evangelii Nuntiandi*, our very beloved Paul VI put it this way:

> The gospel that has been entrusted to us is the word of truth. This truth sets us free, and it alone provides peace of heart. It is what people are looking for when we announce the Good News. The truth about God, the truth about human beings and their mysterious destiny, the truth about the world. . . . The preacher of the gospel will be someone who, even at the cost of renunciation and sacrifice, is always seeking the truth to be transmitted to others. Such a person never betrays or misrepresents the truth out of a desire to please people, to astonish or shock people, to display originality, or to strike a pose. . . . We are pastors of the people of God; our pastoral service bids us to preserve, defend, and communicate the truth, whatever sacrifices may be entailed [78].

THE TRUTH ABOUT JESUS CHRIST

I, 2. From you, pastors, the faithful of your countries expect and demand first and foremost a careful and zealous transmission of the truth about Jesus Christ. This truth is at the core of evangelization and constitutes its essential content: "There is no authentic evangelization so long as one does not announce the name, the teaching, the life, the promises, the kingdom, the mystery of Jesus of Nazareth, the Son of God" (EN:22).

The vigor of the faith of millions will depend on a lively knowledge of this truth. On such knowledge will also depend the strength of their adhesion to the church and their active presence as Christians in the world. From it will flow options, values, attitudes, and behavior patterns that can give direction and definition to our Christian living, that can create new human beings, and then a new humanity through the conversion of the individual and social conscience (EN:18).

It is from a solid christology that light must be shed on so many of the doctrinal and pastoral themes and questions that you propose to examine in the coming days.

I, 3. So we must profess Christ before history and the world, displaying the same deeply felt and deeply lived conviction that Peter did in his profession: "You are the Messiah, . . . the Son of the living God" (Matt. 16:16).

This is the Good News, unique in a real sense. The church lives by it and for it, even as the church draws from it all that it has to offer to all human beings, regardless of nation, culture, race, epoch, age, or condition. Hence "on the basis of that profession [Peter's], the history of sacred salvation and of the people of God should take on a new dimension" (John Paul II, inaugural homily of his pontificate, October 22, 1978).

This is the one and only gospel. And as the apostle wrote so pointedly, "Even if we, or an angel from heaven, should preach to you a gospel not in accord with the one we delivered to you, let a curse be upon him" (Gal. 1:8).

I, 4. Now today we find in many places a phenomenon that is not new. We find "rereadings" of the gospel that are the product of theoretical speculations rather than of authentic meditation on the word of God and a genuine evangelical commitment. They cause confusion insofar as they depart from the central criteria of the church's faith, and people have the temerity to pass them on as catechesis to Christian communities.

In some cases people are silent about Christ's divinity, or else they indulge in types of interpretation that are at variance with the church's faith. Christ is alleged to be only a "prophet," a proclaimer of God's kingdom and love, but not the true Son of God. Hence he allegedly is not the center and object of the gospel message itself.

In other cases people purport to depict Jesus as a political activist, as a fighter against Roman domination and the authorities, and even as someone involved in the class struggle. This conception of Christ as a political figure, a revolutionary, as the subversive from Nazareth, does not tally with the church's catechesis. Confusing the insidious pretext of Jesus' accusers with the attitude of Jesus himself—which was very different—people claim that the cause of his death was the result of a political conflict; they say nothing about the Lord's willing self-surrender or even his awareness of his redemptive mission. The Gospels show clearly that for Jesus anything that would alter his mission as the servant of Yahweh was a temptation (Matt. 4:8; Luke 4:5). He does not accept the position of those who mixed the things of God with merely political attitudes (Matt. 22:21; Mark 12:17; John 18:36). He unequivocally rejects recourse to violence. He opens his message of conversion to all, and he does not exclude even the publicans. The perspective of his mission goes much deeper. It has to do with complete and integral salvation through a love that brings transformation, peace, pardon, and reconciliation. And there can be no doubt that all this imposes exacting demands on the attitude of any Christians who truly wish to serve the least of their brothers and sisters, the poor, the needy, the marginalized: all those whose lives reflect the suffering countenance of the Lord (LG:8).

I, 5. Against such "rereadings," therefore, and against the perhaps brilliant but fragile and inconsistent hypotheses flowing from them "evangelization in Latin America's present and future" cannot cease to affirm the church's faith: Jesus Christ, the Word and son of God, becomes human to draw close to human beings and to offer them, through the power of his mystery, the great gift of God that is salvation (EN: 19, 27).

This is the faith that has informed your history, that has shaped what is best in the values of your peoples, and that must continue to animate the dynamics of their future in the most energetic terms. This is the faith that reveals the vocation to concord and unity that must banish the danger of warfare from this continent of hope, a continent in which the church has been such a potent force for integration. This, in short, is the faith that has found such lively and varied expression among the faithful of Latin America in their religiosity or popular piety.

Rooted in this faith in Christ and in the bosom of the church, we are capable of serving human beings and our peoples, of penetrating their culture with the gospel, of transforming hearts, and of humanizing systems and structures.

Any form of silence, disregard, mutilation, or inadequate emphasis on the whole of the mystery of Jesus Christ that diverges from the church's faith cannot be the valid content of evangelization. "Today, under the pretext of a piety that is false, under the deceptive appearance of a preaching of the gospel message, some people are trying to deny the Lord Jesus," wrote a great bishop in the midst of the hard crises of the fourth century. And he added: "I speak the truth, so that the cause of the confusion that we are suffering may be known to all. I cannot keep silent" (St. Hilary of Poitiers, *Ad Auxentium*, 1-4). Nor can you, the bishops of today, keep silent when this confusion occurs.

This is what Pope Paul VI recommended in his opening address at the Medellín Conference: "Speak, speak, preach, write, take a position, as is said, united in plan and intention, for the defense and elucidation of the truths of the faith, on the relevance of the gospel, on the questions that interest the life of the faithful and the defense of Christian conduct."

To fulfill my duty to evangelize all of humanity, I myself will never tire of repeating: "Do not be afraid. Open wide the doors for Christ. To his saving power open the boundaries of state, economic, and political systems, the vast fields of culture, civilization, and development" (John Paul II, inaugural homily of his pontificate, October 22, 1979).

THE TRUTH ABOUT THE CHURCH'S MISSION

I, 6. As teachers of the truth, you are expected to proclaim unceasingly, but with special vigor at this moment, the truth about the mission of the church, an object of the creed we profess, and a basic, indispensable area of our fidelity. The Lord instituted the church "as a fellowship of life, charity, and truth" (LG:9); as the body, *pleroma*, and sacrament of Christ, in whom dwells the fullness of divinity (LG:7).

The church is born of our response in faith to Christ. In fact it is by sincere acceptance of the Good News that we believers gather together "in

Jesus' name to seek the kingdom together, build it up, and live it" (EN:13). The church is the gathering together of "all those who in faith look upon Jesus as the author of salvation and the source of unity and peace" (LG:9).

But on the other hand we are born of the church. It communicates to us the riches of life and grace entrusted to it. The church begets us by baptism, nourishes us with the sacraments and the word of God, prepares us for our mission, and leads us to God's plan—the reason for our existence as Christians. We are the church's children. With just pride we call the church our mother, repeating a title that has come down to us through the centuries from the earliest days (Henri de Lubac, *Méditation sur l'Église*, pp. 211ff.).

So we must invoke the church, respect it, and serve it because "one cannot have God for one's Father if one does not have the church for one's mother" (St. Cyprian, *De catholicae ecclesiae unitate*, 6, 8). After all, "how can one possibly love Christ without loving the church, since the most beautiful testimony to Christ is the following statement of St. Paul: 'He loved the church and gave himself up for it'?" (EN:16). Or, as St. Augustine puts it: "One possesses the Holy Spirit to the extent that one loves the church of Christ" (*In Ioannis evangelium*, 32, 8).

Love for the church must be composed of fidelity and trust. In the first address of my pontificate, I stressed my desire to be faithful to Vatican II, and my resolve to focus my greatest concern on the area of ecclesiology. I invited all to take up once again the Dogmatic Constitution *Lumen Gentium* and "to ponder with renewed earnestness the nature and mission of the church, its way of existing and operating, . . . not only to achieve that communion of life in Christ among all those who believe and hope in him, but also to help broaden and tighten the oneness of the whole human family" (John Paul II, Message to the Church and the World, October 17, 1978).

Now, at this critical moment in the evangelization of Latin America, I repeat my invitation: "Adherence to this conciliar document, which reflects the light of tradition and contains the dogmatic formulas enunciated a century ago by Vatican I, will provide all of us, both pastors and faithful, a sure pathway and a constant incentive—to say it once again—to tread the byways of life and history" (ibid.).

I, 7. Without a well-grounded ecclesiology, we have no guarantee of a serious and vigorous evangelizing activity.

This is so, first of all, because evangelizing is the essential mission, the specific vocation, the innermost identity of the church, which has been evangelized in turn (EN:14-15; LG:5). Sent out by the Lord, the church in turn sends out evangelizers to preach "not themselves or their personal ideas, but a gospel that neither they nor the church owns as their own absolute property, to dispose of as they may see fit" (EN:15). This is so, in the second place, because "for no one is evangelizing an isolated, individual act; rather, it is a profoundly ecclesial action, . . . an action of the church"

(EN:60). Far from being subject to the discretionary authority of individualistic criteria and perspectives, it stands "in communion with the church and its pastors" (EN:60). Hence a correct vision of the church is indispensable for a correct view of evangelization.

How could there be any authentic evangelization in the absence of prompt, sincere respect for the sacred magisterium, a respect based on the clear realization that in submitting to it, the people of God is not accepting the word of human beings but the authentic word of God? (1 Thess. 2:13; LG:12). "The 'objective' importance of this magisterium must be kept in mind and defended against the insidious attacks that now appear here and there against some of the solid truths of our Catholic faith" (John Paul II, Message to the Church and the World, October 17, 1978).

I am well aware of your attachment and availability to the See of Peter and of the love you have always shown it. In the Lord's name I express my heartfelt thanks for the deeply ecclesial outlook implied in that, and I wish you yourselves the consolation of counting on the loyal adherence of your faithful.

I, 8. In the abundant documentation that went into the preparation of this conference, and particularly in the contributions of many churches, one sometimes notices a certain uneasiness in interpreting the nature and mission of the church. Allusion is made, for example, to the separation that some set up between the church and the kingdom of God. Emptied of its full content, the kingdom of God is understood in a rather secularist sense: that is, we do not arrive at the kingdom through faith and membership in the church but rather merely by structural change and socio-political involvement. Where there is a certain kind of commitment and praxis for justice, there the kingdom is already present. This view forgets that "the church . . . receives the mission to proclaim and to establish among all peoples the kingdom of Christ and of God. It becomes on earth the initial budding forth of that kingdom" (LG:5).

In one of his beautiful catechetical instructions, Pope John Paul I alludes to the virtue of hope. He says: "By contrast, it is a mistake to state that political, economic, and social liberation coincide with salvation in Jesus Christ; that the *regnum Dei* is identified with the *regnum hominis*" (John Paul I, Catechetical Lesson on the Theological Virtue of Hope, September 20, 1978).

In some instances an attitude of mistrust is fostered toward the "institutional" or "official" church, which is described as alienating. Over against it is set another, people's church, one which "is born of the people" and is fleshed out in the poor. These positions could contain varying and not always easily measurable degrees of familiar ideological forms of conditioning. The council has called our attention to the exact nature and mission of the church. It has reminded us of the contribution made to its deeper oneness and its ongoing construction by those whose task is to minister to the community and who must count on the collaboration of all the people of God. But let us face the fact: "if the gospel proclaimed by us seems to be rent by doctrinal disputes, ideological polarizations, or mutual condemnations among Christians, if it is at the mercy of their differing views about Christ and the church, and even of their differing conceptions of human society and its institutions, . . . how can those to whom we address our preaching fail to be disturbed, disoriented, and even scandalized?" (EN:77).

THE TRUTH ABOUT HUMAN BEINGS

I, 9. The truth we owe to human beings is, first and foremost, a truth about themselves. As witnesses to Jesus Christ, we are heralds, spokesmen, and servants of this truth. We cannot reduce it to the principles of some philosophical system, or to mere political activity. We cannot forget it or betray it.

Perhaps one of the most glaring weaknesses of present-day civilization lies in an inadequate view of the human being. Undoubtedly our age is the age that has written and spoken the most about the human being; it is the age of various humanisms, the age of anthropocentrism. But paradoxically it is also the age of the deepest anxieties about identity and destiny; it is the age when human beings have been debased to previously unsuspected levels, when human values have been trodden underfoot as never before.

How do we explain this paradox? We can say that it is the inexorable paradox of atheistic humanism. It is the drama of people severed from an essential dimension of their being—the Absolute—and thus confronted with the worst possible diminution of their being. *Gaudium et Spes* goes to the heart of the problem when it says: "Only in the mystery of the incarnate word does the human mystery take on light" (GS:22).

Thanks to the gospel, the church possesses the truth about the human being. It is found in an anthropology that the church never ceases to explore more deeply and to share. The primordial assertion of this anthropology is that the human being is the image of God and cannot be reduced to a mere fragment of nature or to an anonymous element in the human city (GS: 12, 14). This is the sense intended by St. Irenaeus when he wrote: "The glory of the human being is God; but the receptacle of all God's activity, wisdom, and power is the human being" (St. Irenaeus, *Adversus Haereses*, III, 20, 2-3).

I made especially pointed reference to this irreplaceable foundation of the Christian conception of the human being in my Christmas message: "Christmas is the feast of the human being. . . . Viewed in quantitative terms, the human being is an object of calculation. . . . But at the same time the human being is single, unique, and unrepeatable, someone thought of and chosen from eternity, someone called and identified by name" (John Paul II, Christmas Message, December 25, 1978).

Faced with many other forms of humanism, which frequently are locked into a strictly economic, biological, or psychological view of the human being, the church has the right and the duty to proclaim the truth about the human being that it received from its teacher, Jesus Christ. God grant that no external coercion will prevent the church from doing so. But above all, God grant that the church itself will not fail to do so out of fear or doubt, or because it has let itself be contaminated by other brands of humanism, or for lack of confidence in its original message.

So when a pastor of the church clearly and unambiguously announces the truth about the human being, which was revealed by him who knew "what was in the human heart" (John 2:25), he should be encouraged by the certainty that he is rendering the best service to human beings.

This complete truth about human beings is the basis of the church's social teaching, even as it is the basis of authentic liberation. In the light of this truth we see that human beings are not the pawns of economic or political processes, that instead these processes are geared toward human beings and subject to them.

I have no doubt that this truth about human beings, as taught by the church, will emerge strengthened from this pastoral meeting.

PUEBLA FINAL DOCUMENT, "EVANGELIZATION, LIBERATION, AND HUMAN PROMOTION"

This section of the Puebla document (nos. 470-562) contains the most explicit attention given to many of the fundamental themes of liberation theology, both in its theory and practice. Most liberation theologians considered it a very fruitful dialogue and praised this section, perhaps with a feeling of relief that the theology had not been condemned. There was some disagreement with the document's social analysis as, for example, in the statement that the social doctrine of the church is completely free of ideologies. This text may be found in Puebla and Beyond, *pp. 189-202.*

4.1. A WORD OF ENCOURAGEMENT

We fully recognize the efforts undertaken by many Latin American Christians to explore the particularly conflict-ridden situations of our peoples in terms of the faith and to shed the light of God's word on them. We encourage all Christians to continue to provide this evangelizing service and to consider the criteria for reflection and investigation; and we urge them to put special care into preserving and promoting ecclesial communion on both the local and the universal levels.

We are also aware of the fact that since the Medellín Conference pastoral agents have made significant advances and encountered quite a few difficulties. Rather than discouraging us, this should inspire us to seek out new paths and better forms of accomplishment.

4.2. THE SOCIAL TEACHING OF THE CHURCH

The contribution of the church to liberation and human promotion has gradually been taking shape in a series of doctrinal guidelines and criteria for action that we now are accustomed to call "the social teaching of the church." These teachings have their source in sacred Scripture, in the teaching of the fathers and major theologians of the church, and in the magisterium (particularly that of the most recent popes). As is evident from their origin, they contain permanently valid elements grounded in an anthropology that derives from the message of Christ and in the perennial values of Christian ethics. But they also contain changing elements that correspond to the particular conditions of each country and each epoch.

Following Paul VI (OA:4), we can formulate the matter this way: attentive to the signs of the time, which are interpreted in the light of the gospel and the church's magisterium, the whole Christian community is called upon to assume responsibility for concrete options and their effective implementation in order to respond to the summons presented by changing circumstances. Thus these social teachings possess a dynamic character. In their elaboration and application lay persons are not to be passive executors but rather active collaborators with their pastors, contributing their experience as Christians, and their professional, scientific competence (GS:42).

Clearly, then, it is the whole Christian community, in communion with its legitimate pastors and guided by them, that is the responsible subject of evangelization, liberation, and human promotion.

The primary object of this social teaching is the personal dignity of the human being, who is the image of God, and the protection of all inalienable human rights (PP:14-21). As the need has arisen, the church has proceeded to spell out its teaching with regard to other areas of life: social life, economics, politics, and cultural life. But the aim of this doctrine of the church, which offers its own specific vision of the human being and humanity (PP:13), is always the promotion and integral liberation of human beings in terms of both their earthly and their transcendent dimensions. It is a contribution to the construction of the ultimate and definitive kingdom, although it does not equate earthly progress with Christ's kingdom (GS:39).

If our social teachings are to be credible and to be accepted by all, they must effectively respond to the serious challenges and problems arising out of the reality of Latin America. Human beings who are diminished by all sorts of deficiencies and wants are calling for urgent efforts of promotion on our part, and this makes our works of social assistance necessary. Nor can we propose our teaching without being challenged by it in turn insofar as our personal and institutional behavior is concerned. It requires us to display consistency, creativity, boldness, and total commitment. Our social conduct is an integral part of our following of Christ. Our reflection on the church's projection into the world as a sacrament of communion and salvation is a part of our theological reflection. For "evangelization would not be complete if it did not take into account the reciprocal appeal that arises in the course of time between the gospel on the one hand and the concrete personal and social life of human beings on the other" (EN:29).

Human promotion entails activities that help to arouse human awareness in every dimension and to make human beings themselves the active protagonists of their own human and Christian development. It educates people in living together, it gives impetus to organization, it fosters Christian sharing of goods, and it is an effective aid to communion and participation.

If the Christian community is to bear consistent witness in its efforts for liberation and human betterment, each country and local church will organize its social pastoral effort around ongoing and adequate organisms. These organisms will sustain and stimulate commitment to the community, ensuring the needed coordination of activities through a continuing dialogue with all the members of the church. Caritas and other organisms, which have been doing effective work for many years, can offer valuable help to this end.

If they are to be faithful and complete, theology, preaching, and catechesis must keep in mind the whole human being and all human beings. In timely and adequate terms they must offer people today "an especially vigorous message concerning liberation" (EN:29), framing it in terms of the "overall plan of salvation" (EN:38). So it seems that we must offer some clarifying remarks about the concept of liberation itself at this present moment in the life of our continent.

4.3. DISCERNING THE NATURE OF LIBERATION IN CHRIST

At the Medellín Conference we saw the elucidation of a dynamic process of integral liberation. Its positive echoes were taken up by *Evangelii Nuntiandi* and by John Paul II in his message to this conference. This proclamation imposes an urgent task on the church, and it belongs to the very core of an evangelization that seeks the authentic realization of the human being.

But there are different conceptions and applications of liberation. Though they share common traits, they contain points of view that can hardly be brought together satisfactorily. The best thing to do, therefore, is to offer criteria that derive from the magisterium and that provide us with the necessary discernment regarding the original conception of Christian liberation.

There are two complementary and inseparable elements. The first is liberation from all the forms of bondage, from personal and social sin, and from everything that tears apart the human individual and society; all this finds its source to be in egotism, in the mystery of iniquity. The second element is liberation for progressive growth in being through communion with God and other human beings; this reaches its culmination in the perfect communion of heaven, where God is all in all and weeping forever ceases.

This liberation is gradually being realized in history, in our personal history and that of our peoples. It takes in all the different dimensions of life: the social, the political, the economic, the cultural, and all their interrelationships. Through all these dimensions must flow the transforming treasure of the gospel. It has its own specific and distinctive contribution to make, which must be safeguarded. Otherwise we would be faced with the situation described by Paul VI in *Evangelii Nuntiandi*: "The church would lose its innermost significance. Its message of liberation would have no originality of its own. It would be prone to takeover or manipulation by ideological systems and political parties" (EN:32).

It should be made clear that this liberation is erected on the three great pillars that John Paul II offered us as defining guidelines: that is, the truth about Jesus Christ, the truth about the church, and the truth about human beings.

Thus we mutilate liberation in an unpardonable way if we do not achieve liberation from sin and all its seductions and idolatry, and if we do not help to make concrete the liberation that Christ won on the cross. We do the very same thing if we forget the crux of liberative evangelization, which is to transform human beings into active subjects of their own individual and communitarian development. And we also do the very same thing if we overlook dependence and the forms of bondage that violate basic rights that come from God, the Creator and Father, rather than being bestowed by governments or institutions, however powerful they may be.

The sort of liberation we are talking about knows how to use evangelical means, which have their own distinctive efficacy. It does not resort to violence of any sort, or to the dialectics of class struggle. Instead it relies on the vigorous energy and activity of Christians, who are moved by the Spirit to respond to the cries of countless millions of their brothers and sisters.

We pastors in Latin America have the most serious reasons for pressing for liberative evangelization. It is not just that we feel obliged to remind people of individual and social sinfulness. The further reason lies in the fact that since the Medellín Conference the situation has grown worse and more acute for the vast majority of our population.

We are pleased to note many examples of efforts to live out liberative evangelization in all its fullness. One of the chief tasks involved in continuing to encourage Christian liberation is the creative search for approaches free of ambiguity and reductionism (EN:32) and fully faithful to the word of God. Given to us in the church, that word stirs us to offer joyful proclamation to the poor as one of the messianic signs of Christ's kingdom.

John Paul II has made this point well: "There are many signs that help us to distinguish when the liberation in question is Christian and when, on the other hand, it is based on ideologies that make it inconsistent with an evangelical view of humanity, of things, and of events" (EN:35). These signs derive from the content that the evangelizers proclaim or from the concrete attitudes that they adopt. At the level of content one must consider how faithful they are to the word of God, to the church's living tradition, and to its magisterium. As for attitudes, one must consider what sense of communion they feel, with the bishops first of all, and then with the other sectors of God's people. Here one must also consider what contribution they make to the real building up of the community; how they channel their love into caring for the poor, the sick, the dispossessed, the neglected, and the oppressed; and how, discovering in these people the image of the poor and suffering Jesus, they strive to alleviate their needs and to serve Christ in them (LG:8). Let us make no mistake about it: as if by some evangelical instinct, the humble and simple faithful spontaneously sense when the gospel is being served in the church and when it is being eviscerated and asphyxiated by other interests (OAP:III,6).

Those who hold to the vision of humanity offered by Christianity also take on the commitment not to measure the sacrifice it costs to ensure that all will enjoy the status of authentic children of God, and brothers and sisters in Jesus Christ. Thus liberative evangelization finds its full realization in the communion of all in Christ, as the Father of all persons wills.

4.4. LIBERATIVE EVANGELIZATION FOR A HUMAN SOCIETAL LIFE WORTHY OF THE CHILDREN OF GOD

Other than God, nothing is divine or worthy of worship. Human beings fall into slavery when they divinize or absolutize wealth, power, the state, sex, pleasure, or anything created by God—including their own being or human reason. God is the source of radical liberation from all forms of idolatry, because the adoration of what is not adorable and the absolutization of the relative leads to violation of the innermost reality of human persons: that is, their relationship with God and their personal fulfillment. Here is the liberative word par excellence: "You shall do homage to the Lord your God; him alone shall you adore" (Matt. 4:10; cf. Deut. 5:6ff.). The collapse of idols restores to human beings their essential realm of freedom. God, who is supremely free, wants to enter into dialogue with free beings who are capable of making their own choices and exercising their responsibilities on both the individual and communitarian levels. So we have a human history that, even though it possesses its own consistency and autonomy, is called upon to be consecrated to God by humanity. Authentic liberation frees us from oppression so that we may be able to say yes to a higher good.

Humanity and earthly goods. By virtue of their origin and nature, by the will of the creator, worldly goods and riches are meant to serve the utility and progress of each and every human being and people. Thus each and every one enjoys a primary, fundamental, and absolutely inviolable right to share in the use of these goods, insofar as that is necessary for the worthy fulfillment of the human person. All other rights, including the right of property and free trade, are subordinate to that right. As John Paul II teaches: "There is a social mortgage on all private property" (OAP:III,4). To be compatible with primordial human rights, the right of ownership must be primarily a right of use and administration; and though this does not rule out ownership and control, it does not make these absolute or unlimited. Ownership should be a source of freedom for all, but never a source of domination or special privilege. We have a grave and pressing duty to restore this right to its original and primary aim (PP:23).

Liberation from the idol of wealth. Earthly goods become an idol and a serious obstacle to the kingdom of God (Matt. 19:23-26) when human beings devote all their attention to possessing them or even coveting them. Then earthly goods turn into an absolute, and "you cannot give yourself to God and money" (Luke 16:13).

Turned into an absolute, wealth is an obstacle to authentic freedom. The cruel contrast between luxurious wealth and extreme poverty, which is so visible throughout our continent and which is further aggravated by the corruption that often invades public and professional life, shows the great extent to which our nations are dominated by the idol of wealth.

These forms of idolatry are concretized in two opposed forms that have a common root. One is liberal capitalism. The other, a reaction against liberal capitalism, is Marxist collectivism. Both are forms of what can be called "institutionalized injustice."

Finally, as already noted, we must take cognizance of the devastating effects of an uncontrolled process of industrialization and a process of urbanization that is taking on alarming proportions. The depletion of our natural resources and the pollution of the environment will become a critical problem. Once again we affirm that the consumptionist tendencies of the more developed nations must undergo a thorough revision. They must take into account the elementary needs of the poor peoples who constitute the majority of the world's population.

The new humanism proclaimed by the church, which rejects all forms of idolatry, "will enable our contemporaries to enjoy the higher values of love and friendship, of prayer and contemplation, and thus find themselves. This is what will guarantee humanity's authentic development — its transition from less than human conditions to truly human ones" (PP:20). In this way economic planning will be put in the service of human beings rather than human beings being put in the service of economics (PP:34). The latter is what happens in the two forms of idolatry mentioned above (liberal capitalism and Marxist collectivism). The former is the only way to make sure that what human beings "have" does not suffocate what they "are" (GS:35).

Human beings and power. The various forms of power in society are a basic part of the order of creation. Hence in themselves they are essentially good, insofar as they render service to the human community.

Authority, which is necessary in every society, comes from God (Rom. 13:1; John 19:11). It is the faculty of giving commands in accordance with right reason. Hence its obligatory force derives from the moral order (PT:47), and it should develop out of that ground in order to oblige people in conscience: "authority is before all else a moral force" (PT:48; GS:74).

Sin corrupts humanity's use of power, leading people to abuse the rights of others, sometimes in more or less absolute ways. The most notorious example of this is the exercise of political power. For this is an area that involves decisions governing the overall organization of the community's temporal welfare, and it readily lends itself to abuses. Indeed it may lead not only to abuses by those in power but also to the absolutizing of power itself (GS:73) with the backing of public force. Political power is divinized when in practice it is regarded as absolute. Hence the totalitarian use of power is a form of idolatry; and as such, the church completely rejects it (GS:75). We grieve to note the presence of many authoritarian and even oppressive regimes on our continent. They constitute one of the most serious obstacles to the full development of the rights of persons, groups, and even nations.

Unfortunately, in many instances this reaches the point where the political and economic authorities of our nations are themselves made subject to even more powerful centers that are operative on an international scale. This goes far beyond the normal range of mutual relationships. And the situation is further aggravated by the fact that these centers of power are ubiquitous, covertly organized, and easily capable of evading the control of governments and even international organisms.

There is an urgent need to liberate our peoples from the idol of absolutized power so that they may live together in a society based on justice and freedom. As a youthful people with a wealth of culture and tradition, Latin Americans must carry out the mission assigned to them by history. But if they are to do this, they need a political order that will respect human dignity and ensure harmony and peace to the community, both in its internal relations and its relations with other communities. Among all the aspirations of our peoples, we would like to stress the following:

— Equality for all citizens. All have the right and the duty to participate in the destiny of their society and to enjoy equality of opportunity, bearing their fair share of the burdens, and obeying legitimately established laws.

— The exercise of their freedoms. These should be protected by basic institutions that will stand surety for the common good and respect the fundamental rights of persons and associations.

— Legitimate self-determination for our peoples. This will permit them to organize their lives in accordance with their own genius and history (GS:74) and to cooperate in a new international order.

— The urgent necessity of reestablishing justice. We are not talking only about theoretical justice recognized merely in the abstract. We are talking also about a justice that is effectively implemented in practice by institutions that are truly operative and adequate to the task.

5. EVANGELIZATION, IDEOLOGIES, AND POLITICS

5.1. INTRODUCTION

Recent years have seen a growing deterioration in the socio-political life of our countries.

They are experiencing the heavy burden of economic and institutional crises, and clear symptoms of corruption and violence.

The violence is generated and fostered by two factors: (1) what can be called institutionalized injustice in various social, political, and economic systems; and (2) ideologies that use violence as a means to win power.

The latter in turn causes the proliferation of governments based on force, which often derive their inspiration from the ideology of National Security.

As a mother and teacher whose expertise is humanity, the church must examine the conditions, systems, ideologies, and political life of our continent — shedding light on them from the standpoint of the gospel and its own social teaching. And this must be done even though it knows that people will try to use its message as their own tool.

So the church projects the light of its message on politics and ideologies, as one more form of service to its peoples and as a sure line of orientation for all those who must assume social responsibilities in one form or another.

5.2. EVANGELIZATION AND POLITICS

The political dimension is a constitutive dimension of human beings and a relevant area of human societal life. It has an all-embracing aspect because its aim is the common welfare of society. But that does not mean that it exhausts the gamut of social relationships.

Far from despising political activity, the Christian faith values it and holds it in high esteem.

Speaking in general, and without distinguishing between the roles that may be proper to its various members, the church feels it has a duty and a right to be present in this area of reality. For Christianity is supposed to evangelize the whole of human life, including the political dimension. So the church criticizes those who would restrict the scope of faith to personal or family life; who would exclude the professional, economic, social, and political orders as if sin, love, prayer, and pardon had no relevance in them.

The fact is that the need for the church's presence in the political arena flows from the very core of the Christian faith. That is to say, it flows from the lordship of Christ over the whole of life. Christ sets the seal on the definitive fellowship of humanity, wherein every human being is of equal worth: "All are one in Christ Jesus" (Gal. 3:28).

From the integral message of Christ there flows an original anthropology and theology that takes in "the concrete personal and social life of the human being" (EN:29). It is a liberating message because it saves us from the bondage of sin, which is the root and source of all oppression, injustice, and discrimination.

These are some of the reasons why the church is present in the political arena to enlighten consciences and to proclaim a message that is capable of transforming society.

The church recognizes the proper autonomy of the temporal order (GS:36). This holds true for governments, political parties, labor unions, and other groups in the social and political arena. The purpose that the Lord assigned to his church is a religious one; so when it does intervene in the socio-political arena, it is not prompted by any aim of a political, economic, or social nature. "But out of this religious mission itself come a function, a light, and an energy which can serve to structure and consolidate the human community according to the divine law" (GS:42).

Insofar as the political arena is concerned, the church is particularly interested in distinguishing between the specific functions of the laity, religious, and those who minister to the unity of the church—that is, the bishop and his priests.

5.3. Notions of Politics and Political Involvement

We must distinguish between two notions of politics and political involvement. First, in the broad sense politics seeks the common good on both the national and international plane. Its task is to spell out the fundamental values of every community—internal concord and external security—reconciling equality with freedom, public authority with the legitimate autonomy, and participation of individual persons and groups, and national sovereignty with international coexistence and solidarity. It also defines the ethics and means of social relationships. In this broad sense politics is of interest to the church, and hence to its pastors, who are ministers of unity. It is a way of paying worship to the one and only God by simultaneously desacralizing and consecrating the world to God (LG:34).

So the church helps to foster the values that should inspire politics. In every nation it interprets the aspirations of the people, especially the yearnings of those that society tends to marginalize. And it does this with its testimony, its teaching, and its varied forms of pastoral activity.

Second, the concrete performance of this fundamental political task is normally carried out by groups of citizens. They resolve to pursue and exercise political power in order to solve economic, political, and social problems in accordance with their own criteria or ideology. Here, then, we can talk about "party politics." Now even though the ideologies elaborated by such groups may be inspired by Christian doctrine, they can come to differing conclusions. No matter how deeply inspired in church teaching, no political party can claim the right to represent all the faithful because its concrete program can never have absolute value for all (cf. Pius XI, *Catholic Action and Politics*, 1937).

Party politics is properly the realm of lay persons (GS:43). Their lay status entitles them to establish and organize political parties, using an ideology and strategy that is suited to achieving their legitimate aims.

In the social teaching of the church lay people find the proper criteria deriving from the Christian view of the human being. For its part the hierarchy will demonstrate its solidarity by contributing to their adequate formation and their spiritual life, and also by nurturing their creativity so that they can explore options that are increasingly in line with the common good and the needs of the weakest.

Pastors, on the other hand, must be concerned with unity. So they will divest themselves of every partisan political ideology that might condition their criteria and attitudes. They then will be able to evangelize the political sphere as Christ did, relying on the gospel without any infusion of partisanship or ideologization. Christ's gospel would not have had such an impact on history if he had not proclaimed it as a religious message: "The Gospels show clearly that for Jesus anything that would alter his mission as the servant of Yahweh was a temptation (Matt. 4:8; Luke 4:5). He does not accept the position of those who mixed the things of God with merely political attitudes (Matt. 22:21; Mark 12:17; John 18:36)" (OAP:I,4).

Priests, also ministers of unity, and deacons must submit to the same sort of personal renunciation. If they are active in party politics, they will run the risk of absolutizing and radicalizing such activity; for their vocation is to be "men dedicated to the Absolute." As the Medellín Conference pointed out: "In the economic and social order . . . and especially in the political order, where a variety of concrete choices is offered, the priest, as priest, should not directly concern himself with decisions or leadership nor with the structuring of solutions" (Med-PR:19). And the 1971 Synod of Bishops stated: "Leadership or active militancy on behalf of any political party is to be excluded by every priest unless, in concrete and exceptional circumstances, this is truly required by the good of the community and receives the consent of the bishop after consultation with the priests' council and, if circumstances call for it, with the episcopal conference" ("The Ministerial Priesthood," part 2, no. 2). Certainly the present thrust of the church is not in that direction.

By virtue of the way in which they follow Christ, and in line with the distinctive function that is theirs within the church's mission because of their specific charism, religious also cooperate in the evangelization of the political order. Living in a society that is far from fraternal, that is taken up with consumptionism, and that has as its ultimate goal the development of its material forces of production, religious will have to give testimony of real austerity in their lifestyle, of interhuman communion, and of an intense relationship with God. They, too, will have to resist the temptation to get involved in party politics, so that they do not create confusion between the values of the gospel and some specific ideology.

Close reflection upon the recent words of the Holy Father addressed to bishops, priests, and religious will provide valuable guidance for their service in this area: "Souls that are living in habitual contact with God and that are operating in the warm light of God's love know how to defend themselves easily against the temptations of partisanship and antithesis that threaten to create painful divisions. They know how to interpret their options for the poorest and for all the victims of human egotism in the proper light of the gospel, without succumbing to forms of socio-political radicalism. In the long run such radicalism is untimely, counterproductive, and generative of new abuses. Such souls know how to draw near to the people and immerse themselves in their midst without calling into question their own religious identity or obscuring the 'specific originality' of their own vocation, which flows from following the poor, chaste, and obedient Christ. A measure of real adoration has more value and spiritual fruitfulness than the most intense activity, even apostolic activity. This is the most urgent kind of 'protest' that religious should exercise against a society where efficiency has been turned into an idol on whose altar even human dignity itself is sometimes sacrificed" (RMS).

Lay leaders of pastoral action should not use their authority in support of political parties or ideologies.

5.4. REFLECTIONS ON POLITICAL VIOLENCE

Faced with the deplorable reality of violence in Latin America, we wish to express our view clearly. Condemnation is always the proper judgment on physical and psychological torture, kidnapping, the persecution of political dissidents or suspect persons, and the exclusion of persons from public life because of their ideas. If these crimes are committed by the authorities entrusted with the task of safeguarding the common good, then they defile those who practice them, notwithstanding any reasons offered.

The church is just as decisive in rejecting terrorist and guerilla violence, which becomes cruel and uncontrollable when it is unleashed. Criminal acts can in no way be justified as the way to liberation. Violence inexorably engenders new forms of oppression and bondage, which usually prove to be more serious than the ones people are allegedly being liberated from. But most importantly violence is an attack on life, which depends on the creator alone. And we must also stress that when an ideology appeals to violence, it thereby admits its own weakness and inadequacy.

Our responsibility as Christians is to use all possible means to promote the implementation of nonviolent tactics in the effort to reestablish justice in economic and socio-political relations. This is in accordance with the teaching of Vatican II, which applies to both national and international life: "We cannot fail to praise those who renounce the use of violence in the vindication of their rights and who resort to methods of defense which are otherwise available to weaker parties too, provided that this can be done without injury to the rights and duties of others or of the community" (GS:78).

"We are obliged to state and reaffirm that violence is neither Christian nor evangelical, and that brusque, violent structural changes will be false, ineffective in themselves, and certainly inconsistent with the dignity of the people" (Paul VI, address in Bogotá, August 23, 1968). The fact is that "the church realizes that even the best structures and the most idealized systems quickly become inhuman if human inclinations are not improved, if there is no conversion of heart and mind on the part of those who are living in those structures or controlling them" (EN:36).

5.5. EVANGELIZATION AND IDEOLOGIES

Here we shall consider the exercise of discernment with regard to the ideologies existing in Latin America and the systems inspired by them.

Of the many different definitions of ideology that might be offered, we apply the term here to any conception that offers a view of the various aspects of life from the standpoint of a specific group in society. The ideology manifests the aspirations of this group, summons its members to a certain kind of solidarity and combative struggle, and grounds the legitimacy of these aspirations on specific values. Every ideology is partial because no one group can claim to identify its aspirations with those of society as a whole. Thus an ideology will be legitimate if the interests it upholds are legitimate and if it respects the basic rights of other groups in the nation. Viewed in this positive sense, ideologies seem to be necessary for social activity, insofar as they are mediating factors leading to action.

But in themselves ideologies have a tendency to absolutize the interests they uphold, the vision they propose, and the strategy they promote. In such a case they really become "lay religions." People take refuge in ideology as an ultimate explanation of everything: "In this way they fashion a new idol, as it were, whose absolute and coercive character is maintained, sometimes unwittingly" (OA:28). In that sense it is not surprising that ideologies try to use persons and institutions as their tools in order to achieve their aims more effectively. Herein lies the ambiguous and negative side of ideologies.

But ideologies should not be analyzed solely in terms of their conceptual content. In addition, they are dynamic, living phenomena of a sweeping and contagious nature. They are currents of yearning tending toward absolutization, and they are powerful in winning people over and whipping up redemptive fervor. This confers a special "mystique" on them, and it also enables them to make their way into different milieus in a way that is often irresistible. Their slogans, typical expressions, and criteria can easily make their way into the minds of people who are far from adhering voluntarily to their doctrinal principles. Thus many people live and struggle in practice within the atmosphere of specific ideologies, without ever having taken cognizance of that fact. This aspect calls for constant vigilance and reexamination. And it applies both to ideologies that legitimate the existing situation and to those that seek to change it.

To exercise the necessary discernment and critical judgment with regard to ideologies, Christians must rely on "a rich and complex heritage, which *Evangelii Nuntiandi* calls the social doctrine, or social teaching, of the church" (OAP:III,7).

This social doctrine or teaching of the church is an expression of its "distinctive contribution: a global perspective on the human being and on humanity" (PP:13). The church accepts the challenge and contribution of ideologies in their positive aspects, and in turn challenges, criticizes, and relativizes them.

Neither the gospel nor the church's social teaching deriving from it are ideologies. On the contrary, they represent a powerful source for challenging the limitations and ambiguities of all ideologies. The ever-fresh originality of the gospel message must be continually clarified and defended against all efforts to turn it into an ideology.

The unrestricted exaltation of the state and its many abuses must not, however, cause us to forget the necessity of the functions performed by the modern state. We are talking about a state that respects basic rights and freedoms; a state that is grounded on a broad base of popular participation involving many intermediary groups; a state that promotes autonomous development of an equitable and rapid sort, so that the life of the nation can withstand undue pressure and interference on both the domestic and international fronts; a state that is capable of adopting a position of active cooperation with the forces for integration into both the continental and the international community; and finally, a state that avoids the abuse of monolithic power concentrated in the hands of a few.

In Latin America we are obliged to analyze a variety of ideologies:

(a) First, there is capitalist liberalism, the idolatrous worship of wealth in individualistic terms. We acknowledge that it has given much encouragement to the creative capabilities of human freedom, and that it has been a stimulus to progress. But on the other side of the coin it views "profit as the chief spur to economic progress, free competition as the supreme law of economics, and private ownership of the means of production as an absolute right, having no limits or concomitant social obligations" (PP:26). The illegitimate privileges stemming from the absolute right of ownership give rise to scandalous contrasts, and to a situation of dependence and oppression on both the national and international levels. Now it is true that in some countries its original historical form of expression has been attenuated by necessary forms of social legislation and specific instances of government intervention. But in other countries capitalist liberalism persists in its original form, or has even retrogressed to more primitive forms with even less social sensitivity.

(b) Second, there is Marxist collectivism. With its materialist presuppositions, it too leads to the idolatrous worship of wealth—but in collectivist terms. It arose as a positive criticism of commodity fetishism and of the disregard for the human value of labor. But it did not manage to get to the root of that form of idolatry, which lies in the rejection of the only God worthy of adoration: the God of love and justice.

The driving force behind its dialectics is class struggle. Its objective is a classless society, which is to be achieved through a dictatorship of the proletariat; but in the last analysis this really sets up a dictatorship of the party. All the concrete historical experiments of Marxism have been carried out within the framework of totalitarian regimes that are closed to any possibility of criticism and correction. Some believe it is possible to separate various aspects of Marxism—its doctrine and its method of analysis in particular. But we would remind people of the teaching of the papal magisterium on this point: "It would be foolish and dangerous on that account to forget that they are closely linked to each other; to embrace certain elements of Marxist analysis without taking due account of their relation with its ideology; and to become involved in the class struggle and the Marxist interpretation of it without paying attention to the kind of violent and totalitarian society to which this activity leads" (OA:34).

We must also note the risk of ideologization run by theological reflection when it is based on a praxis that has recourse to Marxist analysis. The consequences are the total politicization of Christian existence, the disintegration of the language of faith into that of the social sciences, and the draining away of the transcendental dimension of Christian salvation.

Both of the aforementioned ideologies—capitalist liberalism and Marxism—find their inspiration in brands of humanism that are closed to any transcendent perspective. One does because of its practical atheism; the other does because of its systematic profession of a militant atheism.

(c) In recent years the so-called Doctrine of National Security has taken a firm hold on our continent. In reality it is more an ideology than a doctrine. It is bound up with a specific politico-economic model with elitist and verticalist features, which suppresses the broad-based participation of the people in political decisions. In some countries of Latin America this doctrine justifies itself as the defender of the Christian civilization of the West. It elaborates a repressive system, which is in line with its concept of "permanent war." And in some cases it expresses a clear intention to exercise active geo-political leadership.

We fully realize that fraternal coexistence requires a security system to inculcate respect for a social order that will permit all to carry out their mission with regard to the common good. This means that security measures must be under the control of an independent authority that can pass judgment on violations of the law and guarantee corrective measures.

The Doctrine of National Security, understood as an absolute ideology, would not be compatible with the Christian vision of the human being as responsible for carrying out a temporal project, and to its vision of the state as the administrator of the common good. It puts the people under the tutelage of military and political elites, who exercise authority and power; and it leads to increased inequality in sharing the benefits of development.

We again insist on the view of the Medellín Conference: "The system of liberal capitalism and the temptation of the Marxist system would appear to exhaust the possibilities of transforming the economic structures of our continent. Both systems militate against the dignity of the human person. One takes for granted the primacy of capital, its power, and its discriminatory utilization in the function of profit-making. The other, although it ideologically supports a kind of humanism, is more concerned with collective humanity, and in practice becomes a totalitarian concentration of state power. We must denounce the fact that Latin America finds itself caught between these two options and remains dependent on one or the other of the centers of power that control its economy" (Med-JU:10).

In the face of this situation, the church chooses "to maintain its freedom with regard to the opposing systems, in order to opt solely for the human being. Whatever the miseries or sufferings that afflict human beings, it is not through violence, power-plays, or political systems but through the truth about human beings that they will find their way to a better future" (OAP:III,3). Grounded on this humanism, Christians will find encouragement to get beyond the hard and fast either-or and to help build a new civilization that is just, fraternal, and open to the transcendent. It will also bear witness that eschatological hopes give vitality and meaning to human hopes.

For this bold and creative activity Christians will fortify their identity in the original values of Christian anthropology. The church "does not need to have recourse to ideological systems in order to love, defend, and collaborate in the liberation of the human being. At the center of the message of which the church is the trustee and herald, it finds inspiration for acting in favor of brotherhood, justice, and peace; and against all forms of domination, slavery, discrimination, violence, attacks on religious liberty, and aggression against human beings and whatever attacks life" (OAP:III,2).

Finding inspiration in these tenets of an authentic Christian anthropology, Christians must commit themselves to the elaboration of historical projects that meet the needs of a given moment and a given culture.

Christians must devote special attention and discernment to their involvement in historical movements that have arisen from various ideologies but are distinct from them. The teaching of *Pacem in Terris* (PT:55 and 152), which is reiterated in *Octogesima Adveniens*, tells us that false philosophical theories cannot be equated with the historical movements that originated in them, insofar as these historical movements can be subject to further influences as they evolve. The involvement of Christians in these movements imposes certain obligations to persevere in fidelity, and these obligations will facilitate their evangelizing role. They include:

(a) Ecclesial discernment, in communion with their pastors, as described in *Octogesima Adveniens* (OA:4).

(b) The shoring up of their identity by nourishing it with the truths of faith, their elaboration in the social teaching or doctrine of the church, and an enriching life of prayer and participation in the sacraments.

(c) Critical awareness of the difficulties, limitations, possibilities, and values of these convergences.

5.6. THE DANGER OF THE CHURCH AND ITS MINISTERS' ACTIVITY BEING USED AS A TOOL

In propounding an absolutized view of the human being to which everything, including human thought, is subordinated, ideologies and political parties try to use the church or deprive it of its legitimate independence. This manipulation of the church, always a risk in political life, may derive from Christians themselves, and even from priests and religious, when they proclaim a gospel devoid of economic, social, cultural, and political implications. In practice this mutilation comes down to a kind of complicity with the established order, however unwitting.

Other groups are tempted in the opposite direction. They are tempted to consider a given political policy to be of primary urgency, a precondition for the church's fulfillment of its mission. They are tempted to equate the Christian message with some ideology and subordinate the former to the latter, calling for a "rereading" of the gospel on the basis of a political option (OAP:1,4). But the fact is that we must try to read the political scene from the standpoint of the gospel, not vice versa.

Traditional integrism looks for the kingdom to come principally through a stepping back in history and reconstructing a Christian culture of a medieval cast. This would be a new Christendom, in which there was an intimate alliance between civil authority and ecclesiastical authority.

The radical thrust of groups at the other extreme falls into the same trap. It looks for the kingdom to come from a strategic alliance between the church and Marxism, and it rules out all other alternatives. For these people it is not simply a matter of being Marxists, but of being Marxists in the name of the faith (see nos. 543-46 above).

5.7. CONCLUSION

The mission of the church is immense and more necessary than ever before, when we consider the situation at hand: conflicts that threaten the human race and the Latin American continent; violations of justice and freedom; institutionalized injustice embodied in governments adhering to opposing ideologies; and terrorist violence. Fulfillment of its mission will require activity from the church as a whole: pastors, consecrated ministers, religious, and lay people. All must carry out their own specific tasks. Joined with Christ in prayer and abnegation, they will commit themselves to work for a better society without employing hatred and violence; and they will see that decision through to the end, whatever the consequences. For the attainment of a society that is more just, more free, and more at peace is an ardent longing of the peoples of Latin America and an indispensable fruit of any liberative evangelization.

PUEBLA FINAL DOCUMENT, "BASE-LEVEL ECCLESIAL COMMUNITIES (CEBs), THE PARISH, AND THE LOCAL CHURCH"

There was some apprehension before the Puebla Conference that two key elements of the practice of liberation theology—the pastoral strategy of forming basic ecclesial communities and the preferential option for the poor—might be condemned or completely ignored. However, Puebla gave a clear and enthusiastic approval, as may be seen in the following selections. The text on the basic ecclesial communities may be found in Puebla and Beyond, *pp. 210-14.*

Besides the Christian family, the first center of evangelization, human beings live their fraternal vocations in the bosom of the local church, in communities that render the Lord's salvific design present and operative, to be lived out in communion and participation.

Thus within the local church we must consider the parishes, the CEBs, and other ecclesial groups.

The church is the people of God, which expresses its life of communion and evangelizing service on various levels and under various historical forms.

2.1. THE SITUATION

In general we can say that in our Latin American church today we find a great longing for deeper and more stable relationships in the faith, sustained and animated by the word of God. We see an intensification in common prayer and in the effort of the people to participate more consciously and fruitfully in the liturgy.

We note an increase in the co-responsibility of the faith, both in organization and in pastoral action.

There is more wide-ranging awareness and exercise of the rights and duties appropriate to lay people as members of the community.

We notice a great yearning for justice and a sincere sense of solidarity, in a social milieu characterized by growing secularism and other phenomena typical of a society in transformation.

Bit by bit the church has been dissociating itself from those who hold economic or political power, freeing itself from various forms of dependence, and divesting itself of privileges.

The church in Latin America wishes to go on giving witness of unselfish and self-denying service in the face of a world dominated by greed for profit, lust for power, and exploitation.

In the direction of greater participation, there has been an increase of ordained ministries (such as the permanent diaconate), nonordained ministries, and other services such as celebrators of the word and community animators. We also note better collaboration between priests, religious, and lay people.

More clearly evident in our communities, as a fruit of the Holy Spirit, is a new style of relationship between bishops and priests, and between them and their people. It is characterized by greater simplicity, understanding, and friendship in the Lord.

All this is a process, in which we still find broad sectors posing resistance of various sorts. This calls for understanding and encouragement, as well as great docility to the Holy Spirit. What we need now is still more clerical openness to the activity of the laity and the overcoming of pastoral individualism and self-sufficiency. On the other hand, the impact of the secularized milieu has sometimes produced centrifugal tendencies in the community and the loss of an authentic ecclesial sense.

We have not always found effective ways to overcome the meager education of our people in the faith. Thus they remain defenseless before the onslaughts of shaky theological doctrines, sectarian proselytism, and pseudo-spiritual movements.

In particular we have found that small communities, especially the CEBs, create more personal interrelations, acceptance of God's word, reexamination of one's life, and reflection on reality in the light of the gospel. They accentuate committed involvement in the family, one's work, the neighborhood, and the local community. We are happy to single out the multiplication of small communities as an important ecclesial event that is peculiarly ours, and as the "hope of the church" (EN:58). This ecclesial expression is more evident on the periphery of large cities and in the countryside. They are a favorable atmosphere for the rise of new lay-sponsored services. They have done much to spread family catechesis and adult education in the faith, in forms more suitable for the common people.

But not enough attention has been paid to the training of leaders in faith education and Christian directors of intermediate organisms in neighborhoods, the world of work, and the rural areas. Perhaps that is why not a few members of certain communities, and even entire communities, have been drawn to purely lay institutions or have been turned into ideological radicals, and are now in the process of losing any authentic feel for the church.

The parish has been going through various forms of renewal that correspond to the changes in recent years. There is a change in outlook among pastors, more involvement of the laity in pastoral councils and other services, ongoing catechetical updating, and a growing presence of the priest among the people, especially through a network of groups and communities.

In the area of evangelization the parish embodies a twofold relationship of communication and pastoral communion. On the diocesan level, parishes are integrated into regions, vicarages, and deaneries. And within the parish itself pastoral work is diversified in accordance with different areas, and there is greater opening to the creation of smaller communities.

But we still find attitudes that pose an obstacle to the dynamic thrust of renewal. Primacy is given to administrative work over pastoral care. There is routinism and a lack of preparation for the sacraments. Authoritarianism is evident among some priests. And sometimes the parish closes in on itself, disregarding the overall apostolic demands of a serious nature.

On the level of the local church we note a considerable effort to arrange the territory so that greater attention can be paid to the people of God. This is being done by the creation of new dioceses. There is also concern to provide the churches with organisms that will foster co-responsibility through channels suited for dialogue: that is, priest councils, pastoral councils, and diocesan committees. These are to inspire a more organic pastoral effort suited to the specific reality of a given diocese.

Among religious communities and lay movements we also see a greater awareness of the necessity of being involved in the mission of the local church and evincing an ecclesial spirit.

On the national level there is a noticeable effort to exercise greater collegiality in episcopal conferences, which are continuously being better organized and fitted with subsidiary organisms. Deserving of special mention is the growth and effectiveness of the service that CELAM offers to ecclesial communion throughout Latin America.

On the worldwide level we note the fraternal interchange promoted by the sending of apostolic personnel and economic aid. These relationships have been established with the episcopates of Europe and North America, with the help of CAL; their continuation and intensification offer ampler opportunities for interecclesial participation, which is a noteworthy sign of universal communion.

2.2. DOCTRINAL REFLECTION

The Christian lives in community under the activity of the Holy Spirit. The Spirit is the invisible principle of unity and communion, and also of the unity and variety to be found in states of life, ministries, and charisms.

In their families which constitute domestic churches, the baptized are summoned to their first experience of communion in faith, love, and service to others.

In small communities, particularly those that are better organized, persons grow in their experience of new interpersonal relationships in the faith, in deeper exploration of God's word, in fuller participation in the eucharist, in communion with the pastors of the local church, and in greater commitment to justice within the social milieu that surrounds them.

One question that might be raised is: When can a small community be considered an authentic base-level ecclesial community (CEB) in Latin America?

As a community, the CEB brings together families, adults and young people, in an intimate interpersonal relationship grounded in the faith. As an ecclesial reality, it is a community of faith, hope, and charity. It celebrates the word of God and takes its nourishment from the eucharist, the culmination of all the sacraments. It fleshes out the word of God in life through solidarity and commitment to the new commandment of the Lord; and through the service of approved coordinators, it makes present and operative the mission of the church and its visible communion with the legitimate pastors. It is a base-level community because it is composed of relatively few members as a permanent body, like a cell of the larger community. "When they deserve their ecclesial designation, they can take charge of their own spiritual and human existence in a spirit of fraternal solidarity" (EN:58).

United in a CEB and nurturing their adherence to Christ, Christians strive for a more evangelical way of life amid the people, work together to challenge the egotistical and consumeristic roots of society, and make explicit their vocation to communion with God and their fellow humans. Thus they offer a valid and worthwhile point of departure for building up a new society, "the civilization of love."

The CEBs embody the church's preferential love for the common people. In them their religiosity is expressed, valued, and purified; and they are given a concrete opportunity to share in the task of the church and to work committedly for the transformation of the world.

The *parish* carries out a function that is, in a way, an integral ecclesial function because it accompanies persons and families throughout their lives, fostering their education and growth in the faith. It is a center of coordination and guidance for communities, groups, and movements. In it the horizons of communion and participation are opened up even more. The celebration of the eucharist and the other sacraments makes the global reality of the church present in a clearer way. Its tie with the diocesan community is ensured by its union with the bishop, who entrusts his representative (usually the parish priest) with the pastoral care of the community. For the Christian the parish becomes the place of encounter and fraternal sharing of persons and goods; it overcomes the limitations inherent in small communities. In fact, the parish takes on a series of services that are not within the reach of smaller communities. This is particularly true with respect to the missionary dimension and to the furthering of the dignity of the human person. In this way it reaches out to migrants, who are more or less stable, to the marginalized, to the alienated, to nonbe-lievers, and in general to the neediest.

In *the local church*, which is shaped in the image of the universal church, we find the only, holy, catholic, and apostolic church of Christ truly existing and operating (LG:23; CD:11). The local church is a portion of the people of God, defined by a broader socio-cultural context in which it is incarnated. Its primacy in the complex of ecclesial communities is due to the fact that it is presided over by a bishop. The bishop is endowed, in a full, sacramental way, with the threefold ministry of Christ, the head of the mystical body: prophet, priest, and pastor. In each local church the bishop is the principle and foundation of its unity.

Because they are the successors of the apostles, bishops—through their communion with the episcopal college and, in particular, with the Roman pontiff—render present the apostolicity of the whole church. They guar-antee fidelity to the gospel. They make real the communion with the uni-versal church. And they foster the collaboration of their presbytery and the growth of the people of God entrusted to their care.

It will be up to the bishop to discern the charisms and promote the ministries that are needed if his diocese is to grow toward maturity as an evangelized and evangelizing community. That means his diocese must be a light and leaven in society as well as a sacrament of unity and integral liberation. It must be capable of interchange with other local churches and animated by a missionary spirit that will allow its inner evangelical richness to radiate outside.

2.3. PASTORAL LINES OF APPROACH

As pastors, we are determined to promote, guide, and accompany the CEBs in the spirit of the Medellín Conference (Med-JPP:10) and the guide-lines set forth by *Evangelii Nuntiandi* (no. 58). We will also foster the dis-covery and gradual training of animators for these communities. In particular, we must explore how these small communities, which are flour-ishing mainly in rural areas and urban peripheries, can be adapted to the pastoral care of the big cities on our continent.

We must continue the efforts at parish renewal: getting beyond the merely administrative aspects; seeking greater lay participation, particularly in pastoral councils; giving priority to organized forms of the apostolate; and training lay people to assume their responsibilities as Christians in the community and the social milieu.

We must stress a more determined option for an overall, coordinated pastoral effort, with the collaboration of religious communities in particu-lar. We must promote groups, communities, and movements, inspiring them to an ongoing effort at communion. We must turn the parish into a center for promoting services that smaller communities cannot surely provide.

We must encourage experiments to develop the pastoral activity of all the parish agents, and we must support the vocational pastoral effort of ordained ministers, lay services, and the religious life.

Worthy of special recognition and a word of encouragement are priests and other pastoral agents, to whom the diocesan community owes support, encouragement, and solidarity. This holds true also for their fitting sustenance and social security, within the spirit of poverty.

Among priests we want to single out the figure of the parish priest. He is a pastor in the likeness of Christ. He is a promoter of communion with God, his fellow humans to whose service he dedicates himself, and his fellow priests joined around their common bishop. He is the leader and guide of the communities, alert to discern the signs of the time along with his people.

In the realm of the local church, efforts should be made to ensure the ongoing training and updating of pastoral agents. Spirituality and training courses should be provided by retreat centers and days of recollection. It is urgent that diocesan curias become more effective centers of pastoral promotion on three levels: that of catechetics, liturgy, and services promoting justice and charity. The pastoral value of administrative service should also be recognized. A special effort should be made to coordinate and integrate pastoral diocesan councils and other diocesan organisms. For even though they present problems, they are indispensable tools in planning, implementing, and keeping up with the pastoral activity in diocesan life.

The local church must stress its missionary character and its aspect of ecclesial communion, sharing values and experiences as well as fostering the interchange of personnel and resources.

Through its pastors, episcopal collegiality, and union with the Vicar of Christ, the diocesan community ought to intensify its intimate communion with the center of church unity. It should also shore up its loyal acceptance of the service that is offered through the magisterium, nurturing its fidelity to the gospel and its concrete life of charity. This would include collaboration on the continental level through CELAM and its programs.

We pledge to make every effort to ensure that this collegiality—of which this conference in Puebla and the two previous conferences are privileged instances—will be an even stronger sign of credibility for our proclamation of the gospel and our service to it; that it will thereby foster fraternal communion in all of Latin America.

PUEBLA FINAL DOCUMENT, "A PREFERENTIAL OPTION FOR THE POOR"

As noted in the previous section, the bishops at Puebla gave a ringing endorsement to the option for the poor, thus following in the footsteps of the Medellín Conference. This text may be found in Puebla and Beyond, *pp. 264-67.*

1.1. FROM MEDELLÍN TO PUEBLA

With renewed hope in the vivifying power of the Spirit, we are going to take up once again the position of the Second General Conference of the Latin American episcopate in Medellín, which adopted a clear and prophetic option expressing preference for, and solidarity with, the poor. We do this despite the distortions and interpretations of some, who vitiate the spirit of Medellín, and despite the disregard and even hostility of others (OAP:Intro.). We affirm the need for conversion on the part of the whole church to a preferential option for the poor, an option aimed at their integral liberation.

The vast majority of our fellow humans continue to live in a situation of poverty and even wretchedness that has grown more acute. We wish to take note of all that the church in Latin America has done, or has failed to do, for the poor since the Medellín Conference. This will serve as a starting point for seeking out effective channels to implement our option in our evangelizing work in Latin America's present and future.

We see that national episcopates and many segments of lay people, religious men and women, and priests have made their commitment to the poor deeper and more realistic. This witness, nascent but real, led the Latin American church to denounce the grave injustices stemming from mechanisms of oppression.

The poor, too, have been encouraged by the church. They have begun to organize themselves to live their faith in an integral way, and hence to reclaim their rights.

The church's prophetic denunciations and its concrete commitments to the poor have in not a few instances brought down persecution and oppression of various kinds upon it. The poor themselves have been the first victims of this oppression.

All this has produced tensions and conflicts both inside and outside the church. The church has frequently been the butt of accusations, either of being on the side of those with political or socio-economic power, or of propounding a dangerous and erroneous Marxist ideology.

Not all of us in the Latin American church have committed ourselves sufficiently to the poor. We are not always concerned about them, or in solidarity with them. Service to them really calls for constant conversion and purification among all Christians. That must be done if we are to achieve fuller identification each day with the poor Christ and our own poor.

1.2. DOCTRINAL REFLECTION

Jesus evangelizes the poor. As the pope has told us, the evangelical commitment of the church, like that of Christ, should be a commitment to those most in need (Luke 4:18-21; OAP:III,3). Hence the church must look to Christ when it wants to find out what its evangelizing activity should be like. The Son of God demonstrated the grandeur of this commitment when he became a human being. For he identified himself with human beings by becoming one of them. He established solidarity with them and took up the situation in which they find themselves — in his birth and in his life, and particularly in his passion and death where poverty found its maximum expression (Phil. 2:5-8; LG:8; EN:30; Med-JU:1,3).

For this reason alone, the poor merit preferential attention, whatever may be the moral or personal situation in which they find themselves. Made in the image and likeness of God (Gen. 1:26-28) to be the children of God, this image is dimmed and even defiled. That is why God takes on their defense and loves them (Matt. 5:45; James 2:5). That is why the poor are the first ones to whom Jesus' mission is directed (Luke 4:18-21), and why the evangelization of the poor is the supreme sign and proof of his mission (Luke 7:21-23).

This central feature of evangelization was stressed by Pope John Paul II: "I have earnestly desired this meeting because I feel solidarity with you, and because you, being poor, have a right to my special concern and attention. I will tell you the reason: the pope loves you because you are God's favorites. In founding his family, the church, God had in mind poor and needy humanity. To redeem it, God sent the Son specifically, who was born poor and lived among the poor to make us rich with his poverty (2 Cor. 8:9)" (Address in the Barrio of Santa Cecilia, January 30, 1979).

In her Magnificat (Luke 1:46-55), Mary proclaims that God's salvation has to do with justice for the poor. From her, too, "stems authentic commitment to other human beings, our brothers and sisters, especially to the poorest and neediest, and to the necessary transformation of society" (HZ:4).

Service to our poor brothers and sisters. When we draw near to the poor in order to accompany them and serve them, we are doing what Christ taught us to do when he became our brother, poor like us. Hence service to the poor is the privileged, though not the exclusive, gauge of our following of Christ. The best service to our fellows is evangelization, which disposes them to fulfill themselves as children of God, liberates them from injustices, and fosters their integral advancement.

It is of the utmost importance that this service to our fellow human beings take the course marked out for us by Vatican II: "The demands of justice should first be satisfied, lest the giving of what is due in justice be represented as the offering of a charitable gift. Not only the effects but also the causes of various ills must be removed. Help should be given in such a way that the recipients may gradually be freed from dependence on others and become self-sufficient" (AA:8).

Commitment to the poor and oppressed and the rise of grassroots communities have helped the church to discover the evangelizing potential of the poor. For the poor challenge the church constantly, summoning it to conversion; and many of the poor incarnate in their lives the evangelical values of solidarity, service, simplicity, and openness to accepting the gift of God.

Christian poverty. For the Christian, the term "poverty" does not designate simply a privation and marginalization from which we ought to free ourselves. It also designates a model of living that was already in evidence in the Old Testament, in the type known as "the poor of Yahweh" (Zeph. 2:3; 3:12-20; Isa. 49:13; 66:2; Ps. 74:19; 149:4), and that was lived and proclaimed by Jesus as blessedness (Matt. 5:3; Luke 6:20). St. Paul spelled out this teaching, telling us that the attitude of the Christian should be that of a person who uses the goods of this world (whose makeup is transitory) without absolutizing them, since they are only means to reach the kingdom (1 Cor. 7:29-31). This model of the poor life is one that the gospel requires of all those who believe in Christ; so we can call it "evangelical poverty" (Matt. 6:19-34). Religious live this poverty, required of all Christians, in a radical way when they commit themselves by vows to live the evangelical counsels (see nos. 733-35 above).

Evangelical poverty combines the attitude of trusting confidence in God with a plain, sober, and austere life that dispels the temptation to greed and haughty pride (1 Tim. 6:3-10).

Evangelical poverty is also carried out in practice through the giving and sharing of material and spiritual goods. It is not forced on others but done out of love, so that the abundance of some might remedy the needs of others (2 Cor. 8:1-15).

The church rejoices to see many of its children, particularly the more modest members of the middle class, living this Christian poverty in concrete terms.

In today's world this poverty presents a challenge to materialism, and it opens the way for alternative solutions to a consumer society.

1.3. PASTORAL GUIDELINES

Objective. The objective of our preferential option for the poor is to proclaim Christ the savior. This will enlighten them about their dignity, help them in their efforts to liberate themselves from all their wants, and lead them to communion with the Father and their fellow human beings through a life lived in evangelical poverty. "Jesus Christ came to share our human condition through his sufferings, difficulties, and death. Before transforming day-to-day life, he knew how to speak to the heart of the poor, liberate them from sin, open their eyes to a light on the horizon, and fill them with joy and hope. Jesus Christ does the same thing today. He is present in your churches, your families, and your hearts" (AWM:8).

This option, demanded by the scandalous reality of economic imbalances in Latin America, should lead us to establish a dignified, fraternal way of life together as human beings and to construct a just and free society.

The required change in unjust social, political, and economic structures will not be authentic and complete if it is not accompanied by a change in our personal and collective outlook regarding the idea of a dignified, happy human life. This in turn disposes us to undergo conversion (Med-JU:1,3; EN:30).

The gospel demand for poverty, understood as solidarity with the poor and as a rejection of the situation in which most people on this continent live, frees the poor person from being individualistic in life, and from being attracted and seduced by the false ideals of a consumer society. In like manner the witness of a poor church can evangelize the rich whose hearts are attached to wealth, thus converting and freeing them from this bondage and their own egotism.

Means. To live out and proclaim the requirement of Christian poverty, the church must reexamine its structures and the life of its members, particularly that of its pastoral agents, with the goal of effective conversion in mind.

Such conversion entails the demand for an austere lifestyle and a total confidence in the Lord, because in its evangelizing activity the church will rely more on the being and power of God and God's grace than on "having more" and secular authority. In this way it will present an image of being authentically poor, open to God and fellow human beings, ever at their disposal, and providing a place where the poor have a real chance for participation and where their worth is recognized.

Concrete actions. Committed to the poor, we condemn as antievangelical the extreme poverty that affects an extremely large segment of the population on our continent.

We will make every effort to understand and denounce the mechanisms that generate this poverty.

Acknowledging the solidarity of other churches, we will combine our efforts with those of people of good will in order to uproot poverty and create a more just and fraternal world.

We support the aspirations of laborers and peasants, who wish to be treated as free, responsible human beings. They are called to share in the decisions that affect their lives and their future, and we encourage all to improve themselves (AO; AWM).

We defend their fundamental right "to freely create organizations to defend and promote their interests, and to make a responsible contribution to the common good" (AWM:3).

The indigenous cultures have undeniable values. They are the peoples' treasure. We commit ourselves to looking on them with sympathy and respect and to promoting them. For we realize "how important culture is as a vehicle for transmitting the faith, so that human beings might progress in their knowledge of God. In this matter there can be no differences of race or culture" (AO:2).

With its preferential but not exclusive love for the poor, the church present in Medellín was a summons to hope for more Christian and humane goals, as the holy father pointed out (AWM). This Third Episcopal Conference in Puebla wishes to keep this summons alive and to open up new horizons of hope.

23

Pope John Paul II
"Address to the Indians of Oaxaca and Chiapas"
(January 29, 1979)

Many observers at Puebla believe that Pope John Paul was tremendously influenced by the eighty-mile drive from Mexico City to Puebla, when hundreds of thousands of Mexico's poorest stood in the searing heat to catch a glimpse of him. At any rate, reliable reports asserted that the pope rewrote his planned speech to the poor Indians in the village of Cuilapan in the state of Oaxaca. Perhaps he felt he had been too ambiguous or had been influenced by articles in the press to that effect. At any rate, he was much more forthright, even passionate, as he spoke about the human rights of the poor and insisted that there was a "social mortgage" on all property, so that it could even be expropriated if that was demanded by the common good. The text of his speech is taken from Puebla and Beyond, *pp. 81-83.*

I am glad to meet you, and I thank you for your enthusiastic presence and your words of welcome to me. I can find no better greeting, to express to you the sentiments that now fill my heart, than the words of St. Peter, the first pope of the church: "Peace to you who are in Christ." Peace to you who make up this crowded throng.

You too, you the inhabitants of Oaxaca, Chiapas, Cuilapan, and other places represented here, heirs of the blood and culture of your noble ancestors—particularly the Mixtecs and the Zapotecs—have been "called to be a holy people, as . . . all those who, wherever they may be, call on the name of our Lord Jesus Christ" (1 Cor. 1:2).

The Son of God "dwelt among us" to make those who believe in his name the children of God (John 1:11ff.); and he entrusted the church with the continuation of this saving mission wherever human beings might be. So it is not surprising that one day, in the now distant seventeenth century, intrepid missionaries arrived here out of fidelity to the church. They were anxious to assimilate your lifestyle and customs so as to better reveal and give living expression to the image of Christ. We remember with gratitude the first bishop of Oaxaca, Juan José López de Zárate, and numerous other missionaries—Franciscans, Dominicans, Augustinians, and Jesuits. They were men to be admired for their faith and their humane generosity.

They knew very well how important culture is as a vehicle for transmitting the faith, so that human beings might progress in their knowledge of God. In this matter there can be no differences of race or culture: "There is no Greek or Jew, ... slave or freeman. Rather, Christ is everything in all of you" (Col. 3:11). This constitutes a challenge and a stimulus for the church. For, in being faithful to the Lord's genuine and complete message, the church must be open and interpret all human reality in order to impregnate it with the power of the gospel (EN: 20,40).

Very beloved brothers and sisters: my presence in your midst is meant to be a living, authentic sign of this universal preoccupation on the part of the church. The pope and the church are with you and they love you. They love your persons, your culture, your traditions. They admire your marvelous past, encourage you in the present, and have great expectations for the future.

But that is not all I want to talk about. Through you, peasants and indigenous peoples, there comes before my eyes the vast multitude of the agricultural world. It is still the prevalent sector on the Latin American continent, and it is still a very large sector today on our planet.

Before this imposing spectacle reflected in my eyes, I cannot help but think of the same scene that was contemplated ten years ago by my predecessor Paul VI in his memorable visit to Colombia, and more specifically in his meeting with the peasants.

With him I would like to reiterate—with an even stronger emphasis in my voice, if that were possible—that the present pope wishes to be "in solidarity with your cause, which is the cause of the humble people, the poor people" (Address to Peasants, August 23, 1968). I wish to reiterate that the pope is with these masses of people who are "almost always left behind in an ignoble standard of living and sometimes harshly treated and exploited" (ibid.).

I adopt the view of my predecessors, John XXIII and Paul VI, and of Vatican II (see MM; PP; GS:9,71; etc.). Seeing a situation that remains alarming, that is seldom better and sometimes even worse, the pope chooses to be your voice, the voice of those who cannot speak or who have been silenced. He wishes to be the conscience of consciences, an invitation to action, to make up for lost time, which has frequently been a time of prolonged sufferings and unsatisfied hopes.

The disheartened world of field work, the laborers whose sweat waters their disheartened state as well, cannot wait any longer for their dignity to be recognized really and fully—a dignity no whit inferior to that of any other social sector. They have a right to be respected. They have a right not to be deprived of the little they have by maneuvers that sometimes amount to real plunder. They have a right not to be blocked in their desire to take part in their own advancement. They have a right to have the barriers of exploitation removed. These barriers are frequently the product of intolerable forms of egotism, against which their best efforts at advancement are dashed. They have a right to effective help, which is neither a handout nor a few crumbs of justice, so that they may have access to the development that their dignity as human beings and as children of God merits.

For their sake we must act promptly and thoroughly. We must implement bold and thoroughly innovative transformations. Without further delay, we must undertake the urgently required reforms (PP:32).

It should not be forgotten that the measures taken have to be suitable. The church defends the legitimate right to private property in itself; but it is no less clear in teaching that there is always a social mortgage on all private property, so that goods may serve the general assignment that God has given them. And if the common good demands it, there is no need to hesitate at expropriation itself, done in the right way (PP:24).

The realm of agriculture has great importance and great dignity. It is this realm that offers society the products it needs for its nourishment. It is a task that merits appreciation and grateful esteem from all, which are a recognition of the dignity of those who work at it.

This dignity can and should be enhanced by contemplating God. God encourages contact with nature, which mirrors the divine activity. God looks after the grass of the fields, nurtures its growth, and makes the earth fruitful. He sends the rain and the wind so that it may also feed the animals, who are the helpmates of human beings, as we read in the beginning of Genesis.

Work in the fields entails no small difficulties. There is the effort it takes, the scorn in which it is sometimes held, and the obstacles encountered. Sometimes only long-term effort can surmount the problems. Without that, the flight from countryside to the cities will continue. And that frequently creates problems: the extensive, anxiety-ridden proletarianization of human beings, their overcrowding in native dwellings, and so forth.

A fairly widespread evil is the tendency toward individualism among field workers. By contrast, a more coordinated and solidary effort could be a big help. Think about that, beloved children.

Despite everything, the peasant world possesses enviable human and religious riches: deeply rooted love for the family; a sense of friendship; helping those most in need; a deep humanism; love for peace and shared civic life; a vital religious life; trust in God and openness to God; a cultivation of love for the Virgin Mary; and many other things.

What the pope wishes to express to you is a well deserved tribute of thanks, which society owes you. Thank you, peasants, for your valuable contribution to the social welfare. Humanity owes you much. You can be proud of your contribution to the common good.

To you, responsible officials of the people, power-holding classes who sometimes keep your lands unproductive when they conceal the food that so many families are doing without, the human conscience, the conscience of the peoples, the cry of the destitute, and above all the voice of God and the church join me in reiterating to you that it is not just, it is not human, it is not Christian to continue certain situations that are clearly unjust. You must implement real, effective measures on the local, national, and international levels, following the broad line marked out by the encyclical *Mater et Magistra* (part 3). And it is clear that those who can do most are the ones most obligated to collaborate in this effort.

Most beloved brothers and sisters and children: work for your advancement as human beings. But do not stop there. Improve yourself more and more in morality and religion. Do not harbor sentiments of hatred and violence, but look to the Lord and Master of all, who gives to all the recompense their acts deserve. The church is on your side. It urges you to live out your status as children of God united in Christ, under the gaze of Mary, our most holy mother.

The pope asks you for your prayers, and he offers you his. And as I bless you and your families, I bid you farewell with words of St. Paul the Apostle: "Give a greeting and a good kiss to all the brethren." May this be a call to hope. Amen.

PART V

PUEBLA AND THE POLISH POPE
(1979–1986)

In the immediate aftermath of the Puebla Conference, a fierce controversy erupted over who had "won" at Puebla, the liberationists or their opponents. I think the most important comments on it were made by Pope John Paul himself in his weekly audience in Rome just a week after the conference ended (Feb. 21, 1979; no. 24). Another article by a North American critic of liberation theology, Michael Novak, provides a different interpretation of the conference and of John Paul's role in it (no. 25).

The Latin Americans who supported Medellín and liberation theology were satisfied if not delighted with the results. One theologian asserted that Medellín was a leap, while Puebla was an elegant step forward. Another said it was like achieving a tie in a game played on the opponents' field. In an article in *America*, I compared Puebla to a gigantic patchwork quilt, in sharp contrast to the clean lines of Medellín, and predicted that analysts of varying ideological tendencies would be selecting from the mélange and designing their own quilts for years to come. But the major point is that Medellín and liberation theology were *not* repudiated, and that in fact all the major positions of those movements were actually incorporated into the documents, usually without attribution. A number of other opposed positions are scattered throughout Puebla's sprawling canvas, but none of them provide a coherent positive alternative to the Medellín-liberation position.

Granted the momentous importance of the Puebla Conference, the last years of the 1970s and early 80s are remarkable for a startling series of surprises that would continue to exert a powerful influence on the church and society in Latin America, as well as on the world church. It was surprise enough that the Puebla Conference continued along the main directions of Medellín and liberation theology, despite the formidable odds and the truly awesome forces marshaled against them. But before this, in quick succession, had come the death of Pope Paul VI on August 6, 1978, the selection of his successor, Albino Luciani (who took the name Pope John Paul), followed by his own sudden death less than two months later on September 28, 1978. Perhaps the greatest surprise of all occurred when the white smoke poured from the Vatican chimney on October 16, 1978, and the name of the new pope was announced: Karol Wojtyla, archbishop of Krakow, Poland, who took the name of John Paul II and thus became the first non-Italian to mount the throne of Peter since 1522.

As regards liberation theology, it was also a surprise to find the prefect of the Congregation for the Doctrine of the Faith, Cardinal Joseph Ratzinger, becoming a leading actor in the liberation dialogue, not only in his official Instructions, but also in secular press interviews and appearances on the international lecture circuit. Another unusual phenomenon regarding liberation theology was that it began in the 80s to reverse the flow of theology from Europe outward; rather, there began the export of Spanish and Portuguese theological tomes northward, where they were soon translated for eager readers into English, German, French, and other languages.

Again in the late 70s, other surprises were taking place in the arena of politics. In July 1979 a ragtag band of Sandinista guerrillas triumphantly entered Managua, Nicaragua, after routing the fearsome National Guard and deposing the military dictator, Anastasio Somoza. Somoza was so extreme an example of corruption and greed that he had united the Nicaraguan people as never before against him. However, the socialist or Marxist government that emerged was bound to create difficulties with the United States, which for over a century had regarded Central America as its "back yard." This probability became a certainty in November 1980 when Jimmy Carter, who had waged an effective campaign for human rights in Latin America, lost reelection to Ronald Reagan. Reagan and the Sandinistas were doomed from the start to become mortal enemies, which indeed happened and continued up to the very end of the Reagan presidency, with considerable damage to U.S. relations with Latin America.

Finally, more gruesome and bloody developments began to surface in this period. The infamous "death squads" of El Salvador began to increase their brutal assassinations, reaching into the thousands, with no killer ever brought to justice. The only change was in the shocking escalation of violence: in March 1977 Fr. Rutilio Grande, S.J., was machine-gunned to death in Aguilares, on his way to celebrate the eucharist, and in March 1980 the archbishop of San Salvador, Oscar Romero, was shot through the heart as he preached at Mass. But the public in the United States did not seem to notice the slaughter until December 1980, when four North American church women were raped and shot on the road from the airport in San Salvador. Films that were taken of the retrieval of the women's disheveled and torn bodies from the pit where they had been hastily buried opened many eyes to the deadly plague that had descended on El Salvador.

Aside from the events just mentioned, however, it soon became perfectly apparent that a new and powerful figure had entered the Latin American scene: the enormously gifted, charismatic, and supremely self-confident personality of the first Polish pope. One evidence of his self-confidence is the fact that he is "his own theologian"—that is, he composes his own theological and social publications, without trying to present a consensus of opinions from around the world, as his predecessors had done.

A number of analysts, however, have pointed out some limitations of his approach, especially with regard to his social teaching. On the one hand, Wojtyla's social analysis is clearly progressive and even radical on the theoretical level, as was demonstrated in 1981 when he critically integrated Marxist concepts into his basically phenomenological synthesis in the encyclical letter "On Human Work" (*Laborem Exercens*). On the level of social praxis, however, such as the need for profound social change, he often seems cautious and even ambivalent; he is often more severe in his prescriptions for society than for the church, as in the case of human rights. Finally, the question has been raised whether the pope tends to elevate the value of unity in the church, especially based on obedience and conformity, to a position of greater importance than that of self-giving love of neighbor, the struggle for justice for the poor, and the freedom of the human spirit to imagine new futures and to create history.

This question of unity seems to have been at the core of the problem in his turbulent and finally unsuccessful visit to Nicaragua in 1983. In his letter to the bishops in June 1982 and in his homily in the gigantic *Plaza de 19 de julio* (nos. 32 and 33), the pope concentrated on the need for unity in the church, ignoring the war that was costing many lives, including those of civilians and even children, and the revolution itself, which many thought was the high point in the history of Nicaragua. The result was even greater disunity than had been present before his visit.

His approach seems to have influenced the Nicaraguan bishops, who indicated critical support for a socialist government as they understood it (see no. 26) in 1979. However, in 1984 in their "Call for Dialogue" the bishops appeared firmly hardened in their opposition to the Sandinista regime (no. 41).

The pope also appears to have approved Cardinal Ratzinger's investigation of two of the best-known liberation theologians, Gustavo Gutiérrez of Peru (no. 37) and Leonardo Boff of Brazil (no. 48). A number of other documents in this section refer to the reactions to these moves by observers around the world, and also include an excerpt from Boff's defense of his book, *Church: Charism and Power* (no. 49). It is also very interesting to note that two prestigious international journals, *Concilium* and *Communio* (Latin American edition) entered into the debate with public statements that predictably took contradictory positions on the liberation issue (no. 44 and no. 51, known as the "Declaration of Los Andes").

During this period, Cardinal Ratzinger continued to become more and more actively involved in the debate, especially in a widely publicized article in the Italian monthly, *Trenta Giorni*, in 1984, where he stated flatly that "with the analysis of the phenomenon of liberation theology, we are clearly facing a fundamental danger for the faith of the church" (no. 40). Later, in August of the same year, he published through the Congregation of the Doctrine of the Faith an instruction on liberation theology, which many thought was excessively critical, while others embraced it as a definitive condemnation of liberation theology (no. 45). My own opinion, given the excellent training and long experience of Cardinal Ratzinger as a professional theologian, was that this document was a poor theological essay, in its content, in its organization, and in its stylistic expression. A sample of Latin American reactions is presented in nos. 46–47.

With regard to the increasing level of persecution mentioned earlier, especially in Central America, the Louvain address and last homily of Archbishop Oscar Romero (nos. 27 and 28) remain as eloquent testimonies of a life totally dedicated to the defense of the rights of the poor. Unfortunately, his murder was followed by an unseemly debate in the church as to whether his death was due to religious or socio-political reasons, when obviously both were involved, as would be true in any action that would actively advance the kingdom of God. Jon Sobrino's brief reflection on the death of four church women in El Salvador (no. 30) is also a poignant tribute to a new generation of North American martyrs.

The article by Juan Luis Segundo (no. 39) is included here for two reasons. First, it points to fundamental divisions on theological sources and method in the ranks of the liberation theologians themselves, which would warrant attention and serious dialogue to resolve. Also, although Segundo has been accused of being too critical of other liberation theologians, I think that constructive criticism is a salutary development and its acceptance a sign of theological maturity. Finally, an article is included here which traces the history and present situation of the relationship of feminism and liberation theology (no. 43). It seems clear that reflection of this type by women will be one of the major areas of development of liberation theology in the years ahead.

At this point, I will refer briefly to some of the developments in liberation theology itself during this period. It will be possible here to make only a selection from a vast and steadily increasing production of books. I would characterize the liberation theology of this period as in the state of maturity that belongs to young adulthood—that is to say, it has real quality and profundity, but the more substantive and comprehensive works still lie in the future.

An excellent example of this early maturity is the rather astonishing decision, taken in 1985, to produce a series of no less than fifty-five volumes, entitled *Theology and Liberation*, which would cover all the basic themes of theology and pastoral practice from the viewpoint of liberation. The first volumes have already been published. Foreign publishers, including Orbis Books in the United States, have begun to issue translations of these stimulating works from Latin America, a convincing proof of the assertion made earlier that the direction of theological influence now flows from the nations of the south to the nations of the north.

Otherwise, this period witnessed a number of solid works by three of the leading figures of liberation theology: Gustavo Gutiérrez, Leonardo Boff, and Juan Luis Segundo. In 1979 Gutiérrez produced *The Power of the Poor in History* (Orbis Books, 1983), which gathered together a number of essays on the role of the poor in their own liberation and the role of the church as it accompanies them. This was followed in 1983 by *We Drink from Our Own Wells: The Spiritual Journey of a People* (Orbis Books, 1984), which consisted of a long-awaited expansion and deepening of the spiritual insights that have marked his writing from the beginning. A book-length reflection on Scripture appeared next in 1985 with the publication of *On Job: God-Talk and the Suffering of the Innocent* (Orbis Books, 1987), which discovered some fascinating parallels between the suffering of Job and that of the poor in Latin America.

During this period, Leonardo Boff continued his amazing productivity on a variety of subjects. With considerable courage, he produced in 1979 *The Maternal Face of God: The Feminine and Its Religious Expressions* (New York: Harper and Row, 1987). In 1981 he published the now famous *Church: Charism and Power* (New York: Crossroad, 1985), which called for an emphasis on nurturing the charisms of service of all members of the church with a consequent deemphasis on the structures of power. The same year saw the publication of *Saint Francis: A Model for Human Liberation* (Crossroad, 1984), which he divides into five great questions to which Francis responded throughout his whole life and which have startling relevance for liberation in Latin America today. *When Theology Listens to the Poor* (Harper and Row, 1988) appeared in 1984, and presents a variety of approaches to the question of what theology should be from the standpoint of the poor, stating flatly that the renewal of the church and the revitalization of theology will both depend on our approach to the issue of the poor.

Juan Luis Segundo completed his most important work thus far in 1982, with the publication of a three-volume Spanish work, *Jesus Christ Yesterday and Today* (Orbis Books, 5 volumes, 1984–1988). In this erudite and profound work, he stresses the need for creative christologies for different epochs and cultural contexts, and at the end presents his own evolutionary christology as an example. In 1985 he also replied at length to the Instruction on Certain Aspects of the "Theology of Liberation" by showing that the instruction's theology was contrary to that of Vatican II, and more generally by mounting an attack against all attempts to reverse the direction of the council (see *Theology and the Church* [Minneapolis: Winston Press, 1985]). It was in this period that Jon Sobrino of El Salvador decisively emerged as a leading exponent of liberation theology. In 1982 he continued the clarification and deepening of his earlier work on christology with *Jesus in Latin America* (Orbis Books, 1987). He also moved into a different area in 1981 with his treatment of the foundational theology of a church with, for, and of the poor in *The True Church and the Poor* (Orbis Books, 1984). Perhaps most importantly, in 1985 he assembled the many creative ideas he had published in articles over the years regarding a liberation spirituality and put them together in a brilliant and inspiring synthesis in *Spirituality of Liberation: Toward Political Holiness* (Orbis Books, 1988).

Three other books stand out in a variety of important areas. Ricardo Antoncich, S.J., has for years been a specialist in the social teaching of the church and its relationship to the church in Latin America and especially to the documents of the Puebla Conference. In 1980 he presented a remarkable survey of this research in *Christians in the Face of Injustice: A Latin American Reading of Catholic Social Teaching* (Orbis Books, 1987). Also in 1980 a collection of the works of Oscar Romero, the martyred archbishop of San Salvador, was assembled with the title *Voice of the Voiceless: The Four Pastoral Letters and Other Statements* (Orbis Books, 1985), reminding the church that the ultimate purpose of liberation theology is a praxis like that of Romero. Finally, a great deal of information and theological reflection on the building blocks of the church of the poor—the basic ecclesial communities—was made available in *The Challenge of Basic Christian Communities* (Sergio Torres and John Eagleson, eds.; Orbis Books, 1981).

24

Pope John Paul II
General Audience on Evangelization
and Liberation
(Rome, February 21, 1979)

This papal audience took place three weeks after the conclusion of the Puebla Conference. It is a very interesting document when it is kept in mind that many media reports asserted that the pope had condemned liberation theology definitively in his opening address at Puebla. Using the explicit term ("theology of liberation") Pope John Paul says it is sometimes "too exclusively" connected with Latin America, and goes on to state flatly that he agrees with the great contemporary theologian, Hans Urs von Balthasar, when he demands a theology of liberation on a universal scale. "Only the contexts are different, the reality itself of the liberty 'for which Christ freed us' (Gal. 5:1) is universal." This idea reoccurs later in both the "Instruction on Christian Freedom and Liberation" (1986) and the pope's encyclical letter "On Social Concerns" (1988). The text is taken from Origins, 8 *(March 1979, pp. 594–98).*

Today, too, I wish to refer to the subject of the third conference of the Latin American episcopate: evangelization. It is a fundamental subject, a subject that is always topical. The conference, which ended its work at Puebla on February 13, bears witness to this. It is, moreover, the subject "of the future": the subject that the church must live continually and prolong in the future. The subject, therefore, constitutes the permanent perspective of the church's mission.

To evangelize means making Christ present in human life as a person and, at the same time, in the life of society. To evangelize means doing everything possible, according to our capacities, in order that human beings "may believe," in order that they may find themselves again in Christ, in order that they may find again in him the meaning and the adequate dimension of their own lives. This finding again is, at the same time, the deepest source of human liberation. St. Paul expresses this when he writes,

"It was for liberty that Christ freed us" (Gal. 5:1). So liberation, then, is certainly a reality of faith, one of the fundamental biblical themes which are a deep part of Christ's salvific mission, of the work of redemption, of his teaching. This subject has never ceased to constitute the content of the spiritual life of Christians.

The conference of the Latin American episcopate bears witness that this subject returns in a new historical context; therefore it must be taken up again in the teaching of the church, in theology and in the apostolate. It must be taken up again in its own depth and in its evangelical authenticity.

There are many circumstances that make it such a relevant subject today. It is difficult, here, to mention them all. Certainly it is recalled by that "universal desire for dignity" on the part of humankind, of which the Second Vatican Council speaks. The "theology of liberation" is often connected (sometimes too exclusively) with Latin America; but it must be admitted that one of the great contemporary theologians, Hans Urs von Balthasar, is right when he demands a theology of liberation on a universal scale. Only the contexts are different, the reality itself of the liberty "for which Christ freed us" (cf. Gal. 5:1) is universal. The task of theology is to find its real significance in the different concrete historical and contemporary contexts.

Christ himself links liberation particularly with knowledge of the truth: "You will know the truth, and the truth will set you free" (John 8:32). This sentence testifies above all to the intimate significance of the freedom for which Christ liberates us. Liberation means inner human transformation, which is a consequence of the knowledge of truth. The transformation is, therefore, a spiritual process, in which humankind matures "in true justice and holiness" (Eph. 4:24). The human person, inwardly mature in this way, becomes a representative and a spokesman of this "justice and holiness" in the various environments of social life. Truth is important not only for the growth of human knowledge, deepening one's interior life in this way; truth has also a prophetic significance and power. It constitutes the content of testimony and it calls for testimony.

We find this prophetic power of truth in the teaching of Christ. As a prophet, as a witness to truth, Christ repeatedly opposes nontruth; he does so with great forcefulness and decision, and often he does not hesitate to condemn falsehood. Let us reread the gospel carefully; we will find in it a good many severe expressions, for example, "white-washed tombs" (Matt. 23:27), "blind guides" (Matt. 23:16), "frauds" (Matt. 23:13, 15, 23, 25, 27, 29)—which Christ utters, aware of the consequences that are in store for him.

So this service of truth as participation in Christ's prophetic service is a task of the church, which tries to carry it out in the various historical contexts. It is necessary to call by name injustice and exploitation, whether by the state, institutions, mechanisms, or systems and regimes which sometimes operate without sensitivity. It is necessary to call by name every social injustice, discrimination, or violence inflicted on human beings against their bodies, against their spirits, against their consciences, and against their convictions.

Christ teaches us a special sensitivity for humankind, for the dignity of the human person, for human life, for the human spirit and body. It is this sensitivity which bears witness to the knowledge of that "truth which makes us free" (John 8:32). It is not permitted for humans to conceal this truth from themselves. It is not permitted to falsify it. It is not permitted to make this truth the object of barter. It is necessary to speak of it clearly and simply, not to condemn humankind, but to serve its cause. Liberation in the social sense also begins with knowledge of the truth.

Let us stop at this point. It is difficult to express in a short speech everything involved in this great subject, which has many aspects and, above all, many levels. I stress: many levels, because it is necessary in this subject to see humankind according to all different elements of the riches of personal and social being; "historical" and at the same time, in a certain way, "supertemporal" being. (History, among other things, bears witness to this human "supertemporality.") The being which is a "thinking reed" (cf. B. Pascal, *Pensées*, 347)—everyone knows how frail a reed is—just because its "thinking" always goes beyond itself; it bears within it the transcendental mystery and a "creative restlessness" which springs from the latter.

We will stop for the present at this point. The theology of liberation must, above all, be faithful to the whole truth about humankind, in order to show clearly, not only in the Latin American context but also in all contemporary contexts, what in reality this liberty is "for which Christ freed us."

Christ! It is necessary to speak of our liberation in Christ; it is necessary to proclaim this liberation. It must be integrated in the whole contemporary reality of human life. Many circumstances, many reasons, demand this. In these times, when it is claimed that the condition for "human liberation" is liberation "from Christ," that is, from religion, the reality of our liberation in Christ must become for us all more and more evident and more and more full.

"The reason I was born, the reason why I came into the world, is to testify to the truth" (John 18:37). The church, looking to Christ, who bears witness to the truth, must always and everywhere ask itself and, in a certain sense, the contemporary "world" too, how to make good emerge from humankind, how to liberate the dynamism of the good that is in human nature, so that it will be stronger than evil, any moral, social evil, etc. The third conference of the Latin American episcopate bears witness to the readiness to undertake this effort. We want not only to recommend this effort to God, but also to follow it for the good of the church and of the whole human family.

25

Michael Novak
"Liberation Theology and the Pope"
(June 1979)

Michael Novak holds the chair of religion and public policy at the American Enterprise Institute, Washington, D.C., and has published a large number of books and articles in that field. He is one of the main representatives of a very strong and broad opposition to liberation theology that has gradually developed in conservative intellectual circles in the United States and continues to expand today. The article appeared originally in the June 1979 issue of Commentary. *This text is from Quentin Quade, ed.,* The Pope and Revolution: John Paul II Confronts Liberation Theology *(Washington, D.C.: Ethics and Public Policy Center, 1982), pp. 73–85. A more recent elaboration of Novak's critique of liberation theology may be found in* Will It Liberate? Questions About Liberation Theology *(Mahwah, N.J.: Paulist Press, 1986).*

On his highly publicized voyage to Mexico late in January 1979, Karol Wojtyla, only recently become Pope John Paul II, faced two systems of authoritarianism. He faced Latin American feudal regimes of a cruelty well-known to the bishops he was about to address, some of whom had experienced prison themselves. And he faced a rising enthusiasm, particularly on the part of foreign trained Latin American clergymen, for "Marxist liberation."

The pope addressed the Conference of Latin American Bishops (CELAM) at Puebla on January 28. At first his 8,000-word sermon drew words of disappointment and sarcasm from many of the "liberation theologians" he was taken to be attacking. Then began a process by which the pope's straight sentences were gradually softened and transmuted until, we were told by the *New York Times* (February 18), the theologians in question celebrated the end of the conference by drinking beer, singing "folk songs from all over the continent," so that "well past midnight their songs echoed through the streets ... sounding suspiciously like a victory celebration." What had actually happened? Had the pope attacked "liberation theology" or had he given it official sanction?

The meeting at Puebla was the third major meeting of CELAM in twenty-five years. At the first one in Rio de Janeiro, the bishops of Latin America had established a continentwide organization. Over the years, they formulated some fairly clear views about their own special needs and the general need for a reorganization of the international church. Thus, at the Second Vatican Council (1961–65), their regional unity was already conspicuous, and their interventions helped the "progressive" forces at the council do much more than expected. Then in 1968 — the year of vast student unrest in the United States, Mexico, France, and elsewhere — the bishops met for the second time, at Medellín, Colombia, and produced a document that addressed the public-policy needs of the continent. Tinged with Marxist rhetoric, that document gave rise, two years later, to the first writings self-described as "liberation theology" — that is, formal attempts to translate Christianity into Marxist categories. Works in this genre have multiplied since.

Pope John Paul II went straight to the heart of all this in the opening paragraphs of his address at Puebla. He said immediately that his "point of departure" was "the conclusions of Medellín" as well as the sympathetic support of those conclusions by Pope Paul VI in *Evangelii Nuntiandi*. But he did not hesitate to qualify his praise of "all the positive elements" that the Medellín conclusions contained, with the warning that he was not about to ignore the "incorrect interpretations at times made and which call for calm discernment, opportune criticism, and clear choices of position."

The misconception, the confusion the pope wished to sweep away, was that Christianity is reducible to Marxist categories. He opposed those "re-readings" of the gospel that "cause confusion by diverging from the central criteria of the faith of the church." He opposed those for whom "the kingdom of God is emptied of its full content and is understood in a rather secularist sense," as if it were to be reached "by mere changing of structures and social and political involvement, and as being present wherever there is a certain type of involvement and activity for justice." And he particularly opposed those who "claim to show Jesus as politically committed, as one who fought against Roman oppression and the authorities, and also as one involved in the class struggle. This idea of Christ as a political figure, a revolutionary, as the subversive man from Nazareth, does not tally with the church's catechesis."

The pope observed that "our age is the one in which humankind has been most written and spoken of," yet it is also "the age of human abasement to previously unsuspected levels, the age of human values trampled on as never before." Like Solzhenitsyn in his commencement address at Harvard in 1978, Pope John Paul II attributed this to "the inexorable paradox of atheistic humanism." By contrast, "the primordial affirmation of [Catholic] anthropology is that humankind is God's image and cannot be reduced to a mere portion of nature or a nameless element in the human city." He rejected a "strictly economic, biological, or psychological view" of humankind, insisting instead that "the complete truth about the human being constitutes the foundation of the church's social teaching and the basis of true liberation. In the light of this truth, humankind is not a being subjected to economic or political processes; these processes are instead directed to and subjected to humankind." It is necessary, in short, to reject a materialistic interpretation of history and to defend the primacy of the spiritual.

At this point, Pope John Paul II showed himself in consonance with the traditional political philosophies of Western civilization. Tocqueville, for example, had made a similar observation: "There is no religion which does not place the object of human desire above and beyond the treasures of the earth, and which does not naturally raise the soul to regions far above those of the senses. Nor is there any which does not impose on man some sort of duties to his mind, and thus draws him at times from the contemplation of himself." Correspondingly, the pope discerned in "human dignity a gospel value that cannot be despised without greatly offending the Creator," and then launched one of his two explicit condemnations of Latin American practices:

This dignity is infringed on the individual level when due regard is not had for values such as freedom, the right to essential goods, to life. . . . It is infringed on the social and political level when humankind cannot exercise its right of participation, or when it is subjected to unjust and unlawful coercion, or submitted to physical or mental torture, etc. I am not unaware of how many questions are being posed in this sphere today in Latin America.

The pope then turned to problems of action. This mission of the church, he said, "although it is religious and not social or political, cannot fail to consider humankind in the entirety of its being." This mission "has as an essential part action for justice and the tasks of human advancement." But the church "does not need to have recourse to ideological systems in order to love, defend, and collaborate in human liberation . . . acting in favor of brotherhood, justice, and peace, and against all foes of domination, slavery, discrimination, violence, attacks on religious liberty, and aggression against humankind, and whatever attacks life." The church has a commitment, like Christ's, "to the most needy. In fidelity to this commitment, the church wishes to stay free with regard to the competing systems, in order to opt only for humankind."

The pope then went on to define liberation in a Christian way, first positively, and then with this negative: "Liberation . . . in the framework of the church's proper mission is not reduced to the simple and narrow economic, political, social, or cultural dimension, and is not sacrificed to the demands of any strategy, practice, or short-term solution." The important thing is "to safeguard the originality of Christian liberation," and "to avoid any form of curtailment or ambiguity" which would cause the church to "lose its fundamental meaning" and leave it open to "manipulation by ideological systems and political parties."

THE LIBERATION CENTER

What is the liberation theology to which the pope so clearly addressed himself? The headquarters for liberation theology in the United States, and perhaps in the entire world, are located near the Hudson River at Maryknoll, New York, international center of America's most active missionary order, the Maryknoll Fathers and Sisters. In a bibliography of Third World theologies, 32 of 82 titles were published by Maryknoll's Orbis Books. Founded in 1970, Orbis announced that it "draws its imperatives from and orders its priorities on the fact that the majority of Christians live in the affluent countries of the North Atlantic community, which controls almost 80 percent of the world's resources but accounts for only 20 percent of the world's population. . . . Christians bear a heavy responsibility for a world that can annually 'afford' to spend $150 billion on arms, but can scarcely scrape together $10 billion for economic and social development." At the heart of the matter, according to the initial Orbis release, was the need for a change in intellectual focus: "Total development will demand the restructuring of oppressive political and social orders wherever they exist, in Calcutta or Chicago, New York or Recife. For this reason, the word *development* should be replaced by *liberation*."

It is quite remarkable that the list of cities requiring liberation did not include Cracow or Leningrad, Havana or Peking, Hanoi or Prague. The complete Orbis catalogue of 141 titles, as of the end of 1978, maintains this distinction intact. Thirty-nine titles are concentrated on Latin America, a few on Africa and other places, none on communist lands.

The focus on Latin America is not accidental. Liberation theology is mainly, although not entirely, a product of the Spanish-speaking world. Father Sergio Torres of Chile, lecturer at Maryknoll, describes his worldview and that of his fellow Latin American theologians in this way:

> What we understand is that we are at the end of a stage in the history of the world. Europe and Western society is no longer making the history of the world as it has been since the Roman empire. We understand that history is now being made by the peoples of the Third World. The oil crisis is getting that through here in the United States. . . . We in Latin America are the only continent that is both Christian and underdeveloped, so we are in a special place. We will start a new understanding of the faith because we belong to the churches, Catholic and Protestant, and are living in a situation which makes them functional to the systems. . . . The process of colonization, liberation, and organization is best understood in Marxist terms.

Father Miguel D'Escoto, a Nicaraguan, the director of communications at Maryknoll, adds:

> As Latin Americans, we know capitalism in a way young people here don't know it. We had no New Deal, no Roosevelt to come along and soften it up. Capitalism is intrinsically wrong at its base. The basic concept is that man is selfish, and being realistic, we should accept this and cater to it rather than change it.

The chief systematizer of liberation theology, Father Juan Luis Segundo, whose five-volume treatise *Theology for Artisans of a New Humanity* has sold 64,000 copies, told a group of American Jesuits:

> There is no perfect solution. The only way is for us to choose between two oppressions. And the history of Marxism, even oppressive, offers right now more hope than the history of existing capitalism. . . . Marx did not create the class struggle; international capitalism did.

The most widely read of all the liberation theologians is Father Gustavo Gutiérrez of Peru, whose *A Theology of Liberation* (Orbis) has sold 45,000 copies. He writes:

> It is undeniable that the class struggle plants problems for the universality of Christian love and church unity. But every consideration on this matter ought to begin with two elemental attestations: class struggle is a fact and neutrality in this matter is impossible.

But it is not merely the theologians and the priests of Latin America who have looked upon Marxism with favor. Distinguished bishops, like the bishop of Cuernavaca, Arceo Mendez, and the archbishop of Recife, Dom Helder Camara, have been unambiguous in their preference for Marxism. Archbishop Camara, for example, addressed the University of Chicago's celebration of the seventh centenary of St. Thomas Aquinas in these terms:

> When a man, whether philosopher or not, attracts irresistibly millions of human beings, especially young people; when a man becomes the inspiration for life and for death of a great part of humanity, and makes the powerful of the earth tremble with hate and fear, this man deserves to be studied. . . . As the University of Chicago chose to take upon herself the responsibility of celebrating St. Thomas Aquinas's Seventh Centenary, we have the right to suggest that the best way to honor the centenary . . . should be for the University of Chicago to try to do with Karl Marx what St. Thomas, in his day, did with Aristotle.

The social and intellectual background of the liberation theologians is germane to their views. When I was studying theology in Rome at the Gregorian University in 1956–58, I became familiar with some of the Latin American and Spanish seminarians, and several clear impressions about their political-theological culture fixed themselves in my mind. First, it was obvious that they chafed under the image of Latin cultures which prevailed in the English-speaking world. They were, they felt, the victims of an Anglo-Saxon ethnocentric bias, a Protestant bias to boot, and a bias informed by the sort of individualism, pragmatism, and materialism they found especially abhorrent. Some seemed, in effect, to be still carrying in mind the long-ago defeat of the Spanish Armada in much the same way some Southerners recall the humiliation of defeat in the Civil War.

Many of these bright young men studied not only in Rome but in Belgium and France and Germany as well. There they shared in what was then known as *nouvelle théologie* — that contemporary reaction against Thomism, strong on scriptural studies and "salvation history," intensely preoccupied with the renewal of the church from biblical and patristic sources (and hostile to the theory of Christian democracy developed by Thomists like Jacques Maritain). On their return to Latin America, many of them became involved in the movements organizing peasants in credit unions and agrarian cooperatives. Much of their earlier training seemed far too theological, and they reacted with a veritably oedipal vehemence against their European teachers.

Yet in their work among the peasants, many found themselves already upstaged by Marxist organizers; as for the sophisticated French and German theology they brought to the peasants, it served little useful purpose. So the younger clergy began to attend more intently to the indigenous piety of the people. They discovered the power of popular religion. In its quiet endurance and strength, they found new theological resources — resources, moreover, which served to differentiate them from the despised Yankee experts and technicians who imported into Latin America the strange and threatening concepts of "development" capitalist-style. In expressing their resentment of the Northern experts, such activists have had no better spokesman than the brilliant but erratic Ivan Illich of Cuernavaca, whose anti-institutional reflections have become so popular in radical circles in North America.

THE LATIN AMERICAN CONTEXT

When the Latin American liberation theologians speak of "class struggle," they are thinking primarily of the struggle within feudalism of landholders and peasants, hardly at all of the classic Marxist picture of an industrial proletariat. (What Latin Americans persist in calling "capitalism" is, in Latin America, largely a form of syndicalism or corporatism, which descends from the rights given by the Spanish or Portuguese crown to certain large landholders or adventurers, and constitutes virtual monopoly or state mercantilism.) Both the industrial revolution and the social revolution that would have broken the power of the traditional landholders, as the Glorious Revolution did in Great Britain, have hardly been known among them. In most of Latin America, the middle class is quite small, and "bourgeois values," of the sort well established in the North Atlantic world, scarcely exist.

The full effect of the Protestant spirit of dissent and individual conscience has thus not been felt in Latin cultures. By the same token, the compensating social forces of pragmatic compromise, voluntary association, and cooperative fellow-feeling that characterize Anglo-American individualism are equally missing in Latin American politics. Latin forms of idealism and romanticism make for acute political fractionalization. There is in Latin America little scope for the entrepreneur, for invention, for enterprise. There are few Horatio Algers. The virtues most celebrated — honor, nobility, dignity — are the opposite of bourgeois.

The system confronted by Latin American Catholics is one of entrenched inequality, in which powerful landholders (often of early Spanish stock) have power and privileges far removed from those of peasants and workers (often of Amerindian stock). The Latin American elites lack those traditions of service, stewardship, and public-spiritedness that within the United States have softened the impact of economic elites upon political life. The lower classes in Latin America have had little opportunity to develop the political consciousness which has characterized the Anglo-Saxon yeoman for several centuries, and have scarcely shared in the traditions of "the rights of Englishmen" which have affected Anglo-Saxon consciousness.

The picture is further clouded by the powerful traditions of a strong, authoritarian military. In many Latin American countries, a military career has offered ambitious youngsters more opportunities for higher education and advancement than any other profession. Not infrequently, the military provides leaders of idealistic tendencies both on the socialist and on the democratic side. In recent years, however, military regimes have grown more "modern" in precisely the least humane ways: in the techniques of cruel repression.

All this, moreover, takes place in an environment in which European ideologies — both the fascism of the World War II era and the Marxism of Stalin's time — exist not merely as abstract theories but as embodied political forces. In such an environment, the theological idealist is often forced to take sides, to throw in his lot with one or another active organization. In many places there are few organized alternatives of the middle, democratic way.

Thus it was that in 1968, the second Conference of Latin American Bishops at Medellín legitimized not only the normal preaching of the church about social conscience ("the formation of Christian conscience") and not only the classical, peaceful tactics of social reform (labor unions, credit unions, cooperatives, and the like), but also the bald use of Marxist categories. It did so in a context in which instances of armed insurrection by a few "guerilla priests"—not simply as chaplains but as active combatants—were occurring, and in which the public-policy elites of the continent, especially the university intelligentsia, were already deeply immersed in Marxist thought.

But in what sense are the liberation theologians Marxist? None of them shows evidence that he has actually studied Marx, the social systems derived from Marxist thought, or the literature assessing socialist experiments. They do not, apparently, believe in the total abolition of private property (the principle Marx offered as a pithy summary of his theory). They claim not to be materialists. They are not atheists. They say that they are not totalitarians, as Castro is. They surely do not hold—since few Marxists today do—that economic gains for the poor are empirically to be achieved through the nationalization of major industries. It is doubtful whether they believe in the humane quality of the authoritarian, bureaucratic state which is the natural outgrowth of socialism. It is not clear that they are ready to impose equality, to command choices of what society and individuals "need," to insist upon planning by technical experts, or to repress private initiatives.

Nevertheless, there do seem to be two senses in which they are Marxists. Repeatedly, liberation theologians insist that they are Marxists "because the people are." By this they do not mean that "the people" have ever read Marx or know much about him but a few slogans. But the slogans are the point. If it is difficult to take liberation theologians seriously as theoreticians of Marxism, one can grant that they are "populist Marxists," using Marxist slogans to ventilate some of the frustrations and aggressions of people whose aspirations have long been colored by external propaganda.

There is a second sense in which they are Marxists. Marxism in Latin America is not just a theory. It is a well-financed, well-organized political institution, with parties, officials, printing presses, secret agents, operatives, intellectual sympathizers, international connections, and designated politicians. To be a Marxist, as the liberation theologians say, is not merely to hold a theory but to be committed to a "praxis." Yet the innocence with which the liberation theologians are committed to the Marxist "praxis" speaks volumes.

Marxist "praxis" is something of which the world has had some experience—but one would not know it from the writings of the liberation theologians. The literature of liberation theology, which is rich in general allegations about "capitalist" practice, is silent when it comes to the empirical evidence of how Marxist regimes operate. Since almost three-quarters of the world's nations are, officially, Marxist in design, and since most have had upward of thirty years to prove themselves, it should not have been beyond the capacity of theologians to work out an assessment, even a theological assessment, of their actual daily "praxis," and judge these in

the light of the gospels. But this the liberation theologians have conspicuously not done.

THE MISSING MEASUREMENTS

In recounting the experience of the "poor and the oppressed" of the
Third World, strange gaps appear in the empirical reasoning of liberation
theologians. No notice is taken of those Third World nations whose annual
rate of economic growth borders on 10 percent—nations like Taiwan, Hong
Kong, South Korea, Singapore, whose secrets in overcoming poverty are
open to inspection. No empirical survey of the comparative inequalities
between elites and the poor is made as between socialist and capitalist
regimes. Little attention is paid to measurements of institutional respect
for human dignity and liberties, as, for example, between South Korea and
North Korea.

There are other strange gaps in empirical knowledge. Bishop Helder
Camara, in his youth a Fascist as in his maturity a Marxist, is constant in
his criticism of liberal democracies. He is especially fond of the suggestion
that a small fraction of humankind uses a large fraction of the earth's
resources, and that poverty results for millions. Is this in fact true? A special
kind of human culture is required for the production of wealth. Not every
organization of society or culture is suited to such production. Indeed, only
a small fraction of the earth's population *produces* the larger part of the
world's wealth. Besides, many of the earth's resources were unknown even
a century ago, or no use for them—hence no value—had yet been found.
In fact, Latin America is immensely rich in resources, now that other cultures have discovered their secrets and learned their uses.

It is not empirically true, either, that "the poor are getting poorer." In
longevity, medical care, and nutrition, the modern production of wealth
has raised the levels of the entire population of the world by unprecedented
annual increments over the last fifty years. Average personal incomes have
also risen annually, in Latin America even more than in Asia or Africa. If
the present organization of the production of wealth is "sinful," what shall
we say of rival Marxist systems, which are not raising the levels of the poor
by so much?

Catholic theologians, especially those who claim to speak for "liberation," have a duty to study how liberation has, in fact, been attained in
human history, and by what empirical and practical means its scope can be
extended. If such a study were undertaken dispassionately and in good faith,
I believe it would show that the greatest chances for improving the concrete
daily life of human beings everywhere lie not with the forces of Marxist
"liberation" but with the forces of democratic capitalism. Others may dis-
agree; but that Catholic social theory has so far failed even to raise the
necessary intellectual questions is a sign of its bankruptcy in this area, and

of the extent to which too much of it has, in fact, already fallen hostage to Marxist categories of thought.

In the writings of liberation theologians, the contradictions of Marxist theory and practice go unnoted. And this tells us something about the liberation theologians: they are Marxists not by reason or by experience, but by faith. As Leszek Kolakowski, who (like Pope John Paul II) has lived through the Marxist phenomenon in Poland, has observed:

> Almost all the prophecies of Marx and his followers have already proved to be false, but this does not disturb the spiritual certainty of the faithful, any more than it did in the case of chiliastic sects: for it is a certainty not based on any empirical premises or supposed "historical laws," but simply on the psychological need for certainty. In this sense Marxism performs the function of a religion, and its efficacy is of a religious character.

In the real world, Marxism has been immobilized for decades as the ideological superstructure of totalitarian states and of parties aspiring to that status. As an explanatory system, Marxism "explains" little. There is nothing in the Latin American system, to which the liberation theologians point, for which Marxism affords the only or the best explanation. It offers no "method" either of inquiry or of action by which modern life is to be better understood, its future predicted, or its utopian hopes realized. Contemporary Marxist literature, as Kolakowski shows, is dogmatic, sterile, helpless, out of touch both with modern economics and with cultural life. But what Marxism does do very well today is to inspire with fantasies of utopian fulfillment, and to license the identification of some malevolent enemy as the only roadblock to that fulfillment. In a quite literal sense, the works of liberation theologians are innocent both of empirical verification and of sophistication about Marxist theory. Their originality lies chiefly in their openness to fantasy.

It is thus hardly surprising that Pope John Paul II's clear-eyed account of Marxism in Puebla proved to have a stronger bite than many Catholics could accept. He attempted to staunch the unthinking fantasies of theologians bent on the creation of totalitarian processes whose consequences they do not allow themselves to foresee and whose dynamics they cannot control. As against this, the pope maintained the independence and integrity of the church. He based himself on sound political philosophy. He spoke for the authentic interests of the poor and the oppressed, against those who would transmute their sufferings into envy, hatred, and coercion. He refused to adopt the role of Dostoevsky's Grand Inquisitor, offering bread in exchange for liberty. For this, even those who are secular have reason to be grateful.

26

Bishops of Nicaragua
"Christian Commitment
for a New Nicaragua"
(November 17, 1979)

*This pastoral letter was written four months after the overthrow of the dicta-
torship of General Anastasio Somoza in Nicaragua on July 19, 1979, by the
FSLN (Frente Sandinista de Liberación Nacional). It is a remarkable document because of its openness to and endorsement of a socialist society to
establish justice, especially for the poor. It should be recalled that the Nicaraguan bishops had taken another unprecedented step when they declared on July
2, 1979, that the Nicaraguan people had the right to join in the revolutionary
struggle. As succeeding letters of the bishops will show, this policy of collaboration was to change drastically. This is taken from* LADOC, 10 *(March-April
1980), pp. 1-4.*

To the clergy, men and women religious, basic Christian communities,
Delegates of the Word, and all people of good will, peace and blessings in
the Lord.

INTRODUCTION

We address the Nicaraguan community, of which we are a part, which
is searching for the path of truth and for justice during the current stage
of the revolutionary process in our country, a process that is being watched
by many people in the world today. We wish to speak with the clarity
demanded in the gospel (Matthew 5:37) and by the Catholic community
and all the people of Nicaragua to whom we have an obligation. We speak
as ministers of the church, aware that many Christians participated actively
in the insurrection and work today for the consolidation of its triumph. We
believe that this message can be of service to the people of God by encouraging them in their commitment and helping them to discern that which

is the role of the Holy Spirit in the revolutionary process. As a church we are convinced that there is much to be done and that we have not always been fully aware of the needs of our people.

We cannot make this discernment alone. We recall and make our own the wise words of Pope Paul VI: "In Christian communities it is necessary to determine, with the help of the Holy Spirit, in communion with the bishops involved, and in dialogue with our fellow Christians and all people of good will, the options and commitments that must be made in order to carry out the social, political, and economic changes that are felt to be urgently needed in each case" (OA, 4). For this reason, this pastoral letter is also an appeal to continue the dialogue with the Christian communities and a request that these communities, which are in closest touch with our realities, will be able to find the true spirit "to join Christ in effectively moving the history of our peoples toward the kingdom" (Puebla, 274). We know that what we have to offer is not "silver and gold" (Acts 3:6) nor to provide political and economic solutions, but to proclaim the Good News.

We wish to speak humbly and simply because we are ministers and members of a church that is "holy and at the same time in need of purification" (LG, 8; EN, 15).

We will discuss the following points in this letter:

1. Christian commitment for a new Nicaragua.
2. Evangelical motivation.
3. The responsibility and challenge of today.

PART I: CHRISTIAN COMMITMENT FOR A NEW NICARAGUA

ACCOMPLISHMENTS

We would like to begin with a few remarks about the achievements of the revolutionary process that help us to:

(a) Realize that through years of suffering and social marginalization, our people have been accumulating the experience necessary to transform this situation into a broad and profoundly liberating action.

Our people fought bravely to defend their right to live with dignity in a peaceful and just society. This struggle has given profound significance to the activities conducted against a regime that violated and repressed human, personal, and social rights. As in the past we denounced this situation as one that was contrary to the demands of the gospel, so now we wish to reaffirm that we accept the profound motivation of this struggle for justice and for life.

(b) Realize that the blood of those who gave lives in this lengthy struggle, the devotion of youth who want to build a just society, and the outstanding role of women in this whole process — elsewhere in the world postponed — signals the development of new forces for constructing a new Nicaragua. All of this underscores the originality of the historic process we are now living through. At the same time, our people's struggle to control their own future has been strongly affected by the thought and work of Augusto César Sandino, which emphasize the uniqueness of the Nicaraguan revolution, giving it its own style and its clearly defined banner of social justice, of affirmation of national values, and of international solidarity.

(c) Observe in the joy of an impoverished people who, for the first time in many years, feel that they are masters in their own country, an expression of revolutionary creativity that opens up broad and fruitful opportunities for a commitment by all who seek to fight against an unjust, oppressive system and build a new humanity.

(d) Appraise the determination to start on the first day of victory to institutionalize the revolutionary process by providing a legal basis. This was evident in the decision to keep the programs announced prior to victory. Some examples are the promulgation of the Statute on the Rights and Guarantees of Nicaraguans, the consequent practice of freedom of information, of partisan political organization, of worship, and of movement, nationalizations to recover the country's wealth, the first steps in land reform, etc. Other examples include the ability to start, on the first days of the process, to plan and organize a national literacy campaign to ennoble the spirit of our people and make them more capable of guiding their own destinies and participating more responsibly and with greater farsight in the revolutionary process.

(e) Recognize the existence in Nicaragua of conflicts between opposing interests brought about by land reform, expropriations of large estates, etc., conflicts which can be aggravated by changes in the economic, social, political, and cultural structures.

(f) Recognize also the risks, dangers, and errors in this revolutionary process, aware that there is no absolutely pure human undertaking in history and, with this in mind, to consider freedom of expression and criticism as an invaluable means of pointing out and correcting mistakes and improving the accomplishments of the revolutionary process.

TASKS

We believe that the present revolutionary moment is an opportune time to truly implement the church's option for the poor. We must remember that no historical revolutionary event can exhaust the infinite possibilities for justice and absolute solidarity of the kingdom of God. We must state that our commitment to the revolutionary process does not imply naiveté, blind enthusiasm, or the creation of a new idol before which everyone must bow down unquestioningly. Dignity, responsibility, and Christian freedom are essential attributes for active participation in the revolutionary process.

During this process, as in all other human undertakings, mistakes may be made and abuses may occur. Many Nicaraguans have certain concerns and fears. It is our pastoral duty to listen to the anxieties of the people whom we have served and discern the reasons behind these concerns. We must report those that are caused by abuse or negligence, and we must make certain that concerns arising from a lack of material resources and current conditions are not used demagogically.

The government has created channels that we believe will increasingly become more useful for collecting complaints about the revolutionary process. This creates the need for a dialogue, although it may be brief and we know that not everyone shares our point of view on some concerns that we have heard and that we think are important.

(a) Although the policy followed by the authorities has been that of avoiding executions or mistreatment of prisoners and appealing to the people not to take justice into their own hands, abuses have still occurred.

These distressing situations have been caused by some local leaders. Our task will be to give national authorities the evidence of such abuse that we have received, confident that they will know how to correct it as the possibilities for effective control and national integration increase.

(b) There is much talk about the disorder and even administrative chaos of the country, but we must remember that we are living in a time of creativity and of transition, and that reconstruction is everyone's work, not that of just certain sectors.

(c) Insofar as the freedom of political parties is concerned, it seems to us that responsible, active participation by a majority of Nicaraguans in our current revolutionary process is most important and should occur both through the existing organizations for direct popular democracy as well as through organizations that will be created out of national dialogue. Various forces have contributed generously to the historic process, and no one should prevent their continued contribution.

Leading all these forces, the *Frente Sandinista de Liberación Nacional* has clearly earned a place in history. In order to strengthen that position, the Frente's principal task is to continue calling on the whole people to make their own history through strong participation by the many in the life of the nation. This requires absolute faithfulness to the community of the poor on the part of the present leaders so as to maintain unsullied the principles of justice and the name "Sandinista" earned in the struggle for freedom.

SOCIALISM

The fear is expressed, at times with anguish, that the current process in Nicaragua is heading toward socialism. We bishops have been asked for our opinion of the matter.

If socialism, as some imagine, becomes distorted, denying persons and communities the right to decide their own destinies, and if it attempts to force persons to submit blindly to the manipulation and dictates of individuals who have arbitrarily and unlawfully seized power, then we cannot accept such false socialism. We cannot accept a socialism which oversteps its limits and attempts to take away individuals' right to a religious motivation in their life or their right to express this motivation and their religious beliefs publicly, regardless of their faith.

Equally unacceptable would be a denial of parents' right to educate their children according to their convictions or a denial of any other right of the human person.

If, on the other hand, socialism means, as it should, that the interests of the majority of Nicaraguans are paramount and if it includes a model of an economic system planned with national interests in mind, in solidarity with and providing for increased participation by the people, we have no objections. Any social program that guarantees that the country's wealth and resources will be used for the common good and that improves the quality of human life by satisfying the basic needs of all the people seems to us to be a just program. If socialism means the injustice and traditional inequalities between the cities and the country, and between remuneration for intellectual and manual labor, will be progressively reduced, and if it means the participation of workers in the fruit of their labors, overcoming economic alienation, then there is nothing in Christianity that is at odds with this process. Indeed Pope John Paul II has just drawn attention at the U.N. to the concern arising from the radical separation of labor and ownership.

If socialism implies that power is to be exercised by the majority and increasingly shared by the organized community, so that power is actually transferred to the popular classes, then it should meet nothing in our faith but encouragement and support.

If socialism leads to cultural processes that awaken the dignity of the masses and give them the courage to assume responsibility and demand their rights, then it promotes the same type of human dignity proclaimed by our faith.

Insofar as the struggle between social classes is concerned, we think that a dynamic class struggle that produces a just transformation of the social structure is one thing, while class hatred directed against individuals is another matter, which goes completely against the Christian duty to be guided by love.

Our faith tells us of the urgent Christian responsibility to subdue the earth, and transform the land and all other means of production in order to allow everyone to live fully and make of Nicaragua a land of justice, solidarity, peace, and freedom in which the Christian message of the kingdom of God can take on its full meaning.

We are further confident that our revolutionary process will be something original, creative, truly Nicaraguan, and in no sense imitative. For what we, together with most Nicaraguans, seek is a process that will result in a society completely and truly Nicaraguan, one that is neither capitalistic, nor dependent, nor totalitarian.

PART II: EVANGELICAL MOTIVATION

On various occasions in the past, we have sought to address the situation of our country in the light of the gospel (see our messages of 1/8/77 and 1/8/78). More recently, on June 2, 1979, we proclaimed the right of the Nicaraguan people to engage in revolutionary insurrection. Each time, we have relied on fidelity to the gospel and the traditional teaching of the church.

It now falls to us again, in this new situation, to offer a word of faith and of hope concerning the present revolutionary process and how, through it, we can accomplish what the gospel requires of us.

We would like, therefore, to recall a fundamental truth of our Christian faith, one which we are rediscovering and seeing again as central in the present situation of our country and in the orientation of the process of revolutionary change.

ANNOUNCEMENT OF THE KINGDOM OF GOD

The heart of Jesus' message is the announcement of the kingdom of God, a kingdom founded on the Father's love for all humankind and in which the poor hold a special place. "Kingdom" signifies universality; nothing is outside it. Proclaiming the kingdom of God means proclaiming the God of the kingdom and God's fatherly love, the foundation of solidarity among all peoples.

Jesus tells us that the kingdom means liberation and justice (Luke 4:16-20), because it is a kingdom of life. Our need to build this kingdom is the basis for our accepting and participating in the current process, whose purpose is to ensure that all Nicaraguans truly live. Our faith in this God moves us to emphasize what we have always preached but which has now moved urgently to the fore. To believe in this God is to give life to others, to love them in truth and to do justice. The particular life which God wants for Nicaraguans can only be achieved by radically overcoming the selfishness and casting aside the self-interest which have festered in our country for so many years and have, we must tragically recall, caused the deaths of our brothers and sisters. Each of us must be made to live a life of love and justice, to forget about ourselves and to consider what we can contribute.

EVANGELICAL COMMITMENT

To announce the kingdom means that we have to bring it into our lives. On that effort, the authenticity of our faith in God is staked, establishing what the holy Scriptures call "justice and right" for the poor. It is commitment which tests our faith in Christ, who gave his life to proclaim the kingdom of God. There is no life of faith unless there is witness to it, which is given in our acts. Only then can the announcement through the word be understood and be confirmed. In our commitment to help the poor and to fight against social injustice, our faith becomes truly productive, for others as well as for ourselves. By acting as Christians, we become Christians. Without such solidarity, our announcement of the Good News is but an empty phrase. An evangelical movement of liberation implies a commitment to the liberation of our people. In the words of the bishops at Puebla, "Confronted with the realities that are part of our lives today, we must learn from the gospel that in Latin America we cannot truly love our fellow beings, and hence God, unless we commit ourselves on the personal level, and on the structural level as well" (327). After a long and patient wait, our people have committed themselves to the struggle for their full and total liberation.

LIBERATION IN JESUS CHRIST

Liberation in Jesus Christ encompasses the various aspects of human existence, because God wants people to live and to live fully. God thus created humanity according to a plan in which our relationships with nature, with our fellows, and with God are linked closely together. First is the relationship with nature, whereby human beings can satisfy their most elemental needs. Harnessing it through a planned economy to the benefit of humankind forms the basis for a just society. There is also the relationship between individuals in society, which must be marked by fellowship implying genuine unity and effective participation by all in the society to which they belong. For us today, this must be primarily the work of justice for the oppressed and an effort to liberate those who need it most (Puebla, 327). Yet liberation also signifies a relationship with God. As children who accept and live in the light of God's freely given love, we are inextricably linked to nature and to society. When we reject our fellows, we reject God. The act of love for the poor and oppressed is an act of love for the Lord (Matthew 25:31-46). Complete liberation encompasses these three, mutually inclusive, aspects. In neglecting one of them, we diminish the rights and the potential of the human person. In accepting the free gift of the Father, we are committing ourselves to the struggle for justice and the establishment of brotherhood. This, in turn, acquires its full significance in the acknowledgment of the presence in history of God's liberating love.

SOCIAL COMMITMENT

The kingdom of God, the heart of Christ's message, is at the same time a requirement for social commitment which incorporates a critical judgment of history and refuses to deny change. It is open to human creativity and to the outpouring of the Lord's grace.

The situation in our country today offers an exceptional opportunity for announcing and for bearing witness to God's kingdom. If, through fear and mistrust, or through the insecurity of some in the face of any radical social change, or through the desire to defend personal interests, we neglect this crucial opportunity to commit ourselves to the poor, urged by both Pope John Paul II and the bishops at Puebla, we would be in serious violation of the gospel's teachings.

This commitment implies the renunciation of old ways of thinking and behaving, and the dramatic conversion of our church. Indeed, the day when the church fails to present the appearance of poverty and to act as the natural ally of the poor, will be the day it has betrayed its divine creator and the coming of God's kingdom. Never before has Nicaragua been faced with such an urgent need to persuasively confirm this commitment to the poor.

The poor of whom Jesus speaks and who surround him are the truly poor, the hungry, the afflicted, the oppressed, and all those for whom society has failed to provide a place. Through this solidarity with the poor, Jesus proclaimed his Father's love for all humankind, was persecuted, and died.

PREFERENTIAL OPTION FOR THE POOR

Brothers and sisters of Nicaragua, our faith in Jesus and in the God of life must enlighten our Christian commitment in the current revolutionary process. The first contribution of the church and each Nicaraguan is the preference for the poor; thus, each should support the measures and laws which bring the poor out of their oppression, restoring their rights and strengthening the institutions which assure their freedom. We cannot and must not close our eyes to the dangers and possible errors inherent in any historical process of change; indeed, we believe that we must clearly and boldly lay them bare, working from the gospel, whose word it is our task and responsibility to spread. But we are convinced that this commitment will be authentic only if we listen humbly and perceptively to what the Lord is telling us through the signs of our times.

We wish to share this discernment and this commitment with the entire Nicaraguan ecclesial community, where we hope to encounter a spirit and a vocation in unity with the poor, whose "evangelizing potential" we have discovered and who call the whole church to conversion (Puebla, 1147).

PART III: THE RESPONSIBILITY AND CHALLENGE OF TODAY

The eyes of Latin America and of the Latin American church are on Nicaragua. Our revolution is occurring at a time when the Catholic Church, through the experiences of Vatican II, Medellín, and Puebla, is becoming increasingly aware of the fact that the cause of the poor is its own.

Many are the church members of this continent who have lately given clear witness to this solidarity. Aware that the revolutionary process demands generosity and sacrifice, we urge all of you, our brothers and sisters, to join with us in finding the motivation and strength in our faith so that we will be the first to accept the sacrifice and to devote ourselves to the task of building a new Nicaragua.

In the first place, the revolution requires us to undergo a profound change of heart. It also demands austerity in our lives. The war, and above all the previous social order, have left us with a legacy of economic poverty, despite the richness of our country. The exodus of competent administrative personnel and the inevitable confusion when any such radical change in systems occurs, only worsen the problem.

We must be prepared to support the lean years with austerity and prevent those who must bear the consequences from being in the majority. As Christians aware of the Lord's exhortation to poverty, we must be the first to accept, joyfully and generously, this period of austerity. We are certain that it will lead to a more fully human and fraternal way of life. In this way we will learn, as John Paul II has maintained repeatedly, that peoples' fulfillment and the satisfaction of needs are not predicated upon abundance and still less on consumerism. The human person rather finds fulfillment as an individual from the solidarity which enables each to satisfy basic material needs and to create a higher level of culture, to labor more productively and humanistically, and to achieve a peace more receptive each day to spiritual progress. At the same time, we appeal for a halt to capital flight and for increased repatriation and reinvestment. We call for more equitable international trade practices and fairer conditions for renegotiating Nicaragua's foreign debt, in the certainty that this will help alleviate shortages and prevent much human suffering.

GENEROSITY OF OUR YOUNG PEOPLE

The hope of this revolution lies above all in the youth of Nicaragua. They have shown an outpouring of generosity and valor which has astonished the world, and henceforth will be the principal architects of this new "civilization of love" (Puebla, 1188) which we hope to build. It is up to them to incarnate in the revolutionary process the authentic values of the gospel. The evangelical effort of the whole church must be channelled to them with special care.

FREEDOM IN OUR APOSTOLIC MISSION

We Nicaraguan bishops want no special privileges for the church other than the ability to accomplish its evangelical mission of humble but valued service to the people. To do so, the church desires only "that broad area of freedom that will enable it to carry out its apostolic work without interference. That work includes the practice of cultic worship, education in the faith, and the fostering of those many and varied activities that lead the faithful to implement the moral imperatives deriving from the faith in their private, family, and social life" (Puebla, 144). The people of God must become revitalized through the basic Christian communities which create a growing sense of fellowship. The church must learn and teach others to see things from the perspective of the poor, whose cause is that of Christ. By adopting the cause of all Nicaraguans as its own, the church believes that it will be able to make an important contribution to the process which the country is now experiencing.

May the Virgin of the Magnificat, who sings of the fall of the powerful and the exaltation of the humble (Luke 2:52), guide us and help us in fulfilling our role in the arduous and exciting task of building a new Nicaragua in this hour when the commitment to the poor makes it possible to "create new horizons of hope" (Puebla, 1165).

Managua, November 17, 1979.

Archbishop Miguel Obando y Bravo, Managua
Bishop-Prelate Pablo A. Vega M., Juigalpa
Bishop Ruben López Ardón, Estelí
Bishop Manuel Salazar Espinosa, León
Bishop Leovigildo López Fitoria, Granada
Bishop Julián Barni, Matagalpa
Bishop Salvador Schlaefer, Bluefields Vicariate

27

Archbishop Oscar Romero
"The Political Dimension of the Faith
from the Perspective of the Option
for the Poor"
(University of Louvain, February 2, 1980)

As archbishop of San Salvador, the capital of El Salvador, Romero took the side of poor peasants and others against the forces of the military government and death squads. On the day before his death, he preached to soldiers of the army to cease killing their own fellow citizens, and this seems to have been the immediate reason for his assassination. Because of his prophetic boldness and serene courage in defending the rights of the poor, he has become a symbol and martyr, not only for El Salvador, but for all Latin America. His address was on the occasion of the conferral of a doctorate, Honoris Causa, by the University of Louvain, Belgium, February 2, 1980. The text is taken from Archbishop Oscar Romero, Voice of the Voiceless: The Four Pastoral Letters and Other State- ments *(Maryknoll, N.Y.: Orbis Books, 1985), pp. 177–87.*

I come from the smallest country in faraway Latin America. I come bringing in my heart, which is that of a Salvadoran Christian and pastor, greetings, gratitude, and the joy of sharing the experiences of life.

I first of all greet with admiration this noble alma mater of Louvain. Never did I imagine the enormous honor of being thus linked with a Eu- ropean center of such academic and cultural prestige, a center where were born so many of the ideas that have contributed to the marvelous effort being made by the church and by society to adapt themselves to the new times in which we live.

Therefore I come also to express my thanks to the University of Louvain, and to the church in Belgium. I want to think of this honorary doctorate as something other than an act of homage to me personally. The enormous disproportion of such a great weight being attributed to my few merits would overwhelm me. Let me rather interpret this generous distinction awarded by the university as an affectionate act of homage to the people of El Salvador and to their church, as an eloquent testimony of support for, and solidarity with, the sufferings of my people and for their noble struggle for liberation, and as a gesture of communion, and of sympathy, with the apostolic work of my archdiocese.

I could not refuse to accept the privilege of this act of homage if, by coming to receive it, I could come to thank the church of Belgium for the invaluable pastoral help it has given to the church of El Salvador. It would not, indeed, have been possible to find a more suitable time and place to say "thank you" than this one, so courteously provided for me by the University of Louvain. So, from the depths of my heart, many thanks to you—bishops, priests, religious, and lay persons—for so generously uniting your lives, your labors, the hardships, and the persecution involved in our pastoral activities.

And in the same spirit of friendship as that in which I expressed my greetings and my gratitude, I want to express the joy I have in coming to share with you, in a fraternal way, my experience as a pastor and as a Salvadoran, and my theological reflection as a teacher of the faith.

In line with the friendly suggestion made by the university, I have the honor of placing this experience and reflection within the series of conferences taking place here upon the theme of the political dimension of the Christian faith.

I shall not try to talk, and you cannot expect me to talk, as would an expert in politics. Nor will I even speculate, as someone might who was an expert, on the theoretical relationship between the faith and politics. No, I am going to speak to you simply as a pastor, as one who, together with his people, has been learning the beautiful but harsh truth that the Christian faith does not cut us off from the world but immerses us in it, that the church is not a fortress set apart from the city. The church follows Jesus who lived, worked, battled, and died in the midst of a city, in the *polis*. It is in this sense that I should like to talk about the political dimension of the Christian faith: in the precise sense of the repercussions of the faith on the world, and also of the repercussions that being in the world has on the faith.

A CHURCH AT THE SERVICE OF THE WORLD

We ought to be clear from the start that the Christian faith and the activity of the church have always had socio-political repercussions. By commission or omission, by associating themselves with one or another social group, Christians have always had an influence upon the socio-political makeup of the world in which they lived. The problem is about the "how" of this influence in the socio-political world, whether or not it is in accordance with the faith.

As a first idea, though still a very general one, I want to propose the intuition of Vatican II that lies at the root of every ecclesial movement of today. The essence of the church lies in its mission of service to the world, in its mission to save the world in its totality, and of saving it in history, here and now. The church exists to act in solidarity with the hopes and joys, the anxieties and sorrows, of men and women. Like Jesus, the church was sent "to bring good news to the poor, to heal the contrite of heart . . . to seek and to save what was lost" (Luke 4:18, 19:10).

THE WORLD OF THE POOR

You all know these words of Scripture, given prominence by Vatican II.[1] During the 1960s several of your bishops and theologians helped to throw light on the essence and the mission of the church understood in these terms. My contribution will be to flesh out those beautiful declarations from the standpoint of my own situation, that of a small Latin American country, typical of what today is called the Third World. To put it in one word — in a word that sums it all up and makes it concrete — the world that the church ought to serve is, for us, the world of the poor.

Our Salvadoran world is no abstraction. It is not another example of what is understood by "world" in developed countries such as yours. It is a world made up mostly of men and women who are poor and oppressed. And we say of that world of the poor that it is the key to understanding the Christian faith, to understanding the activity of the church and the political dimension of that faith and that ecclesial activity. It is the poor who tell us what the world is, and what the church's service to the world should be. It is the poor who tell us what the *polis* is, what the city is and what it means for the church really to live in that world.

Allow me, then, briefly to explain from the perspective of the poor among my people, whom I represent, the situation and the activity of our church in the world in which we live, and then to reflect theologically upon the importance that this real world, this culture, this socio-political world, has for the church.

In its pastoral work, our archdiocese in recent years has been moving in a direction that can only be described and only be understood as a turning toward the world of the poor, to their real, concrete world.

INCARNATION IN THE WORLD OF THE POOR

Just as elsewhere in Latin America, the words of Exodus have, after many years, perhaps centuries, finally resounded in our ears: "The cry of the sons of Israel has come to me, and I have witnessed the way in which the Egyptians oppress them" (Exod. 3:9). These words have given us new eyes to see what has always been the case among us, but which has so often been hidden, even from the view of the church itself. We have learned to see what is the first, basic fact about our world and, as pastors, we have made a judgment about it at Medellín and at Puebla. "That misery, as a collective fact, expresses itself as an injustice which cries to the heavens."[2] At Puebla we declared, "So we brand the situation of inhuman poverty in which millions of Latin Americans live as the most devastating and humiliating kind of scourge. And this situation finds expression in such things as a high rate of infant mortality, lack of adequate housing, health problems, starvation wages, unemployment and underemployment, malnutrition, job uncertainty, compulsory mass migrations, etc."[3] Experiencing these realities, and letting ourselves be affected by them, far from separating us from our faith has sent us back to the world of the poor as to our true home. It has moved us, as a first, basic step, to take the world of the poor upon ourselves.

It is there that we have found the real faces of the poor, about which Puebla speaks.[4] There we have met landworkers without land and without steady employment, without running water or electricity in their homes, without medical assistance when mothers give birth, and without schools for their children. There we have met factory workers who have no labor rights, and who get fired from their jobs if they demand such rights; human beings who are at the mercy of cold economic calculations. There we have met the mothers and the wives of those who have disappeared, or who are political prisoners. There we have met the shantytown dwellers, whose wretchedness defies imagination, suffering the permanent mockery of the mansions nearby.

It is within this world devoid of a human face, this contemporary sacrament of the suffering servant of Yahweh, that the church of my archdiocese has undertaken to incarnate itself. I do not say this in a triumphalistic spirit, for I am well aware how much in this regard remains to be done. But I say it with immense joy, for we have made the effort not to pass by afar off, not to circle round the one lying wounded in the roadway, but to approach him or her as did the good Samaritan.

This coming closer to the world of the poor is what we understand both by the incarnation and by conversion. The changes that were needed within the church and in its apostolate, in education, in religious and in priestly life, in lay movements, which we had not brought about simply by looking inward upon the church, we are now carrying out by turning ourselves outward toward the world of the poor.

PROCLAIMING THE GOOD NEWS TO THE POOR

Our encounter with the poor has regained for us the central truth of the gospel, through which the word of God urges us to conversion. The church has to proclaim the Good News to the poor. Those who, in this-worldly terms, have heard bad news, and who have lived out even worse realities, are now listening through the church to the word of Jesus: "The kingdom of God is at hand; blessed are you who are poor, for the kingdom of God is yours." And hence they also have Good News to proclaim to the rich: that they, too, become poor in order to share the benefits of the kingdom with the poor. Anyone who knows Latin America will be quite clear that there is no ingenuousness in these words, still less the workings of a soporific drug. What is to be found in these words is a coming together of the aspiration on our continent for liberation, and God's offer of love to the poor. This is the hope that the church offers, and it coincides with the hope, at times dormant and at other times frustrated or manipulated, of the poor of Latin America.

It is something new among our people that today the poor see in the church a source of hope and a support for their noble struggle for liberation. The hope that our church encourages is neither naive nor passive. It is rather a summons from the word of God for the great majority of the people, the poor, that they assume their proper responsibility, that they undertake their own conscientization, that, in a country where it is legally or practically prohibited (at some periods more so than at others) they set about organizing themselves. And it is support, sometimes critical support, for their just causes and demands. The hope that we preach to the poor is intended to give them back their dignity, to encourage them to take charge of their own future. In a word, the church has not only turned toward the poor, it has made of the poor the special beneficiaries of its mission because, as Puebla says, "God takes on their defense and loves them."[5]

COMMITMENT TO THE DEFENSE OF THE POOR

The church has not only incarnated itself in the world of the poor, giving them hope; it has also firmly committed itself to their defense. The majority of the poor in our country are oppressed and repressed daily by economic and political structures. The terrible words spoken by the prophets of Israel continue to be verified among us. Among us there are those who sell others for money, who sell a poor person for a pair of sandals; those who, in their mansions, pile up violence and plunder; those who crush the poor; those who make the kingdom of violence come closer as they lie upon their beds of ivory; those who join house to house, and field to field, until they occupy the whole land, and are the only ones there.

Amos and Isaiah are not just voices from distant centuries; their writings are not merely texts that we reverently read in the liturgy. They are everyday realities. Day by day we live out the cruelty and ferocity they excoriate. We live them out when there come to us the mothers and the wives of those who have been arrested or who have disappeared, when mutilated bodies turn up in secret cemeteries, when those who fight for justice and peace are assassinated. Daily we live out in our archdiocese what Puebla so vigorously denounced: "There are the anxieties based on systematic or selective repression; it is accompanied by accusations, violations of privacy, improper pressures, tortures, and exiles. There are the anxieties produced in many families by the disappearance of their loved ones, about whom they cannot get any news. There is the total insecurity bound up with arrest and detention without judicial consent. There are the anxieties, felt in the face of a system of justice that has been suborned or cowed."[6]

In this situation of conflict and antagonism, in which just a few persons control economic and political power, the church has placed itself at the side of the poor and has undertaken their defense. The church cannot do otherwise, for it remembers that Jesus had pity on the multitude. But by defending the poor it has entered into serious conflict with the powerful who belong to the monied oligarchies and with the political and military authorities of the state.

PERSECUTED FOR SERVING THE POOR

This defense of the poor in a world deep in conflict has occasioned something new in the recent history of our church: persecution. You know the more important facts. In less than three years over fifty priests have been attacked, threatened, calumniated. Six are already martyrs—they were murdered. Some have been tortured and others expelled. Nuns have also been persecuted. The archdiocesan radio station and educational institutions that are Catholic or of a Christian inspiration have been attacked, threatened, intimidated, even bombed. Several parish communities have been raided.

If all this has happened to persons who are the most evident representatives of the church, you can guess what has happened to ordinary Christians, to the campesinos, catechists, lay ministers, and to the ecclesial base communities. There have been threats, arrests, tortures, murders, numbering in the hundreds and thousands. As always, even in persecution, it has been the poor among the Christians who have suffered most.

It is, then, an indisputable fact that, over the last three years, our church has been persecuted. But it is important to note why it has been persecuted. Not any and every priest has been persecuted, not any and every institution has been attacked. That part of the church has been attacked and persecuted that put itself on the side of the people and went to the people's defense.

Here again we find the same key to understanding the persecution of the church: the poor. Once again it is the poor who bring us to understand what has really happened. That is why the church has understood the persecution from the perspective of the poor. Persecution has been occasioned by the defense of the poor. It amounts to nothing other than the church's taking upon itself the lot of the poor.

Real persecution has been directed against the poor, the body of Christ in history today. They, like Jesus, are the crucified, the persecuted servant of Yahweh. They are the ones who make up in their own bodies that which is lacking in the passion of Christ. And for that reason when the church has organized and united itself around the hopes and the anxieties of the poor, it has incurred the same fate as that of Jesus and of the poor: persecution.

THE POLITICAL DIMENSION OF THE FAITH

This has been a brief sketch of the situation, and of the stance, of the church in El Salvador. The political dimension of the faith is nothing other than the church's response to the demands made upon it by the de facto socio-political world in which it exists. What we have rediscovered is that this demand is a fundamental one for the faith, and that the church cannot ignore it. That is not to say that the church should regard itself as a political institution entering into competition with other political institutions, or that it has its own political processes. Nor, much less, is it to say that our church seeks political leadership. I am talking of something more profound, something more in keeping with the gospel. I am talking about an authentic option for the poor, of becoming incarnate in their world, of proclaiming the good news to them, of giving them hope, of encouraging them to engage in a liberating praxis, of defending their cause and of sharing their fate.

The church's option for the poor explains the political dimension of the faith in its fundamentals and in its basic outline. Because the church has opted for the truly poor, not for the fictitiously poor, because it has opted for those who really are oppressed and repressed, the church lives in a political world, and it fulfills itself as church also through politics. It cannot be otherwise if the church, like Jesus, is to turn itself toward the poor.

MAKING THE FAITH REAL IN THE WORLD OF THE POOR

The course taken by the archdiocese has clearly issued from its faith conviction. The transcendence of the gospel has guided us in our judgment and in our action. We have judged the social and political situation from the standpoint of the faith. But it is also true, to look at it another way, that the faith itself has been deepened, that hidden riches of the gospel have been opened, precisely by taking up this stance toward socio-political reality such as it is.

Now I should just like to put forward some short reflections on several fundamental aspects of the faith that we have seen enriched through this real incarnation in the socio-political world.

A CLEARER AWARENESS OF SIN

In the first place, we have a better knowledge of what sin is. We know that offending God is death for humans. We know that such a sin really is mortal, not only in the sense of the interior death of the person who commits the sin, but also because of the real, objective death the sin produces.

Let us remind ourselves of a fundamental datum of our Christian faith: sin killed the Son of God, and sin is what goes on killing the children of God.

We see that basic truth of the Christian faith daily in the situation in our country. It is impossible to offend God without offending one's brother or sister. And the worst offense against God, the worst form of secularism, as one of our Salvadoran theologians has said, is:

> to turn children of God, temples of the Holy Spirit, the body of Christ in history, into victims of oppression and injustice, into slaves to economic greed, into fodder for political repression. The worst of these forms of secularism is the denial of grace by the objectivization of this world as an operative presence of the powers of evil, the visible presence of the denial of God.[7]

It is not a matter of sheer routine that I insist once again on the existence in our country of structures of sin. They are sin because they produce the fruits of sin: the deaths of Salvadorans—the swift death brought by repression or the long, drawn out, but no less real, death from structural oppression. That is why we have denounced what in our country has become the idolatry of wealth, of the absolute right, within the capitalist system, of private property, of political power in National Security regimes, in the name of which personal security is itself institutionalized.

No matter how tragic it may appear, the church through its entrance into the real socio-political world has learned how to recognize, and how to deepen its understanding of, the essence of sin. The fundamental essence of sin, in our world, is revealed in the death of Salvadorans.

GREATER CLARITY ON THE INCARNATION AND REDEMPTION

In the second place we now have a better understanding of what the incarnation means, what it means to say that Jesus really took human flesh and made himself one with his brothers and sisters in suffering, in tears and laments, in surrender. I am not speaking of a universal incarnation. This is impossible. I am speaking of an incarnation that is preferential and partial: incarnation in the world of the poor. From that perspective the church will become a church for everybody. It will offer a service to the powerful, too, through the apostolate of conversion—but not the other way around, as has so often been the case in the past.

The world of the poor, with its very concrete social and political characteristics, teaches us where the church can incarnate itself in such a way that it will avoid the false universalism that inclines the church to associate itself with the powerful. The world of the poor teaches us what the nature of Christian love is, a love that certainly seeks peace but also unmasks false pacifism—the pacifism of resignation and inactivity. It is a love that should certainly be freely offered, but that seeks to be effective in history. The world of the poor teaches us that the sublimity of Christian love ought to be mediated through the overriding necessity of justice for the majority. It ought not to turn away from honorable conflict. The world of the poor teaches us that liberation will arrive only when the poor are not simply on the receiving end of handouts from governments or from the church, but when they themselves are the masters of, and protagonists in, their own struggle and liberation, thereby unmasking the root of false paternalism, including ecclesiastical paternalism.

The real world of the poor also teaches us about Christian hope. The church preaches a new heaven and a new earth. It knows, moreover, that no socio-political system can be exchanged for the final fullness that is given by God. But it has also learned that transcendent hope must be preserved by signs of hope in history, no matter how simple they may apparently be — such as those proclaimed by the Trito-Isaiah when he says "they will build houses and inhabit them, plant vineyards and eat their fruit" (Isa. 65:21). What in this is an authentically Christian hope — not reduced, as is so often said disparagingly, to what is merely of this world or purely human — is being learned daily through contact with those who have no houses and no vineyards, those who build for others to inhabit and work so that others may eat the fruits.

A DEEPER FAITH IN GOD AND IN CHRIST

In the third place, incarnation in the socio-political world is the locus for deepening faith in God and in Christ. We believe in Jesus who came to bring the fullness of life, and we believe in a living God who gives life to men and women and wants them truly to live. These radical truths of the faith become really true and truly radical when the church enters into the heart of the life and death of its people. Then there is put before the faith of the church, as it is put before the faith of every individual, the most fundamental choice: to be in favor of life or to be in favor of death. We see, with great clarity, that here neutrality is impossible. Either we serve the life of Salvadorans, or we are accomplices in their death. And here what is most fundamental about the faith is given expression in history: either we believe in a God of life, or we serve the idols of death.

In the name of Jesus we want, and we work for, life in its fullness, a life that is not reduced to the frantic search for basic material needs, nor one reduced to the sphere of the socio-political. We know perfectly well that the superabundant fullness of life is to be achieved only in the kingdom of the Father. In human history this fullness is achieved through a worthy service of that kingdom, and total surrender to the Father. But we see with equal clarity that in the name of Jesus it would be sheer illusion, it would be an irony, and, at bottom, it would be the most profound blasphemy, to forget and to ignore the basic levels of life, the life that begins with bread, a roof, a job.

With the Apostle John we believe that Jesus is "the Word who is life" (1 John 1:1), and that God is revealed wherever this life is to be found. Where the poor begin to really live, where the poor begin to free themselves, where persons are able to sit around a common table to share with one another—the God of life is there. When the church inserts itself into the socio-political world it does so in order to work with it so that from such cooperation life may be given to the poor. In doing so, therefore, it is not distancing itself from its mission, nor is it doing something of secondary importance or something incidental to its mission. It is giving testimony to its faith in God; it is being the instrument of the Spirit, the Lord and giver of life.

This faith in the God of life is the explanation for what lies deepest in the Christian mystery. To give life to the poor, one has to give of one's own life, even to give one's life itself. The greatest sign of faith in a God of life is the witness of those who are ready to give up their own life. "A man can have no greater love than to lay down his life for his friends" (John 15:13). And we see this daily in our country. Many Salvadorans, many Christians, are ready to give their lives so that the poor may have life. They are following Jesus and showing their faith in him. Living within the real world just as Jesus did, like him accused and threatened, like him laying down their lives, they are giving witness to the word of life.

Our story, then, is a very old one. It is Jesus' story that we, in all modesty, are trying to follow. As church, we are not political experts, nor do we want to manipulate politics through its own internal mechanisms. But entrance into the socio-political world, into the world where the lives and deaths of the great mass of the population are decided upon, is necessary and urgent if we are to preserve, not only in word but in deed, faith in a God of life, and follow the lead of Jesus.

CONCLUSION

In conclusion, I should like to sum up what is central to the things I have been saying. In the ecclesial life of our archdiocese the political dimension of the faith—or, if one prefers, the relationship between faith and politics—has not been discovered by purely theoretical reflection, reflection made before the church has acted. Such reflection is important—but not decisive. Such reflection becomes important *and* decisive when it does indeed reflect the real life of the church. The honor of putting my pastoral experience into words in this university setting has obliged me today to undertake theological reflection. But it is rather in the actual practice of service to the poor that the political dimension of the faith is to be found, and correctly found. In such practice one can discover the relationship between the two, and what distinguishes them. It is the faith that provides the first impulse to incarnate oneself in the socio-political world of the poor, and gives encouragement to actions that lead to liberation and are also socio-political. And in their own turn that praxis and that incarnation make concrete the basic aspects of the faith.

In what I have here laid out, I have sketched only a broad outline of this double movement. Naturally, there are many more topics to be discussed. I might have talked about the relationship between the faith and political ideologies—in particular Marxism. I could have dwelt upon the question of violence and its legitimacy—a burning issue for us. Such topics are frequent subjects for reflection, and we face them without preconceptions and without fear. But we face them to the extent that they become real problems, and we are learning to provide solutions within the same process.

In the short period it has fallen to me to guide the archdiocese, there have been four different governments with distinctive political programs. Over these years other political forces, revolutionary and democratic, have been growing and developing. So the church has had to go on making judgments about politics from within a changing scene. At the present time the outlook is ambiguous. On the one hand all the projects emanating from the government are collapsing, and the possibility of popular liberation is growing.

But rather than listing for you all the fluctuations in the politics of El Salvador, I have chosen to explain what lies at the root of the church's stance in our explosive socio-political world. I have tried to make clear to you the ultimate criterion, one which is theological and historical, for the church's involvement in the world of the poor. In accordance with its own specific nature the church will go on supporting one or another political program to the extent that it operates in favor of the poor among the people.

I believe that this is the way to maintain the church's identity and transcendence. We enter into the real socio-political development of our people. We judge it from the point of view of the poor. We encourage all liberation movements that really lead to justice and peace for the majority of the people. We think this is the way to preserve the transcendence and the identity of the church, because in this way we preserve our faith in God.

Early Christians used to say *Gloria Dei, vivens homo* ("the glory of God is the living person"). We could make this more concrete by saying *Gloria Dei, vivens pauper* ("the glory of God is the living poor person"). From the perspective of the transcendence of the gospel, I believe we can determine what the life of the poor truly is. And I also believe that by putting ourselves alongside the poor and trying to bring life to them we shall come to know the eternal truth of the gospel.

NOTES

1. *Lumen Gentium,* 8.
2. "Justice," 1.

3. Final Document, 29.

4. See ibid., 31–39.

5. Ibid., 1142.

6. Ibid., 42.

7. I. Ellacuría, "Entre Medellín y Puebla," *Estudios Centroamericanos*, March 1978, n. 353, p. 123.

28

Archbishop Oscar Romero
Last Homily
(March 24, 1980)

On the above date, Archbishop Romero celebrated Mass on the first anniversary of the death of Sara Meardi de Pinto, mother of Jorge Pinto, editor of El Independiente, *a weekly journal that fought for human rights in El Salvador. The Mass began at about six in the evening in the chapel of the Divine Providence Hospital in San Salvador. During the homily, Romero was shot once through the heart by an assassin standing in the doorway of the chapel. The homily is taken from* Voice of the Voiceless, *pp. 191–93.*

Because of the manifold relationship I have had with the editor of the newspaper *El Independiente*, I am able to share to some extent his feelings on the anniversary of his mother's death. Above all, I can appreciate her noble spirit, how she put all of her educated upbringing, all her graciousness, at the service of a cause that is so important now: our people's true liberation.

My dear brothers and sisters, I think we should not only pray this evening for the eternal rest of our dear Doña Sarita, but above all we should take to ourselves her message, one that every Christian ought to want to live intensely. Many do not understand; they think Christianity should not be involved in such things. But, to the contrary, you have just heard in Christ's gospel that one must not love oneself so much as to avoid getting involved in the risks of life that history demands of us, and that those who try to fend off the danger will lose their lives, while those who out of love for Christ give themselves to the service of others will live, like the grain of wheat that dies, but only apparently. If it did not die, it would remain alone. The harvest comes about only because it dies, allowing itself to be sacrificed in the earth and destroyed. Only by undoing itself does it produce the harvest.

Now in eternity, Doña Sarita gives us the same wonderful message that Vatican II gives us in the following passage, which I have chosen on her behalf:

304

We do not know the time for the consummation of the earth and of humanity. Nor do we know how all things will be transformed. As deformed by sin, the shape of this world will pass away. But we are taught that God is preparing a new dwelling place and a new earth where justice will abide, and whose blessedness will answer and surpass all the longings for peace which spring up in the human heart.

Then, with death overcome, the sons of God will be raised up in Christ. What was sown in weakness and corruption will be clothed with incorruptibility. While charity and its fruits endure, all that creation which God made on our account will be unchained from the bondage of vanity.

Therefore, while we are warned that it profits us nothing if we gain the whole world and lose ourselves, the expectation of a new earth must not weaken but rather stimulate our concern for cultivating this one. For here grows the body of a new human family, a body which even now is able to give some kind of foreshadowing of the new age.

Earthly progress must be carefully distinguished from the growth of Christ's kingdom. Nevertheless, to the extent that the former can contribute to the better ordering of human society, it is of vital concern to the kingdom of God.

For after we have obeyed the Lord, and in his Spirit nurtured on earth the values of human dignity, brotherhood, and freedom, and indeed all the good fruits of our nature and enterprise, we will find them again, but freed of stain, burnished and transfigured. This will be so when Christ hands over to the Father a kingdom eternal and universal: "a kingdom of truth and life, of holiness and grace, of justice, love, and peace." On this earth that kingdom is already present in mystery. When the Lord returns, it will be brought into full flower [*Gaudium et Spes*, 39].

This is the hope that inspires us Christians. We know that every effort to better society, especially when injustice and sin are so ingrained, is an effort that God blesses, that God wants, that God demands of us. Doña Sarita was that kind of generous person, and her attitude was embodied in her son Jorge and in all those who work for these ideals. Of course, we must try to purify these ideals, Christianize them, clothe them with the hope of what lies beyond. That makes them stronger, because it gives us the assurance that all that we cultivate on earth, if we nourish it with Christian hope, will never be a failure. We will find it in a purer form in that kingdom where our merit will be in the labor we have done here on earth.

As we celebrate this anniversary, I think we do not aspire in vain in these times of hope and struggle. We remember with gratitude this generous woman who was able to sympathize with the concerns of her husband and her son and of all those who work for a better world, and who added her own grain of wheat through her suffering. I have no doubt this will guarantee that her heavenly reward will be in proportion to her sacrifice and to her sympathy—self-sacrifice and sympathy that many lack at this moment in El Salvador.

Dear brothers and sisters, let us all view these matters at this historic moment with that hope, that spirit of giving and of sacrifice. Let us all do what we can. We can all do something, at least have a sense of understanding and sympathy. The holy woman we remember today could not do many things directly perhaps, but she did encourage those who can work, sympathized with their struggle, and above all prayed. Even after her death, she sends a message from eternity that it is worthwhile to labor, because all those longings for justice, peace, and well-being that we experience on earth become realized for us if we enlighten them with Christian hope. We know that no one can go on forever, but those who have put into their work a sense of very great faith, of love of God, of hope among human beings, find it all results in the splendors of a crown that is the sure reward of those who labor thus, cultivating truth, justice, love, and goodness on the earth. Such labor does not remain here below, but purified by God's Spirit, is harvested for our reward.

This holy Mass, now, this eucharist, is just such an act of faith. To Christian faith at this moment the voice of diatribe appears changed for the body of the Lord, who offered himself for the redemption of the world, and in this chalice the wine is transformed into the blood that was the price of salvation. May this body immolated and this blood sacrificed for humans nourish us also, so that we may give our body and our blood to suffering and to pain—like Christ, not for self, but to bring about justice and peace for our people.

Let us join together, then, intimately in faith and hope at this moment of prayer for Doña Sarita and ourselves.

[At this moment, a shot rang out in the chapel and Archbishop Romero fell mortally wounded. He died within minutes, on arriving at a nearby hospital emergency room.]

29

Pedro Arrupe, S. J.
"Marxist Analysis by Christians"
(December 8, 1980)

This carefully thought out letter of the Superior General of the Society of Jesus was addressed to Jesuit superiors in Latin America. It does not reject the use of elements of Marxist analysis, an issue that was to surface again in the "Instruction on Certain Aspects of the 'Theology of Liberation'" (1984). It was first published in the Jesuit review, Civiltà Catolica, *on April 4, 1981. The text here is from* Origins 10 *(April 16, 1981), pp. 689–93.*

1. Last year you requested my help in discussing at greater depth the problem of "Marxist analysis," on which the bishops of Latin America had just published important guidelines (Puebla Document, nos. 544–45). This letter, based on wide consultation, attempts to meet your request. I am also sending a copy of it to other provincials in the society since I believe it will be of service to some of them as well.

2. I shall not deal with the whole problem of the relationship between Marxism and Christianity. This is too large a theme and it has already been developed in many documents, both of the sovereign pontiffs and of several episcopal conferences. The question I shall treat is more specific and limited: Can a Christian, a Jesuit, adopt Marxist analysis as long as he distinguishes it from Marxist philosophy or ideology and also from Marxist praxis, at least considered in its totality?

3. The first thing to note in this question is that not everybody understands the same thing by the words "Marxist analysis." Whenever the expression is used, it is necessary to seek a precise explanation of its content. In addition, there are sociological or even philosophical aspects of this problem which are outside my competence as superior general. However, bearing in mind the way the question is generally raised today, I have no hesitation in offering some guidelines and directives which are needed for the good government of the society as an apostolic body.

4. I am well aware that some may not recognize themselves right away

in the way I have often heard it expressed in your provinces. But there are some Jesuits, few enough in Latin America but more in some European countries, who find themselves immersed straightaway in an atmosphere of convinced Marxism and sometimes of long Marxist tradition.

For example, some priest-workers feel that for the sake of inculturation and solidarity they cannot avoid sharing a number of viewpoints in common with their fellow workers. It is only out of such a situation that they enter into a faith discernment to which, moreover, they attach great importance. They note that it is often a far cry from theoretical Marxism to the actual behavior and attitudes of Marxist workers. Thus they put us on guard against giving too much weight to the intellectual aspects of the problem.

These observations are very helpful. However, we must acknowledge that even in a more intuitive type of faith discernment, problems continue to arise at the level of reflection, which is where I wish to locate my discussion here. And so, in the case of the priest-workers as well, the guidelines given here are important.

5. First, it seems to me that in our analysis of society we can accept a certain number of methodological viewpoints which to a greater or lesser extent arise from Marxist analysis, as long as we do not attribute an exclusive character to them. For instance, an attention to economic factors, to property structures, to economic interests which motivate this or that group; or again, a sensitivity to the exploitation that victimizes entire classes, attention to the role of class struggle in history (at least of many societies), attention to ideologies which can camouflage vested interests and even injustice.

6. In practice, however, the adoption of Marxist analysis is rarely the adoption of only a method or an "approach." Usually it means accepting the substance of the explanations Marx provided for the social reality of his time and applying them to that of our time.

And so we come to our first observation: In the area of social analysis, we cannot admit any a priori. There is room for hypotheses and theories, but everything should be verified, nothing can be presupposed. Now it can happen that someone will adopt Marxist analysis or elements of it as a set of a priori principles which need no verification, but at the most some illustration. At times these are identified in an unwarranted way with an evangelical option for the poor. They certainly do not flow directly from the gospel. In matters of sociological and economic interpretation, we Jesuits must carefully verify facts and be outstanding in our efforts at objectivity.

7. We come now to the heart of the question: Can one accept the set of explanations that constitute Marxist analysis without subscribing to Marxist philosophy, Marxist ideology, Marxist politics? To answer this question we must bear some important points in mind.

8. According to a good number of Christians who are themselves sympathetic to Marxist analysis, even if it does not imply either "dialectical

materialism" or, a fortiori, atheism, it nonetheless encompasses "historical materialism" and, in the view of some, is even identical with it. All social reality, therefore, including the political, the cultural, the religious, and the area of conscience, is seen to be determined by the economic factor.

Admittedly, even in Marxism itself, the terms thus employed are poorly defined and open to a variety of interpretations. However, historical materialism is most frequently understood in a reductionist sense. Politics, culture, religion lose their own substance and are perceived only as realities wholly dependent on that which occurs in the sphere of economic relations. This view of reality is prejudicial to Christian faith, at least to the Christian concept of humankind and to Christian ethics.

Thus even if it remains true that we Christians should be particularly attentive to economic factors in every account we give of social reality, we must keep our distance from an analysis which entails the idea of economic determination in this reductionist sense.

9. Furthermore, a criticism of religion and of Christianity is connected with historical materialism, and Marxist analysis generally does not succeed in freeing itself from it. Of course, such a criticism can have the effect of opening our eyes to cases in which the abuse of religion conceals situations that are socially indefensible. Nevertheless, if one's reasoning assumes that everything is intimately a function of productive relations, as if these determined reality, then the content of religion and Christianity is very quickly relativized and diminished. Belief in God the creator and in Jesus Christ the savior is left fragile or at least regarded as serving no useful purpose. A sense of gratuity gives way to that of utility. Christian hope tends to become unreal.

10. Sometimes an attempt is made to distinguish direct faith in Jesus Christ himself, to be preserved from its various concrete doctrinal and social expressions which do not survive the onslaught of such an analysis. But then the danger often arises of a radical criticism of the church quite beyond the limits of appropriate fraternal correction within the *ecclesia semper reformanda*. At times there even appears a tendency to judge the church as if from the outside and even to refuse any longer to recognize it as the true source of one's faith. In this way it is not a rare occurrence that the adoption of Marxist analysis leads to judgments about the church which are extremely severe and even unjust.

11. Even in cases where it is not taken as implying a rigorous historical materialism, Marxist social analysis contains as an essential element a radical theory of antagonism and class struggle. It is no exaggeration to say that it is social analysis in the service of class struggle.

The fact of antagonisms and class struggles should be realistically and fully recognized — the Christian sees here some relationship between this evil and sin. It should not, however, be generalized. It has nowhere been proved that all human history, past and present, can be reduced to a struggle, still less to a class struggle in the precise meaning of the expression.

Social reality cannot be understood solely in light of the master-slave dialectic: there have been and still are other factors in human history (alliance, peace, love), other deep forces which influence it.

12. We must also take note here of the fact that Marxist analysis often does not remain mere analysis but leads to action programs and strategies. Recognition of the class struggle does not necessarily imply that the means to end it should also be a struggle — that between the working class and the bourgeoisie. But it often happens that those who adopt the analysis also adopt this strategy. And such a strategy cannot be fully understood apart from the messianic role of the proletariat which belongs to Marx's ideology and already formed part of his philosophy before he undertook his systematic economic analysis.

In addition, even when Christians recognize the legitimacy of certain struggles and do not exclude revolution in situations of extreme tyranny that have no other solution, they cannot accept that the privileged method for ending struggle is struggle itself. They will rather seek to promote other methods of social transformation, calling for persuasion, witness, reconciliation, and never losing hope in conversion. Only as a means of last resort will they have recourse to struggle, especially if it involves violence, in order to combat injustice. There is a whole philosophy — and for us, theology — of action that is at stake here.

13. In brief, although Marxist analysis does not directly imply acceptance of Marxist philosophy as a whole — and still less of dialectical materialism as such — as it is normally understood it implies in fact a concept of human history which contradicts the Christian view of humankind and society, and leads to strategies which threaten Christian values and attitudes.

The consequences have often been disastrous, even though perhaps not always or immediately. Moral considerations are of great importance here. Christians who have for a time tended to adopt Marxist analysis and praxis have confessed they have been led bit by bit to accept any means to justify the end. There are many instances which still today corroborate what Paul VI wrote in *Octogesima Adveniens* (n. 34): "It would be illusory and dangerous ... to accept the elements of Marxist analysis without recognizing their relationships with ideology." To separate one from the other is more difficult than is sometimes imagined.

14. In this context the bishops of Latin America meeting at Puebla noted that theological reflection based on Marxist analysis runs the risk of leading to "the total politicization of Christian existence, the disintegration of the language of faith into that of the social sciences and the draining away of the transcendental dimension of Christian salvation" (Puebla Document, n. 545). This triple risk becomes evident in light of the observations I have just made.

15. To adopt therefore not just some elements or some methodological insights, but Marxist analysis as a whole, is something we cannot accept. Even supposing someone, with a whole series of careful distinctions, could

legitimately speak of Marxist analysis without accepting a reductive historical materialism or the theory and strategy of a generalized class struggle[1] —
but would this still be Marxist analysis? — most people, including the majority of Jesuits, would be incapable of doing this. So there is real danger
in defending the position that it is possible to undertake a Marxist analysis
separate from its philosophy, ideology, or political praxis. This is all the
more true in that, with a few exceptions, Marxists themselves reject any
separation between the analysis and a Marxist worldview or principles of
action. We have to make this practical discernment, as well as the theoretical one. We must, however, give young Jesuits in training instruments
for critical study and serious Christian reflection so that they can understand the problems of Marxist analysis. This analysis certainly cannot be
offered them during formation as a basis for understanding reality.

16. I wish to mention another point which I would like our specialists to
study in greater depth. It is the question of property structures (specifically,
the means of production), which occupy such a key position in Marxist
analysis. There is no doubt that a bad distribution of property, uncompen-
sated by other factors, leads to and facilitates the exploitation pointed out
by Marx and also denounced by the church.

All the same, is not the institution of property itself confused with its
bad distribution? It is important to continue investigating, with the help of
experience, what forms of distribution of property rights, as of other powers
(political, trade union), will bring about greater justice and more development for all people in different types of societies. Far from forgetting
the contributions of the church's social teaching in this practical field, we
should study them in greater depth, work out their applications, and help
in their development.

17. Finally, before concluding I would like to make four observations.
First, whatever the reservations with regard to Marxist analysis, we should
always understand well and appreciate the reasons that make it attractive.
Christians readily and rightly sympathize with the aim and ideal of liberating humankind from domination and oppression, of doing the truth while
condemning the ideologies that conceal it, of ending class divisions. What
we cannot admit is that this can be achieved by means that are facile or in
contradiction with the final aim; but neither can we ever allow ourselves to
be discouraged in the continuing quest for these objectives, for they are
intimately related to the charity that characterizes the Christian enterprise.
Besides, we must have compassion for those who are suffering in their own
flesh the degradation of social injustices.

18. In the second place, it should be very clear that in our day Marxist
analysis is not unique in being affected by ideological or philosophical presuppositions that have permeated its system. In particular, the type of social
analysis used in the liberal world today implies an individualistic and materialistic vision of life that is destructive of Christian values and attitudes.
In this connection, are we giving enough attention to the content of text-

books used in our schools? In using elements of social analysis of whatever type, if we want to remain faithful to the gospel, we must be critical of them, trying always to purify them before selecting what genuinely helps us to understand and describe without prejudice existing reality. Our efforts should be guided by the criteria of the gospel, not by ideologies incompatible with it.

19. Third, as regards Marxists themselves, we should remain fraternally open to dialogue with them. However, true to the spirit of *Gaudium et Spes* (21, para. 6), we ought not to refuse practical cooperation in concrete cases where the common good seems to call for it.[2] Naturally we must keep in mind our own special role as priests and religious, and never act like lone rangers in our dealings with the Christian community and its responsible leaders.

We must ensure that any collaboration on our part is only concerned with activities acceptable to a Christian. In this whole area we always have the obligation to maintain our own identity; because we accept some points of view that are valid, we should not allow ourselves to be carried as far as approval of the analysis in its totality; we must ever act in accordance with our faith and the principles of action that it inspires. So let us behave in such a way that Christianity can be seen to be a message that has greater value for humankind than any concept, however useful, of Marxist analysis.

20. Finally, we should also firmly oppose the efforts of anyone who wishes to take advantage of our reservations about Marxist analysis in order to condemn as Marxist or communist, or at least to minimize esteem for, a commitment to justice and the cause of the poor, the defense of their rights against those who exploit them, the urging of legitimate claims. Have we not often seen forms of anticommunism that are nothing but means for concealing injustice? In this respect as well, let us remain true to ourselves and not permit anyone to exploit our critical assessment of Marxism and Marxist analysis.

21. I ask you all to act with limpid clarity and fidelity. I ask you to strive with all your energy, in the context of our vocation, on behalf of the poor and against injustice, but without allowing indignation to obscure your vision of the faith and always maintaining, even in the heat of conflict, a Christian attitude that is characterized by love and not hardness of heart.

22. To conclude: I appreciate that the presentation of Marxist analysis may eventually be modified on one point or another in the future.[3] Besides, there is still room for further theoretical studies and empirical investigations concerning the various problems on which I have touched. At the present moment I want everyone to observe the indications and directives contained in this letter. I hope it will allow you and other superiors to help more effectively those of ours whose ministry puts them in contact with men and women of Marxist conviction, among whom I include those Christians who refer to themselves as "Christian Marxists." More generally, I hope this letter will help all Jesuits who feel the need to analyze society

and cannot avoid facing the problem of Marxist analysis.

Along these lines we can do better work in the promotion of justice, which is inseparable from our service of the faith.

Very fraternally yours,
Pedro Arrupe, S.J.
Superior General

NOTES

1. Cf. *Populorum Progressio*, 31 (AAS, LXIX, 1969, p. 272).
2. Cf. *Mater et Magistra*, IV (AAS, LIII, 1961, pp. 456–57).
3. *Pacem in Terris* (AAS, LV, 1963, pp. 299–300).

30

Jon Sobrino
"Martyrdom of Maura, Ita, Dorothy, and Jean" (January 1981)

This short article is a moving tribute to the four American church women who were murdered by the Salvadoran military on the road from the airport to San Salvador on December 2, 1980. The dead included two Maryknoll sisters, Maura Clarke and Ita Ford, one Ursuline sister, Dorothy Kazel, and a Maryknoll lay missioner, Jean Donovan. The article was originally published in Estudios Centroamericanos *(January-February 1981), pp. 51–53. This translation is from Jon Sobrino,* Spirituality of Liberation: Toward Political Holiness *(Maryknoll, N.Y.: Orbis Books, 1988), pp. 153–56.*

I have stood by the bodies of Maura Clarke, Ita Ford, Dorothy Kazel, and Jean Donovan. Once more I felt what I have felt so often since the murder of Rutilio Grande in 1977. Then, the martyrs had been a Jesuit priest — my friend and comrade — and two Aguilares campesinos. This time the martyrs were four American women missionaries: two Maryknoll sisters, an Ursuline sister, and a social worker from the diocese of Cleveland, Ohio. Between those two dates — March 12, 1977, and December 2, 1980 — there has been martyrdom upon martyrdom — an endless procession of priests, seminarians, students, campesinos, teachers, workers, professionals, and intellectuals murdered for the faith in El Salvador.

Death has come to be the inseparable, dismal companion of our people. And yet, each time we gather to bid our martyrs farewell, the same feelings well up inside, surge to the surface again. First we are filled with indignation and grief, and we cry with the psalmist: "How long, O Lord? How long?" Then comes that feeling of determination and high resolve, and we pray with the psalmist: "Rejoice, Jerusalem. Your deliverance is at hand!"

This time, however, things are different. No one can conceal the new sensation we have. Not since the murder of Archbishop Romero (March

24, 1980) has there been a commotion like the one occasioned by this latest martyrdom. Neither within the country nor abroad has there been such a universal repudiation, such a feeling that God's patience must be exhausted and that this martyrdom is telling us that liberation is in the offing.

There were three hundred of us priests and sisters gathered in the chancery to hear Archbishop Rivera. His voice had a new and different ring, as he denounced the security forces of the Christian Democractic Junta. He tore the masks from their faces. He pointed the finger of shame and guilt. Once again the truth was crystal clear. And with the truth came courage, and the Christian resolve to keep on, shoulder to shoulder with a massacred people, even if it meant that the church must march once more to the cross.

It was the first Christian Easter all over again. The horror, the abandonment, the solitude of Jesus' cross had driven the disciples to their refuge in the upper room. But Jesus' spirit was mightier than death, and it flung the doors wide apart. The disciples emerged stronger than before, determined to preach resurrection and life, determined to proclaim the good news of the reign of the poor. The archbishop's residence had been transformed into a latter-day upper room. The God of life was there. And that God was stronger than death, stronger than oppression and repression, stronger than ourselves and our fears and terrors. There, in the presence of four corpses, the Christian paradox came to life. Yes, where sin and crime had abounded, life and grace abounded even more.

This past Easter was a special celebration indeed. With this last murder the reservoirs of iniquity have overspilled their limits. The dams of evil have burst. We have seen everything in El Salvador. No barbarity would surprise us, we thought. But this time we were overwhelmed. Once more we witnessed the murder of the just, the innocent. But this time the murdered Christ was present in the person of four women, four missionaries, four Americans. This time the thick clouds of crime were pierced by a brand-new light.

The murdered Christ is here in the person of four *women*. In the drama of the world, and the drama of the church, all the actors are human beings. We are all of us equal, as well as different, in God's eyes. And yet, the two together—equality and difference—are hard to come by in our history. Then suddenly, with these four dead bodies, we see something of it. Men and women are oppressed and repressed in El Salvador. Men and women have raised their lamentation to God and begged God to hear the cries wrung from them by their exploiters. Men and women have thrown in their lot with the struggle for liberation. And men and women have fallen in that struggle. Here is the most profound equality of all: equality in suffering and in hope.

By making themselves one with the archetypical Salvadoran woman, these four sisters made themselves one with the whole Salvadoran people. Woman is the procreator of humankind. But she is the creator of humanity—of humanness and humaneness—as well, in a specific manner all her own: in the delicacy of her service, her limitless self-donation, her affective and effective contact with the people, and that compassion of hers that simply will not rationalize the suffering of the poor. Woman is the creator of a courage that will never abandon the suffering, as these four sisters did not abandon their people when they saw the danger. Woman is more defenseless physically. This fact points up the singular barbarity of their murder. It shows that barbarity for what it is. And it demonstrates the simplicity and gratuity of these women's self-sacrifice.

The murdered Christ is present here in the person of four *religious*. We hear a great deal about the renewal of the religious life today, in El Salvador as elsewhere. We hear a great deal about charisms and vows. And now these four dead bodies show us what a life of consecration to God today is all about. They make no fuss. They hold no grandiloquent harangues. They show us, simply, the basic element of all religious charism: service. Religious women today have been moving out more and more, reaching the most abandoned places, places where others cannot or will not go. They have drawn close to the poor, in genuineness and in truth, the poor of the slums, the poor of the working-class neighborhoods, and especially the poor campesinos. Consecration to God today means service and dedication to the poor.

Just as quietly, women religious have exercised their prophetic charism, which is part and parcel of the religious life. By their presence, by their activity, they have denounced the petrification of other echelons of the church. They have denounced the alienation of the hierarchy from Christian peoples. Above all, they have denounced the death-dealing sin that decimates the Salvadoran population. Therefore they have suffered the fate of the prophets, and shared the people's own lot: martyrdom. And so religious women, too, have their representatives among the martyrs of all social classes. They too have made an option for the poor, and therefore they too had to die.

The dead Christ is present among us in the person of four *Americans*. The United States is everywhere in El Salvador. We have U.S. businessmen and military experts. We have a U.S. embassy here to decide the fate of Salvadorans without consulting them. We have U.S. arms, we have U.S. helicopters to pursue and bombard the civilian population. But we have something else from the United States, too. We have American Christians, priests and nuns. These have given us the best the United States has to offer: faith in Jesus instead of faith in the almighty dollar; love for persons instead of love for an imperialist plan; a thirst for justice instead of a lust for exploitation. With these four Americans, Christ, although he came from a far-off land, was no stranger in El Salvador. He was a Salvadoran, through and through.

In these four religious women, the churches of El Salvador and of the United States have become sister churches. After all, Christian action is helping others for their own sake, not blackmailing them with economic aid or babying them with paternalism. El Salvador gave these four sisters new eyes, and they beheld the crucified body of Christ in our people. El Salvador gave these four sisters new hands, and they healed Christ's wounds in the people of our land. The United States of America gave us four women who left their native land to give. And they gave all, in utter simplicity. They gave their very lives.

What has brought these two churches together? What has enabled the churches of El Salvador and the United States to contribute so much to the upbuilding of the world church? The poor. Service to the poor. How moved I was to hear from Peggy Healy, the Maryknoll sister who was a friend of the murdered sisters, that the high-ranking officials sent here by President Carter were to investigate not only the death of four American citizens, but the genocide of ten thousand Salvadorans.

Today as yesterday, there is no other Christian formula for building the church or unifying the various churches throughout the world: we must emerge from ourselves, we must devote ourselves to others—to the very poorest, to the oppressed, to the tortured, to the "disappeared," to the murdered. If this is the attitude with which Christians of the church of the United States come to their fellow Christians of the church of El Salvador, then the church of El Salvador can only say: "Welcome." And if that attitude leads Christians of the church of the United States down the path of martyrdom, we can only say: "Thank you, from the bottom of our hearts."

Christ lies dead here among us. He is Maura, Ita, Dorothy, and Jean. But he is risen, too, in these same four women, and he keeps the hope of liberation alive. The world is moved, and indignant, and so are we Christians. But to us Christians, this murder tells us something about God as well. We believe that salvation comes to us from Jesus. And perhaps this is the moment to take seriously something that theology has been telling us in its too spiritualistic and too academic way: salvation comes by way of a woman—Mary, the virgin of the cross and of the Magnificat. Salvation comes to us through all women and men who love truth more than lies, who are more eager to give than to receive, and whose love is that supreme love that gives life rather than keeping it for oneself. God is here today. Yes, their dead bodies fill us with sorrow and indignation. And yet, our last word must be: Thank you. In Maura, Ita, Dorothy, and Jean, God has visited El Salvador.

31

Sandinista National Liberation Front (FSLN) "Communiqué of the National Directorate of the FSLN concerning Religion" (February 1981)

This statement by the Sandinista government of Nicaragua was published in the magazine Envío *(English translation) in its first issue (February 1981, vol. 1, no. 1). There has been a great deal of controversy as to whether these directives have been carried out in practice. Nevertheless, the document is a remarkable and perhaps unprecedented example of a Marxist regime's willingness to collaborate and engage in dialogue with Christians.*

For some time, the enemies of the people, definitively put out of power, have been developing a pertinacious campaign of misrepresentations and lies concerning certain aspects of the revolution in order to confuse the people. This ideological confusionism tries to promote anti-Sandinista fears and attitudes in the hearts of the people, while trying to wear down the FSLN politically with interminable polemics that never look for the just position, rather the opposite.

In these confusionist campaigns the topic of religion occupies a preferential place, since a high percentage of the Nicaraguan people have deeply rooted religious sentiments. In this manner the reactionary forces have undertaken to advance the view that the FSLN is manipulating religion for the moment in order to try to suppress it later. It is clear that the purpose of this propaganda is to manipulate the simple faith of our people in order to promote a political reaction against the FSLN and the Revolution.

This campaign is particularly perverse since it refers to matters that touch deep sentiments of many Nicaraguans. Given the importance of the subject and in order to give our militancy the proper perspective, in order to clarify it for our people and to avoid that they continue to be manipulated in this area, the National Directorate of the FSLN has decided to publish the official position on religion in this document.

CHRISTIANS IN THE POPULAR SANDINISTA REVOLUTION

The Christian patriots and revolutionaries are an integral part of the Popular Sandinista Revolution, not just now but for many years past. The participation that Christians, as much laity as religious, had in the Revolution and in the National Reconstruction Government (GRN) is a logical consequence of their outstanding participation at the side of the people during the long struggle against the dictatorship.

Large numbers of militants and combatants of the FSLN found the motivation for joining the revolutionary struggle and thus the FSLN in the interpretation of their faith. Many of them not only made a very valuable contribution to our cause, but also were striking examples, to the point of shedding their blood to germinate the seed of liberty. How could we forget our beloved martyrs Oscar Pérez Cassar, Oscar Robelo, Sergio Guerrero, Arlen Siu, Guadalupe Moreno, and Leonardo Matute, the dozens of Delegates of the Word assassinated in the mountains of the country by Somocista National Guards, and so many more of our brothers and sisters?

The revolutionary work and heroic sacrifice of the Catholic priest and militant Sandinista Gaspar García Laviana requires special mention. In him the Christian vocation and the revolutionary conscience were synthesized to the maximum degree. All of these were humble people who knew how to fulfill their patriotic and revolutionary duties without becoming entangled in long philosophical discussions. Now they will live eternally in the memory of the people who will never forget their sacrifice.

But the contribution of Christians was not limited to that of combatants in the Sandinista front. Many Christians, laity and religious, who never fought in the ranks of the FSLN, even though some were tied to it, preached and practiced their faith in accordance with the needs for liberty of our people. This includes the Catholic Church and some evangelical churches, as institutions, which participated in the popular victory against the regime of Somoza.

The Catholic bishops on various occasions have valiantly denounced the crimes and abuses of the dictatorship, especially Bishop Obando y Bravo and Bishop Salazar y Espinosa who, among others, suffered harassment by the Somocista bands. It was a group of priests and sisters who denounced to the world the disappearances of three thousand campesinos in the northern mountains of our country. Many Christians of different denominations brought the message of liberation to the people. There were even some who gave refuge and food to the Sandinistas who were being pursued to be killed by the Somocistas. It was in the churches that the people met to hear the underground news when Somocista repression prohibited broadcasts by independent radio stations.

For this valiant participation in the struggle, the Catholic Church and Christians in general suffered persecution and death; in the same way many religious suffered maltreatment, many were expelled from the country, many were impeded in a thousand ways from practicing their Christian faith. Many churches like Calvary Church in León and the chapels in the mountains, were violated, sacked, bombed, and assaulted in order to assassinate people inside.

Thus Christians have been an integral part of our revolutionary history to a degree unprecedented in any other revolutionary movement in Latin America and possibly in the world. This fact opens new and interesting possibilities for the participation of Christians in other regions, not only in the period of the struggle for power, but also in the period of building a new society.

Christians and non-Christians must meet the task of giving continuity and projection into the future to this valuable experience under the new conditions that the revolutionary process gives us. We should perfect the forms of conscious participation among all Nicaraguan revolutionaries, regardless of their philosophical position or their religious beliefs.

POSITIONS OF THE FSLN CONCERNING RELIGION

1. For the FSLN, the right to profess a religious faith is an inalienable right of the people that the Revolutionary Government fully guarantees. This principle was inscribed in our Revolutionary Program a long time ago and we will have to effectively sustain it in the future. In addition, no one can be discriminated against in the new Nicaragua for publicly professing or spreading his/her religious beliefs. Those who do not profess any religion have the same rights.

2. Some authors have stated that religion is a mechanism that alienates people and serves to justify the exploitation of one class by another. This affirmation undoubtedly has historic value in relation to the distinct historical periods in which religion served as a theoretical support for political domination. Suffice it to mention the role that missionaries played in the process of domination and colonization of the indigenous people of our country.

Nevertheless, the Sandinistas affirm that our experience shows that when Christians, relying on their faith, are capable of responding to the needs of the community and of history, their same beliefs push them toward revolutionary militancy. Our experience shows us that one can be a believer and at the same time a consistent revolutionary, and that there is no contradiction between the two.

3. The FSLN is the organization of the Nicaraguan revolutionaries who have voluntarily come together in order to transform the social, economic, and political reality of our country in accordance with a well-known program and strategy. All those who are in agreement with our goals and objectives and bring the personal qualities demanded by our organization have every right to militantly participate in our ranks, regardless of their

religious beliefs. A proof of this is that there are three Catholic priests participating in the Sandinista Assembly. Many Christians serve within the FSLN and as long as there are Christian revolutionaries in Nicaragua, there will be Christians within the Sandinista Front.

4. As the vanguard, conscious of the immense responsibilities that have fallen on its shoulders, the FSLN jealously guards the unity and force of its organization around the objectives for those for whom it is expressly responsible. Religious proselytizing does not fit within the partisan framework of the FSLN because it perverts the specific character of our vanguard and introduces disunifying factors, as there are members of distinctive religious beliefs and no beliefs in the Sandinista Front.

5. The FSLN has a profound respect for all religious celebrations and traditions of our people and makes an effort to recover the true meaning of these celebrations, opposing the vice and manifestations of corruption that marked them in the past. We consider that that respect ought to express itself not only in guaranteeing the conditions which allow those traditions to be freely expressed, but also that they not be used for political or commercial ends. If any Sandinista militant in the future departs from this principle, we want to state right now that that action does not represent the FSLN position.

Clearly, if other political parties or individuals try to turn their celebrations or popular religious activities into political acts contrary to the Revolution (as has happened on past occasions), the FSLN has the right to defend the people and also the Revolution in these same circumstances.

6. No militant Sandinistas, in their capacity as such, should express their opinion about the interpretation of religious questions that are only contentions for the different churches. These questions should be elucidated by Christians themselves. If Sandinistas who are, at the same time, Christians intervene in the polemics that are stirred up in this sense, they do it as individuals and not in their role as Sandinistas.

7. Some reactionary ideologists have accused the FSLN of trying to divide the church. Nothing is more false or malicious than this accusation. If division exists within the religions this is something that is completely independent from the volition and action of the FSLN. An examination of history is sufficient for one to realize that concerning large political issues, the members of the Catholic Church have always taken distinct and even contradictory positions. Alongside the Spanish conquerors, the missionaries came to finish with the cross the work of enslavement that the sword had begun. But the firmness of Bartolomé de Las Casas, the defender of the Amerindians, rose up opposing them. At the beginning of the last century there were many priests who fought for the independence of Central America, even bearing arms. At the other extreme, there were priests who with equal vehemence defended the privileges of the Crown in Latin America.

Once liberated from the colonial yoke, we encounter the anti-interventionist position of Bishop Pereira y Castellon, calling for the defense of the national interests against North American invasion. During the Somoza regime, the figure of Bishop Calderon y Padilla stands out, lashing out at vice, corruption, and the abuse of power by the Somozas against the humble. Thus it continues up to the massive military commitment we find today in Christian revolutionaries.

We have mentioned the extensive participation by many Christians in the revolutionary struggle of the people; but we also have to say that there were some like León Pallais and others who were at Somoza's side until the end.

Let us not forget that in that period there were priests who held military rank and official positions—certainly it was never demanded of them that they abandon their posts—but before those sad examples, the immense figure of Gaspar García L. stands out along with so many other Sandinista martyrs of Christian background.

In the present period that situation persists. There is an immense majority of Christians who actively support and participate in the Revolution, but there is also a minority who maintain political positions contrary to the Revolution. Logically, the Sandinistas are good friends of the Christian revolutionaries but not of the counterrevolutionaries, although they call themselves Christians. Nevertheless the FSLN maintains communications with the different churches at all levels, the base level and the hierarchical level, without paying attention to their political positions.

We do not encourage or provoke activities to divide the churches. If there is division, the churches ought to look for the causes within themselves and not attribute responsibility to supposedly evil outside influences. Yes, we are frank in saying that we would look favorably upon a church that, without prejudice, with maturity and responsibility, worked in common effort to develop more and more avenues for dialogue and participation that our revolutionary process has opened.

8. Another matter that is being debated lately is that of the participation of priests and religious in the Government of National Reconstruction. In that respect we state that it is a right of all Nicaraguan citizens to participate in conducting the political affairs of the country, whatever their civil status, and that the Government of National Reconstruction guarantees this right, which is endorsed by law after 150 years of plunder, repression, and dependence. To construct the future of Nicaragua is a historic challenge that transcends our borders and encourages other peoples in their struggle for liberation and the integral formation of the new person. That is a right and duty of all Nicaraguans regardless of their religious beliefs.

32

Pope John Paul II
"The Bishop: Principle of Unity"
(June 29, 1982)

As indicated in this message to the bishops of Nicaragua, the pope was obviously very worried about unity among the bishops in Nicaragua, and also unity in the church itself, which was deeply divided regarding support or opposition to the Nicaraguan government. This text is from The Pope Speaks, *27 (Winter 1982), pp. 338-43.*

While in obedience to the mysterious call which made him Peter's successor, he willingly spends what he has and even spends himself for the good of all,[1] the pope does not forget his special obligations toward those who in the particular churches of the whole world carry out their ministry as pastors in the midst of many difficulties.

A special bond unites them. Special because of its roots in the gospel, since to Peter, on whom he had conferred the first place among the Twelve, Jesus wished to confide, at a solemn moment of his life, the mission of confirming his brethren in the faith and in apostolic service.[2]

Special also because of its theological nature: the Second Vatican Council deepened the ancient doctrine of episcopal collegiality and emphasized with a richness of concepts and expressions that the episcopal college, "insofar as it is composed of many members, is the expression of the multifariousness and universality of the people of God; and of the unity of the body of Christ, insofar as it is assembled under one head."[3]

By reason of this bond, which nonetheless is deeply affective because of its dogmatic aspect, and given the peculiar circumstances in which you are called to carry out your episcopal ministry, I want you to know that I am very close to you. Close, I say, insofar as "I do not cease to thank God for you and to remember you in my prayers."[4] Close, too, because of the care and interest with which I keep myself informed about your pastoral activities.

Close, also, through my spiritual support of your work, a work that is as devoted as it is demanding and delicate, in favor of the human, personal, and collective promotion of peoples. Close, finally, because of my fraternal solicitude concerning your duty as pastors and teachers in the churches confided to you.

COMMUNION AMONG YOURSELVES

Besides, since today's feast of the Apostles Peter and Paul renews in us the sense of collegiality, it provides me with an opportunity of writing to you, "for I long to see you, that I may impart to you some spiritual gift to strengthen you."[5]

I want to find in these preceding considerations the first and fundamental expression of the support and encouragement I desire to communicate to you.

A bishop is never alone, since he finds himself in living and dynamic communion with the pope and with his brother bishops of the whole world. You are not alone: you are sustained by the spiritual presence of this your elder brother, and you are surrounded by the affective communion of thousands of brothers.

However, I wish to invite you to reflect on another, more reduced, but not less important dimension of communion: the communion among yourselves, members of that beloved episcopal conference of Nicaragua.

This communion, which finds its origin in the fullness of the priesthood of Jesus Christ, is not merely external, nor is it brought about by human arrangements or protocol. It is a sacramental communion and, as such, ought to be acted upon.

I must confess that nothing can give me greater joy than that of knowing that there prevails among you, over and above all that could divide you, this essential unity in Christ and in the church. It is a unity which is all the more demanding and necessary since on it will depend, on the one hand, the credibility of your preaching and the effectiveness of your apostolate, and on the other, that communion which in view of the well-known difficulties, it is your mission to build up among the faithful.

SIGN AND INSTRUMENT OF UNITY

Now it seems to us that this unity of the faithful is perhaps the most precious quality—because it is fragile and threatened—of this church, yours and ours, of Nicaragua.

That which the Second Vatican Council declared about the universal church—namely, that it is both a sign and instrument of the unity which is to be built up in the world and among all persons[6]—can be applied in due measure to the ecclesial communities at all levels.

Wherefore the church in Nicaragua has the great responsibility of being a sacrament, that is, a sign and instrument of unity in the country. For this reason it, as a community, should be a true unity and an image of unity.

In this respect it must be remembered that the more ferments of discord, disunion, and separation that are to be found in a particular place, the more must the church be a sphere of unity and cohesion. But it will be this only if it gives witness to being *cor unum et anima una* through the use of the supernatural principles of unity which are sufficiently strong and clear so as to overcome the forces of division to which it also finds itself subject.

Since, by divine vocation, you are visible signs of unity, would that the Christians of your land were not divided by reason of opposing ideologies, gathered together as they are by "one only Lord, one only faith, one only baptism, one only God and Father," as they are in the habit of singing, taking their inspiration from the words of the Apostle Paul. Would that your Christians, united by the same faith, would reject all that is contrary to or destroys that unity; and would meet one another joined together by the gospel ideals of justice, peace, solidarity, communion, and participation, without being divided irremediably by contingent options arising from certain systems, currents, parties, or organizations.

From this point of view your responsibility grows since it is around the bishop that the unity of the faithful should be built up in the concrete.

You know the great importance of the letters of St. Ignatius of Antioch, both because of the authority of the writer — a disciple of the beloved apostle — and because of their antiquity, which makes of them a testimony to a vital moment in the history of the church, and also because of the richness of their doctrinal content.

Now it is Ignatius who, with forceful terms, shows in these letters, certainly in reply to the earliest difficulties that had arisen in this matter, that there is not, nor can there be, any valid or lasting communion in the church except through the union of mind and heart of respect and obedience, of sentiments and action, with the bishop. The cords of the lyre are a beautiful image and suggest a deeper reality: the bishop is like Jesus Christ made present in the midst of his church as the living and dynamic principle of unity. Without him this unity does not exist or is falsified and, therefore, is inconsistent and ephemeral.

From this we can see how absurd and dangerous it is to imagine that there exists alongside of — without actually saying contrary to — the church built up around the bishop, another church regarded as "charismatic" and not institutional, "new" and not traditional, an alternative and, as has been recently advocated, a "popular church."

I am not unaware that one can attribute to this last name — synonymous with "a church that takes its origin from the people" — a meaning that is acceptable. By it one wishes to emphasize that the church comes into being when a community of persons, especially of persons who by their littleness, humility, and poverty are open to the Christian message, welcomes the Good News of Jesus Christ, and begins to live according to it in a continuum of faith, love, hope, prayer, of celebration of the participation in the Christian mysteries, especially in the eucharist.

But you are aware that the concluding document of the Third Episcopal Conference of Latin America at Puebla declared that this title "popular church" is not a happy one.[7] This was done after mature study and reflection among the bishops of the entire continent, because they were aware that this title, in general, conceals another reality.

"Popular church," in its most common acceptation, as can be seen in the writings of a certain theological trend, means a church that takes its origin much rather from the so-called values of a certain strata of the population than from the free and gratuitous initiative of God. It means a church that ends with the autonomy of the so-called *bases*, without reference to the legitimate pastors or teachers; or at least puts the "rights" of these former above the authority and charisms perceived through faith in the latter.

It means also — since the term "people" lends itself easily to a content that is markedly sociological and political — the church incarnate in the popular organizations characterized by ideologies. These organizations are put at the service of their claims, their programs, and groups which are considered as not belonging to the people.

It is easy to see — and the document of Puebla indicates this — that the concept "popular church" can scarcely avoid the infiltration of strongly ideological connotations, along the lines of a certain political radicalization, of class warfare, of the acceptance of violence to attain certain ends, etc.

PASTORAL WARNING

When I myself in my inaugural address to the assembly at Puebla made serious reservations about the title "church that takes its origin from the people," I had in mind the dangers that I have just recalled. For this reason I feel it my duty now to repeat, using your voices for the purpose, the same pastoral warning with affection and with clarity. It is a call to your faithful through your intermediary.

A "popular church" as opposed to the church presided over by its legitimate pastors is — from the point of view of the teaching of the Lord and of the apostles in the New Testament, and also in the ancient and recent teaching of the solemn magisterium of the church — a serious departure from the will and plan of salvation of Jesus Christ. It is besides, a principle of division and rupture of that unity which he left as a characteristic sign of the church itself, and which he wished to confide precisely to those whom "the Holy Spirit established to rule the church of God."[8]

I entrust, therefore, to you, beloved brethren in the episcopate, the assignment and task of making this call of fundamental importance to your faithful people with patience and firmness.

None of us can forget the dramatic concept of my predecessor Paul VI, when he wrote in his memorable exhortation *Evangelii Nuntiandi* that the most insidious dangers and the most deadly attacks against the church are not those that come from without—these can only strengthen it in its mission and its work—but rather those that come from within.

Let all the sons of the church then, in this historic moment for Nicaragua and for the church in that country, strive to preserve intact the communion around their pastors while avoiding anything that may be a seed of rupture or division.

Let this call find an echo, above all, in the conscience of the priests, be they either from the country or missionaries, who for years have consecrated their lives to the pastoral ministry in that nation, or volunteers wishing to give their help to their Nicaraguan brothers at a time of the greatest consequence.

Let them be aware that if they really wish to serve the people as priests, this people is hungering and thirsting for God and full of love for the church, and expects of them the announcement of the gospel, the proclamation of the fatherhood of God, the administration of the sacramental mysteries of salvation. The people want to have them near, not with a political role, but with their priestly ministry.

AVAILABLE TO SERVE

Let this call find an echo also in the consciences of religious men and women whether they be natives of the country or have come from outside. The people of this country want to see them united with the bishops in an unbreakable ecclesial communion and bearers of a message that is not parallel to or, worse still, opposed to that of lawful pastors, but rather in harmony with it and consistent with it.

May this message be welcomed by all those who by any title find themselves at the sincere service of the mission of the church, especially if they are in a position of particular responsibility as, for example, in the university, the centers of study and research, the media of social communications, etc.

Let them make themselves available to serve in conformity with the equally generous and resolute arrangements of their bishops and of the very large portion of the people who with the bishops are seeking the good of the country while taking as their inspiration the directives of the church.

Finally, I exhort you, beloved brothers, to persevere even in the midst of no small difficulties with your untiring work to ensure the active presence of the church in this historic moment through which the country is going.

CONVINCING WITNESS

Under your direction as solicitous pastors, may the Catholic faithful of Nicaragua constantly give a clear and convincing witness of love and a capacity for service to their country, second in nothing, not even in efficiency, to that of the rest. It should be a witness of farsightedness in facing events and situations, a witness of full availability to serve the authentic cause of the people, of courage to propose, in every situation, the thought and directives—what I have often called *the way*—of the church, even when these are not in agreement with other proposed ways.

I desire, I hope, I ask you to do all that lies in your power to bring it about that fidelity to Christ and to the church among yourselves and your people, far from diminishing, will strengthen and enrich loyalty to the earthly homeland.

I am very happy on this occasion to impart to you fraternally, as a pledge of abundant divine graces for yourselves and your ministry, my cordial apostolic blessing, which I extend also to all your faithful.

NOTES

1. See 2 Cor. 12:15.
2. See Luke 22:32.
3. *Lumen Gentium*, 22; see *Christus Dominus*, 4.
4. Eph. 1:16.
5. Rom. 1:10.
6. See *Lumen Gentium*, 1.
7. See n. 263.
8. Acts 20:28.

33

Pope John Paul II
"Unity of the Church"
(Managua, Nicaragua, March 4, 1983)

*This sermon was delivered in the huge Plaza 19 de Julio by Pope John Paul,
and again he repeated the message on church unity. It appears that a number
of people in the enormous crowd expected the pope to mention the war waged
by the U.S.-supported contras and to offer consolation for a number of men
killed in the war. There were cries for peace, and the pope shouted "Silence!"
several times. It is doubtful that this was planned, for such an attempt to disrupt
a Mass would bring down the opprobrium of the entire world. The text is from*
The Pope Speaks, *28 (Fall 1983), pp. 206–10.*

Beloved Brothers in the episcopate, dear brothers and sisters:
We are assembled here beside the altar of the Lord. What joy to be with
you, my dear priests, men and women religious, seminarians and laity —
gathered together around your pastors — of this dear land of Nicaragua, so
tried, so heroic in the face of natural disasters which have struck it, so
vigorous in responding to the challenges of history and in seeking to build
up a society in proportion to the material needs and the transcendent
dimension of humankind!

Above all, with sincere affection and esteem, I greet the pastor and
archbishop of this city of Managua, the other bishops and all of you, old
and young, rich and poor, workers and businessmen, since in all of you is
present Jesus Christ, "firstborn of many brothers";[1] "you have been
clothed" by him in your baptism;[2] thus, "all of you are one in Jesus Christ."[3]

The scriptural texts which have just been proclaimed during this eucharist speak to us of unity.

Above all, it is a matter of the unity of the church, of the people of God,
of the "flock" of the one shepherd, but also, as the Second Vatican Ecumenical Council teaches, of the "unity among all persons" as the "communion" of every person "with God," of which the church is a "sign and
instrument."[4]

The sad legacy of the separation among persons caused by the sin of pride[5] endures over the centuries. The consequences are wars, oppression, persecutions, hatred, and conflicts of every kind.

Instead, Jesus Christ came to reestablish the lost unity so that there would be "one flock" and "one shepherd,"[6] a shepherd whose voice the sheep "know," while they do not know that of a stranger;[7] he who is the one "door" through which it is necessary to enter.[8]

Unity is the reason for the ministry of Jesus to the point that he came to die "to gather into one all the dispersed children of God."[9] This is what St. John the Evangelist teaches us, showing us Christ praying to the Father for the union of the community he was entrusting to his apostles.[10]

Jesus Christ, by his death and resurrection and with the gift of his Spirit, reestablished unity among persons, gave it to his church and made of the latter, according to what the council tells us, a "sacrament—a sign and instrument, that is, of communion with God and of unity among all persons."[11]

CHURCH: GOD'S FAMILY

The church is the family of God,[12] and just as in a family unity in order must reign, so likewise in the church. In it, no one has a greater right to citizenship than anyone else: neither Jews, nor Greeks, nor slaves, nor freed men, nor men, nor women, nor the poor, nor the rich, since all "are one in Jesus Christ."[13]

This unity is based on "one Lord, one faith, one baptism, one God and Father of all, who is over all, and works through all, and is in all," as is stated in the text of the Letter of the Ephesians, which we have just heard,[14] and which you often sing during your celebrations.

We must appreciate the profundity and the solidity of the foundations of this unity which we enjoy in the universal church, in that of all of Central America, and to which this local church in Nicaragua must steadfastly aspire. Precisely for this reason we must give due value also to the dangers which threaten it and to the need to maintain and deepen this unity, a gift of God in Christ Jesus.

As I wrote in my letter to the bishops of Nicaragua last August,[15] this "gift" is perhaps more precious precisely because it is "fragile" and "threatened."

In effect, the unity of the church is called into question when the powerful factors which constitute and maintain it—faith itself, the revealed word, the sacraments, *obedience to the bishops and to the pope*, the sense of vocation and mutual responsibility in Christ's mission in the world—are relegated to a position inferior to earthly considerations, unacceptable ideological commitments, temporal options, even concepts of the church which supplant the true one.

Yes, dear Central American and Nicaraguan brothers and sisters, when

Christians, whatever their condition may be, prefer any other doctrine or ideology to the teaching of the apostles and of the church, when these doctrines are made the criterion of our vocation, when an attempt is made to reinterpret according to their categories the catechesis, religious teaching and preaching, when "parallel magisteria" are established, as I said in my inaugural address at the Puebla Conference,[16] then the unity of the church is weakened, the exercise of its mission of being the "sacrament of unity" for all is made more difficult.

The unity of the church means and demands from us the radical overcoming of all these tendencies toward separation; it means and demands the reexamination of our scale of values: it means and requires the *submission of our doctrinal concepts* and of our pastoral projects to the *magisterium of the church*, represented by the pope and the bishops. This also applies to the field of the social teaching of the church set out by my predecessors and by myself.

No Christian, and still less any person who has a special title of consecration in the church, may become responsible for the rupture of this unity, by *acting beyond or against the will of the bishops* "placed by the Holy Spirit to shepherd the church of God."[17]

This is valid in every situation and country, and no process of development or social progress which may have been undertaken can lawfully compromise the religious identity and freedom of a people, the transcendent dimension of the human person and the sacred nature of the mission of the church and its ministers.

WORK AND GIFT OF CHRIST

The unity of the church is the work and gift of Christ. It is built up with reference to him and around him. But Christ *entrusted to the bishops a very important ministry of unity* in their local churches.[18] In communion with the pope and never without him,[19] it is their task to foster the church's unity and, in this way, to build up in this unity the communities, groups, various currents, and classes of individuals who exist in a local church and in the great community of the universal church. I support you in this unitary effort, which will be strengthened during your next *ad limina* visit.

Evidence of the unity of the church in a specific place is the respect for the pastoral directions given by the bishops to their clergy and to the faithful. This organic pastoral action is a great guarantee of ecclesial unity: a duty which falls especially on priests, religious, and the other pastoral workers.

But the duty to build up and maintain unity is also *a responsibility of all the members of the church*, joined by the bond of one baptism, in the same profession of faith, in obedience to their bishop and faithful to the successor of Peter.

Dear brothers: keep well in mind that there are cases in which unity is saved only when everyone is able to renounce one's own ideas, plans, and commitments, even if they are good—all the more so when they lack the necessary ecclesial reference!—for the higher good of communion with the bishop, with the pope, with the entire church.

In effect, as I said earlier in my letter to your bishops, a divided church cannot fulfill its mission "of sacrament, that is, sign and instrument of unity in the country." Therefore I warned how *"absurd and dangerous" it is "to imagine"* alongside—not to say against—the church built up around the bishop *another church* conceived only as "charismatic" and not institutional, "new" and not traditional, alternative and, as lately announced, a popular church. Today I want to reaffirm these words here, before you.

The church must remain united in order to resist the various forms, direct or indirect, of materialism which its mission encounters in the world.

It must remain united to proclaim the true message of the gospel— according to the norms of tradition and of the magisterium—and to be free of distortions due to whatever human ideology or political program.

The gospel thus understood leads to the spirit of truth and of freedom of the children of God, so that they do not allow themselves to be confused by propaganda which is contrary to true education or dependent on current circumstances, but rather educates for eternal life.

The eucharist that we are celebrating is in itself a sign and cause of unity. We are all one single thing although we are many, "for we all partake of the one bread,"[20] which is the body of Christ. In the Eucharistic Prayer which we will recite in a few moments, we will ask the Father that, through the sharing in the body and blood of Christ, he make of us "one body and one spirit."[21]

The obtainment of this requires a serious and explicit commitment to respect the fundamental nature of the eucharist as a sign of unity and bond of charity.

NO LONGER CHURCH'S EUCHARIST

Therefore the eucharist is not celebrated without the bishop (or the lawful minister—that is, the priest), who in his own diocese is the natural president of a eucharistic celebration worthy of the name.[22] Nor is the eucharist suitably celebrated when this ecclesial reference is lost or is perverted because the liturgical structure of the celebration is not respected, as has been established by my predecessors and by myself. *The eucharist which is placed at the service of one's own ideas* and opinions, or ends foreign to it, *is no longer a eucharist of the church*. Instead of uniting, it divides.

May this eucharist which I myself, successor of St. Peter and "foundation of visible unity"[23] am presiding over and in which your bishops are participating around the pope, serve you as an example and renewed inspiration in your behavior as Christians.

Dear priests, renew in this way the unity among you and with your bishops in order to preserve and make it grow in your communities. And you religious, always be united to the person and to the directives of your bishops. May the service of everyone to unity be a true pastoral service to the flock of Jesus Christ and in his name. And you, bishops, always remain close to your priests.

COMMITMENT FOR UNITY

In this context must likewise be included true ecumenism — that is, the commitment for unity among all Christians and all Christian communities. Once more I say to you that this unity can be based only on Jesus Christ, on one baptism,[24] and on the common profession of faith. The task of building up again full communion among all Christians can have no other reference or other criteria, and must always use methods of loyal collaboration and research. It can serve no other purpose but to give witness to Jesus Christ "so that the world may believe."[25]

Any other end or other use of the ecumenical commitment can only lead to the creation of an illusory unity and, finally, to the causing of new divisions. How sad it would be if what should help to reconstruct Christian unity, which constitutes one of the pastoral priorities of the church in this historic moment, should become, through shortsightedness, because of erroneous criteria, the source of new and worse divisions!

In the passage just read, St. Paul exhorts us to "preserve unity of the Spirit through the bond of peace."[26]

I repeat this exhortation to you and once more I point out the basis and the goal of such unity. "One body, one Spirit, just as there is but one hope given to all of you by your call, one Lord, one faith, one baptism, one God and Father of us all, who is over all, and works through all, and is in all."[27]

Beloved brothers, I have opened my heart to you. I have warmly commended to you this vocation and this mission of ecclesial unity. I am certain that you, people of Nicaragua, who have always been faithful to the church, will continue to be so also in the future.

The pope, the church, expect this from you. This I ask of God for you, with great affection and confidence. May the intercession of Mary, the *Most Pure*, your beautiful name for her, she who is the patroness of Nicaragua, help you to be ever constant in this vocation of ecclesial unity and fidelity. Amen.

NOTES

1. Rom. 8:29.
2. See Gal. 3:27.
3. Gal. 3:28.
4. See *Lumen Gentium*, 1.
5. See Gen. 4:9.

6. John 10:16.
7. John 10:4–5.
8. John 10:7.
9. John 11:52.
10. John 17:11–12.
11. *Lumen Gentium*, 1.
12. See Puebla, 238–49.
13. See Gal. 3:28.
14. Eph. 4:5.
15. See *L'Osservatore Romano*, Spanish ed., August 8, 1982, p. 9.
16. January 28, 1979.
17. See Acts 20:28.
18. See *Lumen Gentium*, 26.
19. Ibid., 22.
20. 1 Cor. 10:17.
21. Eucharistic Prayer, III.
22. See *Sacrosanctum Concilium*, 41.
23. See *Lumen Gentium*, 18.
24. See Eph. 4:5.
25. See John 17:21.
26. Eph. 4:3.
27. Eph. 4:5–6.

34

International Observers
"Open Letter regarding the Papal Mass"
(March 1983)

This letter was signed by six well-known theologians, social scientists, and jour-
nalists who had been present during the pope's visit to Nicaragua and had
followed the preparations for the visit. The letter attempted to correct some false
news reports that had circulated during the visit. The text is from a mimeo-
graphed version distributed by the Instituto Histórico Centroamericano, which
is based in the Jesuit-run Universidad Centroamericana in Managua.

We, the undersigned, priests and laity, theologians, social scientists, writers, and journalists were present during the visit of his holiness John Paul
II to Nicaragua, and we have closely followed all the preparations for the
visit. We feel obliged to write you to correct the versions which some international media have published about these events, and particularly about
what happened during the open air Mass of the pope in the 19th of July
Plaza in Managua, Friday, March 4th.

1. It has been repeatedly stated that the Nicaraguan Catholics who
wanted to attend the two major religious services at which the pope offi-
ciated met with obstacles from the civil authorities and that only persons
selected by the government were able to attend the Mass in the 19th of
July Plaza. We can personally verify that approximately 700,000 persons,
one fourth of the population, attended the two liturgical ceremonies in
León and Managua. Almost all of Nicaragua's collective transportation and
almost every road in the country were used to assure the greatest mobilization possible, and the possibility of participating was officially offered to
all.

2. It has also been said that Nicaraguan civil authorities imposed press
censorship on his holiness's visit to the country. This is not correct. We
have read the various Nicaraguan papers for the month before the papal
visit and we have seen that after the pope's visit to Nicaragua was officially
announced, the newspapers were able to give broad, varied, and, in recent
weeks, continuous information.

3. We have also read that the Vatican commission which prepared his holiness's trip to Nicaragua was not able to dialogue with the Government Junta of National Reconstruction about placing a large cross on the platform on which the holy father would celebrate the eucharist and that instead the government decorated the 19th of July Plaza with a large revolutionary billboard. We wish to clarify that everyone in Nicaragua knows that the three murals located there, which are paintings of General Augusto C. Sandino and the founders of the Sandinista National Liberation Front, have been there since July 1981. On the other hand, it seems strange to us that almost no one has mentioned the mural that the parishioners of Managua painted a week prior to the arrival of the holy father, which depicts a procession of the Nicaraguan people receiving the pope with the statues of the Immaculate Conception of Mary, the patron of Nicaragua, and Saint Dominic of Guzman, the patron of Managua. Before we left Managua, it was public knowledge in the country that Nicaraguan civil authorities in a meeting with the Vatican commission offered to place a cross on the stage. The reaction of the commission was one of indifference.

4. Similarly we have seen that some of the international cables have reported an "electronic piracy" on the part of the government in the celebration of the open air Mass in the 19th of July Plaza. These same cables have described a manipulation "of the microphones during the pope's Mass in Managua, so that the voice of John Paul II could not be heard, only that of the political propaganda." Those of us who personally attended that Mass are witnesses to the fact that at no time was the voice of the holy father not heard over the loudspeaker system. Those who followed this event on radio or television, including persons in other Central American countries, can confirm that the voice of the pope was never silenced due to a manipulation of the sound system in the plaza.

5. In almost all of the international press it was insistently stated that during the afternoon of March 4th, the Nicaraguan Government, using "Sandinista mobs," transformed a religious celebration into a political one by means of political slogans. We who attended that celebration maintain that the public liturgical celebration developed normally until almost the end of the holy father's homily. At that point from different places in the plaza, but especially from the area where many of the mothers of Nicaraguan heroes and martyrs were sitting, the tension was palpable. This was expressed in cries to the holy father asking that he speak a word of peace and say a prayer for their dead. These women were located close to the transmission center and even though the sound technicians tried to control this unexpected development, they could not prevent the women either from expressing themselves through the plaza microphones or that their anguish spread to broad sectors of those in attendance. To this request others were added, some clearly religious and others of a political nature, which are customary at Nicaraguan public events. Once this social-

psychological phenomenon occurred, practically everyone lost control over what was happening.

6. In the international press, it has been reported that the Nicaraguan government planned this boycott of the papal Mass. Although we profoundly regret that no one was able to effectively restore the tenor of the celebration, we never had the impression that it involved something which had been arranged beforehand. We feel that most of those in attendance would be able to say with certainty that they were both surprised and overwhelmed when the phenomenon occurred, a phenomenon which is difficult to comprehend outside the current Nicaraguan situation. No Nicaraguan deliberately tried to be disrespectful to the holy father, and much less in a moment as solemn as the Mass. The preparations for the visit demonstrated the effort, the affection, and the cooperation with which all sectors of Nicaragua prepared to receive the holy father.

These clarifications have arisen from our honest desire to make the truth known, and to avoid more unjust damage from outside the country to a people who have already suffered considerably. We hope that you will take these into consideration.

Managua, March 6, 1983

Cordially,

Javier Solís, Costa Rican journalist, works at IDOC International Christian Documentation Center in Rome.

Father François Houtart, sociologist, coordinator of Tricontinental Center (Africa, Asia, Latin America) at the Catholic University in Louvain, Belgium.

Father Miguel Concha Malo, journalist and professor of theology at the National Autonomous University of Mexico.

Dr. Pedro A. Riveiro de Oliveira, sociologist and author of various books on Catholicism in Brazil, professor at the Superior Institute of Religious Studies at Rio de Janeiro, Brazil.

Dr. Pablo Richard, professor of theology at the National University of Heredia, Costa Rica.

Dr. Cayetano de Lella, expert in sociology of communications, professor in the Department of Social Communications at the National Autonomous University of Mexico.

35

Latinamerica Press
"Central Americans Respond
to Papal Visit"
(March 24, 1983)

This report on the pope's Central American trip points out the tension and ambiguity in Pope John Paul's speeches between a preferential option for the poor and the pastoral option for Christian base communities. This is taken from the issue of March 24, 1983, of Latinamerica Press, *which is the English version of* Noticias Aliadas, *published in Lima, Peru.*

Mexico City. Early on in his journey, the primary objective of Pope John Paul II's visit to Central America became clear. He was interested above all in consolidating an institutionally strong church opposed to all forms of materialism, a church guided by the gospel message as traditionally understood, and free of ideological and political distortions.

From the beginning it was evident that the pope was deeply concerned over the growth of new church movements in Central America, especially the Christian base communities, that have led people to actively participate not only in theological and liturgical change, but also—and often with great intensity—in political movements. In the face of these developments, the pope consistently expressed his concerns throughout the trip. Speaking in Costa Rica, Nicaragua, El Salvador, and Haiti, he gave clear support to local church hierarchies generally viewed as reactionary, and repeatedly warned against the dangers of what he called the "popular church."

CENTRAL AMERICAN CHURCH CONFLICT

The pope's journey brought him into the heart of a Catholic Church in crisis, and he addressed the age-old dilemma of the relationship between religious practice and political activism. He made it clear to Catholics in Nicaragua and El Salvador that they should respect church institutionality and channel their struggles in the directions indicated by their bishops.

There are few regions and churches in the world today that are experiencing such intense conflict. In Central America, as in the rest of Latin America, most of the population is both Catholic and subject to multiple forms of oppression. In a certain sense, John Paul saw the situation as an ideological contest. According to Guatemalan theologian Juan Hernández Pico, John Paul reaffirmed his own vision of the church, in which the pope must reinforce the church's institutional identity through the exercise of firm authority. In addition, John Paul has a traditional Catholic attitude toward socialist societies, and fears the upsurge of atheistic tendencies that could threaten church unity.

Arriving in Costa Rica, the pope declared that the church should become an instrument of unity: "Its power does not lie in arms. It should promote harmony and avoid political activism."

He warned priests that representatives of the church should remember that they "cannot turn to violent means that are repugnant to Christian practice or to ideologies based on a narrow understanding of the human person that ignores the dimension of transcendence. The clergy should keep these things in mind, remembering that their specific mission is to preach Christ's salvation." A day later, he enjoined women religious "not to be deceived by sectarian ideologies or tempted by options that go against freedom."

In Managua's Plaza 19 de Julio, John Paul pointed out that responsibility to the church should come before "earthly considerations and unacceptable ideological commitments, as well as temporal options, including ideas of a church that would take the place of the true church itself." He called for a unified church opposed to the various forms of materialism. He warned of the absurdity and danger of another church, understood "only as 'charismatic' and not institutional, 'new' and not traditional, 'alternative' and, as it is envisaged lately, a 'popular church.'" The latter phrases repeat themes contained in his July 1982 letter to the Nicaraguan church (cf. *LP,* Sept. 9, 1982). Speaking in the Plaza 19 de Julio, which commemorates the 1979 revolutionary victory over the Somoza regime, the pope spoke warmly of Archbishop Obando y Bravo of Managua, who is considered by the Sandinista government to be a counterrevolutionary. The pope then exhorted priests to obedience, and urged them to rally around their bishops.

According to Dominican Father Miguel Concha, a Mexican journalist and theologian present during the papal visit, the pope's speech was disappointing to Nicaraguans and extremely difficult for them to comprehend. Concha noted two incidents in particular: first, although junta member, Daniel Ortega, reaffirmed, in the presence of the pope, the October 1980 declaration of the Sandinista leadership supporting religious freedom, John Paul felt impelled, in a speech in León, to insist on the "strict right of religious parents not to have their children subjected to school programs inspired by atheism." Second, during his homily on church unity, he conspicuously made no reference to the "preferential option for the poor" preached by the Latin American church since Medellín and confirmed as a principle for the whole church by the pope himself in his encyclical *Laborem Exercens*.

MESSAGE TO SALVADORANS

In El Salvador, where the hierarchy is divided and predominantly conservative, and Christian communities have formed what they call a "popular church" (cf. *LP,* Feb. 24 and March 3, 1983), John Paul spoke positively of a church that, through the witness of martyrdom, is experiencing "the pains of giving birth to a new humanity." In his San Salvador homily he lamented "how many children have been orphaned, how many noble and innocent lives have been cut short. Among the martyrs are priests, sisters, and brothers, faithful servants of the church, and a dedicated and venerable shepherd, the archbishop of his flock, Oscar Romero."

Nevertheless, he balanced these words with what was generally understood as an admonition directed toward the "popular church": "Remembering [Archbishop Romero], I ask that no ideological interest attempt to manipulate this shepherd's sacrifice."

In a country where Christians have joined the armed struggle and several priests (including a former assistant of Archbishop Romero, Fr. Rutilio Sanchez) are active in zones under guerilla control, the pope reminded the clergy of his words four years ago to the Latin American bishops at Puebla: "You are not to be social or political leaders or functionaries of a temporal power." He called priests to serve as a "bridge" between the various contending factions and to facilitate dialogue. He said they must be united with their bishops, and once again condemned ideologies that are "cooptations, or mutilations" of the gospel.

Celia Ramirez, a spokesperson in Mexico for the Comité Cristiano Oscar Arnulfo Romero, expressed the group's concern over "missing elements" in the pope's message. "He made no mention of the preferential option for the poor," she said.

"In Central America, to opt for the poor is to take risks and break new ground. It demands a pastoral approach that means being where the people are and accompanying them in the commitments they make."

36

Fernando Cardenal
"A Letter to My Friends"
(December 1984)

Fernando Cardenal worked for many years for the cause of the poor in Nicaragua as an educator and charismatic speaker. A Jesuit priest, he was a supporter of the Sandinista revolution, and also of the reconstruction, where he led a successful literacy campaign with the help of young persons from all over the nation. In 1984 he accepted the post of minister of education, seeing this as a fulfillment of his life work as an educator. Continuing pressure was brought to bear on him and other priests working with the Sandinista government, by religious superiors and especially by the Vatican, to leave their posts. On December 10, 1984, he was expelled by the Society of Jesus. The following letter, which was written shortly before his dismissal, gives Cardenal's views on the entire process. This text is taken from The National Catholic Reporter *(January 11, 1985), pp. 1, 6-8.*

In these last years of my life (1979-1984), a great number of friends from various countries, Christians or Christian at heart, cardinals, bishops, priests, brother Jesuits, religious, both men and women, and lay friends have written to me, have taken an interest in me. In these last few months I have not answered these letters. Though grateful, I have kept silent, waiting for the time when I could tell the whole truth.

On various occasions the national and international press has referred to me, making affirmations sometimes true and sometimes false. Now is the time to speak. I want to give a simple and fraternal answer (without being antagonistic, for this would be senseless in the present situation of Nicaragua), giving at the same time my honest view of what has happened and is happening. It is a limited and painful view of only one person, but it is my view and I believe I ought to share it with those who are interested in me. It is above all a letter full of gratitude. Not one of your names will be forgotten. . . .

Not long after the triumph of the Nicaraguan revolution, the bishops of

Nicaragua began to pressure us priests who were part of the revolution to abandon our commitment to it. That meant (Maryknoll) Father Miguel D'Escoto, minister of external affairs; my (Trappist) brother Ernesto, minister of culture; Father Edgar Parrales, minister of social welfare; and myself, in charge of the literacy campaign. After long months of tension, finally, in June of 1981, the conference of bishops of Nicaragua granted us permission to continue in our work as an exception because of the emergency our country was experiencing; on our part, we were to voluntarily renounce celebrating any of the sacraments in public or in private. Since that time, they have never again granted us a meeting, even though we have asked for one many times.

Before the end of the first year of this agreement, the bishops once again began to pressure us to completely leave our work in the revolution. They did not pressure us personally, but always used the mass media. In these last two years, the Vatican began to participate in the pressure, but it also did not do so personally or directly. Ever since I accepted the nomination as minister of education, the pressure through the media has intensified much more, to the point where I see clearly in these last weeks of 1984 that I will now be faced with the final alternative of either abandoning my commitment to the Nicaraguan revolution or being expelled from the Society of Jesus and receiving the priestly sanctions of suspension and interdict.

I thought that I could nourish the hope that the church would see in my work a missionary type of apostolic service along the lines of gospel presence and inculturation into a new historical process, which has taken an option for the poor. Because of this, I thought I would be able to keep hoping that a conflict between a desire and command of the church and my conscience would never arise.

Throughout these last months, I have dedicated a lot of time to discernment and spiritual direction, always involving much prayer for a greater confirmation in my decision. I have reflected on the whole of my situation with people of deep spiritual experience who love the church and know the spirit of the Society of Jesus.

Because of this, I can responsibly state that honestly, objectively, and seriously I conscientiously object to the pressures of the ecclesiastical authorities. In all sincerity I consider that before God I would be committing serious sin if in the present circumstances I were to abandon my priestly option for the poor, which is presently being concretized through my work in the Sandinista people's revolution.

My conscience grasps, as if in a global intuition, that my commitment to the cause of the poor of Nicaragua comes from God, that my desire not to abandon my work comes from God, and that for me today to be faithful to the gospel and to do God's will in my life is to continue with my present responsibilities. I cannot conceive of a God who asks me to abandon my commitment to the people.

If I do an analysis, I easily discover many reasons which reinforce the conviction of my conscience. Here are a few, briefly stated:

1. This revolutionary process of Nicaragua, in spite of the mistakes inherent in every human enterprise, which I, because I am on the inside of it, see very clearly, is a process which places the interests of the poor above everything else. Politically, therefore, it is a legitimate translation of the Latin American church's preferential option for the poor.

2. I can verify that this process, once again in spite of errors, is trying to create an original model of revolution, one of whose most characteristic features is respect for the Christian religion of the majority of the Nicaraguan people and the active participation of religious leaders in the construction of a new society.

3. I have experienced that, in the midst of tendencies toward unbelief, my priestly presence, as a religious and as a Christian among the revolutionaries, is an important testimony to the value and role of the faith. I see this activity of mine in the context of Decree IV of the 32nd General Congregation and in the special mission against atheism given the society by his holiness Paul VI.

4. Since the end of my tertianship, in 1970, I promised to live my priesthood in service of the poor, leaving its concrete applications to the impulse of the Spirit. Since then I believe that, with the grace of God, I have fulfilled this promise—always in consultation with my religious community, in its widest sense, and with my superiors in the Society of Jesus. This promise is fulfilled today in Nicaragua by working in the revolution.

5. Since then, I encouraged as a priest many, many young people and many adults both from the moneyed as well as from the popular classes that, moved by this faith, they might dedicate themselves in the most efficacious manner possible to the cause of the poor. In Nicaragua this cause was being carried forward by the FSLN. Not a few of these followed my words and inserted themselves as yeast in the dough and into our history; thousands were assassinated, among whom were my brother-in-law and three nephews. A bond of blood that has been shed also unites me to this cause, to this people.

6. I am convinced that our presence in the Nicaraguan revolution in these times brings a great transcendence not only to this process, but also to all the processes of social transformation that will take place in Latin America. One has to be blind not to see this. We do not believe in models, but these experiences enlighten and, above all, inspire.

7. I am under the impression that our revolutionary model is so novel and original that it is difficult to understand from outside. I personally feel that the challenge which (without trying to and without taking personal credit for it) we are carrying forward, the responsibility which weighs on our shoulders, and the repercussions this involves in these times in whatever definitive decisions we take, are not well understood. The hundreds of

letters written to us from all over are a tangible proof of what we are affirming.

8. Our little Nicaragua is almost totally defenseless against the avalanche of calumny and clever manipulation of every type which try to delegitimize and denigrate it, thus more easily justifying military aggression against it. The cause of the people and the truth of this cause has to face so much mud-slinging and infamy. That is why we are going to accompany the people in revolution with all our strength, shouting to all who care to listen, with all the force of our priestly credibility and with all the moral authority we have with our friends: "Don't believe the calumnies against Nicaragua; like all human beings, we make mistakes as we go along, but not as our detractors claim. Our goals are just, noble, beautiful and holy." Nicaragua, now more than ever, needs qualified witnesses to the truth and justice of its cause. And this is where we should be.

9. To leave the revolution precisely at this time would be like deserting my commitment to the poor, and I would have difficulty convincing myself that at this time my withdrawal from the cause could be anything but a betrayal of the cause of the poor and even a betrayal of my country. A very careful analysis of the international situation indicates to us that at any moment we could move from being a nation besieged by counterrevolutionaries officially and publicly supported by the U.S. government, to becoming a nation suffering more direct intervention by the military forces of the U.S. government precisely because the present U.S. administration does not want to accept the Sandinista people's revolution.

10. At a time when the whole country is in a state of "general alert" and the Sandinista army ready for combat and waiting for military aggression, I am ordered to leave the revolution. The task I have been given for the eventuality of intervention is a dangerous one. I know clearly that my life is in greater danger than during the struggle against the dictatorship of Somoza, but I cannot abandon my people. I will never abandon them. I love this cause more than my life, and they are asking me to abandon it precisely when my people are in critical danger, calumniated and accosted by the most powerful country in the world.

11. The order I am being given obliges me to make decisions of conscience but I have come to realize that the pressures that are provoking this order do not originate in theological reflection, or in evangelical inspiration of pastoral necessity. In communion with the church, I have the right to say that some bishops of Nicaragua have taken a political stance which yesterday and today continues to show that they are in open contradiction with the interests of the poor majority of Nicaragua.

Also the Holy See, in the case of Nicaragua, appears to be imprisoned by conceptions in the political sphere that it has received from the traumatic experiences of East European conflicts which have nothing to do with the history of the people of God in our Latin American countries and much less with the revolutionary process in Nicaragua. From our vantage point, the political stance of the Vatican toward Nicaragua coincides with that of President Reagan. With my withdrawal they are trying to delegitimize the revolutionary process. Here there is no question of a dogma of the Christian faith, neither a Catholic doctrine nor a Christian moral imperative; there is only political confrontation. The bishops have publicly shown themselves to be united to those who are attacking the revolution, to those who wish the destruction of this regime in order to return to the past. The rigid application of canon 285-3 cannot help but appear to be in line with a series of acts of aggression which the U.S. government and its allies are directing against our little country. They want to facilitate the work of Goliath in the destruction of David.

Moreover, this whole incident was carried out by the bishops in a manner that is scarcely pastoral. Six times I asked the episcopal conference to meet with me in order to dialogue, but they did not even answer my letters. It hurts to feel permanently rejected by one's pastors.

On July 8 this year, before making public my nomination as minister of education, I wrote the president of the conference (with a copy to each of the bishops) asking that they give me an opportunity to dialogue with them, and I terminated my letter with this paragraph: "Henceforth, I wish to point out that I am ready to broach with you or with the entire episcopal conference any concern, problem, or perspective that you have on your mind in the area of education."

This letter had the same fortune as the previous ones; it was not answered.

This whole combination of reasons makes up some of the elements that have resulted—for the first time in thirty-two years of Jesuit life—in my having problems with a command of obedience. In the situation we are considering, I have a serious objection in conscience to obeying. . . .

Today, two years after making this testimony, I confirm it with greater conviction.

I believe that canon 285 is valid, and I am not against it. I also believe that today more than ever the exception for the priests in Nicaragua ought to be renewed because, today more than ever, the church ought to give witness to being on the side of the poor at a time when there is a desire to relentlessly attack and destroy their hopes.

I maintain my objection in conscience. My religious community continues to bear witness to the fact that it is sincere and that its motivation is evangelical. I believe that it would be a sin to abandon my people and even more so when they are being attacked militarily, economically, politically, and even through worldwide news agencies. I feel that God could not put me on the side of those who want to devour the people like bread.

At no time will I ask to leave the Society of Jesus. As far as possible, expulsion from it, something I think is the result of pressure, I consider to be the same as those the bishops want to impose on me—that is, unjust and abusive. I accept the fact that there is authority in the church, but I also know that it is not arbitrary or without its limits. For this reason, I protest against what seems to me to be an abuse of authority.

I will continue to live as a religious, and, with God's grace, I will try to keep my vow of celibacy. No one can take my priesthood away from me. With the Lord's help and in communion with the church, I hope to continue being a spiritual leader for my people—that is to say, I hope to continue being its servant even to the point of giving my life for the increase of conditions leading to its total liberation.

I consider myself to be a sinner. I have a deep awareness of this. I do not want anyone to idealize me, because this would be a big mistake. But the interesting thing in this situation is that they are not punishing me for my sins, but for what I experience as God's call to me, and to this call I cannot say no.

I am grateful for the support, the advice, and the deep friendship of the Jesuit community at Bosques de Altamira, especially of its superior, Father Peter Marchetti, S.J. All these years, they have been my brothers and best friends.

I am grateful to Fr. Provincial's delegate for Nicaragua, Father Inaki Zubizarreta, S.J., who always took an interest in my situation. A great friend and a man of God.

The provincial of the Central American Province, Father Valentin Menéndez, S.J., accompanied me with genuine kindness, understanding, and support. I also thank Father Peter-Hans Kolvenbach, S.J., superior general of the Society of Jesus, for respecting my conscientious objection, for his personal appreciation, and for the interest he has taken in positively resolving my situation.

The one who has categorically refused to grant an exception to the priests in Nicaragua so that they might continue working in the revolutionary government has been Pope John Paul II. It hurts me to say this, but as a Christian I cannot keep quiet.

When in 1982 the then papal legate to the Society of Jesus, Father Paolo Dezza, S.J., was ordered to tell me to withdraw from my work with the Sandinista youth, I wrote asking for the reasons in writing so that I could reflect on them. Father Dezza answered me on January 12, 1983. There were not any reasons. It was an order from the pope. Here is a transcription of the principal paragraphs of the text of this letter:

"I very much admire what you have been able to do for the good of your Nicaraguan brothers in many various ways, especially the National Literacy Crusade, and how you have tried to give clear witness to your priestly and Jesuit identity, even rejecting posts that did not appear compatible with your religious vocation, even though on the other hand they could have rendered service to the country. In the name of the Society I wish to express a deep recognition and gratitude, and at the same time clearly describe the present situation.

"As you know, I have communicated to Fr. Provincial the confirmed desire of the Holy Father that all the priests, not only the Jesuits, withdraw from the type of collaboration with the government in which they are committed to being part of official organisms. The post you are holding, though not directly part of the government, is very closely aligned to it because it deals with a political organization of the Sandinistas. And though it is possible to exercise a real apostolate in a position like the one you hold, the Holy Father has over and over manifested his will that such offices are not to be performed by priests, and he hopes that the Jesuits will be an example of obedience in this matter. It is necessary, therefore, that we follow the will of the Holy Father promptly and in a spirit of faith.

"As you can see, my dear Father Cardenal, we are dealing with a delicate and difficult situation, but I believe that God will give us the light and the grace needed to respond with complete trust in the Lord, who by his example revealed to us an obedience that seemed like madness to men, but was a love that brought redemption to men of all times.

"I realize I am asking you for a very difficult act of obedience, one in which the human reasons appear to be insufficient; but I am sure that God will reward your faith and make it apostolically fruitful. You can count on my prayers for this, on my admiration and my help in all that is within my hands."

It is perhaps clear to those who have read this text up to this point that, "the love that brings about redemption" through the passion and death of Jesus Christ is the love that leads me to follow my conscience and to continue serving this revolution calumniated and attacked and which in Nicaragua, I believe, is concretized in the cause of the poor. As this is a decision in conscience, I am not trying to set it up as an example or a norm. Others could experience fidelity and its demands in another way, but equally according to their conscience. For me, it would be a serious sin before God not to follow this hard and painful road, which is only softened by the hope that my permanent communion with the church and my obedience to God in my conscience must justify the Lord of history and the same church in the eyes of the people.

I need the prayer and the solidarity of all of you, of those who have written me and are in solidarity in this conflict, and with the cause of the poor in Nicaragua and with the revolution. I need your prayer, and I trust in it to sustain me in the rest of my life so that I might help to also sustain the long suffering and the courage of my people.

37

Congregation for the Doctrine of the Faith "Ten Observations on the Theology of Gustavo Gutiérrez" (March 1983)

The congregation here makes very serious charges against the theology of Gutiérrez, for example, that he makes the Marxist understanding of class struggle "the determining principle, from which he goes on to reinterpret the Christian message" (no. 2). This is clearly a false interpretation of Gutiérrez's theology; perhaps that is why very little publicity was given to this document by the congregation. Although Gutiérrez has replied to these and other charges, constant pressure has been kept up against him. Some of the same charges were made again the following year in an instruction from the Congregation of the Doctrine of the Faith, against unspecified "theologies of liberation." I was able to obtain a French text in the periodical Dial *(March 22, 1984); the English translation is my own.*

Facing the situation of poverty and oppression of millions of Latin Americans, the church has the duty of proclaiming the liberation of humankind and of helping this liberation to come to birth. But it also has the duty of proclaiming liberation in its integral and profound meaning, in the same way that Jesus announced it and realized it. In order to protect the originality and the specific contribution of Christian liberation, it is important to avoid all reductionism and all ambiguity (cf. John Paul II, Opening Address at the Puebla Conference).

In accord with this principle, we present below some observations on the theology of liberation as it has been interpreted by one of its principal adherents, Gustavo Gutiérrez. For the most part he does this in two books, entitled respectively *A Theology of Liberation* and *The Power of the Poor in History*. Although these two works are separated in time, they share the same internal coherence and give the theology of liberation a clearly distinctive orientation.

1. The urgent attention focused on the scandal of the masses of Latin America and the uncritical acceptance of the Marxist interpretation of this situation explain the seductiveness of the theology of Gustavo Gutiérrez and the extreme ambiguity which characterizes it.

2. Because of its "scientific" character, Gutiérrez accepts the Marxist conception of history, which is a history of conflict, structured around the class struggle and requiring commitment on behalf of the oppressed in their struggle for liberation. This is the determining principle from which he goes on to reinterpret the Christian message.

3. In the first place, this approach leads him to a selective rereading of the Bible. He emphasizes the theme of Yahweh as the God of the poor as well as the theme of Matthew 25, but does not consider all the dimensions of evangelical poverty. He then proceeds to form a unity between the poor of the Bible and the exploited victims of the capitalist system. From this follows his justification of revolutionary commitment on behalf of the poor.

4. This same selective reading highlights certain texts, which are given an exclusively political meaning. The exodus, considered as a political event, becomes a paradigm: liberation means political liberation. The Magnificat of Mary (Luke 2:46ff.) is interpreted in the same way. Genesis is taken to mean a promethean glorification of liberating work.

5. As an excuse for eliminating every "dualism," the author proposes a dialectical relationship between liberation-salvation and liberation-politics along the same lines as the relation between the whole and the part. Although he does not admit it, he falls into a temporal messianism and reduces the growth of the kingdom to the increase in justice (what kind of justice?) in society.

6. The same thing occurs with regard to sin as a radical alienation, which is conceived as merely the bias of political alienations in the socio-political sphere. Consequently, the struggle against injustice in the ranks of class struggle is a struggle against sin. In the real world there is no sin except "social sin."

One hopes also that further clarifications will be forthcoming on what is meant by a just society.

7. The influence of Marxism is clear both in the understanding of truth and the notion of theology. Orthodoxy is replaced by orthopraxy, for truth does not exist except within praxis—that is, in the commitment to revolution. A number of positions flow from this.

a) The lamp which enlightens us is that of the experience gained in the struggle for liberation; this experience is an encounter with the Lord, and is marked by the presence of the Holy Spirit. A concept such as this mounts an attack on the transcendence of revelation and on its normative value, as well as on the specific character of theological faith.

b) A formula such as "God becomes history" leads, in this perspective, to relativism: theology, with its roots in historical experience, has the task of leading each epoch to a rereading of the Bible and a reformulation of doctrine. This approach puts in question the unity that exists between the meaning of God's word and the reality of tradition.

c) If God becomes history, it is the human person who makes history through struggle and work. One can only emphasize the Pelagianism contained in such a concept.

d) The Marxist theory of praxis aggravates matters. Like every ideology, theology is viewed as the reflection of class interests. It follows that liberation theology is a class theology in opposition to the "dominant theology," which takes over the gospel in order to profit the rich of the world. The theologian is the "organic intellectual" of the "historic bloc" of the proletariat (phrases taken from Gramsci).

e) The experience mentioned above appears by itself to provide the criteria for truth. It has never taken account of the normative function of the church and particularly of the Second Vatican Council.

8. The kingdom is constructed by means of struggles for liberation. Ecclesiology has to be understood in this sense, and it is also necessary to be able to change the "structures" of the church.

a) The church is seen merely as a sign of unity and love, which will be the result of struggle. The class struggle is the way of living which leads to fraternity (a reference to Girardi and to the "concrete universal" of Hegel).

b) This calls into question the reconciliation already realized in the redemptive sacrifice of Christ as well as the fact that salvation is already offered in Jesus Christ. The transcendent grace within the mystery of the church is not recognized, and a partisan church is advocated. It follows that there is only one history, that of the salvation (liberation) that is coming; this is its understanding of eschatology.

c) Thus, class struggle traverses the whole church. In opposition to those who belong to a church collaborating with power is a church of the poor, the church at the base, which is the authentic people of God. Such an understanding leads logically to rejection of the hierarchy and its legitimacy.

d) The church of the poor is now in the process of realization in the base communities involved in struggles for liberation. Nowhere are these class struggles described, a surprising reticence that should attract the attention of genuine pastors.

e) The same must be said with regard to allusions to the eucharist as a celebration and announcement of liberation. Is the true nature of the sacrament thus respected? There is cause for serious doubts about this.

9. The author, who says so much about the poor, never examines the Beatitudes in their true meaning. A theological reflection on violence is missing from his work. The class struggle is presented as a fact and as a necessity for Christians, who are thus invited to join the struggle without any doubt as to the legitimacy of a battle inspired by Marxism.

10. Therefore, the objective is to make of Christianity a means of mobilizing for the sake of the revolution. By its recourse to Marxism, this theology can pervert an inspiration that is evangelical: the consciousness and the hopes of the poor.

38

Karl Rahner, S. J.
"Letter to Cardinal Juan Landázuri Ricketts of Lima, Peru"
(March 16, 1984)

Fr. Karl Rahner was undoubtedly one of the greatest theologians of the twentieth century. In his Theological Investigations *and prolific articles he illuminated most of the key theological and pastoral issues that confronted the church in these turbulent times. Like Gutiérrez, he had also experienced investigation and censorship by Rome, but he persevered in his work and was justified by his many important contributions to the Second Vatican Council. This letter was written just two weeks before his death. In it he steadfastly maintains the orthodoxy of Gutiérrez, and the need for pluralism in theology. A German text of the letter may be found in Norbert Greinacher,* Konflikt um die Theologie der Befreiung: Diskussion und Dokumentation *(Cologne: Benziger Verlag, 1985), pp. 184-86. This English translation is my own.*

Innsbruck, March 16, 1984

Your Eminence,

Because of various circumstances of a personal nature which need not be mentioned here, I consider myself obliged to testify to the high esteem I have for the theological work of Gustavo Gutiérrez.

I am convinced of the orthodoxy of the theological work of Gustavo Gutiérrez. The liberation theology he represents is thoroughly orthodox and is aware of its limits within the whole context of Catholic theology. Moreover, it is deeply convinced (correctly, in my opinion) that the voice of the poor must be listened to by theology in the context of the Latin American church. This means that a theology which must serve the concrete task of evangelization cannot prescind from the social and cultural context in which it must take place, so that it occurs in the situation in which the hearer actually lives.

In agreement with the letter on Marxism of my highly esteemed former General Superior, Pedro Arrupe [see no. 32], I am convinced that the social sciences are of great significance for contemporary theology. The social sciences are not the norm for theology, since the latter is based on the message of Jesus Christ in the gospels and on the teaching of the Catholic Church; today, however, it is impossible to practice any kind of theology without taking the secular sciences into account.

I am fully convinced that a condemnation of Gustavo Gutiérrez would have extremely unfortunate consequences for the whole climate that is necessary today for the very existence of a theology that is alive and serving the task of evangelization. At the present time there are a number of different schools and movements in theology, that at times take part in heated controversies. But this has always been true, and a legitimate pluralism in Catholic theology existed even in the Middle Ages and the Baroque period. It would be deplorable, then, if such a legitimate pluralism were to be excessively restricted by means of administrative measures.

If I may allude to a personal matter, I would like to point out that I am as controversial in my own theology as Gustavo Gutiérrez is. But this did not prevent the Holy Father [Pope John Paul II] from congratulating me in a most friendly manner on my eightieth birthday; the German bishops' conference did the same thing. I have also had serious public controversies with Cardinal Joseph Hoeffner of Cologne, but that did not prevent him from congratulating me on my birthday on behalf of the German bishops' conference and from thanking me for my theological labors.

It goes without saying that I would be happy to express my views on more specific questions in this matter, if you should so desire.

With my best wishes, I remain at the service of your eminence.

Fr. Karl Rahner, S.J.

39

Juan Luis Segundo, S.J.
"Two Theologies of Liberation"
(Toronto, March 22, 1983)

This talk by Segundo is concerned with changes of direction taken by the best-known liberation theologians, and is quite critical of some of his colleagues. Such honest self-criticism may be very helpful for the future elucidation of liberation theology. This English text is from The Month, *17 (October 1984), pp. 321–27.*

I

There are so many and at times such ridiculous myths about Latin American theology, especially about so-called liberation theology. It should be clear from the beginning that I do not want to bore you by trying to correct them. For instance, I will not try to show that this theology has nothing more to do with violence than the traditional theology one learns, and which was used in the northern hemisphere to allow Christians to kill without regret millions of people in the Second World War as well as in other battlefields subsequent. I do not pretend either, for it would be naive and unrealistic, to deny that, within what is labeled Latin American liberation theology, there could be and surely often are superficial, boastful, and excessive features.

Rather, I prefer to deal with an important shift which, after the middle or even the early 1970s, has clearly divided theologians and, more generally speaking and taking account of the receptivity and creativity of lay people, has changed the method of developing a liberating theology in our continent.

I will speak then of at least two theologies of liberation coexisting now in Latin America. And, given the fact that they did not appear simultaneously, I will try to give a historical account of their respective causes, the context of their appearance, their aims, their methods, and their results.

In so doing, it is my hope that this historical view may help to avoid a superficial view of what is happening in Latin America, as well as global misconceptions about the development of theology in our continent during the past twenty years.

Contrary to the most common assumption, Latin American theology, without any precise title, began to show clearly distinctive features at least ten years before Gustavo Gutiérrez's well-known book *A Theology of Liberation*. This was a kind of baptism, but the baby had already grown old. The real beginning came simultaneously from many theologians working in different countries and places in Latin America, even before the first session of Vatican II. In any case, these developments began some years before the Constitution *Gaudium et Spes* in 1965, which, to a great extent, was used afterward as an official support for the main views of this liberation theology. Let us, therefore, go back to the early 1960s. Something was happening, more or less at the same time, all over Latin America, something which established a new context for understanding our Christian faith and, hence, for doing theology. It is, I believe, of great importance to understand precisely the social, political and theological context of this event.

Until 1964, when the military takeover of Brazil began to foreshadow a reversal of privileges afforded to universities within society, the state universities at least were ruled by a students' movement created at the beginning of this century in Argentina. This movement, which was successful in almost every Latin American country, was aimed at giving the university the freedom it needed in the face of political governments and other pressures.

It did not mean a depoliticization of universities. On the contrary, by making students the principal rulers of university life (together with faculty members and groups of professionals), and by gaining political autonomy, the state university became a sort of parallel power in politics. It was so to speak a state within the state. It became free to support any kind of political ideas, and above all to unmask, through all kinds of intellectual tools, the mystifying ideologies used by governments to hide and to justify the inhuman situation of the majority of our population.

It was precisely in this context, however one may evaluate it, that a new approach to Christian faith developed among students. It involved a kind of Christian conversion as far as the social consequences of our faith were concerned. Without taking this context into account, one easily falls into the mistaken notion that liberation theology is a specific branch of theology, recently created and somehow inflated, dealing with "liberation," whatever this term may mean. Another mistake coming from the lack of knowledge of this context consists in believing that liberation theology in Latin America came from a particular understanding of European political theology. Before knowing anything about political theology, if it existed at all at this time, the university student, using above all the option of the social function of *ideologies*, had already discovered that our whole culture, whatever the intention in constructing it may have been, was working for the benefit of the ruling classes. It was not, of course, necessary to be a Marxist to make such a commonsense discovery, but it is also true that many Christian students at the university were led by their Marxist fellows to this realization and to be concerned with this fact.

Furthermore, Christian students could do nothing except include *theology* — the understanding of Christian faith — in the ideological mechanisms structuring the whole of our culture. And when I say "the whole of our culture" I mean by that, that even though ideologies are consciously or unconsciously developed in the ruling classes which benefit from them, they also pervade the whole of society, since they are injected even into the minds of those who are their victims. Unlearned and so incapable of utilizing developed tools of ideological suspicion in a culture considered impartial and the same for all social classes, poor and marginalized people were led by their culture to accept distorted and hidden oppressive elements which "justified" their situation, and, among all these elements, a distorted and oppressive theology.

From Christian students to theologians working with them, this ideological suspicion thus became a source of a new vision about what theology should become and about how a theologian was supposed to work to unmask the anti-Christian elements hidden in a so-called Christian society. In order to give some concrete flesh to this quite abstract reflection, let me give you an example. Among thousands of possible examples, I will choose one, since the same example will be helpful later on to show the shift between the first trend in liberation theology and the second. I suppose that all are familiar with the name of at least one of the outstanding Latin American theologians today, Leonardo Boff, a Franciscan from Brazil. In an article written two years ago after a month of pastoral experience in one of Brazil's poorest states, the state of Acre on the frontier between Brazil and Bolivia, Boff, trying to reflect on the Christian faith, that is, trying to theologize with the poor and uncultivated members of the Basic Christian Communities, experienced some difficulties in dialogue and communication between such different levels of culture. But he tells us in his article that once, at least, the dialogue was set in motion when he asked: How did Jesus redeem us? Many people answered: "through the cross." Others put the same idea in slightly different terms: "through his suffering."

At this point Boff recalls his reflection on those answers of grassroots Christians. His reflection can be meaningful for us since it shows, in a particular *theological* case, the global attitude of suspicion which a university student is supposed to have about popular religion and its function in an oppressive society like ours. Boff writes:

> I asked myself: why do [grassroots] people immediately associate redemption with the cross? Undoubtedly because they have not learned the historical character of redemption, that is, of the process of lib-

eration. Perhaps it is so because their own life is nothing but suffering and crosses, the cross society has managed to make them carry on their shoulders.

And the consequence for theology develops in this article: "A Jesus who only suffers is not liberating; he generates the cult of suffering and fatalism. It is important to *relocate within the mind of (common) persons the cross in its true place.*"[1]

I think that this example can provide a good indication of both the method and the aim of this first theology of liberation.

No amount of subtle argument can conceal that the only relevant methodological feature of Latin American theology is, as a matter of fact, to start thinking not from a systematic listing of theological problems linked by an inner logic for the sake of orthodox and credible answers to every problem, but instead in the precise context I am describing, to start both from a commitment to think for the sake of poor and oppressed people, and from a consideration of their praxis every time we perceive that this praxis is linked, through theology, to the oppressive mechanisms of the whole culture. This consideration of praxis aims at reformulating a Christian theology capable of transforming this praxis into a more liberative one, that is to say, aiming at orthopraxis: in this example, it aims at preventing passivity and fatalism.

The context I am describing should prevent one from falling into two superficial and mistaken preconceptions. The first one is that liberation theology comes out of practice. And the second one is that it makes orthopraxis, instead of orthodoxy, the main criterion for its solutions. In the example I presented, one can see the true role of praxis in theologizing. Of course, as we understand it, the passivity and fatalism of common people belong indeed to the practical side of their lives, insofar as they are not intellectual problems about their faith calling for theoretical solutions. Praxis means, therefore, a starting point based on a systematic suspicion which tries to perceive any possible link between some oppressive and inhuman behavior and a similarly oppressive and inhuman understanding of Christian faith. In this sense, and only in this sense, has the first line of liberation theology stressed the relevance of the hermeneutic function of praxis. And I am not trying to belittle it. But at least serious theologians in Latin America, as one can see from the example proposed, do not aim at reducing theology to more or less superficial and spontaneous answers to the problems which Christian people *perceive* in their everyday life and which they bring forward when they meet in Basic Christian Communities.

Secondly and accordingly, when theologians in our continent stress the relevance of orthopraxis over against orthodoxy, they are not saying that they prefer the former to the latter, or that they are not concerned with the historical development of Christian dogmas as a true criterion in theology. They are as concerned with orthodoxy as everybody else. They cannot, however, deny that the starting point of their task as theologians is closely connected with the concrete facts of *heteropraxis* that are clearly discernible, like the cult of suffering and fatalism Boff was alluding to in the example. Do not forget that we live at the same time in one of the most Christian lands and in one of the most inhuman ones. We cannot escape the question of the connection between both facts. And, of course, what appears at the beginning as a heuristic starting point, leading our theological inquiries, must also appear at the end as a relevant though always vague and elusive focus, namely, orthopraxis. Humanization and liberation in real people should measure to some extent our theological achievements, no matter how provisional and ambiguous these achievements are.

That is why the aim of this first theology of liberation from the beginning was to remake, to the extent of what was possible for us, the whole of theology. Being faithful to both, orthodoxy and orthopraxis, we felt the necessity of deideologizing our language and our message about God, the church, the sacraments, grace, sin, the meaning of Jesus Christ, and so on. We were not interested at all in creating a new kind of branch of theology that *spoke of liberation,* or in making liberation the explicit center of the whole of theology, instead of any other theological theme. In this sense, the title this theological trend received after Gustavo Gutiérrez's famous book *A Theology of Liberation*[2] made us perhaps quite fashionable, but helped also to distort to some extent our aim and to push us toward a useless battle against many European and North American theologians, and finally to create suspicion among church authorities about our supposed intention of substituting "supernatural and vertical salvation" with historical and political liberation.

In any case, deideologizing our customary interpretation of Christian faith was, for us, the necessary task in order to get the whole church to carry to our people an understanding of our faith both more faithful to Jesus' gospel and more capable of contributing to the humanization of all people and social classes in our continent.

Of course, this theological liberation was supposed, through pastoral activities and agents, to reach at a *different pace* different social classes, thus becoming universal with the same kind of universality that can be attributed to the gospel of Jesus. As I have already said, the context for this new trend in Latin American theology was the university, or, in other words, middle-class people. Now, the middle class are usually considered by sociologists as the most mobile and creative part of society, inclined either to provoke rightist upheavals when they feel their interests or social order threatened, or to be involved in restructuring and liberating society when they feel guilty.

Thus it was not the oppressed people, but the middle classes, beginning with students, who received the first features of this liberation theology as a joyful conversion and a new commitment. As middle class, they clearly perceived that they themselves belonged to the side of our oppressors and were more or less linked with an ideology fostering their interests. As Christians, they felt increasingly concerned with fighting for the liberation of poor and marginalized people, but also blocked by many oppressive elements which they had always considered constituent parts of their faith. A new theological vision of faith was thus assumed by a wide range of middle-class Christians as a liberating force so that they accepted and fulfilled a new type of Christian commitment to liberation, even against their own material interests and privileges.

As theologians, we believed at that time, and some of us still believe, that this movement among the most active and creative members of the church could reach, sooner or later, all oppressed people on our continent, through the pastoral activities of a church following a new line and carrying out a new message. Thus the first theology of liberation was committed to a long-term and far-reaching goal.

But something different happened.

II

Now as I examine the second line in liberation theology, I believe that it would be useful to recall the elements we have brought forward in the first line, namely: the origin of a theology of conversion among middle-class groups, the methodological trend to suspect that the customary way of understanding Christian faith was distorted at all levels of society by ideological bias that concealed and justified the status quo, and, finally, the long-term aim of providing the pastoral activities of the church with a new and deideologized theology capable of speaking about the common themes of Christian faith as they were at the beginning—that is, a revelation of the humanizing and liberating will of God and of God's own being.

Let me briefly look at a new context for theologizing: the common people. This context was already there in most Latin American countries, but it was discovered, so to speak, with the help of some popular or populist movements, which came to public attention in the early 1970s and still more openly in the late 1970s. I would like to call attention to the fact that in this new context for theologizing it is important to depart from the customary view of two things: the intellectual foundation for theologizing and the usual and culturally simplistic view of Third World countries as only economically underdeveloped and poor societies.

Let us follow very briefly one of these powerful popular movements in Latin America, the so-called Peronism of Argentina. As you know, perhaps, Perón was freely elected and reelected president of Argentina, and his government lasted for more than ten years until a military takeover in the late 1950s. Perón went into exile and remained in Spain for almost twenty years. And, then, another free election gave him the presidency again for a new term, one which terminated with his death. This is the rough historical outline of political events which will provide us with a central fact and an excellent example of the shift among Latin American intellectuals in general and within the theology of liberation in particular.

What happened among intellectuals and theologians during those twenty years of Perón's exile? When Perón went into exile, Argentina was deeply divided politically. For different and understandable reasons, the upper classes, the upper-middle class, intellectuals, and the majority of the Catholic hierarchy were utterly anti-Peronist. The lower-middle class and the working classes, both in urban and rural areas, remained fervently Peronist during these two decades. It is perhaps worth noting that the intellectuals' disaffection with Perón during his first presidential period was clearly caused by the liberal ground of Perón's vague political ideology, rightist nationalism, linked with elements akin to fascism and anti-Semitism. Intellectuals were against Perón for the sake of democracy and for the sake of the people themselves. In any case, the successive failures of many military and some civilian non-Peronist governments made both intellectuals in general and Catholics in particular reflect on their former political position. They seemingly discovered the mechanism of their political mistake, and they were converted to Peronism for the sake of the same popular majority, which suffered oppression from every regime but was always faithful to its old leader. Thus when Perón came back from exile, he had at his disposal beside the old and monolithic popular support the new support of the majority of intellectuals and particularly of a "new" theology of liberation.

I guess that this conversion of intellectuals and, hence, of theologians (since the latter belong by definition to the former by their task, *intellectus fidei*) had its roots in a painful experience intellectuals often have. In Latin America and everywhere else, they try to think and to create ideas for the sake of the common good. They sometimes speak against their own interests in the name of a voiceless people supposedly incapable of recognizing where their actual interest is. And finally they discover not only that they are not understood by the people for the sake of whom they have tried to think and to speak, but also that the main stream of history cuts them off from popular victories.

Conversion means, then, for many intellectuals, a kind of self-negation. Instead of teaching, they should learn. And in order to learn from common people, they should incorporate themselves, even mentally, with these common people, and give up the chronic suspicion among intellectuals that common people are always wrong. Given this background, let us consider, from this example, the crisis of the mid-1970s in the Latin American theology of liberation, and the following shift from the first to the second one.

One thing was obvious: the rise of popular or populist movements either outside or inside the church had shown that common people had neither understood nor welcomed anything from the first theology of liberation, and had actually reacted against its criticism of the supposed oppressive elements of popular religion. They resisted the new pastoral trends trying to correct it. The first theology of liberation had raised hopes, enthusiasm, and conversion only among the middle classes, which were integrated into a European culture. It is true that their concern for the poor and oppressed had made them dangerous for the status quo, but the persecution of middle-class leftists all over Latin America did not close the gap between them and grassroots people.

It appeared then that if theologians were still to be the "organic intellectuals" of the common people, that is to say, useful as intellectuals charged with the understanding of popular faith, they were obliged to learn how oppressed people lived their faith. Thus Enrique Dussel coined for theologians and pastoral agents the expression, *the discipleship of the poor*. And Leonardo Boff spoke about a new "ecclesiogenesis," a church born from the poor.[3] And Gustavo Gutiérrez chose as the title of his new book *The Power of the Poor in History*.[4] Theologians, wanting to be in religious matters the "organic intellectuals" of poor and uncultivated people, began then to understand their function as one of unifying and structuring people's understanding of their faith, as well as grounding and defending the practices coming from this faith. Of course, not all Latin American theologians agreed with this shift. Some still refuse to give up the first critical function, which comes out of a suspicion that theology, like other all-pervasive cultural features, can and perhaps should be considered an instrument of oppression and, hence, as a non-Christian theology. Facts point so obviously in that direction that theologians belonging explicitly to the second line cannot but raise the same central suspicion.

Let us recall here as an example the experience of Leonardo Boff trying to dialogue with members of Basic Christian Communities in Acre about Jesus' redemption. He cannot but conclude that theologians must (in his own words) "relocate in the mind of (common) people the cross in its true place." In saying that, Leonardo seems to act naturally as a theologian of the first line of Latin American liberation theology. But at the beginning of his article we find a brief introduction containing the methodological principle of the second one. He writes there:

> In a church that has opted for the people, for the poor and for their liberation, the *principal learning of theology* comes from the contact with (grassroot) people. Who evangelizes the theologian? The faith witnessed by faithful people, their capacity to introduce God in all their struggling, their resistance against the oppression they customarily have to suffer.[5]

I do not know if you perceive that there is an undoubtedly involuntary contradiction here between the claim of having been evangelized by the poor and taught by them, and, on the other hand, the pretension of relocating in people's minds the true meaning of the cross and suffering. How can a passive and fatalistic conception of God evangelize the theologian?

I believe that at this point we both grasp the meaning and appreciate the difficulty in the shift in Latin American liberation theology I was alluding to in the title of this paper. No doubt, both share the same global intention of liberating and humanizing those who suffer the most from unjust structures on our continent; but this cannot conceal the fact that we are faced here with two different theologies under the same name: different in scope, different in method, different in presuppositions, and different in pastoral consequences.

III

Let me now list some of the opposite characteristics of both liberation theologies now existing and working simultaneously in Latin America.

If we look at their scope, both lines seem to have failed, to a considerable extent, to fulfill the expectations raised by them. It is clear by now that the first line of liberation theology failed in providing the Latin American church with a new and deideologized theology dealing, in a liberating way, with the customary themes of pastoral activities: God, sacraments, grace, and so forth. I think that three principal causes were influential in this failure.

The first was the *title*. Instead of taking over the old theology by slowly giving a new content to every field of theology, the new title sounded as if it were pointing to a new and dangerous kind of theology more concerned with politics than with a serious improvement of theology taught in universities and seminaries. To this inner danger was soon added the pressures and threats of civilian or military authorities against the church to make it avoid any activities explicitly connected with the theology of liberation.

Secondly, the new theology, identified by its title, to the extent that it reached not only theologians but also large segments of the middle-class lay population, raised all over Latin America a wave of doubt and strong criticism about *popular religion* (otherwise and perhaps more aptly called "popular Catholicism") as being oppressive and, all in all, non-Christian. It provoked a growing reaction against liberation theology among church officials striving to keep the masses within the church. The accusation of being more or less influenced by Marxism in this analysis of the relationship between religion and oppression was an easy although unfair reason for preventing the majority of theologians in this line of thought from teaching in institutes, seminaries, and faculties destined to prepare pastoral agents for the church in Latin America.

Thirdly, many Latin American theologians, under this banner, which made them fashionable in the international market, if not fully appreciated in their particular churches, engaged in relentless and quite useless battle with their European and North American peers comparing methods and theological *loci*. As a result, twenty years later, Latin American liberation theology is more a repetitive apology for itself than a constructive theological discourse.

It is far more difficult to determine to what extent the second line of liberation theology has achieved its objective, not only because it has been functioning for a more limited time on the continent, but, above all, because of a certain modesty in the very objective proposed. Actually, I believe it should be clear that this modesty is part of the conversion which is required of the intellectual confronted with the interests and way of thinking of the people themselves. To some extent this conversion demands a renunciation of critical and creative characteristics which the intellectual can draw out of himself or herself, in order to be freely engaged as an instrument of the people.

It is not odd, then, that a theologian in this precise context cannot present serious works, or better, works which would be considered weighty by other intellectuals who are working in the same area of thought. Thus, for example, the second theological work of Gustavo Gutiérrez, his book *The Power of the Poor in History*, could not be considered, even by a long shot, to be of the same intellectual quality that characterized *A Theology of Liberation*. Anyone who ignores the context and shift we are studying would think that the theological quality of Gustavo had markedly diminished and that the work does not rise above a certain sort of debatable propaganda, although it is of a quality beyond that which characterizes ordinary people and what they do. The same comparison could be made of certain books of Leonardo Boff such as *Jesus Christ Liberator*, but above all, *Passion of Christ, Passion of the World*,[6] in relation to more recent works such as those which deal with new ecclesial forms and a church born of the people.

As a result, trying to indicate exactly to what extent the second line of liberation theology has succeeded or not in its own quest, I would say that, considering the context, it can only be said that it has only half achieved its objective and that on two levels.

In the first place, it is true that this second line of thought has had more success in winning over for liberation theology an important part of the ecclesiastical hierarchy. We have already indicated that the resistance to the first line came from a criticism of it vis-à-vis popular religiosity, or simply, because of its way of conceiving Christian religiosity in Latin America. In that regard, the second line dissipated many suspicions when it accepted the religion of ordinary people as a generally liberating element. Where the church felt itself strongest in protecting ordinary people, even against two governments and their repression, as in the case of Brazil, the second line was widely accepted. From this point of view, the Puebla Conference would have been, if not an acceptance of this line, at least a compromise between it and those who wanted a global condemnation of liberation theology.

Nevertheless, it is impossible to ignore, whatever our opinion about the justification of popular religiosity might be, the political aspect of this second line which is just as or even more accentuated than that of the first. Actually, the first line of liberation theology came in contact with political concerns through a redefinition of faith which paid close attention to the influence of faith on the political activity of Christians. However, the second line accepts, up to a certain point, the control and design of a political posture for liberation from the people themselves. When the theologian becomes part of the people, he or she lends even more political support for the political vindication of the people. It is not in vain that a theology linked with Peronism is even more political than an attempt to reformulate theology in general in a deideologized way. The same thing could be said about Brazil where the bishops of several dioceses distributed political guidelines for the last election to teach people how to make a political option among different parties. And the same thing could be said about the relationship between Basic Christian Communities and politics in the whole process which characterizes the present situation in Nicaragua.

Furthermore, there is another level where the objectives achieved by the second line of liberation theology should be considered, although as very modest achievements. As intense as the theologian's conversion to ordinary people might be, this intellectual cannot totally renounce the exercise of a certain criticism. We have already seen that sort of "lapse" or contradiction between the pretension of learning theology from common people and the attempt of relocating in people's minds the true meaning of suffering in the example of Leonardo Boff. But generally speaking, this second line of theology has tried to provide more balanced principles despite its seeming lack of criticism toward popular phenomena. It sees the issue as one "of rescuing and promoting Christian values in popular culture." To that end, obviously, one has to be immersed in it, but not with closed eyes. Beyond doubt there are negative elements in a culture, while at the same time a theologian discovers magnificent liberating aspects. It is a question, then, of distinguishing one from the other and, to the extent possible, of promoting some while restraining or repressing others.

I think it is imperative to explain briefly why the results on this level have been much less than were expected. And I believe this explanation is all the more necessary in countries where the Latin American context at the cultural level could be unfamiliar.

As opposed to North America, Latin America is a veritable mosaic of cultures to a degree and depth difficult to imagine outside that context. It is not a question of the existence of immigrants from Western or Central Europe—they certainly exist as well—or even of immigrants from cultures developed for centuries in Asia. Rather it is a question of very ancient cultures from the time of the conquest and colonization by Spain and Portugal, pre-Columbian cultures like the civilizations of the Aztecs, Mayas, Incas, and lesser indigenous civilizations (like that of the Guaraní, who once formed the old Jesuit "reductions"), who have remained as enclaves in a Western civilization introduced and imposed by occidental conquerors. And to this we should add the introduction in many countries of African slaves who were violently deprived of their own religion and obliged to accept Christianity.

The most important thing here is to recognize that these African or American indigenous people managed to preserve for centuries under Christian names, rites, and creed, their ancient cultures and religions. These enormous efforts of the ancient cultures to survive the growing impact of modern Western culture, supported by a market economy which does not recognize any cultural differences, have only very recently been acknowledged by the church. And this struggle has been given a liberating character: it is, in reality, the right of these peoples to maintain their own cultures. Furthermore, those cultures, closed in on themselves, display certain values which can be considered very Christian as opposed to the consumerism and growing individualism of Western urban culture.

The second liberation theology we have spoken about has given great importance to those values. But perhaps it has not taken account of an important anthropological element of these cultures—namely, their monolithic character. They are such, partly because they are primitive, and partly in order to defend themselves better. Many efforts to "rescue Christian values" from values in these cultures which are not Christian, and especially the religions of these peoples, have failed because they have not realized that everything is bound to a unitary understanding of existence. It is a question of survival where any change (for example, in religion) is considered terribly dangerous.

Thus, partly as a result of this second liberation trend, we now see a great amount of energy unleashed in pastoral work with these people from ancient cultures. But in trying to modify slightly rites, places and instruments of worship, the idea of the religious, and so on, all in the name of rescuing the most valuable and liberating Christian elements, this energy is not generally producing the hoped for results. Let us consider certain elements relative to the *method* in both lines of liberation theology. For this purpose it will be interesting to consider some observations of Jon Sobrino, another of the liberation theologians who has passed through the same shift from the first to the second position.

In an article given as an address to a meeting precisely on theological method which took place in Mexico in 1975,[7] Sobrino refers to the context in which liberation theology was born—namely, the Latin American university—as something closely related with its methodology. He says that the founders of this theology were not professional theologians, but rather people that "had become theologians as counselors of action groups, such as priests involved in pastoral work." From this context arises an important methodological characteristic to which we have already referred and which Sobrino introduces with these words: "We think that Latin American theology is more conscious than European theology of its very status as *aware-*

ness. Obviously, *this is the problem of the ideologization of theology*, in regard to which Latin American theology is more sensitive than European theology."[8] And precisely because of this sensitivity, according to Sobrino himself the *social sciences* are used in a way similar to the use theology made of philosophy in past centuries. The social sciences provide the theologian who wants to carry out a deideologizing task with valuable cognitive tools, but tools which, because of their complexity and subtlety, are beyond the grasp of the majority of people.

In a later article Sobrino goes on to the second line of liberation theology. The subtitle of this article is quite interesting: "The poor: the theological *locus* of ecclesiology." And there he writes: "Thus the church of the poor finds the historical site of conversion, *the place of the other and the force to become the other*. And the most important thing, although it is apparently trivial in terms of mere conceptual reflection, is that it consequently happens in good measure."[9]

The process of becoming the other in the church thus occupies the theological position that the social sciences and their instrumentality for deideologization held in the first variety of liberation theology. Up to a certain point it is interesting that the second line returns to philosophy in a certain way, because it finds in philosophy the means to establish the theological rationale for becoming other among common people. One can observe, for example, the profound influence of the philosopher Emmanuel Levinas as much in Enrique Dussel as in Juan Carlos Scanone, two of the outstanding theologians of the second line.[10]

To conclude, I realize that many central questions are still unanswered. And it is true that I have no answer for many of them. For example, are these two lines complementary? Are they opposed? Of course, as attempts to liberate and humanize the same people through the same Christian faith, they should be considered as complementary. Nevertheless, they are based on opposite presuppositions, they have different strategies, and their methods are not easily compatible in reality. Perhaps the only thing we can take for granted is that, after twenty years at work, liberation theology is profoundly alive on our continent, although taking different forms in different classes or groups of society. It is our common hope that those different forms will prove to be convergent. In any case, with this amount of data, one can perhaps have a better and more accurate picture of what is happening in Latin America with liberation theology or, more simply, with theology.

But in trying to focus attention on the important shift which took place on our continent in the middle of the 1970s, my aim has been not only to provide a surer, more complex and balanced account of something abstract and remote. My purpose, whether or not I have succeeded in accomplishing it, was also from the beginning to challenge. The challenge is not to do the same thing as we are doing, for this would not make sense. But certainly it is to fight creatively for the same cause in your own context, with your own tools and, above all, with your own hearts.

NOTES

1. Leonardo Boff, "Teologia a Escuta do Povo," *Revista Eclesiástica Brasileira*, 41 (March, 1981), 65.

2. Gustavo Gutiérrez, *A Theology of Liberation* (Maryknoll, N.Y.: Orbis Books, 1973). Original Spanish version: *Teología de la Liberación: Perspectivas* (Lima: CEP, 1971).

3. Cf. Leonardo Boff, *Ecclesiogénese* (Petrópolis: Vozes, 1977). English trans., *Ecclesiogenesis* (Maryknoll, N.Y.: Orbis, 1986).

4. Gustavo Gutiérrez, *La Fuerza Histórica de los Pobres: Selección de Trabajos* (Lima: CEP, 1979). English trans., *The Power of the Poor in History* (Maryknoll, N.Y.: Orbis, 1983).

5. Boff, *Ecclesiogénese*, p. 55.

6. Leonardo Boff, *Paixâo de Cristo — Paixâo de Mundo* (Petrópolis: Vozes, 1977). English trans., *Passion of Christ, Passion of the World* (Maryknoll, N.Y.: Orbis, 1987).

7. Jon Sobrino, *Resurrección de la Verdadera Iglesia: Los Pobres, Lugar Teológico de la Eclesiología* (Santander: Sal Terrae, 1981), chapter 1, "El conocimiento teológico en la teología europea y latinoamericana," pp. 21–53. English trans., *The True Church and the Church of the Poor* (Maryknoll, N.Y.: Orbis, 1984).

8. Ibid., p. 34.

9. Ibid., p. 163.

10. See in the collection edited by the Instituto Fe y Secularidad entitled *Fe Cristiana y Cambio Social en América Latina* (Salamanca: Sígueme, 1973), E. Dussel, "Historia de la fe cristiana y cambio social en América Latina," especially pp. 91 and 97, as well as the explicit reference to Levinas, p. 69, note. See also citations of Levinas in the collections edited by R. Gibellini, *La Nueva Frontera de la Teología en América Latina* (Salamanca: Sígueme, 1977), by Dussel and Scannone, "Supuestos histórico-filosóficos de la teología desde América Latina," p. 183, and "Teología, cultura popular y discernimiento," p. 215; English trans., *Frontiers of Theology in Latin America* (Maryknoll, N.Y.: Orbis, 1979).

40

Cardinal Joseph Ratzinger
"Liberation Theology"
(March 1984)

There was considerable surprise that the prefect of the Congregation for the Doctrine of the Faith should publish an article in the public press while an instruction on the subject was being prepared and awaited. In general, the critique is much more carefully done than the "Ten Observations" (no. 37). This text is taken from the September 1984 edition of Catholicism in Crisis. *A different translation of the article may be found in* The Ratzinger Report: An Exclusive Interview on the State of the Church *(San Francisco: Ignatius Press, 1985), pp. 174-86.*

The theology of liberation is an extraordinarily complex phenomenon. Any concept of liberation theology has to be able to span positions ranging from the radically Marxist to those that stress necessary Christian responsibility toward the poor and the oppressed in the context of a sound ecclesiology, as did the documents of CELAM from Medellín to Puebla. Here, I am using the concept of "liberation theology" in a more restricted sense, a sense which includes only those theologians who in some way have espoused a Marxist fundamental option. Even here, there are many differences that are impossible to describe in detail in a general reflection such as this. In this context I can only try to consider some fundamental lines which, without ignoring the different points of origin, are very widespread and exercise a certain influence even where a theology of liberation does not exist in the strict sense.

With the analysis of the phenomenon of liberation theology we are clearly facing a fundamental danger for the faith of the church. Undoubtedly one must realize that an error cannot exist unless it contains a nucleus of truth. In fact, an error is much more dangerous to the extent that it contains a greater proportion of truth. Moreover, the error could never appropriate that portion of the truth if this truth were sufficiently lived and witnessed where it is in its place, that is, in the faith of the church. For this reason, alongside the demonstration of error, and the danger of liberation theology, we have to also consider the question, what truth is hidden in the error, and how do we recover it completely.

The theology of liberation is a universal phenomenon for three reasons:

This theology does not pretend to construct a new treatise alongside the others that already exist, for example, to develop some new aspects of the social teaching of the church. It is conceived, rather, as a new hermeneutic of the Christian faith, which means it is a new form of understanding and a realization of Christianity in its totality. For this reason, it changes all the aspects of ecclesial life, ecclesiastical structures, liturgy, catechesis, and moral options.

Liberation theology certainly has its center of gravity in South America, but it is not exclusively restricted to Latin and South America. It is unthinkable without the important influence of Europeans and North American theologians, but it also exists in India, Sri Lanka, the Philippines, Taiwan, and Africa, even though there the research for an "African theology" is foremost. The association of theologians of the Third World is strongly characterized by the amount of attention they give to themes that belong to the theology of liberation.

The theology of liberation goes beyond confessional boundaries. One of the most well-known representatives of the theology of liberation, Hugo Assman, was a Catholic priest who today teaches as a Protestant in a Protestant department of theology, but continues to present himself with the claim of being above and beyond confessional boundaries. Liberation theology seeks to create from its premises a new universality by which the classical separations of the churches should lose their importance.

THE CONCEPT OF THE THEOLOGY OF LIBERATION AND THE SUPPOSITIONS OF ITS GENESIS

These preliminary observations have introduced us to the heart of the question. They have left open the question, What exactly is liberation theology? In a first effort to reply, we can say that liberation theology claims to give a new global interpretation of Christianity. It explains Christianity as a praxis of liberation and claims to be itself a guide to such a praxis. As according to this theology all reality is political, so liberation is a political concept and the guide to liberation must be a guide to political action.

Gutiérrez says: "Nothing remains outside political commitment. All exists with a political coloration." A theology that would not be "practical," that is to say, essentially political, is considered "idealistic" and condemned as unreal or as a vehicle to maintain the oppressors in power. For theologians who have learned their theology in the classical tradition and who accept their spiritual vocation, it is difficult to imagine how we can seriously empty the global reality of Christianity into a scheme or study of the sociopolitical practice of liberation. This is even more difficult, however, as many theologians of liberation continue, in great measure, to use the ascetical and dogmatic language of the church in a new key in such a way that the person from another background who reads and listens can have the impression of finding the traditional patrimony with the addition of a few affirmations that seem somewhat strange, but which, however, joined to such religious fervor, cannot be dangerous. It is exactly the radical nature of the theology of liberation that makes one very often miss its gravity, its seriousness, because it does not enter into any existing treatment of heresy. Its starting point is found outside what is usually accepted as a starting point for traditional methods of discussion. For this purpose, I would like to try to determine the fundamental direction of liberation theology in two steps. First, it will be necessary to say something about the presuppositions that have made it possible. Next, I would like to explain some of the basic concepts that allow us to know something of the structure of liberation theology. How did we reach such a completely new direction in theological thought as expressed in liberation theology? I see principally three factors which made it possible.

First, after the council there was a new theological situation. The opinion was created that the existing theological tradition was no longer acceptable and, as a consequence, one must attempt, starting from scripture and the signs of the times, to develop totally new theological and spiritual directions.

The idea of openness to the world and of commitment to the world was often transformed into a naive faith in science, a faith which accepted human sciences as a new gospel without trying to recognize their limits and their own particular problems. Psychology, sociology, and the Marxist interpretation of history were considered as scientifically certain and as instances of Christian thought that are no longer debatable.

The criticism of the tradition starting with the modern New Testament exegesis, especially that of Bultmann and of his school, became an indispensable theological method that closed the door on forms that up to now were valid in theology, and encouraged totally new constructions.

In the second place, this changed theological situation coincided with a changed situation of spiritual history. At the end of the reconstruction after World War II, a phase which coincided with the beginning of the council, there was produced in the Western world an obvious void of meaning to which existential philosophy, then in vogue, was not able to give any reply. In this situation, the different forms of neo-Marxism supplied a moral impulse and, at the same time, a promise of achieving meaning that appeared almost irresistible to university youth. Marxism, with the religious accents of Bloch and the totally unscientific philosophies of Adorno, Horkheimer, Habermas, and Marcuse, offered a model of action which one believed to offer a way to respond to the challenge of misery and poverty in the world and, at the same time, to realize the correct meaning of the biblical message.

Finally, the moral challenge of poverty and oppression was not able to be ignored after Europe and North America reached an opulence until then unknown. This challenge evidently demanded new replies that until then could not be found in the existing tradition. The changed theological and philosophical situation expressly invited seeking the reply in a Christianity that would be guided by models of hope taken from Marxist philosophies and seemingly scientifically established.

THE FUNDAMENTAL EPISTEMOLOGICAL STRUCTURE OF LIBERATION THEOLOGY

We can find quite a different reply in the different forms of liberation theology, in the theology of revolution, political theology, etc. Liberation theology cannot be presented globally. However, some fundamental concepts are constantly repeated in the different variations that express common fundamental intentions. Before we pass to fundamental concepts of content, it is necessary to make an observation on the structural elements that hold liberation theology together. For this purpose, we can go to what we have already said about the changed theological situation after the council. As was said, the exegesis of Bultmann and of his school was read as a proclamation of a "science" about Jesus; a science which must obviously be considered valid. The "Jesus of history" of Bultmann is presented, however, as separated by an abyss (Bultmann speaks of a grave) from the Christ of faith. According to Bultmann, Jesus belongs to the presuppositions of the New Testament remaining, however, contained in the world of Judaism. The final result of this exegesis consists in shaking the historical credibility of the Gospels. The Christ of ecclesial tradition and the historical Jesus presented by science belong, apparently, to two different worlds. The figure of Jesus was uprooted from its position in the tradition by means of science, considered as the supreme method. In this way, on the one hand, the tradition was considered as something unreal in a void, and on the other, one was obliged to seek a new interpretation and a new meaning for the figure of Jesus. Moreover, Bultmann was important not so much for his positive affirmations as for the negative results of his critique; the nucleus of faith, christology, remained open to new interpretations because those which had been used until then disappeared as historically unsustainable. In the meantime, the magisterium of the church was abolished because it was bound to an unsustainable scientific theory, therefore, deprived of all value as a source of knowledge about Jesus. Its pronouncements can only be considered as the frustrated pronouncements of a previous scientific position.

Moreover, Bultmann was important for the further development of a second key concept. He brought back the ancient concept of hermeneutics, giving it a new dynamic. The word "hermeneutic" contains the idea that a real understanding of historical texts is not given only by means of historic interpretation, but that every historic interpretation includes certain preliminary decisions. This was included in his use of the word "hermeneutic." Hermeneutic has the task of "realizing," in connection with the determination of the historical data. In it, according to the classical terminology, one deals with a "fusion of horizons" between the "then" and the "now." As a consequence, it raises the question, What does the "then" mean for today? Bultmann himself replies to this question using the philosophy of Heidegger and interpreting the Bible in an existentialist sense. This reply does not have any interest any longer. In this way present-day exegesis has gone beyond Bultmann. There has remained the separation between the figure of Jesus in the classical tradition and the idea that one can and should transfer this figure into the present by means of a new hermeneutics.

At this point we meet a second element of our situation, the new philosophical climate of the late 1960s. The Marxist analysis of history and of society was considered as the only one with a scientific character. This meant that the world was interpreted in the light of a structure of class struggle and that the only possible choice was between capitalism and Marxism. It also meant that all reality is political and must be justified politically.

The biblical concept of "the poor" offered a starting point for the confusion between the biblical image of history and Marxist dialectic. This concept, interpreted according to the idea of the proletariat in a Marxist sense, justifies Marxism as a legitimate hermeneutic for an understanding of the Bible. According to this understanding, only two options exist or can exist. Moreover, to contradict this interpretation of the Bible means nothing less than an expression of the dominant class to preserve its power. Gutiérrez affirms: "If class struggle is an actual fact, then neutrality on this point is absolutely impossible." From this point of view, any intervention of the ecclesial magisterium is impossible. In the case in which it is opposed to such an interpretation of Christianity, it would only show that it was on the side of the rich and the dominators against the poor and the suffering, that is, against Jesus himself, who in the dialectic of history would have been on the side of criticism.

This apparently "scientific" and "hermeneutically" unavoidable decision determines by itself the way for further interpretation of Christianity both for what concerns the interpretive work as well as for the contents that are interpreted. Concerning the methods of interpretation, the decisive concepts are people, community, experience, and history. If up to now the Catholic Church was the fundamental hermeneutical instance, in its totality transcending time and space, embracing laity (*sensus fidei*) and hierarchy (*magisterium*), today it has become the community. The lived reality and the experiences of the "community" determine now the understanding and the interpretation of Scripture. Again, one can say, apparently in a rigorously scientific way, that the figure of Jesus presented in the Gospels constitutes a synthesis of events and interpretations of the experience of particular communities where, however, the interpretation is much more important than the event, which in itself is no longer determinable. This original synthesis of the event and of its interpretation can be dissolved and restructured over and over again. The community "interprets" with its "experience" the events and finds in this way its "praxis."

We find this idea in a slightly different form in the concept of people, according to which one transforms the conciliar emphasis on the idea of the "people of God" into a Marxist myth. The experiences of the people explain the Scriptures. "People" becomes a concept opposed to that of "hierarchy," and in antithesis to all the institutions that are indicated as forces of oppression. Finally, it is the people who participate in the "class struggle"; the popular church (*Iglesia popular*) is in opposition to the hierarchical church.

Finally, the concept of "history" becomes a decisive hermeneutical aspect. The opinion, considered scientifically sound and irrefutable, that the Bible reasons exclusively in terms of the history of salvation and therefore in an antimetaphysical way, allows the fusion of the biblical horizon with the Marxist idea of history which proceeds dialectically as authentic bearer of salvation. History is the authentic revelation and, therefore, the true hermeneutical instance of the interpretation of the Bible. Such a dialectic is sometimes supported by reference to pneumatology. In any case, it sees in the magisterium that insists upon permanent truths an instance that is hostile to progress since it thinks "metaphysically" and, in this way, contradicts "history." One can say that the concept of history absorbs the concept of God and revelation. The "historicity" of the Bible should justify its absolutely predominant role and must at the same time justify its passage to a Marxist, materialist philosophy in which history has assumed the role of God.

FUNDAMENTAL CONCEPTS OF A THEOLOGY OF LIBERATION

We have now reached the fundamental concepts of the content of the new interpretation of Christianity. Because the context in which the different concepts appear are diverse, I would like to quote some without any claims of a synthesis. We can begin with the new interpretation of faith, hope, and charity. Concerning faith, for example, J. Sobrino affirms that the experience that Jesus had of God is radically historical. "His faith is converted into fidelity." Sobrino, however, fundamentally substitutes "fidelity to history" for faith. "Jesus is faithful to the profound conviction that the mystery of the life of men . . . is really ultimate. . . ." Here one sees the fusion between God and history which gives Sobrino the possibility of preserving for Jesus the formula of Chalcedon, even if it has a completely changed meaning. One sees how classical criteria of orthodoxy are not applicable to the analysis of this theology. Ignacio Ellacuría, on the dust jacket of his book on the same topic, affirms that Sobrino "says again . . . that Jesus is God, adding, however, immediately that the true God is only the one who is revealed historically and scandalously in Jesus and in the poor who continue his presence. Only one who maintains these two affirmations together is orthodox. . . ."

Hope is interpreted as "confidence in the future" and as work for the future; in that way, it is subordinated again to the domination of the history of the classes.

Love consists in an "option for the poor," that is, it coincides with an option for class struggle. Theologians of liberation underline very strongly, in opposition to "false universalism," the partiality and partial character of the Christian option; to take sides is, according to them, a fundamental requisite for a correct hermeneutics of the biblical witness. In my opinion one can recognize very clearly here the mixture of the fundamental truth of Christianity and the fundamental non-Christian option which makes this thought so seductive. The Sermon on the Mount is, in reality, a choice on the part of God in favor of the poor. But the interpretation of the poor in the sense of Marxist, dialectical history and the interpretation of the choice of a party in terms of class struggle, is a move toward "other genres" (*eis allo genos*) in which the contrary is presented as identical.

The fundamental concept of the preaching of Jesus is the "kingdom of God." This concept is found again at the center of the theologies of liberation, read, however, against the background of Marxist hermeneutics. According to Sobrino, the kingdom cannot be understood spiritually or universally in the sense of an abstract eschatological reserve. It must be understood in a party form and turned toward practice. Only if we start with the praxis of Jesus, and not theoretically, is it possible to say what the kingdom means — that is, to work in the historical reality that surrounds us, to transform it into the kingdom. Here one must mention also the fundamental idea of a certain kind of postconciliar theology that has moved in this direction. Many have maintained that according to the council one must overcome every form of dualism, dualism of body and soul, of natural and supernatural, of imminence and transcendence, of present and future. After the dismantling of these dualisms, there remains only the possibility of working for a kingdom which is realized in this history and in its political and economic reality.

But it is precisely here that one has stopped working for the person of today and one begins to destroy the present in favor of a hypothetical future. In this way one immediately produces a true dualism.

In this context I would like to mention a surprising and fearful interpretation that Sobrino has given of the death and resurrection. Above all, he establishes, against the universalist concepts, that the resurrection is first a hope for those who have been crucified, and they constitute the majority of humankind, those millions on whom structural justice is imposed like a slow crucifixion. The believer, however, participates in the lordship of Jesus over history through the building of the kingdom, that is, in the struggle for justice and for integral liberation and the transformation of unjust structures into more human structures. This lordship over history is exercised, repeating in history the action of God who raised Jesus, that is, giving life again to the crucified over history. Humankind has assumed God's role and here the total transformation of the biblical message is shown in an almost tragic way, if one thinks of how this attempt at imitating God is explicit and is also explained.

I would like to cite another concept: the *exodus* is transformed into a central image of the history of salvation; the *paschal mystery* is understood as a revolutionary symbol and therefore the *eucharist* is interpreted as a liberation feast in the sense of a political, messianic hope and of its practice. The word "redemption" is generally replaced by "liberation," which in turn is understood against the background of history and class struggle as a process of liberation that moves forward.

Finally, the emphasis placed on *praxis* is fundamental. The truth cannot be understood in a metaphysical way; this is "idealism." The truth must be realized in history and in practice. Action is truth. Consequently, even the ideas that are used for action are, in the last analysis, interchangeable. The only decisive thing is praxis. Orthopraxis becomes the only true orthodoxy. An enormous distance from the biblical texts is thus justified; critical history liberates from traditional interpretation which appears as nonscientific. Concerning the tradition, the liberation theologian gives importance to the greatest scientific rigor, along the lines of Bultmann. But, in turn, the historically determined contents of the Bible cannot be binding in an absolute way. The instrument for interpretation is not, in the final analysis, historical research, but the hermeneutic of history experienced in the community, that is, in political groups above all, given the fact that the greater part of the same biblical contents are considered as a product of this community hermeneutic.

If one seeks to offer a global judgment, one must say that when we try to understand the fundamental options of liberation theology, one cannot deny that the whole theology contains an almost irrefutable logic. On the one hand, with the premises of biblical criticism and of hermeneutics founded upon experience, and on the other hand, with the Marxist analysis of history, one succeeds in creating a global vision of Christianity which seems to respond fully to the demands of science and of the moral challenges of our day. Moreover, people of today have the obligation to make of Christianity an instrument for the transformation of the world, which seems united to all the progressive forces of our era. One can understand, then, how this new interpretation of Christianity attracts more and more theologians, priests, and religious, especially in the light of the problems of the Third World. To abstain from it must necessarily appear in their eyes to be an evasion of the real and a renunciation of reason and moral thought. On the other hand, if one thinks how radical this interpretation of Christianity that derives from it really is, the problem of what one can and must do about it becomes even more urgent.

41

Bishops of Nicaragua
"Call to Dialogue"
(April 22, 1984)

After the first year of the revolution, the middle and upper classes in Nicaragua perceived that the Sandinista government was not favoring their interests, and they became increasingly hostile to the Sandinistas. At this time, also, counter-revolutionaries (contras), trained and equipped by the United States, began to invade the country and attack both military posts and villages.

This letter was not successful in establishing dialogue, because it seemed to many to be siding with the contra forces, a position the Sandinista government regarded as treasonous. Other difficulties and issues are discussed in the following article (no. 42). The English text is from Origins, *14 (July 26, 1984), pp. 131–134.*

At this solemn Easter celebration, the ultimate expression of God's love for humankind through the redemption, we invite you to share more fully in the spiritual wealth of the holy year, which will be extended in Nicaragua by a special concession from Pope John Paul II until June 17, 1984, the feast of the Holy Trinity.

This extension and the urgent need in our society for sincere and brotherly reconciliation through individual conversion have moved us to send you this exhortation.

I. DOCTRINAL SECTION

SIN, THE ROOT OF ALL EVIL

When sin came into the world, all things were changed profoundly; the soil yielded brambles; civilizations and institutions passed away; human beings rebelled against fellow humans, and the empire of tyranny and death began (cf. Gen. 3:16–19; 4:7–8).

Human beings created in the image of God (Gen. 1:26), did not wish to acknowledge or glorify God; they became vain in their imagination, and their foolish hearts darkened (Rom. 1:21). There were also those who, like Satan, disguised themselves as angels of light to deceive others and lead them to perdition (cf. 2 Cor. 11:14–15). A false anthropocentrism plunged humankind into the heavy bondage of sin.

REDEMPTION BY CHRIST

Christ, by his death and resurrection, has reconciled us to God, to ourselves, and to our brothers and sisters, has freed us from the bondage of sin (cf. Col. 1: 20–22; 2 Cor. 5:18) and has given his church the mission of transmitting his message, pardon, and grace (cf. Matt. 28:18–20; Mark 16:15).

All this should be for us a call to conversion; it should be the beginning of a radical change of spirit, mind, and life (cf. John Paul II, bull, "Open the Doors to the Redeemer," 5).

There are three aspects to this conversion, which redeems our individual and collective lives:

A. We must avoid personal sin, any act that disrupts our baptismal alliance with God.

B. We must banish any sinful attitudes from our hearts, that is, any habitual rejections, whether conscious or unconscious, of Christian standards and moral values.

C. We must put an end to such social sins as participation in injustice and violence.

SIN AFTER THE REDEMPTION

Nonetheless, sin has persisted in the world since our redemption by Christ, because:

A. Human beings abuse their freedom and do not accept God's grace.

B. Society has become secularized and is no longer oriented toward God; it does not heed the church, the universal sacrament of salvation, but considers it an alienating institution.

C. At times it claims to accept Christ and his teachings, but it repudiates the church and thereby falls into the temptation of establishing other "churches" than the one founded by the apostles and their successors, the legitimate bishops.

D. We forget that community can only be based on an accurate perception of the individual as an intelligent, free, and religious human being, with rights and duties devolving from his very nature (cf. John XXIII, *Pacem in Terris,* 9–10).

E. Materialistic concepts of mankind distort the person and teachings of Christ, reduce human beings to merely physical terms without taking account of their spiritual nature, so they remain subject to material forces called the "dialectics of history." And human beings, alienated from God and from themselves, become disoriented, without moral and religious reference points, without a higher nature, insecure and violent.

II. OUR SITUATION

THE PROBLEM OF SIN IN THE WORLD

Pope John Paul II, in his message for the 17th World Day of Peace, January 1, 1984, expressed his concern about the current world situation, a concern which we, too, share: "Peace is truly precarious, and injustice abounds. Relentless warfare is occurring in many countries, continuing on and on despite the proliferation of deaths, mourning, and destruction, without any apparent progress toward a solution. It is often the innocent who suffer while passions become inflamed and there is the risk that fear will lead to an extreme situation."

IN NICARAGUA

A. Belligerent situation: Our country too is plagued by a belligerent situation pitting Nicaraguan against Nicaraguan, and the consequence of this situation could not be sadder:

—Many Nicaraguan youths and men are dying on the battlefields.

—Many others look toward the future with the fear of seeing their own lives prematurely ended.

—A materialistic and atheistic educational system is threatening the consciences of our children.

—Many families are divided by political differences.

—The suffering of mothers who have lost their children, which should merit our great respect, is instead exploited to incite hatred and feed the desire for vengeance.

—Farmworkers and Indians, for whom the church reserves a special love, are suffering, living in constant anxiety, and many of them are forced to abandon their homes in search of a peace and tranquility that they do not find.

—Some of the mass media, using the language of hate, encourage a spirit of violence.

B. The church: One, albeit small, sector of our church has abandoned ecclesial unity and surrendered to the tenets of a materialistic ideology. This sector sows confusion inside and outside Nicaragua through a campaign extolling its own ideas and defaming the legitimate pastors and the faithful who follow them. Censorship of the media makes it impossible to clarify the positions and offer other points of view.

FOREIGN INTERFERENCE

Foreign powers take advantage of our situation to encourage *economic and ideological* exploitation. They see us as a support for their power, without respect for our persons, our history, our culture, and our right to decide our own destiny.

Consequently, the majority of the Nicaraguan people live in fear of their present and uncertainty of their future. They feel deep frustration, clamor for peace and freedom. Yet their voices are not heard, muted by belligerent propaganda on both sides.

THE ROOT OF THESE EVILS

This situation is rooted in the sin of each and every one, in injustice and oppression, in exploitive greed, in political ambition and abuse of power, in disregard for moral and religious values, in lack of respect for human dignity, in forgetting, abandoning, and denying God.

III. THE CHURCH'S RESPONSE

CONVERSION AND RECONCILIATION

The church ardently desires and encourages peace and tranquility, and believes that there is only one path to that end, conversion. This means that we must all turn our eyes and heart to God, our Father, who through Christ offers us the true path to reconciliation, forgiveness, and peace.

"It is not behavior alone that needs to be changed, but the heart that guides our lives. At the community level it is important to examine ourselves as persons, as groups and social units, not only as victims but also as authors of certain collective deviations from God's plan, in order to implement together God's plan for constructive human endeavor" ("Peace and Conversion," Pontifical Commission Justice and Peace, Sept. 30, 1983).

The entire universe is the object of redemption since it also reveals the glory of God and must be sanctified and consecrated to God (cf. Vatican Council II, *Lumen Gentium,* 34). Christ resurrected is at the center of history and of the world, leading us toward its full maturity and its final liberation from all the forces of evil (cf. ibid., 48).

CONFESSION: PATH TO CONVERSION

"To assist such conversion, the Lord instituted the sacrament of reconciliation. In it Christ himself goes to meet the oppressed by the awareness of his own weakness, he raises them and gives them the necessary strength to continue their path. With the sacrament the life of the resurrected Christ enters the spirit of the believer, bringing forth renewed generosity of purpose and an enhanced capacity to live by the gospel" (John Paul II, address, Nov. 26, 1983).

Jesus reconciled all things, bringing peace through the cross (Col. 1:20) and transmitted this power to his disciples (cf. John 4:21; 13:34–35; 12–17).

Preparing to receive the benefits of the sacrament of confession is an important step in conversion. A sincere examination of our sins, self-criticism of our attitudes and our life, reveal to us our faults and make us abhor sin, which is an offense against God, an affront to the church, and damage or injury to our neighbor. It encourages us to turn totally to God and to reform our lives; it brings us back to the church and closer to our brothers and sisters.

DIALOGUE

The road to social peace must necessarily pass through dialogue, sincere dialogue that seeks truth and goodness. "That [dialogue] must be a meaningful and generous offer of a meeting of good intentions and not a possible justification for continuing to foment dissension and violence" (John Paul II, Greeting to Nicaragua, March 4, 1983).

It is dishonest to constantly blame internal aggression and violence on foreign aggression.

It is useless to blame the evil past for everything without recognizing the problems of the present.

All Nicaraguans inside and outside the country should participate in this dialogue, regardless of ideology, class, or partisan belief. Furthermore, we think that Nicaraguans who have taken up arms against the government should also participate in this dialogue. If not, there will be no possibility of a settlement, and our people, especially the poorest among them, will continue to suffer and die.

The dialogue of which we speak "is not a tactical truce to strengthen positions for further struggle, but a sincere effort to seek appropriate solutions to the anguish, pain, exhaustion, and fatigue of the many, many people who long for peace, the many, many people who want to live, to rise from the ashes, to see the warmth of a smile on a child's face, far from terror, in a climate of democratic harmony.

"The terrible chain of reactions inherent in friend-enemy dialectics is halted by the word of God, who demands that we love even our enemies and that we forgive them. God urges us to move from distrust and aggressiveness to respect and harmony, in a climate conducive to true and objective deliberation on our problems and a prudent search for solutions. The solution is reconciliation" (John Paul II, Address in El Salvador, March 6, 1983).

If we are not open to objective acknowledgment of our situation and events that distress our people ideologically, politically, and militarily, then we are not prepared, in a true and Christian way, for reconciliation for the sake of the real, living wholeness of our nation.

Considering that freedom of speech is a vital part of the dignity of a human being, and as such is indispensable to the well-being of the nation, inasmuch as a country progresses only when there is freedom to generate new ideas, the right to free expression of one's ideas must be recognized.

The great powers, which are involved in this problem for ideological or economic reasons, should leave Nicaraguans free from coercion.

CONCLUSION

If we want our conversion to find true expression in the life of our national community, we must strive to lead lives worthy of the gospel (cf. Phil. 1:27, Eph. 4:1), reject all lies, all harmful or offensive words, all anger and evil utterance, and be benevolent and forgive generously as God forgave us through Christ (cf. Eph. 4:25–32, Col. 3:12–14).

It behooves us to value each life as a gift of God, help the young to find meaning and value in their lives, and prepare themselves for their future roles in society, forgive enemies and adversaries, facilitate the return of those who have left their country and welcome them with an open heart, free those imprisoned for ideological differences, create a climate of friendship and peace conducive to social harmony.

"In the great task of bringing peace and reconciliation to the nation, the family as the basic unit of society cannot be ignored." Nor can respect for its rights (cf. *Gaudium et Spes,* 52, quoted by John Paul II in his address to the bishops of El Salvador, Feb. 24, 1984).

May the Holy Virgin, who played her part in our redemption with such exemplary fortitude, provide us with the necessary strength to perform our Christian duty of love and peace.

And may the Lord of peace grant us all, always and in all our endeavors, the peace and tranquility which we seek (cf. 2 Thess. 3:16).

42

Patricia Hynds
"Bishops' Letter Deepens Church-State Estrangement"
(May 24, 1984)

Patricia Hynds is a Maryknoll lay missioner who has worked for a number of years in Nicaragua. Basically, she feels that the bishops' letter speaks of dialogue but is really taking sides with the internal opposition and the Reagan administration. The text is taken from the May 24, 1984, issue of Latinamerica Press.

The Nicaraguan Bishops' Pastoral Letter on Reconciliation, which was read in most parishes on Easter Sunday and included a call to dialogue with those who have taken up arms against the government, has provoked a wave of protest here and has heightened already tense church-state relations. Many were angered by the fact that the bishops, when they address the theme of reconciliation, fail to mention that the suffering and violent death of so many Nicaraguans is a direct consequence of U.S. support for the counter-revolutionary movement and its persistent efforts (like the mining of Nicaraguan ports) to destabilize the Sandinista government.

The omissions provoked a heated response. Sandinista leaders made thinly-veiled references to the bishops, using phrases like *vendepatrias* (traitors) and "CIA collaborators," while Managua's opposition daily *La Prensa* strongly backed the bishops' position. The progovernment press dug out old archive photos of several bishops greeting former dictator Anastasio Somoza, and published copies of their letters thanking him for lavish gifts. The archdiocesan office came back with a warning that any harm that might come to the bishops would be laid on the shoulders of those responsible for the campaign.

Equally strong but more measured was the response of many Christian groups. A number of them released critiques of the letter. After the publication of the letter, Managua's Archbishop Miguel Obando y Bravo was called to Rome, where he had a long conversation with Pope John Paul. As yet, the contents of their meeting have not been disclosed.

CONTENTS OF THE LETTER

The pastoral letter is divided into three parts. The first is a doctrinal treatise on the roots of sin and redemption in Christ. The second part offers the bishops' interpretation of what is happening in the country today. They see Nicaragua ever more deeply divided, and insist that essential values are being undermined. This second part has provoked considerable criticism, not the least of which concerned the timing of the letter. During the very weeks when the media were denouncing the role of the CIA in the mining of Nicaragua's ports and criticizing the Reagan administration for thumbing its nose at the International Court of Justice at the Hague, the bishops chose to issue their attack on the Sandinistas and call them to repent.

But it was the section on "dialogue" in the third part of the letter that provoked the most consternation. The bishops call upon the Sandinistas to ask forgiveness, to repent, and to dialogue with all involved, including the armed *contras* invading the country's northern and southern borders. Nowhere do the bishops suggest that the *contras* lay down their arms, repent of their sins, or seek forgiveness and make amends. According to critics, the one-sidedness of the appeal makes the bishops' letter look like a political document in support of the opposition.

OMISSIONS

Criticism of the letter has centered especially on its very noteworthy omissions. No mention is made of the U.S. role in the hostilities — a role acknowledged by the U.S. government itself and criticized by many European countries, by the Contadora group and in the United Nations. There is no mention of efforts by the Sandinistas in the search for peace and reconciliation in Nicaragua. Last December, for example, the Sandinistas extended an amnesty to all Miskito prisoners and to any peasants who had, for whatever reason, taken up arms and been fighting with the *contras* (*LP*, Dec. 29, 1983). Neither is there recognition of the electoral process under way in Nicaragua, a process that, for all its limitations, is open to all except the heads of armed counterrevolutionary groups or persons who have led acts of sabotage against the economy or the people of the country (*LP*, Apr. 26, 1984).

There is no protest against the violence, brutality, and suffering inflicted by the *contras* on the civilian population, and no call for repentance or conversion by either the U.S. government or the *contras*. And there is no admission of the need for dialogue and reconciliation within the conflict-torn Nicaraguan church itself. Instead, the bishops lash out against "a small sector of the church that has abandoned ecclesial unity, subjecting itself to the norms of a materialistic ideology and breeding confusion within and without our borders in a campaign that exalts their own ideas and defames their legitimate pastors and the faithful united to them." The letter also creates the image of a complete absence of freedom of expression in Nicaragua. The letter's critics point out that this impression is refuted by the fact that the bishops' views are widely published in Nicaragua.

The pastoral speaks of "the manipulation of the sorrows of mothers" whose sons or daughters have been killed in the fighting, but has no word to say to the authors of the killings that have occasioned the mothers' grief. And when the prelates lament that "materialistic and atheistic education is undermining the consciences of children and young people," the choice of the Spanish verb *minar* (to "mine," or to "undermine") offends many Nicaraguans who are deeply distressed by the mining of the country's harbors—an act the bishops also fail to repudiate.

RESPONSE OF NICARAGUAN JESUITS

One of the most detailed responses to the letter came from Nicaragua's Jesuit community. In a letter published on May 9 in two Managua dailies, the Jesuits compare the present pastoral letter with one published by the bishops in November 1979. In the earlier letter, the bishops maintained that "the duty of the followers of Christ includes being a leaven in a likely journey toward a socialism that is compatible with faith" and indicated that the Nicaraguan revolution could provide the opportunity, within a new structural situation, to make real the church's preferential option for the poor. The present letter, the Jesuits point out, has an entirely different tone.

For the Jesuits, "the letter ignores the fact that Nicaraguans who are not in agreement with the revolutionary process and go to the extreme of carrying out an armed counterrevolution, could do so only because in December 1981 the president of the United States authorized a covert operation that finances, trains and gives logistical support to the counter-revolutionary movement."

The Jesuits express a fear that is being heard more and more frequently in Nicaragua today: "We believe that what is at stake is the relationship between Christian faith and an imperfect process that is, nevertheless, an attempt to structure society in a way that is more just." They wonder whether the bishops' call for dialogue with those who have taken up arms against the government and their failure to condemn the attackers with equal force, have not made the bishops an obstacle to the faith of many Nicaraguans.

In the final analysis, argue many critics, the bishops' letter is not conciliatory either in tone or in content. It uses theological language and speaks of dialogue while defending the interests of the internal opposition as well as that of the Reagan administration.

Most observers agree that the letter has deepened the gulf between the hierarchy and the progressive sector of the Nicaraguan church, increased confusion among ordinary people, and heightened the Sandinistas' mistrust of the bishops.

43

Mary Judith Ress
"Feminist Theologians Challenge Churches"
(May 31, 1984)

*The author traces the beginning of the feminist challenge in Latin America to
a meeting in October 1979, in Mexico, and comments on its progress since then.
This movement seems destined to have an enormous impact on liberation theology and the Latin American church. This article is taken from the May 31,
1984 issue of* Latinamerica Press.

In the United States and Europe, feminist theologians have been working for over a decade on the reinterpretation of theological and biblical
themes from a woman's point of view. However, this process is just beginning in Latin America, where a feminist perspective is all but absent from
an otherwise vibrant theological climate. Latin American feminist theologians are few, but all insist that sexism must be seen within, not apart from,
the overall situation of oppression suffered by the continent's poor. Most
would agree with the position of Mexican feminist theologian Elsa Támez:
"What absorbs our attention is how to speak of God with genocide being
committed against Guatemalan Indians, and torture, disappearances, and
death in El Salvador and under the dictatorship of the Southern Cone; it
is how to nourish the struggles of human beings whose daily survival is
precarious, who risk uncertainty and death to resist unjust structures. In
this context, theological reflection of necessity centers on the meaning of
life and death—for women, men, children, old people, the indigenous, etc."

At the same time, feminist theologians here insist that this overriding
concern for the liberation struggles of the continent's poor cannot excuse
church people or theologians from addressing the violence of Latin American *machismo*. They challenge liberation theologians and those who facilitate the growing Christian base community movement to make the struggle
against patriarchy—both within the church and in society as a whole—an
essential item on their agendas. Only if women's oppression is dealt with
seriously, they argue, can the liberation to which all aspire become a reality.

NEWNESS OF CHRISTIAN FEMINISM

Feminist theology is very new in Latin America. For the first time, in October 1979 in Mexico, a small group of women came together to discuss the issue. In the meeting sponsored by the Mexican-based Women for Dialogue, participants concluded that traditional church structures have reinforced women's oppression by imposing moral norms that sacralize the domination of men over women. "The church is a patriarchal structure allied with the powerful," they declared. "Women do not participate on the decision-making level in the church. Furthermore, hierarchical, masculine church structures serve as a model for the oppressive male-female relationships found throughout Latin American society where men dictate, in terms binding on faith and conscience, what women should believe and practice."

The meeting's concluding document notes that while it is women who most faithfully participate in the church's liturgies and social and pastoral programs, and who are the main transmitters of religious values and beliefs, these same women are expected to be passive receivers and unquestioning participants in these activities. Women are almost totally excluded from the process of systematizing pastoral and theological thought, notes the document. Particularly galling to those present was the church's failure to support movements for women's liberation.

Costa Rican feminist theologian Cora Ferro charges that the church has traditionally defined woman as "a being for others, a receiver; her role is to accompany man. As such, she must be married to God (virgin) or to a man (wife). If not, she is considered to be married to the devil. The church offers us the model of Mary as virgin and mother. Sanctity, we are told, is found not in anything we do, but in the acceptance of one or other state in life. This attitude overlooks Mary's defiant song of liberation in the Magnificat and her stance at the foot of the cross, which was a courageous political act." Ferro and others point out that the church has constantly dealt with women by focusing on problems of "morality" — exalting women's role as mother and in the family — or by issuing moral prohibitions.

CEB: NEW MODEL OF CHURCH

In spite of this history, most Christian feminists are enthusiastic about the new, more community-based model of church evolving in Latin America, and celebrate the renewed vitality present in the continent's Christian base community (CEB) movement. Since the hallmark of this new model of church is participation, patriarchal structures are of necessity relativized. Members discover new definitions for God, who is present with them in community, in *vivencia* a God who, by the incarnation, became poor before becoming a man or a woman. Women are very much present in these communities and hear God speaking in their favor—something most men do not hear because, although equally poor, they still live in the patriarchal context of privilege.

But feminist theologians also deplore the frequent absence of women in charting the course the CEB movement is to take. For the most part, women are still second-class citizens in the CEBs, where male-centered traditions continue to persist. For instance, CEB leadership is usually male, as are those who represent the community to the larger church. It is most often a man who leads the liturgy in the absence of a priest or pastor. Male opinions tend to be given more weight in community reflection, and women are more often than not assigned the tasks that have to do with childcare, the preparation of food, setting up the chapel for worship, and clean-up afterwards.

Nevertheless, these local CEB structures are not rigid; it is hoped that they will continue to evolve into more deeply communitarian structures that will, in turn, call the larger church to conversion. But, notes Támez, "the specific concerns of women will be expressed in the CEBs to the extent that women themselves insist on making them present."

Feminist theologians also note that the CEBs are producing theology in a much more spontaneous and experiential (feminist) way that confronts and challenges more traditional, masculine-oriented, and systematic models. This theology is made explicit during liturgical celebrations, in bible study groups, and in the wealth of community bulletins, songs, poems, and popular theater presentations the CEB movement has generated. But while women participate in these forms of expression and contribute their experience and reflection to them, there is little evidence that this contribution is well reflected in theological writings that attempt to capture the CEB experience. Latin America can count its feminist liberation theologians on the fingers of one hand, and women's presence in theological or pastoral conferences is also very limited.

CHALLENGE TO LIBERATION THEOLOGIANS

It is here that feminist liberation theologians offer a challenge to their male counterparts. They argue that the very methodology of liberation theology—reflection on the praxis of liberation within a faith perspective—demands that the situation of women be a *constitutive element*, not just one more theme, within liberation theology. They maintain that to make the situation of poor women a central concern is indispensable to liberation theology if it is to be lifegiving to all the continent's marginated people. A workshop, "Patriarchy and the Church," held here in Lima last July as part of the Second Latin American Feminist Conference declared: "While liberation theologians recognize that women are marginalized within society as *poor people*, they do not address patriarchal structures as such, either within society as a whole or within church structures. It is imperative that liberation theologians actively challenge the structure of patriarchy in both their own practice and their methodology, and make a specific option for women among the poor and oppressed."

NEW ROLE FOR WOMEN

Christian feminists are just beginning to make explicit their intuitions on the specific role of women in the liberation struggle. When some 150 women gathered in Managua last May for the Second Meeting of Christian Women for Peace in Latin America, they concluded that "the greatest enemy of life is an unjust social system that places profit over the satisfaction of basic human needs. We have discovered this because we are bearers of life." They declared, "We know that it is precisely this task of giving birth—to new men and to new women and to a new society—that reveals a new place in which to find ourselves and a source of our identity as women."

Just as Christian men have done, women also discover that sanctity is bound up in the liberation struggle. But more than men, women understand that struggle in terms of the life-death motif. They discover that their faith gives certainty to the final victory of life over death. And they begin to discover the collective experience of women who, both in the past and present, have put their lives on the line for the liberation of their people.

More and more, poor Christian women are holding up the many militant women who have been tortured, imprisoned, and killed for their vision of this new society. They see as decisive to the building of that society the "feminine" virtues women bring to the struggle: generosity, steadfastness, openness to universal love, courage, capacity to endure suffering, forgiveness.

And they are also beginning to reflect on the Scriptures from the point of view of oppressed women. Poor women know by experience that the God of life could never legitimate any kind of oppression, including sexism. They are discovering that, despite the ways in which the Bible reflects the patriarchal culture of its milieu, the witness of biblical women could not be silenced. They find it necessary to rescue these forgotten heroines from oblivion: to reappropriate the role of Miriam in the Israelites' exodus journey, that of the prophetess Anna and of Deborah and Judith in their struggles to keep God's people faithful and free; to look again at that nameless mother in the book of Maccabees who gives her seven sons over to be tortured and killed—and is then killed herself rather than violate Jewish law. And above all, they are impelled to recapture and hold up Mary, that woman totally committed to the coming of the kingdom; to reflect on her fidelity, her resistance, her role in strengthening and encouraging the first Christian community. As the women gathered in Mexico stressed, "In Mary, we see the only true meaning that motherhood can have for us; the generation and creation of a new humanity. Mary's fidelity to the human community is seen in her generous relinquishing of her own son for the birth of that humanity."

"Like Mary, I, too, had to flee when they persecuted my family," recalls a Salvadoran peasant woman. "They cut my husband and my two oldest sons to pieces because they said they were learning communism in religion classes. . . . I believe Mary deeply understands the mothers of our country because she underwent what we are suffering today. She now pleads with her son for our children when we no longer have the strength to do so. And she joins her voice to that of Archbishop Romero when she declares in her Magnificat that the rich will no longer oppress the lowly."

44

Editorial Board of Concilium
"Statement of Solidarity
with Liberation Theologians"
(June 24, 1984)

The article of Cardinal Ratzinger about liberation theology (see no. 40) was the major reason for the publication of this statement of support by a very influential international publication. This text is from Origins, *14 (July 26, 1984), pp. 134-35.*

Liberation theology is in the public eye. It has been the subject of comment by high ecclesiastical authorities, of articles in various newspapers and reviews, and of questions put to several individual theologians. We consider it our duty to take a position on this problem.

BIRTH OF BASIC CHRISTIAN COMMUNITIES
AND OF THE THEOLOGY OF LIBERATION

Since Vatican II, we have witnessed a real renewal in the life of the churches in poor countries. This has shown itself in the flourishing of numerous basic ecclesial communities and of groups of biblical reflection, in a new vitality of faith among the people and in the involvement of Christians (laity, priests, and bishops) in the struggle for the defense of the right of the poorest to life.

In this way the church has begun to enter the world of the poor and to share their destiny, while at the same time the people have assumed new responsibilities within its communion. From the moment that the people of God committed itself to this road, there began a critical reflection whose purpose has been to address the problem of the oppressed in the light of the faith and to promote their full liberation.

Simultaneously, in other contexts but as part of the same vital movement, there has been a process of liberation and reflection among women, finding themselves marginal to the life of society and of the church, and among races and cultures conscious of their position as minorities in church and society.

CURRENT TENSIONS

These developments, and the hopes and claims which they embody, have provoked contrary reactions, incomprehension, and even hostility on the part of those who hold political and economic power. We have seen men and women disappear, forced into exile, tortured, and assassinated. These things are absolutely unacceptable. Within the church, while some holding positions of authority have sometimes supported and accepted these movements of liberation, we have also seen people defamed, forbidden to teach theology, rendered suspect of infidelity to the Christian message, and accused of substituting ideologies for the gospel, under the influence of Marxism. Against such procedures we register a strong and vigorous protest.

There are tensions necessary to the life of the church, but today these are exacerbated by integrist and neoconservative groups. Resisting all social change and holding that religion has nothing to do with politics, they fight against movements of liberation and make choices that constitute an offense against the poor and oppressed.

All these factors have created a climate unfavorable to the search for new ways of being church and of proclaiming the gospel.

THE POSITION OF THE THEOLOGIANS OF *CONCILIUM*

Wishing to remain always faithful to the orientations and inspirations of Vatican II, in line with a preferential option for the poor and in keeping with its own distinctive theological identity, *Concilium* expresses its solidarity with these new movements, with the local churches affected by them, and with the theologians of liberation both within the Catholic Church and in other Christian churches. The theologians of *Concilium* wish to express our solidarity not only with their theological thought, but also with the concrete positions that they take.

In doing this, we are pursuing an orientation taken within recent years, as evidenced by the creation of new sections (Third World theology, feminist theology) and by the line taken in several recent numbers of the review. A future number of *Concilium* will be devoted to the ecclesial context within which these tensions have to be situated.

Certainly it is not our pretension to possess the fullness of truth, and we are conscious of being but one voice among several, a voice, however, that is fully ecclesial. In fact, it is a sign of the fecundity of the gospel today that it is lived in different contexts in different ways. Theology is but an expression of and a reflection upon this situation, a situation that is cause for joy and not for alarm. This is the dimension of pluralism inherent to catholicity. To fulfill its role, theology needs that freedom of research and expression which we claimed for it in our declaration of 1971.

CONCLUSION

As these movements are a sign of hope for the whole church, any premature intervention from higher authorities risks stifling the Spirit, which animates and guides local churches. We express our strong solidarity with these movements of liberation and with their theology. We protest against the suspicions and unjust criticisms registered against them. We firmly believe that the future of the church, the coming of the kingdom, and the judgment of God on the world are tied up with these movements.

45

Congregation for the Doctrine of the Faith "Instruction on Certain Aspects of the 'Theology of Liberation'" (Vatican City, August 6, 1984)

This is the first official Vatican statement that was wholly concerned with the theology of liberation. It was roundly applauded in some quarters, while others considered it too negative, largely because there seems to have been no input from liberation theologians themselves. Some criticisms by these theologians are included below (nos. 46–47). The text is taken from Origins, *14 (September 13, 1984), pp. 194–204.*

The gospel of Jesus Christ is a message of freedom and a force for liberation. In recent years this essential truth has become the object of reflection for theologians, with a new kind of attention which is itself full of promise.

Liberation is first and foremost liberation from the radical slavery of sin. Its end and its goal is the freedom of the children of God, which is the gift of grace. As a logical consequence, it calls for freedom from many different kinds of slavery in the cultural, economic, social, and political spheres, all of which derive ultimately from sin and so often prevent people from living in a manner befitting their dignity. To discern clearly what is fundamental to this issue and what is a by-product of it is an indispensable condition for any theological reflection on liberation.

Faced with the urgency of certain problems, some are tempted to emphasize, unilaterally, the liberation from servitude of an earthly and temporal kind. They do so in such a way that they seem to put liberation from sin in second place, and so fail to give it the primary importance it is due. Thus, their very presentation of the problems is confused and ambiguous. Others, in an effort to learn more precisely what are the causes of the slavery they want to end, make use of different concepts without sufficient critical caution. It is difficult, and perhaps impossible, to purify these borrowed concepts of an ideological inspiration which is incompatible with Christian faith and the ethical requirements which flow from it.

The Sacred Congregation for the Doctrine of the Faith does not intend to deal here with the vast theme of Christian freedom and liberation in its own right. This it intends to do in a subsequent document which will detail in a positive fashion the great richness of this theme for the doctrine and the life of the church.

The present instruction has a much more limited and precise purpose: to draw the attention of pastors, theologians, and all the faithful to the deviations and risks of deviation, damaging to the faith and to Christian living, that are brought about by certain forms of liberation theology which use, in an insufficiently critical manner, concepts borrowed from various currents of Marxist thought.

This warning should in no way be interpreted as a disavowal of all those who want to respond generously and with an authentic evangelical spirit to the "preferential option for the poor." It should not at all serve as an excuse for those who maintain an attitude of neutrality and indifference in the face of the tragic and pressing problems of human misery and injustice. It is, on the contrary, dictated by the certitude that the serious ideological deviations which it points out tend inevitably to betray the cause of the poor. More than ever, it is important that numerous Christians, whose faith is clear and who are committed to live the Christian life in its fullness, become involved in the struggle for justice, freedom, and human dignity because of their love for their disinherited, oppressed, and persecuted brothers and sisters. More than ever, the church intends to condemn abuses, injustices, and attacks against freedom, wherever they occur and whoever commits them. It intends to struggle, by its own means, for the defense and advancement of the rights of humankind, especially of the poor.

I. AN ASPIRATION

1. The powerful and almost irresistible aspiration that people have for liberation constitutes one of the principal signs of the times which the church has to examine and interpret in the light of the gospel.[1] This major phenomenon of our time is universally widespread, though it takes on different forms and exists in different degrees according to the particular people involved. It is, above all, among those people who bear the burdens of misery and in the heart of the disinherited classes that this aspiration expresses itself with the greatest force.

2. This yearning shows the authentic, if obscure, perception of the dignity of the human person, created "in the image and likeness of God" (Gen. 1:26-27), ridiculed and scorned in the midst of a variety of different oppressions: cultural, political, racial, social, and economic, often in conjunction with one another.

3. In revealing to them their vocation as children of God, the gospel has elicited in the hearts of humankind a demand and a positive will for a peaceful and just fraternal life in which everyone will find respect and the conditions for spiritual as well as material development. This requirement is no doubt at the very basis of the aspiration we are talking about here.

4. Consequently humankind will no longer passively submit to crushing poverty with its effects of death, disease, and decline. It resents this misery as an intolerable violation of its native dignity. Many factors, and among them certainly the leaven of the gospel, have contributed to an awakening of the consciousness of the oppressed.

5. It is widely known even in still illiterate sections of the world that, thanks to the amazing advances in science and technology, humankind, still growing in numbers, is capable of assuring all human beings the minimum of goods required by their dignity as persons.

6. The scandal of the shocking inequality between the rich and the poor—whether between rich and poor countries, or between social classes in a single nation—is no longer tolerated. On one hand, people have attained an unheard-of abundance which is given to waste, while on the other hand so many live in such poverty, deprived of the basic necessities, that one is hardly able even to count the victims of malnutrition.

7. The lack of equity and of a sense of solidarity in international transactions works to the advantage of the industrialized nations so that the gulf between the rich and the poor is ever-widening. Hence derive the feeling of frustration among Third World countries and the accusations of exploitation and economic colonialism brought against the industrialized nations.

8. The memory of crimes of a certain type of colonialism and of its effects often aggravates these injuries and wounds.

9. The apostolic see, in accord with the Second Vatican Council and together with the episcopal conferences, has not ceased to denounce the scandal involved in the gigantic arms race which, in addition to the threat it poses to peace, squanders amounts of money so large that even a fraction of it would be sufficient to respond to the needs of those who want for the basic essentials of life.

II. EXPRESSIONS OF THIS ASPIRATION

1. The yearning for justice and for the effective recognition of the dignity of every human being needs, like every deep aspiration, to be clarified and guided.

2. In effect, a discernment process is necessary which takes into account both the theoretical and the practical manifestations of this aspiration. For there are many political and social movements which present themselves as authentic spokesmen for the aspiration of the poor and claim to be able, though by recourse to violent means, to bring about the radical changes which will put an end to the oppression and misery of people.

3. So the aspiration for justice often finds itself the captive of ideologies which hide or pervert its meaning and which propose to people struggling for their liberation goals which are contrary to the true purpose of human life. They propose ways of action which imply the systematic recourse to violence, contrary to any ethic which is respectful of persons.

4. The interpretation of the signs of the times in the light of the gospel requires, then, that we examine the meaning of this deep yearning of people for justice, but also that we study with critical discernment the theoretical and practical expressions which this aspiration has taken on.

III. LIBERATION, A CHRISTIAN THEME

1. Taken by itself, the desire for liberation finds a strong and fraternal echo in the heart and spirit of Christians.

2. Thus, in accord with this aspiration, the theological and pastoral movement known as "liberation theology" was born, first in the countries of Latin America, which are marked by the religious and cultural heritage of Christianity, and then in other countries of the Third World, as well as in certain circles in the industrialized countries.

3. The expression "theology of liberation" refers first of all to a special concern for the poor and the victims of oppression, which in turn begets a commitment to justice. Starting with this approach, we can distinguish several often contradictory ways of understanding the Christian meaning of poverty and the type of commitment to justice it requires. As with all movements of ideas, the "theologies of liberation" present diverse theological positions. Their doctrinal frontiers are badly defined.

4. The aspiration for liberation, as the term suggests, repeats a theme fundamental to the Old and New Testaments. In itself, the expression "theology of liberation" is a thoroughly valid term: it designates a theological reflection centered on the biblical theme of liberation and freedom, and on the urgency of its practical realization.

The meeting, then, of the aspiration for liberation and the theologies of liberation is not one of mere chance. The significance of this encounter between the two can be understood only in light of the specific message of revelation, authentically interpreted by the magisterium of the church.[2]

IV. BIBLICAL FOUNDATIONS

1. Thus a theology of liberation correctly understood constitutes an invitation to theologians to deepen certain essential biblical themes with a concern for the grave and urgent questions which the contemporary yearning for liberation and those movements which more or less faithfully echo it pose for the church. We dare not forget for a single instant the situations of acute distress which issue such a dramatic call to theologians.

2. The radical experience of Christian liberty[3] is our first point of ref-

erence. Christ, our liberator, has freed us from sin and from slavery to the law and to the flesh, which is the mark of the condition of sinful humankind. Thus it is the new life of grace, fruit of justification, which makes us free. This means that the most radical form of slavery is slavery to sin. Other forms of slavery find their deepest root in slavery to sin. That is why freedom in the full Christian sense, characterized by the life in the Spirit, cannot be confused with a license to give in to the desires of the flesh. Freedom is a new life in love.

3. The "theologies of liberation" make wide use of readings from the Book of Exodus. The exodus, in fact, is the fundamental event in the formation of the chosen people. It represents freedom from foreign domination and from slavery. One will note that the specific significance of the event comes from its purpose, for this liberation is ordered to the foundation of the people of God and the covenant cult celebrated on Mt. Sinai.[4] That is why the liberation of the exodus cannot be reduced to a liberation which is principally or exclusively political in nature. Moreover, it is significant that the term freedom is often replaced in scripture by the very closely related term *redemption.*

4. The foundational episode of the exodus will never be effaced from the memory of Israel. Reference is made to it when, after the destruction of Jerusalem and the exile to Babylon, the Jewish people lived in the hope of a new liberation and, beyond that, awaited a definitive liberation. In this experience God is recognized as the liberator. God will enter into a new covenant with the people. It will be marked by the gift of God's Spirit and the conversion of hearts.[5]

5. The anxieties and multiple sufferings sustained by those who are faithful to the God of the covenant provide the theme of several Psalms: laments, appeals for help, and thanksgivings all make mention of religious salvation and liberation. In this context, suffering is not purely and simply equated with the social condition of poverty or with the condition of the one who is undergoing political oppression. It also includes the hostility of one's enemies, injustice, failure, and death. The Psalms call us back to an essential religious experience: it is from God alone that one can expect salvation and healing. God, and not humankind, has the power to change the situations of suffering. Thus the "poor of the Lord" live in a total and confident reliance upon the loving providence of God.[6] Moreover, throughout the whole crossing of the desert, the Lord did not fail to provide for the spiritual liberation and purification of the people.

6. In the Old Testament, the prophets after Amos keep affirming with particular vigor the requirements of justice and solidarity and the need to pronounce a very severe judgment on the rich who oppress the poor. They come to the defense of the widow and the orphan. They threaten the powerful: the accumulation of evils can only lead to terrible punishments.

Faithfulness to the covenant cannot be conceived of without the practice of justice. Justice as regards God and justice as regards humankind are inseparable. God is the defender and the liberator of the poor.

7. These requirements are found once again in the New Testament. They are even more radicalized, as can be shown in the discourse on the Beatitudes. Conversion and renewal have to occur in the depths of the heart.

8. Already proclaimed in the Old Testament, the commandment of fraternal love extended to all humankind thus provides the supreme rule of social life.[7] There are no discriminations or limitations which can counter the recognition of everyone as neighbor.[8]

9. Poverty for the sake of the kingdom is praised. And in the figure of the poor, we are led to recognize the mysterious presence of the Son of Man, who became poor himself for love of us.[9] This is the foundation of the inexhaustible words of Jesus on the judgment in Matthew 25: 31-46. Our Lord is one with all in distress; every distress is marked by his presence.

10. At the same time, the requirements of justice and mercy, already proclaimed in the Old Testament, are deepened to assume a new significance in the New Testament. Those who suffer or who are persecuted are identified with Christ.[10] The perfection that Jesus demands of his disciples (Matt. 5:18) consists in the obligation to be merciful "as your heavenly Father is merciful" (Luke 6:36).

11. It is in light of the Christian vocation to fraternal love and mercy that the rich are severely reminded of their duty.[11] St. Paul, faced with the disorders of the church of Corinth, forcefully emphasizes the bond between participation in the sacrament of love and sharing with the brother or sister in need.[12]

12. New Testament revelation teaches us that sin is the greatest evil, since it strikes humankind in the heart of its personality. The first liberation, to which all others must make reference, is that from sin.

13. Unquestionably, it is to stress the radical character of the deliverance brought by Christ and offered to all, be they politically free or slaves, that the New Testament does not require some change in the political or social condition as a prerequisite for entrance into this freedom. However, the Letter to Philemon shows that the new freedom procured by the grace of Christ should necessarily have effects on the social level.

14. Consequently, the full ambit of sin, whose first effect is to introduce disorder into the relationship between God and humankind, cannot be restricted to "social sin." The truth is that only a correct doctrine of sin will permit us to insist on the gravity of its social effects.

15. Nor can one localize evil principally or uniquely in bad social, political, or economic "structures" as though all other evils came from them so that the creation of the "new person" would depend on the establishment of different economic and socio-political structures. To be sure, there are structures which are evil and which cause evil and which we must have the courage to change. Structures, whether they are good or bad, are the result of human actions and so are consequences more than causes. The root of evil, then, lies in free and responsible persons who have to be converted

by the grace of Jesus Christ in order to live and act as new creatures in the love of neighbor and in the effective search for justice, self-control, and the exercise of virtue.[13]

To demand first of all a radical revolution in social relations and then to criticize the search for personal perfection is to set out on a road which leads to the denial of the meaning of the person and personal transcendence, and to destroy ethics and its foundation, which is the absolute character of the distinction between good and evil. Moreover, since charity is the principle of authentic perfection, that perfection cannot be conceived without an openness to others and a spirit of service.

V. THE VOICE OF THE MAGISTERIUM

1. In order to answer the challenge leveled at our times by oppression and hunger, the church's magisterium has frequently expressed its desire to awaken Christian consciences to a sense of justice, social responsibility, and solidarity with the poor and the oppressed, and to highlight the present urgency of the doctrine and imperatives contained in revelation.

2. We would like to mention some of these interventions here: the papal documents *Mater et Magistra, Pacem in Terris, Populorum Progressio,* and *Evangelii Nuntiandi.* We should likewise mention the letter to Cardinal Roy, *Octogesima Adveniens.*

3. The Second Vatican Council in turn confronted the questions of justice and liberty in the pastoral constitution *Gaudium et Spes.*

4. On a number of occasions the holy father has emphasized these themes, in particular in the encyclicals *Redemptor Hominis, Dives in Misericordia,* and *Laborem Exercens.* These numerous addresses recall the doctrine of human rights and touch directly on the problems of the liberation of the human person in the face of the diverse kinds of oppression of which of which each is the victim. It is especially important to mention in this connection the address given before the 26th General Assembly of the United Nations in New York, October 2, 1979.[14] On January 28 of that same year, while opening the Third Conference of CELAM in Puebla, John Paul II affirmed that the complete truth about humanity is the basis for any real liberation.[15] This text is a document which bears directly upon the theology of liberation.

5. Twice the Synod of Bishops treated subjects directly related to a Christian conception of liberation: in 1971, justice in the world, and in 1974, the relationship between freedom from oppression and full freedom, or the salvation of humankind. The work of the synods of 1971 and 1974 led Paul VI in his apostolic exhortation *Evangelii Nuntiandi* to clarify the connection between evangelization and human liberation or advancement.[16]

6. The concern of the church for liberation and for human advancement was also expressed in the establishment of the Pontifical Commission on Justice and Peace.

7. Numerous national episcopal conferences have joined the Holy See in recalling the urgency of authentic human liberation and the routes by which to achieve it. In this context, special mention should be made of the documents of the general conferences of the Latin American episcopate at Medellín in 1968 and at Puebla in 1979.

Paul VI was present at the Medellín conference and John Paul II was at Puebla. Both dealt with the themes of conversion and liberation.

8. Following Paul VI, who had insisted on the distinctive character of the gospel message,[17] a character which is of divine origin, John Paul II, in his address at Puebla, recalled the three pillars upon which any authentic theology of liberation will rest: truth about Jesus Christ, truth about the church, and truth about humankind.[18]

VI. A NEW INTERPRETATION OF CHRISTIANITY

1. It is impossible to overlook the immense amount of selfless work done by Christians, pastors, priests, religious, or lay persons, who, driven by a love for their brothers and sisters living in inhuman conditions, have endeavored to bring help and comfort to countless people in the distress brought about by poverty. Among these, some have tried to find the most effective means to put a quick end to the intolerable situation.

2. The zeal and the compassion which should dwell in the hearts of all pastors nevertheless run the risk of being led astray and diverted to works which are just as damaging to human beings and their dignity as is the poverty being fought, if one is not sufficiently attentive to certain temptations.

3. The feeling of anguish at the urgency of the problems cannot make us lose sight of what is essential nor forget the reply of Jesus to the tempter: "It is not on bread alone that man lives, but on every word that comes from the mouth of God" (Matt. 4:4; cf. Deut. 8:3).

Faced with the urgency of sharing bread, some are tempted to put evangelization into parentheses, as it were, and postpone until tomorrow: first the bread, then the word of the Lord. It is a fatal error to separate these two and even worse to oppose the one to the other. In fact, the Christian perspective naturally shows they have a great deal to do with one another.[19]

4. To some it even seems that the necessary struggle for human justice and freedom in the economic and political sense constitutes the whole essence of salvation. For them, the gospel is reduced to a purely earthly gospel.

5. The different theologies of liberation are situated between the preferential option for the poor forcefully reaffirmed without ambiguity after Medellín at the conference of Puebla[20] on the one hand, and the temptation to reduce the gospel to an earthly gospel on the other.

6. We should recall that the preferential option described at Puebla is twofold: for the poor and for the young.[21] It is significant that the option

for the young has in general been passed over in total silence.

7. We noted above (cf. 3) that an authentic theology of liberation will be one rooted in the word of God, correctly interpreted.

8. But from a descriptive standpoint, it helps to speak of theologies of liberation, since the expression embraces a number of theological positions or even sometimes ideological ones, which are not simply different but more often incompatible with one another.

9. In this present document, we will only be discussing developments of that current of thought which, under the name "theology of liberation," proposes a novel interpretation of both the content of faith and of Christian existence, which seriously departs from the faith of the church, and, in fact, actually constitutes a practical negation.

10. Concepts uncritically borrowed from Marxist ideology and recourse to theses of a biblical hermeneutic marked by rationalism are at the basis of the new interpretation which is corrupting whatever was authentic in the general initial commitment on behalf of the poor.

VII. MARXIST ANALYSIS

1. Impatience and a desire for results have led certain Christians, despairing of every other method, to turn to what they call "Marxist analysis."

2. Their reasoning is this: an intolerable and explosive situation requires effective action which cannot be put off. Effective action presupposes a scientific analysis of the structural causes of poverty. Marxism now provides us with the means to make such an analysis, they say. Then one simply has to apply the analysis to the Third World situation, especially in Latin America.

3. It is clear that scientific knowledge of the situation and of the possible strategies for the transformation of society is a presupposition for any plan capable of attaining the ends proposed. It is also a proof of the seriousness of the effort.

4. But the term *scientific* exerts an almost mythical fascination even though everything called "scientific" is not necessarily scientific at all. That is why the borrowing of a method of approach to reality should be preceded by a careful epistemological critique. This preliminary critical study is missing from more than one "theology of liberation."

5. In the human and social sciences it is well to be aware above all of the plurality of methods and viewpoints, each of which reveals only one aspect of reality, which is so complex that it defies simple and univocal explanation.

6. In the case of Marxism, in the particular sense given to it in this context, a preliminary critique is all the more necessary since the thought of Marx is such a global vision of reality that all data received from observation and analysis are brought together in a philosophical and ideological structure, which predetermines the significance and importance to be at-

tached to them. The ideological principles come prior to the study of the social reality and are presupposed in it. Thus no separation of the parts of this epistemologically unique complex is possible. If one tries to take only one part, say, the analysis, one ends up having to accept the entire ideology. That is why it is not uncommon for the ideological aspect to be predominant among the things which the "theologians of liberation" borrow from Marxist authors.

7. The warning of Paul VI remains fully valid today: Marxism as it is actually lived out poses many distinct aspects and questions for Christians to reflect upon and act on. However, it would be "illusory and dangerous to ignore the intimate bond which radically unites them, and to accept elements of the Marxist analysis without recognizing its connections with the ideology, or to enter into the practice of class struggle and of its Marxist interpretation while failing to see the kind of totalitarian society to which this process slowly leads."[22]

8. It is true that Marxist thought ever since its origins, and even more so lately, has become divided and has given birth to various currents which diverge significantly from one another. To the extent that they remain fully Marxist, these currents continue to be based on certain fundamental tenets which are not compatible with the Christian conception of humanity and society. In this context certain formulas are not neutral, but keep the meaning they had in the original Marxist doctrine. This is the case with "class struggle." This expression remains pregnant with the interpretation that Marx gave it, so it cannot be taken as the equivalent of "severe social conflict," in an empirical sense. Those who use similar formulas, while claiming to keep only certain elements of the Marxist analysis and yet to reject this analysis taken as a whole, maintain at the very least a serious confusion in the minds of their readers.

9. Let us recall the fact that atheism and the denial of the human person, liberty, and rights are at the core of Marxist theory. The theory, then, contains errors which directly threaten the truths of the faith regarding the eternal destiny of individual persons. Moreover, to attempt to integrate into theology an analysis whose criterion of interpretation depends on this atheistic conception is to involve oneself in terrible contradictions. What is more, this misunderstanding of the spiritual nature of the person leads to a total subordination of the person to the collectivity and thus to the denial of the principles of a social and political life in keeping with human dignity.

10. A critical examination of the analytical methods borrowed from other disciplines must be carried out in a special way by theologians. It is the light of faith which provides theology with its principles. That is why the use of philosophical positions or of human sciences by the theologian has a value which might be called instrumental, but yet must undergo a critical study from a theological perspective. In other words, the ultimate and decisive criterion for truth can only be a criterion which is itself theological. It is only in the light of faith and what faith teaches us about the truth of

humankind and the ultimate meaning of human destiny, that one can judge the validity or degree of validity of what other disciplines propose, often rather conjecturally, as being the truth about humankind, its history and its destiny.

11. When modes of interpretation are applied to the economic, social, and political reality of today, which are themselves borrowed from Marxist thought, they can give the initial impression of a certain plausibility to the degree that the present-day situation in certain countries is similar to what Marx described and interpreted in the middle of the last century. On the basis of these similarities, certain simplifications are made which, abstracting from specific essential factors, prevent any really rigorous examination of the causes of poverty and prolong the confusion.

12. In certain parts of Latin America the seizure of the vast majority of the wealth by an oligarchy of owners bereft of social consciousness, the practical absence or the shortcomings of a rule of law, military dictators making a mockery of elementary human rights, the corruption of certain powerful officials, the savage practices of some foreign capital interests constitute factors which nourish a passion for revolt among those who thus consider themselves the powerless victims of a new colonialism in the technological, financial, monetary, or economic order. The recognition of injustice is accompanied by a pathos which borrows its language from Marxism, wrongly presented as though it were scientific language.

13. The first condition for any analysis is total openness to the reality to be described. That is why a critical consciousness has to accompany the use of any working hypotheses that are being adopted. One has to realize that these hypotheses correspond to a particular viewpoint, which will inevitably highlight certain aspects of the reality while leaving others in the shade. This limitation, which derives from the nature of human science, is ignored by those who, under the guise of hypotheses recognized as such, have recourse to such an all-embracing conception of reality as the thought of Karl Marx.

VIII. SUBVERSION OF THE MEANING OF TRUTH AND VIOLENCE

1. This all-embracing conception thus imposes its logic and leads the "theologies of liberation" to accept a series of positions which are incompatible with the Christian vision of humanity. In fact, the ideological core borrowed from Marxism which we are referring to exercises the function of a determining principle. It has this role in virtue of its being described as "scientific," that is to say, true of necessity.

In this core we can distinguish several components.

2. According to the logic of Marxist thought, the "analysis" is inseparable from the praxis and from the conception of history to which this praxis is linked. The analysis is for the Marxist an instrument of criticism, and criticism is only one stage in the revolutionary struggle. This struggle is that

of the proletarian class, invested with its mission in history.

3. Consequently, for the Marxist, only those who engage in the struggle can work out the analysis correctly.

4. The only true consciousness, then, is the partisan consciousness.

It is clear that the concept of truth itself is in question here, and it is totally subverted: there is no truth, they pretend, except in and through partisan praxis.

5. For the Marxist, the praxis and the truth that comes from it are partisan praxis and truth because the fundamental structure of history is characterized by class struggle. There follows, then, the objective necessity to enter into the class struggle, which is the dialectical opposite of the relationship of exploitation, which is being condemned. For the Marxist, the truth is a truth of class: there is no truth but truth in the struggle of the revolutionary class.

6. The fundamental law of history, which is the law of the class struggle, implies that society is founded on violence. To the violence which constitutes the relationship of the domination of the rich over the poor, there corresponds the counterviolence of the revolution, by means of which this domination will be reversed.

7. The class struggle is presented as an objective, necessary law. Upon entering this process on behalf of the oppressed, one "makes" truth, one acts "scientifically." Consequently, the conception of the truth goes hand in hand with the affirmation of necessary violence, and so, of a political amorality. Within this perspective, any reference to ethical requirements calling for courageous and radical institutional and structural reforms makes no sense.

8. The fundamental law of class struggle has a global and universal character. It is reflected in all the spheres of existence: religious, ethical, cultural, and institutional. As far as this law is concerned, one of these spheres is autonomous. In each of them this law constitutes the determining element.

9. In particular, the very nature of ethics is radically called into question because of the borrowing of these theses from Marxism. In fact, it is the transcendent character of the distinction between good and evil, the principle of morality, which is implicitly denied in the perspective of the class struggle.

IX. THE THEOLOGICAL APPLICATION OF THIS CORE

1. The positions here in question are often brought out explicitly in certain of the writings of "theologians of liberation." In others, they follow logically from their premises. In addition, they are presupposed in certain liturgical practices, as for example a "eucharist" transformed into a celebration of the people in struggle, even though the persons who participate in these practices may not be fully conscious of it. We are facing, therefore,

a real system, even if some hesitate to follow the logic to its conclusion. As such, this system is a perversion of the Christian message as God entrusted it to the church. This message in its entirety finds itself then called into question by the "theologies of liberation."

2. It is not the fact of social stratification with all its inequity and injustice, but the theory of class struggle as the fundamental law of history which has been accepted by these "theologies of liberation" as a principle. The conclusion is drawn that the class struggle thus understood divides the church itself, and that in light of this struggle even ecclesial realities must be judged.

The claim is even made that it would maintain an illusion with bad faith to propose that love in its universality can conquer what is the primary structural law of capitalism.

3. According to this conception, the class struggle is the driving force of history. History thus becomes a central notion. It will be affirmed that God makes history. It will be added that there is only one history, one in which the distinction between the history of salvation and profane history is no longer necessary. To maintain the distinction would be to fall into "dualism." Affirmations such as these reflect historicist immanentism. Thus there is a tendency to identify the kingdom of God and its growth with the human liberation movement and to make history itself the subject of its own development, as a process of the self-redemption of humankind by means of the class struggle.

This identification is in opposition to the faith of the church as it has been reaffirmed by the Second Vatican Council.[23]

4. Along these lines, some go so far as to identify God with history and to define faith as "fidelity to history," which means adhering to a political policy suited to the growth of humanity, conceived of as a purely temporal messianism.

5. As a consequence, faith, hope, and charity are given a new content: they become "fidelity to history," "confidence in the future," and "option for the poor." This is tantamount to saying they have been emptied of their theological reality.

6. A radical politicization of faith's affirmations and of theological judgments follows inevitably from this new conception. The question no longer has to do with simply drawing attention to the consequences and political implications of the truths of faith, which are respected beforehand for their transcendent value. In this new system every affirmation of faith or of theology is subordinated to a political criterion which in turn depends on the class struggle, the driving force of history.

7. As a result, participation in the class struggle is presented as a requirement of charity itself. The desire to love everyone here and now, despite their class, and to go out to meet them with the nonviolent means of dialogue and persuasion, is denounced as counterproductive and opposed to love.

If one holds that a person should not be the object of hate, it is claimed nevertheless that if one belongs to the objective class of the rich, one is primarily a class enemy to be fought. Thus the universality of love of neighbor and brotherhood become an eschatological principle, which will only have meaning for the "new person" who arises out of the victorious revolution.

8. As far as the church is concerned, this system would see it only as a reality interior to history, itself subject to those laws which are supposed to govern the development of history in its immanence. The church, the gift of God and mystery of faith, is emptied of any specific reality by this reductionism. At the same time it is disputed that the participation of Christians who belong to opposing classes at the same eucharistic table still makes any sense.

9. In its positive meaning the "church of the poor" signifies the preference given to the poor, without exclusion, whatever the form of their poverty, because they are preferred by God. The expression also refers to the church of our time, as communion and institution, and on the part of its members, becoming more fully conscious of the requirement of evangelical poverty.

10. But the "theologies of liberation," which deserve credit for restoring to a place of honor the great texts of the prophets and of the gospel in defense of the poor, go on to a disastrous confusion between the poor of Scripture and the proletariat of Marx. In this way they pervert the Christian meaning of the poor, and they transform the fight for the rights of the poor into a class fight within the ideological perspective of the class struggle. For them, the "church of the poor" signifies the church of the class which has become aware of the requirements of the revolutionary struggle as a step toward liberation and which celebrates this liberation in its liturgy.

11. A further remark regarding the expression "church of the people" will not be out of place here. From the pastoral point of view, this expression might mean the favored recipients of evangelization to whom, because of their condition, the church extends its pastoral love first of all. One might also refer to the church as people of God, that is, people of the new covenant established in Christ.[24]

12. But the "theologies of liberation" of which we are speaking mean by church of the people a church of the class, a church of the oppressed whom it is necessary to "conscientize" in the light of the organized struggle for freedom. For some, the people, thus understood, even become the object of faith.

13. Building on such a conception of the church of the people, a critique of the very structures of the church is developed. It is not simply the case of fraternal correction of pastors of the church whose behavior does not reflect the evangelical spirit of service and is linked to old fashioned signs of authority which scandalize the poor. It has to do with a challenge to the sacramental and hierarchical structure of the church, which was willed by

the Lord himself. There is a denunciation of members of the hierarchy and the magisterium as objective representatives of the ruling class which has to be opposed. Theologically, this position means that ministers take their origin from the people, who therefore designate ministers of their own choice in accord with the needs of their historic revolutionary mission.

X. A NEW HERMENEUTIC

1. The partisan conception of truth, which can be seen in the revolutionary praxis of the class, corroborates this position. Theologians who do not share the theses of the "theology of liberation," the hierarchy, and especially the Roman magisterium are thus discredited in advance as belonging to the class of the oppressors. Their theology is a theology of class. Arguments and teachings thus do not have to be examined in themselves since they are only reflections of class interests. Thus the instruction of others is decreed to be, in principle, false.

2. Here is where the global and all-embracing character of the theology of liberation appears. As a result, it must be criticized not just on the basis of this or that affirmation, but on the basis of its classist viewpoint, which it has adopted a priori and which has come to function in it as a determining principle.

3. Because of this classist presupposition, it becomes very difficult, not to say impossible, to engage in a real dialogue with some "theologians of liberation" in such a way that the other participant is listened to and his arguments are discussed with objectivity and attention. For these theologians start out with the idea, more or less consciously, that the viewpoint of the oppressed and revolutionary class, which is their own, is the single true point of view. Theological criteria for truth are thus relativized and subordinated to the imperatives of the class struggle. In this perspective, orthodoxy, or the right rule of faith, is substituted by the notion of orthopraxy as the criterion of the truth. In this connection it is important not to confuse practical orientation, which is proper to traditional theology in the same way that speculative orientation is, with the recognized and privileged priority given to a certain type of praxis. For them, this praxis is the revolutionary praxis, which thus becomes the supreme criterion for theological truth. A healthy theological method no doubt will always take the praxis of the church into account and will find there one of its foundations, but that is because the praxis comes from the faith and is a lived expression of it.

4. For the "theologies of liberation," however, the social doctrine of the church is rejected with disdain. It is said that it comes from the illusion of a possible compromise, typical of the middle class, which has no historic destiny.

5. The new hermeneutic inherent in the "theologies of liberation" leads to an essentially political rereading of the scriptures. Thus a major impor-

tance is given to the exodus event inasmuch as it is a liberation from political servitude. Likewise, a political reading of the Magnificat is proposed. The mistake here is not in bringing attention to a political dimension of the readings of scripture, but in making of this one dimension the principal or exclusive component. This leads to a reductionist reading of the Bible.

6. Likewise, one places oneself within the perspective of a temporal messianism, which is one of the most radical of the expressions of secularization of the kingdom of God and of its absorption into the immanence of human history.

7. In giving such priority to the political dimension, one is led to deny the radical newness of the New Testament and above all to misunderstand the person of our Lord Jesus Christ, true God and true man, and thus the specific character of the salvation he gave us, that is above all liberation from sin, which is the source of all evils.

8. Moreover in setting aside the authoritative interpretation of the church, denounced as classist, one is at the same time departing from tradition. In that way one is robbed of an essential theological criterion of interpretation and, in the vacuum thus created, one welcomes the most radical theses of rationalist exegesis. Without a critical eye, one returns to the opposition of the "Jesus of history" vs. the "Jesus of faith."

9. Of course the creeds of the faith are literally preserved, especially the Chalcedonian creed, but a new meaning is given to them, which is a negation of the faith of the church. On one hand, the christological doctrine of tradition is rejected in the name of class; on the other hand, one claims to meet again the "Jesus of history" coming from the revolutionary experience of the struggle of the poor for their liberation.

10. One claims to be reliving an experience similar to that of Jesus. The experience of the poor struggling for their liberation, which was Jesus' experience, would thus reveal, and it alone, the knowledge of the true God and of the kingdom.

11. Faith in the incarnate word, dead and risen for all, and whom "God made Lord and Christ"[25] is denied. In its place is substituted a figure of Jesus who is a kind of symbol who sums up in himself the requirements of the struggle of the oppressed.

12. An exclusively political interpretation is thus given to the death of Christ. In this way its value for salvation and the whole economy of redemption is denied.

13. This new interpretation thus touches the whole of the Christian mystery.

14. In a general way this brings about what can be called an inversion of symbols. Thus instead of seeing, with St. Paul, a figure of baptism in the exodus,[26] some end up making of it a symbol of the political liberation of the people.

15. When the same hermeneutical criterion is applied to the life and to the hierarchical constitution of the church, the relationship between the

hierarchy and the "base" becomes the relationship of obedient domination to the law of the struggle of the classes. Sacramentality, which is at the root of the ecclesial ministries and which makes of the church a spiritual reality which cannot be reduced to a purely sociological analysis, is quite simply ignored.

16. This inversion of symbols is likewise verified in the area of the sacraments. The eucharist is no longer to be understood as the real sacramental presence of the reconciling sacrifice and as the gift of the body and blood of Christ. It becomes a celebration of the people in their struggle. As a consequence, the unity of the church is radically denied. Unity, reconciliation, and communion in love are no longer seen as a gift we receive from Christ.[27] It is the historical class of the poor who by means of their struggle will build unity. For them, the struggle of the classes is the way to unity. The eucharist thus becomes the eucharist of the class. At the same time they deny the triumphant force of the love of God, which has been given to us.

XI. ORIENTATIONS

1. The warning against the serious deviations of some "theologies of liberation" must not at all be taken as some kind of approval, even indirect, of those who keep the poor in misery, who profit from that misery, who notice it while doing nothing about it or who remain indifferent to it. The church, guided by the gospel of mercy and by the love for humankind, hears the cry for justice[28] and intends to respond to it with all its might.

2. Thus a great call goes out to all the church: with boldness and courage, with farsightedness and prudence, with zeal and strength of spirit, with a love for the poor which demands sacrifice, pastors will consider the response to this call a matter of the highest priority, as many already do.

3. All priests, religious, and lay people who hear this call for justice and who want to work for evangelization and the advancement of humankind will do so in communion with their bishop and with the church, each in accord with his or her own specific ecclesial vocation.

4. Aware of the ecclesial character of their vocation, theologians will collaborate loyally and with a spirit of dialogue with the magisterium of the church. They will be able to recognize in the magisterium a gift of Christ to his church[29] and will welcome its word and its directives with filial respect.

5. It is only when one begins with the task of evangelization understood in its entirety that the authentic requirements of human progress and liberation are appreciated. This liberation has as its indispensable pillars the truth about Jesus the savior, the truth about the church, and the truth about humankind and its dignity.[30]

It is in light of the Beatitudes, and especially the Beatitude of the poor of heart, that the church, which wants to be the church of the poor throughout the world, intends to come to the aid of the noble struggle for truth and justice. It addresses each person, and for that reason every person. It is the "universal church. The church of the incarnation. It is not the church of one class or another. And it speaks in the name of truth itself. This truth is realistic." It leads to a recognition "of every human reality, every injustice, every tension and every struggle."[31]

6. An effective defense of justice needs to be based on the truth of humankind, created in the image of God and called to the grace of divine filiation. The recognition of the true relationship of human beings to God constitutes the foundation of justice to the extent that it rules the relationships between people. That is why the fight for human rights, which the church does not cease to reaffirm, constitutes the authentic fight for justice.

7. The truth of humankind requires that this battle be fought in ways consistent with human dignity. That is why the systematic and deliberate recourse to blind violence, no matter from which side it comes, must be condemned.[32] To put one's trust in violent means in the hope of restoring more justice is to become the victim of a fatal illusion: violence begets violence and degrades humankind. It mocks human dignity in the person of the victims, and it debases that same dignity among those who practice it.

8. The acute need for radical reforms of the structures which conceal poverty and which are themselves forms of violence should not let us lose sight of the fact that the source of injustice is in the human heart. Therefore it is only by making an appeal to the moral potential of the person and to the constant need for interior conversion that social change will be brought about which will truly be in the service of humankind.[33] For it will only be in the measure that they collaborate freely in these necessary changes through their own initiative and in solidarity that people, awakened to a sense of their responsibility, will grow in humanity.

The inversion of morality and structures is steeped in a materialist anthropology which is incompatible with the dignity of humankind.

9. It is therefore an equally fatal illusion to believe that these new structures will of themselves give birth to a "new person" in the sense of the truth of humankind. The Christian cannot forget that it is only the Holy Spirit, who has been given to us, who is the source of every true renewal and that God is the Lord of history.

10. By the same token, the overthrow by means of revolutionary violence of structures which generate violence is not ipso facto that beginning of a just regime. A major fact of our time ought to evoke the reflection of all those who would sincerely work for the true liberation of their brothers: millions of our own contemporaries legitimately yearn to recover those basic freedoms of which they were deprived by totalitarian and atheistic regimes, which come to power by violent and revolutionary means, precisely in the name of the liberation of the people. This shame of our time cannot be ignored: while claiming to bring them freedom, these regimes keep whole nations in conditions of servitude, which are unworthy of humankind. Those

who, perhaps inadvertently, make themselves accomplices of similar enslavements betray the very poor they mean to help.

11. The class struggle as a road toward a classless society is a myth which slows reform and aggravates poverty and injustice. Those who allow themselves to be caught up in fascination with this myth should reflect on the bitter examples history has to offer about where it leads. They would then understand that we are not talking here about abandoning an effective means of struggle on behalf of the poor for an ideal which has no practical effects. On the contrary, we are talking about freeing oneself from a delusion in order to base oneself squarely on the gospel and its power of realization.

12. One of the conditions for necessary theological correction is giving proper value to the social teaching of the church. This teaching is by no means closed. It is, on the contrary, open to all the new questions which are so numerous today. In this perspective, the contribution of theologians and other thinkers in all parts of the world to the reflection of the church is indispensable today.

13. Likewise the experience of those who work directly for evangelization and for the advancement of the poor and the oppressed is necessary for the doctrinal and pastoral reflection of the church. In this sense it is necessary to affirm that one becomes more aware of certain aspects of truth by starting with praxis, if by that one means pastoral praxis and social work which keeps its evangelical inspiration.

14. The teaching of the church on social issues indicates the main lines of ethical orientation. But in order that it be able to guide action directly, the church needs competent people from a scientific and technological viewpoint, as well as in the human and political sciences. Pastors should be attentive to the formation of persons of such capability who live the gospel deeply. Lay persons, whose proper mission is to build society, are involved here to the highest degree.

15. Theses of the "theologies of liberation" are widely popularized under a simplified form in formation sessions or in what are called "base groups" which lack the necessary catechetical and theological preparation as well as the capacity for discernment. Thus these theses are accepted by generous men and women without any critical judgment being made.

16. That is why pastors must look after the quality and the content of catechesis and formation, which should always present the whole message of salvation and the imperatives of true liberation within the framework of this whole message.

17. In this full presentation of Christianity, it is proper to emphasize those essential aspects, which the "theologies of liberation" especially tend to misunderstand or to eliminate, namely: the transcendence and gratuity of liberation in Jesus Christ, true God and true man; the sovereignty of grace; and the true nature of the means of salvation, especially of the church and the sacraments. One should also keep in mind the true meaning of

ethics, in which the distinction between good and evil is not relativized, the real meaning of sin, the necessity for conversion and the universality of the law of fraternal love.

One needs to be on guard against the politicization of existence, which, misunderstanding the entire meaning of the kingdom of God and the transcendence of the person, begins to sacralize politics and betray the religion of the people in favor of the projects of the revolution.

18. The defenders of orthodoxy are sometimes accused of passivity, indulgence, or culpable complicity regarding the intolerable situations of injustice and the political regimes which prolong them. Spiritual conversion, the intensity of the love of God and neighbor, zeal for justice and peace, the gospel meaning of the poor and of poverty, are required of everyone and especially of pastors and those in positions of responsibility. The concern for the purity of the faith demands giving the answer of effective witness in the service of one's neighbor, the poor and the oppressed in particular, in an integral theological fashion. By the witness of their dynamic and constructive power to love, Christians will thus lay the foundations of this "civilization of love" of which this conference of Puebla spoke, following Paul VI.[34] Moreover there are already many priests, religious, and lay people who are consecrated in a truly evangelical way for the creation of a just society.

CONCLUSION

The words of Paul VI in his "Profession of Faith" express with full clarity the faith of the church, from which one cannot deviate without provoking, besides spiritual disaster, new miseries and new types of slavery.

"We profess our faith that the kingdom of God, begun here below in the church of Christ, is not of this world, whose form is passing away, and that its own growth cannot be confused with the progress of civilization, of science, of human technology, but that it consists in knowing ever more deeply the unfathomable riches of Christ, to hope ever more strongly in things eternal, to respond ever more ardently to the love of God, to spread ever more widely grace and holiness among humankind. But it is this very same love which makes the church constantly concerned for the true temporal good of humankind as well. Never ceasing to recall to its children that they have no lasting dwelling here on earth, it urges them also to contribute, each according to their own vocation and means, to the welfare of their earthly city, to promote justice, peace, and fellowship among humans, to lavish their assistance on their brothers, especially on the poor and the most dispirited. The intense concern of the church, the bride of Christ, for the needs of humankind, their joys and their hopes, their pains and their struggles, is nothing other than the great desire to be present to them in order to enlighten them with the light of Christ and join them all to him, their only savior. It can never mean that the church is conforming to the things of this world or that it is lessening the earnestness with which it awaits its Lord and the eternal kingdom."[35]

This instruction was adopted at an ordinary meeting of the Sacred Congregation for the Doctrine of the Faith and was approved at an audience granted to the undersigned cardinal prefect by his holiness Pope John Paul II, who ordered its publication.

Given at Rome, at the Sacred Congregation for the Doctrine of the Faith, August 6, 1984, the feast of the Transfiguration of our Lord.

Cardinal Joseph Ratzinger
Prefect

Archbishop Alberto Bovone
Secretary

NOTES

1. Cf. *Gaudium et Spes,* 4.
2. Cf. *Dei Verbum,* 10.
3. Cf. Gal. 5:1ff.
4. Cf. Ex. 24.
5. Cf. Jer. 31:31–34; Ez. 36:26ff.
6. Cf. Zec. 3:12ff.
7. Cf. Dt. 10:18–19.
8. Cf. Lk. 10:25–37.
9. Cf. 2 Cor. 8:9.
10. Cf. Mt. 25:31–46; Acts 9:4–5; Col. 1:24.
11. Cf. Jas. 5ff.
12. Cf. 1 Cor. 11:17–34.
13. Cf. Jas. 2:14–26.
14. Cf. *Acta Apostolicae Sedis,* 71 (1979) pp. 1144–60.
15. Cf. *AAS,* 71 (1979) p. 196.
16. Cf. *Evangelii Nuntiandi,* 25–33, *AAS,* 68 (1976) pp. 23–28.
17. Cf. *Evangelii Nuntiandi,* 32, AAS, 68 (1976) p.27.
18. Cf. *AAS,* 71 (1979) pp. 188–196.
19. Cf. *Gaudium et Spes,* 39; Piux XI, *Quadragesimo Anno: AAS,* 23 (1931) p. 207.
20. Cf. nos. 1134–65 and nos. 1166–1205.
21. Cf. Puebla Document, IV, 2.
22. Cf. Paul VI, *Octogesima Adveniens,* 34, *AAS,* 63 (1971) pp. 424–25.
23. Cf. *Lumen Gentium,* 9–17.
24. Cf. *Gaudium et Spes,* 39.
25. Cf. Acts 2:36.
26. Cf. 1 Cor. 10:1–2.
27. Cf. Eph. 2:11–22.
28. Cf. Puebla Document I, II, 3.3.
29. Cf. Lk. 10:16.

30. Cf. John Paul II, Address at the Opening of the Conference at Puebla, *AAS,* 71 (1979) pp. 188–96; Puebla Document, II P, c.1.

31. Cf. John Paul II, Address to the Favela Vidigal at Rio de Janeiro, July 2, 1980, *AAS,* 72 (1980) pp. 852–58.

32. Cf. Puebla Document. II, c. II, 5.4.

33. Cf. ibid., IV, c.3. 3.1.

34. Cf. ibid., IV, II, 2.3.

35. Cf. Paul VI, Profession of Faith of the People of God, June 30, 1968, *AAS,* 60 (1968) pp. 443–444.

46

Leonardo Boff
"Vatican Instruction Reflects
European Mind-Set"
(August 31, 1984)

Leonardo Boff's comments were originally published in the Brazilian newspaper,
Folha de São Paulo. *The English text included here is from* LADOC, *15
(January-February 1985), pp. 8–12.*

The Roman document on liberation theology makes it necessary to raise
an issue fundamental and decisive for an accurate understanding of the
meaning of liberation theology. Is the liberation of which this theology
speaks a theoretical topic of urgent importance, to be examined along with
other pertinent topics (work, sexuality, the demographic explosion) in the
context of the present situation of great poverty suffered by the Third
World? Or is it above all else a historical process, a social phenomenon
that touches the entire social and historical reality lived by the oppressed
in their conscious and organized struggle for bread, for work, for participation, for dignity—in a word, for full liberation? The way we understand
liberation, whether we see it as a topic of study and discussion or as action
that liberates captives (thus, liber-action) will profoundly affect our understanding of the Roman *Instruction*. It is this point that distinguishes the
Central European perspective from that characteristic of the Third World
and of Latin America.

The Central European study of liberation begins with the "topic" as
such. Liberation is a fundamental concept in biblical theology and in the
tradition of emancipation found in modern culture. When dealing with it
theologically, the theologian researches Scripture, tradition, the teachings
of the church, and the recent opinions of theologians. The idea is to systematically reconstruct the idea of liberation and to establish a critical
grounding for the topic; once this is done, its consequences for the everyday
life of the faithful are deduced, and advice and instructions for future action
are drawn up.

415

The Latin American and Third World perspective starts from the opposite pole. First it examines the concrete practice of the oppressed, their progress and their allies; it asks about the participation of individual Christians, base communities and sectors of the church in the overall liberation process. Then it asks a number of questions. What is the relationship of this journey and this practice to the unfolding of God's plan? To what extent is this process an incipient and historical realization of the kingdom of God, which is a kingdom of justice, of fellowship and of peace? What relationship is there between this concrete liberation and salvation in Jesus Christ who, when he was among us, surely made an option for the poor, cured the sick, and liberated the oppressed? Finally, it offers a critical evaluation, in the light of faith, of the presence of Christians and the practice of non-Christians as well, and calls for concrete actions aimed at furthering the struggle for liberation. It attempts to carry out its faith reflection (theology) beginning with this process and from within an ongoing liberation commitment. What image of God emerges? What is the figure of Christ that takes shape for the Christian militant? What are the forms that sin and grace take? What are the signs that embody Christian hope? What forms should the church adopt in order to best carry out its liberating mission, grounded in its inalienable religious identity?

The theology of liberation is born of the effort to answer these questions, which are raised by the practice of liberation. The object of reflection is not just the traditional biblical theme of liberation; it is above all the reality of the liberation of the oppressed. Because God is present in this concrete process, the Christian realizes that liberation is open to the future and to transcendence: to the future, in the sense of not resting on past achievements but rather of engaging in a constant search for the wider exercise of participation and freedom; and to transcendence, turning to a God whose action makes liberation full and whole—a liberation that necessarily includes forgiveness, reconciliation, and the resurrection of the dead, most especially of those fallen and of those martyred for the cause of injustice.

It is this perspective that constitutes the originality of the theology of liberation, and that distinguishes it from other theologies *on* liberation. The basic issue is its essential relationship with liberating action. In order to write on the topic of liberation, all you need is a basic awareness of its relevance (otherwise there would be no interest in dealing with it), an abundance of theological sources (exegesis, history, documents of the church on the subject, the texts of theologians who have written on the matter), and an ability for creative and critical systematization. The task can be carried out at a desk surrounded by the tools necessary for serious research, and apart from the actual practice of liberation. In sum, it is the practice of theory.

To create a theology of liberation based on the practice of liberation it is necessary to participate as an active member in a particular movement, a base community, a center for the defense of human rights, or a trade union. This immersion in the world of the poor and oppressed gives the-ological discourse a passionate edge, an occasional mordancy, a holy wrath—and a sense of the practical. There is an objective concern for efficacy, because in the last analysis what counts is not theological reflection but the concrete liberation of the poor. It is this liberation-in-act rather than liberation-in-thought that anticipates the kingdom and is pleasing to God. Oppression is not so much to be thought about; it is to be overcome.

Where can we place the *Instruction on Some Aspects of the Theology of Liberation* signed by Cardinal Joseph Ratzinger and Archbishop Alberto Bovone? We must situate it squarely within the Central European per-spective, that of reflection on the topic of liberation. The text does not begin with a description of the struggles of the oppressed, of their orga-nizations, and of the presence of Christians within the process. These real-ities are totally ignored. In its introduction, the document starts off with the "essential truth" of liberation. It deals with the topic in the Old and New Testaments, in the teaching of the church, and in the documents of the Latin American hierarchy. From these it derives consequences for prac-tice in the foreseeable and unforeseeable future. Its methodological strat-egy is clearly defined in the introduction: "To clearly discern what is fundamental and what belongs to the realm of consequences is an indis-pensable condition for theological reflection on liberation."

This initial methodological focus guides the development of the entire subject. It is a *Konsequenztheologie*, as the greatest theologian of this cen-tury, the late Karl Rahner, would say: a theology of the consequences deduced from principles and doctrines.

We do not want to express disdain for this method. We merely point it out at the beginning, and note the difference between this way of thinking and the Latin American way. The difference is not without consequences.

The first consequence of this difference is that Latin American theolo-gians will have difficulty recognizing themselves in the text presented by Roman doctrinal authorities. It has a different style, different concerns, a different tone.

The second consequence is that most of the charges of reductionism leveled against the theology of liberation (or better, as the text prefers, theologies of liberation) do not really apply to this type of theology. In no way are these theologians denying the divinity of Christ, or the redemptive value of his death, or the Mass as an actualization of the sacrifice of the Lord and of his eucharistic presence. But the fact that they start from practice gives their work a different tone. They begin with the people's shared faith that Jesus is God, that the Mass has a salvific value, etc. But they emphasize the social dimensions and political components present in these realities. In the last analysis, Jesus was condemned to death in a court under Pontius Pilate, celebrated the last supper in the context of death threats from the religious and ideological powers of the time, lived out certain kinds of relationships with the poor, and assumed a highly critical posture in the face of riches and power/domination. Our medieval teachers taught that *abstractio non est negatio*: to abstract from a given truth is not to deny it. We must see with the emphasis demanded by a reality lived and suffered, not with denials of elements of the faith that are accepted as a given and lived out.

The third criticism concerns Marxism: theologians of liberation who make use of some categories drawn from the Marxist tradition (especially from Althusser and Gramsci) do so for the sake of their practical usefulness in analyzing situations suffered by the people; they are not engaging in systematic, academic reflection on the relationship between Marxism and Christianity. They are not interested in Marx as such. Marx and his comrades interest us to the degree that they help us better understand the reality of exploitation and point to possible ways of overcoming the capitalist system, which is harmful to the people and excludes them from participation. If Rome had dialogued with the theologians of liberation, if it had examined existing texts on this liberating action, it would have given itself the opportunity to grasp the difference between a theoretical approach to the topic and a practical approach to liberating action.

Many other comments would be possible. For the moment, these initial remarks will have to do, along with the hope that a second document promised soon will do more justice to Latin American reflection. This reflection is peripheral, and carried out in conditions of poverty, but it could be a contribution to the church, and principally to those among the oppressed of this world who have a Christian or religious perspective.

47

Gustavo Gutiérrez
"Criticism Will Deepen, Clarify Liberation Theology" (September 14, 1984)

Gutiérrez's comments on the Instruction *are generally more positive and constructive than the judgments of many other liberation theologians. This interview in the Peruvian newspaper* La República *was later translated by* Latinamerica Press. *I have taken the English text from* LADOC, *15 (January-February, 1985), pp. 2-7.*

Liberation theology has not only become the center of debate between progressive and conservative groups within the Catholic Church, it is making headlines around the world. Why is there so much interest in liberation theology, Father?

Gutiérrez: The reason why the debate is so intense, I suspect, is that liberation theology addresses concrete problems that specifically relate to the peoples of Latin America. That it has provoked discussion seems normal to me. At the same time, I believe the debate is important and will help believers and nonbelievers alike to better understand what it means to be a Christian in Latin America today.

What does it mean to be a Christian in Latin America today, and more specifically, in present-day Peru?

One could respond to that question in a variety of ways, of course. But I believe that being a Christian in Latin America today means proclaiming, in action and in word, the message of life—precisely in the face of the reality of the premature and unjust death of so many of this continent's peoples. It implies a firm, Gospel-oriented witness to God's love and, as a concrete expression of that love, a firm commitment to those who are most oppressed and dispossessed.

What does it mean to be a priest in a country as frighteningly violent and unjust as Peru?

I have asked myself that question, as I suspect many others have. I believe it must constantly be reformulated in the face of new realities. I believe that to be a Christian and a priest in Peru today means to reject every violation of the right to life, whatever its source. It also means, as the Peruvian bishops recently said, having the courage to examine the underlying causes of the painful, incredible situation of violence in which we are living. A violence the Latin American bishops gathered at Puebla described as "institutionalized injustice." We must search for the root causes of this violence if we are to eliminate it.

And to be a priest in a country filled with so much violence?

It means not becoming accustomed to seeing the newspapers filled day after day with pictures of mutilated corpses, of mass graves, of innocent people mowed down. It means not getting used to the fact that fellow human beings must search the garbage to find something to eat, that they must trick their stomachs by eating dirt. ... It means maintaining a permanent attitude of shock and rejection in the face of all these indignities. Not to do so would be to compromise one's own human dignity.

Father Gutiérrez, do you fear there will be an official Vatican condemnation of liberation theology? Are the conditions ripe for that? What do you fear will happen?

At no time in the course of the present debate has there been any mention of a condemnation. Furthermore, highly placed, authoritative sources have explicitly rejected the possibility of any sort of condemnation. Cardinal Ratzinger has been very clear about this in his *Instruction on Some Aspects of Liberation Theology*, which he views as one contribution to the dialogue on this delicate topic.

Well then, why all the fuss?

What is taking place is a serious discussion on liberation theology. And as is normal in any discussion, critical points emerge. All together, however, these criticisms will help clarify both the scope and the limitations of this theological reflection on action. And in the long run, above and beyond the give and take of the moment, the present debate will lead the church to a greater and deeper commitment to the people of Peru—especially to the poorest and most outcast.

Criticism centers on the Marxist analysis found in liberation theology. What most bothers people ...

I admit that this is one of the central criticisms. And here I want to respond only for myself and for what I have written, although I think that what I am about to say holds for many other works published in Latin America. It is necessary to be very clear on this point: to deal with the poverty—the inhuman poverty, as Puebla said—lived by the great majority of the inhabitants of our country, and to shed the light of the gospel on it, we must attain the most exact understanding available of the causes of this situation of poverty. It is necessary to make use of whatever tools human thought offers to help us understand our social reality.

You are referring, of course, to the knowledge offered by the social sciences.

Yes. However, we all know that the social sciences are still only in their beginnings, and that their conclusions are still only tentative. Still, they give us a more accurate picture of the social situation, and those of us doing liberation theology make use of them.

How exactly do you use them?

They give us a description and an understanding of poverty. The bishops' conference at Medellín and Puebla used the social sciences to analyze poverty in Latin America. In their documents, for instance, they refer to the dependency theory. We are not speaking here of the use of Marxist analysis.

But the dependency theory is not based on a Marxist analysis.

But the issue is not the use of Marxist analysis. And especially not in what Father Arrupe, former superior general of the Jesuits [in a famous and enlightening letter] called its "exclusive character." In theology, the contemporary social sciences must be used critically, just as any working tool must. Many schools of social thought have influenced theology, and one of them happens to be the social thought of Marx. But one thing is the critical use of the social sciences and another is the adoption of Marxist analysis in its entirety, with all the ideological presuppositions that implies.

What sources does theology use, then?

Theology must go to its own sources, but out of its grounding in faith. It cannot disdain anything that will allow it to more fully understand the situation of those to whom the gospel must be announced. This is a classical point in theology, and I have expressed my views on it on a number of occasions. Let me make a comparison: in contemporary psychology there are many different schools of thought; one of them happens to be that of Freud. We cannot reduce the entire field of psychology to Freud's contribution. And while the Marxist aspect of social analysis used by liberation theology is one of its most striking features, what is important in liberation theology is its treatment of specific theological themes. When treating these themes as such it does not use the social sciences.

Well, Father, there are many people who will call any discussion of the structural causes of poverty "Marxist."

Let us not forget the instances in which the church has legitimately criticized poverty and its structural causes and has been accused of using Marxism. For instance, when Pope Paul VI published his encyclical *On the Progress of Peoples*, the *Wall Street Journal* called it "warmed-over Marxism." The Medellín documents and many other church documents have been criticized in the same way.

Liberation theology is also criticized for what seems to be its exclusive concern about political matters.

That is a point on which I believe I have spoken very clearly. Allow me to say that the first time the term "theology of liberation" was used was in 1971 when my book appeared with that title. I used the term because liberation in Christ is above all liberation from the fundamental root of social injustice: sin. At that time, I clearly stated that liberation cannot be reduced to its socio-political dimensions, no matter how important they are.

What is your response to recent press attacks that accuse liberation theology of fomenting communism and of confusing and dividing Catholics?

Naturally, I respect everyone's convictions. However, I believe it is important to stress the contributions this theological reflection has made to the Peruvian church. But in my own case—and on all this there is very weighty testimony—this theological reflection has been one of the factors (there are doubtless other more important ones) that has encouraged a greater fidelity to the gospel as well as an authentic preferential option for the poor and to the Medellín documents. It has also contributed to a new vitality in the Peruvian church. There are many witnesses to the work of Cardinal Juan Landázuri, who for the last thirty years has lead the Peruvian church with great religious fervor, moderation, and a remarkable sensitivity toward the poor. These witnesses abound, and come from people from very diverse backgrounds. I am not saying that this new vitality in the church is a result of theological reflection. What I am affirming is that liberation theology tries to situate itself within this context of deep fidelity to the church. Liberation theologians are also aware of our limitations and of the new paths we must pursue in order to continue to serve the church.

What is your response to the recently released document from the Sacred Congregation for the Doctrine of the Faith on liberation theology?

Above and beyond all the clamor, I believe it is a very important document, not only because of its source but also for its content. The document declares that the Christian message "is a message of freedom and a force for liberation." It also affirms that aspirations to liberation are a sign of our times that must be analyzed in the light of the gospel. It explicitly states that "the expression 'liberation theology' is a totally valid expression."

And that was never admitted before?

Well, it depends on what level. This is the first time it has been admitted in a document on this level and of this kind. Pope John Paul II did refer to liberation theology in a speech shortly after the bishops' conference in Puebla.

The document refers to certain excesses in liberation theology that lead to confusions in the faith. . . .

I was getting to that. The document contains questions and criticism of what it sees as deviations and excesses. I believe these criticisms are important for a deepening and a clearer formulation of these themes. I believe the document speaks to all of us. At the same time I can say in conscience that the excesses referred to in the *Instruction* are not found in what I have written.

Compared with other liberation theologians, you are considered a moderate. Would you agree?

Well, as they say, comparisons are always odious.

Does the comparison bother you?

Some may consider my contributions to be moderate. Personally, I hope they encourage a greater fidelity to the gospel, to the God of life revealed in Jesus Christ, and in the poor and oppressed of my country. I also believe they are a contribution that flows out of a concrete commitment to bring the gospel to, and stand in solidarity with, those who are denied their most fundamental rights. As the document itself states, "we must start from praxis, if by that we mean our pastoral practice and a social practice inspired by the gospel." Here I believe the document is being very precise; this praxis has been the starting point for all I have been able to contribute to theological reflection in the church at large.

What are you thinking, at this time, when every kind of calumny is being leveled against your work and your motives?

It has been a very intense year, filled with very personal events, discussions on liberation theology, the celebration of my twenty-fifth anniversary as a priest serving in the archdiocese of Lima.

And in the midst of it all, the recent death of your mother. . . .

Yes, helping me, as other events have, to deepen my faith in God and my hope in God who gives us love gratuitously, in communion with the entire church.

Were you ever able to talk with her about all this?

Only with great difficulty, given the state of her health. But there was always a very deep relationship between us. I wouldn't be saying anything new by calling that relationship irreplaceable. From her I learned the importance of simple, gratuitous love and the deep tenderness with which, in spite of everything, we must treat one another as fellow human beings.

Could you tell me, finally, what role she had in influencing your options for the poor?

I think her simple faith made me understand something that I later worked on theologically. That is, that the final basis for an option for the poor is found in the God I believe in. That conviction has led me to live a very deep spiritual experience—one that is not without its sorrow, but that is, in the last analysis, shot through with deep joy—a joy grounded in a firm faith in the Lord's resurrection.

48

Congregation for the Doctrine of the Faith "Notification Sent to Fr. Leonardo Boff regarding Errors in His Book, *Church: Charism and Power*" (March 11, 1985)

This letter from the office of Cardinal Ratzinger is quite critical of Boff's book, especially with regard to its critique of the exercise of power by the church's hierarchy and institutions. In making the letter public, the Congregation also states that the positions of Boff mentioned in the letter "endanger the sound doctrine of the faith" ("Conclusion"). The text here is from Origins, *14 (April 4, 1985), pp. 683–87.*

On February 12, 1982, Leonardo Boff, OFM, took the initiative of sending the Congregation for the Doctrine of the Faith his answer to the archdiocesan commission for the Doctrine of the Faith at Rio de Janeiro, which had criticized his book, *Church: Charism and Power*. He declared that the criticism contained grave errors of reading and of interpretation.

The doctrinal congregation studied the text of the book under its doctrinal and pastoral aspects, and expressed a number of reservations to the author in a letter of May 15, 1984. It invited him to accept them and at the same time offered him the possibility of a dialogue for the sake of clarification. However, considering the influence the book was having on the faithful, the congregation informed L. Boff that the letter would be made public in any case, account being eventually taken of the position he might assume during the dialogue.

On September 7, L. Boff was received by the cardinal-prefect of the Congregation, who was assisted by Msgr. Jorge Mejia (as notary). Included in the conversation were a number of ecclesiological problems, arising from a reading of the book *Church: Charism and Power*, which were pointed out in the letter of May 15, 1984. The conversation was carried on in a fraternal atmosphere and offered the author the opportunity to present his clarifications, which were also conveyed by him in writing. All of that was noted in a final communiqué issued and drawn up in accord with L. Boff. At the end of the talk, the eminent Cardinals Aloisio Lorscheider and Paulo Evaristo Arns, who were in Rome for the occasion, were received by the cardinal-prefect in another place.

According to its practice, the Congregation examined the oral and written clarifications furnished by L. Boff. While it noted the good intentions and repeated testimonies of fidelity to the church and the magisterium he expressed, it stated, however, that the reservations raised in regard to the volume and indicated in the letter could not be considered substantially overcome. It therefore considers it necessary, as was provided, to make the doctrinal content of the aforesaid letter public in its essential parts.

DOCTRINAL PREMISE

The ecclesiology of the book *Church: Charism and Power* is intended to meet the problems of Latin America, particularly Brazil (cf. p. 1), through a series of studies and views. Such an intention demands on the one hand serious and thorough attention to the concrete situations to which the book refers; on the other hand—in order really to achieve its purpose—it requires a concern to enter into the universal church's great task, which is aimed at interpreting, developing, and applying under the guidance of the Holy Spirit the common inheritance of the unique gospel, entrusted once and for all by the Lord to our fidelity.

In such fashion the one single faith in the gospel creates and builds up the Catholic Church over the centuries, and the church remains one throughout the diversities of times and the differences of situations proper to the many particular churches. The universal church develops and lives in the particular churches, and these form a church, while remaining expressions and realizations of the universal church in a determined time and place so that the universal church grows and progresses in the growth and development of the particular churches; whereas the particular church would diminish and decay if unity diminished.

Therefore, true theological reasoning ought never to be content only to interpret and animate the reality of a particular church, but rather should try to penetrate the contents of the sacred deposit of God's word entrusted to the church and authentically interpreted by the magisterium. Praxis and experience always rise out of determined and limited historical situations; they aid the theologian and oblige him to make the gospel accessible in his time. However, praxis neither replaces nor produces the truth, but remains at the service of the truth consigned to us by the Lord. The theologian has therefore to decipher the language of the various situations—the signs of the times—and to open this language up to the understanding of the faith (cf. *Redemptor Hominis*, 19).

When examined in the light of the criteria of an authentic theological method—which has just been briefly outlined—certain options in L. Boff's book appear to be unsustainable. Without claiming to analyze all of them, here are the ecclesiological options which seem decisive: the structure of the church, the concept of dogma, the exercise of sacred power, and the prophetic role.

THE STRUCTURE OF THE CHURCH

L. Boff, according to his own words, sets himself inside an orientation where it is affirmed that "Jesus did not have in mind the church as institution but rather that it evolved after the resurrection, particularly as part of the process of de-eschatologization" (p. 74). Consequently, for him the hierarchy is "a result" of "the powerful need to organize" and the "assuming of societal characteristics" in "the Roman and feudal style" (p. 40). Hence the necessity arises for permanent "change in the church" (p. 64); today a "new church" must arise (p. 62 and passim), which will be "an alternative for the incarnation of new ecclesial institutions whose power will be pure service" (p. 63).

It is in the logic of these affirmations that he also explains his interpretation of the relations between Catholicism and Protestantism: "It would appear that Roman Christianity [Catholicism] is distinguished by its valiant affirmation of sacramental identity while Protestant Christianity has fearlessly affirmed nonidentity" (p. 80; cf. pp. 84ff.).

In this view, both confessions would be incomplete meditations, pertaining to a dialectical process of affirmation and negation. In this dialectic "Christianity is manifested. . . . What is Christianity? We do not know. We only know what is shown in the historical process" (p. 79).

This relativizing concept of the church stands at the basis of the radical criticisms directed at the hierarchic structure of the Catholic Church. In order to justify it, L. Boff appeals to the constitution *Lumen Gentium* (no. 8) of the Second Vatican Council. From the council's famous statement, *Haec ecclesia (sc. unica Christi ecclesia) . . . subsistit in ecclesia Catholica* ("this church [that is, the sole church of Christ] . . . subsists in the Catholic Church"), he derives a thesis which is exactly the contrary to the authentic meaning of the council text, for he affirms: "In fact it (sc. the sole church of Christ) may also be present in other Christian churches" (p. 75). But the council had chosen the word *subsistit*—subsists—exactly in order to make clear that one sole "subsistence" of the true church exists, whereas outside its visible structure only *elementa ecclesiae*—elements of church— exist; these—being elements of the same church—tend and conduct toward the Catholic Church (*Lumen Gentium*, 8). The decree on ecumenism expresses the same doctrine (*Unitatis Redintegratio*, 3–4), and it was restated precisely in the declaration *Mysterium Ecclesiae* (no. 1, AAS, LXV (1973), pp. 396–98).

Turning upside down the meaning of the council text on the church's subsistence lies at the base of L. Boff's ecclesiological relativism, which is outlined above; a profound misunderstanding of the Catholic faith on the church of God in the world is developed and made explicit.

DOGMAS AND REVELATION

The same relativizing logic is found again in the conception of doctrine and dogma expressed by L. Boff. The author criticizes in a very severe way the "doctrinal" understanding of revelation (p. 42). It is true that L. Boff distinguishes between dogmatism and dogma (cf. p. 85), admitting the latter and rejecting the former. However, according to him, dogma in its formulation holds good only "for a specific time and specific circumstances" (p. 76). "In the later stages of the process, the text must be able to give way to a new text of faith proper to today's world" (p. 77).

The relativism resulting from such affirmations becomes explicit when L. Boff speaks of mutually contradictory doctrinal positions contained in the New Testament (cf. p. 77). Consequently, "the truly Catholic attitude" would be "to be fundamentally open to everything without exception" (p. 77). In L. Boff's perspective, the sole authentic Catholic conception of dogma falls under the verdict "dogmatism." "As long as this type of dogmatic and doctrinaire understanding of revelation and salvation continues, there inevitably will be repression of freedom of thought within the church" (p. 42).

In this regard it must be pointed out that the contrary of relativism is not literalism or immobility. The ultimate content of revelation is God — Father, Son, and Holy Spirit — who invites us to communion; all the words refer to the word or — as St. John of the Cross says: "In his Son . . . he told everything to all of us and at one time in that sole word, and he has no more to say" ("Ascent of Mount Carmel," II, 22). But the truth on God and humankind is expressed in a way deserving belief in the always analogical and limited word of Scripture and the authentic belief of the church, based on Scripture. The permanent necessity of interpreting the language of the past, far from sacrificing this truth, renders it accessible and develops the richness of the authentic texts. Walking under the guidance of the Lord, who is the way and the truth (John 14:6), the church, teaching and believing, is sure that the truth expressed in the words of faith not only does not oppress, but liberates, humankind (John 8:32) and is the sole instrument of real communion among persons of various classes and opinions, whereas a dialectical and relativistic conception exposes persons to arbitrary decision-making.

Already in the past this congregation has had to point out that the sense of the dogmatic formulas always remains true and coherent, determined and unalterable, although it may be further clarified and better understood (cf. *Mysterium Ecclesiae*, pp. 403–4).

In order to go on with its function of being the salt of the earth which never loses its savor, the *depositum fidei* (the deposit of faith) must be loyally preserved in its purity, without falling along the line of a dialectical process of history and in the direction of the primacy of praxis.

EXERCISE OF SACRED POWER

A "grave pathology" from which, according to L. Boff, the Roman church ought to liberate itself is constituted by the hegemonic exercise of the sacred power which, besides making the Roman church an asymmetrical society, has also deformed it.

L. Boff takes it for granted that the organizational axis of a society coincides with the specific mode of production proper to it, and he applies this principle to the church. Thus he affirms that there has been a historical process of expropriation of the means of religious production on the part of the clergy and to the detriment of the Christian people; the latter would then have seen itself deprived of its capacity to decide, to teach (cf. pp. 43; 133ff.; 138–43). Moreover, after having suffered this expropriation, the sacred power would also have been gravely deformed, thereby falling into the same defects as profane power in terms of domination, centralization, triumphalism (cf. pp. 72, 56, 60ff.). In order to remedy these unbefitting features, a new model of the church is proposed in which power is conceived without theological privileges, as pure service, articulated according to the community's needs (cf. pp. 161, 63).

One ought not impoverish the reality of the sacraments and the word of God by reducing them to the "production and consumption" pattern, thus reducing the communion of faith to a mere sociological phenomenon. The sacraments are not "symbolic material," their administration is not production, their reception is not consumption. The sacraments are gifts of God, no one "produces" them, all receive the grace of God in them, which are the signs of eternal love. All that lies beyond any production, beyond every human doing and fabrication. The sole measure corresponding to the greatness of the gift is utmost fidelity to the will of the Lord, according to which all — priests and laity — will be judged, all of them being "useless servants" (Luke 17:10). Certainly the danger of abuses always exists. The problem is always present of how access by all the faithful to full participation in the church's life and its sources, the Lord's life, can be guaranteed. But interpreting the reality of the sacraments, of the hierarchy, of the word and the whole life of the church in terms of production and consumption, of monopoly, expropriation, conflict with the hegemonic bloc, rupture and the occasion for an asymmetrical method of production is equivalent to subverting religious reality, and that, far from contributing to a solution of various problems, leads rather to the destruction of the authentic meaning of the sacraments and of the word of faith.

PROPHETIC ROLE IN THE CHURCH

The book *Church: Charism and Power* denounces the church's hierarchy and institutions (cf. pp. 33–34; 57; 154–56). By way of explanation and justification of this attitude, it makes claim to the role of the charisms, particularly of prophecy (cf. pp. 154–56, 162). The hierarchy would have the mere function of "coordinating," of "making way for unity and harmony among the various services," and keeping things flowing and impeding all division and impositions, therefore eliminating from the prophetic function "immediate subordination of the members to those in the hierarchy" (p. 164).

There is no doubt that the whole people of God takes part in the prophetic office of Christ (cf. *Lumen Gentium*, 12). Christ fulfills his prophetic office not only by means of the hierarchy but also by means of the laity (cf. ibid., 35). But it is equally clear that, in order to be legitimate, prophetic denunciation in the church must always remain at the service of the church itself. Not only must it accept the hierarchy and the institutions, but it must also cooperate positively in the consolidation of the church's internal communion; furthermore, the supreme criterion for judging not only its ordinary exercise but also its genuineness pertains to the hierarchy (cf. ibid., 12).

CONCLUSION

In making the above publicly known, the congregation also feels obliged to declare that the options of L. Boff analyzed here endanger the sound doctrine of the faith, which this Congregation has the task of promoting and safeguarding.

The supreme pontiff, John Paul II, in the course of the audience granted to the undersigned prefect, approved the present notification, decided upon in the ordinary meeting of this Congregation, and ordered its publication.

Rome, from the seat of the Congregation of the Doctrine of the Faith, March 11, 1985.

Cardinal Joseph Ratzinger, prefect
Archbishop Albert Bovone, secretary

49

Leonardo Boff
"Defense of His Book,
Church: Charism and Power"
(September 7, 1984)

On September 7, 1984, Leonardo Boff appeared before Cardinal Joseph Rat-
zinger in Vatican City to respond to inquiries that had been made regarding his
book, Church: Charism and Power. *Boff had written a lengthy document in*
defense of his book, and excerpts from it are included here. The text is taken
from the October 4, 1984 issue of Latinamerica Press.

ATTITUDE OF THE THEOLOGIAN

I referred to historical facts and tried to develop my thinking beginning
with them, attempting to discern what might be the meaning behind those
facts. While theology can be criticized, I believe that historical facts cannot
be denied. They are always a challenge to our thinking, and do not allow
us to maintain a smug, triumphalistic attitude when we consider the complex reality that is the church. To admit that the church is *semper refor-*
manda (always in need of reform) is to admit that within the church not
all is correct and in harmony with the gospel. That is why prophecy exists
both inside and outside the church—always on the condition that we admit
that the church is and continues to be holy with the holiness of Christ, with
grace, with the sanctity of its saints and of its divine institutions. A church
that today—through its popes, its many bishops' conferences, its world-
renowned prophets such as Dom Helder Camara and Cardinal Paulo Evaristo Arns—is once again becoming a sign raised up among the nations to
defend the wretched of the earth and to foster the rights of the human
person, especially of the poor. This same church must also bear truthful
witness to its respect for the human person and his or her rights. Just as it
demands that authoritarian states give freedom and participation to its
people, so too must the church itself allow greater participation in those

matters and in pastoral decisions that principally affect the laity. In doing so, the church will become more fraternal, unpretentious, and Gospel-centered. . . .

These criticisms are meant to contribute to the church's pilgrimage, in which I take part and live out my own faith. Certain institutional, doctrinal, and liturgical rigidities hamper the creativity demanded by the church in the face of today's enormous social and pastoral challenges. Theology must address these obstacles and show that they can be overcome within the church by balancing institutional elements (power) with pneumatic ones (charisms). . . .

Ecclesiology is renewed when it confronts new situations such as those we are faced with in Brazil. I have endeavored to carry out this task in a responsible manner. But it is not only the theologian who is involved here: the "prophet" is present, too. Given the gravity of the challenges facing us, the prophet denounces those situations and ways of acting by the church that are less than adequate responses, especially when the cause of the poor is not given the central place assigned to it by the gospel and recent church decisions. And prophetic language, as we shall see later on, does not exhibit the reasonable tone used by a calmer theologian. Prophetic language will always cause discomfort, and thereby provoke misunderstanding and even persecution. Nevertheless, it has its place and its rights within the church, as the [Old Testament] prophets — and Jesus Christ himself — demonstrated. In saying this, I am not trying to defend those occasional excesses I may have committed. However, these should be considered in the context of my daily behavior in trying to contribute positively to the church. . . .

CHALLENGES TO THE CHURCH

The church (in Brazil) has made an explicit preferential option for the poor — against poverty and in favor of social justice. Here the poor cannot be understood as the proletariat defined by Marx, as some would erroneously have us believe. The proletariat is actually quite small in Brazil. What is present is a huge mass of poor and working-class people, a block of social and historical outcasts in the countryside and the cities: the underemployed, the ten million *boias frias* (temporary field hands). In sum, those two-thirds of all Brazilians who live in misery. From among the poor, the church sees with ever greater clarity that society must undergo structural transformation. The church has no concrete political or economic strategy; it simply calls for greater participation by the people in national decision making. It supports those movements that call for greater justice in working conditions and fosters those organizations that struggle for a society that is neither rich nor poor, but is just and fraternal. The church has an undisputed social mission, as Pope John Paul himself stressed when he journeyed to Brazil in 1979. This is far from involving attempts to promote a Marxist-Leninist state or something similar; however, it does involve the fostering of a more democratic society in which all people and not just those social classes that benefit from the present socio-economic system can be makers of their own destiny. . . .

The church in Latin America, and especially that in Brazil, faces a theological challenge of unprecedented historical magnitude. Our continent's races bear witness to great cultures such as those of the Incas, the Mayas, the Aymaras, etc. It is also populated by European immigrants, primitive indigenous peoples, and millions of blacks and mulattos. Brazil, with almost forty million blacks is, after Nigeria, the largest black nation in the world. Very few elements from Afro-Brazilian or Amerindian cultures have been incorporated into Christianity. Blacks are in the process of developing an immensely rich cultural and religious vitality. They want to be Christians within their own cultural milieu, one that will allow their own experiences and worldview to be present. There is now the possibility of the gospel being incarnated in a way that will permit a new model of Latin-Afro-Indigenous Catholicism to be born.

This is why I insist that the charismatic element in the church must be present; and on the positive value of a syncretism that is not vulgar (as most people think) but that is an organic assimilation into the Christian identity of elements of cultures not yet integrated. . . .

PARTICIPATION OF THE PEOPLE

In the last thirty years, the church (in Brazil) has endeavored to become more and more open to the people's participation. The two key words "communion" and "participation" were proposed and lived out here before they were taken up by the Latin American bishops at Puebla: communion with God and participation in the life of the church. As a result of this twofold emphasis, some 150,000 Christian base communities (CEBs) have been formed (according to statistics recently released by the Rio-based Institute for Socio-Economic Analysis), thousands of biblical reflection circles have sprung up, and many other small groups composed of Christians who want to live a life of shared faith have come into existence. In these groups, it is the people themselves who take responsibility for the key tasks of evangelization through newly evolving forms of ministry—always in communion with their pastors. We are seeing a marvelous convergence between these communities, which want their priests and bishops to be present with them, and the priests and the bishops who encourage and support the CEBs.

Until now, thanks to God, we have not had any major conflicts between these two expressions of the ecclesiality of the one church. The communion that exists between the hierarchy and the people safeguards this one church against division. There is no confrontation between the hierarchy and the laity; nor has there been any attempt to establish a parallel power-block outside the bond of communion and participation. . . .

This option for the poor has led our bishops to return to a simple way of living, gospel-centered and closer to the struggles of the people. That option has inspired our religious to leave their center houses and move into marginated slum areas. Theology is no longer simply an academic discipline to be engaged in by seminarians; it has become a tool for enlightenment and critical understanding used by the CEBs to reflect on their journey together as a Christian community.

The frequent accusation that some schools of theology use Marxist analysis must be understood as a challenge to the legitimacy and ecclesiality of this theology. These detractors try to link this theological reflection to elements unacceptable to the faith, such as class struggle and a reduction of the Christian message to its political dimension. The real problem is not the use of Marxist analysis to decipher the mechanisms that generate poverty; it is resistance to the transformation of society so that the people can have more life. Those who seek this transformation are defamed as Marxists or as perverters of the Christian faith. What these critics do not want is the freedom of the people, progress toward more worthy forms of social organization, and social and political participation.

50

Harvey Cox
"Oneness and Diversity"
(1988)

This is an excerpt from Harvey Cox's recent book, The Silencing of Leonardo Boff: The Vatican and the Future of World Christianity *(Oak Park, Ill.: Meyer Stone Books, 1988), pp. 178-88. He begins the book on May 9, 1985, when Boff received official notice from the Vatican that he was to begin a period of "obedient silence" for an unspecified period of time. He was told to use the time for "serious reflection" and to refrain from continuing to work as editor of Brazil's foremost theological periodical,* Revista Eclesiástica Brasileira. *He was also told to cease such activities as writing and lecturing. The excerpt constitutes the end of the book, where Cox provides some very interesting theological reflections on the practice of "silencing" in the modern church.*

ONENESS AND DIVERSITY

The riddle of the one and the many antedates the birth of Christianity by many centuries. But, since the church's earliest years, it has been a major preoccupation of theologians as well. The world is so obviously many. It is peopled by many tongues and nations, many classes and conditions, many philosophies and faiths. Yet Christians confess that God is one and that the church is, or should be, one. But this is exactly what troubles the conscientious critics of liberation theology most: they are genuinely fearful that it threatens the church's unity. They are afraid its partisan stance could tear the flesh of the body of Christ.

It would be idle to belittle their apprehensiveness as totally unfounded. To many observers, the rift that has appeared during the Boff case reveals all the elements of a major schism, such as the ones that devastated the visible unity of the church when Constantinople separated from Rome in 1054, or when the Protestant Reformation erupted in the sixteenth century. Once again, today—as then—geography, theology, politics, and personality clashes all seem to be conspiring to drive a divisive wedge into the visible body of the church.

But there are also significant differences between today's situation and the previous schisms. Unlike the earlier instances, both sides in this present conflict accept — at least in principle — the role of the bishops and the pope in maintaining the church's unity. The patriarch of the Orthodox Church once excommunicated the bishop of Rome. Martin Luther publicly burned the papal bull that excommunicated him. But nothing of the kind is going on today. When Pope John Paul II's prefect silenced Leonardo Boff, the friar accepted the silencing and said he preferred to "walk with his church." When Gutiérrez and Sobrino and Boff defend their theologies today, they do so by insisting their ideas are "ecclesial," that they have worked them out in cooperation with the bishops and in service to them. The liberation theologians sometimes differ with the pope, but they accept the principle of papal authority. There seems to be little likelihood that the kind of division that rent the church on those previous occasions will occur again.

But will the visible unity that the church manages to maintain through all the tumult of dissent and diversity, political division and liturgical innovation, be anything more than a facade? If Christian base communities led by lay people, including unordained women, continue to multiply at their current rate, how will bishops actually exercise any real authority over them? If the Vatican is reluctant to excommunicate anyone today, but its public warnings and disciplining of theologians succeed only in getting their ideas a wider hearing, what does that mean for the church's unity? If, as Ratzinger claims, the problem is that old-fashioned styles of heresy have been replaced by heterodox forms of inculturation that strenuously claim to be orthodox, where will it all lead?

The worst possible scenario says that the Catholic Church is headed for even more retrenchment and repression, that we have seen only the beginning of a massive attempt at controlling dissent and consolidating hierarchical control, that the worst is yet to come. According to this grim script, lifting the silencing of Leonardo Boff was merely a temporary respite that will be followed by increasingly draconian measures. Unfortunately, the continued attacks on Boff and the warnings of more punishments to come lend some plausibility to this worst-case scenario. But need it be so?

It might be helpful to sketch out a few ground rules that could help facilitate a genuine rather than a spurious unity, while at the same time encouraging the necessary debate to follow its course.

1. First, all parties should recognize that the argument has gone on for a long time, in one form or another, since before they were born, so it is unlikely it will be settled in the foreseeable future. This recognition almost automatically carries with it the implication that a certain amount of forbearance and patience will be required. It also suggests that various forms of censorship and silencing are inappropriate and should be avoided. The history of Christianity is too replete with the stories of the various Joans of Arc, who were burned in one century, only to be canonized in a later one. The French theologians censored by Pius XII became the heroes of

the council fifteen years later. The theological faculty of the University of Paris once burned the books of Thomas Aquinas, and, as we have noted, Cardinal Ratzinger's view that the church is a post-Resurrection phenomenon might well have been condemned by a previous prefect of his own congregation in Rome eighty-five years ago.

Stifling honest debate is morally wrong and counterproductive. If depriving dissidents of their right to speak and publish is evil in the U.S.S.R., it is also wrong in the church. Nor does an involuntary silencing become more acceptable when it is described by those who impose it as an expression of spiritual discipline for the good of the person silenced, as it was in Leonardo Boff's case. Liberation theologians are not averse to silence. Gustavo Gutiérrez has written that one's first response to the presence of God should always be awe, silence, and contemplation. The second should be loving action toward one's neighbor. At best theology comes in third. There can be little doubt that theologians should sometimes choose to be silent, but prefects should not make that decision for them.

2. On the other hand, theologians who decide to explore new avenues of thought and redefinitions of doctrine should not, at the same time, expect to receive the unqualified sanction and endorsement of the hierarchy for everything they write. Father Charles Curran, the American Catholic moral theologian who has run into serious trouble with Rome for taking issue with what he thinks is a mistaken or ill-conceived teaching by the pope or the bishops, has set a good example. He carefully distinguishes in his writing what is the teaching of the church — as interpreted by the pope — and what he thinks it should be. Of course, he also tries to argue for his own view, but when he does so, though he insists his freedom be respected, he does not expect to be recognized by church authorities to be an official interpreter of the standing teaching.

It is obvious to everyone, including the prefect of the Congregation for the Doctrine of the Faith, that the teaching authorities of the Catholic Church have been mistaken more than once in the past, and that they have eventually conceded their mistake, sometimes in response to the criticism of theologians and others who openly differed with them. Thus, Father Curran does not pretend that his ideas about artificial contraception, for example, are completely in line with the most recent authoritative statement on this issue in *Humanae Vitae*, so he carefully distinguishes his own position from the encyclical's when he presents it. This is only fair. But it also suggests that his competence as a teacher should not be judged on the basis of whether he *holds* a particular view but on whether he presents it fairly and accurately. This is hardly asking for too much.

3. The more difficult case comes, as Cardinal Ratzinger points out, when theologians claim they, and not the pope or the prefect, are presenting the *true* teaching of the church. Some of this problem could be avoided if all parties in the argument gave up the claim to be stating some final, unamendable interpretation, and admitted that all theology, whether of friars

or of prefects or of anyone else, is a matter of approximation, of trying to define a reality that ultimately eludes final definition. Still, even if this degree of modesty is reached, what is needed in a dispute is a careful and bona fide *attempt* by all parties concerned to decide at least what the nature of the disagreement is, and not a silencing. In such a dispute, it is always important, especially for prefects, to maintain with great care the canons of due process and fair procedure. When all else fails, there is nothing wrong with a prefect publicly announcing that a given theologian's teachings are not in conformity with Rome. But this should always be done with respect and dignity. As Boff points out, if higher authorities treat dissenters in the church callously or shabbily, it makes the church's efforts to combat such demeaning practices in the secular world look silly and hypocritical. But this is not the most important reason to respect human rights within the church, for even if their denial had no negative impact on the outside world, violations would be an intrinsic breach of Christian ethics.

4. Perhaps the friars of this age could improve the situation by recognizing that the church will probably always need some prefects. Even St. Francis himself sought the endorsement of the pope (and got it). Leonardo Boff seems to agree with this proposition when he writes, in *Church: Charism and Power*, that there is a charism of leadership, and that the church needs both spirit and structure. Other liberation theologians accept this idea as well, though some more willingly than others. The friars need to give up the fantasy they sometimes indulge in of a church without prefects. Such a thing will never happen this side of the reign of heaven. Even religious institutions, being human, need governance. The question is not how to get rid of prefects but how to keep them honest. Maybe the friars will be able to recognize this more easily when they admit that they themselves have more power *vis-à-vis* the prefects than they admit. At some level the prefects, including the cardinal-prefect of the Congregation for the Doctrine of the Faith, already know this. On their best days they realize full well that dissent and discussion are signs not of sclerosis but of vitality. They know they need the Leonardo Boffs and base communities, or they would eventually have nothing over which to preside as prefects. Religion always requires both spirit and structure. When the friars also recognize how much the prefects need them, they may be able to allow them to exercise the leadership charism Boff says they have, but also to keep them humble while they do it.

5. As for Cardinal Ratzinger and his supporters, the day is not far off when they will have to concede that the basic biblical and theological premises of liberation theology are correct. The church's mission must trace itself back to Jesus himself, or his resurrection means nothing. The prefectural theologians who still make the hours between the crucifixion and Easter Sunday an impassable gap instead of an unbreakable link between Israel and the church are fighting an uphill battle against a growing mass of theological consensus and biblical scholarship. They have taken the

wrong path, and they cannot go on much longer denying the accumulating historical evidence, carefully pieced together by many Catholic as well as Protestant scholars. This evidence says that between the Palestinian rabbi, the risen Christ, and the early church there is far more continuity than hiatus. Nor can they continue to deny that historical evidence has any theological bearing on our understanding of Jesus and the early church, for to do so is to veer perilously close to what was once called Docetism, the heresy that denied the earthly flesh-and-blood reality of Christ's incarnation. Once the prefects make this admission, then the whole debate about liberation theology, which is now stalled because its critics do not consider the "historical Jesus" a relevant datum, will enter a new phase. This does not mean the Latin Americans and their allies will then win all the arguments, but that a serious debate about who Jesus really was and what he means for us today can begin at last.

If both sides in the current dispute could agree to something like these ground rules, then I believe the much-needed argument could proceed. But the question would still remain: How should the participants conduct the argument?

This is where, in my view, the whole theological world has the most to learn from the liberation theologians. They have developed an enormously promising method: "theology as reflection on praxis." This means they do not do their work in the serene atmosphere of arguments with other theologians alone, but in the bruising back-and-forth between acting in the world and careful reflection on that action. This is why liberation theologians are so insistent that their critics do more than read what they have written—which is like overhearing one side of a telephone call—but that they become aware of the actual situation in which they live and work, what they often call "social reality." In their usage, "social reality" means what actual people think and do to shape their political and cultural worlds. It also includes the religious ideas and values that shape the way people see and act. For Latin Americans, theology has a double link with this "reality." First, it *arises* out of reality, pondering and analyzing it in the light of faith. But it has a second link, too. It also *guides* the attempt to shape it. Then the cycle begins again. Action shapes thought and thought informs action. Theology becomes not just a dispute about ideas but a resource for real people on how to see themselves and their world, therefore also on what to do. Theology guides action. Action refocuses theology. This continuous process of acting, reflecting, then acting again—all in the light of faith—*is* "liberation theology."

Once one understands this modus operandi, the liberation theologians' claim that their method is not particular to Latin America becomes more believable, and so does their strong belief in the positive function of dissent. Dissent is not deviation but an integral part of the process. This also explains why liberation theologians sometimes find holding prolonged discussions with their theological critics over the marks of the church (or anything else) so frustrating. The arguments race past each other, because most conventional theologians, including those who teach at seminaries and those who staff the Sacred Congregation for the Doctrine of the Faith, proceed something like *theoretical* physicists. They work with full confidence that, given sufficient time, differences can be resolved at the level of conceptual exchange. Cardinal Ratzinger himself is a particularly good example of this ideational approach to religious and theological dissensus. Or, he also believes, when all else fails, one must resort to various modes of discipline. On the other hand, liberation theologians work in the manner of *experimental* physicists. If there is a difference of opinion, they are inclined to invite a colleague into the laboratory to observe what happens when the procedure is tried out. Here the laboratory is the Christian community itself as it lives in "the social reality," and the procedure is "praxis," the continuous sequence of action and reflection.

In recent years, liberation theologians have suffered unnecessarily. They have had to endure not only the warnings and silencings meted out by short-sighted prefects but also stinging reprimands even from their friends. They have been scolded because — it is said — they are divisive and not sufficiently committed to dialogue, and they should be in closer communication with the worldwide church and the international theological guild. Maybe one positive outcome of the Boff case is that it makes clear why the Latin Americans feel so misrepresented by this critique. They do not oppose dialogue. They welcome it. They are strong advocates of a truly global church and an authentically catholic Christianity. But they insist it must be made up of distinct communities, critically conscious of their own particularity and speaking to each other with that awareness. They are suspicious of the claims of European or Roman theology to be *the* one universal, catholic theology to which all others must adapt. They have never denied the church's apostolicity. They believe that the people they serve are living apostolically, and the number of Latin American Christians who have suffered martyr's deaths, as the first apostles did, provides some substantiation to their claim.

What kind of "oneness" in the church might the approach liberationists represent eventually lead to? Probably never again to the attempt to devise a single, all-encompassing theological formula — however minimal — to which everyone everywhere must subscribe. Rather, it could lead to the culturally and theologically pluralistic church Karl Rahner once foresaw, united not from the past or from the top, but by its hope for that which is yet to be. The Latin Americans believe they have grounds for hope, since signs and portents of just such a church are already appearing on their own continent. It is a church, which though weak and vulnerable by worldly standards, is nonetheless moving toward apostolicity, catholicity, holiness, and unity. It finds the oneness in its stumbling attempt to follow the poor Christ into the depths of diverse cultures in order to demonstrate the beloved community only God makes possible.

It seems that Karl Rahner, too, toward the end of his life, imagined a church bound together more by this venturesome love than by dictums and dogmas. Maybe that is why one of his last acts was to send a warm letter of support for Gustavo Gutiérrez, who was then under attack by Rome. In any case, writing in his *Theological Investigations*, Rahner said in 1974 that he hoped one day, there will "no longer be any one single and universal basic formula of the Christian faith applicable to the whole church." If that day comes, and is welcomed by both the prefects and the friars, by the pope and the Congregation for the Doctrine of the Faith, then the Catholic Church will have taken a decisive step toward an authenticity that now seems so elusive. And if it does, all the nations of the world—and all the other churches—will be greatly blessed.

The trial of Leonardo Boff is not yet over, nor is the trial of liberation theology. When will we learn that within the church we have had quite enough trials? What is beginning now is the trial of the church itself. That trial will test whether the church can in fact "become the people," and whether Christianity, for so many centuries a largely Western and "northern" faith, can live in and speak to the tribes and nations of the whole world. This will require a good deal of venturesome theology. Obviously, some of that theology will be true and faithful, and some will not. What we will need, therefore, is not indictments and censures but patience, humility, and a genuinely open debate. But a debate does not have accusers and defendants. It has partners and protagonists who respect and listen to each other. In a debate no one tries to silence anyone else. Both sides expect to learn from the clash and resolution of ideas. Boff and his fellow liberation theologians know as well as anyone that they are not always right, nor their opponents always wrong. What they ask is not for agreement, but for the opportunity to contribute to the conversation, to speak and to listen.

SILENCING AND COMMUNITY

Indeed, as the conversation continues, it will no doubt become clear that liberation theology, like every other theology, has no final answers. Human life and history being what they are, the time will come when new voices with concerns we cannot now foresee and perspectives we can scarcely imagine will arise in the household of faith and seek to be heard. But whether the church as a whole will hear and respond to such voices tomorrow depends in considerable measure on whether it learns to heed the cries of the voiceless today. This is why someone's right to be heard within the Christian community is not just a procedural question or a matter of fair play. It has to do with the very nature of the religious community itself.

Leonardo Boff is not the only Christian to be silenced. There have been many before him. And it may be well to remember that the first silencing to occur in the church, and in some ways the primal one, was that of women. The "original silencing" made an impact in some ways analogous to that of original sin: it has stained everything since. Why and how did it happen? It is incontestable that women played critical leadership roles in the early Christian church. Priscilla, for example, seems to have been at least the equal of her husband Aquila in the work they did together as teachers (Acts 18:2, 18, 26; 1 Cor. 16:9; Rom. 16:3). The Apostle Paul taught that women could lead worship and that the sexes were equal before God. In some ways the early Christian movement appears to have been a bold experiment in egalitarian inclusiveness. But as the church began to adjust itself to its environing culture, something changed. In the generation that followed Paul, the male leaders surrendered to the pressure they felt to deprive women of the role they had once played (1 Tim. 2:11-12). Most scholars now explain the notorious passage in Paul's 1 Corinthians (14:33-35) in which women are admonished to remain silent in the churches—a blatant contradiction of what he says elsewhere—as an insertion that was placed there during the less venturesome generation that followed him.

Whether this was the case or not, the result of this "original silencing," which antedated Leonardo Boff's by nineteen hundred years, was not just to deprive half of the church's members of their full humanity, a wounding that would be serious enough in its own right. It also set an ugly precedent, and it fundamentally distorted the entire structure of Christian worship and teaching. Insofar as it was actually enforced, it deprived the community's prayer and hymnody of the symbols that could be brought to it only from the lives of women. It impoverished its ethical life and its diaconal service by assigning less weight to those particular forms of pain that women, as the bearers of children and the objects of patriarchal power, bring to expression. It thinned out the celebration, not just for women, but for everyone, by preventing the unique joys and ecstasies women feel from being shared by all.

The deformation that resulted from the silencing of women is that the whole body was crippled and its capacity to hear anything or anybody seriously attenuated. One cannot tune out some without at the same time tuning out others. By muting the sisters, the early church inflicted on itself a form of deafness that has persisted ever since. Women were the first to be silenced, and in many respects that archetypal silencing continues today. But women were not alone. Once silencing found its way into the company of the faithful, there were others whose songs and stories were also stifled. Women share this disallowance of speech, of saying one's word, with many, many others. Their enforced quiet is also the lot of millions of the world's poor, and of those who are rejected or excluded for a variety of other reasons from full participation in the human family. This is probably why women everywhere have responded with enthusiasm to those theologies that take as their starting point the perspective of the voiceless, a preferential option for the silenced.

In the biblical tradition, God is known as the Holy One who speaks to human beings and who expects them to answer. Therefore, to silence someone, it could be said, is a type of blasphemy. It denies that person the opportunity to respond to God's call, and it therefore denies God. To silence is to fashion a kind of idol, a false God who calls everyone but who does not expect everyone to answer, or who expects some to answer for others. The Christian church, however, understands itself to be a community that is constituted by the word which God spoke to it in the life of Jesus and to which a response *must* be given. This is why the practice of silencing and excluding stands in opposition to the spirit that is needed if the church is to become an inclusive world church.

Bishop Casaldáliga said it with elegance when, in the poem he wrote at the time of the silencing, he reminded Leonardo that by becoming silent for awhile, he would partake of the condition in which those who have no voice — either in the church or in the world — live all the time. But the hope to which the church gives voice — or should — is that this unnatural silence will not last forever, that by God's grace the mouths of the mute will be unstopped, and one day all will sing the Lord's song together.

51

Communio (*Latin American Edition*)
"Declaration of Los Andes"
(July 1985)

I have already referred to the statement of support for liberation theologians by the editorial board of the international publication Concilium *(no. 47). This conference in Los Andes, Chile, was sponsored by* Communio, *an international journal which is more conservative than* Concilium *and included bishops and Cardinal Alfonso López Trujillo in the list of participants. The Spanish text of the declaration is from* CELAM: Consejo Episcopal Latinoamericano, *24 (October-November 1985), pp. 5–9. The translation from Spanish to English is my own.*

1. We the undersigned are Christian pastors and laity with training in philosophy, theology, and the social sciences. On July 24 to 28, 1985, we convened in the city of Los Andes at the foot of the Andes mountains in Chile, under the sponsorship of the Latin American edition of *Communio,* which has its office in Santiago. Our purpose was to investigate the response which the so-called theologies of liberation have made to the serious challenge to the Christian conscience created by the misery and marginalization of vast numbers of the people of Latin America.

2. The participants in this international seminar have come from a wide variety of countries and also of experiences, activities, and publications. The common denominator which unites us, which led to our meeting, and which dominated our lengthy meetings is essentially the following: complete fidelity to the gospel, as it is professed by the church's magisterium, by the social teaching of the church, and by the content of the Instruction *Libertatis Nuntius* ["Instruction on Certain Aspects of the 'Theologies of Liberation' "]. In the light of these teachings, we have worked intensively during the workshop, aware of the concerns of our communities and especially of their poorest members.

3. The study of this Instruction, when compared with the theological works which its own authors have called and still call the "theology of

liberation," have led once again to this conclusion. Even if different movements are included under this title, nevertheless the positions described in parts VI to X of the Instruction are not hypothetical constructs, but real pronouncements contained in numerous books, essays, and articles that circulate throughout Latin America, as has been documented in the presentations given at this seminar.

4. The theology of liberation, as the authors just mentioned understand it, claims to be a "new way of doing theology" from the perspective of "the oppressed" and takes a certain interpretation of liberating praxis as its source and as the ultimate criterion of theological truth. This requires an essentially political reading of the word of God, which ends up interpreting the whole of Christian existence, faith, and theology in a political key. This radical politicization is aggravated by the uncritical use of a rationalist biblical hermeneutic, which ignores the basic exegetical criteria of tradition and of the magisterium.

5. We are convinced that the fundamental defect of the theology of liberation is rooted in its very understanding of theological method, that is, in what *Libertatis Nuntius* calls its "determining hermeneutical principle" (X,2), as noted above. We accept fully the two criteria for an authentic theological method indicated by the Congregation of the Doctrine of the Faith in its Notification of March 11, 1985, concerning a book by one of the liberation theologians [Leonardo Boff; see no. 48].

(a) The primacy of our common heritage. The theologian makes use of "the common heritage of the unique gospel, entrusted once and for all by the Lord to our fidelity." The theologian's primary concern must be this common heritage, which he or she must receive, interpret, develop, and apply to different historical circumstances. The particular churches are churches precisely to the extent that they are an expression and actualization of the universal church in a definite time and place. Authentic theological discourse can never imprison itself in the confines of a particular church.

(b) In no case can praxis be the first or foundational act of theological reflection. Praxis and experience always arise from a definite and concrete historical situation. Experiences like this can help theologians adapt their interpretation of Scripture to their own time. But prior to praxis is the truth the divine master has entrusted to us. "Praxis neither replaces nor produces the truth, but remains at the service of the truth consigned to us by the Lord." Faith is not born from praxis; rather it orients and illuminates praxis. It is superior to praxis and precedes it ontologically. This is truly the first act of theology.

6. If the above is valid for any type of praxis, it becomes much more problematic in the concrete case of certain theologies of liberation, since their "liberating praxis" acquires a meaning that is clearly derived from Marxism. Thus we cannot ignore some key aspects of the liberationist phenomenon which, as the Instruction notes in its introduction, become "dam-

aging to the faith and to Christian living," because they "use, in an insufficiently critical manner, concepts borrowed from various currents of Marxist thought." Thus we can see the powerful influence it has had on these theologies and the uncritical manner in which it has been incorporated into their theologico-social discourse. Whatever its subjective intentions were, this theoretical influence tends to betray the true option for the poor in Latin America and eventually becomes a fundamental danger for the faith of the people of God.

7. Theology can and should make use of the social sciences. However, on the one hand it cannot accept the subordination of theological discourse to the discourse of any positive science. On the other hand, it cannot concede scientific validity to the Marxist analysis of society or to the dialectical interpretation of history, since their ideological character is evident. Finally, it must be denied that the Christian people in the name of some science are forced to work in a single socio-political movement, since this ignores their right to legitimate pluralism in temporal matters, where Christian faith does not require only one solution. These three types of confusion are present in the very point of departure of the theologies of liberation mentioned in the preceding paragraph.

8. We are in complete agreement with interpretations of the capital importance of the exodus event and of the preaching of the prophets in the Old Testament. This is also true of the preaching of Jesus himself in the Gospels, which clearly reveal his liberating power and his urgent call for profound changes that are not only individual but historical and social. However, violence is committed against the word of God when it is interpreted in an arbitrary manner, reading it with exegetical criteria that are based on rationalism or on a perspective that is essentially political and even based on class. Such interpretations distort the principal events of salvation history and place them outside the bounds of its genuine ethical and religious point of view.

9. Jesus Christ is presented as the "subversive from Nazareth," who entered into and deliberately committed himself to the "class struggle" of his time. His life and liberating death are seen as simply that of a martyr for the people, who was crushed by the ruling Judeo-Roman establishment. This is undoubtedly an attempt to manifest the historical, social, and even political dimension of the life of Jesus. It is certain that the Lord did move within the social context of his own time and place. The portrait, however, of a "historical Jesus" who died for the poor classes and against the rich ones is not drawn from the New Testament but rather from an a priori dialectic of conflict, which is profoundly at odds with the faith of the church on fundamental issues. For one thing, the mystery of the incarnate word and of the divine nature of Christ is, if not openly denied, at least so obscured and distorted that in this interpretation the church can no longer recognize its own faith as it was defined in the early councils. Furthermore, the sacrificial and salvific dimension of the Lord's death is dissolved in

favor of a political interpretation of his crucifixion, thus bringing into question the salvific meaning of the entire economy of redemption. The profound mystery of the passion and death of Jesus and the unfathomable depths of the love of God the Father revealed therein are thus obscured, as are the radical meaning of sin and the dignity proper to human beings as objects of this boundless divine love.

It is only in the light of these mysteries as proclaimed by the faith of the church that we understand the full meaning of the redemption—namely, that Christ liberated us fundamentally from the radical slavery of sin, and by virtue of this his liberation should extend itself effectively in the effort to remove economic, social, and political forms of slavery, which are derived from sin. Thus the definitive liberation of the kingdom of heaven is both announced and anticipated.

10. As regards the church and without ignoring the love for the poor that can be found in some liberation theologians, we must regretfully assert that in the portrait of the "popular church" presented by these theologies we are unable to recognize the face of the true church of Christ. In fact, it is distorted by the dialectical confrontation between a church supposedly composed of the people and the hierarchical and sacramental church, which is rejected beforehand. At times, the latter church is even attacked by a comprehensive critique that accuses it of being bourgeois-capitalistic and an ally of oppression. In communion with this one, unique church and its present and past history, we declare that there have been moments of crisis and periods of darkness. Always inspired, however, by the Holy Spirit, it has tried to be faithful to the will of its Lord and to the commitment to service that should characterize a community of his disciples, a commitment manifested in numerous acts of love for the poor and the suffering.

11. The expression, "preferential option for the poor," promulgated by the episcopal conferences at Medellín and Puebla (1979), constitutes a privileged landmark that is authentically evangelical. The evangelization of the poor is a messianic sign which looks to liberation from all the sufferings and enslavements of human existence. But this statement has on occasion been interpreted in a unilateral way, which distorts its biblical meaning. Poverty is reduced to its material aspect and even more is interpreted by means of a sociology of conflict. The poor are thus identified with the proletariat and are viewed through the lens of class struggle, which involves inevitable partisanship. The result is a kind of theological reflection and ecclesial preaching centered almost exclusively on socio-economic questions, at times bitterly self-seeking and even more frequently overlooking or forgetting essential dimensions of faith and basic features of human experience. We have observed the uneasiness of many persons who feel abandoned and ignored in their aspirations and religious needs because of a mistaken interpretation of the option for the poor. We have also noted how reductionist approaches to preaching create a religious vacuum which is often filled by religious sects.

12. The presentation of truth as identical with praxis, and the practical equivalence of Christian salvation and socio-political liberation, presuppose a historic monism (cf. Instruction, IX, 3). This is derived from a reductionist anthropology and totalitarian politics, the latter becoming ever more dangerous when it is sacralized. Christian faith reveals the divine vocation of humankind and consequently the profound meaning of history and the whole human condition. Church preaching, therefore, should help to judge every action with reference to God and to inspire action which has an effective impact upon history. At the same time, however, it is necessary to emphasize that human existence is not reducible to its political dimensions, nor does it have its principal axis in the political sphere but in relationship with God. This must be proclaimed with complete clarity, for on it are based the defense of the transcendent vocation of the human person as well as the affirmation of his or her liberty.

13. In our discussion, we have tried to be faithful to the truth, with a desire to prevent any ideologizing of the faith and particularly of the love for the poorest. We are opposed to every economic, social, cultural, or political activity that attacks human aspirations for liberty and justice (Instruction, I and III). We believe it is essential to affirm the latter completely, avoiding every interpretation that tends to pervert rather than implement them. We are certain that the "serious ideological deviations," which the Instruction of the Holy See denounces in some theologians of liberation, "tend inevitably to betray the cause of the poor" (Instruction, Introduction). In communion with the church's hierarchy, we believe that authentic liberation is based on "the truth about Jesus the savior, the truth about the church, and the truth about humankind and its dignity" (Instruction, XI, 5), and that this liberation must be understood in a context that is at the same time perennial, dynamic, and capable of renewing the teaching of the church, especially its social teaching.

14. Some liberation theologians affirm that the social teaching of the church is not an instrument capable of overcoming the poverty and suffering of Latin America; rather, the only instrument capable of doing this is the Marxist analysis of history. On the contrary, we state that the social teaching offers principles capable of effective guidance in the task of building a society based on justice and solidarity. An adequate solution to the present problems of Latin America will not be achieved by simplistic declarations based on Marxist ideology, but rather by vigorous action based on careful analyses of the multiple causes of the poverty of so many individuals and families. These analyses can be fruitful if they are illumined by the Christian concept of the human person, which is the ultimate foundation of a just social order, and if they are guided by the criteria, truths, and experiences contained in that enormously rich and always renewable body of doctrine that is the social teaching of the church. Of particular importance are ethical studies on work, on the relations of production, and on the distribution of goods and services to all members of the community.

15. Every genuine theology must incorporate this joyous and tremendous truth: what is at stake in our historical existence is eternal life, inasmuch as the total and definitive liberation of the human person will only take place in the consummation of the kingdom in heaven and in the vision of God face to face, to which all of us are summoned. This truth, far from legitimating the act of oppression, is actually its most profound condemnation, as is clear in the case of the rich man and Lazarus. And far from causing an evasion of temporal responsibilities, it is the most tremendous historical liberation from the economic, social, political, and cultural enslavements of our peoples. For it is only in this truth that the supreme dignity of the human person shines forth, that person created in the image of God and summoned to sonship with God; it is this alone that grounds the ethical imperative that never allows the human person to be considered a mere object at the mercy of powerful interests or any kind of ideology.

16. A genuine liberation theology supposes the reconciliation of the human person with God, with himself or herself, with others and with the entire creation, as this is taught in the Apostolic Exhortation *Reconciliatio et Poenitentia* and in the related teachings of the councils and popes. It is there that we find a clear teaching regarding the contents and the values of liberation from the slaveries which have their deepest root in sin, and of liberation as the fulfillment of the human person in the definitive encounter with God. It is there, moreover, that we are reminded that there is no true liberation without reconciliation or any true reconciliation without a longing for liberation. In this spirit we wish to encourage dialogue at the service of unity in the church.

We, the participants in this seminar, echoing the final drafts of *Libertatis Nuntius,* invite all Christians to respond to the challenge God issues in the dramatic context of Latin America today with the generosity which the following of Christ demands and the hope which derives from the certainty of the action of the Spirit and of the maternal protection of Mary.

Signers of the Declaration of the Andes:

Señor Humberto Belli
R.P. Estevenao Betancourt, O.S.B.
R.P. Cottier, O.P.
R.P. Bruno Dessi, O.M.D.
Pbro. Danilo Eterovic
R.P. François Francou, S.J.
Señor Joaquin García-Huidobro
Señor Alfredo Garland
Pbro. José Miguel Ibañez Langlois
Pbro. José Luis Illanes
Exmo. Mons. Boaventura Kloppenburg, O.F.M.
R.P. Fintan Lawless

Exmo. Card. Alfonso López Trujillo
Señor Carlos Martínez F.
Exmo. Mons. Jorge Medina E.
Pbro. Antonio Moreno
Señor Ernesto Moreno B.
Señor Fernández Moreno V.
Señor Juan Oses
R.P. Anton Rauscher, S.J.
Señor Miguel Salazar
Señor Miguel Angel Salgado
Señor Gonzalo Sánchez G.H.
Exmo. Mons. Fernando Vargas, S.J.

52

Ronaldo Muñoz
"An Open Letter to
Cardinal Alfonso López Trujillo"
(July 31, 1985)

Ronaldo Muñoz is a Chilean priest who divides his time between theology and pastoral work among the poor. He has published numerous books and articles on theological and pastoral themes. This letter is a response to the declaration of Los Andes (no. 51); Muñoz clearly identifies its views with those of Cardinal López Trujillo. The letter was translated by the Iglesias Press Service *and published in* LADOC, *16 (November-December 1985), pp. 40–43, which is the text used here.*

Dear Alfonso:

Twenty years ago, the Second Vatican Council reminded all of us that "the church stands forth as a sign of that brotherliness which allows honest dialogue and invigorates it. Such a mission requires in the first place that we foster within the church itself mutual esteem, reverence, and harmony, through the full recognition of lawful diversity. Thus all those who compose the one people of God, both pastors and the general faithful, can engage in dialogue with ever-abounding fruitfulness" (*Gaudium et Spes,* no. 92).

In the light of these words of the council—which to me seem urgently topical today—I wish to communicate publicly my surprise and sorrow at the "Declaration of Los Andes," signed by yourself and a group of friends in Chile, and widely published here by the mass media.

In that declaration you repeat the grave accusations of corruption of the Christian faith which you have been attributing to the theology of liberation for many years. Now you repeat those accusations as a "confirmation" for Latin America (and Chile) of the grave errors described in the "Instruction" of the Vatican's Sacred Congregation "On Certain Aspects of the 'Theology of Liberation.'"

Some of those errors, really "ruinous for the Christian faith and practice," are the following:

(a) That "a certain interpretation of the liberating praxis" would be the "supreme source and criterion of theological truth" (4).

(b) That the Bible would be read "from an exegesis based on criterion of a rationalist kind and with basically political, when not classist, eyes" (8).

(c) That there would be a denial of faith in "the mystery of the incarnate word and in the divine nature of Christ," while questioning "the salvific significance of the whole plan of redemption" (9).

(d) "The dialectical conflict between a supposed peoples' church and the hierarchical and sacramental church" (10).

(e) The identification of the poor "with the proletariat as seen from the optic of the class struggle" (11).

(f) "An anthropological reductionism and a political totalitarianism . . . held as sacred" (12).

Faced with such accusations, made with such publicity, I feel it necessary to express publicly and clearly certain points:

1) You present those errors, which in the Vatican "Instruction" seem to take into account different shades of meaning and are attributed to "certain currents of opinion," with no shades of meaning and attribute them globally to Latin American "theologies of liberation."

2) Such an accusation constitutes a grave affront to many Christians. It is like saying that all of us who may ascribe to a "theology of liberation" don't share in the Christian faith or in the communion of the church, but rather are "Marxist wolves" with the "sheep's clothing" of a pseudo theology. That we are perverting or dispersing Christ's flock.

3) You irresponsibly attribute such a radical corruption of the Christian faith to "the theologies of liberation," without stating precisely what authors you are talking about or what in their writings or teachings you are basing your argument on. Thus you make any reply very difficult, and spread a mantle of suspicion on all Latin American theologians who are trying to serve the gospel from closer to the oppressed majorities.

4) You have acted thus while knowing that the three most well-known and read "liberation theologians" among us — G. Gutiérrez, L. Boff, and J. Sobrino — have all had their works most carefully examined by their bishops and by the Vatican, and without finding in them the grave deviations you keep repeating.

5) The public "condemnation," as if we were Marxists who "use" the language and ministry of the faith, leaves us more exposed to the attacks of the dominant groups in our society and constitutes — in countries like Chile — a virtual incitement to repression, even criminal repression.

6) That you elaborated and published that Declaration in Chile, while pretending to theological and even magisterial authority, that you did it behind the backs of our bishops and with a press and television coverage which they don't always enjoy, constitutes a disavowal of the authority of our pastors and a motive for discord among the Christian people of our

country. Our bishops, in fact, opportunely expressed their opinion on the matter, and now the spokesman of the bishops' conference has had to express his surprise at the "Declaration of Los Andes," explaining that it is just another contribution by a group of theologians and reiterating that the grave errors described in the "Instruction" don't exist among us.

7) My sorrow and fraternal protest at such accusations—which without judging intentions, I consider objectively calumnious—don't come so much from any worry about my own credibility as a theologian of the church who could be considered among the "liberation theologians," as much as from the discredit that such accusations bring to ample sectors of the Christian people, whose "sense of faith" sees itself reflected in, and in fact draws its strength from, the ministry of our Latin American theology so closely bound to the life and testimony of the poor.

My fraternal and respectful greetings,

Ronaldo Muñoz

PART VI

HOPES AND CONCERNS
FOR THE FUTURE
(1986–   )

This final part obviously covers the shortest time frame of all the periods discussed in this book. I would stress, however, that it also contains the two most important official church documents published thus far concerning the theology of liberation: the "Instruction on Christian Freedom and Liberation" (see no. 53 below) and Pope John Paul II's encyclical letter "On Social Concerns" (see excerpts in no. 57 below). While not on the same level of official teaching, the pope's letter to the Brazilian bishops (no. 54) was also quite significant.

It must be emphasized that the teaching of these documents from the highest level of church authority provides a major source of hope for the future of liberation theology. More will be said about this in the discussion of the documents themselves, but here I would like to point to an even more significant fact. It has gone largely unnoticed that all the significant themes stressed by various liberation theologians have over the past two decades been gradually incorporated into the social teaching of the Catholic Church, without necessarily referring to the movement by name. Consequently, this is an even stronger basis for hope for the future of liberation theology, for it is difficult to imagine that a corpus of teaching so firmly entrenched and so carefully developed could be ignored or even suddenly reversed. The documents treated in this book, then, are only a part of a much larger edifice of social thought that applies directly to the universal church as well as to each and every local church, with its network of varied communities. I have expressed the rationale for this universality as lucidly as I can in an article below (no. 55).

Granted the significance of the instruction and the encyclical for the moment, there is yet an equally important conclusion to be drawn from them that extends beyond the documents themselves and flows from the

455

very nature of liberation theology. A remarkably lucid liberation theologian, Clodovis Boff, understands this far better than I, for he spends half of each academic year working in the jungles of western Brazil. Boff places great emphasis on the fact that *before* any liberation theology existed "there were the prophetic bishop, the committed lay person, and liberation communities." The theology came later as a second moment, as the *expression* of this liberation practice. Boff's conclusion is momentous both for the understanding of the church and for the definition of liberation theology: "Liberation theology is the *theology of a liberation church*—a church with a preferential option for solidarity with the poor"[1] (Boff's italics).

Some of the Brazilian's further remarks on this issue are well worth quoting at length:

> It is crucial to grasp liberation theology in its locus. Theologians of liberation must be read not in the ivory towers of certain departments of theology (to borrow an image from Pope John Paul II), but in the slums, in the miserable neighborhoods of the destitute, in the factories, on the plantations—wherever an oppressed people live, suffer, struggle, and die.
>
> To pretend to "discuss liberation theology" *without seeing the poor* is to miss the whole point, for one fails to see the central problem of the theology being discussed. For the core and kernel of liberation theology is not theology but liberation.[2]

To sum up, we have now in the two documents of the magisterium of the church an officially endorsed *theory* regarding the importance of liberation theology for the whole church. But there also exists a *practice* of liberation, which has deep roots among the people through the basic ecclesial communities. Since this is rooted in the Bible and stresses a profound personal and social conversion and active involvement at the service of others, a true process of evangelization has been taking place, which gives great promise for the future. Since they have learned the meaning of the good news, these church members are eager to spread this to other communities and to other sectors of the church. The whole process also appears to be relatively independent of pronouncements from higher levels.

Moving to other issues in this final part, I envision in the future developments that are only seeds at present, but give promise of one day becoming giant trees within the liberation movement. One of these comprises the voices and theological reflection of women, which at present are only a trickle (as in nos. 43 and 56 in this volume), but one day will surely become a torrent. In the days to come, when persons use the expression "option for the poor," they will be fully aware that the majority and the poorest of the poor in this world are women and that of all the oppressed people throughout the world the most oppressed are women.

Most of the women in the world, moreover, and the overwhelming majority of the poorest women, are not white but women of color. This question of race appears to me at present to be an even smaller seed than that of the women's movement on the horizon of the consciousness of liberation theology. But in this area, too, I foresee a great expansion of understanding regarding the enormous oppressive force of racist animosity in the world.

One dramatic example of this occurred recently with the publication of a new edition of Gustavo Gutiérrez's *A Theology of Liberation* to mark the fifteenth anniversary of the English translation of the book. This edition also includes a new introduction containing the author's reflections on the development of liberation theology during those years. After noting that many Latin Americans in recent years place an almost exclusive emphasis on the social and economic aspects of poverty, Gutiérrez replies with these two remarkable paragraphs:

> One of our social lies has been the claim that there is no racism in Latin America. There may indeed be no racist laws as in some other countries, but there are very rigid racial customs that are no less serious for being hidden. The marginalization of Amerindian and black populations, and the contempt in which they are held, are situations we cannot accept as human beings, much less as Christians. These populations themselves are becoming increasingly aware of their situations and are beginning to claim their most basic rights; this new attitude carries the promise of fruitful results.
>
> The racial question represents a major challenge to the Christian community, and one to which we are only now beginning to respond. The approaching five hundredth anniversary of the evangelization of America should be the occasion for an examination of conscience regarding the immense human cost historically connected with that evangelization — I mean the destruction of individuals and of cultures. Such an examination will help us define a commitment of the church to races that have for centuries been neglected and mistreated. The bold efforts of Bartolomé de Las Casas and so many others past and present are there to point a way we must follow in accordance with our own historical situation.[3]

Another positive harbinger for the future may be discerned from what I have been doing at the end of these chapters — that is, giving references to the development in each of the stages to theological works that combine scholarship and profound reflection with a very acute social conscience. Perhaps the best example of this at the present time is *Theology and Liberation*, a series of fifty-some volumes that takes up a liberation perspective on many of the most critical issues in contemporary theology. Soon after these are published in Spanish and Portuguese, the volumes are translated into English and the modern European languages, thus ensuring a worldwide diffusion. The high caliber of these works makes them ideal for use in seminary and university courses, thus producing, along with the huge bibliography of works already published, a truly long-range influence on the pastoral activists and theologians who will be the leaders of the church of the future.

From this brief reflection, it should be clear that I am relatively optimistic about the future of liberation theology. That does not signify, however, that there are no storm clouds on the horizon or no urgent "concerns," as stated in the title of this Part.

A major concern, obviously, lies in the fact that the gross disparity in the possession of the goods of the earth between developed nations and the underdeveloped nations has grown significantly larger during the two decades since the Medellín Conference in 1968, as economies throughout Latin America continue to falter. A startling example of this is the almost Kafkaesque situation of inflation (at times over 1,000 percent per year), so that persons are forced to engage in a frantic race each day to spend or invest their money before it loses value. Even more grotesque is the newest version of dependency or domination — that is, the crushing burden of external debt. Here the poor nations are doomed to a Sisyphean future, where each year they have to spend very large portions of their national wealth on the interest payments alone of their debt, while the capital of the debt itself remains inexorably in place.

Other important aspects of this economic decline include the fact that the diagnosis and cure for the diseased economy is prescribed by the ones who primarily caused the disease — that is, the governments, financial institutions, and banks of the West. And this remedy almost always includes strict demands for "austerity," that is, an increase in prices of basic food, goods, and services, a prescription that obviously increases the already intolerable suffering of the poor. Protest in any fashion against this situation leads not to change but to severe repression, as of 1990 still including the scourges of "death squads" and *desaparecidos,* atrocities that continue to occur even in the nations that have followed the trend toward at least formal democracy.

Again as of 1990, the world crisis in Marxist communism, including the Gorbachev revolution and the turn to *glasnost* (openness) and *perestroika* (restructuring), Russian terms that amount to a condemnation of the entire Soviet political and economic system, has removed any doubt: this form of centralized state capitalism provides no salvation for the poor nations. The one "model" of Latin American communism that was often held up as a paradigm for the future, Cuba, has evolved into an economy based on a new form of dependency (with subsidies of $5 billion a year from the Soviet Union) and into a political system dominated in autocratic style by Fidel Castro.

One could say that the one bright spot in this dreary portrait is provided by the churches, who often continue to point clearly at the beast of oppression, while calling for profound changes and aiding the people through conscientization to construct the basic framework for grassroots political organizing and action for social change. If we turn, however, to the inner life of the church itself, asking if it practices what it preaches, a number of phenomena have occurred in recent years that cause serious concerns.

Thus, one wonders whether the investigations of Gustavo Gutiérrez, Leonardo Boff, and Bishop Pedro Casaldáliga were intended as a signal and a warning that this could also happen to other liberation theologians — and to liberation bishops. If this is so, we are confronted today with the highly ironic situation that the Catholic Church, which considers itself to be a "community of freedom" and a "zone of truth," is instituting the silencing of some of its members, while the Kremlin, the bastion of totalitarianism, is issuing clarion calls for *glasnost* — that is, a drive for greater openness and freedom of speech among its citizens.

Certainly more troublesome for the long run, moreover, is the question of certain tendencies in the appointment of bishops during the past decade. Unlike the usual practice of consultation with the local churches and a balancing of appointments between liberal and conservative bishops, so that the local churches could establish a prudent equilibrium, the emphasis has been overwhelmingly on the appointment of conservative prelates, often despite the clear and urgent desire of local hierarchies and people. This is abundantly clear in Brazil, for instance (see no. 58 below), and a similar pattern is obvious to even the most casual observer in the United States, especially in all the major sees. It is important, also, to stress that this kind of appointment has often resulted in Latin America in the cancellation of apostolates among the poor or the dismantling of structures that were instituted to aid or to defend the poor.

A clear indication that this has become a worldwide problem may be seen in the recent protest of distinguished German theologians in what has come to be called "the Cologne Declaration." They first protest that "the Roman Curia is energetically filling episcopal sees around the world without respecting the suggestions of the local churches and neglecting their established rights." With reference to the recent episcopal appointment in Cologne, they consider the procedure "scandalous" and state rather bluntly that "this exercise of domination as expressed in recent episcopal appointments is opposed to the fraternity of the gospel, to the positive experiences of freedom and openness, and episcopal collegiality."[4]

In concluding this final chapter of the book, I was reminded of an idiom that occurs often in Spanish and seems to express our present situation very accurately. We live, I believe, in a time of *luces y sombras,* a time of lights and shadows. We certainly do not know which part, the bright or the dark, of this chiaroscuro will predominate in the years ahead. But I make my own Pascalian wager that the future will be decided according to the answers given to the following questions: (1) What is the correct meaning of authentic human liberation? And (2) What are the most efficacious means of bringing about this authentic human liberation in this decade and in the coming twenty-first century? On the answers to those questions hinges the future of humanity—and the future of the church.

NOTES

1. Clodovis and Leonardo Boff, *Liberation Theology: From Dialogue to Confrontation* (San Francisco: Harper and Row, 1986), p. 9.

2. Ibid., pp. 10–11.

3. Gustavo Gutiérrez, *A Theology of Liberation* (15th anniversary ed., Maryknoll, N.Y.: Orbis Books, 1988), p. xxii.

4. "The Cologne Declaration," *The Tablet* (London), Feb. 4, 1989, pp. 140–42. The declaration was signed by 163 German theologians.

53

Congregation for the Doctrine of the Faith "Instruction on Christian Freedom and Liberation" (March 22, 1986)

The first Vatican instruction on liberation theology, of 1984, had focused on certain "dangers," while promising to take up the constructive task of an authentic Christian approach to freedom and liberation in a future document. The second document did not appear for nearly two years. There was a common opinion that this document was much better organized and balanced in its viewpoint on freedom and liberation than the first instruction. My own views are given in a subsequent article (no. 55). The English text of the Instruction is taken from Origins, *15 (April 17, 1986), pp. 115–28.*

INTRODUCTION

1. Awareness of human freedom and dignity, together with the affirmation of the inalienable rights of individuals and peoples, is one of the major characteristics of our time. But freedom demands conditions of an economic, social, political, and cultural kind, which make possible its full exercise. A clear perception of the obstacles that hinder its development and offend human dignity is at the source of the powerful aspirations to liberation at work in our world.

The church of Christ makes these aspirations its own, while exercising discernment in the light of the gospel, which is by its very nature a message of freedom and liberation. Indeed, on both the theoretical and practical levels, these aspirations sometimes assume expressions that are not always in conformity with the truth concerning humankind as it is manifested in the light of creation and redemption. For this reason the Congregation for the Doctrine of the Faith has considered it necessary to draw attention to "deviations, or risks of deviation, damaging to the faith and to Christian

461

living."[1] Far from being outmoded, these warnings appear ever more timely and relevant.

2. The instruction *Libertatis Nuntius*, on certain aspects of the theology of liberation, stated the intention of the Congregation to publish a second document, which would highlight the main elements of Christian doctrine on freedom and liberation. The present instruction responds to that intention. Between the two documents there exists an organic relationship. They are to be read in the light of each other.

With regard to their theme, which is at the heart of the gospel message, the church's magisterium has expressed itself on many occasions.[2] The present document limits itself to indicating its principal theoretical and practical aspects. As regards applications to different local situations, it is for the local churches, in communion with one another and with the see of Peter, to make direct provision for them.[3]

The theme of freedom and liberation has an obvious ecumenical dimension. It belongs in fact to the traditional patrimony of the churches and ecclesial communities. Thus the present document can assist the testimony and action of all Christ's disciples, called to respond to the great challenges of our times.

3. The words of Jesus, "the truth will make you free" (John 8:32), must enlighten and guide all theological reflection and all pastoral decisions in this area.

The truth, which comes from God, has its center in Jesus Christ, the savior of the world.[4] From him, who is "the way, and the truth, and the life" (John 14:6), the church receives all that it has to offer to humankind. Through the mystery of the incarnate word and redeemer of the world, it possesses the truth regarding the Father and his love for us, and also the truth concerning humanity and its freedom.

Through his cross and resurrection, Christ has brought about our redemption, which is liberation in the strongest sense of the word, for it has freed us from the most radical evil—namely, sin and the power of death. When the church, taught by its Lord, raises to the Father its prayer "deliver us from evil," it asks that the mystery of salvation may act with power in our daily lives. The church knows that the redeeming cross is truly the source of light and life and the center of history. The charity that burns in it impels it to proclaim the Good News and to distribute its life-giving fruits through the sacraments. It is from Christ the redeemer that its thought and action originate when, as it contemplates the tragedies affecting the world, it reflects on the meaning of liberation and true freedom, and on the paths leading to them.

Truth, beginning with the truth about redemption, which is at the heart of the mystery of faith, is thus the root and the rule of freedom, the foundation and the measure of all liberating action.

4. Human moral conscience is under an obligation to be open to the

fullness of truth; it must seek it out and readily accept it when it is presented.

According to the command of Christ the Lord,[5] the truth of the gospel must be presented to all persons, and they have a right to have it presented to them. Its proclamation, in the power of the Spirit, includes full respect for the freedom of each individual and the exclusion of every form of constraint or pressure.[6]

The Holy Spirit guides the church and the disciples of Jesus Christ "into the full truth" (John 16:13). The Spirit directs the course of the centuries and "renews the face of the earth" (Ps. 104:30). It is the Spirit who is present in the maturing of a more respectful awareness of the dignity of the human person.[7] The Holy Spirit is at the root of courage, boldness, and heroism: "Where the Spirit of the Lord is, there is freedom" (2 Cor. 3:17).

CHAPTER 1: THE STATE OF FREEDOM IN THE WORLD TODAY

I. Achievements and Dangers of the Modern Liberation Process

5. By revealing to humankind its condition as free persons called to enter into communion with God, the gospel of Jesus Christ has evoked an awareness of the hitherto unsuspected depths of human freedom.

Thus the quest for freedom and the aspiration to liberation, which are among the principal signs of the times in the modern world, have their first source in the Christian heritage. This remains true even in places where they assume erroneous forms and even oppose the Christian view of humankind and its destiny. Without this reference to the gospel, the history of the recent centuries in the West cannot be understood.

6. Thus it is that from the dawn of modern times at the Renaissance it was thought that by a return to antiquity in philosophy and through the natural sciences humankind would be able to gain freedom of thought and action, thanks to a knowledge and control of the laws of nature.

Luther, for his part, basing himself on his reading of St. Paul, sought to renew the struggle for freedom from the yoke of the law, which he saw as represented by the church of his time.

But it was above all in the age of the Enlightenment and at the French Revolution that the call to freedom rang out with full force. Since that time, many have regarded future history as an irresistible process of liberation inevitably leading to an age in which humankind, totally free at last, will enjoy happiness on this earth.

7. Within the perspective of such an ideology of progress, humankind sought to become master of nature. The servitude which it had experienced up to that point was based on ignorance and prejudice. By wresting from nature its secrets, humanity would subject it to its own service. The conquest of freedom thus constituted the goal pursued through the development of science and technology. The efforts expended have led to remarkable successes. While humanity is not immune from natural disasters, many natural

dangers have been removed. A growing number of individuals are ensured adequate nourishment. New means of transport and trade facilitate the exchange of food resources, raw materials, labor, and technical skills, so that a life of dignity with freedom from poverty can be reasonably envisaged for humankind.

8. The modern liberation movement had set itself a political and social objective. It was to put an end to the domination of humankind by humankind and to promote the equality and fellowship of all. It cannot be denied that in this sphere, too, positive results have been obtained. Legal slavery and bondage have been abolished. The right of all to share in the benefits of culture has made significant progress. In many countries the law recognizes the equality of men and women, the participation of all citizens in political life, and equal rights for all. Racism is rejected as contrary to law and justice. The formulation of human rights implies a clearer awareness of the dignity of all human beings. By comparison with previous systems of domination, the advances of freedom and equality in many societies are undeniable.

9. Finally and above all, the modern liberation movement was supposed to bring humankind inner freedom in the form of freedom of thought and freedom of decision. It sought to free humanity from superstition and atavistic fears, regarded as so many obstacles to development. It proposed to give humanity the courage and boldness to use reason without being held back by fear before the frontiers of the unknown. Thus, notably in the historical and human sciences, there developed a new notion of humankind, professedly to help gain a better self-understanding in matters concerning personal growth and the fundamental conditions for the formation of the community.

10. With regard to the conquest of nature, or social and political life, or human self-mastery on both the individual and collective level, anyone can see that the progress achieved is far from fulfilling the original ambitions. It is also obvious that new dangers, new forms of servitude, and new terrors have arisen at the very time that the modern liberation movement was spreading. This is a sign that serious ambiguities concerning the very meaning of freedom have from the very beginning plagued this movement from within.

11. So it is that the more humankind was freed from the dangers of nature, the more it experienced a growing fear confronting it. As technology gains an even greater control of nature, it threatens to destroy the very foundations of our future in such a way that mankind living today becomes the enemy of the generations to come. By using blind power to subjugate the forces of nature, are we not on the way to destroying the freedom of the men and women of tomorrow? What forces can protect humankind from the slavery of its own domination? A wholly new capacity for freedom and liberation, demanding an entirely renewed process of liberation, becomes necessary.

12. The liberating force of scientific knowledge is objectively expressed in the great achievements of technology. Whoever possesses technology has power over the earth and humanity. As a result of this, hitherto unknown forms of inequality have arisen between those who possess knowledge and those who are simple users of technology. The new technological power is linked to economic power and leads to a concentration of it. Thus, within nations and between nations, relationships of dependence have grown up which within the last twenty years have been the occasion for a new claim to liberation. How can the power of technology be prevented from becoming a power of oppression over human groups or entire peoples?

13. In the field of social and political achievements, one of the fundamental ambiguities of the affirmation of freedom in the age of the Enlightenment had to do with the concept of the subject of this freedom as an individual who is fully self-sufficient and whose finality is the satisfaction of personal interests in the enjoyment of earthly goods. The individualistic ideology inspired by this concept of humankind favored the unequal distribution of wealth at the beginning of the industrial era to the point that workers found themselves excluded from access to the essential goods they had helped to produce and to which they had a right. Hence the birth of powerful liberation movements from the poverty caused by industrialization.

Certain Christians, both lay persons and pastors, have not failed to fight for a just recognition of the legitimate rights of workers. On many occasions the magisterium of the church has raised its voice in support of this cause.

But more often than not the just demands of the worker movement have led to new forms of servitude, being inspired by concepts that ignored the transcendental vocation of the human person and attributed to humankind a purely earthly destiny. These demands have sometimes been directed toward collectivist goals, which have then given rise to injustices just as grave as the ones they were meant to eliminate.

14. Thus it is that our age has seen the birth of totalitarian systems and forms of tyranny that would not have been possible in the time before the technological leap forward. On the one hand, technical expertise has been applied to acts of genocide. On the other, various minorities try to hold in thrall whole nations by the practice of terrorism. Today control can penetrate into the innermost life of individuals, and even the forms of dependence created by early-warning systems can represent potential threats of oppression.

A false liberation from the constraints of society is sought in recourse to drugs, which have led many young people from all over the world to the point of self-destruction and brought whole families to sorrow and anguish.

15. The recognition of a juridical order as a guarantee of relationships within the great family of peoples is growing weaker and weaker. When confidence in the law no longer seems to offer sufficient protection, security and peace are sought in mutual threats, which become a danger for all

humanity. The forces that ought to serve the development of freedom serve instead the increase of threats. The weapons of death drawn up against each other today are capable of destroying all human life on earth.

16. New relationships of inequality and oppression have been established between the nations endowed with power and those without it. The pursuit of one's own interest seems to be the rule for international relations, without the common good of humanity being taken into consideration.

The internal balance of the poor nations is upset by the importation of arms, which introduces among them a divisive element leading to the domination of one group over another. What powers could eliminate systematic recourse to arms and restore authority to law?

17. It is in the context of the inequality of power relationships that there have appeared movements for the emancipation of young nations, generally the poor ones, until recently subjected to colonial domination. But too often peoples are frustrated in their hard-won independence by unscrupulous regimes or tyrannies which scoff at human rights with impunity. The peoples thus reduced to powerlessness merely have a change of masters.

It remains true that one of the major phenomena of our time, of continental proportions, is the awakening of the consciousness of persons who, bent beneath the weight of age-old poverty, aspire to a life in dignity and justice, and are prepared to fight for their freedom.

18. With reference to the modern liberation movement within humankind itself, it has to be stated that the effort to free thought and will from their limits has led some to consider that morality as such constitutes an irrational limit. It is for humankind, now resolved to become its own master, to go beyond it. For many more, it is God who is the specific alienation of humankind. There is said to be a radical incompatibility between the affirmation of God and of human freedom. By rejecting belief in God, they say, humankind will become truly free.

19. Here is the root of the tragedies accompanying the modern history of freedom. Why does this history, in spite of great achievements which also remain always fragile, experience frequent relapses into alienation and see the appearance of new forms of slavery? Why do liberation movements which had roused great hopes result in regimes for which the citizens' freedom,[8] beginning with the first of these freedoms, which is religious freedom,[9] become the major enemy?

When humankind wishes to free itself from moral law and become independent of God, far from gaining such freedom, it destroys it. Escaping the measuring rod of truth, it falls prey to the arbitrary; fraternal relations between persons are abolished and give place to terror, hatred, and fear.

Because it has become contaminated by deadly errors about the human condition and human freedom, the deeply rooted modern liberation movement remains ambiguous. It is laden both with promises of true freedom and threats of deadly forms of bondage.

II. Freedom in the Experience of the People of God

20. It is because of its awareness of this deadly ambiguity that through its magisterium the church has raised its voice over the centuries to warn against aberrations that could easily bring enthusiasm for liberation to bitter disillusionment. The church has often been misunderstood in so doing. With the passage of time, however, it is possible to do greater justice to the church's point of view.

It is in the name of the truth about humankind, created in the image of God, that the church has intervened.[10] Yet it is accused of thereby setting itself up as an obstacle on the path to liberation. Its hierarchical constitution is said to be opposed to equality, its magisterium to be opposed to freedom of thought. It is true that there have been errors of judgment and serious omissions for which Christians have been responsible in the course of centuries,[11] but these objections disregard the true nature of things. The diversity of charisms in the people of God, which are charisms of service, is not opposed to the equal dignity of persons and to their common vocation to holiness.

Freedom of thought, as a necessary condition for seeking the truth in all the fields of human knowledge, does not mean that human reason must cease to function in the light of the revelation which Christ entrusted to this church. By opening itself to divine truth, created reason experiences a blossoming and a perfection that are an eminent form of freedom. Moreover, the Second Vatican Council has recognized fully the legitimate autonomy of the sciences,[12] as well as of activities of a political nature.[13]

21. One of the principal errors that has seriously burdened the process of liberation since the age of the Enlightenment comes from the widely held conviction that it is the progress achieved in the fields of the sciences, technology, and economics that should serve as a basis for achieving freedom. This was a misunderstanding of the depths of freedom and its needs.

The reality of the depth of freedom has always been known to the church, above all through the lives of a multitude of the faithful, especially among the little ones and the poor. In their faith, these latter know that they are the object of God's infinite love. Each of them can say: "I live by faith in the Son of God, who loved me and gave himself for me" (Gal. 2:20). Such is the dignity which none of the powerful can take away from them; such is the liberating joy present in them. They know that to them too are addressed Jesus' words: "No longer do I call you servants, for the servant does not know what his master is doing; but I have called you friends, for all that I have heard from my Father I have made known to you" (John 2:20, 27). They are also aware of sharing in the highest knowledge to which humanity is called.[14] They know that they are loved by God, the same as all other persons and more than all other persons. They thus live in the freedom which flows from truth and love.

22. The same sense of faith, possessed by the people of God in its hope-filled devotion to the cross of Jesus, perceives the power contained in the

mystery of Christ the redeemer. Therefore, far from despising or wishing to suppress the forms of popular piety this devotion assumes, one should take and deepen all its meaning and implications.[15] Here we have a fact of fundamental theological and pastoral significance: it is the poor, the object of God's special love, who understand best, and as it were instinctively, that the most radical liberation, which is liberation from sin and death, is the liberation accomplished by the death and resurrection of Christ.

23. The power of this liberation penetrates and profoundly transforms humanity and its history in its present reality and animates its eschatological yearning. The first and fundamental meaning of liberation that thus manifests itself is the salvific: humankind is freed from the radical bondage of evil and sin.

In this experience of salvation, humankind discovers the true meaning of this freedom, since liberation is the restoration of freedom. It is also education in freedom — that is to say, education in the right use of freedom. Thus to the salvific dimension of liberation is linked its ethical dimension.

24. To different degrees, the sense of faith, which is at the origin of a radical experience of liberation and freedom, has imbued the culture and the customs of Christian peoples.

But today, because of the formidable challenges that humanity must face, it is in a wholly new way that it has become necessary and urgent that the love of God and freedom in truth and justice should mark relations between individuals and peoples, and animate the life of cultures.

For where truth and love are missing, the process of liberation results in the death of a freedom which will have lost all support.

A new phase in the history of freedom is opening before us. The liberating capacities of science, technology, work, economics, and political activity will produce results only if they find their inspiration and measure in the truth and love which are stronger than suffering: the truth and love revealed by Jesus Christ.

CHAPTER 2: THE HUMAN VOCATION TO FREEDOM AND THE TRAGEDY OF SIN

I. Preliminary Approaches to Freedom

25. The spontaneous response to the question, What does being free mean, is this: Persons are free when they are able to do whatever they wish without being hindered by an exterior constraint and thus enjoy complete independence. The opposite of freedom would therefore be the dependence of one will upon the will of another.

But do persons always know what they want? Can they do everything they want? Is closing in on oneself and cutting oneself off from the will of others in conformity with human nature? Often the desire of a particular moment is not what a person really wants. And in one and the same person there can exist contradictory wishes. But above all, one comes up against the limits of human nature: one's desires are greater than one's abilities. Thus the obstacles that oppose one's will do not always come from outside, but from the limits of one's own being. That is why, under pain of self-destruction, one must learn to harmonize one's will with one's nature.

26. Furthermore, every individual is oriented toward others and needs their company. It is only by learning to unite one's will to the others for the sake of true good that one will learn rectitude of will. It is thus harmony with the exigencies of human nature which makes the will itself human. This in fact requires the criterion of truth and a right relationship to the will of others. Truth and justice are therefore the measure of true freedom. By discarding this foundation and taking oneself for God, one falls into deception, and instead of realizing oneself, destroys oneself.

Far from being achieved in total self-sufficiency and an absence of relationships, freedom truly exists only where reciprocal bonds, governed by truth and justice, link persons to one another. But for such bonds to be possible, each person must live in the truth.

Freedom is not the liberty to do anything whatsoever. It is the freedom to do good, and in this alone happiness is to be found. The good is thus the goal of freedom. In consequence, humans become free to the extent that they come to a knowledge of the truth, and to the extent that this truth—and not any other forces—guides their will. Liberation for the sake of a knowledge of the truth that alone directs the will is the necessary condition for a freedom worthy of the name.

II. Freedom and Liberation

27. In other words freedom, which is interior mastery of one's own acts and self-determination, immediately entails a relationship with the ethical order. It finds its true meaning in the choice of moral good. It then manifests itself as emancipation from moral evil.

By free action, humans must tend toward the supreme good through lesser goods which conform to the exigencies of their nature and their divine vocation.

In exercising freedom, they decide for themselves and form themselves. In this sense they are their own cause. But they are this only as a creature and as God's image. This is the truth of their being, which shows by contrast how profoundly erroneous are the theories which think they exalt human freedom or "historical praxis" by making this freedom the absolute principle of being and becoming. These theories are expressions of atheism or tend toward atheism by their own logic. Indifferentism and deliberate agnosticism go in the same direction. It is the image of God in the human person which underlies the freedom and dignity of the human person.[16]

28. By creating humankind free, God imprinted on it the divine image and likeness.[17] Humankind hears the call of its creator in the inclination and aspiration of its own nature toward the good and still more in the word of revelation, which was proclaimed in a perfect manner in the Christ. It

is thus revealed to humankind that God created it free so that by grace we could enter into friendship with God and share the divine life.

29. Humankind does not take its origin from its own individual or collective action, but from the gift of God, the creator. This is the first confession of our faith, and it confirms the loftiest insights of human thought.

Human freedom is a shared freedom. Its capacity for self-realization is in no way suppressed by its dependence on God. It is precisely the characteristic of atheism to believe in an irreducible opposition between the causality of a divine freedom and that of human freedom, as though the affirmation of God meant the negation of humankind or as though God's intervention in history rendered vain the endeavors of humankind. In reality, it is from God and in relationship with God that human freedom takes its meaning and consistency.

30. Human history unfolds on the basis of the nature it has received from God and in the free accomplishment of the purpose toward which the inclinations of this nature and of divine grace orient and direct it.

But human freedom is finite and fallible. Its desire may be drawn to an apparent good: in choosing a false good, it fails in its vocation to freedom. By free will, humans are master of their own life: they can act in a positive or a destructive sense.

By obeying the divine law inscribed in their conscience and received as an impulse of the Holy Spirit, human beings exercise true mastery over themselves and thus realize their royal vocation as children of God. "By the service of God one reigns."[18] Authentic freedom is the "service of justice," while the choice of disobedience and evil is the "slavery of sin."[19]

31. This notion of freedom clarifies the scope of temporal liberation: it involves all the processes which aim at securing and guaranteeing the conditions needed for the exercise of an authentic human freedom.

Thus it is not liberation which in itself produces human freedom. Common sense, confirmed by Christian sense, knows that even when freedom is subject to forms of conditioning it is not thereby completely destroyed. Persons who undergo terrible constraints succeed in manifesting their freedom and taking steps to secure their own liberation. A process of achieved liberation can only create better conditions for the effective exercise of freedom. Indeed a liberation which does not take into account the personal freedom of those who fight for it is condemned in advance to defeat.

III. Freedom and Human Society

32. God did not create humans as "solitary beings" but wished them to be "social beings."[20] Social life therefore is not something exterior: one can grow and realize one's vocation only in relation with others. We belong to different communities: the family and professional and political communities. It is inside these communities that we must exercise responsible freedom. A just social order offers us irreplaceable assistance in realizing our free personality. On the other hand, an unjust social order is a threat

and an obstacle which can compromise our destiny.

In the social sphere, freedom is expressed and realized in actions, structures, and institutions, thanks to which people communicate with one another and organize their common life. The blossoming of a free personality, which for every individual is a duty and a right, must be helped, not hindered, by society.

Here we have an exigency of a moral nature, which has found its expression in the formulation of human rights. Some of these have as their object what are usually called "the freedoms," that is to say, ways of recognizing every human being's character as a person responsible for itself and its transcendent destiny, as well as the inviolability of one's conscience.[21]

33. The social dimension of the human being also takes on another meaning: only the vast numbers and rich diversity of persons can express something of the infinite richness of God.

Finally, this dimension is meant to find its accomplishment in the body of Christ, which is the church. This is why social life, in the variety of its forms and to the extent that it is in conformity with the divine law, constitutes a reflection of the glory of God in the world.[22]

IV. Human Freedom and Dominion over Nature

34. As a consequence of its bodily dimension, humankind needs the resources of the material world for personal and social fulfillment. In this vocation to exercise dominion over the earth by putting it at its service through work, one can see an aspect of the image of God.[23] But human intervention is not "creative"; it encounters a material nature which like itself has its origin in God the creator and of which humankind has been constituted the "noble and wise guardian."[24]

35. Technical and economic transformations influence the organization of social life; they cannot help but affect to some extent cultural and even religious life.

However, by reason of its freedom humankind remains the master of its activity. The great and rapid transformations of the present age face us with a dramatic challenge: that of mastering and controlling by the use of reason and freedom the forces we put to work in the service of the true purposes of human existence.

36. It is the task of freedom then, when it is well ordered, to ensure that scientific and technical achievements, the quest for their effectiveness, and the products of work and the very structures of economic and social organization are not made to serve projects which would deprive them of their human purposes and turn them against humankind.

Scientific activity and technological activity each involve specific exigencies. But they acquire their properly human meaning and value only when they are subordinated to moral principles. These exigencies must be respected; but to wish to attribute to them an absolute and necessary autonomy not in conformity with the nature of things is to set out along a path which is ruinous for authentic human freedom.

V. Sin, the Source of Division and Oppression

37. God calls humankind to freedom. In each person there lives a desire to be free. And yet this desire almost always tends toward slavery and oppression. All commitment to liberation and freedom therefore presupposes that this tragic paradox has been faced.

Human sin—that is to say, our breaking away from God—is the radical reason for the tragedies which mark the history of freedom. In order to understand this, many of our contemporaries must first rediscover a sense of sin.

In the human desire for freedom there is hidden the temptation to deny one's own nature. Insofar as we wish to desire everything and to be able to do everything and thus forget that we are finite and created beings, we claim to be a god. "You will be like God" (Gen. 3:5). These words of the serpent reveal the essence of human temptation; they imply the perversion of the meaning of one's own freedom. Such is the profound nature of sin: we reject the truth and place our own will above it. By wishing to free ourselves from God and be a god ourselves, we deceive and destroy ourselves. We become alienated from ourselves.

In this desire to be a god and to subject everything to our own good pleasure, there is hidden a perversion of the very idea of God. God is love and truth in the fullness of the mutual gift of divine persons. It is true that we are called to be like God. But we become like God not in the arbitrariness of our own good pleasure but to the extent that we recognize that truth and love are at the same time the principle and the purpose of our freedom.

38. By sinning, we lie to ourselves and separate ourselves from our own truth. But seeking total autonomy and self-sufficiency, we deny God and deny ourselves. Alienation from the truth of our being as a creature loved by God is the root of all other forms of alienation.

By denying or trying to deny God, who is our beginning and end, we profoundly disturb our own order and interior balance and also those of society and even of visible creation.[25]

It is in their relationship to sin that Scripture regards all the different calamities which oppress humankind in personal and social existence. Scripture shows that the whole course of history has a mysterious link with the action of humankind. From the beginning, it has abused its freedom by setting itself up against God and by seeking to gain its ends without God.[26] Genesis indicates the consequences of this original sin in the painful nature of work and childbirth, in man's oppression of woman and in death. Human beings deprived of divine grace have thus inherited a common mortal nature, incapable of choosing what is good and inclined to covetousness.[27]

39. Idolatry is an extreme form of disorder produced by sin. The re-

placement of adoration of the living God by worship of created things falsifies the relationships between individuals and brings with it various kinds of oppression.

Culpable ignorance of God unleashes the passions, which are causes of imbalance and conflicts in the human heart. From this there inevitably come disorders which affect the sphere of family and society: sexual license, injustice, and murder. It is thus that St. Paul describes the pagan world, carried away by idolatry to the worst aberrations which ruin the individual and society.[28]

Even before St. Paul the prophets and wise men of Israel saw in the misfortunes of the people a punishment for their sin of idolatry; and in the "heart full of evil" (Eccl. 9:3),[29] they saw the source of humanity's radical slavery and of the forms of oppression which their fellow humans endured.

40. The Christian tradition, found in the fathers and doctors of the church, has made explicit this teaching of Scripture about sin. It sees sin as contempt for God (*contemptus Dei*). It is accompanied by a desire to escape from the dependent relationship of the servant to his Lord, or still more of the child to its Father. By sinning, humankind seeks to free itself from God. In reality, it makes itself a slave. For by rejecting God it destroys the momentum of its aspiration to the infinite and of its vocation to share in the divine life. This is why its heart is a prey to disquiet.

Sinful humankind, refusing to accept God, is necessarily led to become attached in a false and destructive way to creatures. In turning toward creatures (*conversio ad creaturam*) it focuses on the latter its unsatisfied desire for the infinite. But created goods are limited; and so the heart rushes from one to another, always searching for an impossible peace.

In fact, when we attribute to creatures an infinite importance, we lose the meaning of our created being. We claim to find our center and our unity in ourself. Disordered love of self is the other side of contempt for God. We then try to rely on ourselves alone; we wish to achieve fulfillment by ourselves and to be self-sufficient in our own immanence.[30]

41. This becomes more particularly obvious when sinners think that they can assert their own freedom only by explicitly denying God. Dependence of the creature upon the creator and dependence of the moral conscience upon the divine law are regarded as an intolerable slavery. Thus sinners see atheism as the true form of emancipation and of human liberation, whereas religion or even the recognition of moral law constitutes forms of alienation. We then wish to make independent decisions about what is good and what is evil, or decisions about values; and in a single step we reject both the idea of God and the idea of sin. It is through the audacity of sin that we claim to become adult and free, and we claim this emancipation not only for ourselves but for the whole of humanity.

42. Having become our own center, we tend to assert ourselves and to satisfy our desire for the infinite by the use of things: wealth, power, and pleasure, despising other persons and robbing them unjustly and treating

them as objects or instruments. Thus we make our own contribution to the creation of those very structures of exploitation and slavery which we claim to condemn.

CHAPTER 3: LIBERATION AND CHRISTIAN FREEDOM

43. Human history, marked as it is by the experience of sin, would drive us to despair if God had abandoned creation to itself. But the divine promises of liberation and their victorious fulfillment in Christ's death and resurrection are the basis of the "joyful hope" from which the Christian community draws the strength to act resolutely and effectively in the service of love, justice, and peace. The gospel is a message of freedom and a liberating force[31] which fulfills the hope of Israel based upon the words of the prophets. This hope relied upon the action of Yahweh, who even before intervention as the *goel*,[32] liberator, redeemer, and savior of the people, had freely chosen that people in Abraham.[33]

I. Liberation in the Old Testament

44. In the Old Testament the liberating action of Yahweh, serving as model and reference for all others, is the exodus from Egypt, "the house of bondage." When God rescues the people from hard economic, political, and cultural slavery, he does so in order to make them, through the covenant on Sinai, "a kingdom of priests and a holy nation" (Exod. 19:6). God wishes to be adored by people who are free. All the subsequent liberations of the people of Israel help to lead them to this full liberty that they can find only in communion with their God.

The major and fundamental event of the exodus therefore has a meaning which is both religious and political. God sets the people free and gives them descendants, a land and a law, but within a covenant and for a covenant. One cannot therefore isolate the political aspect for its own sake; it has to be considered in the light of a plan of a religious nature within which it is integrated.[34]

45. In his plan of salvation God gave Israel its law. This contained, together with the universal moral precepts of the decalogue, religious and civil norms which were to govern the life of the people chosen by God to be a witness among the nations.

Of this collection of laws, love of God above all things[35] and of neighbor as oneself[36] already constitute the center. But the justice which must govern relations between persons and the law which is its juridical expression also belongs to the sum and substance of biblical law. The codes and the preaching of the prophets, as also the Psalms, constantly refer to both of them, very often together.[37] It is in this context that one should appreciate the biblical law's care for the poor, the needy, the widow, and the orphan: they have a right to justice according to the juridical ordinances of the people of God.[38] Thus there already exist the ideal and the outline of a society centered upon worship of the Lord and based upon justice and law inspired by love.

46. Prophets constantly remind Israel of the demands made by the law of the covenant. They condemn the hardened human heart as the source of repeated transgressions, and they foretell a new covenant in which God will change hearts by writing on them the law of the Spirit.[39]

In proclaiming and preparing for this new age, the prophets vigorously condemn injustice done to the poor: they make themselves God's spokesmen for the poor. Yahweh is the supreme refuge of the little ones and the oppressed, and the messiah will have the mission of taking up their defense.[40]

The situation of the poor is a situation contrary to the covenant. This is why the law of the covenant protects them by means of precepts which reflect the attitude of God when God liberated Israel from slavery in Egypt.[41] Injustice to the little ones and the poor is a grave sin, one which destroys communion with God.

47. Whatever the forms of poverty, injustice, and affliction they endure, the "just" and the "poor of Yahweh" offer up their supplications in the Psalms.[42] In their hearts they suffer the servitude to which the "stiff-necked" people are reduced because of their sins. They endure persecution, martyrdom, and death; but they live in hope of deliverance. Above all, they place their trust in Yahweh, to whom they commend their cause.[43]

The "poor of Yahweh" know that communion with Yahweh[44] is the most precious treasure and the one in which humankind finds true freedom.[45] For them, the most tragic misfortune is the loss of this communion. Hence their fight against injustice finds its deepest meaning and its effectiveness in their desire to be freed from the slavery of sin.

48. On the threshold of the New Testament, the "poor of Yahweh" make up the first fruits of a "people humble and lowly" who live in hope of the liberation of Israel.[46]

Mary, personifying this hope, crosses the threshold from the Old Testament. She proclaims with joy the coming of the messiah and praises the Lord, who is preparing to set the people free.[47] In her hymn of praise to the divine mercy, the humble Virgin, to whom the people of the poor turn spontaneously and so confidently, sings of the mystery of salvation and its power to transform. The *sensus fidei*, so vivid among the little ones, is able to grasp at once all the salvific and ethical treasures of the Magnificat.[48]

II. Christological Significance of the Old Testament

49. The exodus, the covenant, the law, the voices of the prophets, and the spirituality of the "poor of Yahweh" achieve their full significance only in Christ. The church reads the Old Testament in the light of Christ, who died and rose for us. It sees a prefiguring of itself in the people of God of the old covenant, made incarnate in the concrete body of a particular nation, politically and culturally constituted as such. This people was part of

the fabric of history as Yahweh's witness before the nations until the fulfillment of the time of preparation and prefiguration. In the fullness of time which came with Christ, the children of Abraham were invited to enter, together with all the nations, into the church of Christ in order to form with them one people of God, spiritual and universal.[49]

III. Christian Liberation

50. Jesus proclaims the good news of the kingdom of God and calls people to conversion.[50] "The poor have the good news preached to them" (Matt. 11:5). By quoting the expression of the prophet,[51] Jesus manifests his messianic action in favor of those who await God's salvation.

Even more than this, the Son of God, who has made himself poor for love of us,[52] wishes to be recognized in the poor, in those who suffer or are persecuted[53]: "As you did it to one of the least of these my brethren, you did it to me."[54]

51. But it is above all by the power of his paschal mystery that Christ has set us free.[55] Through his perfect obedience on the cross and through the glory of his resurrection, the lamb of God has taken away the sin of the world and opened for us the way to definitive liberation.

By means of our service and love, but also by the offering up of our trials and sufferings, we share in the one redeeming sacrifice of Christ, completing in ourselves "what is lacking in Christ's afflictions for the sake of his body, that is, the church" (Col. 1:24), as we look forward to the resurrection of the dead.

52. The heart of the Christian experience of freedom is in justification by the grace received through faith and the church's sacraments. This grace frees us from sin and places us in communion with God. Through Christ's death and resurrection we are offered forgiveness. The experience of our reconciliation with the Father is the fruit of the Holy Spirit. God is revealed to us as the Father of mercy, before whom we can come with total confidence.

Having been reconciled with God[56] and receiving the peace of Christ which the world cannot give,[57] we are called to be peacemakers among all persons.[58]

In Christ, we can conquer sin, and death no longer separates us from God; death will finally be destroyed at our resurrection, which will be like that of Jesus.[59] The "cosmos" itself, of which humankind is the center and summit, waits to be "set free from its bondage to decay and to share in the glorious freedom of the children of God" (Rom. 8:21). Even now Satan has been checked; the power of death has been reduced to impotence by the death of Christ.[60] Signs are given which are a foretaste of the glory to come.

53. The freedom brought by Christ in the Holy Spirit has restored to us the capacity, which sin had taken away from us, to love God above all things and remain in communion with God.

We are set free from disordered self-love, which is the source of contempt of neighbor and of human relationships based on domination.

Nevertheless, until the risen one returns in glory, the mystery of iniquity is still at work in the world. St. Paul warns us of this: "For freedom Christ has set us free" (Gal. 5:1). We must therefore persevere and fight in order not to fall once more under the yoke of slavery. Our existence is a spiritual struggle to live according to the gospel, and it is waged with the weapons of God.[61] But we have received the power and the certainty of our victory over evil, the victory of the love of Christ, whom nothing can resist.[62]

54. St. Paul proclaims the gift of the new law of the Spirit in opposition to the law of the flesh or of covetousness which draws human nature toward evil and makes it powerless to choose what is good.[63] This lack of harmony and this inner weakness do not abolish human freedom and responsibility, but they do have a negative effect on their exercise for the sake of what is good. This is what causes the Apostle to say: "I do not do the good I want, but the evil I do not want is what I do" (Rom. 7:19). Thus he rightly speaks of the "bondage of sin" and the "slavery of the law," for to sinful humankind the law, which cannot be made part of itself, seems oppressive.

However, St. Paul recognizes that the law still has value for the Christian, because it "is holy and what it commands is sacred, just, and good" (Rom. 7:12).[64] He reaffirms the decalogue, while putting it into relationship with that charity which is its true fullness.[65] Furthermore, he knows well that a juridical order is necessary for the development of life in society.[66] But the new thing he proclaims is God's giving us the Son "so that the law's just demands might be satisfied in us" (Rom. 8:1).

The Lord Jesus himself spelled out the precepts of the new law in the Sermon on the Mount: by the sacrifice he offered on the cross and again by his glorious resurrection he conquered the power of sin and gained for us the grace of the Holy Spirit, which makes possible the perfect observance of God's law[67] and access to forgiveness if we fall again into sin. The Spirit who dwells in our hearts is the source of true freedom.

Through Christ's sacrifice, the cultic regulations of the Old Testament have been rendered obsolete. As for the juridical norms governing the social and political life of Israel, the apostolic church, inasmuch as it marked the beginning of the reign of God on earth, was aware that it was no longer held to their observance. This enabled the Christian community to understand the laws and authoritative acts of various peoples. Although lawful and worthy of being obeyed,[68] they could never, inasmuch as they have their origin in such authorities, claim to have a sacred character. In the light of the gospel, many laws and structures seem to bear the mark of sin and prolong its oppressive influence in society.

IV. The New Commandment

55. God's love, poured out into our hearts by the Holy Spirit, involves love of neighbor. Recalling the first commandment, Jesus immediately adds:

"And the second is like it, 'You shall love your neighbor as yourself.' On these two commandments depend all the law and the prophets" (Matt. 22:39–40). And St. Paul says that love is the fulfillment of the law.[69]

Love of neighbor knows no limits and includes enemies and persecutors. The perfection which is the image of the Father's perfection and for which the disciple must strive is found in mercy.[70] The parable of the good Samaritan shows that compassionate love, which puts itself at the service of neighbor, destroys the prejudices which set ethnic or social groups against one another.[71] All the New Testament witnesses to the inexhaustible richness of the sentiments included in Christian love of neighbor.[72]

56. Christian love, which seeks no reward and includes everyone, receives its nature from the love of Christ, who gave his life for us: "Even as I have loved you. . . , you also love one another" (John 13:34–35).[73] This is the "new commandment" for the disciples.

In the light of this commandment, St. James severely reminds the rich of their duty,[74] and St. John says that those who possess the riches of this world but shut their heart to their brother in need cannot have the love of God dwelling in them.[75] Fraternal love is the touchstone of love of God: "He who does not love his brother whom he has seen cannot love God whom he has not seen" (1 John 4:20). St. Paul strongly emphasizes the link between sharing in the sacrament of the body and blood of Christ and sharing with one's neighbor in need.[76]

57. Evangelical love and the vocation to be children of God, to which all are called, have as a consequence the direct and imperative requirement of respect for all human beings in their rights to life and to dignity. There is no gap between love of neighbor and desire for justice. Indeed, the meaning of mercy completes the meaning of justice by preventing justice from shutting itself up within the circle of revenge.

The evil inequities and oppression of every kind, which afflict millions of men and women today, openly contradict Christ's gospel and cannot leave the conscience of any Christian indifferent.

The church, in docility to the Spirit, goes forward faithfully along paths to authentic liberation. Its members are aware of their failings and their delays in this quest. But a vast number of Christians, from the time of the Apostles onward, have committed their powers and their lives to liberation from every form of oppression and the promotion of human dignity. The experience of the saints and the example of so many works of service to one's neighbor are an incentive and a beacon for the liberating undertakings needed today.

V. The Church, People of God of the New Covenant

58. The people of God of the new covenant is the church of Christ. Its law is the commandment of love. In the hearts of its members the Spirit dwells as in a temple. It is the seed and the beginning of the kingdom of God here below, which will receive its completion at the end of time with

the resurrection of the dead and the renewal of the whole of creation.[77]

Thus possessing the pledge of the Spirit,[78] the people of God is led toward the fullness of freedom. The new Jerusalem which we fervently await is rightly called the city of freedom in the highest sense.[79] Then, "God will wipe away every tear from their eyes and death shall be no more, neither shall there be mourning nor crying nor pain any more, for the former things have passed away" (Rev. 21:4). Hope is the certain expectation "of new heavens and of a new earth where justice will dwell" (2 Pet. 3:13).

59. The transfiguration by the risen Christ of the church at the end of its pilgrimage in no way cancels out the personal destiny of each individual at the end of his or her life. All those found worthy before Christ's tribunal for having, by the grace of God, made good use of their free will are to receive the reward of happiness.[80] They will be made like to God, for they will see God, as he is.[81] The divine gift of eternal happiness is the exaltation of the greatest freedom which can be imagined.

60. This hope does not weaken commitment to the progress of the earthly city, but rather gives it meaning and strength. It is of course important to make a careful distinction between earthly progress and the growth of the kingdom, which do not belong to the same order. Nonetheless, this distinction is not a separation; for the human vocation to eternal life does not suppress but confirms the task of using the energies and means received from the creator for developing temporal life.[82]

Enlightened by the Lord's Spirit, Christ's church can discern in the signs of the times the ones which advance liberation and those that are deceptive and illusory. It calls individuals and societies to overcome situations of sin and injustice, and to establish the conditions for true freedom. It knows that we shall rediscover all these good things—human dignity, fraternal union and freedom—which are the result of efforts in harmony with God's will, "washed clean of all stain, illumined and transfigured when Christ will hand over to the Father the eternal and universal kingdom,"[83] which is a kingdom of freedom.

The vigilant and active expectation of the coming of the kingdom is also the expectation of a finally perfect justice for the living and the dead, for persons of all times and places, a justice which Jesus Christ, installed as supreme judge, will establish.[84] This promise, which surpasses all human possibilities, directly concerns our life in this world. For true justice must include everyone; it must bring the answer to the immense load of suffering borne by all generations. In fact, without the resurrection of the dead and the Lord's judgment, there is no justice in the full sense of the term. The promise of the resurrection is freely made to meet the desire for true justice dwelling in the human heart.

CHAPTER 4: THE LIBERATING MISSION OF THE CHURCH

61. The church is firmly determined to respond to the anxiety of contemporary humankind as it endures oppression and yearns for freedom.

The political and economic running of society is not a direct part of its mission.[85] But the Lord Jesus has entrusted to it the word of truth capable of enlightening consciences. Divine love, which is its life, impels it to a true solidarity with everyone who suffers. If its members remain faithful to the mission, the Holy Spirit, the source of freedom, will dwell in them, and they will bring forth fruits of justice and peace in their families and in the places where they work and live.

I. For the Integral Salvation of the World

62. The gospel is the power of eternal life, given even now to those who receive it.[86] But by begetting people who are renewed,[87] this power penetrates the human community and its history, thus purifying and giving life to its activities. In this way it is a "root of culture."[88]

The Beatitudes proclaimed by Jesus express the perfection of evangelical love, and they have never ceased to be lived throughout the history of the church by countless baptized individuals and in an eminent manner by the saints.

The Beatitudes, beginning with the first, the one concerning the poor, form a whole unit which itself must not be separated from the entirety of the Sermon on the Mount.[89] In this sermon Jesus, the new Moses, gives a commentary on the decalogue, the law of the covenant, thus giving it its definitive and fullest meaning. Read and interpreted in their full context, the Beatitudes express the spirit of the kingdom of God which is to come. But, in the light of the definitive destiny of human history thus manifested, there simultaneously appear with a more vivid clarity the foundations of justice in the temporal order.

For the Beatitudes, by teaching trust which relies on God, hope of eternal life, love of justice and mercy which goes as far as pardon and reconciliation, enable us to situate the temporal order in relation to a transcendent order which gives the temporal order its true measure but without taking away its own nature.

In the light of these things, the commitment necessary in temporal tasks of service to neighbor and the human community is both urgently demanded and kept in its right perspective. The Beatitudes prevent us from worshiping earthly goods and from committing the injustices which their unbridled pursuit involves.[90] They also divert us from an unrealistic and ruinous search for a perfect world, "for the form of this world is passing away" (1 Cor. 7:31).

63. The church's essential mission, following that of Christ, is a mission of evangelization and salvation.[91] It draws its zeal from the divine love. Evangelization is the proclamation of salvation, which is a gift of God. Through the word of God and the sacraments, human beings are freed in the first place from the power of sin and the power of the evil one; and they are brought into a communion of love with God. Following its Lord,

who "came into the world to save sinners" (1 Tim. 1:15), the church desires the salvation of all.

In this mission, the church teaches the way which humankind must follow in this world in order to enter the kingdom of God. Its teaching therefore extends to the whole moral order and notably to the justice which must regulate human relations. This is part of the preaching of the gospel.

But the love which impels the church to communicate to all persons a sharing in the grace of divine life also causes it, through the effective action of its members, to pursue the true temporal good, help them in their needs, provide for their education, and promote an integral liberation from everything that hinders the development of individuals. The church desires the good of humankind in all its dimensions, first of all as a member of the city of God and then as a member of the earthly city.

64. Therefore, when the church speaks about the promotion of justice in human societies or when it urges the faithful to work in this sphere according to their own vocation, it is not going beyond its mission. It is, however, concerned that this mission should not be absorbed by preoccupations concerning the temporal order or reduced to such preoccupations. Hence it takes great care to maintain clearly and firmly both the unity and the distinction between evangelization and human promotion: unity, because it sees the good of the whole person; distinction, because these two tasks enter in different ways into its mission.

65. It is thus by pursuing its own finality that the church sheds the light of the gospel on earthly realities in order that human beings may be healed of their miseries and raised in dignity. The cohesion of society in accordance with justice and peace is thereby promoted and strengthened.[92] Thus the church is being faithful to its mission when it condemns the forms of deviation, slavery, and oppression of which human beings are victims.

It is being faithful to its mission when it opposes attempts to set up a form of social life from which God is absent, whether by deliberate opposition or by culpable negligence.[93]

It is likewise being faithful to its mission when it exercises its judgment regarding political movements which seek to fight poverty and oppression according to theories or methods of action contrary to the gospel and opposed to human nature itself.[94]

It is of course true that, with the energy of grace, evangelical morality brings humankind new perspectives and new duties. But its purpose is to perfect and elevate a moral dimension which already belongs to human nature and with which the church concerns itself in the knowledge that this is a heritage belonging to all human beings by their very nature.

II. A Love of Preference for the Poor

66. Christ Jesus, although he was rich, became poor in order to make us rich by means of his poverty.[95] St. Paul is speaking here of the mystery of the incarnation of the eternal Son, who came to take on mortal human

nature in order to save us from the misery into which sin had plunged us. Furthermore, in the human condition Christ chose a state of poverty and deprivation[96] in order to show in what consists the true wealth which ought to be sought, that of communion of life with God. He taught detachment from earthly riches so that we might desire the riches of heaven.[97] The apostles whom he chose also had to leave all things and share his deprivation.[98]

Christ was foretold by the prophets as the messiah of the poor;[99] and it was among the latter, the humble, the "poor of Yahweh," who were thirsting for the justice of the kingdom, that he found hearts ready to receive him. But he also wished to be near to those who, though rich in the goods of this world, were excluded from the community as "publicans and sinners," for he had come to call them to conversion.[100]

It is this sort of poverty, made up of detachment, trust in God, sobriety, and a readiness to share, that Jesus declared blessed.

67. But Jesus not only brought the grace and peace of God; he also healed innumerable sick persons; he had compassion on the crowd who had nothing to eat and he fed them; with the disciples who followed him he practiced almsgiving.[101] Therefore the Beatitude of poverty, which he proclaimed, can never signify that Christians are permitted to ignore the poor, who lack what is necessary for human life in this world. This poverty is the result and consequence of sin and natural frailty, and it is an evil from which human beings must be freed as completely as possible.

68. In its various forms—material deprivation, unjust oppression, physical and psychological illnesses, and finally death—human misery is the obvious sign of the natural condition of weakness in which humankind finds itself since original sin and the sign of its need for salvation. Hence it drew the compassion of Christ the savior to take it upon himself[102] and to be identified with the least of his brethren (cf. Matt. 25:40, 45). Hence also those who are oppressed by poverty are the object of a love of preference on the part of the church, which since its origin and in spite of the failings of many members, has not ceased to work for their relief, defense, and liberation. It has done this through numberless works of charity which remain always and everywhere indispensable.[103] In addition, through its social doctrine which it strives to apply, it has sought to promote structural changes in society so as to secure conditions of life worthy of the human person.

By detachment from riches, which makes possible sharing and opens the gate of the kingdom,[104] the disciples of Jesus bear witness through love for the poor and the unfortunate to the love of the Father manifested in the savior. This love comes from God and goes to God. The disciples of Christ have always recognized in the gifts placed on the altar a gift offered to God.

In loving the poor, the church also witnesses to human dignity. It clearly affirms that the human person is worth more for what one is than for what one has. The church bears witness to the fact that this dignity cannot be destroyed, whatever the situation of poverty, scorn, rejection, or power-lessness to which a human being has been reduced. It shows its solidarity with those who do not count in a society by which they are rejected spir-itually and sometimes even physically. It is particularly drawn with maternal affection toward those children who, through human wickedness, will never be brought forth from the womb to the light of day, as also for the elderly, alone and abandoned.

The special option for the poor, far from being a sign of particularism or sectarianism, manifests the universality of the church's being and mis-sion. This option excludes no one.

This is the reason why the church cannot express this option by means of reductive sociological and ideological categories which would make this preference a partisan choice and a source of conflict.

69. The new basic communities or other groups of Christians which have arisen to be witnesses to this evangelical love are a source of great hope for the church. If they really live in unity with the local church and the universal church, they will be a real expression of communion and a means for constructing a still deeper communion.[105] Their fidelity to their mission will depend on how careful they are to educate their members in the full-ness of the Christian faith through listening to the word of God, fidelity to the teaching of the magisterium, to the hierarchical order of the church and to the sacramental life. If this condition is fulfilled, their experience, rooted in a commitment to the complete human liberation, becomes a treasure for the whole church.

70. Similarly, a theological reflection developed from a particular expe-rience can constitute a very positive contribution, inasmuch as it makes possible a highlighting of aspects of the work of God, the richness of which has not yet been fully grasped. But in order that this reflection may be truly a reading of the Scripture and not a projection onto the word of God of a meaning it does not contain, the theologian will be careful to interpret the experience from which he begins in the light of the experience of the church. This experience of the church shines with a singular brightness and in all its purity in the lives of the saints. It pertains to the pastors of the church, in communion with the successor of Peter, to discern its authen-ticity.

CHAPTER 5: THE SOCIAL DOCTRINE OF THE CHURCH: FOR A CHRISTIAN PRACTICE OF LIBERATION

71. The salvific dimension of liberation cannot be reduced to the socio-ethical dimension, which is a consequence of it. By restoring true human freedom, the radical liberation brought about by Christ assigns a task: Christian practice, which is the putting into practice of the great com-mandment of love. The latter is the supreme principle of Christian social

morality, founded upon the gospel and the whole of tradition since apostolic times and the age of the fathers of the church up to and including the recent statements of the magisterium.

The considerable challenges of our time constitute an urgent appeal to put into practice this teaching on how to act.

I. *Nature of the Social Doctrine of the Church*

72. The church's social teaching is born of the encounter of the gospel message and of its demands summarized in the supreme commandments of love of God and neighbor in justice[106] with the problems emanating from the life of society. This social teaching has established itself as a doctrine by using the resources of human wisdom and the sciences. It concerns the ethical aspect of this life. It takes into account the technical aspects of problems but always in order to judge them from the moral point of view.

Being essentially orientated toward action, this teaching develops in accordance with the changing circumstances of history. This is why, together with principles that are always valid, it also involves contingent judgments. Far from constituting a closed system, it remains constantly open to the new questions which continually arise; it requires the contribution of all charisms, experiences, and skills.

As an "expert in humanity," the church offers by its social doctrine a set of principles for reflection and criteria for judgment[107] and also directives for action[108] so that the profound changes demanded by situations of poverty and injustice may be brought about, and this in a way which serves the true good of humanity.

73. The supreme commandment of love leads to the full recognition of the dignity of each individual, created in God's image. From this dignity flow natural rights and duties. In the light of the image of God, freedom, which is the essential prerogative of the human person, is manifested in all its depth. Persons are the active and responsible subjects of social life.[109]

Intimately linked to the foundation, which is human dignity, are the principle of solidarity and the principle of subsidiarity.

By virtue of the first, human beings are obliged to contribute to the common good of society at all its levels.[110] Hence the church's doctrine is opposed to all forms of social or political individualism.

By virtue of the second, neither the state nor any society must ever substitute itself for the initiative and responsibility of individuals and of intermediate communities at the level on which they can function, nor must they take away the room necessary for their freedom.[111] Hence the church's social doctrine is opposed to all forms of collectivism.

74. These principles are the basis of criteria for making judgments on social situations, structure, and systems.

Thus the church does not hesitate to condemn situations of life which are injurious to human dignity and freedom.

These criteria also make it possible to judge the value of structures.

These are the sets of institutions and practices which people find already existing or which they create on the national and international level, and which orientate or organize economic, social, and political life. Being necessary in themselves, they often tend to become fixed and fossilized as mechanisms relatively independent of the human will, thereby paralyzing or distorting social development and causing injustice. However, they always depend on human responsibility; human beings can alter them, and they are not dependent on an alleged determinism of history.

Institutions and laws, when they are in conformity with the natural law and ordered to the common good, are the guarantees of a people's freedom and of the promotion of that freedom. One cannot condemn all the constraining aspects of law or the stability of a lawful state worthy of the name. One can therefore speak of structures marked by sin, but one cannot condemn structures as such.

The criteria for judgment also concern economic, social, and political systems. The social doctrine of the church does not propose any particular system; but in the light of other fundamental principles it makes it possible at once to see to what extent existing systems conform or do not conform to the demands of human dignity.

75. The church is, of course, aware of the complexity of the problems confronting society and of the difficulties in finding adequate solutions to them. Nevertheless it considers that the first thing to be done is to appeal to the spiritual and moral capacities of the individual and to the permanent need for inner conversion, if one is to achieve the economic and social changes that will truly be at the service of humanity.

The priority given to structures and technical organization over the person and the requirements of human dignity is the expression of a materialistic anthropology, contrary to the construction of a just social order.[112]

On the other hand, the recognized priority of freedom and of conversion of heart in no way eliminates the need for unjust structures to be changed. It is therefore perfectly legitimate that those who suffer oppression on the part of the wealthy or the politically powerful should take action, through morally licit means, in order to secure structures and institutions in which their rights will be truly respected.

It remains true, however, that structures established for human good are of themselves incapable of securing and guaranteeing that good. The corruption which in certain countries affects the leaders and the state bureaucracy, and which destroys all honest social life, is a proof of this. Moral integrity is a necessary condition for the health of society. It is therefore necessary to work simultaneously for the conversion of hearts and for the improvement of structures. For the sin which is at the root of unjust situations is, in a true and immediate sense, a voluntary act which has its source in the freedom of individuals. Only in a derived and secondary sense is it applicable to structures, and only in this sense can one speak of "social sin."[113]

Moreover, in the process of liberation, one cannot abstract from the historical situation of the nation or attack the cultural identity of a people. Consequently, one cannot passively accept, still less actively support, groups which by force or by the manipulation of public opinion take over the state apparatus and unjustly impose on the collectivity an imported ideology contrary to the culture of the people.[114] In this respect, mention should be made of the serious moral and political responsibility of intellectuals.

76. Basic principles and criteria for judgment inspire guidelines for action. Since the common good of human society is at the service of the people, the means of action must be in conformity with human dignity and facilitate education for freedom. A safe criterion for judgment and action is this: there can be no true liberation if from the very beginning the rights of freedom are not respected.

Systematic recourse to violence put forward as the necessary path to liberation has to be condemned as a destructive illusion and one that opens the way to new forms of servitude. One must condemn with equal vigor violence exercised by the powerful against the poor, arbitrary action by the police, and any form of violence established as a system of government. In these areas one must learn the lessons of tragic experience which the history of the present century has known and continues to know. Nor can one accept the culpable passivity of the public powers in those democracies where the social situation of a large number of men and women is far from corresponding to the demands of constitutionally guaranteed individual and social rights.

77. When the church encourages the creation and activity of associations such as trade unions which fight for the defense of the rights and legitimate interests of the workers and for social justice, it does not thereby admit the theory that sees in the class struggle the structural dynamism of social life. The action which the church sanctions is not the struggle of one class against another in order to eliminate the foe. It does not proceed from a mistaken acceptance of an alleged law of history. This action is rather a noble and reasoned struggle for justice and social solidarity.[115] The Christian will always prefer the path of dialogue and joint action.

Christ has commanded us to love our enemies.[116] Liberation in the spirit of the gospel is therefore incompatible with hatred of others, taken individually or collectively, and this includes hatred of one's enemy.

78. Situations of grave injustice require the courage to make far-reaching reforms and to suppress unjustifiable privileges. But those who discredit the path of reform and favor the myth of revolution not only foster the illusion that the abolition of an evil situation is in itself sufficient to create a more humane society; they also encourage the setting up of totalitarian regimes.[117] The fight against injustice is meaningless unless it is waged with a view to establishing a new social and political order in conformity with the demands of justice. Justice must already mark each stage of the establishment of this new order. There is a morality of means.[118]

79. These principles must be especially applied in the extreme case where there is recourse to armed struggle, which the church's magisterium admits as a last resort to put an end to an obvious and prolonged tyranny gravely damaging the fundamental rights of individuals and the common good.[119] Nevertheless, the concrete application of this means cannot be contemplated until there has been a very rigorous analysis of the situation. Indeed, because of the continual development of the technology of violence and the increasingly serious dangers implied in its recourse, that which today is termed "passive resistance" shows a way more conformable to moral principles and having no fewer prospects for success. One can never approve, whether perpetrated by established power or insurgents, crimes such as reprisals against the general population, torture, or methods of terrorism and deliberate provocation aimed at causing deaths during popular demonstrations. Equally unacceptable are detestable smear campaigns capable of destroying a person psychologically or morally.

80. It is not for the pastors of the church to intervene directly in the political construction and organization of social life. This task forms part of the vocation of the laity acting on their own initiative with their fellow citizens.[120] They must fulfill this task conscious of the fact that the purpose of the church is to spread the kingdom of Christ so that all persons may be saved and that through them the world may be effectively ordered to Christ.[121] The work of salvation is thus seen to be indissolubly linked to the task of improving and raising the conditions of human life in this world.

The distinction between the supernatural order of salvation and the temporal order of human life must be seen in the context of God's singular plan to recapitulate all things in Christ. Hence in each of these spheres lay persons, who are at one and the same time members of the church and citizens of their country, must allow themselves always to be guided by their Christian conscience.[122]

Social action, which can involve a number of concrete means, will always be exercised for the common good and in conformity with the gospel message and the teaching of the church. It must be ensured that the variety of options does not harm a sense of collaboration, or lead to a paralysis of efforts or produce confusion among the Christian people.

The orientation received from the social doctrine of the church should stimulate an acquisition of the essential technical and scientific skills. The social doctrine of the church will also stimulate the seeking of moral formation of character and a deepening of the spiritual life. While it offers principles and wise counsels, this doctrine does not dispense from education in the political prudence needed for guiding and running human affairs.

II. Evangelical Requirements for an In-depth Transformation

81. Christians working to bring about a "civilization of love," which will include the entire ethical and social heritage of the gospel, are today faced with an unprecedented challenge. This task calls for renewed reflection on

what constitutes the relationship between the supreme commandment of love and the social order considered in all its complexity.

The immediate aim of this in-depth reflection is to work out and set in motion ambitious programs aimed at the socio-economic liberation of millions of men and women caught in an intolerable situation of economic, social, and political oppression.

This action must begin with an immense effort at education: education for the civilization of work, education of solidarity, access to culture for all.

82. The life of Jesus of Nazareth, a real "gospel of work," offers us the living example and principle of the radical cultural transformation essential for solving the grave problems that must be faced by the age in which we live. He, who though he was God became like us in all things, devoted the greater part of his earthly life to manual labor.[123] The culture our age awaits will be marked by the full recognition of the dignity of human work, which appears in all its nobility and fruitfulness in the light of the mysteries of creation and redemption.[124] Recognized as a form of the person, work becomes a source of creative meaning and effort.

83. Thus the solution of most of the serious problems related to poverty is to be found in the promotion of a true civilization of work. In a sense, work is the key to the whole social question.[125]

It is therefore in the domain of work that priority must be given to the action of liberation in freedom. Because the relationship between the human person and work is radical and vital, the forms and models according to which this relationship is regulated will exercise a positive influence for the solution of a whole series of social and political problems facing each people. Just work relationships will be a necessary precondition for a system of political community capable of favoring the integral development of every individual.

If the system of labor relations put into effect by those directly involved — workers and employers, with the essential support of public powers — succeeds in bringing into existence a civilization of work, then there will take place a profound and peaceful revolution in people's outlooks and in institutional and political structures.

84. A work culture such as this will necessarily presuppose and put into effect a certain number of essential values. It will acknowledge that the person of the worker is the principle, subject, and purpose of work. It will affirm the priority of work over capital, and the fact that material goods are meant for all. It will be animated by a sense of solidarity involving not only rights to be defended but also duties to be performed. It will involve participation aimed at promoting the national and international common good and not just defending individual or corporate interests. It will assimilate the methods of confrontation and of frank and vigorous dialogue.

As a result, political authorities will become more capable of acting with respect for the legitimate freedoms of individuals, families, and subsidiary groups; and they will thus create the conditions necessary for persons to be able to achieve their authentic and integral welfare, including their spiritual goal.[126]

85. A culture which recognizes the eminent dignity of the worker will emphasize the subjective dimension of work.[127]

The value of any human work does not depend on the kind of work done; it is based on the fact that the one who does it is a person.[128] There we have an ethical criterion whose implications cannot be overlooked.

Thus every person has a right to work, and this right must be recognized in a practical way by an effective commitment to resolving the tragic problem of unemployment. The fact that unemployment keeps large sectors of the population, and notably the young, in a situation of marginalization is intolerable. For this reason the creation of jobs is a primary social task facing individuals and private enterprise, as well as the state. As a general rule, in this as in other matters the state has a subsidiary function; but often it can be called upon to intervene directly, as in the case of international agreements between different states. Such agreements must respect the rights of immigrants and their families.[129]

86. Wages, which cannot be considered as a mere commodity, must enable workers and their families to have access to a truly human standard of living in the material, social, cultural, and spiritual orders. It is the dignity of the person which constitutes the criterion for judging work, not the other way round. Whatever the type of work, the workers must be able to perform it as an expression of their personality. There follows from this the necessity of a participation which, over and above a sharing in the fruits of work, should involve a truly communitarian dimension at the level of projects, undertakings, and responsibilities.[130]

87. The priority of work over capital places an obligation in justice upon employers to consider the welfare of workers before the increase of profits. They have a moral obligation not to keep capital unproductive and in making investments to think first of the common good. The latter requires a prior effort to consolidate jobs or create new ones in the production of goods that are really useful.

The right to private property is inconceivable without responsibilities to the common good. It is subordinated to the higher principle which states that goods are meant for all.[131]

88. This teaching must inspire reforms before it is too late. Access for everyone to the goods needed for a human, personal, and family life worthy of the name is a primary demand of social justice. It requires application in the sphere of industrial work and in a particular way in the area of agricultural work.[132] Indeed, rural peoples, especially in the Third World, make up the vast majority of the poor.[133]

III. Promotion of Solidarity

89. Solidarity is a direct requirement of human and supernatural brotherhood. The serious socio-economic problems that occur today cannot be

solved unless new fronts of solidarity are created: solidarity of the poor among themselves, solidarity with the poor to which the rich are called, solidarity among the workers, and with workers. Institutions and social organizations at different levels, as well as the state, must share in a general movement of solidarity. When the church appeals for such solidarity, it is aware that it itself is concerned in a quite special way.

90. The principle that goods are meant for all, together with the principle of human and supernatural fellowship, express the responsibilities of richer countries toward poorer ones. These responsibilities include solidarity in aiding the developing countries, social justice through a revision in correct terms of commercial relationships between North and South, the promotion of a more human world for all, a world in which each individual can give and receive, and in which the progress of some will no longer be an obstacle to the development of others or a pretext for their enslavement.[134]

91. International solidarity is a necessity of the moral order. It is essential not only in cases of extreme urgency but also for aiding true development. This is a shared task, which requires a concerted and constant effort to find concrete technical solutions and also to create a new mentality among our contemporaries. World peace depends on this to a great extent.[135]

IV. Cultural and Educational Tasks

92. The unjust inequalities in the possession and use of material goods are accompanied and aggravated by similarly unjust inequalities in the opportunity for culture, which is the specific mode of a truly human existence to which one gains access through the development of one's intellectual capacities, moral virtues, abilities to relate with other human beings, and talents for creating things that are useful and beautiful. From this flows the necessity of promoting and spreading education, to which every individual has an inalienable right. The first condition for this is the elimination of illiteracy.[136]

93. The right of each person to culture is assured only if cultural freedom is respected. Too often culture is debased by ideology, and education is turned into an instrument at the service of political or economic power. It is not within the competence of public authorities to determine culture. Their function is to promote and protect the cultural life of everyone, including that of minorities.[137]

94. The task of educating belongs fundamentally and primarily to the family. The function of the state is subsidiary: its role is to guarantee, protect, promote, and supplement. Whenever the state lays claim to an educational monopoly, it oversteps its rights and offends justice. It is parents who have the right to choose the school to which they send their children and the right to set up and support educational centers in accordance with their own beliefs. The state cannot, without injustice, merely

tolerate so-called private schools. Such schools render a public service and therefore have a right to financial assistance.[138]

95. The education that gives access to culture is also education in the responsible exercise of freedom. That is why there can be authentic development only in a social and political system that respects freedoms and fosters them through the participation of everyone. This participation can take different forms; it is necessary in order to guarantee a proper pluralism in institutions and in social initiatives. It ensures, notably by the real separation between the powers of the state, the exercise of human rights, also protecting them against possible abuses on the part of public powers. No one can be excluded from this participation in social and political life for reasons of sex, race, color, social condition, language, or religion.[139] Keeping persons on the margins of cultural, social, and political life constitutes in many nations one of the most glaring injustices of our time.

When political authorities regulate the exercise of freedoms, they cannot use the pretext of the demands of public order and security in order to curtail those freedoms systematically. Nor can the alleged principle of national security, or a narrowly economic outlook or a totalitarian concept of social life prevail over the value of freedom and its rights.[140]

96. Faith inspires criteria of judgment, determining values, lines of thought, and patterns of living which are valid for the whole human community.[141] Hence the church, sensitive to the anxieties of our age, indicates the lines of a culture in which work would be recognized in its full human dimension and in which all would find opportunities for personal self-fulfillment. The church does this by virtue of its missionary outreach for the integral salvation of the world, with respect for the identity of each people and nation.

The church, which is a communion uniting diversity and unity through its presence in the whole world, takes from every culture the positive elements it finds there. But inculturation is not simply an outward adaptation; it is an intimate transformation of authentic cultural values by their integration into Christianity and the planting of Christianity in the different human cultures.[142] Separation between the gospel and culture is a tragedy of which the problems mentioned are a sad illustration. A generous effort to evangelize cultures is therefore necessary. These cultures will be given fresh life by their encounter with the gospel. But this encounter presupposes that the gospel is truly proclaimed.[143] Enlightened by the Second Vatican Council, the church wishes to devote all its energies to this task, so as to evoke an immense liberating effort.

CONCLUSION

97. "Blessed is she who believed" (Luke 1:45). At Elizabeth's greeting, the heart of the mother of God would burst into the song of the Magnificat. It tells us that it is by faith and in faith like that of Mary that the people

of God express in words and translate into life the mysterious plan of salvation with its liberating effects upon individual and social existence. It is really in the light of faith that one comes to understand how salvation history is the history of liberation from evil in its most radical form and of the introduction of humanity into the true freedom of the children of God. Mary is totally dependent on her son and completely directed toward him by the impulse of her faith; and, at his side, she is the most perfect image of freedom and of the liberation of humanity and of the universe. It is to her as mother and model that the church must look in order to understand in its completeness the meaning of its own mission.

It is altogether remarkable that the sense of faith found in the poor leads not only to an acute perception of the mystery of the redeeming cross but also to a love and unshakable trust in the mother of the Son of God, who is venerated in so many shrines.

98. Pastors and all those who, as priests, laity, or men and women religious, often work under very difficult conditions for evangelization and integral human advancement should be filled with hope when they think of the amazing resources of holiness contained in the living faith of the people of God. These riches of the *sensus fidei* must be given the chance to come to full flowering and bear abundant fruit. To help the faith of the poor to express itself clearly and to be translated into life through a profound meditation on the plan of salvation as it unfolds itself in the virgin of the Magnificat — this is a noble ecclesial task that awaits the theologian.

Thus a theology of freedom and liberation, which faithfully echoes Mary's Magnificat preserved in the church's memory, is something needed by the times in which we are living. But it would be criminal to take the energies of popular piety and misdirect them toward a purely earthly plan of liberation, which would very soon be revealed as nothing more than an illusion and a cause of new forms of slavery. Those who in this way surrender to the ideologies of the world and to the alleged necessity of violence are no longer being faithful to hope, to hope's boldness and courage, as they are extolled in the hymn to the God of mercy, which the virgin teaches us.

99. The *sensus fidei* grasps the very core of the liberation accomplished by the redeemer. It is from the most radical evil, from sin and the power of death, that he has delivered us in order to restore freedom to itself and to show it the right path. This path is marked out by the supreme commandment, which is the commandment of love.

Liberation in its primary meaning, which is salvific, thus extends into a liberating task, as an ethical requirement. Here is to be found the social doctrine of the church, which illustrates Christian practice on the level of society.

The Christian is called to act according to the truth[144] and thus to work for the establishment of that "civilization of love" of which Pope Paul VI spoke.[145] The present document, without claiming to be complete, has indicated some of the directions in which it is urgently necessary to undertake in-depth reforms. The primary task, which is a condition for the success of all others, is an educational one. The love that guides commitment must henceforth bring into being new forms of solidarity. To the accomplishment of these tasks urgently facing the Christian conscience, all persons of good will are called.

It is the truth of the mystery of salvation at work today in order to lead redeemed humanity toward the perfection of the kingdom which gives true meaning to the necessary efforts for liberation in the economic, social, and political orders, and keep them from falling into new forms of slavery.

100. It is true that before the immensity and the complexity of the task, which can require the gift of self even to a heroic degree, many are tempted to discouragement, skepticism, or the recklessness of despair. A formidable challenge is made to hope, both theological and human. The loving virgin of the Magnificat, who enfolds the church and humanity in her prayer, is the firm support of hope. For in her we contemplate the victory of divine love, which no obstacle can hold back, and we discover to what sublime freedom God raises up the lowly. Along the path which she shows us, the faith which works through love must go forward with great resolve.[146]

During an audience granted to the undersigned prefect, his holiness John Paul II approved this instruction, adopted in an ordinary session of the Congregation for the Doctrine of the Faith, and ordered it to be published.

Given at Rome, from the congregation, March 22, 1986, the solemnity of the annunciation of our Lord.

Cardinal Joseph Ratzinger, prefect
Archbishop Alberto Bovone, secretary

NOTES

1. Congregation for the Doctrine of the Faith, "Instruction on Certain Aspects of the 'Theology of Liberation' " (*Libertatis Nuntius*), Introduction: AAS, 76 (1984), pp. 876–77.

2. Cf. *Gaudium et Spes* and *Dignitatis Humanae* of Vatican Council II; the encyclicals *Mater et Magistra, Pacem in Terris, Populorum Progressio, Redemptor Hominis,* and *Laborem Exercens;* the apostolic exhortations *Evangelii Nuntiandi* and *Reconciliatio et Paenitentia;* the apostolic letter *Octogesima Adveniens.* Pope John Paul II dealt with this theme in his opening address to the Third General Conference of the Latin American Episcopate at Puebla: AAS,71 (1979), pp. 187–205. He has returned to it on numerous other occasions. The theme has also been dealt with at the Synod of Bishops in 1971 and 1974. Latin American episcopal conferences have made it the immediate object of their reflections. It has also attracted the attention of other episcopal conferences—for example, the French: *Libération des hommes et salut en Jésus-Christ,* 1975.

3. Paul VI, apostolic letter *Octogesima Adveniens,* 1–4: AAS,63 (1971), pp. 404ff.

4. Cf. John 4:42; 1 John 4:14.

5. Cf. Matt. 28:18–20; Mark 16:15.

6. Cf. *Dignitatis Humanae,* 10.

7. Paul VI, apostolic exhortation *Evangelii Nuntiandi,* 78–80: AAS,68 (1976), pp. 70–75; *Dignitatis Humanae,* 3; John Paul II, encyclical *Redemptor Hominis,* 12: AAS,71 (1979), pp. 278–81.

8. Cf. *Libertatis Nuntius,* XI, 10.

9. Cf. John Paul II, *Redemptor Hominis,* 17; discourse of March 10, 1984, to the fifth conference of jurists: *L'Osservatore Romano,* March 11, 1984, p.8.

10. Cf. *Libertatis Nuntius,* XI, 5; John Paul II, Opening Address at Puebla.

11. Cf. *Gaudium et Spes,* 36.

12. Cf. ibid.

13. Cf. ibid., 41.

14. Cf. Matt. 11:25; Luke 10:21.

15. Cf. *Evangelii Nuntiandi,* 48.

16. Cf. *Libertatis Nuntius,* VII, 9; VIII, 1–9.

17. Cf. Gen. 1:26.

18. *Redemptor Hominis,* 21.

19. Cf. Rom. 6:6; 7:23.

20. Cf. Gen. 2:18–23, "It is not good that man should be alone....This is flesh of my flesh and bone of my bones"; in these words of Scripture, which refer directly to the relationship between man and woman, one can discern a more universal meaning. Cf. Lev. 19:18.

21. Cf. John XXIII, encyclical *Pacem in Terris,* 5–15: AAS,55 (1963), pp. 259–65; John Paul II, letter to Dr. Kurt Waldheim, secretary general of the United Nations, on the 30th anniversary of the Universal Declaration on Human Rights: AAS,71 (1979), p. 122; the pope's speech to the United Nations, 9: AAS,71 (1979), p. 1149.

22. Cf. St. Augustine, *Ad Macedonium,* II, 7–17 (PL 33, 669–73); CSEL 44, 437–47).

23. Cf. Gen. 1:27–28.

24. Cf. *Redemptor Hominis,* 15.

25. Cf. *Gaudium et Spes,* 13.1.

26. Cf. John Paul II, *Reconciliatio et Paenitentia,* 13: AAS,77 (1985), pp. 208–11.

27. Cf. Gen. 3:16–19; Rom. 5:12; 7:14–24; Paul VI, *Sollemnis Professio Fidei,* June 30, 1968, 16: AAS,60 (1968), p. 439.

28. Cf. Rom. 1:18–32.

29. Cf. Jer. 5:23; 7:24; 17:9; 18:12.

30. Cf. St. Augustine, *De Civitate Dei,* XIV, 28 (PL 41, 435; CSEL 40–2, 56–57; CCL 14–2, 451–52).

31. Cf. *Libertatis Nuntius,* Introduction.

32. Cf. Isa. 41:14; Jer. 50:34. *Goel:* this word implies the idea of a bond of kinship between the one who frees and the one who is freed. Cf. Lev. 25:25, 47–49; Ruth 3:12; 4:1. *Padah* means "to obtain for oneself." Cf. Exod. 13:13; Deut. 9:26; 15:15; Ps. 130: 7–8.

33. Cf. Gen. 12:1–3.

34. Cf. *Libertatis Nuntius,* IV, 3.

35. Cf. Deut. 6:5.

36. Cf. Lev. 19:18.

37. Cf. Deut. 1:16–17; 16:18–20; Jer. 22:3–15; 23:5; Ps. 33:5; 72:1, 99:4.

38. Cf. Exod. 22:20–23; Deut. 24:10–22.

39. Cf. Jer. 31:3–34; Ezek. 36:25–27.

40. Isa. 11:1–5; Ps. 72:4, 12–14; *Libertatis Nuntius,* IV, 6.

41. Cf. Exod. 23:9; Deut. 24:17–22.

42. Cf. Pss. 25, 31, 35, 55; *Libertatis Nuntius.* IV, 5.

43. Cf. Jer. 11:20; 20:12.

44. Cf. Ps. 73:26–28.

45. Cf. Pss. 16, 62, 84.

46. Cf. Zeph. 3:12–20; *Libertatis Nuntius,* IV, 5.

47. Cf. Luke 1:46–55.

48. Cf. Paul VI, apostolic exhortation *Marialis Cultus,* 37: AAS,66 (1974), pp. 148–49.

49. Cf. Acts 2:39; Rom. 10:12; 15:7–12; Eph. 2:14–18.

50. Cf. Mark 1:15.

51. Cf. Isa. 61:9.

52. Cf. 2 Cor. 8:9.

53. Cf. Matt 25:31–46; Acts 9:4–5.

54. Cf. *Libertatis Nuntius,* IV, 9.

55. Cf. Opening Address at Puebla, 1, 5.

56. Cf. Rom. 5:10; 2 Cor. 5:18–20.

57. Cf. John 14:27.

58. Cf. Matt. 5:9; Rom. 12:18; Heb. 12:14.

59. Cf. 1 Cor. 15:26.

60. Cf. John 12:31; Heb. 2:14–15.

61. Cf. Eph. 6:11–17.

62. Cf. Rom. 8:37–39.

63. Cf. Rom. 8:2.

64. Cf. 1 Tim. 1:8.

65. Cf. Rom. 13:8–10.

66. Cf. Rom. 13:1–7.

67. Cf. Rom. 8:2–4.

68. Cf. Rom. 13:1.

69. Cf. Rom. 13:8–10; Gal. 5:13–14.

70. Cf. Matt. 5:43–48; Luke 6:27–38.

71. Cf. Luke 10:25–37.

72. Cf. e.g., 1 Thess. 2:7–12; Phil. 2:1–4; Gal. 2:12–20; 1 Cor. 13:4–7; 2 John 12; 3 John 14; John 11:1–5, 35–36; Mark 6:34; Matt. 9:36; 18:21ff.

73. Cf. John 15:12–13; 1 John 3:16.

74. Cf. Jas. 5:1–4.

75. Cf. 1 John 3:17.

76. Cf. 1 Cor. 11:17–34; *Libertatis Nuntius,* IV, 11. St. Paul himself organizes a collection for the "poor among the saints at Jerusalem" (Rom. 15:26).

77. Cf. Rom. 8:11–21.

78. Cf. 2 Cor. 1:22.

79. Cf. Gal. 4:26.

496   *Congregation for the Doctrine of the Faith*

80. Cf. 1 Cor. 13:12; 2 Cor. 5:10.
81. Cf. 1 John 3:2.
82. *Gaudium et Spes,* 39.2.
83. Cf. ibid., 39.3.
84. Cf. Matt. 24:29–44, 46; Acts 10:42; 2 Cor. 5:10.
85. Cf. *Gaudium et Spes,* 42.2.
86. Cf. John 17:3.
87. Cf. Rom. 6:4; 2 Cor. 5:17; Col. 3:9–11.
88. Cf. *Evangelii Nuntiandi,* 18 and 20.
89. Cf. Matt. 5:3.
90. Cf. *Gaudium et Spes,* 37.
91. Cf. *Lumen Gentium,* 17; *Ad Gentes,* 1; *Evangelii Nuntiandi,* 14.
92. *Gaudium et Spes,* 40.3.
93. Cf. *Reconciliatio et Paenitentia,* 14.
94. Cf. *Libertatis Nuntius,* XI, 10.
95. Cf. 2 Cor. 8:9.
96. Cf. Luke 2:7; 9:58.
97. Matt. 6:19–20, 24–34; 19:21.
98. Cf. Luke 5:11, 28; Matt. 19:27.
99. Cf. Isa. 11:4; 61:1; Luke 4:18.
100. Cf. Luke 19:1–10; Mark 2:13–17.
101. Cf. Matt. 8:6, 14:13–21; John 13:29.
102. Cf. Matt. 8:17.
103. Cf. *Populorum Progressio,* 12 and 46; document of the Third General Conference of the Latin American Episcopate at Puebla, 476.
104. Cf. Acts 2:44–45.
105. Cf. Second Extraordinary Synod, Final Report, II, C, 6: *L'Osservatore Romano,* Dec. 10, 1985, p. 7; *Evangelii Nuntiandi,* 58.
106. Cf. Matt. 22:37–40; Rom. 13:8–10.
107. Cf. *Octogesima Adveniens,* 4; Opening Address at Puebla, III, 7.
108. Cf. *Mater et Magistra,* 235: AAS,53 (1961), p. 461.
109. Cf. *Gaudium et Spes,* 25.
110. Cf. *Mater et Magistra,* 132–133.
111. Cf. Pius XI, encyclical *Quadragesimo Anno,* 79–80: AAS,23 (1931), p. 203; *Mater et Magistra,* 138; *Pacem in Terris,* 74.
112. Cf. *Evangelii Nuntiandi,* 18; *Libertatis Nuntius,* XI, 9.
113. Cf. *Reconciliatio et Paenitentia,* 16.
114. Cf. *Octogesima Adveniens,* 25.
115. Cf. John Paul II, encyclical *Laborem Exercens,* 20: AAS,73 (1981), pp. 629–32; *Libertatis Nuntius,* VII, 8; VIII, 5–9; XI, 11–14.
116. Cf. Matt. 5:44; Luke 6:27–28, 35.
117. Cf. *Libertatis Nuntius,* XI, 10.
118. Cf. Puebla Document, 533–34. Cf. John Paul II, Homily at Drogheda, Sept. 30, 1979: AAS,71 (1979), pp. 1076–85.
119. *Populorum Progressio,* 31. Cf. Pius XI, encyclical *Nos es muy conocida:* AAS,29 (1937), pp. 208–9.
120. Cf. *Gaudium et Spes,* 76.3; *Apostolicam Actuositatem,* 7.
121. Cf. ibid., 20.
122. Cf. ibid., 5.

123. Cf. *Laborem Exercens,* 6.

124. Cf. ibid., chap. 5.

125. Cf. ibid., 3; Address at Loreto, May 10, 1985: AAS,77 (1985), pp. 967–69.

126. Cf. *Octogesima Adveniens,* 46.

127. Cf. *Laborem Exercens,* 6.

128. Cf. ibid.

129. Cf. John Paul II, apostolic exhortation *Familiaris Consortio* 46: AAS,74 (1982), pp. 137–39; *Laborem Exercens,* 23. Cf. Holy See, Charter of Rights of the Family, Art. 12, *L'Osservatore Romano,* Nov. 25, 1983.

130. Cf. *Gaudium et Spes,* 68; *Laborem Exercens,* 15. Discourse of July 3, 1980: *L'Osservatore Romano,* July 5, 1980, pp. 1–2.

131. Cf. *Gaudium et Spes,* 69; *Laborem Exercens,* 12 and 14.

132. Cf. *Quadragesimo Anno,* 72; *Laborem Exercens,* 19.

133. Cf. Document of the Second General Conference of the Latin American Episcopate at Medellín, "Justice," 1, 9; Puebla Document, 31, 35, 1245.

134. Cf. John XXIII, Encyclical *Mater et Magistra,* 163: AAS,53 (1961), p. 443; Paul VI, Encyclical *Populorum Progressio,* 51: AAS,59 (1967), p. 282; John Paul II, *Discourse to the Diplomatic Corps* of January 11, 1986: *L'Osservatore Romano,* January 12, 1986, pp. 4–5.

135. Cf. Paul VI, Encyclical *Populorum Progressio,* 55: AAS,59 (1967), p. 284.

136. Cf. *Gaudium et Spes,* 60; John Paul II, Discourse to UNESCO of June 2, 1980, 8: AAS72 (1980), pp. 739–40.

137. Cf. *Gaudium et Spes,* 59.

138. Cf. Declaration on Christian Education *Gravissimum Educationis,* 3 and 6; Pius XI, Encyclical *Divini illius magistri,* 28, 38 and 66: AAS,22 (1930), pp. 59, 63 and 68. Cf. Holy See, *Charter of Rights of the Family,* art. 5: *L'Osservatore Romano,* November 25, 1983.

139. Cf. Pastoral Constitution *Gaudium et Spes,* 29; John XXIII, Encyclical *Pacem in Terris,* 73–74 and 79: AAS,55 (1963), pp. 294–96.

140. Cf. *Dignitatis Humanae,* 7; *Gaudium et Spes,* 75; *Document of the Third General Conference of the Latin American Episcopate at Puebla,* 311–14, 317–18, 548.

141. Cf. Paul VI, Apostolic Exhortation *Evangelii Nuntiandi,* 19: AAS,68 (1976), p. 18.

142. Cf. Second Extraordinary Synod, *Relatio Finalis,* II, D, 4: *L'Osservatore Romano,* December 10, 1985, p. 7.

143. Cf. Paul VI, Apostolic Exhoration *Evangelii Nuntiandi,* 20: AAS,68 (1976), pp. 18–19.

144. Cf. Jn. 3:21.

145. Cf. Paul VI, *General Audience* of December 31, 1975: *L'Osservatore Romano,* January 1, 1976, p. 1. John Paul II took up this idea again in the *Discourse to the "Meeting for Friendship Between People"* of August 29, 1982: *L'Osservatore Romano,* August 30–31, 1982. The Latin American Bishops also alluded to this idea in the *Message to the Peoples of Latin America,* 8, and in the *Puebla Document,* 1188 and 1192.

146. Cf. Gal. 5:6.

54

Pope John Paul II
"Letter to Brazilian Episcopal Conference"
(Vatican City, April 9, 1986)

The pope had positive things to say about an authentic liberation theology, especially in sections 5 and 6 of this letter, and the bishops were delighted that he highly esteemed their pastoral work. On the other hand, a number of bishops have become increasingly uneasy with regard to the continuing pattern over the past decade of appointing bishops who are moderately to very conservative (with a few exceptions). Since these bishops are by and large indifferent to or even hostile to liberation theology, how is the Brazilian hierarchy going to fulfill its function of developing a liberation theology for all of Latin America, as the pope calls for in his letter? The English text is taken from L'Osservatore Romano *(April 28, 1986; English ed., pp.6-7).*

Beloved Cardinals and Brothers in the Episcopate:
Pax vobis, alleluia!
1. In this simple yet evocative greeting, intimately related to Jesus, risen from the dead (cf. John 20:19, 21 and 26; Luke 24:16), and with the congratulations and good wishes contained in these words, I wish to begin this message addressed to you and through you to the entire church in Brazil.

This expression of personal presence and care comes in the wake of the individual and group gatherings with all of you, as well as the meeting your representatives had with me and my collaborators of the Roman Curia. This message is the third stage and the crowning moment of your *ad limina* visit, an ecclesial event which, over a period of fourteen months, touched the life of the episcopate and the church in Brazil. The framework within which this *ad limina* visit developed was the result of both your and my initiative and was an exercise highly expressive of an authentic collegiality that is at once both affective and effective, harmoniously linked with the correlative exercise of the *ministerium Petri*. The fraternal charity which characterized this experience, united to a relentless search for truth, inspired a dialogue that was not superficial but profound and coherent, a dialogue which, throughout its duration, was an instrument of that communion which, since the church's beginning and throughout its history, but in a special way in the documents of the Second Vatican Council, manifests itself as an essential element in the same church of Jesus Christ.

Surely this *ad limina* visit will be useful for each of you and the entire episcopal conference which together you constitute. The manner in which the *ad limina* visit was conducted was and will continue to be an invaluable service to the church in Brazil and, by extension, to other local churches and to the universal church, a service as well, even though indirect, to Brazilian society and by extension to the entire human family.

2. It would be superfluous to stress that this message has a markedly ecclesial character, given those to whom it is addressed, the context with which it deals and its themes: this message comes at the conclusion of an ecclesial act — namely, the *ad limina* visit; it is directed to persons consecrated to the church as its ministers and pastors; and it will touch on points of considerable interest to the life and mission of the church.

This message, therefore, springs from a precise ecclesiological perception — that of the Second Vatican Council — and, for that reason, responds to clearly felt needs and desires. For was it not you yourselves who, at the various stages of your *ad limina* visit strongly emphasized ecclesiology, explicitly stating that at the basis of the most serious problems confronting you as bishops is an ecclesiological question, and that the solution of these very problems necessarily involves a well-grounded and precise concept of church?

Aware of this, I felt it my duty to stress in all our meetings the basic features of the true church of Jesus Christ, features affirmed with the necessary clarity by the ordinary and extraordinary magisterium of the church — especially by the documents of the Second Vatican Council — and by the *sensus fidelium*.

The Church is, before everything else, a mystery — that is its first feature — a response to the loving and saving plan of the Father, a prolongation of the incarnate word's mission, fruit of the Holy Spirit's creative action. For this reason the church cannot be defined and interpreted beginning with purely rational categories (socio-political or otherwise), the product of a purely human knowledge. Part of the mystery of the church consists in its being: holy, although made up of sinners; pilgrim, contemplative in action and active in contemplation; eschatological, the first fruits of the kingdom but not yet its fullness and consummation; changing in accidental aspects, yet unchanging in being and in mission.

This very mission — and this is the second feature to outline — is that of *evangelization* — that is, to provide for the world the ministry of salvation, by means of the *dialogus salutis* begun with it (cf. the encyclical *Ecclesiam Suam* of Pope Paul VI). The *ministerium salutis* is essentially religious because it is born of God's initiative and finds its completion in the absolute of God. It is at the same time service to humankind — the person and society—to its spiritual and temporal needs, fundamental human rights, and human and civil life in common.

Consequently it is part of the church's mission to *concern itself in a certain way with questions relating to the human person* from womb to the tomb, questions of a social and socio-political nature. The proper exercise of this delicate aspect of the church's evangelizing mission requires that certain conditions be met, among them: a clear-cut distinction between the function of the laity, committed by specific vocation and charism to temporal tasks, and the function of pastors who dedicate themselves to forming the laity to live out those temporal tasks. Another condition is that it be clear that the church as such does not point out technical solutions to temporal problems, but rather illuminates the search for solutions with the light of faith. A final condition is that the exercise of ministry in the socio-political area ought to remain in perfect harmony with the constant teachings of the magisterium.

THE CHURCH: FACED WITH FORMIDABLE CHALLENGES

3. In this regard the church in Brazil as well as in other regions, especially in Latin America, finds itself faced with formidable challenges. It is aware of its limitations and what is lacking in order to confront these challenges; yet the church does not cease to believe that in this task it can count on the help of the Spirit of the Father and of Jesus Christ. This is why it absolutely never loses theological hope.

Some of these challenges are ecclesial in nature. I dealt with several of them with a sense of brotherly trust in my discourses to the various groups during the *ad limina* visit. I encouraged you not to lose sight of these ecclesial challenges and to seek possible solutions with decisiveness and patience. I refer to the shortage of priests, men and women religious, and pastoral workers, the adequate formation of ordained ministers, the threat to faith coming from fundamentalist as well as non-Christian sects, catechesis, family and youth problems, the danger coming from ecclesiologies that distance themselves from that of the Second Vatican Council, and so forth. Once again, beloved brother bishops, I encourage you, with renewed certainty, sustained by convictions in the depths of my soul and reenforced again by this very *ad limina* visit:

—the conviction that the people entrusted to your pastoral care by God are gifted with an authentic hunger and thirst for God, for God's word, God's sacramental mysteries, for the essential truths of faith, realities which they express in their own way in their popular religious devotions. Nor is there lacking in their instinctively Christian and Catholic spirit a deep sense of great filial love of the Mother of Jesus, a sense of reverence toward the successor of Peter, whoever he may be. This is the church's great power, as I never ceased to observe in my pilgrimage throughout this country, and it is a source of comfort for those who govern the church there as pastors.

This force would be even greater if those riches were continually consolidated by a lively and orderly liturgy, by a properly oriented sacramental practice and catechesis, by great attention paid to vocations, which certainly would arise;

—the conviction that despite the above-mentioned deficiencies, these persons preserve by God's grace the seeds of the gospel sown since the first days of evangelization by devoted and hardworking missionaries. The work of these apostles is not eclipsed even at the moment when the church in your country pursues the task of achieving its own proper physiognomy, developing its own resources and even extending a helping hand to needier churches;

—the conviction that you and your collaborators in pastoral service are, in the eyes of the universal church and of the world, giving witness to being pastors who are extraordinarily close to your people, in solidarity with them in joy and in suffering, ready to educate them in the faith and embellish their Christian life as well as assist them in their needs, share in their afflictions and efforts, and inspire hope in them.

In this connection it is more than just to express sincere gratitude to the innumerable bishops, priests, men and women religious, devoted and committed lay persons who, throughout the history of this church—but I refer especially to more recent times—have given proof of admirable apostolic zeal, abnegation, and a spirit of sacrifice, of extreme love for their people, and of an incomparable capacity for selfless service. May these ministers according to the heart of Christ, priest and good shepherd, and their collaborators, continue to be numerous and even grow—this is the greatest grace God can grant a church. To achieve this grace may the ongoing formation of ordained ministers be constantly upgraded. May special care be taken in the preparation of candidates for the priesthood in seminaries and in the period of preparation of permanent deacons, in the formation of young candidates to the religious life, in accord with the vision proposed by the church. May attention likewise continue to be given to the human, spiritual, and apostolic formation of the laity disposed to serve the gospel.

Other challenges are of a cultural, socio-political, or economic nature and show themselves at this historical moment of the nation as demanding attention and requiring a response. It is, speaking in global terms, the challenge of the contrast between two Brazils: one highly developed, dynamic, thrusting toward progress and affluence; the other, reflected in extensive poverty belts, in endemic diseases, illiteracy, and social marginalization. This contrast penalizes with its tremendous imbalances and inequalities great numbers of the population condemned to all sorts of misery.

Grave problems like these cannot be foreign to the church, at least in the light of the ethical aspects they involve, as cause or as effect of material situations. But in this area also the church, led by you, the bishops of Brazil, gives signs of being identified with the people, especially the poor, the suffering, those without influence, resources, and assistance. The church consecrates itself to these with a love that is neither exclusive nor excluding but rather preferential. For the church does not hesitate to defend fearlessly the just and noble cause of human rights and to support courageous reforms, leading to a better distribution of goods, including earthly goods such as education, health services, housing, and so forth. Because the church has taken this courageous stance it enjoys the respect and trust of a broad cross section of Brazilian society.

Well aware of the fact that you cannot abdicate your specific mission as bishops in order to assume temporal tasks, you regret the disturbing lack of laity properly prepared to confront these latter challenges. However, I know that I can vigorously maintain the appeal I had occasion to repeat during the *ad limina* visit to the effect that you do not depart from the important priority you have set for yourselves, that of *forming the laity*, whether among the builders of a pluralist society (cf. Document of Puebla, part 4, chap. 3), or among the popular masses, in workers' or rural environments, or among youth — always with the idea of furthering the laity's active presence in and pursuit of temporal tasks. *To form lay persons* means to assist them in the acquisition of real competence and ability in the field in which they ought to act; but it means, above all, educating them in the faith and in the knowledge of the church's doctrine in that same field.

4. In the context of this human and ecclesial reality, with its challenges, you are called to be pastors in Brazil today. An immense task! A provocative and fascinating one! A task that is possible, with God's help.

On more than one occasion, basing myself on the rich and fertile teaching of the Second Vatican Council, I have tried to define that task. I did it in a special way in the discourse addressed to you in Fortaleza at the close of my unforgettable journey in Brazil. I wanted to do it also on subsequent occasions, in the nine discourses addressed to the regional groups that came for the *ad limina* visit.

This task is derived from a mysterious call of God and corresponds to a *mission* given by God and it obtains its support from the *grace of God* conferred by the sacrament of holy orders. In carrying out the task certain essential aspects cannot be omitted and ought to be properly applied to the concrete conditions of the human and ecclesial situation in Brazil.

God our Father and our Lord Jesus Christ expect, the church in Brazil expects, along with the priests, men and women religious, consecrated persons and laity of all kinds, and to a certain extent, the entire Brazilian people expect that each of its bishops be:

—a convinced and convincing proclaimer of the word of God and, consequently, an educator in the faith, a servant and master of revealed truth, especially the truth about Christ, about the church, and about the human person;

—a builder of ecclesial community and at the same time a sign and visible principle of *continuing communion* which ought to be the soul of that community, above all in the midst of possible divisions and dangers, conflicts and threats of discord and disintegration;

— an example of true unity with his brother priests and faithful in the bosom of the particular church, with his brother bishops in the episcopal conference and in the universal church, and the successor of Peter and his ministry in the service of Catholicity;

— a *perfector* of his priests and consecrated persons, by means of his teaching and life witness and *dispenser of the mysteries of sanctification,* through the sacraments, for all the faithful, without distinction;

— a pastor and guide of the people entrusted to him along life's journey and in the midst of earthly realities, on the way to salvation;

— a spiritual father for all, especially those most in need of guidance and help, defense and protection.

5. Having before your eyes these irreducible demands of episcopal service, you have striven, especially in these recent years, to find *appropriate responses to the challenges* mentioned above, which were never far from your thoughts and desires. The Holy See has not ceased to accompany you in these efforts as it does with all the churches. An expression and proof of the attention with which the Holy See participates in those efforts are the numerous documents recently published, among them the two Instructions provided by the Congregation for the Doctrine of the Faith, with my explicit approval: one, regarding certain aspects of the theology of liberation (*Libertatis Nuntius* of August 6, 1984); the other, on Christian freedom and liberation (*Libertatis Conscientia* of March 22, 1986). These latter two, addressed to the universal church, have an undeniable pastoral relevancy for Brazil.

To the extent that the effort is made to find those appropriate responses—imbued with insight into the rich experience of the church in your country—to that extent will the responses be as effective and constructive as possible and, at the same time, consistent and coherent with the teachings of the gospel of the living tradition and of the ongoing magisterium of the church. As long as all this is observed we are convinced, we and you, that the theology of liberation is not only timely but useful and necessary. It should constitute a new state—in close connection with former ones—of the theological reflection initiated with the apostolic tradition and continued by the great fathers and doctors, by the ordinary and extraordinary magisterium and, in more recent years, by the rich patrimony of the church's social doctrine, expressed in documents from *Rerum Novarum* to *Laborem Exercens.*

I think that in this field the church in Brazil can play an important and at the same time delicate role: that of creating the space and conditions for the development of a theological reflection that fully adheres to the church's constant teaching on social matters and, at the same time, is suitable for inspiring an effective pastoral praxis in favor of social justice, equity, the observance of human rights, the construction of a human society based on brotherhood, harmony, truth, and charity. This theological reflection should also be in perfect accord with the fruitful teaching in the two previously mentioned Instructions. Thus the fatal orientations and tendencies of both unbridled capitalism and collectivism or state capitalism can be broken. Both are incapable of assuring the liberation brought about by Jesus Christ (cf. *Libertatis Conscientia*, nn. 10 and 13). Such a function, if realized, will certainly be a service the church can render to the nation, and to Latin America, as well as to many other world religions where similarly serious challenges present themselves.

There is no substitute for wise and courageous action on the part of pastors—that is, on your part, in the carrying out of this role. May God help you to be unceasingly watchful so that a correct and necessary theology of liberation can develop in Brazil and in Latin America in a homogenous and not heterogeneous fashion with relation to the theology of all times, in full fidelity to church doctrine, attentive to a preferential but not excluding or exclusive love for the poor.

6. At this point it is indispensable to recall the important reflection of the Instruction *Libertatis Conscientia* (nn. 23 and 71) regarding the two constitutive dimensions of liberation in its Christian conception: whether at the level of reflection or of praxis, liberation is, first of all *salvific* (an aspect of the salvation achieved by Jesus Christ, son of God) and afterward *socio-ethical* (or *ethico-political*). To reduce one dimension to the other—practically suppressing them both—or putting the second before the first is to subvert and emasculate true Christian liberation.

It is the duty of pastors, therefore, to announce to all persons, without ambiguities, the *mystery* of *liberation* in the cross and resurrection of Christ. The church of Jesus, in our day as in all times, in Brazil as well as in every part of the world, knows only one wisdom and only one power: that of the cross which leads to the resurrection (cf. 1 Cor. 2:1-5; Gal. 6:14). The poor of this nation, the poor of this continent, are the first to feel the urgent need for this *gospel* of *radical* and *integral liberation*. To deny them would be to defraud and disillusion them.

On the other hand, you—and with you the entire church in Brazil—show yourselves ready to undertake in your own area and in line with your proper charism all that as a consequence is derived from salvific liberation. This is, moreover, what the church, from its very dawn, always tried to do by means of its saints, teachers, and pastors, and by means of the faithful engaged in temporal realities.

REGAIN AND HEAL FREEDOM

Allow me, brothers in the episcopate, with full trust and confidence, to invite you to a task that is less visible but of great relevance besides being profoundly related to our episcopal function: the task of educating for liberation, educating for freedom (cf. *Libertatis Conscientia*, nn. 80, 81, and

94). To *educate for freedom* is to impart those criteria without which that freedom becomes a chimera, if not a dangerous deception.

It is to help reconquer the lost freedom or to heal freedom when it has become adulterated or corrupted. As educators in the faith, as the Second Vatican Council calls us, our task will also consist in educating for freedom.

7. I entrust this message to the hands of my esteemed brother Cardinal Bernardin Gantin, prefect of the Congregation in the Roman Curia which is dedicated, with exemplary availability, to aid all the bishops in their ministry to the churches and to collaborate with the bishop of Rome in his function of "confirming the brethren." Invited as he has been by you to preach a day of spiritual retreat, in the larger context of the General Assembly of the Episcopal Conference, he will kindly tell you, in his own words and with the warmth of his personal presence, the feelings of sincere appreciation and brotherhood with which this message has been written; those very same sentiments, which on my part inspired and animated the meetings we had during the *ad limina* visits.

Evoking once again in my mind those meetings and especially the meeting of March 13-15 with some of you, there spontaneously came to me the feeling of having attained with you a new and deeper form of collegiality: after this *ad limina* visit, the pope and his collaborators surely know better these realities, which pertain to the church in Brazil and its episcopate. In turn, the pope and his collaborators hope they themselves are now more and better known.

I desire to remain in constant contact with you and to participate in *vinculo fraternitatis,* in all the important and demanding tasks of your pastoral ministry, and to remain in contact especially when those tasks weigh more heavily on your shoulders.

On my part, I ask for your prayers for me, especially in the eucharist, so that the name *servus servorum Dei,* given by St. Gregory the Great to the pontifical mission, may be true in regard to me.

In the person of Cardinal Gantin I wish to be reunited with you at the feet of Our Lady Aparecida. May we all be together around the mother of the high priest, Jesus Christ, in the image of the apostles of whom we are the successors, assembled together with Mary in the expectation of the gift of the Holy Spirit of truth and charity. May this Spirit make you watchful pastors of the ecclesial communities of Brazil and ministers of salvation for the entire human community of Brazil.

At the close of this message and the memorable *ad limina* visit, it remains for me, beloved brother bishops, to confer upon you the apostolic blessing, an expression of the divine blessings which I implore God for you and your episcopal ministry. Please communicate this apostolic blessing to the entire church in Brazil, for whom this letter is also intended: to priests, collaborators in the episcopal ministry; to the permanent deacons, numerous, dedicated, and active in several of your dioceses; to the seminarians at this decisive moment on their path toward the priesthood; to all consecrated

persons whether devoted to prayer, to silence, and to penance, or dedicated
to education, to the service of the sick, the poor, or the myriad other forms
of evangelization; to the laity active in movements and associations, in the
basic ecclesial communities, in extraordinary ministries, and in the most
diverse kinds of service to the church; to lay men and women involved as
sons and daughters of the church and in the name of its faith in temporal
endeavors; to the laity who for some reason are not very involved, so that
they may feel themselves motivated to assume their role in the church and
in the world; to those who are separated from the church, that they may
return to the practice of their Christian and Catholic life; to those who
experience doubts and are searching for the way, that light and energy be
not lacking to them; to youth and children who are so numerous in your
nation and so worthy of concern, because they are the hope and the future
of this nation and of the church and because they face so many problems
and threats; to all, finally, especially the poor, those who suffer or weep,
that God may be all in all.

55

Alfred T. Hennelly, S. J.
"The Red-Hot Issue: Liberation Theology"
(May 24, 1986)

This article appeared in the Jesuit weekly America *(May 24, 1986), pp. 425-28. It stresses the positive aspects for the whole church of the "Instruction on Christian Freedom and Liberation" (see no. 53 above).*

For a number of years, I have kept a list of themes in Scripture and tradition that for various reasons appear to be rarely used in the ordinary preaching of the U.S. Catholic Church. A high position on that list has long been occupied by the topic of "Christian freedom," as epitomized in the ringing words of St. Paul: "For freedom Christ has set us free; stand fast therefore and do not submit again to a yoke of slavery" (Gal. 5:1). I could only rejoice, then, to hear that the Vatican Congregation for the Doctrine of the Faith had elaborated this theme in its recent "Instruction on Christian Freedom and Liberation."

Unfortunately, there was a certain delay in my receiving the document, and during that time the secular media (apparently the first recipients) excerpted it, analyzed it, editorialized on it, and quickly moved on to other matters. But let me emphasize from the start that the document was well worth waiting for. Despite a loud chorus of criticism from various sources, it eminently succeeds in providing an excellent brief synthesis of the major themes of a liberating theology. Thus we now have a formal Vatican endorsement (with all the necessary caveats and provisos) of the liberation approach, not merely for Latin America or other parts of the Third World, but for the universal church.

This is pointed out with great clarity in the introduction, which indicates its purpose of presenting the "principal theoretical and practical aspects" of the theme of freedom and liberation, and then goes on to insist: "As regards applications to different local situations, *it is for the local churches,* in communion with one another and with the See of Peter, *to make direct provision for them"* (no. 3; my italics). The publication of "Christian Freedom and Liberation" is, then, a theological event of profound importance with far-reaching implications for the Catholic Church in every part of the world. I will return to this later on, but first let us turn to the Instruction itself.

After a brief introduction, the document may be divided into two principal sections, the first consisting of the first three chapters and emphasizing theoretical and scriptural reflections on freedom, liberation, and sin, while the second section is concerned with mainly practical issues regarding the liberating mission of the church (chap. 4) and a Christian practice of liberation (chap. 5). Since the Instruction is quite long (over 18,000 words) and at times tedious and repetitive, readers with limited time would do well to begin with the fifth chapter, which treats most of the fundamental and controversial issues.

As regards the general method of the work, it has been asserted in the press that it actually represents a synthesis of the teaching of Pope John Paul II. There is some truth to this observation, but only in the sense that the pope has thoroughly assimilated Catholic social and political thought, especially of the past twenty-five years, beginning with Pope John XXIII's *Mater et Magistra* in 1961 and including Vatican II and the writings of Pope Paul VI. His adoption of the names of these two popes as his own was consequently more than merely a symbolic gesture, since it constituted an expression of his commitment to their lifework and teaching. John Paul's major contribution to Catholic social thought, *Laborem Exercens* ("On Human Labor"[1981]), is also his most significant contribution to this Instruction and, in my opinion, is the most original aspect of the document's integration of liberation themes into the mainstream of Catholic social thought. My major disappointment with this new text is that it was not issued as an encyclical letter, which would have given its teaching even greater weight on the world theological scene.

Regarding this method, there has also been criticism that the assimilation of liberation thinking into official or mainstream Catholic thought would blunt the cutting edge of this thinking, and that it would be co-opted, domesticated, and soon forgotten. I do not find this argument convincing, for many liberation theologians I have met have many years of experience resisting such takeovers and appear totally impervious to such machinations. Besides, the text I have quoted above on the applications of liberation themes by local churches seems to me to provide Latin American and other Third World theologians with the carte blanche they need to continue on the paths they have already chosen.

At this point it would be helpful to refer to the Instruction's own understanding of its method, which I found to be extremely interesting. In a section on the church's social teaching, which is said to be born of the encounter of the gospel with the problems of society, we learn that such doctrine is essentially orientated toward practice and that it develops in accordance with the changing circumstances of history. Finally, it is asserted that "far from constituting a closed system, it remains constantly open to the new questions which continually arise; *it requires the contribution of all charisms, experiences, and skills*" (no. 72; my italics). The italicized sentence appears to me to open up a promising new direction in the formation process of Catholic social thought, and I happily take this opportunity to make my own "contribution," in the following reflections on a variety of topics in the Instruction.

The first two chapters are concerned with a history and analysis of freedom and sin. Frankly, it is a rather tedious beginning, and readers should resist being turned away at the start. The outlook is intellectual in the European style. The few references to the poor present a rather idyllic view, with lyrical descriptions of the "liberating joy" and "emancipation from the dominating claims of the learned" that come to the poor because of their knowledge of God (no. 21). I was able to find only one text that seemed to express the yearning of the masses of the Third World for full liberation: "It remains true that one of the major phenomena of our time, of continental proportions, is the awakening of the consciousness of people who, bent beneath the weight of age-old poverty, aspire to a life in dignity and justice and are prepared to fight for their freedom" (no. 17).

A tincture of pessimism regarding freedom pervades this entire section; for example, we read: "God calls humankind to freedom. In each person there lives a desire to be free. And yet this desire *almost always* tends toward slavery and oppression" (no. 37; my italics). Here we are confronted with an attitude that eludes theological argument. The bearers of this and similar views should immediately try anything that might promise relief from such profound *Weltschmerz.*

A refreshing change occurs when we arrive at chapter 3, which contains a good brief survey of liberation themes in the entire Bible. Fortunately, it does not repeat familiar criticisms that liberation theology overemphasizes the exodus or turns it into a political event. Rather, it states the simple fact that exodus is "the liberating action of Yahweh which serves as model and reference for all others" and that it "has a meaning which is both religious and political" (no. 44). The treatment of the New Commandment succinctly weaves together many themes from the New Testament and makes a candid application to the present: "The evil inequities and oppression of every kind which afflict millions of men and women today openly contradict Christ's gospel and cannot leave the conscience of any Christian indifferent" (no. 57). Both here (no. 48) and at the conclusion of the Instruction (no. 97), the role of Mary as model of Christian hope and faith, with a special relationship to the poor, is presented well and integrated gracefully into the biblical history.

Chapter 4, regarding the liberating mission of the church, is dominated by the age-old problem of Christian integration of membership in the city of God with active participation in the earthly city with all its social, political, and economic problems. The document insists that the essential mission of the church is one of evangelization and salvation, and that in this mission its teaching "extends to the whole moral order and notably to the justice that must regulate human relations. This is part of the preaching of the gospel" (no. 63).

With respect to this chapter, too, a certain controversy has arisen in press reports concerning the phrase "a love of preference for the poor"; some accounts held that this was replacing the expression "preferential option for the poor," which had come into common usage through the Latin American Bishops' Conference. Supposedly this was done to avoid the potentially divisive effects implied in a "preferential option." However, the phrase "special option for the poor" is used no less than three times in the pertinent section (no. 68), which clearly refutes the charge that it was being deliberately jettisoned. We may only speculate that the "love of preference" was also used in order to emphasize the Christian motivation of the option.

Another area that has created controversy has been the attitude of the Instruction with regard to basic Christian communities, which are very widespread in Latin America, the Philippines, and many other parts of the Third World. The text states quite approvingly that these small worshiping communities are "a source of great hope," "a real expression of communion," and "a treasure to the whole church," as long as they live in unity with the local and universal church (no. 69). My own experience with Latin America's basic Christian communities has convinced me that they simply did not come into existence without the commitment of the services (e.g., for training lay leaders) and resources (e.g., simple teaching materials, explanations of Scripture) of the local church. Also, their extraordinarily keen sense of belonging to the worldwide church is demonstrated dramatically by their many prayers for that church during worship meetings. As regards the issue of unity, it is abundantly clear that this goal will require a constant commitment and ongoing effort on both sides, people and bishops, in order to construct "a still deeper communion" (no. 69).

The final chapter, chapter 5, on Christian practice for social change, has drawn considerable attention for its discussion of various aspects of violence. These include a description of the stringent requirements for a just rebellion ("as a last resort") and the authors' preference for nonviolent methods ("more conformable to moral principles and have no fewer prospects for success") as a way of achieving social change (no. 79). There is also support for Latin American theology's strong condemnation of systematic violence, including "violence exercised by the powerful against the poor, arbitrary action by the police, and any form of violence established as a form of government" (no. 76).

However, I believe there is a major weakness in this chapter with regard to its treatment of another central notion of liberation theology, and that is the concept of "social sin." The document first asserts that "the sin which is at the root of unjust situations is, *in a true and immediate sense*, a voluntary act which has its source in the freedom of individuals" (no. 75; my italics).

But this statement is immediately followed by what appears to be a non sequitur: "Only *in a derived and secondary* sense is [sin] applicable to structures, and only in this sense can one speak of 'social sin'" (no. 75; my italics). But is it not clear, as in the case of apartheid in South Africa, that though the structures were the creation of individual sinful acts and are continued in existence by individual human acts, nevertheless the oppression and suffering they inflict upon human persons for generations upon generations is immeasurably greater than any individual act of sin? The best depiction I have found of the profound primary evil of social sin is in the following text of Laurenti Magesa of Zambia in the context of an African liberation theology:

> The worst type of sin, in fact the only 'mortal sin' which has enslaved man for the greater part of his history, is the institutionalized sin. Under the institution, vice appears to be, or is actually turned into, virtue. Apathy toward evil is thus engendered; recognition of sin becomes totally effaced; sinful institutions become absolutized, almost idolized, and sin becomes absolutely mortal. . . . Recognition of sin, and therefore repentance for sin, is made practically impossible when sin is idolized as an institution.

With that in mind, I find it impossible to understand why such "social sin" cannot be called sin in a very true and extremely immediate sense.

Finally, the most outstanding feature of this chapter—and the most significant contribution of the entire Instruction—is the integration of Pope John Paul's ground-breaking encyclical *Laborem Exercens* into a liberation context: "Thus the solution of most of the serious problems related to poverty is to be found in a true civilization of work. In a sense, work is the key to the whole social question. It is therefore in the domain of work that priority must be given to the *action of liberation in freedom*" (no. 83; my italics).

Since this part of the Instruction is already a digest of the entire encyclical, it would be impossible to summarize it again, but it seems worthwhile to reiterate certain familiar principles: "The person of the worker is the principle, subject, and purpose of work. . . . Every person has a right to work, and this right must be recognized in a practical way by an effective commitment to solving the tragic problem of unemployment. . . . The creation of jobs is a primary social task facing individuals and private enterprise, as well as the state. . . . The right to private property is inconceivable without responsibilities to the common good" (nos. 84-87). There is much more that deserves careful study in the text, but what is most important is its overarching meaning: the Instruction places human labor—the key to the whole social question—at the heart of the process of liberation in every nation and in every culture and thus provides an *inner* dynamism for a truly universal liberating theology.

A few other general reflections on the Instruction may be added here before concluding. First of all, it has probably occurred to some readers that certain issues which they consider to be absolutely crucial to human liberation have received no mention at all so far. At least this did occur to me, and my response is to reemphasize the importance of the first text I quoted in this article, wherein local churches are told to apply the theory and practice of the Instruction to their different local situations.

Thus, in our own local U.S. situation as a military and economic superpower, I think the application would be to reflect and act even more energetically and courageously about the threat of nuclear weapons and the ending of an insane arms race, to increase the urgency of our reflection on the U.S. economy and its impact, especially on the poor, both at home and abroad, and perhaps to launch a third pastoral that would begin serious reflections on our increasingly belligerent and militaristic foreign policy.

The liberation of women is not alluded to in the document, but, according to the argument above, it should encourage the many talented and dedicated U.S. women who are world leaders in creating a feminist liberating theology. Neither is there mention in the text of the deep roots of racial discrimination and oppression, but it could strengthen this country's many followers of the tradition of Martin Luther King, Jr., who are far advanced in the development of a black theology of liberation, which in turn serves as a model for other minority communities.

The instruction raises a final and very important question that goes to the heart of the theological discipline itself. If my assertion is true—namely, that a *universal significance* has been accorded to a liberating theology—what effect will this have on our reigning centers of theology—that is, the U.S. universities and seminaries that are now busily preparing the next generation of church leaders? In answering this question, it is of primary importance to stress that the implied problem will not be solved by adding a course or two on liberation theology to an already established curriculum. For the key element of any liberating theology, as the Uruguayan Jesuit Juan Luis Segundo has insisted in all his published work, is not its liberating *content* but its liberating *method*. This method, which is explicitly intellectual in the classical sense of "faith seeking *intellectum*," includes a critique of ideology, which critique exposes the alienating or oppressive ideas that legitimate domination in any given society, and a hermeneutical critique, which uncovers the same mechanisms of alienation and legitimation in the interpretation of Scripture and the articulation of theology.

Clearly, then, such a theological method is not restricted to systematic theology, although as a method it should certainly affect every treatise in that field. But it also applies to the exegesis of Scripture, to the methods and subjects of moral theology, to church history and the history of dogma, and, perhaps most of all, to the usually rarefied realms of spirituality, worship, and sacramental theology and practice. In brief, if liberating theology is taken seriously, as the instruction proposes, it must necessarily become central to the theological enterprise, and not remain the fringe phenomenon it is at present. Such a change should not be considered impossible, for to many in the younger generation of theologians it has already become the dominant theological movement for the 1980s and beyond.

So much for my own views. At this writing, I have not seen any Latin American reactions to this document, except for a few brief quotes in the international press. One of these that impressed me deeply was that of Gustavo Gutiérrez. The Peruvian priest referred to the Instruction as a "relaunching" of the movement and insisted that "it closes a chapter; a new, more positive period is beginning." Since Gutiérrez, with his book *A Theology of Liberation,* was primarily responsible for beginning the chapter that is closing, his views should be listened to carefully. Also of great interest to me were the views of Pope John Paul II, which he shared with the bishops of Brazil a short time before the Vatican Instruction was released:

> It would be unrealistic to suppose that in the midst of the intense dialogue of these days the red-hot question of "liberation theology" would not arise. It is not the theme of these days, but neither would it be realistic to avoid it. . . . When purified of elements which can adulterate it, with grave consequences for the faith, this theology is not only orthodox but necessary.

56

Ecumenical Association of Third World Theologians "Final Document: Intercontinental Women's Conference" (Oaxtepec, Mexico, December 6, 1986)

This document is taken from the book, With Passion and Compassion: Third World Women Doing Theology *(Maryknoll, N.Y.: Orbis Books, 1988), pp. 184–90. The editors are Sr. Virginia Fabella, M.M., Asia coordinator of EATWOT, and Mercy Amba Oduyoye, author of* Hearing and Knowing: A Theological Reflection on Africa *and deputy general secretary of the World Council of Churches in Geneva. The document is most impressive, for it is evidence of a women's theology of liberation from oppression that is both worldwide and thoroughly ecumenical.*

An intercontinental conference of women theologians from the Third World was held in Oaxtepec, Mexico, December 1–6, 1986. The theme of the conference was "Doing Theology from Third World Women's Perspective." The conference was sponsored by the Ecumenical Association of Third World Theologians (EATWOT) as part of its commitment to total liberation and the achievement of full humanity for all, women and men alike.

Planned to operate in three stages, the women's project sought:

1. To broaden our understanding of women's situation in our respective socio-economic, political, and religio-cultural realities.

2. To discover the vital aspects of women's experience of God in emerging spiritualities.

3. To reread the Bible from Third World women's perspective in the light of total liberation.

4. To articulate faith reflections on women's realities, struggles, and spirituality.

5. To deepen our commitment and solidarity work toward full humanity for all.

The first two phases of the study took place on the national and continental levels. The present meeting provided a forum of exchange among the women on their findings of the study in their respective continents. Twenty-six delegates from seventeen countries of Africa, Asia, and Latin America took part in the conference.

Mexico—where an affluent minority and a poor majority exist side by side, where signs of its colonial past and neocolonial present were everywhere evident, where *machismo* is still a given—offered a suitable venue for our theological reflections from the perspective of Third World women.

In their address of welcome, the Latin American women pointed out that even though the nameless concubine of the levite in Judges 19 did not speak out against the oppression meted out to her, her cut-up body did. Everyone who saw the outcome of this atrocity was enjoined "to reflect, take counsel, and speak." So Israel stood together united to act for justice. This story moves us to ponder the oppression of women, to discuss it and then give our verdict, acting as Deborah, the judge, would have done, confident that today is the day of Yahweh (Judges 4).

PROCESS

One of the notable features of this meeting was the atmosphere of serious study, sisterhood, and friendliness that prevailed throughout. Worship times saw all the delegates praying together, in the typical styles of each continent, to the God of all nations. The themes (reality of oppression and struggle of women; vital aspects of women's experience of God in emerging spiritualities; women and the church; women and the Bible; women and christology) were presented by skilled panelists from each of the three continents. The open forum that followed each panel presentation gave the participants a chance to question, clarify, or comment on the issues raised.

Variations in the dynamics of the meeting included role-playing, audiovisual presentations, a fishbowl session, small-group discussions, and mural painting by all. Informal exchanges outside the formal sessions strengthened the spirit of friendship and solidarity.

CONTENTS

The panel on each theme brought out some rich commonalities and differences:

1. In all three continents the oppression of women is affirmed as a hard and abiding reality of life, though this varies in form and degree from place to place. Women have an irreplaceable role in society, yet our contribution is not acknowledged, nor are we accorded equal rights with our male counterparts. This oppression is felt in all sectors of life: economic, social, po-

litical, cultural, racial, sexual, religious, and even within the family itself. Having become conscious of our human rights and of the injustices perpetrated against us in all these sectors, as women we are teaming up and organizing various liberating movements and projects to help ourselves.

Some of these movements are motivated by Christian faith; we are aware that our liberation is part and parcel of the liberation of all the poor and oppressed promised by the gospel. Our efforts are rooted in Scriptures. Being created in God's image demands a total rupture with the prevailing patriarchal system in order to build an egalitarian society.

This liberating process happens differently in the three continents. In Latin America, women organize themselves around survival strategies. In Africa, the rebirth of women takes place in their struggle to overthrow the oppressive elements in traditional African cultures and religions, and the evils of colonialism. In Asia, the struggle is centered in rediscovering the pride of being women, in building womanhood and humane communities, and in fighting against political, economic, and sexual injustices.

Nevertheless, we have perceived a common perspective in the three continents. The women's struggle is deeply connected with the efforts of all the poor and the oppressed who are struggling for their liberation in all aspects of life.

2. Among the efforts being made toward liberation from oppression, theologizing emerges as a specific manner in which women struggle for their right to life. Our theologizing arises from our experience of being discriminated against as women and people of the Third World. The emerging spiritualities we perceive in the three continents show that spiritual experience rooted in action for justice constitutes an integral part of our theology. As women we articulate our theology in prayer and worship, in our relationship with our neighbor in whom God lives, and in our ongoing struggle as one with the poor and the oppressed.

Spiritual experience for women of the Third World thus means being in communion with all those who fight for life. This is our motivation for doing theology, which is done with the body, the heart, the mind, the total self— all penetrated by the Holy Spirit. Compassion and solidarity are main elements of this spirituality and this theology, and this is expressed in action: organized, patient and loving action. The divergences in action are due to religious and cultural differences among the continents, to the diversities within the various regions in each continent, and to the varied ways the different churches assimilate these new experiences.

3. The Bible plays a vital role in the lives of women and in our struggle for liberation, because the Bible itself is a book about life and liberation. This liberation is rooted in God's action in history, particularly in the Christ-event. The Gospel restores to women our human dignity as persons loved and cherished by God. New methods of reading the Bible are emerging in the three continents. In Latin America, the poor have rediscovered the Bible and, in it, the liberating God, and this has allowed women, who

are part of the poor and oppressed, to capture the spirit of the text while distancing themselves from the letter. In Asia, where Christians are a minority, the Bible is read in the context of interfaith dialogue as well as in the context of concrete life struggles. In Africa, there is some evidence of openness to new ways of reading the Bible. The fact that there are now some women biblically trained gives us hope that the Bible will be read and interpreted from the perspective of women, especially since the situation of African women has elements similar to that of women in the Old Testament.

In reading the Bible, we women face the constant challenge of interpreting texts that are against us. There is great commonality in considering these texts in their cultural contexts and epochs, not as normative, but as peripheral and not touching the heart of the gospel. The essentially patriarchal nature of the Bible and the interpretations that reinforce the oppressive elements should be acknowledged and exposed.

We participants felt that instead of rejecting the Bible wholesale, as some women do, we should "mine" deeper into it, rejecting all the patriarchal crusts that have obstructed its true meaning over the centuries, and highlighting those neglected elements that portray women as individuals in their own right as well as God's co-workers and agents of life. It was considered imperative to highlight Jesus' relationship with women and his countercultural stand with respect to them. Emphasis should also be laid on God as lover and giver of life, as well as liberator of all the oppressed. The Bible is normative and authoritative insofar as it promotes fullness of life for each person (John 10:10).

4. In all three continents, women constitute a vital and dynamic force within the church. Our strong faith and numerous services of love keep the church alive, especially among the poor and the marginalized. Yet though we constitute a strong labor force within the heavily institutionalized church, we are powerless and voiceless, and in most churches are excluded from leadership roles and ordained ministries. This deplorable condition urgently calls for sustained efforts to discover new ways of being church, of being in the world as the visible presence of God's reign, and of the new creation.

As the New Testament *ecclesia* started with women who were active participants in all areas of its life and mission, we, as women of the Third World, are rediscovering our distinctive role and place in the renewed church today. Our faith in the power of the cross and the resurrection empowers us to live out the vision of God's new creation, where no one is subordinated or enslaved, but where free people take part in God's liberating project to build a true community and a new society. In Latin America and in parts of Africa, a hopeful sign is the increasing leadership roles played by women in basic ecclesial communities. In all Third World continents, the presence of women who stand for justice in all its forms is both challenging and conflictive. But this is the way in which the church will be able to rediscover its true identity.

5. Christology has appeared to be central to women's theology. In the person and praxis of Jesus Christ, women of the three continents find the grounds of our liberation from all discrimination: sexual, racial, social, economic, political, and religious. By reflecting on the incarnation—that is, the life, death, and resurrection of Jesus—we have come to realize the need to contextualize our christology in the oppressed and painful realities of our continents. This means that christology is integrally linked with action on behalf of social justice and the defense of each person's right to life and to a more humane life. Hence in Africa, christology has to do with apartheid, racial discrimination, militarism, deficiency syndromes that come in foreign-aid packages, and genocide perpetrated through family-planning programs. In Asia, with the massive poverty, sexual exploitation, and racial, ethnic, caste, and religious discrimination, christology incorporates the efforts to draw out the humanizing elements in other religions. In Latin America, where poverty and oppression often give rise to a tendency to use religion to reinforce a passive and fatalistic attitude to life, christology is necessarily connected with the preferential option for the poor. In short, to christologize means to be committed to the struggle for a new society.

We remark also that many Christians in our continents are seeking to see in Jesus' suffering, passion, death, and resurrection a meaning for their own suffering. This explains the great devotion our people have to the mysteries of the passion and the cross. Nevertheless, we have a mission to announce that Christ brought a new life for humanity and that this was the whole point of his suffering. Suffering that is inflicted by the oppressor and is passively accepted does not lead to life; it is destructive and demonic. But suffering that is part of the struggle for the sake of God's reign or that results from the uncontrollable and mysterious conditions of humankind is redeeming and is rooted in the paschal mystery, evocative of the rhythm of pregnancy, delivery, and birth. This kind of suffering is familiar to women of all times, who participate in the pains of birth and the joys of a new creation.

6. The passionate and compassionate way in which women do theology is a rich contribution to theological science. The key to this theological process is the word "life." We perceive that in the three continents women are deeply covenanted with life, giving life and protecting life. The woman in our streets always appears surrounded and weighed down with children: children in her body, in her arms, on her back. Thus, even physically, she extends and reaches out to other lives, other human beings born from her body, sustaining their lives. In doing theology, we in the Third World thus find ourselves committed and faithful to all the vital elements that compose human life. Thus without losing its scientific seriousness, which includes analyzing the basic causes of women's multiple oppression, our theologizing is deeply rooted in experience, in affection, in life. We as women feel called

to do scientific theology passionately, a theology based on feeling as well as on knowledge, on wisdom as well as on science, a theology made not only with the mind but also with the heart, the body, the womb. We consider this as a challenge and an imperative not only for doing theology from women's perspective, but also for all theology. The Latin American theology of liberation has already discovered that the rigid, cold, and purely rationalistic theology of the West thirsts to be combined with spiritual flexibility and creativeness. "Minjung theology" and other efforts of contextual theology in Asia, as well as black theology and other emerging theologies in Africa, are also finding their way to a theological reformulation that is firmly and deeply rooted in human life, where the Holy Spirit lives and acts. Thus our theology is people-oriented, not something done in an ivory tower, apart from people.

As women, we have a contribution to make in the effort of Christian communities to rethink and rediscover new expressions of their Christian faith. Moreover, since religious pluralism is a reality in our different situations, we, as Christians and as theologians, need to dialogue and work with women of other faiths, convinced that, in other religious traditions, there too we meet Christ.

In the task of doing theology, our common goal is to bring a new dimension to the struggle for justice and for promoting God's reign, a dimension that is not ours, but is given to us both by the voices of our people clamoring for justice and by God, who inspired and convoked us here. Humanity as a whole, not only women, stands to benefit from the whole endeavor.

RECOMMENDATIONS

Our rich and intensive reflections and exchanges during these past days inspired many possible lines of action, both personal and communal. However, we have made the following specific recommendations:

1. That the Women's Commission continue its program of consultations on the national and continental levels.

2. That the Women's Commission establish a network among the women of the three continents for information-sharing and solidarity work.

3. That EATWOT initiate a dialogue between the Women's Commission and the male members of the association for greater understanding and more effective collaboration toward the attainment of our common goal of achieving full humanity for all.

4. That EATWOT create a joint commission on the Bible, which will:
   a. encourage and organize conferences on the Bible,
   b. provide materials for biblical formation,
   c. facilitate the exchange of personnel and materials.

5. That EATWOT publish in three languages (English, French, and

Spanish) an official bulletin containing works of its members, with adequate contributions from women.

6. That each region of the Women's Commission express its continuing support of and solidarity with the struggles of southern Africa and Central America and direct part of its theological effort to their situations.

CONCLUSION

At the end of our days together, we feel identified with the woman in John 12 and Mark 14, who makes a passionate prophetic action in proclaiming Jesus as messiah, anointing him with the royal ointment. John portrays the woman anointing Jesus' feet, perhaps to show that she is a real disciple, washing Jesus' feet as Jesus himself washed the disciples' feet.

This woman's action is a passionate and compassionate action—passionate, because by anointing Jesus with so expensive a perfume, she shows her extreme love for him; compassionate, because her action gives Jesus the opportunity to direct the community's attention to the poor and to exhort its solidarity with them.

Jesus approves the woman's action and says that it would be proclaimed wherever the Good News is preached. The gospel states that the fragrance spread by her gesture filled the house. As women theologians of the Third World, we are called to do the same. As we commit our lives to the ministry of a passionate and compassionate theology, we shall spread the fragrance of the Good News to all four corners of the world.

57

Pope John Paul II
Excerpts from "On Social Concern"
(Sollicitudo Rei Socialis)
(February 19, 1988)

Sollicitudo Rei Socialis *was issued to mark the twentieth anniversary of Pope Paul VI's encyclical* Populorum Progressio. *As such it deals with the widening gap between the rich and poor nations of the world, laying heavy blame on the ideological struggle between the East and the West. A careful reading of this latter part of Pope John Paul's social encyclical will show that he has incorporated the major themes of liberation theology into a true synthesis with his own creative vision of the world. This is far more important than the fact that he has positive things to say about liberation specifically (as in no. 46). The English text is taken from* Origins, *17 (March 3, 1988), nos. 41–47.*

VI. SOME PARTICULAR GUIDELINES

41. The church does not have technical solutions to offer for the problem of underdevelopment as such, as Pope Paul VI already affirmed in his encyclical.[1] For the church does not propose economic and political systems or programs, nor does it show preference for one or the other, provided that human dignity is properly respected and promoted, and provided it itself is allowed the room it needs to exercise its ministry in the world.

But the church is "an expert in humanity,"[2] and this leads it necessarily to extend its religious mission to the various fields in which men and women expend their efforts in search of the always relative happiness possible in this world, in line with their dignity as persons.

Following the example of my predecessors, I must repeat that whatever affects the dignity of individuals and peoples, such as authentic development, cannot be reduced to a "technical" problem. If reduced in this way, development would be emptied of its true content, and this would be an act of betrayal of the individuals and peoples whom development is meant to serve.

This is why the church has something to say today, just as twenty years ago, and also in the future, about the nature, conditions, requirements, and aims of authentic development, and also about the obstacles which stand in its way. In doing so the church fulfills its mission to evangelize, for it offers its first contribution to the solution of the urgent problem of development, when it proclaims the truth about Christ, about itself, and about humankind, applying this truth to a concrete situation.[3]

As its instrument for reaching this goal, the church uses its social doctrine. In today's difficult situation, a more exact awareness and a wider diffusion of the "set of principles of reflection, criteria for judgment, and directives for action" proposed by the church's teaching[4] would be of great help in promoting both the correct definition of the problems being faced and the best solution to them.

It will thus be seen at once that the questions facing us are above all moral questions; and that neither the analysis of the problem of development as such nor the means to overcome the present difficulties can ignore this essential dimension.

The church's social doctrine is not a "third way" between liberal capitalism and Marxist collectivism, nor even a possible alternative to other solutions less radically opposed to one another; rather, it constitutes a category of its own. Nor is it an ideology, but rather the accurate formulation of the results of a careful reflection on the complex realities of human existence, in society and in the international order, in the light of faith and of the church's tradition. Its main aim is to interpret these realities, determining their conformity with or divergence from the lines of the gospel teaching on human nature and the human vocation, a vocation at once earthly and transcendent; its aim is thus to guide Christian behavior. It therefore belongs to the field, not of ideology, but of theology and particularly of moral theology.

The teaching and spreading of its social doctrine are part of the church's evangelizing mission. And since it is a doctrine aimed at guiding human behavior, it consequently gives rise to a "commitment to justice," according to each individual's role, vocation, and circumstances.

The condemnation of evils and injustices is also part of that ministry of evangelization in the social field, which is an aspect of the church's prophetic role. But it should be made clear that proclamation is always more important than condemnation, and the latter cannot ignore the former, which gives it true solidity and the force of higher motivation.

42. Today more than in the past, the church's social doctrine must be open to an international outlook, in line with the Second Vatican Council,[5] the most recent encyclicals,[6] and particularly in line with the encyclical we are commemorating.[7] It will not be superfluous therefore to reexamine and

further clarify in this light the characteristic themes and guidelines dealt with by the magisterium in recent years.

Here I would like to indicate one of them: the option or love of preference for the poor. This is an option or a special form of primacy in the exercise of Christian charity to which the whole tradition of the church bears witness. It affects the life of each Christian inasmuch as he or she seeks to imitate the life of Christ, but it applies equally to our social responsibilities and hence to our manner of living, and to the logical decision to be made concerning the ownership and use of goods.

Today, furthermore, given the worldwide dimension which the social question has assumed,[8] this love of preference for the poor, and the decisions it inspires in us, cannot but embrace the immense multitudes of the hungry, the needy, the homeless, those without medical care and, above all, those without hope of a better future. It is impossible not to take account of the existence of these realities. To ignore them would mean becoming like the "rich man" who pretended not to know the beggar Lazarus lying at his gate (cf. Luke 16:19–31).[9]

Our daily life as well as our decisions in the political and economic fields must be marked by these realities. Likewise the leaders of nations and the heads of international bodies, while they are obliged always to keep in mind the true human dimension as a priority in their development plans, should not forget to give precedence to the phenomenon of growing poverty. Unfortunately, instead of becoming fewer the poor are becoming more numerous, not only in less developed countries but—and this seems no less scandalous—in the more developed ones too.

It is necessary to state once more the characteristic principle of Christian social doctrine: the goods of this world are originally meant for all.[10] The right to private property is valid and necessary, but it does not nullify the value of this principle. Private property, in fact, is under a "social mortgage,"[11] which means that it has an intrinsically social function based upon and justified precisely by the principle of the universal destination of goods. Likewise, in this concern for the poor, one must not overlook that special form of poverty which consists in being deprived of fundamental human rights, in particular the right to religious freedom and also the right to freedom of economic initiative.

43. The motivating concern for the poor—who are, in the very meaningful term, "the Lord's poor"[12]—must be translated at all levels into concrete actions, until it decisively attains a series of necessary reforms. Each local situation will show what reforms are most urgent and how they can be achieved. But those demanded by the situation of international imbalance, as already described, must not be forgotten.

In this respect I wish to mention specifically: the reform of the international trade system, which is mortgaged to protectionism and increasing bilateralism; the reform of the world monetary and financial system, today recognized as inadequate; the question of technological exchanges and their proper use; the need for a review of the structure of existing international organizations, in the framework of an international juridical order.

The international trade system today frequently discriminates against the products of the young industries of the developing countries and discourages the producers of raw materials. There exists too a kind of international division of labor, whereby the low-cost products of certain countries, which lack effective labor laws or are too weak to apply them, are sold in other parts of the world at considerable profit for the companies engaged in this form of production, which knows no frontiers.

The world monetary and financial system is marked by an excessive fluctuation of exchange rates and interest rates, to the detriment of the balance of payments and the debt situation of the poorer countries.

Forms of technology and their transfer constitute today one of the major problems of international exchange and of the grave damage deriving therefrom. There are quite frequent cases of developing countries being denied needed forms of technology or sent useless ones.

In the opinion of many, the international organizations seem to be at a stage of their existence when their operating methods, operating costs, and effectiveness need careful review and possible correction. Obviously, such a delicate process cannot be put into effect without the collaboration of all. This presupposes the overcoming of political rivalries and the renouncing of all desire to manipulate these organizations, which exist solely for the common good.

The existing institutions and organizations have worked well for the benefit of peoples. Nevertheless, humanity today is in a new and more difficult phase of its genuine development. It needs a greater degree of international ordering, at the service of the societies, economies, and cultures of the whole world.

44. Development demands above all a spirit of initiative on the part of the countries which need it.[13] Each of them must act in accordance with its own responsibilities, not expecting everything from the more favored countries and acting in collaboration with others in the same situation. Each must discover and use to the best advantage its own area of freedom. Each must make itself capable of initiatives responding to its own needs as a society. Each must likewise realize its true needs as well as the rights and duties which oblige it to respond to them. The development of peoples begins and is most appropriately accomplished in the dedication of each people to its own development, in collaboration with others.

It is important, then, that as far as possible the developing nations themselves should favor the self-affirmation of each citizen through access to a wider culture and a free flow of information. Whatever promotes literacy and the basic education which completes and deepens it is a direct contribution to true development, as the encyclical *Populorum Progressio* proposed.[14] These goals are still far from being reached in so many parts of the world.

In order to take this path, the nations themselves will have to identify their own priorities and clearly recognize their own needs according to the particular conditions of their people, their geographical setting, and their cultural traditions.

Some nations will have to increase food production in order to have always available what is needed for subsistence and daily life. In the modern world—where starvation claims so many victims, especially among the very young—there are examples of not particularly developed nations which have nevertheless achieved the goal of food self-sufficiency and have even become food exporters.

Other nations need to reform certain unjust structures and in particular their political institutions, in order to replace corrupt, dictatorial, and authoritarian forms of government by democratic and participatory ones. This is a process which we hope will spread and grow stronger. For the "health" of a political community—as expressed in the free and responsible participation of all citizens in public affairs, in the rule of law, and in respect for and promotion of human rights—is the *necessary condition and sure guarantee* of the development of "the whole individual and of all persons."

45. None of what has been said can be achieved without the collaboration of all—especially the international community—in the framework of a solidarity which includes everyone, beginning with the most neglected. But the developing nations themselves have the duty to practice solidarity among themselves and with the neediest countries of the world.

It is desirable, for example, that nations of the same geographical area should establish forms of cooperation which will make them less dependent on more powerful producers; they should open their frontiers to the products of the area; they should examine how their products might complement one another; they should combine in order to set up those services which each one separately is incapable of providing; they should extend cooperation to the monetary and financial sector.

Interdependence is already a reality in many of these countries. To acknowledge it in such a way as to make it more operative represents an alternative to excessive dependence on richer and more powerful nations as part of the hoped-for development, without opposing anyone, but discovering and making best use of the country's own potential. The developing countries belonging to one geographical area, especially those included in the term *South* can and ought to set up new regional organizations inspired by criteria of equality, freedom, and participation in the comity of nations—as is already happening with promising results.

An essential condition for global solidarity is autonomy and free self-determination, also with associations such as those indicated. But at the same time solidarity demands a readiness to accept the sacrifices necessary for the good of the whole world community.

VII. CONCLUSION

46. Peoples and individuals aspire to be free: their search for full development signals their desire to overcome the many obstacles preventing them from enjoying a "more human life."

Recently, in the period following the publication of the encyclical *Populorum Progressio,* a new way of confronting the problems of poverty and underdevelopment has spread in some areas of the world, especially in Latin America. This approach makes liberation the fundamental category and the first principle of action. The positive values as well as the deviations and risks of deviation, which are damaging to the faith and are connected with this form of theological reflection and method, have been appropriately pointed out by the church's magisterium.[15]

It is fitting to add that the aspiration to freedom from all forms of slavery affecting the individual and society is something noble and legitimate. This in fact is the purpose of development, or rather liberation and development, taking into account the intimate connection between the two.

Development which is merely economic is incapable of setting persons free; on the contrary, it will end by enslaving them further. Development that does not include the cultural, transcendent, and religious dimensions of the individual and society, to the extent that it does not recognize the existence of such dimensions and does not endeavor to direct its goals and priorities toward the same, is even less conducive to authentic liberation. Human beings are totally free only when they are completely themselves, in the fullness of their rights and duties. The same can be said about society as a whole.

The principal obstacle to be overcome on the way to authentic liberation is sin and the structures produced by sin as it multiplies and spreads.[16]

The freedom with which Christ has set us free (cf. Gal. 5:1) encourages us to become the servants of all. Thus the process of development and liberation takes concrete shape in the exercise of solidarity—that is to say, in the love and service of neighbor, especially of the poorest: "For where truth and love are missing, the process of liberation results in the death of a freedom which will have lost all support."[17]

47. In the context of the sad experiences of recent years and of the mainly negative picture of the present moment, the church must strongly affirm the possibility of overcoming the obstacles which by excess or by defect stand in the way of development. And it must affirm its confidence in a true liberation. Ultimately, this confidence and this possibility are based on the church's awareness of the divine promise guaranteeing that our present history does not remain closed in upon itself but is open to the kingdom of God.

The church has confidence also in humankind, though it knows the evil of which humankind is capable. For it well knows that—in spite of the heritage of sin and the sin which each one is capable of committing—there exist in the human person sufficient qualities and energies, a fundamental "goodness" (cf. Gen. 1:31), because humankind is the image of the creator, placed under the redemptive influence of Christ, who "united himself in some fashion with every person,"[18] and because the efficacious action of the Holy Spirit "fills the earth" (Wis. 1:7).

There is no justification then for despair or pessimism or inertia. Though it be with sorrow, it must be said that just as one may sin through selfishness and the desire for excessive profit and power, one may also be found wanting with regard to the urgent needs of multitudes of human beings submerged in conditions of underdevelopment, through fear, indecision, and basically through cowardice. We are all called, indeed obliged, to face the tremendous challenge of the last decade of the second millennium, also because the present dangers threaten everyone: a world economic crisis, a war without frontiers, without winners or losers. In the face of such a threat, the distinction between rich individuals and countries and poor individuals and countries will have little value, except that a greater responsibility rests on those who have more and can do more.

This is not, however, the sole motive or even the most important one. At stake is the dignity of the human person, whose defense and promotion have been entrusted to us by the creator, and to whom the men and women at every moment of history are strictly and responsibly in debt. As many people are already more or less clearly aware, the present situation does not seem to correspond to this dignity. Every individual is called upon to play his or her part in this peaceful campaign, a campaign to be conducted by peaceful means in order to secure development in peace, in order to safeguard nature itself and the world about us. The church too feels profoundly involved in this enterprise and it hopes for its ultimate success.

Consequently, following the example of Pope Paul VI with his encyclical *Populorum Progressio,*[19] I wish to appeal with simplicity and humility to everyone, to all men and women without exception. I wish to ask them to be convinced of the seriousness of the present moment and of each one's individual responsibility, and to implement—by the way they live as individuals and as families, by the use of their resources, by their civic activity, by contributing to economic and political decisions, and by personal commitment to national and international undertakings—the measures inspired by solidarity and love of preference for the poor. This is what is demanded by the present moment and above all by the very dignity of the human person, the indestructible image of God the creator, which is identical in each one of us.

In this commitment, the sons and daughters of the church must serve as examples and guides, for they are called upon, in conformity with the program announced by Jesus himself in the synagogue at Nazareth, to "preach good news to the poor ... to proclaim release to captives and recovering of sight to the blind, to set at liberty those who are oppressed, to proclaim the acceptable year of the Lord" (Luke 4:18–19). It is appropriate to emphasize the preeminent role that belongs to the laity, both men and women, as was reaffirmed in the recent assembly of the synod. It is their task to animate temporal realities with Christian commitment, by which they show that they are witnesses and agents of peace and justice.

NOTES

1. Cf. *Populorum Progressio,* 13, 81.

2. Cf. ibid., 13.

3. Cf. Address at the opening of the Third General Conference of Latin American Bishops (Jan. 28, 1979): *AAS,* 71 (1979), pp. 189–96.

4. *Libertatis Conscientia,* 72; *Octogesima Adveniens,* 4.

5. *Gaudium et Spes,* 83–90: "Building Up the International Community."

6. Cf. *Mater et Magistra; Pacem in Terris,* part 4; *Octogesima Adveniens,* 2–4.

7. *Populorum Progressio,* 3, 9.

8. Ibid., 3.

9. Ibid., 47; *Libertatis Conscientia,* 68.

10. Cf. *Gaudium et Spes,* 69; *Populorum Progressio,* 22; *Libertatis Conscientia,* 90; St. Thomas Aquinas, *Summa Theol.,* IIa-IIae, q. 66, art. 2.

11. Cf. Address at the Opening of the Third General Conference of the Latin American Bishops (Jan. 28, 1979): *AAS,*71 (1979), pp. 189–96; *Ad Limina* Address to a group of Polish Bishops (Dec. 17, 1987), 6: *L'Osservatore Romano,* Dec. 18, 1987.

12. Because the Lord wished to identify himself with them (Matt. 25:31–46) and takes special care of them (cf. Ps. 12[11]:6; Luke 1:52f.).

13. *Populorum Progressio,* 55: "These are the men and women that need to be helped, that need to be convinced to take into their own hands their development, gradually acquiring the means"; cf. *Gaudium et Spes,* 86.

14. *Populorum Progressio,* n. 35: "Basic education is the first objective of a plan of development."

15. Cf. Congregation for the Doctrine of the Faith, Instruction on Certain Aspects of the "Theology of Liberation," *Libertatis Nuntius* (Aug. 6, 1984), Introduction: *AAS,*76 (1984), pp. 876f.

16. Cf. *Reconciliatio et Paenitentia* (December 2, 1984), 16: *AAS,*77 (1985), pp. 213–17; Congregation for the Doctrine of the Faith, Instruction on Christian Freedom and Liberation, *Libertatis Conscientia* (March 22, 1986), 38, 42: *AAS,*79 (1987), pp. 569, 571.

17. Congregation for the Doctrine of the Faith, *Libertatis Conscientia,* 24: *AAS,* 79 (1987), p. 564.

18. Cf. *Gaudium et Spes,* 22; John Paul II, *Redemptor Hominis* (March 4, 1979), 8: *AAS,*71 (1979), p. 272.

19. *Populorum Progressio,* 5: "We believe that all men of good will, together with our Catholic sons and daughters and our Christian brethren, can and should agree on this program"; cf. also 81–83, 87.

58

Alan Riding
"Pope Shifts Brazilian Church to Right"
(June 8, 1988)

This news report in the New York Times *is the tip of an iceberg; many dedicated and committed Catholics wonder how the appointment of an overwhelming number of conservative bishops (in Brazil and throughout the world) is going to provide leadership for social change and a real, concrete option or preferential love for the poor. They wonder whether the inspiring theory or "social concern" of the encyclical is going to be put into practice by church leadership—that is, whether it is going to remain merely words or will lead to real action for the liberation of the poor and oppressed of the world.*

Pope John Paul II is quietly using his authority to name new cardinals and bishops as a way of reasserting Vatican control over Brazil's powerful and outspoken Roman Catholic hierarchy, church experts here say.

The experts said this was seen to be the pope's goal when he included two conservative Brazilian prelates, Archbishops Lucas Moreira Neves of Salvador in the state of Bahia and José Freire Falcão of Brasília, among twenty-five new cardinals just named.

The strategy of promoting clergymen who unquestioningly accept Rome's authority and share the pope's interpretation of church doctrine was also behind the recent choice of new Brazilian bishops and the transfer of others to new dioceses, they added.

One consequence has been new friction between the Vatican and dominant figures in this country's Conference of Bishops who believe that, as representative of the world's most populous Catholic nation, the Brazilian church should have considerable independence from Rome.

GREATER ROLE IS ASKED

"There should be more effective participation by Brazilian bishops in the selection of new bishops," said a prominent Brazilian bishop who asked not be identified. "At present, it's all done through the apostolic nuncio, who has no way of knowing the church in a country of Brazil's size."

The bishop said it is important for Rome to recognize what he described as the "originality" of the church in Latin America and other regions where widespread poverty often obliges bishops, priests, and nuns to become involved in social and even political affairs.

"The Vatican is in Europe," he noted. "It's very difficult, no matter how hard it tries, for the holy see to understand what is happening in the third world. Overcentralization in Rome just doesn't work."

Until now, the Vatican and the Brazilian Conference of Bishops have disagreed principally over a doctrine known as liberation theology, which emphasizes the social role of the church among the poor and which, in the view of Rome, at times veers dangerously close to Marxism.

GRADUAL APPROACH SEEN

Leading Brazilian prelates have not shied from defending the local church against criticism, notably in the case of a left-leaning Brazilian theologian, the Rev. Leonardo Boff, who was summoned to Rome in 1985 and punished after attacking what he described as the "authoritarianism" of the Vatican.

Having failed to bring the Brazilian church into line, the pope is now believed to have chosen a more gradual approach: using more conservative prelates as a counterweight to the left-of-center group that now controls the 358-member Conference of Bishops.

"The quality of the individual as well as local considerations come into play with any appointment," a senior Vatican official said when asked about recent Brazilian nominations. "But there is no doubt the pope looks for men who are going to lead the church in the direction he thinks it ought to go."

The pope's most significant recent appointment in Brazil occurred last September, when he named a longtime Vatican aide, Bishop Neves, to become archbishop of Salvador and, as such, Primate of Brazil. The archbishop's elevation to Cardinal thus came as no surprise.

Archbishop Neves, who served in the Vatican both as vice-president of the Congregation of Bishops and secretary of the College of Cardinals, is widely regarded as being uniquely suited both to represent the pope's interest in Brazil and to build a bloc of more conservative prelates within the Conference of Bishops.

The Pope's decision to elevate the archbishop of Brasília to cardinal was also interpreted as a way of giving a prelate known for his loyalty to Rome greater prestige and authority before the government. Brasília will now have its first cardinal since the new capital was inaugurated twenty-seven years ago.

REPLACED BY CONSERVATIVES

Similarly, when bishops have died or retired in recent years in Brazil, they have invariably been replaced by men with more conservative views than their predecessors. The most notable example of this was the replacement of a legendary defender of the poor, Archbishop Helder Câmara of Recife, who retired in 1985, with Archbishop José Cardoso Sobrinho.

More recently, the Vatican appears to have set its sights on weakening the power of Cardinal Paulo Evaristo Arns. As Archbishop of São Paulo, he not only controls church affairs in Brazil's largest city and a corps of nine auxiliary bishops, but is also a strong defender of human rights and an advocate of social change, exercising enormous influence over the Conference of Bishops.

59

Bishop Pedro Casaldáliga
"Letter to Brazilian Bishops"
(June 1988)

Pedro Casaldáliga, bishop of São Felix, is known throughout Latin America and in many other nations for his heroic work among the poorest Amerindians in Brazil, for his books of theology and poetry, and—not least—for his ebullient and joyous personality. In September 1988 he was censured by Roman authorities with restrictions imposed on his travel and speech. This took place after he had gone to Rome and spoken with Cardinals Joseph Ratzinger and Bernardin Gantin as well as with Pope John Paul. While this case has yet to be resolved, the following account of his trip, written for the Brazilian bishops, speaks for itself. The text is from the National Catholic Reporter *(Nov. 11, 1988), pp. 9–11.*

Until now, I had not made the *ad limina* visit to Rome, which we bishops are obliged to make every five years. I had already been a bishop for seventeen years. I received two quite tough letters from the Congregation for Bishops insisting on this visit, and reminding me—nine years after the event—of alleged unpaid "debts" stemming from apostolic visitations made to the prelature after accusations made by an ultraconservative bishop.

I decided to appeal to the pope—the bishop of São Felix to the bishop of Rome—and wrote to him February 22, 1986, pouring my heart out in a long, ecclesial letter. "If you find it suitable," I said, "you can suggest a date upon which I could visit you personally."

That date was now, in the month of June [1988].

I traveled to Rome by Alitalia, surrounded by boisterous Italo-Argentinians who were also returning to their roots. Traveling in the same plane were forty sisters of St. Joseph—among them our Sister Irene—who were going as pilgrims to the place where their religious congregation had originated.

I felt myself sustained by many prayers, much friendly advice, and promises of support. For their part, the curia and nunciature have asked me to observe the greatest discretion about this journey.

In my extremely intermittent diary, I noted: "I am going to Rome as a pilgrim. *Videre Petrum, videre martyres, videre Franciscum* ("to see Peter, to see the martyrs, to see Francis"). Rome and Assisi. The stone, the blood of Latin America, with the ear of corn made fertile by so much martyrs' blood, and fraternally united in its desire for liberation.

After twenty years, waiting for me in Rome, were the historical stones, the basilicas, the catacombs, obelisks brought from other peoples; ruins patrolled by sacred cats, sun-filled piazzas with their happy-go-lucky tourists; the hills and their country houses; the cornfields; the cherry trees and good wine; the olive trees; the native gorse—my Catalan *ginesta*.

Also the *gelati*, of course, and that Roman traffic so familiar in its madness; the posters proclaiming ecology, politics, art; reporters, especially those from Spain and Catalonia, accompanying me only too eagerly. Christian communities of radical commitment; old friends; my Claretian confreres, more than eager to help me, especially José Fernando Tobón and Angel Calvo of the general prefecture of the apostolate; and my family— reunions, nostalgic encounters, roots. At the end of the day, a European as well as a Latin American.

And, as I said, the apostolic stone, sealed with the blood of the first martyrs. We have something, Rome, of the Romans, all those of us who inherited the milk of Latin, the faith of Peter. Despite the empire, behind the Vatican, in the shared stone and blood, all of us have much of the Romans.

On [June] 16, wearing a borrowed jacket, I was received in the anteroom by Monsignor Giovanni Ré, secretary of the Congregation for Bishops, who had already been in the nunciature of Panama. *"Cum Petro et sub Petro"* (with Peter and under Peter), he cautioned me insistently. And "only one Lord, one faith, one baptism," I added, so that the confession might be fuller.

He also reminded me that, on Saturday, in the joint interview with Cardinals Bernardin Gantin and Joseph Ratzinger, I would have to appear in the appropriate dress. (In this case, it would be the cassock and the Claretian girdle kindly lent to me by the veteran Father Garde, and the [South American] Indian collar of *tucum* and the Franciscan cross.)

Cardinal Gantin, prefect of the congregation (for the bishops) told me in advance, "It will be a meeting of complete sincerity, liberty, and brotherhood."

I felt at once that I would be submitted to an ecclesiastical entrance examination on discipline by the Congregation for Bishops, on theology by the Congregation for the Doctrine of the Faith.

This took place on Saturday, June 18. It lasted one and a half hours, at the Congregation for Bishops. With Cardinal Gantin were his secretary, Monsignor Ré, and an undersecretary; with Cardinal Ratzinger, his secretary, Monsignor Alberto Bovone and Monsignor Américo, a Portuguese from the secretariat of state. The monsignori noted everything and had in their hands photocopies of my texts. Expectation, seriousness, and tact. No aggression.

Personally, I think I spoke freely. Ratzinger smiled often. I made a point of saying, thank God, I had no problem of faith, although I had theological differences with them; nor did I have a problem of communion with the church, although I did have reservations regarding minor aspects of ecclesiastical discipline.

Cardinal Gantin began reading a text, which reminded me of the solemnity of the occasion and of all *ad limina* visits. He recognized our sufferings and our dedication to the people (at times I felt as if we were being collectively challenged; who knows, perhaps this was because of the Italian collective *voi*). "Cardinal Ratzinger and I will give you certain warnings," he said. And he mentioned the anxiety about the (Archbishop Marcel) Lefebvre case, which was coming to a head at that time.

First question asked by Ratzinger: Do you accept the documents of the Holy See on liberation theology?

My reply: I accept the three complementary texts in substance: the two documents together with the letter sent by the pope to the Brazilian bishops in which he affirms that "liberation theology is not only opportune but also useful and necessary." Where I differ is on certain aspects of theology and sociology, and in respect of certain statements concerning our theologians made in the first document. In fact, we are dealing with "instructions" here.

The pope himself, I reminded them, asked that to the first instruction, which was so negative, should be added five introductory sections. Moreover, the pope declined to acknowledge his paternity of this instruction, saying: "It is Cardinal Ratzinger's." "Just jokes," replied the cardinal.

Second question: You wrote that the option for the poor should be understood in a "class-based" sense. We prefer to speak of a preferential love of the poor. "Class-based" is a word charged with meaning, and one which cannot be gotten away from.

My reply: Indeed, the word is charged with meaning, and a valid meaning, as I see it. If you do not want to call it a "class struggle," we can call it a "conflict of classes," as do the instructions. But the conflict is there. We in Latin America wish to avoid people thinking of our poor as spontaneously poor, isolated, existing outside a structure that exploits and marginalizes them; this is why we speak of the "impoverished."

The pope himself has said on several occasions that, precisely in Latin America "the rich are becoming richer and richer at the expense of the poor who are always poorer thereby." This "at the expense of" is structural and, if you permit me the scandalous term, "dialectical."

Third question: You and your colleagues speak of social sin. And what about personal sin?

My reply: It is my custom always to call to mind simultaneously both aspects of sin. In the Pilgrimage of the Martyrs, in Ribeirão Bonito, we burn in the penitential pyre social sins as well as personal sins, explicitly listed, the one and the other.

The New Testament denounces "the sin of the world." There was something of social structure in this sin: the synagogue, the empire, slavery. Obviously, it is persons who sin, but within structures, which they render sinful and which in a way make these persons what they are. We are at once creators of structures and subject to them.

Fourth question: You and your colleagues celebrate the eucharist as a social rite. . . .

My reply: I very much doubt whether you can accuse me of reductionism in this case. Indeed, I always say expressly that the Mass is "the pasch of Jesus, our pasch, the pasch of the world." Death and life, passion and resurrection. In presenting the host to the eucharistic assembly, it is my custom to say, "This is the Lamb of God, who takes away sin, slavery, and the death of the world."

We also speak of the passion, death, and resurrection of each one of us and of the people, yes, indeed. The eucharist exists also for this. In order that we might have life, Christ gave his own. Traditionally, the church makes us repeat at the offertory: "this bread we offer, which earth has given and human hands have made." There is something social in the earth and in this work referred to in the prayer.

I reminded the cardinals of the Mass of the Land without Ills and the Mass of the Quilombos (places where the runaway black slaves took refuge), which the Vatican banned, and I took the opportunity of defending them. I quoted with special emphasis to African Cardinal Gantin the Mass of the Quilombos, a prayer for the Negro cause. I observed how difficult it is for the church to "inculturate itself," to be indigenized in the other cultures of the Third World.

Fifth question: Your colleagues and you easily give the names of martyrs to Archbishop Oscar Romero and Camilo Torres. It is good to call to mind certain people who dedicated themselves to the people, but to call them martyrs. . . .

My reply: We are quite capable of making the distinction between "canonical" martyrs, officially recognized by the church, and those many other martyrs whom we call martyrs of the kingdom, who gave their lives for justice, for liberation, the majority of those Christians who died expressly for the cause of the gospel. Yes, I wrote a poem to "Saint Romero of America," and I consider him thus: a saint, a martyr, ours.

Sixth question: You spoke of "revolutionizing" the church.

My reply: The complete phrase cropped up on the occasion of the "evangelical" insurrection of Nicaragua: "It is imperative to revolutionize oneself constantly, in one's personal life, through metanoia, or conversion; it is essential to revolutionize society, no matter what the system or regime, and it is also imperative constantly to revolutionize the church itself, in order that it may be ever more evangelical." I was addressing the less "ecclesiastical" world. I could have said the church is *semper renovanda* (always to be renewed). We mentioned, in the course of our conversation, pluralism, our (liberation) theology, the episcopal conferences, the appointments of bishops.

"You have been referring to Praetorium and Sanhedrin," Ratzinger said to me, jestingly. And I agreed, in the same tone.

Monsignor Bovone read me the telegram that ten of us Brazilian bishops sent to Rome on the occasion of the first public censure of Leonardo Boff. He added: "You wrote that the second document on liberation theology corrects the first."

I wrote that this is true. It corrects it because it completes it. Had the first been complete, the second would have been unnecessary.

At a certain point, Cardinal Ratzinger observed that all words can be justified, suggesting, as it were, that it is easy to give subsequently correct interpretations of things previously incorrect.

Cardinal Gantin referred gravely to the problem concerning my visits to Nicaragua. "This is already a 'fact,' " he stressed the word. "To leave one's diocese to go to another country to interfere with another episcopate. . . ." I tried to explain myself. But, in the course of those Vatican encounters, I saw that Nicaragua is the last thing that can be "explained" there.

I told them I went to Nicaragua during the fast against violence, and with the support of twenty-three fellow bishops; I quoted my previous friendship with Nicaraguans, my letters to the bishops of this country, my journeys to other Central American countries, and the warm welcome of my brother bishops of these countries.

I spoke of solidarity, of what Nicaragua means for the whole of Latin America. I recalled that there are Christians, Catholics more specifically, on both sides of the church, and that the church, like the hierarchy, is also obliged to take into account the other side. I quoted the scandal suffered by this other side. We were not all equally "convinced" of this!

"You said the *ad limina* visit was useless," Gantin said. I said it was "almost" useless, I joked. And I repeated the complaint of so many [bishops] throughout the world on this matter. I recognized that there was a new form of visit, as was seen during the last visit of the Brazilian episcopate, when twenty-one bishops journeyed to Rome for three days in which they and the dicasteries openly discussed in front of the pope.

I reminded them of how John Paul II himself, in his letter to the National Conference of Brazilian bishops, recognized this new form of visit as being more collegial and one which could serve as a model for other episcopates.

"You are being used in what you say, write, and do," said Gantin.

We are all used, I answered. You are also used; the pope is used. Besides, we must see by whom and how we are used. I spoke about communication, public opinion—within the church itself—of collegiality and coresponsibility. I lamented the fact that we stress obsessive secrecy.

Right from the beginning of the interview, they had hinted at the possibility of a text of propositions I would have to sign. Now they formulated this proposal more specifically. I answered that I would sign nothing without sufficient time in which to think and consult. I answered that I would never ask anyone for such a signature. They reacted: "It is not a question of a tribunal, no. You will have time to think about this."

I reminded Cardinal Gantin that, in his letter, he had promised me a meeting with the Pope. He confirmed this. He would be meeting with Pope John Paul II that very afternoon. I understood that this would be to brief him on our interview.

We got up. I asked if we might pray together, that we might always be faithful to the kingdom, in order to help the church to be even more evangelical. "To revolutionize it," intervened Ratzinger, smiling. "Yes, to revolutionize it evangelically," I added.

I told them about the recent threat by the UDR (União Democrática Ruralista: the National Landowners' Organization), of which I have been the target, and assured them that if I am killed it will be for the kingdom and also for the church. ... We said the Our Father in Latin and made a prayer to Mary, mother of the church.

When I was already on the stairs, one of the monsignori came to ask me not to report any of our conversations to journalists. I said that I would only speak to the press after my audience with the pope and that, if we do not tell journalists the truth, they have to invent it, or perhaps even lies. I insisted on my right and duty of communication. Subsequently, I found out that Vatican Radio had received orders to say nothing about my stay in Rome.

In the waiting room, before the audience, there was a calendar dedicated to refugees. I recalled with special affection the Guatemalan refugees. The caption on the calendar said, "It is very easy to be a refugee; your different race and your different opinions can suffice."

In the waiting room, after the interview, there were three fine ink drawings with royal peacocks, lions devouring a lamb, and serpents wound around a column; a painting of Our Lady of Guadalupe and a crucifix. Fellini would have had a malicious feast.

The private audience with Pope John Paul II took place June 21 and lasted approximately fifteen minutes, after I had passed by some eight guards, presented the *biglietto* (ticket) of the prefecture of the pontifical household four times, crossed patios, and passed through corridors and sitting rooms.

The pope gestured for me to speak, both of us seated around a table.

"I had the interviews with Cardinals Gantin and Ratzinger, and they gave me a series of warnings. You have already read the letter I sent you containing my preoccupations and explaining to you why I had not made my *ad limina* visit."

The pope nodded.

"I am here to hear whatever you have to say to me," I added.

He wished us to speak in Portuguese. He speaks fluently, a true polyglot.

He dwelt on the importance of unity in the church; of communion, and not only communication, with the pope but also with his collaborators. He reminded me that the *ad limina* visit is not a mere question of bureaucracy. I agreed.

I insisted upon the benefits of communion on both sides, upon the advantages of this new form of *ad limina* visit initiated with his agreement by the Brazilian Bishops' Conference, advantages he himself had since recognized in the letter that he wrote us and that was so warmly welcomed by us. He praised the loyalty of the Bishops' Conference in communicating everything to him promptly.

I explained to him how the different reality of our latitudes and the situations we have to live out oblige us to adopt positions possibly not understood by other members of the church. He recognized this and stated several times that "the church must take on social issues." "They are human problems," he said.

Many inside and outside the church, I said, were grateful to him for his encyclical *Sollicitudo Rei Socialis,* which was, in our opinion, very precise and clear. Satisfied, he added: "They even call it the charter of the Third World."

He showed that he knows of our suffering and repeated, several times, that he was aware of the great injustice taking place in Brazil, above all in the north of the country.

"It seemed to us most opportune," I said, "for you to have reminded President Sarney that, without agrarian reform, there will be no democracy in Brazil. Unfortunately, the National Constituent Assembly has already forbidden us agrarian reform in the text of the new constitution so far voted."

On the table was a folder with my name on the cover and a map of our region. The pope bent over it. We spoke of the prelature, of the situation of the people—Amerindians, land squatters, farmhands, tenant farmers; we spoke of the pastoral team: priests, sisters, lay people, seminarians.

He asked me whether the lay people could read. I explained the various types of lay people who work on the team and in the communities and the many reading and writing courses and schools which have been in operation in the area for some time. And I asked:

"You are thinking of returning to Brazil, possibly next year, aren't you?"

"I wish to. I hope the Lord will permit me this visit."

"It would be very good if you visited these inland areas; the sanctuary of Trinidad, for example, near Goiania, would be a most suitable place; it is an extremely popular and much frequented sanctuary."

"Trinidade, Trinidade," he repeated, as if to engrave the name upon his mind.

I mentioned the proposal of the cardinals about certain propositions that I would have to sign, and confessed that, as I saw it, this appeared to me to be a lack of trust.

"It can also be a sign of confidence," he replied. "Cardinal Arns, when he comes here, likes to have everything in writing."

Afterward, he sat down, opened his arms and half warning and half jesting said to me:

"So you see that I am no wild beast. . . !"

At first, I was a bit astonished, then I found his gesture funny.

"I didn't think that for one moment," I smiled.

(But in truth, being so much nearer the Vatican, I felt just how this Vatican resembles a cage, albeit a golden one. Before the bronze statue of St. Peter, I remembered—how could I not—Alberti's verses about St. Peter's longing to be free as a simple fisherman.)

I asked John Paul II for his blessing on the entire prelature, and we went on listing groups of people. I asked, above all, his blessing on those who were persecuted.

"Above all, the persecuted," he repeated.

On Thursday, June 27, in the morning, the last day of my stay in Rome, I had another meeting with Cardinal Gantin and his secretary Monsignor Ré.

The cardinal looked tense: "You have been with the pope, haven't you?"

"Yes, I was with him for about fifteen minutes."

"Useless!"

Faced with my astonishment, he grimly wanted to know why parts of my letter to Pope John Paul had already been published in Spain. "The whole world," he said, "will see your differences with the Holy Father." He and the secretary insinuated that this letter showed a lack of respect.

"The letter," I replied, "appeared to me to be extremely respectful and ecclesial. It is a letter based upon thoughtful, prayerful consultation with others. It did, indeed, express preoccupations and even differences felt by many of us Catholics, and which we have the right to feel and express, as the church which we are. The letter did not deal with private matters."

Afterward, the cardinal once again reproached me very strongly for my visits to Nicaragua, and this in the name of the Congregation for Bishops.

"I shall pray, reflect, and consult with my companions," I replied.

He asked me to examine my conscience about the way in which I related to public opinion.

"I am also a bishop of the church," I said. "And I am aware of my duty of coresponsibility. The pope himself insisted on communication. I believe that we had to facilitate dialogue, pluralism, the greater good of the church, the work of all of us."

The Lefebvre case cropped up again. And I said I thought it most evangelical that the curia had shown so much understanding toward the aged bishop but that I would like them to show the same understanding toward other sectors of the church. The cardinal answered that they treated all bishops equally.

I also had an extremely warm meeting with the Latin American Cardinal Eduardo Pironio outside the official program.

During those days, my thoughts turned many times in faith but with sadness and with hope to our binding obligation of communion and communication between local churches and the church of Rome; between the pope and his curia and the bishops and their conferences; between our church and the other churches, ecumenically speaking; between the churches and the world.

Amid those stones and filled with reverence in the face of so much tradition, I dreamed of another type of Roman curia for another type of papal ministry. I felt, and this not without a tinge of guilt, the distances which set us in contradiction with each other when they ought to bring about Catholicity, to make us united in our plurality, faithful yet free, evangelical and historical....

Assisi was another obligatory stop in this ecclesial pilgrimage. I went with the staunch companions Fernando and Angel [fellow Claretians] and with a crowd of pilgrims on foot, who did not leave me for one moment, to those haunts of the Poverello.

In Assisi all was bathed in light, like Umbria, like the soul of Francis. The bare stones, the fiery geraniums, the doves, the frescoes, the sepulchers, the "little garden of Sister Clare," in which brother Francis burst into his "Canticle of Creatures."

All was conducive to poverty, to liberty, to peace, to *fraternura* (fraternal tenderness). We celebrated the eucharist at Sam Damiano on the very day on which the city was dedicated to St. Clare.

Ah, Francis of the flowers and nature, of the gospel "without gloss"; Francis of the crucified, perfect happiness. What good you do us, and how all of us, followers of the Lord Jesus, miss you!

And I am back in São Felix do Araguaia, more ecclesial, I hope, and also more Latin American. To the glory of the Father, and of the Son, and of the Holy Spirit!

Index